Scrutinizing Internal and External Dimensions of European Law

Les dimensions internes et externes du droit européen à l'épreuve

Liber Amicorum Paul Demaret

Vol. I

P.I.E. Peter Lang

Bruxelles • Bern • Berlin • Frankfurt am Main • New York • Oxford • Wien

Inge GOVAERE & Dominik HANF (eds.)

Scrutinizing Internal and External Dimensions of European Law

Les dimensions internes et externes du droit européen à l'épreuve

Liber Amicorum Paul Demaret

Vol. I

College of Europe Studies/Cahiers du Collège d'Europe
No. 17

Cover picture/illustration de couverture : Paul Demaret, © College of Europe, 2007.

Éditions scientifiques internationales
Brussels/Bruxelles, 2013
1 avenue Maurice, B-1050 Brussels, Belgium
www.peterlang.com; info@peterlang.com

ISSN 1780-9665
ISBN 978-2-80761-151-1
D/2013/5678/67

CIP available from the British Library and the Library of Congress, USA.

Bibliographic information published by "Die Deutsche Nationalbibliothek"

"Die Deutsche Nationalbibliothek" lists this publication in the "Deutsche Nationalbibliografie"; detailed bibliographic data is available on the Internet at <http://dnb.d-nb.de>.

Information bibliographique publiée par « Die Deutsche Bibliothek »

« Die Deutsche Bibliothek » répertorie cette publication dans la « Deutsche Nationalbibliografie » ; les données bibliographiques détaillées sont disponibles sur le site http://dnb.ddb.de.

Table des matières/Contents

III. Aspects institutionnels de l'intégration européenne/Institutional Aspects of European Integration

IV. Marché intérieur et politiques d'accompagnement/ Internal Market and Related Policies

Préface

Dans sa préface, le président du Conseil européen, Herman Van Rompuy, nous rappelle l'importance de la contribution du Collège d'Europe pour l'intégration européenne moyennant, d'une part, l'analyse de ce processus politique, économique et juridique passionnant et, d'autre part, la création continue de liens de solidarité interpersonnels à travers et au-delà des différents pays européens.

La contribution de Paul Demaret au développement du Collège d'Europe est exceptionnelle, et ceci non seulement en raison du fait qu'elle s'étend sur 33 des 64 années de vie de cette institution.

D'une part, c'est sous la responsabilité du directeur d'études Demaret (1981 à 2003) que le programme des études juridiques du Collège a été fermement établi comme une des premières adresses pour tout jeune juriste européen désirant se spécialiser en matière de droit européen.

Il a lui-même décrit les différentes étapes franchies au cours de ce processus de modernisation, de professionnalisation et de développement continu du programme d'études juridiques.[1] Nombreux anciens étudiants – tout comme la liste des enseignants – de ce programme travaillant dans la magistrature, au barreau, dans l'administration publique ou encore en tant qu'universitaires témoignent de cette réussite remarquable.

D'autre part, c'est sous le double mandat du recteur Demaret (2003 à 2013) que le Collège dans son ensemble a été davantage professionnalisé et préparé pour répondre à des nouveaux défis. L'on soulignera, sans être exhaustif, en premier lieu une ouverture accrue du Collège au-delà de l'Europe, notamment la création du nouveau programme sur les relations internationales de l'Union européenne, le renforcement continu du programme d'études interdisciplinaire à Natolin ainsi que le renforcement du corps académique non-visiteur (professeurs à temps plein et titulaires de chaires). Son nom restera également associé au nouveau site « Verversdijk », à Bruges, qu'il a réalisé en dépit de difficultés qui paraissaient insurmontables en 2003.

---

1 Voir Paul Demaret, « Les études juridiques au Collège d'Europe (Bruges) », in P. Demaret, I. Govaere, D. Hanf, *Trente ans d'études juridiques européennes au Collège d'Europe*, Bruxelles, PIE Peter Lang, 2005, pp. 15-26.

Tout cela est d'autant plus remarquable car le recteur Demaret a appliqué avec succès au Collège les principes de comptabilité que le professeur Demaret avait été obligé d'enseigner à ses étudiants liégeois dans les années 1980. Il s'inscrit ainsi dans la ligne du recteur Lukaszewski qui l'avait invité à s'investir au Collège.

Finalement, nous rendons également hommage au professeur Demaret, un universitaire exceptionnel.

D'une part, il a formé des générations de juristes européens et en provenance d'autres régions du monde moyennant ses enseignements à Liège (ou il dirigeait également un programme de DEA/DES en droit européen) et à Bruges ainsi que dans nombreuses autres universités du monde. Ni les cours (qui débutaient généralement à 8 heures ou 8 heures 30) ni les examens du professeur Demaret n'étaient réputés d'être faciles. Mais l'on apprenait toujours quelque chose même – et surtout – lorsque l'on connaissait, ou croyait déjà connaître, la matière. Ce n'est donc pas surprenant que la note d'un candidat obtenue « chez Demaret » constituait un critère de sélection de poids pour nombreux employeurs.

D'autre part, Paul Demaret a contribué de manière significative au développement de la recherche du droit européen et international, et ceci non seulement moyennant ses propres publications dont nombreuses restent toujours des textes de référence. En sa fonction de directeur de l'Institut d'études juridiques européennes « Fernand Dehousse », il a également sans cesse activement encouragé des chercheurs, jeunes et expérimentés, à conduire et publier des recherches, notamment dans le cadre d'un grand projet de recherche en réseau de portée européen (« PAI »). Il n'est donc pas surprenant qu'une des premières mesures prises par le recteur Demaret était d'encourager les assistants académiques du Collège, moyennant l'introduction d'une clause spécifique dans les contrats d'emploi, à publier du moins un article par an.

Dans tous ces domaines, l'action de Paul Demaret était caractérisée par une rigueur sur le plan académique et conceptuelle, une ouverture exceptionnelle envers des nouveaux développements, une flexibilité d'accommoder des difficultés et situations imprévues et un sens très marqué pour l'intérêt de son institution pour laquelle il n'hésitait jamais à prendre ses responsabilités lorsque ceci s'imposait. En même temps, et ceci explique sans doute pourquoi autant de personnes ont eu le plaisir et l'honneur de travailler avec lui, Paul n'hésite pas à faire confiance aux autres et de leur accorder des responsabilités – même lorsqu'il existe un risque d'en être déçu. En règle générale, et le grand nombre d'amis et collègues ayant favorablement répondu à notre initiative de rendre hommage à Paul en témoigne, les déceptions on fait exception.

Ceci nous a confrontés au problème que le nombre des personnes susceptibles de contribuer au présent ouvrage en honneur de Paul était à un tel point élevé qu'il risquait de mettre en péril la réalisation même de ce projet. Un critère de sélection s'imposait. Nous avons finalement retenu celui des amis et collègues, professeurs de droit et directeurs d'études, du Collège car cette *Festschrift* est offerte à Paul Demaret à l'occasion de l'achèvement de son rectorat au Collège d'Europe.

Last but not least, nous souhaitons remercier très chaleureusement Valérie Hauspie qui a assuré de manière particulièrement engagée et efficace le secrétariat ainsi que la mise en page du manuscrit final. De même nous remercions Marc Abenhaïm, Sara Benedi Lahuerta, Svetlana Chobanova, Ziva Nendl, Kletia Noti, Julie Probst et Laurence Van Mullem, assistants au département juridique du Collège, pour leur aide ce qui concerne la première lecture très attentive des épreuves.

Ad multos annos !

Bruges et Alicante, le 15 janvier 2013

Inge Govaere

Director of European Legal Studies,
College of Europe
Professor of European Law,
Jean Monnet Chair in EU
Legal Studies,
Ghent University

Dominik Hanf

Administrator, First Board of Appeal
Office for Harmonization
in the Internal Market
Visiting (and former permanent) Professor,
European Legal Studies, Former Director
of European Interdisciplinary and of
European General Studies, College of Europe

Foreword

Among our Union's founding moments, the Hague Congress of 1948, which saw the foundation of the College of Europe, holds a very special place. Bringing together hundreds of delegates from many countries, only three years after the end of the Second World War, it inspired Europeans all over the continent, and opened some perspectives for the future.

Speaking in the margins of the Congress, Winston Churchill captured the energy that united the supporters of this new Europe. Addressing a crowd of some 40,000 people on Dam Square in Amsterdam on 9 May – by a happy coincidence two years to the day before the Schuman declaration – he called for "*a Europe in which men will be proud to say, 'I am a European'.*" He continued: "*We hope to see a Europe where men of every country will think as much of being a European as of belonging to their native land, and that without losing any of their love and loyalty of their birthplace. We hope wherever they go in this wide domain, to which we set no limits in the European Continent, they will truly feel 'Here I am at home. I am a citizen of this country too'. Let us meet together. Let us work together. Let us do our utmost – all that is in us – for the good of all.*"

The College of Europe, which was conceived that very week in The Hague by some of Europe's prominent founding figures, remains one of the most lasting legacies of this "Congress of Europe". There could have been no better birthplace for an institution devoted to deepening not only the understanding of Europe but also understanding between Europeans.

Though I have not myself had the chance of studying at the College of Europe, I have always felt close to what many refer to as the "*Spirit of the College*". A culture of openness and of curiosity, a layered sense of belonging and of identity, of feeling at home in any place that other Europeans call home. I became familiar with this spirit in 1965 thanks to Father Verleye, one of the founding fathers of the College and a close friend of Rector H. Brugmans. When I was 17, Father Verleye spent three full days teaching us about Europe.

A haven for unexpected encounters and discoveries, the College of Europe has always fostered solidarity and mutual understanding among its students. As a pioneer in the field of European studies, it has continuously broadened our knowledge of this political work in progress that is our Union, examining it from an ever increasing range of perspectives, and mobilising new tools to deepen our understanding of who we are and what we do together.

Paul Demaret spent thirty years at the service – and at the helm – of this unique institution. He invited me to Bruges to deliver my first major speech as President of the European Council, to speak about a common European foreign policy. I still remember the enthusiastic reaction from this audience of young people. It was a great start of my mandate.

What the College has achieved in over six decades since its creation is truly exceptional. By pursuing excellence in European matters, may it continue to teach generation after generation of excellent Europeans.

Herman Van Rompuy
President of the European Council

Curriculum Vitae Paul Demaret

Personal

Born 24 September 1941, Ostend, Belgium, Belgian citizen, four children

Education

1975, J.S.D., U.C. Berkeley

1971, LL.M., Columbia University

1969, "D.E.S. en droit économique" (graduate degree in Economic Law), University of Liège

1967, "Licencié en sciences économiques" (B.A. in economics), University of Liège

1963, Docteur en droit (J.D.), University of Liège

Present Position

Since 1 February 2003 (until 31 August 2013), Rector of the College of Europe (Bruges/Warsaw, Natolin)

Previous Positions

2003-2006, "Professeur extraordinaire" (Part-time professor), University of Liège

1982-2003, "Professeur ordinaire" (Full-time professor), School of Law, University of Liège, Jean Monnet chair in European Economic Law (1990)

1981-2003, Director of European legal studies (bilingual programme French/English), College of Europe, Bruges

1984-2004, Director, Institut d'études juridiques européennes, Fernand Dehousse, University of Liège

1978-1982, "Chargé de cours" (Lecturer), School of Law, University of Liège

1978-1982, "Senior Research Associate", National Foundation for Scientific Research, Belgium

1973-1978, "Research Associate", National Foundation for Scientific Research, Belgium

1969-1973, "Research Fellow", National Foundation for Scientific Research, Belgium

1964-1969, "Research Fellow", National Foundation for Scientific Research (1965-66: military service), Belgium

1963-1964, "Research Assistant", Professor Ch. del Marmol, University of Liège

Visiting Positions

1981-2003, Visiting professor, College of Europe (1981-1985: European Law and Intellectual Property; 1982-2003: European Economic Law)

2001, Visiting professor, World Trade Institute, Bern, (Environmental Protection, Public Health and EU Law) (May 2001)

2000, Visiting professor, Center for European Studies, Peking University, December 2000, (EU and WTO law)

1999-2001, Visiting professor, Pontificia Universidad Catolica del Peru, Lima, (The Single European Market – Internal and External Aspects)

1999, Visiting professor, University of Coimbra (The External Dimension of the Internal Market and WTO)

1998-1999, Robert Schuman professor (EU-China Higher Education Cooperation Programme), Peking University, (EU & WTO law), 15 May-15 June 1999

1999, Visiting professor, University of Paris II (The External Dimension of the Internal Market)

1999, Visiting professor, Institut universitaire international Luxembourg (The Extra-territorial Application of European Competition Law)

1994-1996, Visiting professor, Colegio de Mexico (The Single European market – Internal and External Aspects) (Regional Integration from a Comparative Perspective)

1993-2000, Visiting professor, Barcelona autonomous University (The External Dimension of the Internal Market)

1992, Academy of European Law, European University Institute, Florence (The External Dimension of the Internal Market)

1989, Director and visiting professor, Session juridique, Institut International Universitaire, Luxembourg (European and International Aspects of Industrial Property)

1989-1996, Visiting professor, University of Lusiada, Lisbon, (European Economic Law and Free Movement of Goods)

1988-1993-1994-1995, Visiting professor, Catholic University of Lisbon (The External Dimension of the Internal Market)

1990-1991-1992, Visiting professor, University of Geneva (Introduction to the Four Freedoms of the Common Market)

1987-1988, Visiting professor, University of Fribourg, Switzerland (Free Movement of Goods and Persons in the European Community) (December 1987 and February 1988)

1977 and 1980, Visiting professor, European Centre, University of Nancy (European Competition Law)

Selected Service and other Activities

1999-2000, Member of the WTO panel Korea – Measures Affecting Imports of Fresh, Chilled and Frozen Beef

1999, Co-organisor, Workshop on "Legal Issues in EU-China Trade Relations", Center for European Studies, Peking University, 6-10 December 1999

1998-1999, Member of the WTO panel India BOP Measures

1999-2003, Member, Collège doctoral européen, Université Robert Schuman, Strasbourg

1998 to date, Member of the editorial board, Journal of International Economic Law, Oxford University Press

1997-2007, Member and then Chairman, Legal Science Committee, National Foundation for Scientific Research, Brussels

1990-2004, Coordinator of a research programme sponsored by the Belgian federal government, Law of European Economic Integration, (together with Professor M. Maresceau, Universiteit Gent and Professor M. Dony, Brussels Free University) (twice renewed)

1995-1999, Member, Curatorium de l'Institut Universitaire International Luxembourg

1995-2003, Member, Board of directors and Executive Committee, College of Europe

1994-1996, Executive Director, Association internationale pour l'étude de l'intégration européenne, Responsible for the Organization on behalf of the European Commission of a month-long programme of European Studies at the Colegio de Mexico destined to Latin American graduates and civil servants. Also responsible for the organization of conferences in Lima and La Paz in October 1995

1992, Co-director, Seminar "Legal and economic aspects of regional integration. The European experience", Colegio de Mexico, 25-29 May 1992 (ULB – ULg. – European Commission)

1991-1995, Member, Administrative Board, University of Liège

1987-1991, Co-chairman, Belgian Society for European Law

1990, External consultant, "Cellule de prospective", European Commission, (External relations in the environmental field, trade policy and investments)

1985-86, Chairman, Selection Boards A 408 et A 409 (Recruitment of lawyers), European Commission

Subjects Previously Taught (University of Liege and College of Europe)

1982-2006, European Economic Law

1979-2003, Economic Law in a Comparative Perspective (US Federal law and European Economic Law)

1993-2003, The External Dimension of the Single European Market

1991-2003, The Law of European Integration (course for economists)

1982-1989, Accounting for Lawyers – Introduction

1976-1990, International Economic Law

1981-1985, European Law and Intellectual Property

Languages

French: mother tongue

English: fluent

Dutch: oral and written

Spanish: passive knowledge

German: reading

Publications

A. Books and monographies

- Author

Concurrence et distribution en droit communautaire, Fasc. 510, Juris-Classeurs concurrence, Paris 1984, Editions techniques

Patents, Territorial Restrictions and EEC Law, "IIC Studies", Max-Planck Institute for Foreign and International Patent Copyright and Competition Law, Munich, Vol. 2, Verlag Chemie Weinheim-New York, 1978

- Editor

30 Years of European Legal Studies at the College of Europe (Liber Professorum 1973-74 – 2003-2004), PIE Peter Lang, Brussels 2005 (Co-eds. – I. Govaere & D. Hanf)

Regionalism and Multilateralism After the Uruguay Round: Convergence, Divergence and Interaction, Bruxelles, Presses Interuniversitaires Européennes, 1997, (Co-eds. J.F. Bellis & G. Garcia Jimenez), 862 p.

Trade and the Environment – The Search for a Balance, Cameron May, London 1994, Vol. 2 (Co-eds. J. Cameron & D. Géradin)

Trade laws of the European Community and the United States in a Comparative Perspective, College of Europe, Vol. 47, Story Scientia, 1992 (Co-ed. J. Bourgeois et I. Van Bael)

Relations extérieures de la Communauté européenne et marché intérieur: aspects juridiques et fonctionnels, Collège d'Europe, Vol. 45, Story-Scientia, 1988

"Aides et mesures de sauvegarde en droit international économique/Aids and Safeguard Measures in International Trade Law", Paris, FEDUCI, 1980 (XXXIIe Séminaire de la "Commission Droit et Vie des Affaires")

"Aspects juridiques de la recherche scientifique", Liège et Martinus Nijhoff, 1965 (XVe Séminaire de la "Commission Droit et Vie des Affaires")

B. Articles

L'accès au marché des services réglementés: la libéralisation du commerce des services dans le cadre du traité CE, in *Revue internationale de droit économique* 2002, No. 2-3, pp. 259-291.

Parallel Imports, Free Movement and Competition Rules: The European Experience and Perspective, (co-author Inge Govaere), in Th. Cottier & P. Mavroidis (eds.), *Intellectual Property: Trade Competition and Sustainable Development*, The World Trade Forum, Vol. 3, University of Michigan Press, 2002, pp. 147-175.

L'application du droit communautaire de la concurrence dans une économie globalisée. La problèmatique de l'extraterritorialité, in J.F. Bellis (ed.), *La politique communautaire de concurrence face à la mondialisation et à l'élargissement de l'Union européenne*, Session d'études 1999 de l'Institut universitaire international Luxembourg, Vol. 32, Nomos Verlag, 2001, pp. 13-52.

The TRIPs Agreement: A Response to Global Regulatory Competition or an Exercise in Global Regulatory Coercion? (coauthor I. Govaere), Yale conference of 21-22 October 1999, in D. Esty & D. Géradin (eds.), *Regulatory Competition and Economic Integration: Comparative Perspectives*, Oxford University Press, 2001, pp. 368-385.

The Respective Powers of the European Community and Member States in the External Relations of the European Union (with particular reference to Transatlantic Relations), in G. Bermann (ed.), *Transatlantic Regulatory Cooperation*, Columbia conference, 17-18 April 1999, Oxford University Press, 2000, pp. 431-449.

The Non-Discrimination Principle and the Removal of Fiscal Barriers to Intra-Community Trade in Th. Cottier & P. Mavroidis (eds.), *Regulatory Barriers and the Principle of Non-Discrimination, World Trade Law*, The World Trade Forum, Vol. 2, University of Michigan Press, 2000, pp. 171-190.

Politique extérieure de la Communauté européenne (ou la face communautaire de la politique extérieure de l'Union européenne), in *Droit et politique étrangère*, Conseil de l'Europe, Commission européenne pour la démocratie par le droit (Commission de Venise), 1998, pp. 149-177.

The Reciprocal Influence of Multilateral and Regional Rules: A Framework of Analysis, in *Regionalism and Multilateralism* (*supra*), 1997, pp. 805-838.

Le juge et le jugement dans l'Europe d'aujourd'hui: la Cour de justice des Communautés européennes, in R. Jacob (ed.), *Le juge et le jugement dans les traditions juridiques européennes*, L.G.D.J., Paris 1996, pp. 307-380.

A Short Walk in the Realm of Subsidiarity, in R.M. Buxbaum, G. Hertig, A. Hirsch, K.J. Hopt (eds.), *European Economic and Business Law (1996)*, Vitznau Conference, Institut d'études juridiques européennes, Université de Genève, 1996, pp. 13-31.

The Working of E.C. Policies on Competition, Industry and Trade: A Legal Analysis, in P. Buygues, A. Jacquemin & A. Sapir (eds.), *E.C. Policies on*

Competition, Industry and Trade: Complementarities and Conflicts, Edward Elgar, Publishing Ltd, 1995, pp. 65-114.

Les métamorphoses du GATT: de la Charte de La Havanne à l'OMC, in *Journal des Tribunaux Droit européen*, 1994, pp. 121-134 et pp. 174-178, English version, The Metamorphoses of the GATT: From the Havana Charter to the World Trade Organization, 34 *Columbia Journal of Transnational Law*, 1995, No. 1, pp. 123-171.

Border Tax Adjustments under GATT and EC Law and General Implications for Environmental Taxes, in 28 *Journal of World Trade*, 1994, No. 2, pp. 5-65 (co-author R. Stewardson).

L'égalité de traitement, in "1993, le marché unique et l'Europe des personnes", *Actualités du droit*, 1994, No. 2, pp. 165-209.

TREM's, Multilateralism, Unilateralism and the GATT, in J. Cameron, P. Demaret & D. Géradin (eds.), *Trade and the Environment – The Search for a Balance*, Cameron May, London, 1994, Vol. I, pp. 52-68.

The Emergence of Trade-Related Environmental Measures (TREMs) in the External Relations of the European Community, in M. Maresceau (ed.), *The European Community's Commercial Policy After 1992: The Legal Dimension*, Martinus Nijhoff, 1993, pp. 305-386.

El establecimiento del mercado unico europeo. Aspectos internos y externos, in *Foro Internacional (Revista Trimestral publicada por el Colegio de Mexico)*, 1993, Vol. XXXIII, num. 2, pp. 221-274, Hungarian version "As Egyseges Europai Piac megtermtésének belsö es külso összefüggései" in "A Magyar-EK Tarsulasi Megallapodas végrehajtasa; jogi és szabalyozasi Kérdések" c. projekt anyagai, 1. füzet, Omikk, Budapest, 1993, pp. 11-49.

The Treaty Framework, in *Legal Issues of the Maastricht Treaty*, D. O'Keeffe and P.M. Twomey (eds.), London 1993, pp. 3-11, French version, Le traité de Maastricht ou les voies diverses de l'Union, in *The Maastricht Treaty on European Union, Legal Complexity and Political Dynamic*, J. Monar, W. Ungerer and W. Wessels (eds.), Bruges, 1993, pp. 37-48.

Marché unique – Significations multiples, *Journ. Trib.*, 1992, pp. 137-141 (co-author F. Dehousse).

Le droit européen et la propriété intellectuelle, in *La protection de la propriété intellectuelle: aspects juridiques européens et internationaux*, Institut universitaire international Luxembourg, 1990, pp. 83-96.

Les droits de propriété intellectuelle et la circulation des marchandises et des services, *ibid.*, pp. 97-130.

Les exceptions à la libre circulation des diplômés: les articles 48 § 3, 55 et 48 § 4 du Traité CEE, in El mercat interior i les professions liberales, VI Jornades Europeas de Pasqua, Barcelona 1989.

La politique commerciale: perspectives d'évolution et faiblesses présentes, in Schwarze und Schermers (eds.), *Structures and Dimensions of European Community Policy*, Nomos Verlag, 1988, pp. 69-110

Industrial Property Rights, Compulsory Licences and the Free Movement of Goods under Community Law, 16 *International Review of Industrial Property and Copyright Law*, (IIC), 1987, pp. 161-191, German version, Patent-und Urheberrechtsschutz Zwangslizenzen und freier Warenverkehr im Gemeinschaftsrecht, GRUR Int. 1987, pp. 1-14.

Les affirmations américaines de compétence extraterritoriale, in *L'application extraterritoriale du droit économique*, Centre de droit international de Nanterre, 1987, pp. 41-50, 87-88, 100-101.

Selective Distribution and EEC Law after the Ford, Pronuptia and Metro II Judgments, in 1986 FORDHAM CORP. L. INST., B. Hawk (ed.), *United States and Common Market Antitrust Policies*, 1987, pp. 149-184.

Le régime des échanges internes et externes de la Communauté à la lumière des notions d'union douanière et de zone de libre-échange, in Capotorti *et al.* (ed.), *Du droit international au droit de l'intégration, Liber Amicorum Pierre Pescatore*, Nomos Verlag, 1987, pp. 139-165.

The EEC Rules Governing State Aids to Enterprises, in Madl (ed.), *Legal Structures of the Enterprise*, Budapest 1986, Vol. 1, pp. 183-208.

L'arrêt Pronuptia et les contrats de franchise en droit européen de la concurrence: innovation et tradition, J.C.P., ed. Entreprises, 1986, II, 14816.

The Extraterritoriality Issue in the Transatlantic Context: A Question of Law or Diplomacy? in Tsoukalis (ed.), *Euro-American Relations and Global Economic Interdependence*, Blackwell 1986, pp. 124-148.

L'extraterritorialité des lois dans les relations transatlantiques: une question de droit ou de diplomatie?, *Revue Trimestrielle de droit européen*, 1985, 1-39 (enlarged French version of the previous article)

L'Europe et les moyens de communication, Rapport belge, 32 p., in Vol. 1, *Europe and the Media*, 11e Congrès FIDE, La Haye, 1984 (co-author P. Lewalle).

Mesures nationales d'ordre public et circulation des personnes entre Etats membres – A propos de l'arrêt Adoui, *Cahiers de droit européen*, 1983, pp. 261-303 (co-author B. Ernst de la Graete).

L'utilisation de la propriété industrielle comme cartel clandestin, in *Rapports belges au XIe Congrès de l'Académie internationale de droit comparé*, 1982, pp. 509-526.

L'état du droit européen des ententes et des positions dominantes, in *Concurrence et distribution*, Montpellier 1981, pp. 93-120.

"Les répercussions de la crise économique sur l'organisation du commerce international", in *Aides et mesures de sauvegarde en droit international économique*, cited *supra*, 1980, pp. 6-16.

Compulsory Working of Patents in the EEC: Past, Present and Future, 13 *Les Nouvelles (Journal of the Licensing Executive Society)*, 1978, pp. 102-106.

L'application de l'article 85 du Traité de Rome aux contrats de propriété industrielle, in *L'incidence du droit communautaire de la concurrence sur le droit de propriété industrielle*, Lyon, 1977, pp. 89-105 (co-author R. Joliet).

Le brevet communautaire après Centrafarm: un instrument dépassé ou inachevé?, *Revue Trimestrielle de droit européen*, 1977, pp. 1-52.

The European and Common Market Patent Conventions, in "The Law of the European Economic Community", Smit & Herzog (ed.), (Columbia Law School Project on European Institutions), New York, 1976 et 1977.

Circulation des produits et loi uniforme Benelux sur les marques, *Revue Trimestrielle de droit européen*, 1972, pp. 523-557.

Justification et problèmes d'élaboration d'un droit européen des brevets, *Revue Trimestrielle de droit européen*, 1970, pp. 215-271.

La condition des auteurs étrangers en Belgique, Annales de la Faculté de droit de Liège, 1968, pp. 39-61.

Techniques modernes de reproduction graphique et droit d'auteur, *Revue de droit intellectuel "L'ingénieur-Conseil"*, 1968, pp. 302-318, and 1969, pp. 1-33.

La forme juridique des sociétés de recherche sous contrat, *Revue Trimestrielle de droit commercial*, 1967, pp. 719-742.

Analyse de quelques contrats de recherche, in *Aspects juridiques de la recherche scientifique*, cité *supra*, pp. 59-114.

C. Short Notes and Miscellaneous Works

Les études juridiques au Collège d'Europe (Bruges), in *30 Years of European Legal Studies at the College of Europe*, PIE Peter lang, Brussels 2005, pp. 15-26.

Introduction. Quelques observations sur la signification de l'arrêt "Bosman", in *Revue du Marché unique européen*, A. Mattera (ed.), 1996, pp. 11-15.

General Report, Committee II (GATS, Financial Services, Audiovisual Sector, TRIM4s), in Bourgeois, Berrod & Gippini Fournier (eds.), "The Uruguay Round Results: A European Lawyers' Perspective", European Interuniversity Press, Brussels, 1995, pp. 493-499.

La Communauté de 1958 à l'Acte unique Bilan, promesses et limites, in "Devenez Européens", Liège 1989, pp. 15-38.

Introduction à "L'avenir institutionnel des Communautés", Annales de Droit de Liège, 1984, pp. 271-273.

Book Review, B. Günzel, Territorial beschränkte Lizenzen bei parallelen Patenten im Gemeinsamen Markt, in 12 IIC, 1978, pp. 740-742.

Note pratique, Article 85 et licences: inventaire des clauses examinées par la Commission, Droit et Pratique du Commerce international, 1977, pp. 369-375.

Tableaux analytiques de la jurisprudence relative à la loi uniforme Benelux sur les marques de produits: 1971-1976, *Revue de droit intellectuel "L'ingénieur-Conseil"*, 1976, pp. 403-439 (co-author M. Sequaris-Deliège).

D. Main Unpublished Reports and Speeches

Václav Havel, Patron of the Academic Year 2012-2013, College of Europe, 17 October 2012.

Marie Curie, Patron of the Academic Year 2011-2012, College of Europe, 26 October 2011.

Albert Einstein, Patron of the Academic Year 2010-2011, College of Europe, 2 November 2010.

Charles Darwin, Patron of the Academic Year 2009-2010, College of Europe, 4 November 2009.

Marcus Aurelius, Patron of the Academic Year 2008-2009, College of Europe, 18 November 2008.

Anna Politkovskaja/Hrant Dink, Patrons of the Academic Year 2007-2008, 15 November 2007.

Esprit fondateur des Communautés européennes, Bilan après cinquante ans, enseignements pour le futur, Consell Català del Moviment Europeu, Catalan Parliament, Barcelona, 29 January 2007.

Copernicus, Patron of the Academic Year 2006-2007, College of Europe, 30 October 2006.

The European Union and its Role in the World, Kokkalis Foundation, Athens, 30 March 2006.

The Role of the European Union as a Global Actor, University Sains Malaysia, Penang, 22 February 2006.

Ludwig van Beethoven, Patron of the Academic Year 2005-2006, College of Europe, 19 October 2005.

Le Traité constitutionnel: vraie constitution ou simple révision des traités? Centro de Estudios internacionales, Barcelona, 19 January 2005.

Montesquieu, Patron of the Academic Year 2004-2005, College of Europe, 23 November 2004.

Challenges Facing European Integration in 2004: Enlargement and the Draft Constitution, University of Waseda (Tokyo) and University of Kobe, March 2004.

John Locke, Patron of the Academic Year 2003-2004, College of Europe, 1 December 2003.

European Integration in 2003: Successes and Challenges Ahead, Congreso Bienal, Organización Universitaria Americana, Universidad Veracruzana, Veracruz, Mexico, 10 November 2003.

The Draft Constitutional Treaty, International Conference "The European Constitution – A Vision for Europe", Budapest, Hungarian Parliament, 28 October 2003.

The External Relations of the European Union on the Eve of Enlargement, Columbia Law School Reunion, Paris, 28 June 2003.

The Agreement on Trade-Related Aspects of Intellectual Property Rights (TRIPS), International Conference on WTO and Legal Services, Bejing, 19 September 2002.

GRAN-MERCOSUR: A European Perspective, Report for the "Junta de Cartagena", Lima, 1997.

Environmental Taxes and Border Tax Adjustments, Report for the O.E.C.D. (Co-author R. Stewardson), 1994.

La Communauté et la protection de l'environnement sur le plan international, Report for the European Commission, 1990, (co-author F. Dehousse).

Le droit de l'intégration européenne et la protection de l'environnement, Inaugural address, University of Liège, 1 October 1990.

La question de la réparation par les Etats membres des dommages causés aux particuliers par une violation de l'article 30 au regard du droit communautaire, Report for the European Commission, 1987.

Le traité de Rome et la circulation des marchandises, European Law Session, Liège Bar, 22-23 April, 1983.

Examen de la compatibilité de la législation et de la réglementation belge avec la directive 79/409/CEE relative à la conservation des oiseaux, Report for the ICBP and the European Commission, 1982.

La clause d'exclusivité et la clause territoriale, in "L'évolution des contrats de transfert de technologie", C.D.V.A., Liège, 5 May 1977.

Non-Academic Activities

A. In the legal field (before February 2003)

Occasional consultant (licensing contracts, European competition law, State aids, internal market, EC external relations, GATT /WTO law)

President of an international arbitral tribunal in a case opposing a State and a foreign business firm (1996-1997)

B. In the environmental field

Member of the board, Domaine de Virelles (Aves-R.N.O.B. – W.W.F.), (1983-1995)

Member, Conseil consultatif de gestion, Réserves domaniales du Plateau des Tailles (since 1986)

Member of the board, (1978 to 1985) and later chairman (1990-1995), Aves a.s.b.l. (Ornithological society)

Co-author of "Pollution Wallonie", survey made on behalf of the Walloon Region (1978)

Author of articles on birds

C. In the political field

Member of the International Advisory Board for Bulgaria set up by the Prime Minister of Bulgaria in order to advise the Government of Bulgaria concerning its relations with the European Union (2008-2009)

I

L'enseignement/On Education

On Transnational Education

Some Options and Questions

Jan De Groof

Professor at the University of Tilburg,
Government Commissioner for Universities
(Belgium, Flemish Community)

1. The development of the concept of transnationality is not the first attempt ever made to break though the boundaries set by the practice of using the nation to justify political power. The classic approach may be seen in the international law concept of internationality. However, internationality presupposes the nation; after all, it refers to the relations between nations. The concept transnationality goes much further; it means in effect abandoning the concept of the nation. Yet "*trans*" means, first and foremost, nothing more than "*beyond*", and 'transnational' must therefore be understood to mean "beyond the national".[1]

The concept of national sovereignty will acquire a fundamentally different meaning:

> Recent thinking revises earlier distinctions based on legal ownership and challenges the notion that the "public good" can be defined on a national basis. It focuses on the social character of the "goods" whether public or private. It argues that higher education in one nation has the potential to create positive and negative externalities in another; and all higher education systems and institutions can benefit from collective systems e.g. that facilitate cross-border recognition and mobility.[2]

Under "transnational education" is understood all types of higher education study programmes, or sets of courses of study, or educational services including those of distance education in which the learners are

---

1. Richter I., Berking S. and Müller-Schmid, R., Introduction, Richter I., Berking S. and Müller-Schmid, R. (eds.), *Building a Transnational Civil Society. Global Issues and Global Actions*, Palgrave, 2006, pp. 8-9.
2. Margison S., "The Public/Private divide in Higher Education: A Global Revision", *Higher Education*, Vol. 53, No. 3, 2007, pp. 307-333.

located in a country different from the one where the awarding institution is based. In the case of transnational education, an educational institution or the programme may belong to the national education system of another country, or it may be independent of any national system, which has consequences on the legal aspects of the recognition of qualifications granted under such programmes.

In the "*Education & Training 2010*" work programme, transnational learning in other Member States is becoming an essential component. In 2003 a set of policy recommendations on access to mobility, quality in mobility and the opening up of Europe to the wider world was prepared by the Commission. A second recommendation of the European Parliament and the Council in 2005 on transnational mobility within the EU for education and training purposes is in progress. The recommendation invites the Member States to adopt the "European Quality Charter for mobility". The charter lays down a set of principles in the field of mobility for education and training purposes to be implemented by the Member States on a voluntary basis. The Charter is intended to become a reference instrument to help increase exchanges, develop the recognition of study periods spent in other countries and establish mutual trust between authorities, organisations and all mobility stakeholders concerned.

A study produced by the Academic Cooperation Association on behalf of the European Commission in July 2008 named: *Transnational education in the European context – provision, approaches and policies*, stipulated:

> For the moment, transnational education has not made it to the core of the internationalisation debate in Europe: little attention is given to its potential or impact in either the Bologna Process or the Education and Training 2010 programme of the European Commission. However, transnational education should be seen as an integral part of the European higher education offer, and a central tool for the achievement of several common objectives: internationalisation, research cooperation, brain gain and access.[3]

2. The rise of transnational education is closely linked to the new possibilities offered by information and communication technologies or for-profit companies. It responds to a demand for higher education to which the national system does not respond, e.g.: a kind of programme that does not exist in the national system, the national system is elite higher education that excludes the participation of qualified applicants, the national system does not provide HE in minority languages or has restrictions on access for specific groups (e.g. women).

---

3 http://ec.europa.eu/education/erasmus-mundus/doc/studies/tnesum_en.pdf.

In the case of student mobility, students move to study in another country and return with their credentials that are obtained in another country. The recognition of the qualifications falls under the *Lisbon Convention*. The *Lisbon Recognition Convention* is an agreement between States that covers qualifications issued by national higher education systems.

In the case of transnational education, the students do not move – they study in their home country or even at home – but the credentials are awarded in the name of a foreign institution. In is not the student but the diploma that "travels" across the borderline.

3. What Is the Main Agenda, Dealing with Legal Issues?[4]

A. Joint Programmes

Joint programmes such as programme twinning, joint or double degrees, are the result of co-operation among higher education institutions in different countries. If both higher education institutions and/or the programmes are recognised in their own countries, this kind of transnational education should not lead to too many problems.

B. Branch Campus

When higher education institutions establish branch campuses in other countries and the mother institution is a recognised institution in its own country, the questions arise whether the recognition/accreditation of the mother institution can be transferred to the branch, which quality assurance bodies check the quality of the mother institution, and the branch, in what way is it ensured that quality is the same as in mother institution, are the programmes in the branch campus identical to the ones in the mother institution or adapted to the needs of the receiving country, if the programmes are adapted to the needs of host country, are they still the same degrees/qualifications as in the sending country, is the teaching staff in the mother institution and in the branch campus the same, is it a professor of the mother institution visiting branch campus or is education provided by a well trained local who teaches the branch campus, if it is a well-trained local, is it guaranteed that the students feel the culture of the foreign institution in whose name the qualification will be awarded, what quality of education is ensured if the person teaching is an external?

---

4 A review on the literature shows the minor interest to legal issues: VLK, A., *Higher Education and GATS. Regulatory Consequences and Stakeholders' Responses*, Enschede, CHEPS, 2006; see also De Groof J., Lauwers G. and Dondelinger G., *Globalisation and Competition in Education*, Nijmegen, Wolf Legal Publishers, 2003.

C. Franchised Programmes

In the case of franchising, the foreign institution allows some institution in the receiving country to deliver its programmes and award qualifications in the name of the foreign sending institution. The franchisee can be a recognised or a non-recognized higher education institution of the host country, a non-higher education institution, a company running courses or established with the purpose to run franchised programmes.

The same questions asked about a branch of a foreign institution are also valid for franchising. Additional questions are whether the franchised programmes are provided in compliance with the laws of the receiving country and of the sending country, is there any quality check at all from the side of the sending country, do the authorities of the receiving country have enough reliable information to judge about the quality of the franchised programmes, do the students studying in a franchised programme get any impression about the culture and education system of the sending country at all, if provided in the language of the receiving country, do the programmes still resemble the equally named programmes in the sending country.

D. Offshore Institutions

Offshore institutions do not have a mother institution in the country, they claim to belong to. In the case of offshore institutions it is unclear to which education system it belongs to.

E. International Institutions

International institutions do not belong to the education system of any particular country and no particular country is responsible for the quality of education provided. As a result, qualifications awarded by international institutions are not recognised within the framework of the Lisbon Recognition Convention.

F. Distance Education

Recognition of a credential awarded through distance education by a foreign institution requires answers to the same questions as in the case of a branch campus or offshore institution such as: are the students at the end familiar enough with the traditions of awarding institution, if the programme is adapted to the receiving country's needs, does it still resemble the same programme provided in the sending country, is there an evidence that the awarding institution fully controls the quality of provision, etc.

4. Transnational arrangements should be so elaborated, enforced and monitored as to comply with the national legislation regarding higher education in both receiving and sending countries. Whenever possible, there should be written and legally binding agreements or contracts setting out the rights and obligations of all partners.

Academic quality and standards of transnational education programmes should be comparable to those of the awarding institution as well as to those of the receiving country. Awarding institutions as well as the providing institutions are fully responsible for quality assurance and control based on specific criteria, which are transparent, systematic and open to scrutiny.

Information given by the awarding institution, providing organization, to students should be consistent and reliable. The nature of a collaborative arrangement and the responsibilities of the parties should be clearly outlined.

The admission of students, the examination and assessment requirements for educational services for transnational education should be equivalent to those of the same or comparable programmes delivered by the awarding institution. The academic workload in transnational study programmes should be that of comparable programmes in the awarding institution.

If transnational programmes comply with the provisions of the legal framework, the qualifications issued through transnational education should be assessed in accordance with the stipulations of the *Lisbon Recognition Convention*.[5]

5. Could the adoption of the Regulation establishing "*The European Grouping of Territorial Cooperation – EGTC*" in July 2006 cause a major change in the legal framework for territorial cooperation?[6]

---

5 See also: De Groof J., "European Higher Education in Search of a New Legal Order", in B.M. Kehm, J. Huisman and B. Stensaker, *The European Higher Education Area: Perspectives on a Moving Target*, Rotterdam, Sense, 2009, pp. 79-104.

6 Regulation (EC) No. 1082/2006 of the European Parliament and of the Council of 5 July 2006 on a European grouping of territorial cooperation (EGTC), *Official Journal of the European Union*, L 210, pp. 19-24; Report from the Commission to the European Parliament and the Council, The application of the Regulation (EC) No. 1082/2006 on a European Grouping of Territorial Cooperation (EGTC), COM(2011)462 final, dd. 29-07-2011; Proposal for a regulation of the European Parliament and of the Council amending Regulation (EC) No. 1082/2006 of the European Parliament and of the Council of 5 July 2006 on a European grouping of territorial cooperation (EGTC) as regards the clarification, simplification and improvement of the establishment and implementation of such groupings, COM(2011)610 final, dd. 6-10-2011.

The Regulation was the first EU instrument with regulatory scope in the field. It focused on cooperation between authorities located in different European states. It allows for possible involvement of states, alongside local and regional authorities and territorial cooperation entities with their own legal personality.

In recent decades, there has been a rapid internationalisation in European higher education and research. An international market for higher education and research is developing in which universities compete to attract students, researchers and the scant resources for research. Besides this international competition – for various reasons – there is also an increasing need for international collaboration. With regard to research, scale is becoming an important factor in the competition for research projects and funds. Within the framework of the *Bologna process*, collaboration in the field of education has moved up a gear.

The way in which universities give shape to this collaboration has many modalities. Institutes collaborate at many levels and to varying degrees. There are also more and more collaborative links between universities from different countries. Although the introduction of collaboration regarding the Bachelor-Master-PhD structure in Europe (between programmes) does facilitate this to a certain extent, there are still many obstacles to collaboration. *Transnational collaboration cannot always develop optimally in education and research due to restrictions on collaborative arrangements*. These obstacles relate to matters such as student registration, programme accreditation/quality assessment, the length of the programme, the award of diplomas, the recognition of academic and professional qualifications, social security and student loans of grants.

Universities hoping to become leading institutions for education and research in Europe in the coming years will have to rely on international collaboration, for example in consortiums. The obstacles they meet on their way must be removed. Universities themselves have some control over this, particularly with regard to the removal of internal obstacles. There are, however, also restrictions that cannot be influenced (or only with difficulty) by either individual institutions or in collaboration with other institutions. Such (sometimes insoluble) problems for collaboration are caused by differences in national legal frameworks.

A specific factor in the creation of collaborative arrangements is geographical distance. It is easier to finance and share facilities such as education and student facilities when institutions are relatively close to each other. It also means that programmes can be offered and supplemented, even if there is no critical mass in an individual institution. This is why governments encourage *cross-border collaboration*. Until 2000, for example, the Dutch and Belgian (Flemish) governments actively stimulated transnational collaboration with the "*Grenslandenbeleid*" ("Border Lands policy"). The 2001 evaluation of this policy showed that measures aimed at internationalisation in the border lands or in *Euregions* can have a different character from internationalisation over longer distances; according to the respondents from the evaluation, both forms have their own right to exist. As regards cross-border collaboration, shorter distances and (with Flanders) the language similarity are important factors. They reduce the transaction costs of collaboration projects and student and teacher mobility compared with more distant internationalisation partners. More frequent exchange or closer collaboration is therefore possible in border areas.

6. The "*transnational Universiteit Limburg*" was created in order to take an important step in collaboration. This university (*tUL*) is a unique collaborative arrangement between *Universiteit Maastricht* (UM) and *Universiteit Hasselt* (UHasselt, Hasselt/Diepenbeek, formerly "Limburgs Universitair Centrum"). The *tUL* can be considered as one university with a base in two countries, providing an interesting example of transnational collaboration and of internationalisation and regional collaboration in higher education and research in Europe. One university conglomerate combines research and education – especially in the field of life sciences, law and ICT – on two campuses in two different Member States. UM and UHasselt invest resources and complementarity of mutual expertise in the *tUL* to start new programmes and research lines.

Combining the strengths of the two universities with regard to education and research capacity not only adds value to the quality of education and research, but also to the effectiveness of investment of resources by the two institutions. However, operating within two different legal systems creates specific problems, a fact that was also recognised at the start of *tUL* and the drawing up of the *tUL* Convention between the Netherlands and Flanders. Partly for this reason, an evaluation provision was incorporated in the *tUL* Convention. Pursuant to Article II of the *Convention between the Kingdom of the Netherlands and the Flemish Community of Belgium regarding "transnationale Universiteit Limburg"*,[7] the governments of the parties to the Convention appointed a Joint Committee whose task was to evaluate the operation of the Convention. This should have taken place five years after the implementation of the Convention, i.e. in January 2006. Although the evaluation – as confirmed by both governments – stressed the unique opportunities and the concrete progress made within the *tUL* framework, not all

7 Signed in Maastricht (The Netherlands) on 18 January 2001.

areas had the benefit of long experience, for example, the research resources.

But the *tUL "experiment"* revealed that several crucial questions could not get relevant answers. What interesting collaborative arrangements currently exist, what are their goals, what problems do they encounter and what can their potential be for the *tUL* with regard to the optimisation of education and research? *The aggregated question is what obstacles exist for the creation of international collaboration*? This is further operationalised and developed into collaboration at institutional level and at programme level. Where possible, a bottom-up approach should be proposed.

Instead of binding tUL and similar institutions to national regulations, a research project, decided by both governments, should study what instruments should be used to promote the achievement of the collaboration objectives.

Both universities, UM and UHasselt, committed themselves to a research project with formal support of both governments.

The aim will then be to produce recommendations that are important to European higher education as a whole. This also makes the project interesting to other institutions and countries. What kind of collaboration would offer a solution to the problems identified? Experiences with tUL should provide the necessary information, but there are also other collaborative arrangements in Europe that could provide an important contribution. In France, for example, there are various collaborative arrangements with neighbouring countries (including the French-Netherlands, the French-Italian and the French-German University) and Germany works together with Poland in Frankfurt an der Oder. Remember too the collaboration that has been achieved in multilateral European context with the European University Institute in Florence.

7. Based on these findings, recommendations can be formulated that result in a framework for transnational collaboration. This framework – or "Statute" – should study the relationships between the legal systems and the position of this kind of collaboration. It might also be possible to include joint education programmes (and perhaps even joint degrees, which often have a very complex position in national legislation). This would allow the Statute to be used by other institutions striving for far-reaching collaboration or even a (partial) merger. The "Statute" can thus act as a boost for internationalisation and transnational university collaboration, eventually strengthening the regional and Euregional imbedding of higher education and research in Europe.

Such a structure also makes the project interesting for parties like the European Commission, the Council of Europe and the European University Association. In consultation with the national governments, the research will be brought to the attention of the Committee, focussing on the strengths and weaknesses of the *European Grouping of Territorial Cooperation* as a concrete vehicle for transnational cooperation in the domain of higher education and research.

The research must not only focus on an evaluation of the past and offer a clear analysis of the problems; it seemed also important that the findings are translated into solutions and concrete recommendations, perhaps also with regard to the *tUL Convention*.

The critical findings of this report ought to lead also to a review of the EGTC Regulation. Opportunities for trans-border university cooperation would be strengthened if the practical consequences of such a rethinking will be put on the agenda in the short term by all concerned authorities.

8. An "official" review of the EGTC Regulation has already been a joint initiative of the Committee of the Regions, the Trio of Presidencies of the Council of the European Union (Spain-Belgium-Hungary), the European Commission and the INTERACT programme. The consultation focuses mainly on the legislative aspects that should be improved or modified for the next revision, and also considers the added value and potentialities of this legal instrument.

The principal legal issue concerns the differences in the legislation of the individual Member States. In particular, this relates to the diverse legal status of existing EGTCs, which stem from the divergent decisions taken by Member States as part of the national implementation process, as permitted under the Regulation. Difficulties have also been reported with defining the content of conventions and statutes as well as their approval procedures. In general, there is a need to simplify procedures. Information, communication and technical assistance are also needed at European and national level. Respondents are in favour of a European structure and support the networking, communication and support carried out by the Committee of the Regions.

The issue of third country participation reveals a stark difference between the position of the Member States, which believe that the participation of third countries should be limited, and that of the other stakeholders (EGTCs, LRAs, Associations and experts) who are in favour of revising the present rule and introducing less stringent provisions.

The conclusions of this review are very positive about EGTCs acting as a managing authority and joint technical secretariat, as this embodies the principle of subsidiarity. Some national authorities are reluctant to delegate programme management. There are many advantages to using

EGTCs to implement European Territorial Cooperation (ETC) projects; the main problem, however, concerns EGTC eligibility.

The overall research consider the EGTC to be the EU's main legal instrument for territorial cohesion. It is also a laboratory for multi-level governance,[8] creating a two-tier communication channel and acting via a bottom-up approach. It may act as facilitators in solving various border issues.

---

8 De Groof J., "Multi-level Governance in the EU and the role of CoR", at the Round Table on Multi-Level Governance, European Training Foundation (ETF), Torino (Italy).

Teaching Environmental Law in Europe

A Luxury?

Ludwig KRÄMER

Former Head of the Legal Unit of DG Environment, European Commission; Visiting Professor University College London

When Paul Demaret served and lectured at the College of Europe, he decided that the College should also offer a course on European and international environmental law. Thus, he might find some interest in these lines which try to plead for a strengthened role of environmental law in the legal teaching in the European Union.

Historically, environmental law teaching shared the development of environmental policy in Europe. While water management and nature protection policy and law had a relatively long history, due to their neighbourhood to economic development and agriculture/land use in general, other aspects of environmental concern such as air pollution, noise impairment or waste management only came gradually into the focus of policy makers, and a coherent view that there was a policy topic such as "environment" was building up not earlier than in the 1960s. From there it might not be exaggerated to consider the publication of Rachel Carson's book on "The Silent Spring" (1962) as the birthday of environmental concerns of the public, policy makers, journalists and academics.

Academic teaching of environmental law started at the end of the 1960s or in the beginning of the 1970s at several universities in Europe, again with a strong emphasis on nature protection and water law. Several factors contributed to this development, in particular: the creation of ministries for the environment, environmental agencies and other administrative structures at national or regional level in several European countries; the emergence of EU environmental legislation which required concertation at this level and common planning of environmental policies; the growing awareness of the public of environmental problems (nuclear concerns, petrol accidents, waste management scandals, *Waldsterben*); and the beginning of discussions on globalization (tropical forests, human rights of indigenous people, post-colonization and the misery of developing policy). Environmental law teachers very quickly discovered the immense broadness of the subject and enlarged their classes by more or less all facets of environmental law. At the same time, the number of universities and other academic institutions which offered courses in environmental law increased rapidly and spread to all Western European countries. In the countries under the influence of Soviet Union, this evolution went at a much slower pace, since the State and State-owned companies were the biggest polluters and it was, for ideological reasons, not possible or not opportune to address environmental concerns and the imperfections of environmental law too openly.

Environmental law courses were offered on an optional basis: the students could choose such courses, but were not obliged to do so. This was, of course, different where environmental law was taught as part of public or administrative law, as these topics were compulsory in all universities. However, normally environmental law was not subject of (final) examination of students and whether students opted for participating in classes on environmental law, remained their choice. And this situation has not changed until today, 2013. With very few exceptions (Finland, Estonia and some individual universities or other academic institutions in some countries), environmental law is optional but is not part of the topic which a law student needs to know, when he leaves the *alma mater*.

It is submitted that this is no longer up to date, not even under the Bologna straitjacket which intends to streamline academic lawyers into smoother legal managers for economic purposes. I see good reasons for making courses on environmental law compulsory. A young lawyer who has finished his legal education, should in any circumstance know at least the basic elements of environmental law and policy, whether he later goes into private business or public administration, whether he becomes an independent lawyer or whether he chooses an academic or yet another professional career. Institutions that train young lawyers should therefore revise their programmes and make environmental law courses compulsory for a successful study of the law. There are, in my view, a good number of reasons for changing the present, voluntary, approach.

1. Environmental Law deals with Fundamental Issues of State and Society

Environmental problems are omnipresent and influence political, administrative and private decisions every day more. The "big five" of environmental concern are – without this being a list of priorities.

Climate change. The warming up of this planet with its consequences on sea level rising, change of temperatures, food production and human migration, to name but a few, will have dramatic influences already on the life of the next two or three generations – thus our children and grandchildren. It will influence private housing, production and consumption, energy use and life in agglomerations and will therefore interfere with our daily life in unimagined dimensions. Knowledge about ways and means to fight climate change and to mitigate its effects appears elementary for a lawyer.

Loss of biodiversity. The disappearance of species of fauna and flora, caused by human activities, has reached a worrying speed. A planet that will host, within thirty to forty years, nine billion people, will see this development continue, with considerable economic and human consequences. Soil erosion and desertification are just the most obvious consequences, but one should also realize what a world without elephants, whales or tigers will mean for humans.

The omnipresence of chemicals. Chemicals are everywhere, in food and feed, in cosmetics and pharmaceuticals, in houses and outdoors. They have beneficial effects and create new risks for human, animal and plant health. Many undesirable side effects or cumulative effects provoke problems, and frequently persons are not sufficiently warned of risks linked to the use of chemicals. New technologies – nanotechnology, fracking – raise new problems, where first the chemicals are used and then their impact on human health and the environment is gradually discovered.

Resource management. The departure from fossil fuels, required by the fight against climate change, is but one of the numerous problems. Nine billion people will need food, shelter, energy, water and a decent way of living. Resources are limited, and waste generation and treatment, the recycling and a more efficient way of production and consumption will inevitably lead to new forms of resource management.

Poverty. While concern for the natural environment will have to remain great, it must not be forgotten that humans are in the centre of any environmental concern. Climate change and other environmental events led to predictions that within forty years there might be 200 to 250 million environmental migrants in the world; their destination will, first of all, be the rich countries. Pure egotistical considerations should thus lead policy-makers and lawyers to re-think the present post-mercantilistic development policy strategy and try to prevent migration by reducing the gap between rich and poor on this planet.

The protection of the environment includes, of course, the protection of humans. This brings the discussions on environmental law into close neighbourhood of human rights issues, in particular the right to life and to health of persons. Next to the above-mentioned over-arching concerns, there are more local concerns concerning water quantity and quality, air pollution, in particular in urban agglomerations, noise levels, waste management and the conservation of nature. These concerns are almost all linked to human health and safety rights; they are diversified enough to ensure that literally every lawyer will be confronted with such problems during his or her professional life.

2. The Originality of Environmental Law

Already these specific environmental concerns might raise the reflection, whether it is not appropriate to ensure that any lawyer has some basic knowledge about environmental issues and the legal problems which they raise. However, this is not all. Indeed, environmental law developed, during the some fifty years of its existence, a remarkable number of features which are specific to environmental law, but are not encountered in general administrative or public law:

A. Environmental Law tries to Protect an Interest without a Voice

Agricultural law is the law of farmers; fishery law is the law of fishermen; transport law of those who transport persons or goods or those, who are transported; industry law is the law of persons active in industrial undertakings; competition law the law of competitors, and energy the law of person who produce, supply and demand energy. In all these sectors there are powerful, well-organized vested interest groups, which shape and influence the making of the provisions, lobby parliaments, governments, advisory and scientific bodies, campaign for changes of the rules, when these rules contradict their interests, and work on public opinion, in order to create a climate of law-making and law-application that is favourable to their interests – however these are defined.

There is no comparable social group behind environmental law. Environmental organizations – Greenpeace, Friends of the Earth, World Wildlife Foundation, etc. – are too scattered, too poor in human and financial resources and not numerous enough to be a factor in political elections, the main concern of politicians. Moreover, environmental organizations typically act altruistically, not for increasing their profit.

This is a marked difference to vested-interest groups and their bargaining power in discussions with administrations or policy. In power terms, thus, the environment is weak; this is why it needs the protection of the law. Social groups with power do not need the law that much, as they influence, shape and implement it themselves.

B. Environmental Law is Horizontal in Nature

The environment knows no national frontiers. The above-mentioned concerns are, in one way or the other, concerns that are encountered in any organized society. For this reason, legal instruments to help solving these problems, are very often similar in the different legal systems. European examples are:

- The huge number of international agreements concerning environmental issues which were developed over the last fifty years, and which reach into all environmental sectors, water and air, products and waste, noise and nature;
- environmental impact assessments which examine the effects of infrastructure or other projects on the environment, the search for alternatives and for minimizing negative effects, before the construction permit is granted and which since spread from the environmental sector to law-making in general and to other parts of policy-making;
- the development of transboundary water management structures, such as river basin management for international waters; common management of transnational rivers and of regional seas;
- the development of common networks for nature conservation, such as Natura 2000.

The horizontal character of environmental law has two other dimensions. First, environmental law is inter-generational. The environmental commonplace, that we did not inherit this planet from our parents, but borrowed it from our children and grandchildren, materializes more and more in the recognition that the effects of our present action must also be assessed with regard to their impact on future generations. The realization that the Via Appia in Italy, built some 2,300 years ago, impacted on the location of villages and cities and influenced the shaping of the Italian cultural landscape, might influence our considerations on the impact which the construction of a new motorway might have in the future. And the US and German policy on the location of nuclear waste disposals requires a site which is stable against seismic events, landslides and other events for one million years – knowing quite well the effect of nuclear energy production on future generations. Norbert Elias mentioned once that the unborn have no lobby and that future generations are not represented in today's discussions: the environmental lawyer could and should bring into discussions also such elements.

Also, environmental law is an integrated policy which is trans-sectoral. It impinges on almost all sectors of economic activity within countries, requires

– When policy-makers develop a strategy on *transport* issues, they are nowadays unable to do so without taking into considerations the environmental impact, such as noise, air pollution, impact on climate change, land use, etc.

– *Energy* policy planning will have to discuss the departure from fossil fuels, the role and importance of renewable sources of energy, the impact on climate change, the issues of transporting energy or electricity, the role of nuclear energy, waste issues, etc.

– *Agricultural* policy cannot properly be conceived, elaborated and implemented without taking into consideration the use of chemicals (pesticides and herbicides, fertilizers), the impact of biotechnology, land use, agriculture effects on water and groundwater, soil protection and nature conservation.

– *Fisheries* policy strategies will have to address the diminishing fish stocks, the impact of fishing methods on the marine environment, the protection of non-target species, third countries concerns and other issues.

– *Industrial* policy strategies need to address air, water and soil pollution, waste generation and handling, accident prevention, the location of industrial plants, climate change issues and corporate environmental responsibility, product-related issues such as eco-design or the use of dangerous materials (ozone-depleting substances, greenhouse gases, heavy metals, dangerous chemicals), and the use of energy and water during production and use.

– *Competition* policy will have to deal with environmental standards of competitors, State aid for environmental-friendly activities, or public procurement.

– *Development* policy will have to be aware of the global environmental problems mentioned above and likely to increase the population pressure on the industrialized countries. It will have to try to enable developing countries to ensure a future for their people and develop a sustainable policy which reduces the development distance to richer countries. This in turn has – better, should have – implications on the agricultural, fisheries or industrial policies of European countries. Indeed, neither Europeans nor Americans have as yet any strategy how to prevent the genesis of some 200 million environmental migrants which scientists expect by 2050.

– *Trade* policy strategies need to recognize that a policy which consists in claiming that each euro invested in the third world should bring a profit of three euros just has no future and needs replacement by a better-balanced policy. Some twenty years ago, Paul Demaret discussed the importance of trade-related environmental matters, and these legal problems have not diminished in importance since then.

For a young lawyer, it is an added value, not to remain restrained in his or her national legal system, but to become aware of the concrete implications which the progressive globalization has and will have on daily practical work. Hardly any other sector of public law offers similar perspectives, while being connected to environmental civil law and environmental criminal law.

C. Environmental Law Has Specific Features

Environmental law in Europe generated, over the years, a considerable amount of original and rather unique features which are normally not encountered in other administrative law sectors. Among these features are:

– The fact that in all Member States of the European Union, national environmental law is derived, to 70-80 per cent on average from EU environmental law; in more than half of the 28 EU Member States, this figure is very close to 100 per cent (the thirteen countries which adhered since 2004; Greece, Portugal, Ireland, Spain, Italy, Luxemburg). National environmental law cannot be understood and taught without proper reference to EU environmental law.

– New economic technologies – nuclear technology, biotechnology, nanotechnology, carbon capture and storage, shale gas production and others – mainly raise human health and environmental problems which common administrative law does not full assess.

– The precautionary principle and the polluter-pays-principle are legal principles which were developed in environmental law and apply, at present, horizontally in several sectors of law.

– Emission limit values and concentration values – terminology differs – are specific instruments to assess and control pollution;

– Trade in greenhouse gas emission allowances introduced a new concept to administrative law in Europe.

– (Environmental) impact assessments for plans, programmes and projects were largely unknown in administrative law, until environmental law introduced these concepts.

– Access to information on the environment was constructed as a procedural human right and generated the political request in several

States that general access to information should be granted widely; environmental law stands for openness, transparency and accountability of public administration, principles which are and should be leading principles for any open society.

– Application of the regulatory provisions in practice is the most important legal problem, as the environmental protection rules are not applied by themselves, and administrative inertia all too often leaves the environment without protection. Unless practical application and enforcement of existing environmental provisions receive the necessary attention, environmental law risks sharing the fate with the ten commandments or other religious provisions: they are abundantly quoted in official speeches, but neglected, forgotten or despised in day-to-day life.

– As the environment is not the property of the administration, administrative acts – permitting, infrastructure planning, monitoring data, enforcement measures – need to be controlled by civil society forces. This requires information, participation and judicial procedural rights for citizens and environmental organizations, in order to protect the environment against administrative abuse.

The present trend in legal education undoubtedly goes towards a stronger accentuation of economic issues. Perhaps has the financial and economic crisis since 2008 demonstrated that economic profitability is not the miraculous solution to the numerous global problems. In October 1972, when the Heads of State and Government of the then EEC decided to set up a European environmental policy, they stated:

> Environmental expansion is not an end in itself. Its first aim should be to enable disparities in living conditions to be reduced. It must take place with the participation of all the social partners. It should result in an improvement in the quality of life as well as in standards of living. As befits the genius of Europe, particular attention will be given to intangible values and to protecting the environment, so that progress may really be put at the service of mankind.

These words keep their importance, even forty years later. They also might be useful, when academic institutions reflect on legal curricula and on the question whether environmental law teaching should not be made compulsory. Such a compulsory teaching of the most horizontal of all public law sectors would also be an acknowledgment of the fact that the environment can survive without humans, but humans cannot survive without the environment. This is illustrated by the comparison between the present financial crisis and climate change: we are able to overcome the financial crisis, but we will not be able to overcome climate change, once it has become a reality.

The objective of environmental law teaching is not the economic-oriented streamlined law-manager, but a democratic citizen, who is aware of the public interest and able to apply and promote the rule of law, in particular in favour of the weak; and who would doubt that the environment is a weak partner in our society?

A basic knowledge of environmental law should be in the luggage of any young lawyer in Europe, who enters into the legal profession. Compulsory environmental law teaching is not a luxury, but simply an adaptation to the legal, political and economic reality of the 21st century.

Teaching Law in Bruges

Ole LANDO

Professor Emeritus, Copenhagen Business School

From 1989 till 2000 I taught a course at the Legal Studies Department of the College of Europe. The subjects were first comparative contract law and later European private international law.

Paul Demaret was then head of the Department. He has a peculiar aptitude for inspiriting confidence among those who work with him. I was always looking forward to the meetings we had with him on organizing the teaching. They were pleasant and encouraging. It is partly due to him that teaching in Bruges was a pleasure. Another reason was the students. I have seldom taught students, who were more motivated than the law students of the College of Europe.

1. Teaching Law and Teaching Justice

What is the law? In order not to make it too complicated, you may use the famous definition of *Oliver Wendell Holmes*: *The prophesies of what the courts will do and nothing more pretentious are what I understand by law.*[1] There are professors, many of them in the Latin Countries, who instead teach their own ideas of what the law should be. They do the same in their writings.[2] Their doctrine is sometimes far away from the law as it is practiced by the courts, and which the professors, who are at the same time practicing lawyers, invoke when they plead their cases and advise their clients.

If you teach law, you must teach the students what the law is.

Prophesies of what the courts will do. Is that always the law? If in class you embark upon international commercial arbitration, this definition of law is not very accurate. Then you have to focus on the arbitrators. However, the prophesy of what the arbitrators will do is difficult to

1 "The Path of the Law", *Harvard Law Review*, Vol. 10, 1897, pp. 457f.

2 See on this habit David, R. & Jauffret-Spinosi, C., *Les grands systèmes de droit contemporains*, 11th ed., 2002, No. 111.

make. The only thing you can tell your students is that in international commercial arbitration, the arbitrators have to operate within the limits of different standards of public policy, but that they have an extensive freedom to do whatever they like. In many cases, they apply the law, but they often use their freedom to render awards that differ from what a court would do. That is not always bad. In some cases, they use their freedom to disregard law rules that are ancient relics of a dead past.

Should you also tell the students what you think that the law should be, teach them your conception of justice? That has been discussed. Some Nordic writers[3] have maintained that a scholar should not disclose his own attitude. He should state the various views and then let the reader or the audience take their stand. This attempt at objectivity is connected with the view that law and justice are based on value judgments that are neither false nor true. The legal science is not a science if it makes value judgments.

I agree with the assertion that value judgments are neither true nor false, and that you should focus more upon the law as it is than on your own pronouncements, but that has not prevented me from now and then expressing my view as to what the law should be. As *Ernst Rabel* once said: "*We lawyers... obsessed by the wish to improve the law as we are, are simply not capable of denying us the prospects of the better law*".[4]

I do not care whether I am a scientist or not, when I state my attitude.

However, when you do that, you must tell the students that there are other views, and you should give them a fair account of the other views. To do that often requires self-mastery, because the temptation to disclose your contempt for some of these views is sometimes very strong.

When teaching the students your conception of justice, you should not hide from them that you express a political view. Some professors pretend that their view is the objective truth and that they do not attempt to politicize. That, in my view, is not correct. As mentioned above, law is based on value judgments, and so is justice. There is no law that expresses any objective truth.

There are, however, some legal values that are commonly accepted by most lawyers. On certain points, there is a considerable universal agreement.

---

3 One was the prominent Swedish professor *Knut Rohde* (1909-1999), see for instance his *Lärobok I obligationsrätt (Textbook on the law of obligations)*, 4 ed., Stockholm, 1975.

4 Here cited from Drobnig, "Die Geburt der modernen Rechtsvergleichung. Zum 50. Todestag von Ernst Rabel", *Zeitschrift für europäisches Privatrecht*, 2005, pp. 822, 830.

For example: Several rules of the United Nations Convention on Contracts for the International Sale of Goods (CISG), of the Principles of European Contract Law (PECL) and of the Unidroit Principles of International Commercial Contracts are identical. Many of these rules have been adopted in the Proposal for a Common European Sales Law, which the EU Commission published in October 2011, and they also appear in several recent national legislations. Considering that one may think that after all there is a number of principles expressing a common core and having a lasting value. Maybe those who invented Natural Law were not so silly after all. I know that colleagues share this double feeling of sympathy for and rejection of Natural Law. But one should not forget that those who framed these common rules were perennial figures. The Unidroit Group and the Commission on European Contract Law worked on these texts at the same time. Five scholars were members of both groups, and three of them worked as reporters in both Groups. So the two Groups influenced each other. In PECL, for example, we had introduced a rule that set-off should only have an *ex nunc* effect. Set-off discharges the obligations as from the time of notice by one party. That was contrary to most continental laws where it has an *ex tunc* effect. Set off discharges the obligations *ipso jure* from the time at which being suitable for set-off they first confront each other. When the issue came up in the Unidroit Group, the reporter had proposed an *ex tunc* rule, but *Arthur Hartkamp* made a strong plea for the *ex nunc* effect, and referred to the PECL solution. When a group of European lawyers, he said, could select that solution, it must be right. And he convinced the Unidroit group.

If you teach the students comparative law, you should tell them about these signs of something which might be called the "Modern Natural Law", but you should, of course, add that there is no such thing as a law arising from nature.

2. *Cour Magistral* or Socratic Method

In 1955-56 I spent a year as a student of the University of Michigan Law School in Ann Arbor. There I saw how the case method was applied in the teaching of law and became convinced of its merits.

Christopher Columbus Langdell (1826-1906) was a professor at Harvard Law School, and is said to have invented the case method, although historians have found out that others were teaching by this method before him. *Langdell*, however, made the case method famous.

He said: "Mr. Jones, will you state the facts in the case of *Hadley v. Baxendale?*" In 1870, *Langdell* forever changed the way lawyers learned the law in the United States. No longer would American law students, as many students in Europe still do, sit passively and take notes, while their professor lectured or read out of a legal treatise. The case method makes the student read the reports of actual court cases and requires him/her to discuss them in class. In a Socratic dialogue the professor and the student distill the rule of law.

The case method activates the students, and active students are generally motivated students. It trains their fluency in law. It confronts them with the different views of the parties to litigation, and of the majority and minority among the judges, and it shows them the complexity of life and the shortcomings of the doctrines. It also gives the student an insight into the bad habits of some courts, see on this below.

When I told the then rector of the College of Europe *Jerzy Lukaszewski* about the method I intended to apply to my teaching, he told me to adopt the *cour magistral*. I would talk sense, he said, whereas the students would talk nonsense. However, I did not obey the rector.

Most of the students did not talk nonsense, and some even threw new light on the problems we discussed. It happened that the teaching went both ways.

However, it was not unproblematic to use the case method in Bruges. I taught in English, and several students came from countries, where the teaching of English in the schools had been inadequate. It was therefore a great effort for them to prepare a case. I could not, as does the American professor, expect all the students to be able to present all the cases for each class. I had to select the students who in the following lesson were to make the presentation of the cases.

The case method also has certain shortcomings. The pedagogical value of the published judgments of many Continental European courts is often limited. Their rendering of facts is very short, and their reasons are incomprehensible for the normal student. They have to be accompanied by notes explaining their meaning.

To this must be added that there are statutory provisions and doctrines which the students must learn, and they must get an overview of the main principles of a subject. The cases cannot teach them that. They must be taught in a lecture and in a textbook. So the best method is to combine the case method with the lecture and with a text. Today, many of the case books are no longer case books in the strict sense of the word. They contain *Cases, Materials and Texts* and the materials and texts are often analyses and doctrine.

3. Should You Teach the Students to Be Critical?

Most legislators, courts and writers try to establish harmony and to avoid anomalies, and many legal scholars represent their legal system as a harmonious and consistent whole.

That is, however, an illusion. That is shown by the way the courts make their decisions. There are two typical ways in which courts have solved a legal problem. The first is the loyal way that obeys statute and precedent. The second is the creative and imaginative way. Those who take the first way follow the rules, even when their sense of justice tells them not to. They are the true servants of the law, and they see it as their task to be loyal to the legislator, to obey the precedent and to provide certainty and predictability. Those who take the second way follow their sense of justice, and now and then they bend or disobey the existing rules. They see it as their task to renew or amend the law when they feel that there is a social need to do so.

Should you teach the students that the legal systems are imperfect, and should you encourage them to be critical of the authorities and to be disobedient? If you teach them that, their criticism may become a boomerang. Can you teach them what the law is and at the same time teach them to be critical of it?

Yes you can. There are important cases in which a court is expressing its own political views, rather than basing its decision on law or prior precedent. They are often cases in which the court realizes that the development of society has called upon them to act, or where the court faces an unforeseen situation to which it would be unacceptable to apply the law. If you teach EU law, you cannot avoid these cases. The European Court of Justice (ECJ) is famous for its judicial activism. Without any legal basis in the Treaty Establishing the European Community, it has held that the European Community Law took priority over national law, and that the Community Law replaces national laws that deviate from Community law.[5] It has entered rules into force which the Community legislature should have, but has failed to enter into force before a prescribed date.[6] It has made directly applicable provisions of directives conferring rights on citizens which, under the directives, national authorities should have conferred on them, but where they had failed to do so at the due date. It has established that European Union Member States may be liable to pay compensation to individuals, who have

5 *Van Gend en Loos v. Nederlande Administratie der Belastingen*, Case 26/62, ECR 1. 1962.375.

6 *Defrenne mod Sabena* (No. 2), Case C-43/75, ECR. 1976.455.

suffered a loss by reason of the Member State's failure to transpose an EU directive into national law.[7]

On several occasions, the Court has claimed that the European Communities has established a new and independent legal order and invoked the purpose of the Treaty to support its policy. It has in this way made these premises into a kind of basic norms. When *Hjalte Rassmussen*[8] showed this activism in 1986, the Members of the ECJ protested loudly; they were not disobedient, they followed the law. If you teach EU law, you should point out that *Hjalte Rasmussen* was right, but you may then add that by its activism, the Court has repaired the shortcomings in the functioning of the EC, which the passivity of the EC legislature and the Member states had caused.

All this the students must learn. And students who study the Constitution of the United Sates will also face judicial activism. It has been practiced by the German courts and it has in a way been canonized in the Dutch Civil Code Art 6(2) providing: "*A rule binding upon (the parties) by virtue of* law, *usage or judicial act does not apply to the extent that, in the given circumstances, this would be unacceptable according to the criteria of reasonableness or equity*". Disobedience and activism are widespread phenomena.

4. Do You Have to Reveal the Bad Habits of Some Courts?

In Europe, many courts render their decisions in a language that is incomprehensible for the average citizen and even for lawyers. Sometimes a case note in a law review is necessary in order to make it possible for lawyers to understand a decision and its relationship with previous decisions and the literature.

Private international law has been a favourite playground for covert techniques. In the latter half of the 19th and the first half of the 20th century, the courts in England, France, Germany and other countries professed the rule that in the absence of an express or tacit choice of law by the parties, a contract was to be governed by the law, which the parties must be presumed to have intended. It was obvious that in many of the decided cases, the parties had not given a thought to which law they would apply, and that it was impossible to tell which law they would have agreed upon if they had reached agreement. The presumed intention of the parties, which the courts invoked, was (a) fiction. This was confirmed by the fact that the courts very often found that the parties had intended the law of the forum country to govern their contract. The

7 *Frankovic v Bonifaci*, Sagerne C-6 og 9/90, ECR. 1991. 1 5357.

8 Rasmussen, H., *On law and policy in the European Court of Justice*, Kluwer, 1986.

courts used the presumed intention of the parties as window dressing.[9] By applying the law of the forum country, the courts or the parties were relieved of the often difficult task of acquiring and assessing the information that they could get on the contents of foreign law.

A teacher should not hide these phenomena. And if you tell the students about the disobedience and the bad manners of some courts, you should not dissuade them from being critical themselves.

9 See *Lando* in the International Encyclopaedia of Comparative Law, Vol. III Private International Law, 1976, Chapter 24, Contracts No. 115ff, and Lando, *Kontraktstatuttet*, (1962) 34 f (France), 85f (Germany) and 121 (England).

Constructing Europe

On the Role of the College of Europe United in Diversity

Wolfgang WESSELS

Jean Monnet Chairholder for Political Science at Cologne University; Former Director, European Political and Administrative Studies, College of Europe

1. Elites and the European Construction

A. On the Relevance of Topic: Socialisation Matters

There are many ways to tell the story of how the European integration developed over sixty years from a limited scope of common policies among six founding members to a state like agenda (see Article 2-6 TFEU) of 27 states. Political narratives and theories of many academic disciplines offer a differentiated set of descriptions, analyses and assessments. We observe a rich menu of explanations and evaluations of the EU polity in the making.

I would like to take up the issue of "elites" and the "construction" of the EU system. This Article does not want to test the often simplistic claim that the European integration is just elite driven and ruled by a closed group of unaccountable bureaucrats who were weakly legitimized for a longer period by a permissive consensus. Also the definition and typologies of elites is not my specific topic.

The term "construction" is chosen on purpose as it implies two dimensions of European integration. On one side "construction" relates to the creation and revisions of the constitutional and institutional architecture of the EU-polity. This dimension focuses on building the EU by Treaty making and by accessions. On the other side the use of the term "construction" is inspired by the ontological view that stresses the importance of shaping and framing the understanding of the European Union. This position is based on the assumption that the European integration process was and is not just an automatic spill-over (Schmitter following an automatic *Sachlogik* (Hallstein) determined by functional needs. It is also more than just a reaction to exogenous shocks and pressures from global markets or a reaction to geo-political structures and challenges of the international system, even though they might be important factors and forces in certain historical constellations. The forming of the EU polity is also more than just the result of logics of domestic preference building and of the dynamics of intergovernmental bargaining (Moravcsik). I assume that real actors play a prominent role. In this view activities and actions of persons are based on perceptions and evaluations of the process of European integration. "*Leitbilder* for Europe", "visions of the finality", and "mental maps" of where to locate the EU need to be taken into account. These factors are a necessary ingredient of studying past developments and designing future strategies.

Of course, both dimensions are closely interrelated. The construction of the constitutional and institutional architecture is not independent from the perception of players active in the EU-system like the views of generations of constitutional architects are influenced by the developments in the EU system. Following these assumptions such sets of personal attitudes, of appropriate norms and of normal behaviour are socially constructed. For my argument it implies that a socialisation via a year in the College of Europe has an impact on the students' attitudes, skills and behaviour and with that on their later profile in their professional life.

B. On the College of Europe

Based on the relevance of the two dimensions of constructing Europe I want to discuss the role of an institution which – since the late forties of the last century – offers a specific programme for advanced pre-professional studies on Europe. The College of Europe, now with two campuses in Bruges and Natolin (Warsaw), is a specific set up in which generations of later policy makers, civil servants and academics spent one year of their postgraduate education. When mentioning the College of Europe, the discourse on European elites refers mostly to alumni and alumnae who made their career in prestigious positions shaping and constructing in some way or another and on different levels the European and international polity, politics and policies. We find graduates of the College in high positions in political institutions and regional, national, European and international administrations, in law firms, multinational companies and in academia. Records of many years show that graduates from the College had and have a high success rate in the selection process, the *Concours*, of EU institutions including newer ones like the European Central Bank. Beyond this carrier pattern we find former College students all over the Brussels arena in many NGO think tanks and law firms, but also in Foreign Offices and other ministries of Member States, in regional administrations and in multinational companies. Some have also made a political carrier. Looking at political leadership only in 2012, we find that one prime minister, one vice prime minister and a European minister have passed a year in Bruges. Some graduates also went into academia and contributed significantly to the development of integration studies. Of course, many students have gone also into other professions.

Regularly the value of the College's intergenerational network is mentioned. The often used term "Bruges mafia" claims that the socialisation into the European group has a positive effect on further careers. Early architects of the College have liked to call the College the 'ENA of Europe or a European "*Kaderschmiede*".

When referring to political and administrative elites in the European constructions we should be however aware that there is significant difference to elites formation in national political systems. In most EU Member States we can identify certain patterns of getting into the higher and closer circle(s) of political and administrative power. Well-known cases are the French carrier pattern via *les grandes écoles*, *Sciences Po* and ENA or elite universities in the UK. In each country the access to higher positions in the hierarchy is different, some are more open and pluralistic, some more restricted, as it has been the case with the lawyers' nearly exclusive dominance in German administrations for a long time.

From decade long experiences I would like to offer some insights, experiences and lessons on the ways the College of Europe contributes to the construction of Europe. These considerations are certainly not all-inclusive but they might serve as a point of departure for a later, richer empirical study which needs to take up individual carriers of a larger number of College graduates of several generations. Thus I cannot offer any impact study but I start from the assumption that a year spent at the College had an influence on the motivations, attitudes, behaviour and skills of the students.

This essay is a specific homage to Paul Demaret who has like no other influenced fundamental features of this set up *sui generis* in the last decades, first as head of the legal department and then as a rector, whose profile and performance is characterized by a rare mix of academic excellence, entrepreneurial spirit and administrative skills.

2. Contributions to constructing Europe

A. Professional skills and personal experiences

Thus the basic question is if and in what way this postgraduate set up has contributed to the making and working of the EU polity. I claim that there is no College doctrine or ideology in a narrow sense, but that a year at the College of Europe either on the Bruges or on the Natolin Campus had and has a considerable impact though certainly different from person to person. With a considerable degree of variations we observe the forming of a certain group spirit and of norms of working with sustainable impact.

For many students the College year was a memorable and important year of their education. Leading European figures claim that they had a "truly unique experience"[1] in Bruges. For many it had a lasting impact on their further professional and personal life. It opened the gate to new job opportunities especially in and around Brussels (but not only there). In a considerable number of cases students found friends for their life – including also many marriages.[2]

Of course, without an extensive empirical research it is rather difficult to assess how and in how far the College year has really contributed to the personality of the student and their future perceptions and work.

Let me point at certain factors.

One remarkable feature of forming elites for the on-going construction of the EU polity has been an early involvement and integration of students from applicant countries. It socialised young students from future members into European affairs.

One specific and illustrative case was my group of German students in the fifties who saw themselves (re-)integrated in the Western European family. Some played later a significant role in the German Foreign office and EU institutions; two of them later returned to the College as rectors in difficult times.

In the following decades, students from southern and then from eastern European countries on their way to "return to Europe" went through the College education and started from there a European carrier. With the necessary caveats, it might be argued that the administrative integra-

---

1 See e.g. Prime Minister Helle Thorning-Schmid at the Opening Ceremony of the 63rd Academic Year, available at http://www.coleurope.eu/sites/default/files/speech-files/statsministeriet_-_the_danish_prime_ministers_address_at_the_opening_ceremony_of_the_college_of_europe_bruges_17_october_2012.pdf, last access 15 November 2012.

2 *Ibid.*

tion of many accession states went smoothly because of the experiences representatives of these states gained at the College (and, of course, in other academic institutions). A similar function is currently pursued with extending scholarships for students from the EU's neighbouring countries.

Following one theoretical perspective, prominent in the study of international relations, the College might even be seen as one of the Union's most successful instruments to exercise "soft power" (Nye). It has been useful to spread the Unions *acquis* to coming elites in future Member States and in the "ring of friends" in the near neighbourhood. It serves to shape the regional milieu.

B. Mix of Academic Cultures

The College's concept for the formation of European elites is based on a diversified academic programme with experts from all over the world. One major advantage is the system of visiting professors, which enables the College to get leading academics from different national backgrounds and experienced civil servants from EU institutions. As they get one-year contracts the programme can be swiftly adapted to upcoming subjects and new approaches. Compared with traditional universities the flexibility is much larger. During the absence of the teaching personal the assistants play an essential role in helping the students to fulfil the academic requirements.

Its privileged geographical position – close to Brussels or to Warsaw – makes it easier for the College to involve European policy-makers into its academic life. Organizing conferences with e.g. European Commissioners discussing on-going challenges is a long tradition of the College. This also guarantees a formation of elites which corresponds to the "*Zeitgeist*" of the Union's development. Another particularity in this aspect is the role of the Development Office offering "executive education" for students and professionals.

Thus one significant feature is the multi-disciplinary and multi-cultural nature of the institution. There is no dominance of students or professors from one nation. The College is not a department within a larger national university, which would dominate directly or indirectly the respective academic culture.

This advantage leads to the co-existence of several academic cultures: from the "*cours magistral*" to workshops and seminars and simulation games. Each of the professors pursues her or his own teaching style – strongly influenced by their own academic education. Students are offered a large variation of methods to which they have to adapt. Some of them have difficulties to face these challenges. As part of this challenge the College demands students to attend courses in several disciplines and two languages. For later working in multi-national institutions or networks such a learning process is highly useful.

Perhaps even more important than the impact of the variations in the academic programme are socialisation processes in the annual "promotion", which is each year dedicated to a European personality. Students are confronted with fellow students from different academic and national backgrounds. The shared daily life in the residencies, canteens, library, lectures, simulation games and seminars has an intensive impact on most students. Shared anxieties about examinations add to this group building process. The smaller Natolin campus even leads to an even higher intensity of contacts.

Such an intensive living together leads to life-long memories of their year at the College. Promotions then meet in fixed intervals to celebrate specific decades of their graduations. Most students identify with the patron and name of their respective promotion. Sport competitions such as football games between different promotions reflect the College spirit in its real sense.

C. United in Diversity

One persistent critic about European institutions is that their civil servants lose their national roots and turn into bloodless technocrats without "*patrie*" in their national background.

One characteristic, which you might not expect in this European set up, is the way national background comes to the forefront. Social highlights during the year are national parties – in earlier decades starting with a Vienna style ball. Quite often students of different national backgrounds are proud to show cultural properties of their countries. Also in the daily cooperation you see personal characteristics, which are, perhaps sometimes too easily, attributed to traditional notions of national political and social cultures.

At the same time I discover some kind of European spirit – difficult to define, describe and operationalise. Varying from promotion to promotion, the feeling to belong to a group of young Europeans working for some kind of shared and common future develops during the year. Often this spirit is detected only later. At first we see an on-going interest in dealing with EU affairs. Some came already with this interest to the College. Others were infected with the "Brussels Virus" during that year. Though difficult to prove, it seems that also idealistic motivations and a certain feeling of belonging to a group are elements of that kind of European spirit.

As a *sui generis* academic institution, the College of Europe provides the very fundament for developing such a spirit and lifestyle. It offers the opportunities of a multicultural and multinational community based on the constitutional Treaty's motto of "United in Diversity". Mental and societal structures of the students change throughout the academic year. National reservations and past assumptions towards one or the other nation – either historically pre-given or personally influenced – are put into perspective with the European spirit the College offers.

D. Constructing a Polity in Full Change

The challenges for qualifying future elites were and are considerable. The College has regularly pursued a strategy to mix continuity and adaptations in an adequate form.

As a child of the Congress of Europe in The Hague 1948 and directed by a prominent member of the Dutch resistance the College had a certain federal vocation to bring young Europeans together. With the growth to the EU system the agenda for the *curriculum* has become much broader. Treaty revisions, legislative processes in the institutional triangle, rulings of the Court of Justice of the EU, as well as activities and actions in internal crises and facing external shocks have each year led to a considerable increase in the relevant *acquis* of the EU. Changes in the topics taught are considerable. At the same time the disciplinary state of the art, the *acquis académique*, has evolved. Students and professors alike are confronted with a differentiated set of often contradictory approaches. The academic debate is lively and full of controversies. Thus, also the teaching in the College reflects a pluralistic and fragmented state of the art. The College is thus not a closed shop of just old and perhaps out-dated theories and insights. However, as it can be seen in academia as well, keeping older events, developments and theories in the *curriculum* is part of the agenda. The vocation, as documented by the College's library, is to preserve and conserve earlier state of the arts. It is also a special quality and skill to take up to latest political and academic developments without letting heritages disappear.

At the same time, in a close look at the moving realities of the EU polity the College has taken up new programmes. Thus, with a view to the European External Actions Service, created by the Lisbon Treaty, the College introduced even before the instalment of this service a new International Relations Department.

The evolution of the Union has led to major changes in the academic landscape in which the College is moving. Many national universities have created programmes, some also transnational, which offer well based promotions. A certain exclusivity for inter-disciplinary debates about features and trends of the European construction, which the "*semaine de Bruges*" offered in the early decades, got lost. Other set ups like the European University Institute in Florence, but also many think tanks, Erasmus and EU financed programmes offer a rich debate in lively discourses which increases the competition.

The Bologna university reforms have changed the academic landscape too. The Erasmus programme and other forms of inter-university contacts have led to a Europeanization of many relevant study programmes which form a good pre-requisite for a deeper study later on in the College.

E. Constructing Europe: Increasing Challenges

European leaders – recently the Danish Prime Minster Helle-Thorning-Schmidt – raise great expectations in their speeches at the Opening Ceremonies of the respective Academic Year. The reminder by the Danish Prime Minister "dear students, don't forget to serve. You must do your part to forge the EU of tomorrow" indicates that the "leaders of tomorrow"[3] (this is how students of the College of Europe are often called) face considerable challenges when coming to the College of Europe: academic formation and professional orientation go hand in hand, which is one of the College's main success recipes.

Also the challenges for the College increase. To build-up on the success story so far, the College of Europe will have to keep and diversify the level of academic formation. At the same time, it will have to meet the expectations of a constantly moving European and global political and academic landscape. The need for more skilled European elites has even increased given the consequences of the Great crisis years from 2008 onwards.

---

3 *Ibid.*

II

Droits de l'homme et citoyenneté/ Human Rights and Citizenship

Les institutions nationales de défense des droits de l'homme et la Cour européenne des droits de l'homme

Vincent BERGER

Ancien jurisconsulte de la Cour européenne des droits de l'homme ; Avocat au barreau de Paris

1. Introduction

Les institutions nationales de défense des droits de l'homme (« les INDH ») jouent un rôle important dans la promotion et la protection des droits de l'homme, notamment en œuvrant pour la bonne application des normes internationales en matière de droits de l'homme au niveau national. Ces dernières décennies en particulier, elles ont activement contribué à cette promotion et à cette protection à l'échelle mondiale comme à l'échelle régionale. Cette interaction entre les INDH et les mécanismes internationaux de protection des droits de l'homme a bien sûr pour origine les « Principes de Paris » adoptés en 1993 par l'Assemblée générale des Nations unies.[1] Ceux-ci indiquent entre autres que les INDH ont parmi leurs attributions celle de coopérer avec l'Organisation des Nations unies et tout autre organisme des Nations unies ainsi qu'avec les institutions régionales et les institutions nationales d'autres pays qui ont compétence dans les domaines de la promotion et de la protection des droits de l'homme.[2]

À l'échelle européenne, les INDH collaborent avec les principaux mécanismes régionaux, dont ceux du Conseil de l'Europe.[3] Conscient de

1 Résolution 48/134 de l'Assemblée générale des Nations unies (20 décembre 1993) sur les institutions nationales pour la promotion et la protection des droits de l'homme.

2 *Ibid.*

3 Pour une vue d'ensemble de la relation entre les institutions nationales de défense des droits de l'homme et les mécanismes internationaux de protection des droits de l'homme à l'échelle mondiale et à l'échelle européenne, voir Mac Aodha, É., et

l'importance croissante de ces institutions pour ce qui est de la promotion et du respect au niveau national des normes internationales de protection des droits de l'homme, le Conseil de l'Europe encourage ses États membres à mettre en place des INDH conformément aux Principes de Paris. Il a progressivement établi des structures formelles de coopération avec les INDH et d'assistance à celles-ci.[4]

La situation est assez différente en ce qui concerne la relation entre les INDH et la Cour européenne des droits de l'homme (« la Cour »). Si elle fait partie des mécanismes de protection des droits de l'homme du Conseil de l'Europe, la Cour est une juridiction internationale établie par la Convention européenne des droits de l'homme (« la Convention »).[5] Elle statue sur les requêtes dont la saisissent des particuliers ou des États contractants relativement à l'interprétation et à l'application des garanties des droits de l'homme énoncées dans la Convention et ses protocoles.[6] Elle peut aussi émettre des avis consultatifs.[7] Étant une juridiction indépendante supranationale, elle n'entretient pas de relations structurelles ou institutionnelles avec les INDH.

En outre, à la différence du système interaméricain,[8] le système européen ne reconnaît pas aux INDH la qualité pour agir devant la Cour au nom d'une victime alléguée : en vertu de l'Article 34 de la Convention, qui garantit le droit de recours individuel, il faut que la personne qui introduit la requête devant la Cour soit directement touchée par l'acte ou l'omission allégués dont elle se plaint ou qu'elle ait avec la

---

Roberts, K., « National Human Rights Institutions in Europe », *European Yearbook on Human Rights*, 2011, pp. 527-537 ; de Beco, G., « National Human Rights Institutions in Europe », *Human Rights Law Review*, 2007, pp. 331-370 ; Carver, R., « A New Answer to an Old Question. National Human Rights Institutions and the Domestication of International Law », *Human Rights Law Review*, 2010, pp. 1-32, et le manuel publié par le PNUD et le HCR : *Toolkit for Collaboration with National Human Rights Institutions*, chapitre 3, Roles and Responsibilities of NHRIs, décembre 2010, pp. 31-50.

4 Voir, en particulier, la recommandation R (97) 14 du Comité des ministres aux États membres relative à l'établissement d'institutions nationales indépendantes pour la promotion et la protection des droits de l'homme (30 septembre 1997), la résolution (97) 11 sur la coopération entre les institutions nationales pour la promotion et la protection des droits de l'homme des États membres et entre celles-ci et le Conseil de l'Europe (30 septembre 1997) et la résolution (99) 50 sur le commissaire aux droits de l'homme du Conseil de l'Europe (7 mai 1999).

5 Article 19 de la Convention, tel que modifié par le Protocole n° 11.

6 Article 32 de la Convention, tel que modifié par le Protocole n° 11.

7 Article 47 de la Convention, tel que modifié par le Protocole n° 11.

8 Voir *Janet Espinoza Feria et al. c. Pérou*, affaire 12 404, décision du 10 octobre 2002, où la Commission interaméricaine des droits de l'homme a déclaré recevable une communication présentée notamment par le médiateur péruvien au nom de victimes potentielles alléguées.

victime directe un lien personnel et spécifique. De fait, la Cour a toujours déclaré irrecevables *ratione personae* les requêtes ou les griefs que lui ont soumis des organisations non gouvernementales (ONG).[9] Il en irait de même de tout grief présenté par des INDH au nom d'une victime alléguée.

De plus, en règle générale, la Cour ne considère pas les recours devant les INDH tels que les médiateurs comme des recours effectifs qu'il est nécessaire d'exercer pour épuiser les voies de droit internes avant de la saisir d'une requête comme l'exige l'article 35 de la Convention, car les médiateurs n'ont pas le pouvoir de rendre des décisions contraignantes permettant de remédier à une éventuelle violation.[10]

Il n'y a donc pas entre la Cour et les INDH une interaction semblable à celle qui peut exister entre les INDH et les mécanismes de protection des droits de l'homme des Nations unies. Pourtant, les INDH ne sont pas désarmées et disposent de plusieurs moyens pour jouer un rôle ou exercer une influence à l'égard du système de la Convention : contribuer au développement de la jurisprudence ; collaborer à la surveillance de l'exécution des arrêts ; participer aux projets relatifs à l'avenir de la Cour.

---

9 Voir par exemple *Van Melle et autres c. Pays-Bas* (déc.), n° 19221/08, 29 septembre 2009, *Association du « 21 décembre 1989 » et autres c. Roumanie*, n°s 33810/07 et 18817/08, 24 mai 2011, et *Ligue des musulmans de Suisse et autres c. Suisse* (déc.), n° 66274/09, 28 juin 2011.

10 Voir par exemple *Janatuinen c. Finlande* (déc.), n° 4692/04, 20 janvier 2009. Dans l'affaire *Ananyev et autres c. Russie* (n° 42525/07 et 60800/08, § 106, 10 janvier 2012), relative aux conditions de détention, la Cour a expliqué sa logique dans les termes suivants :

« Pour qu'un recours soit considéré comme effectif, il doit être propre à redresser les griefs de celui qui l'exerce. Or les médiateurs, qu'ils soient régionaux ou fédéraux, n'ont pas le pouvoir de rendre une décision juridiquement contraignante qui soit de nature à apporter une amélioration à la situation de ceux qui les saisissent ou qui puisse servir de base pour l'obtention d'une indemnité. Leur tâche est différente : ils repèrent différents problèmes de droits de l'homme à partir des plaintes individuelles et des autres informations dont ils disposent, ils en rendent compte dans leurs rapports annuels et ils s'efforcent d'y trouver des solutions en coopération avec les autorités régionales et fédérales (…). Si leur action peut contribuer utilement à l'amélioration générale des conditions de détention, ils demeurent incapables, du fait des fonctions qui leur sont attribuées, de redresser les griefs de particuliers comme l'exige la Convention. Il s'ensuit que la plainte devant un médiateur ne constitue pas un recours effectif. »

2. Les INDH et le développement de la jurisprudence de la Cour

Les INDH contribuent au développement de la jurisprudence de Strasbourg de deux manières : indirectement, en établissant des rapports qui pourront être utilisés par la Cour et, directement, en se portant tiers intervenant dans certaines affaires.

A. Les rapports des INDH

Lorsque l'affaire s'y prête, la Cour s'appuie sur les rapports et les informations du domaine public provenant des INDH, notamment lorsqu'elle examine les circonstances factuelles d'une affaire. Cela vaut en particulier pour les travaux des ombudsmen ou médiateurs, qui existent aujourd'hui dans de nombreux pays du Vieux Continent, y compris dans des pays d'Europe centrale et orientale où ils sont apparus après la chute du Mur de Berlin.

De surcroît, il arrive qu'une affaire ou une question ait été examinée par une INDH avant d'être portée devant la Cour. En pareil cas, celle-ci tient dûment compte de l'évaluation qui en a été faite par l'institution. Elle ne peut non plus ignorer que l'affaire ou question en cause est souvent révélatrice d'une situation de caractère général.

Par exemple, dans l'affaire *Rantsev c. Chypre et Russie*,[11] qui concernait le décès d'une jeune femme russe âgée de vingt ans et venue de Russie pour travailler à Chypre en tant qu'artiste de cabaret, la Cour s'est appuyée sur les rapports du commissaire aux droits de l'homme du Conseil de l'Europe et de la médiatrice chypriote sur le régime d'entrée et d'emploi des femmes étrangères en tant qu'artistes dans des lieux de divertissement à Chypre pour relever qu'il y avait dans le pays un grave problème de traite et d'exploitation sexuelle des artistes de cabaret. Les informations figurant dans ces rapports lui ont permis de conclure que les autorités chypriotes avaient connaissance du fait qu'un nombre important de femmes étrangères étaient introduites à Chypre au moyen de visas d'artistes dans le seul but d'être exploitées sexuellement par des propriétaires et des directeurs de cabaret.

Dans une autre affaire récente, *Mandić et Jović c. Slovénie*,[12] qui posait le problème des conditions de détention dans une prison slovène, la Cour s'est appuyée sur les conclusions du médiateur slovène des droits de l'homme pour juger crédibles les allégations des requérants selon lesquelles les températures dans les cellules de l'établissement étaient excessivement élevées en été.

---

11 *Rantsev c. Chypre et Russie*, n° 25965/04, 7 janvier 2010.

12 *Mandić et Jović c. Slovénie*, n°s 5774/10 et 5985/10, 20 octobre 2011.

Dans une affaire antérieure, qui concernait des allégations de mauvais traitements par la police, la Cour avait reproché à l'État chypriote de ne pas avoir mené d'enquête pénale sur les allégations « défendables » de mauvais traitements.[13] En effet, le procureur général, qui était responsable de l'ouverture des poursuites pénales, n'avait pas agi malgré le rapport du médiateur, où celui-ci concluait que le requérant avait été maltraité en deux occasions, et citait nommément certains des agents responsables.

Ces exemples démontrent que la Cour considère les INDH comme une source d'informations fiable et utile et qu'elle est disposée à s'appuyer sur leurs rapports ou autres documents.

B. Les tierces interventions des INDH

L'article 36 de la Convention, tel que modifié par les Protocoles n°s 11 et 14, est ainsi libellé :

> 1. Dans toute affaire devant une chambre ou la Grande Chambre, une Haute Partie contractante dont un ressortissant est requérant a le droit de présenter des observations écrites et de prendre part aux audiences.
>
> 2. Dans l'intérêt d'une bonne administration de la justice, le président de la Cour peut inviter toute Haute Partie contractante qui n'est pas partie à l'instance ou toute personne intéressée autre que le requérant à présenter des observations écrites ou à prendre part aux audiences.
>
> 3. Dans toute affaire devant une chambre ou la Grande Chambre, le commissaire aux droits de l'homme du Conseil de l'Europe peut présenter des observations écrites et prendre part aux audiences.

Cette disposition permet aux INDH de jouer un rôle important dans l'interprétation et l'évolution de la jurisprudence des organes de la Convention, soit en soumettant en leur propre nom des observations de tiers intervenant soit en apportant au commissaire aux droits de l'homme du Conseil de l'Europe leur collaboration et leur assistance pour l'élaboration de ses propres observations de tiers intervenant.[14] Au

---

13 *Egmez c. Chypre*, n° 30873/96, 21 décembre 2000. Cette affaire est aussi intéressante en ce que, exceptionnellement, la Cour y a admis qu'en portant ses griefs devant une institution nationale de défense des droits de l'homme, le requérant s'était acquitté de son obligation d'épuiser les voies de recours internes.

14 Le commissaire aux droits de l'homme du Conseil de l'Europe a présenté des observations en qualité de tiers intervenant dans les affaires suivantes : *Mamasakhlisi c. Géorgie et Russie*, n° 29999/04 (affaire pendante), *Ahmet Ali* (n° 26494/09) *et treize autres requêtes c. Pays-Bas et Grèce* (affaires déclarées par la suite irrecevables), *M.S.S. c. Belgique et Grèce* [GC], n° 30696/09, 21 janvier 2011, et *Centre de ressources juridiques (Despre Centrul de Resurse Juridice) au nom de Valentin Campeanu c. Roumanie*, n° 47848/08 (affaire pendante).

cours des vingt dernières années, des INDH se sont portés tiers intervenants en de rares occasions. On ne peut donc pas dire qu'elles aient été particulièrement dynamiques dans ce domaine, en particulier si l'on compare le nombre de leurs interventions avec celui des ONG. On peut cependant relever plusieurs exemples fort éclairants.

L'une des premières interventions par une INDH fut celle de la Commission des droits de l'homme d'Irlande du Nord (*Northern Ireland Human Rights Commission*). En 2000, celle-ci se porta tiers intervenant dans plusieurs affaires[15] concernant un défaut allégué d'enquête de la part des autorités britanniques après le décès de proches des requérants en Irlande du Nord. Dans ses observations, elle s'appuya notamment sur les normes internationales applicables en matière de droit à la vie pour soutenir que l'État était dans l'obligation de mener une enquête officielle effective lorsque l'un de ses agents était impliqué dans une situation où le recours à la force avait entraîné mort d'homme. Elle pointa également les failles des mécanismes d'investigation en Irlande du Nord et pria la Cour de saisir cette occasion pour préciser quelle forme devaient prendre les enquêtes menées sur le recours à la force meurtrière par des agents de l'État.[16]

Plus récemment, une autre INDH, la Commission britannique pour l'égalité et les droits de l'homme (*Equality and Human Rights Commission*), a présenté des observations en qualité de tiers intervenant dans plusieurs affaires dirigées contre le Royaume-Uni et relatives à différents sujets (logement, immigration, droit de la famille, emploi). C'est ainsi que dans l'affaire *Bah c. Royaume-Uni*, qui concernait le refus d'une autorité locale d'accorder à une mère et à son fils mineur, tous deux ressortissants de Sierra Leone, une place prioritaire dans la liste d'attribution des logements sociaux, elle a critiqué le droit interne et dénoncé ses points faibles.[17] Dans l'affaire *Greens et M.T. c. Royaume-Uni*, qui portait sur le manquement continu du Royaume-Uni à modifier la législation imposant aux détenus condamnés une interdiction générale de voter aux élections nationales et européennes, elle a présenté des observations visant à expliquer les dispositions concernées du droit interne.[18] Elle n'a pas hésité non plus à intervenir dans une affaire politiquement très délicate, *Al-Saadoon et Mufdhi c. Royaume-Uni*, où les requérants – deux Irakiens accusés d'avoir participé au meurtre de deux

---

15 *McKerr c. Royaume-Uni*, n° 28883/95, *Kelly et autres c. Royaume-Uni*, n° 30054/96, *Shanaghan c. Royaume-Uni*, n° 37715/97, et *Hugh Jordan c. Royaume-Uni*, n° 24746/94, 4 mai 2001.

16 *Hugh Jordan c. Royaume-Uni*, *supra*, § 101.

17 *Bah c. Royaume-Uni*, n° 56328/07, 27 septembre 2011, §§ 33-34.

18 *Greens et M.T. c. Royaume-Uni*, n° 6004/08 et 60054/08, § 65.

soldats britanniques en Irak – se plaignaient de leur remise par les autorités britanniques aux autorités irakiennes, au risque selon eux que celles-ci les fassent exécuter ; elle a considéré que lorsque les obligations de l'État en vertu de la Convention se trouvaient en concurrence ou en conflit avec ses obligations en vertu du droit international, il ressortait de la jurisprudence de la Cour qu'il y avait lieu d'accorder la priorité aux premières sur les secondes.[19]

Une évolution positive s'est dessinée récemment avec l'intervention dans deux affaires du Groupe européen des institutions nationales de promotion et de protection des droits de l'homme (« le Groupe européen des INDH »),[20] lequel représente trente-quatre INDH existant dans des États membres du Conseil de l'Europe. Il a d'ailleurs été relevé que ces affaires étaient les premières dans lesquelles un groupement régional d'INDH intervenait en qualité de tiers devant une juridiction internationale. Dans l'affaire *D.D. c. Lituanie*,[21] où la requérante se plaignait d'avoir été internée contre son gré dans un hôpital psychiatrique, le Groupe européen des INDH a présenté des observations sur les changements normatifs quant à la notion de capacité juridique en droit international des droits de l'homme et en droit comparé. Dans l'affaire *Gauer et autres c. France* (n° 61521/08), qui concernait la stérilisation de cinq femmes handicapées mentales en l'absence de leur consentement éclairé, il a présenté des observations portant sur les normes internationales des droits de l'homme applicables, en particulier la Convention des Nations unies relative aux droits des personnes handicapées.

3. Les INDH et l'exécution des arrêts de la Cour

L'effectivité du système de la Convention et la confiance des justiciables dans ce dernier dépendent dans une large mesure d'une exécution complète et rapide des arrêts de Strasbourg, en tout cas de ceux qui contiennent un constat de violation. Les INDH peuvent jouer un rôle à cet égard, aussi bien au niveau européen qu'au niveau national.

A. Devant le Comité des ministres du Conseil de l'Europe

Organe politique du Conseil de l'Europe, le Comité des ministres est chargé par la Convention de surveiller l'exécution des arrêts de la Cour. Il reconnaît que les INDH peuvent l'aider à cet égard, en lui fournissant

19 *Al-Saadoon et Mufdhi c. Royaume-Uni*, n° 61498/08, 2 mars 2010, § 113.

20 Le Groupe européen des INDH est l'un des quatre réseaux régionaux d'institutions nationales de défense des droits de l'homme au sein du Comité international de coordination des institutions nationales pour la promotion et la protection des droits de l'homme, qui coordonne ces institutions au niveau européen.

21 *D.D. c. Lituanie*, n° 13469/06, 14 février 2012.

des informations pertinentes et actualisées. En effet, la règle 9 § 2 des Règles du Comité des ministres pour la surveillance de l'exécution des arrêts et des termes des règlements amiables prévoit ceci :

> Le Comité des ministres est en droit de prendre en considération toute communication transmise par des organisations non gouvernementales, ainsi que par des institutions nationales pour la promotion et la protection des droits de l'homme, concernant l'exécution des arrêts conformément à l'article 46, paragraphe 2, de la Convention.

Le dialogue avec le Comité des ministres sur l'exécution de l'arrêt ou du règlement amiable dans une affaire donnée est une manière constructive d'informer le Comité pour l'aider à contrôler la suite donnée à l'affaire au niveau national. Cela revêt d'autant plus d'importance que le requérant n'a pas voix au chapitre, puisqu'il est tenu à l'écart de la procédure de surveillance. En outre, l'INDH présente l'avantage d'être une institution publique mais en principe indépendante de l'exécutif de l'État défendeur.

La plupart des arrêts dans lesquels la Cour constate une ou plusieurs violations de la Convention ont des conséquences « réparatrices ». Celles-ci ont d'ordinaire une portée individuelle : l'octroi d'une « satisfaction équitable » à la victime consistera dans une indemnité d'un montant plus ou moins élevé, ou dans le retrait d'une mesure, etc. Elles ont parfois une portée générale : l'arrêt provoquera ou accélérera une réforme législative ou réglementaire, un changement de politique ou de pratique, une évolution de la jurisprudence, etc. En pareil cas, la règle 9 paraît fort opportune, dans la mesure où elle devrait permettre au Comité des ministres de prendre de la hauteur et du champ.

Il faut cependant noter – et regretter – que jusqu'à présent rares sont les INDH qui ont exploité la procédure prévue par la règle 9. En l'absence d'explications officielles, il est très malaisé, voire impossible, de connaître les motifs de cette passivité ou de ce désintérêt. On peut seulement en imaginer certains : manque d'information sur l'existence de cette faculté et sur la marche à suivre ; insuffisance de la publicité sur les actions entreprises dans le passé par des INDH ; absence d'illusions quant aux chances d'être pris en considération par le Comité des ministres ; souci de laisser les coudées franches au gouvernement de l'État défendeur face à ses pairs.

Cela dit, la procédure en question n'est pas restée lettre morte. Parmi les récents exemples de son utilisation, on trouve les rapports présentés par la Commission des droits de l'homme d'Irlande du Nord sur les affaires précitées concernant l'action des forces de sécurité en Irlande du Nord. À signaler aussi le rapport présenté en mars 2011 par la Commission britannique pour l'égalité et les droits de l'homme sur l'affaire

Gillan et Quinton c. Royaume-Uni,[22] laquelle mettait en cause les pouvoirs d'interpellation et de fouille conférés à la police par la législation antiterroriste. La Cour avait estimé que les pouvoirs en question étaient trop larges et dépourvus de garanties adéquates contre les abus, au mépris de l'Article 8 de la Convention (droit au respect de la vie privée). À noter enfin le rapport soumis en juillet 2011 par la Commission irlandaise des droits de l'homme (*Irish Human Rights Commission*) sur l'affaire *McFarlane c. Irlande*.[23] Le requérant dénonçait l'absence dans son pays de recours effectif pour se plaindre de la durée d'une procédure pénale, et la Cour avait conclu à la violation de l'article 13 de la Convention (droit à un recours effectif devant une instance nationale).

On remarquera qu'à ce jour chaque INDH qui s'est prononcée l'a toujours fait à propos de « son » État, même si bien des arrêts de la Cour ont une portée qui dépasse le cadre purement national.

B. Dans l'ordre juridique interne

Le principe de subsidiarité veut que les États soient en première ligne pour prévenir, constater et réparer les violations de la Convention, la Cour n'intervenant qu'en cas de défaillance ou de manquement à leurs obligations internationales. Sans cesse mis en avant par les gouvernements européens – parfois de manière obsessionnelle –, il devrait pousser les INDH à s'intéresser de très près au « service après-vente » des arrêts de Strasbourg. Leur contribution semble, pour l'instant et dans la plupart des pays, relativement modeste. Elle pourrait pourtant s'avérer très utile. Les domaines d'action ne manquent pas. On songe à la traduction dans la langue nationale des arrêts les plus importants. On pense aussi à l'information des milieux judiciaires (juges, procureurs et avocats) et des médias, notamment audiovisuels. On évoque surtout les interventions auprès des autorités gouvernementales et législatives pour que soit rapidement tarie la source des violations. Cela est d'autant plus nécessaire quand la Cour a constaté un dysfonctionnement systémique ou structurel et a recouru à la procédure de l'arrêt pilote.

4. Les INDH et l'avenir de la Cour

Deux questions relatives à l'avenir de la Cour et plus généralement celui de la Convention et de sa mise en œuvre suscitent un vif intérêt auprès des INDH, et parfois des préoccupations de leur part : celle de la réforme de la Cour et celle de l'adhésion de l'Union européenne à la Convention.

---

22 *Gillan et Quinton c. Royaume-Uni*, n° 4158/05, 12 janvier 2010.

23 *McFarlane c. Irlande* [GC], n° 31333/06, 10 septembre 2010.

A. La réforme de la Cour

La portée jurisprudentielle, institutionnelle et géographique de la Convention s'est étendue depuis l'adoption de cet instrument le 4 novembre 1950.[24] Victime de son succès, la Cour voit son efficacité sérieusement menacée par le nombre de requêtes toujours très important dont elle est saisie (128 100 étaient pendantes au 31 décembre 2012). Au cours des vingt dernières années, elle a fait l'objet de différentes réformes, issues des efforts qu'elle a déployés conjointement avec le Conseil de l'Europe et les États contractants pour tenter de réduire le nombre d'affaires en souffrance.

Tout naturellement, les INDH se sont intéressées au processus et ont entrepris des démarches consistant à soumettre aux gouvernements des États membres du Conseil de l'Europe des observations écrites par l'intermédiaire du Groupe européen des INDH.[25] Ce dernier a d'ailleurs eu le statut d'observateur aux conférences ministérielles de haut niveau sur l'avenir de la Cour, tenues à Interlaken en février 2010, puis à Izmir en avril 2011 et enfin à Brighton en avril 2012. Par la bouche de son président, il a ainsi eu l'occasion d'exprimer non seulement la volonté des INDH de contribuer à la réforme de la Cour mais aussi leurs préoccupations à ce sujet.

D'une manière générale, le Groupe européen des INDH a adopté des positions empreintes d'ouverture. Il s'est montré hostile à tout ce qui pourrait limiter le droit de recours individuel, comme le raccourcissement du délai pour introduire une requête (de six à quatre mois après la décision interne définitive), l'instauration de nouveaux critères de recevabilité ou la modification du critère du « préjudice important » introduit par le Protocole n° 14 (suppression de l'exigence d'un examen préalable par un tribunal interne), ou encore l'obligation pour les requérants de payer des frais de justice. De même, il s'est dit opposé à ce qui pourrait restreindre la compétence de la Cour, comme la mention de la marge d'appréciation dans le préambule de la Convention, la limitation et a fortiori la suppression du pouvoir d'accorder une « satisfaction équitable » aux victimes de violations de la Convention, le droit de regard des agents des gouvernements sur les amendements au règlement de la Cour. En outre, le Groupe européen s'est déclaré réservé quant à la possibilité pour la Cour de donner des avis consultatifs, sans pour autant

---

24 Helfer, L.R., « Redesigning the European Court of Human Rights : Embeddedness as a Deep Structural Principle of the European Human Rights Regime », *The European Journal of International Law*, 2008, p. 126.

25 Voir les commentaires écrits du Groupe européen des INDH sur le deuxième projet de déclaration de la Conférence d'Interlaken (13 octobre 2010) et sur le premier projet de déclaration de la Conférence de Brighton (16 mars 2012).

en rejeter l'idée. Par ailleurs, il a beaucoup insisté sur le devoir des autorités et juridictions nationales d'appliquer la jurisprudence de Strasbourg et de traiter les problèmes structurels ou systémiques qui génèrent de très nombreuses requêtes répétitives. À ce propos, il a plaidé pour que les INDH soient associées aux mécanismes parlementaires mis en place pour contrôler l'exécution des arrêts de la Cour.

À noter enfin que le rôle des INDH dans l'application de la Convention au niveau national a été reconnu dans la déclaration d'Interlaken : les États parties sont appelés « à s'engager à (...) continuer à renforcer, le cas échéant en coopération avec leurs institutions nationales des droits de l'homme ou d'autres organes, la sensibilisation des autorités nationales aux standards de la Convention et d'assurer l'application de ceux-ci ».

B. L'adhésion de l'Union européenne à la Convention

De même, le Groupe européen des INDH, qui a aussi le statut d'observateur au Comité directeur pour les droits de l'homme (CDDH)[26] du Conseil de l'Europe, a communiqué au Groupe de travail informel du CDDH sur l'adhésion de l'Union européenne à la Convention (CDDH-UE) des commentaires écrits (29 novembre 2010 et 9 mars 2011) dans lesquels il exprimait ses préoccupations et présentait ses propositions. Il regrettait le manque de transparence du processus de négociation dans la mesure où ni les INDH ni les organisations de la société civile n'avaient la qualité d'observateurs. Il formulait des réserves quant à la possibilité pour la Cour de justice de l'Union européenne de donner à la Cour des avis consultatifs sur des matières relevant du droit de l'Union dans le cadre du mécanisme de codéfendeur, et quant à la possibilité pour la Cour de surseoir à statuer en attendant une décision de la Cour de justice. Par ailleurs, le Groupe européen des INDH faisait plusieurs recommandations : que le requérant ne soit pas tenu, quand l'Union européenne serait codéfendeur, de démontrer qu'il y avait eu épuisement des voies de recours offertes par l'Union européenne ou d'entreprendre des démarches procédurales supplémentaires ; que le règlement de la Cour tienne compte de l'inégalité des armes entre le requérant et le codéfendeur et prévoit des délais plus longs pour le premier ; que la procédure de tierce intervention se déroule après la communication de la requête au défendeur ; que les arrêts de la Cour

---

26 Le Comité directeur pour les droits de l'homme, qui est composé de représentants des États membres du Conseil de l'Europe, vise à développer et à promouvoir les droits de l'homme et à améliorer les procédures de protection de ces droits aux niveaux national et européen.

identifient lequel des codéfendeurs serait responsable d'une violation de la Convention.

Un projet d'accord a vu le jour en juillet 2011. Cependant, de nouvelles négociations ont été jugées nécessaires. Elles ont repris en juin 2012, avec un format différent, entre le Groupe de négociation *ad hoc* du CDDH et la Commission européenne. Le Groupe européen des INDH n'y est pas associé et n'a pas encore soumis d'observations.

5. Conclusion

Ces dernières années, les INDH ont été davantage enclines à intervenir devant la Cour et le Comité des ministres sur les affaires soulevant des questions importantes. Elles se sont ainsi familiarisées avec le système de contrôle de la Convention. On ne peut que se féliciter de cette évolution, qui doit être encouragée. De plus, l'implication du Groupe européen des INDH dans le processus de réforme de la Cour est particulièrement importante, malgré d'évidentes réticences de plusieurs gouvernements. Ces tendances récentes démontrent la volonté des INDH européennes de jouer un rôle accru dans la protection et la promotion des normes relatives aux droits de l'homme énoncées dans la jurisprudence de Strasbourg, tant au niveau national qu'au niveau régional.

Il n'en demeure pas moins que les possibilités offertes par la Convention sont loin d'être pleinement exploitées. L'approche des INDH est encore souvent timide, et exclusivement nationale si l'on ne tient pas compte de l'action du Groupe européen des INDH. Cette situation s'explique peut-être par la grande hétérogénéité des INDH, dont l'ancienneté, la composition, les moyens, l'indépendance, le prestige et l'influence varient – parfois beaucoup – d'un pays à l'autre. Sans oublier que treize États membres du Conseil de l'Europe ne sont pas encore dotés d'une INDH.

On pourrait imaginer que les INDH aient à cœur de conseiller les requérants potentiels sur les possibilités mais aussi les limites des ressources offertes par la Convention. Ainsi, il serait naturel qu'elles les éclairent sur les conditions de recevabilité, en particulier celle de l'épuisement des voies de recours internes, sans même parler de la notion malaisée à saisir du défaut manifeste de fondement. D'aucuns considèrent même qu'elles pourraient servir de filtre national afin de soulager la Cour, mais une telle idée se heurterait à des obstacles juridiques et pratiques sans doute insurmontables si l'on entend préserver le droit de recours individuel, véritable pierre angulaire du système de Strasbourg.

Le préambule de la Convention affirme que les libertés fondamentales « constituent les assises mêmes de la justice et de la paix dans le monde ». Dans cet esprit, les INDH ont vocation à relayer ou à amplifier les efforts souvent remarquables des organisations non gouvernementales de défense des droits de l'homme. Les unes et les autres ont beau avoir un statut différent, elles poursuivent en réalité le même but, un but intrinsèquement lié à la mission de la Cour et à la construction de l'Europe.

The European Union, its Citizens and its Foreigners

Elspeth GUILD

Jean Monnet Professor ad personam Radboud University, Nijmegen

1. Introduction

It is a pleasure to be included in this volume in honour of Paul Demaret. His contribution to the European Union's development has been outstanding. In my area, citizens of the Union and their transformations, the work of Professor Demaret has been very important. The objects of my research are the beneficiaries of the efforts of Professor Demaret and our colleagues to take forward the EU integration agenda.

This chapter focuses on how our understanding in the European Union regarding who is a migrant has changed from 1957 to the present. Starting with the EU fundamental freedom, the right of free movement of persons, I examine how EU nationals themselves moved from being perceived as migrants in the territory of other Member States to EU citizens while at the same time the EU enlarged to include an ever wider number of countries. The importance of the creation of EU rights which individuals could access and claim even against the volition of a Member State's authorities plays a key role in this development. In the second part of this chapter, I will examine how the EU has developed its powers in respect of third country nationals and pose the question whether in the process of legislating on the admission and residence of third country nationals in the EU a parallel process is now occurring as regards these persons as has taken place in respect of EU national migrants.

2. The Time Line of Workers' Rights

The acquisition of rights for migrant workers who were also nationals of the Member States takes place incrementally from 1957 until the current time. The EEC Treaty 1957 provided for free movement of workers in what is now Article 39 EC. However, transitional provisions applied to workers until 1968. Article 40 EEC (as it then was) required the Council to take progressive steps to achieve free movement of workers (the right of free movement for establishment and services was not subject to limitations indicating the difference in perspective between workers as agents of market upheaval and the self employed or service providers as a relatively benign group of actors). In 1961 the EU first adopted implementing legislation towards free movement of workers – Regulation 15/61. This was followed in 1964 by a deepening of the rights of workers in Regulation 38/64. According to the recital of the first regulation, the objective is the abolition of all discrimination based on nationality between workers of the Member States as regards work, pay and other conditions of work. The objective requires also the elimination of waiting periods and other restrictions which constituted an obstacle to free movement by the end of the transitional period in 1968. The first stage of the transitional period lasted two years (similarly to that of the transitional arrangements for nationals of the 2004 Member States).[1]

The second stage of the transitional period for free movement of workers arrived two years later and was accompanied by the adoption of a new Regulation 38/64 which was designed to take forward the integration of the EU labour market. In the preamble to this Regulation, one finds references to different categories of workers – permanent, seasonal and frontier. For the first time the situation of workers who are the employees of service providers and as such sent across EU borders is mentioned (an issue which is still, in 2012, a matter of concern in some Member States).[2]

At the end of the transitional period, 1968, Regulation 1612/68 was adopted which replaced the previous rules providing a clear set of rights for migrant workers. At the same time, Directive 68/360 was adopted which provided the rules on procedures for the treatment of EU migrant workers. Interestingly, Directive 64/221 which sets out the rules of exclusion and expulsion of migrant workers was adopted in 1964 and continued to apply until the citizens of the Union Directive was adopted in 2004 (2004/38).[3]

---

1 Guild, E., *European Immigration Law*, The Hague, Kluwer Law International, 2000, pp. 110-120. I examine in depth there the Regulation in comparison with the subsidiary legislation.

2 Carlier, J.Y., *La condition des personnes dans l'Union européene*, Brussels, Larcier, 2007.

3 Condinanzi, M., Lang, A. and Nascimbene, B., *Citizenship of the Union and Freedom of Movement of Persons*, The Hague, Martinus Nijhoff, 2008.

In 1993, EU nationals were designated as citizens of the Union through changes to the EC Treaty which came into effect then. While this change had little immediate impact on the rights of EU nationals, over the 20 years since its introduction it has become a central part of the right to move and reside of EU nationals. The most important EU measure providing for entry and residence rights of EU nationals and their third country national family members has been adopted under this power – Directive 2004/38 – which builds on the rights gradually acquired by EU nationals over the time line described above. While it may be something of a misnomer to call EU nationals citizens of an entity which is not a state, nonetheless the legal framework provides them rights which approximate those of nationals, at least as long as they can find work or support themselves. EU nationals and their third country national family members are entitled to move and reside in any Member State for three months, no questions asked. Thereafter, if they are workers or self employed they are entitled to residence and access to social benefits if they qualify for them; if they are economically inactive or students they have at least to declare themselves self sufficient. After five years residence they acquire permanent residence which gives full access to all social rights which may have been limited before. After 10 years residence an additional protection against expulsion applies. EU nationals, through the acquisition of rights, most importantly to move, reside, exercise economic activities, equal treatment with own nationals and protection from expulsion, have moved from being foreigners or immigrants in the eyes of most citizens of the Union to being fellow citizens.

3. Who are Immigrants in the EU?

The power to decide who is an immigrant and who is not remained a national prerogative until 1999 when the Amsterdam Treaty was adopted giving competence to the EU to adopt legislation in the area. Since then, in the area of legal migration, the EU has adopted a series of measures which regulate the longer term entry and residence of third country nationals. Ireland and the UK have opted out of these measures. The first and most important measure is the Directive on Family Reunification. This was adopted in 2003 and had to be transposed by the Member States by October 2005. The objective of the Directive is to create a right to family reunification for third country nationals who reside legally in the Member States. The way this is pursued is by establishing minimum standards for the admission and treatment of third country national family members. Family reunification is an EU right, according to the Directive, for spouses and minor children. The conditions for its exercise are:

- Stable and regular resources to support the family;
- Adequate housing;
- Comprehensive sickness insurance.

Member States are permitting to apply an integration measures condition to family members either before or after admission to the state. This is a derogation from the right to family reunification.[4]

In October 2008, the Commission published the first report on implementation of the Directive in the Member States (COM (2008) 610 final). In general, the Commission expressed concern that the Directive, which is aimed at creating a level playing field for third country nationals' family reunification, in fact seems to be resulting in very substantial variations in access to the right.

The CJEU has been asked on a number of occasions by 2012 to give an interpretation of the Directive. By September 2012 the most important decision has been one in response a reference from a Dutch court.[5] The key issues were two fold: what income could Member States require of a third country national seeking family reunification with his or her spouse and what constitutes social assistance for the purposes of the Directive. The relevant Dutch law which transposed the Directive requires a sponsor to have an income equivalent to 120% of the minimum wage. However, Dutch law provides that there are two categories of social assistance – a lower level called general assistance which is the minimum wage – and special assistance which is the equivalent of 120% of the minimum wage. Which level then was applicable for the application of the Directive? If only the general social assistance level, then Mr Chakroun's income was sufficient, if the special assistance level applied then it was not.

The problem was compounded by another specificity of Dutch law – where a couple marry before either of them move to the Netherlands, then the applicable rate for income for family reunification is the lower general assistance level. But if the couple marries after one of them has moved to the Netherlands (as Mr and Mrs Chakroun had done) then the higher special assistance level is applicable to the income requirement. The couple complained that this constituted unlawful discrimination in light of the Directive's objectives. The CJEU pointed out that the Directive creates a right of family reunification which an individual can rely upon. There is no margin of appreciation for the Member States. Because the Directive creates this, the conditions for the exercise of the

4 Van Oers, R., Ersboll, E. & Kostakopoulou, D., *A Re-definition of Belonging? Language and Integration Tests in Europe*, The Hague, Brill, 2010.

5 C-578/08, *Chakroun*, 4 March 2010.

right must be restrictively interpreted. In other words the Dutch legislation was found fully incompatible with the Directive. In its finding the CJEU relied not only on the European Convention on Human Rights for guidance but refers to the EU Charter of Fundamental Rights on numerous occasions as a source of interpretation.

The second substantial measure which the EU has adopted in this field is the Long Term Residents' Directive. The Commission will produce a report on the implementation of the Directive in 2011.[6] A number of studies which have been undertaken by academics indicate substantial variations across the Member States.[7] The principle of the Directive is that any third country national, not coming within an excluded group (such as students or diplomats), who has resided lawfully in a Member State for five years will obtain a long term residence status in EU law so long as three conditions are fulfilled:

- The individual fulfills the residential requirement;
- The individual has stable and regular resources to support him or herself and dependents;
- The individual has fully comprehensive sickness insurance.

However, similar to the Family Reunification Directive, a fourth condition may be applied by the Member States – that the individual complies with integration conditions. It is this requirement which has been the source of most concern among academic researchers regarding the implementation of the Directive.[8] Once an individual acquires EU long term residence status under the Directive this can only be lost in accordance with the terms of the Directive, which are very limited. Further the person is entitled to full equal treatment with own nationals within the Member State where the status was acquired (with exceptions for political rights and economic activities which are not open to EU nationals). Finally the status gives an entitlement to move and exercise activities, economic and otherwise in other Member States subject to a (fairly limited) labour market conditions test. With this Directive, the EU has made very important progress towards the objective it stated in Tampere in 1999 to treat third country nationals resident in the EU fairly and consistently.

6 This report was issued on 28 September 2011 COM(2011)585 final.

7 Halleskov, L., "The Long Term Residents' Directive: A Fulfilment of the Tampere Objective of near Equality?", *European Journal of Migration and Law*, Vol. 7, No. 5, 2005, pp. 203-211.

8 Guild, E., Groenendijk, K., Carrera, S., *Illiberal Liberal States: Immigration, Citizenship and Integration in the EU*, Farnham, Ashgate, 2009.

The third measure which has been adopted and provides immigration rights for third country nationals is Directive 2009/50 on the conditions of entry and residence of third country nationals for the purposes of highly qualified employment (the Blue Card Directive). This Directive seeks to regulate highly qualified migration to the EU in pursuit of the EU's objective of becoming the most competitive and dynamic knowledge-based economy in the world. It only applies to highly qualified employment which is defined as that which requires adequate and specific competence as proven by high professional qualifications. These are attested by means of any diploma, certificate or other evidence of formal qualifications issued by a competent authority attesting the successful completion of a post-secondary higher education programme on condition that the studies lasted at least three years. Professional experience of at least five years can be substituted. In order to qualify for a Blue Card, the individual must hold the necessary qualification and the employment proposed in the Member State must pay at least 1.5 times the average gross annual salary in the Member State concerned. After 18 months employment in one Member State, the Blue Card holder is privileged in the movement to another Member State for highly qualified employment.

The fourth measure which the EU has adopted regarding long stay migration for economic activities is regarding researchers. In October 2005 the Directive on admission of third country nationals for the purpose of scientific research was adopted.[9] According to the preamble, it is intended to contribute to achieving the goal of "opening up the Community to third-country nationals who might be admitted for the purposes of research".[10] By doing this, the institutions believe that the EU will be more attractive to researchers from around the world, which in turn will boost its position as an international centre for research. Attention is paid in the preamble to the question of brain drain and back up measures to support researchers' reintegration in their countries of origin. In accordance with the Lisbon process, fostering mobility within the EU is also an objective.[11]

The Directive defines research, researcher and research institution in wide terms. Research means creative work undertaken on a systematic basis in order to increase the stock of knowledge of humanity, culture and society, and the use of this stock of knowledge to devise new applications. A researcher is someone who holds higher education

---

9 Directive 2005/71.

10 The goal does not appear to have been reached.

11 The Lisbon Process, http://www.eu2005.lu/en/actualites/documents_travail/2005/-03/22lisboa/index.html.

qualifications which give access to doctoral programmes. A research organisation must have been approved for the purposes of the Directive by a Member State in accordance with legislation or administrative practice. As the Directive is written in terms of a research institution holding the key to mobility, Member State control over access to the territory for researchers takes place through the qualification of a research institution. According to the Directive, the research institution must initiate the procedure.

As set out above regarding legal immigration, before the adoption of the TFEU, a number of key areas have been the subject of harmonizing measures which are based on the principle of minimum standards. Specifically, family reunification, long term resident status, highly qualified migration and admission of researchers have all enjoyed some degree of harmonization in this way. Further proposals are outstanding as at September 2012 regarding other areas of first admission for labour market access, specifically, seasonal workers and inter-corporate transferees. When these measures are adopted, the EU will have fulfilled much of its objective of creating a common EU migration system composed of legal instruments which provide clarity and certainty to individuals, businesses and state authorities.

4. Who is an Irregular Migrant in the EU?

The EU institutions prefer to use the term "illegal" immigration rather than irregular or undocumented migration favoured by other international organisations and institutions.[12] This is notwithstanding the fact that not only has the Council of Europe's Parliamentary Assembly called on the EU institutions to use more neutral language, but also the European Parliament has similarly done so with noticeably little effect.[13] In this area the EU institutions have been quite active, adopting over twenty measures since acquiring competence to do so. The most controversial of the measures has been the Returns Directive (2008/115) which, for instance, has been denounced by the heads of state of all countries in South America.[14] What the Directive seeks to do is establish clear, transparent and fair rules for an effective return policy which the

12 Council of Europe High Commissioner for Human Rights, *Criminalization of Migration in Europe: Human Rights Implications Council of Europe*, Strasbourg 2009.

13 Carrera, S. and Merlino, M., *Undocumented Immigrants and Rights in the EU: Addressing the Gap between Social Science Research and Policy-Making*, Centre for European Policy Studies, Brussels, 2009.

14 Acosta Arcarazo, D., *Latin American Reactions to the Adoption of the Returns Directive*, Centre for European Policy Studies, Brussels, 2009.

EU considers to be a necessary element of a well managed migration policy. The ending of an irregular stay by a third country national is to occur through a fair and transparent procedure culminating in expulsion.

The objective of the Directive is to set out common standards and procedures to be applied by the Member States when returning irregularly staying third country nationals to other countries. It is required to be in compliance with fundamental rights and international law including refugee protection and human rights obligations. "Illegal stay" which is a key concept of the Directive means the presence on the territory of a Member State of a third country national who does not fulfil or no longer fulfils the conditions of entry as set out in Article 5 of the Schengen Borders Code (on short stay entry for three months or less) or other conditions for entry, stay or residence in that Member State. Return is defined as voluntary or enforced compliance with an obligation to return to either his or her country of origin or a country of transit in accordance with Union or bilateral readmission agreements or other arrangements or another third country to which the third country national concerned voluntarily decides to return and in which he or she will be accepted.

The first step that the Returns Directive requires a Member State to take is to decide whether to issue an individual with an autonomous residence permit or other authorization offering a right to stay for compassionate, humanitarian or other reasons or not (Article 6(4)). If the Member State decides not to issue some sort of authorization then it is obliged under the Directive to issue a return decision. Return can be voluntary which the Directive appears to promote or enforced if the individual does not leave (Article 8). Where a Member State enforces a return decision it must also issue an entry ban on the individual which in principle should be for a five years period (Article 11). The most controversial part of the Directive is that relating to detention. In Chapter IV of the Directive, detention is incorporated as a normal part of the return process although it is specifically stated to be a final resort where there is a risk of absconding or the individual is hampering the return procedure. Detention is subject to a series of safeguards regarding the making of the decision, the right to remedies against the decision and judicial supervision of the detention. The initial limit to the length of detention is six months, but this can be extended for a further twelve months (Article 15).

Like the Family Reunification Directive, the Returns Directive has already been the subject of judicial consideration by the CJEU on a number of occasions.[15] The first time was in one of the last judgments of

15 C-357/09 PPU, *Kadzoev (Huchbarov)*, 30 November 2009.

the CJEU before the entry into force of the Lisbon Treaty and it was subject to the urgent procedure in view of the fact that the individual was in detention. The case revolved around a Mr Kadzoev or Huchbarov whose identity is never fully certain. He had been arrested by the Bulgarian authorities near their border with Turkey. He was detained from 3 November 2006 and was still in detention when the case was heard by the CJEU in 2009. The man stated he was Mr Huchbarov, a Chechen, but he did not wish the assistance of the Russian authorities. The Bulgarian authorities decided that he was Mr Kadzoev a Chechen with a Georgian mother. The Bulgarian authorities sent the identity documents which they had in respect of Mr Kadzoev to the Russian authorities but the latter stated that the documents were from persons and authorities unknown to the Russian Federation and thus no proof of Russian nationality. Various applications for the man to be released from detention failed, not least as he had no address in Bulgaria. In 2007 he applied for asylum. The authorities continued to detain him and eventually in 2009 refused his application definitively without any further appeal right.

In the meantime, the Bulgarian authorities were having no luck in finding a country to send the man to. They struck out with the Russians, tried and failed with the Georgians and even approached the Austrian authorities to see if they would take him, again without success. Finally, a Bulgarian court, once again faced with an application for the man's release from custody, asked the CJEU whether the 18 months maximum period of detention under the Return Directive applied in this case. The CJEU found that the Directive was applicable in light of the Bulgarian law which transposed it (notwithstanding the fact that the period for transposition had not yet expired). Two central issues arose – first, could the man's detention while he was seeking asylum count towards the 18 month maximum on detention, secondly could periods of detention during judicial review count towards the 18 months maximum.

On the first question the CJEU looked long and hard at the Asylum Procedures Directive (2004/85). It held that if the requirements of the procedures which permit limits to be placed on an individual's freedom of movement were followed (and which provide substantial guarantees and freedoms to the individual) then that time when liberty is restricted does not count towards the 18 month maximum under the Return Directive. But if the detention continued to be on the basis of national rules which effectively correspond to detention under the Return Directive then it does count (para. 47). On the second question, the CJEU held that 18 months means 18 months, irrespective of whether judicial review or other legal challenges were launched by the individual. After 18 months the state must release the individual. In no case can the maximum period be exceeded irrespective of whether the individual is aggressive, has no means of supporting himself or has no travel or identity documents (para. 68-69). Further the CJEU held that the possibility of detaining a person on grounds of public order and public safety cannot be based on the Return Directive (para. 70). Since, this first decision, the CJEU has interpreted a number of very important aspects of the Directive, providing Member States with clarity about their common rules on the treatment of persons irregularly present in the EU. This has been a big step forward in the creation of the common Area of Freedom, Security and Justice as it provides the foundations for Member State authorities to have confidence in the rules which apply across the EU and must be implemented regarding the treatment of third country nationals whose residence is not or is no loner permitted.

5. The EU Charter of Fundamental Rights and the Lisbon Treaty

Article 6 TEU provides that the EU Charter of Fundamental Rights, adopted in 2000, shall have the same legal value as the Treaties. The Charter was drafted and adopted in 2000 but it was denied legal effects as a result of disagreements among the Member States (primarily the UK in disaccord with the others) about the added value of a legally binding Charter. According to its preamble, the Charter sets out the Union's foundation on indivisible, universal values of human dignity, freedom, equality and solidarity. It confirms that the EU is based on the principles of democracy and rule of law. In order to promote the four freedoms of the EU, free movement of goods, persons, services and capital, the Charter states that it is necessary to strengthen the protection of fundamental rights and thus recognises the rights, freedoms and principles set out. A protocol to the Lisbon Treaty provides that the legal effect of the Charter is limited in the UK and Poland.

The Charter includes the rights contained in the European Convention on Human Rights (ECHR) and the Charter's Article 52(3) provides that Charter rights which correspond to ECHR rights shall have the same meaning and scope on those in the ECHR. Thus the way in which the ECtHR has interpreted the ECHR rights in immigration matters becomes a subject of substantial importance for the EU. This is not the place now to set out the jurisprudence of the ECtHR in immigration matters which has been extensively examined elsewhere.[16] Nor is it the place to examine how the CJEU has incorporated the ECHR into its

[16] Blake, N.Q.C. & Husain, R., *Immigration, Asylum and Human Rights*, Oxford University Press, Oxford, 2003; Sikuta, J. & Hubalkova, E., *The European Court of Human Rights: Case Law of the Grand Chamber*, Amsterdam, TMC Asser, 2007.

jurisprudence,[17] though it is worth noting that both the Lisbon Treaty and the Stockholm Programme mandate the accession of the EU to the ECHR. The point which I want to make here is that immigration measures in the EU are no longer self-referential. All of the EU immigration measures contain a standard preamble which confirms their compatibility with the ECHR and EU fundamental rights standards. Most of the measures, when they were proposed, were subject to a fundamental rights impact assessment which the Commission carried out. But there was no external assessment of the human rights and fundamental rights consequences for individuals of the measures. Further within the EU system there was no obvious way consistent across the Member States in which an individual could lay claim to fundamental rights in light of the implementation of an EU measure on immigration. Now with the legal effect of the Charter within the scope of EU law this ambiguity has been cleared up.

Bearing in mind the importance of the ECHR as interpreted by the European Court of Human Rights in immigration and asylum cases over the past twenty years, the capacity to absorb into the EU's Common European Asylum System and immigration measures the fundamental rights obligations of the ECHR through the application of the Charter is a great step forward.

6. Conclusions

In this chapter I have sought to examine who is a migrant in the EU, first by looking at the position of EU nationals and their acquisition of hard rights in EU law which resulted in them ceasing to be considered as immigrants as such but as co-citizens at least in the main and then by looking at the EU's developing competences over third country nationals. At the outset, I posed the question whether one could see a parallel in the development of rights of EU nationals and third country nationals in EU law. Having examined the measures which have been adopted, I must make an assessment. Clearly there is some way to go before the rights of third country nationals will approximate those of EU nationals. While this road has been partially covered for third country nationals who have completed five years lawful residence in the EU, for others there is still a distance between the rights of EU nationals and third country nationals. Family reunification remains a contentious issue for third country nationals who must jump through many more hoops to be joined by their third country national family members than EU nation-

17 Guild, E. & Lesieur, G. (eds.), *The European Court of Justice on the European Convention on Human Rights: Who said what when*, The Hague, Kluwer Law International, 1997.

als. Worryingly, even among third country nationals there are now differences in family reunification as those who hold Blue Cards do not have integration conditions to fulfill, while those third country nationals who have lived and worked in the EU for much longer may be subjected to this obstacle to family reunification.

Security of residence for EU nationals and third country nationals who have completed five years residence in the EU are approximated to a fairly high degree. But the capacity to allocate the characteristic of irregular or illegal to an individual remains primarily a matter of national law. Once a state designates the individual as not within the scope of legality according to national rules, a panoply of EU measures provide for the treatment of the individual, from detention to expulsion. For EU nationals, becoming irregularly present on the territory of another Member State is a matter of substantial dispute. To what extent there is a gap between an EU national enjoying an EU right to move and reside and the application of national rules on migration has yet to be ultimately determined by the Court of Justice. However, it does seem clear that it is that court which will have the last word on the subject.

L'autonomie conceptuelle de la citoyenneté de l'Union

Koen Lenaerts

Vice-président de la Cour de justice de l'Union européenne et professeur extraordinaire à la Katholieke Universiteit Leuven

José A. Gutiérrez-Fons

Membre du cabinet du vice-président

Ayant vocation à être « le statut fondamental des ressortissants des États membres »,[1] la citoyenneté de l'Union européenne devait, tôt ou tard, devenir plus que la liberté de circulation des citoyens européens n'exerçant aucune activité économique. C'est ainsi que dans les affaires ayant donné lieu aux arrêts Ruiz Zambrano,[2] McCarthy,[3] Dereci[4] et Iida,[5] la Cour de justice de l'Union européenne (la « Cour ») a jugé que, même en l'absence d'un élément transfrontalier, « l'Article 20 TFUE s'oppose à des mesures nationales ayant pour effet de priver les citoyens de l'Union de la jouissance effective de l'essentiel des droits conférés par leur statut de citoyen de l'Union ».[6] Cette jurisprudence ouvre donc une nouvelle étape pour la citoyenneté de l'Union, dans la mesure où cette citoyenneté s'est émancipée des limites inhérentes aux libertés fondamentales.[7]

---

1 Voir, par exemple, arrêts du 11 juillet 2002, *D'Hoop*, C-224/98, Rec. p. I-6191, point 27, et du 2 octobre 2003, *Garcia Avello*, C-148/02, Rec. p. I-11613, point 21.

2 Arrêt du 8 mars 2011, *Ruiz Zambrano*, C-34/09, non encore publié au Recueil.

3 Arrêt du 5 mai 2011, *McCarthy*, C-434/09, non encore publié au Recueil.

4 Arrêt du 15 novembre 2011, *Dereci e.a.*, C-256/11, non encore publié au Recueil.

5 Arrêt du 8 novembre 2012, *Iida*, C-40/11, non encore publié au Recueil.

6 Ruiz Zambrano, *supra*, note 2, point 42.

7 Voir, en ce sens, Lenaerts, K., et Gutiérrez-Fons, J.A., « Ruiz-Zambrano (C-34/09) o de la emancipación de la Ciudadanía de la Unión de los límites inherentes a la libre circulación », *Revista Española de Derecho Europeo*, 2011, p. 493, et Lenaerts, K., « "Civis europaeus sum" : from the cross-borderlink to the status of citizen of the Union », in P. Cardonnel, A. Rosas, N. Wahl (dir.), *Constitutionalising the EU Judi-*

Étant donné que la « citoyenneté de l'Union » a ainsi obtenu une autonomie conceptuelle par rapport aux libertés fondamentales du marché intérieur, la question se pose de savoir comment la définir et préciser son champ d'application. Dans la présente contribution, nous proposons, dans un premier temps, d'examiner brièvement chacun des arrêts susmentionnés (1.). Il sera déduit de cette lecture que, afin d'appliquer la nouvelle approche issue de l'arrêt Ruiz Zambrano, la mesure nationale doit, *de iure* ou *de facto*, avoir pour effet de priver le citoyen de l'Union en cause d'un des droits conférés par son statut de citoyen. Dans un deuxième temps, nous ferons valoir que des mesures nationales qui limitent l'exercice d'un droit fondamental d'un tel citoyen, mais qui ne le privent pas de la jouissance effective de l'essentiel des droits conférés par son statut de citoyen de l'Union ni n'entravent l'exercice desdits droits, ne relèvent pas du champ d'application des traités, au motif que de telles mesures ne constituent pas « une mise en œuvre du droit de l'Union », au sens de l'Article 51, paragraphe 1, de la charte des droits fondamentaux de l'Union européenne[8] (la « charte ») (2.). Enfin, en guise de conclusion, nous nous efforcerons d'expliquer que cette autonomie conceptuelle ne bouleverse aucunement la répartition verticale et horizontale des compétences au sein de l'Union envisagée par les auteurs des traités (3.).

1. Le critère relatif à la privation de l'essentiel des droits conférés par le statut de citoyen

Les origines de l'autonomie conceptuelle de la citoyenneté de l'Union remontent à l'affaire ayant donné lieu à l'arrêt Rottmann.[9] Dans cette affaire, la question était de savoir si l'Article 20 TFUE devait être interprété en ce sens qu'il s'opposait à ce qu'un État membre, en l'occurrence l'Allemagne, retire à un citoyen de l'Union la nationalité de cet État membre acquise par naturalisation lorsque celle-ci avait été obtenue de manière frauduleuse, dans la mesure où ce retrait privait l'intéressé de son statut de citoyen de l'Union et du bénéfice des droits y attachés en le rendant apatride. En effet, l'acquisition de la nationalité de cet État membre par naturalisation avait entraîné, dans le chef de la personne concernée, la perte de la nationalité de son État membre d'origine, en l'espèce l'Autriche. Contrairement à l'avis des gouvernements allemand et autrichien, la Cour a estimé que la situation du citoyen de l'Union concerné n'était pas purement interne, en dépit du

---

cial System : Essays in Honour of Pernilla Lindh, Oxford, Hart Publishing, 2012, p. 213.

8 *JO* C 83 du 30 mars 2010, p. 389.

9 Arrêt du 2 mars 2010, *Rottmann*, C-135/08, Rec. p. I-1449.

fait que la décision de retrait attaquée avait été prise par des autorités allemandes à l'encontre d'un ressortissant allemand qui résidait en Allemagne. À la différence de l'avocat général Poiares Maduro, la Cour n'a pas cherché à trouver un élément transfrontalier en considérant « l'origine de la situation » du Dr Rottmann, à savoir le fait qu'il avait exercé son droit à la libre circulation avant de devenir ressortissant allemand,[10] mais elle a centré son analyse sur les effets prospectifs de la décision de retrait. La Cour a ainsi jugé que

> la situation d'un citoyen de l'Union qui, tel le requérant au principal, est confronté à une décision de retrait de la naturalisation adoptée par les autorités d'un État membre le plaçant, après qu'il a perdu la nationalité d'un autre État membre qu'il possédait à l'origine, dans une situation susceptible d'entraîner la perte du statut conféré par l'Article [20 TFUE] et des droits y attachés relève, par sa nature et ses conséquences, du droit de l'Union.[11]

Toutefois, en se référant aux principes du droit international général, la Cour a estimé qu'il est légitime pour un État membre de retirer la nationalité à un citoyen de l'Union acquise par naturalisation lorsque celle-ci a été obtenue de manière frauduleuse,[12] pour autant que la décision de retrait respecte le principe de proportionnalité.[13]

Il ressort de l'arrêt Rottmann que, en dépit de l'absence d'un élément transfrontalier, l'Article 20 TFUE s'oppose, en principe, à une mesure nationale qui entraîne juridiquement la perte du statut de citoyen de l'Union et des droits y attachés.

Se posait alors la question de savoir si l'approche retenue par la Cour dans cette affaire était transposable à une mesure nationale qui, sans entraîner la perte *de iure* du statut de citoyen de l'Union, produisait *de facto* les mêmes effets. Dans l'affaire ayant donné lieu à l'arrêt Ruiz Zambrano, la Cour, après avoir estimé que la directive 2004/38[14] n'était pas applicable en l'espèce,[15] a répondu par l'affirmative à cette question en constatant que

---

10 Conclusions de l'avocat général Poiares Maduro dans Rottmann, *supra*, note 9, point 11.

11 Rottmann, *supra*, note 9, point 42.

12 *Ibid.*, points 51-53.

13 *Ibid.*, points 55-56.

14 Directive 2004/38 du Parlement européen et du Conseil du 29 avril 2004 relative au droit des citoyens de l'Union et des membres de leurs familles de circuler et de séjourner librement sur le territoire des États membres, modifiant le règlement (CEE) n° 1612/68 et abrogeant les directives 64/221/CEE, 68/360/CEE, 72/194/CEE, 73/148/CEE, 75/34/CEE, 75/35/CEE, 90/364/CEE, 90/365/CEE et 93/96/CEE, *JO* L 158 du 30 avril 2004, p. 77.

15 Ruiz Zambrano, *supra*, note 2, point 39. S'agissant de l'article 3 de la directive 2004/38, la Cour a jugé qu'« il y a lieu de constater que, aux termes du paragraphe 1

l'Article 20 TFUE s'oppose à des mesures nationales ayant pour effet de priver les citoyens de l'Union de la jouissance effective de l'essentiel des droits conférés par leur statut de citoyen de l'Union.

Pour M. Ruiz Zambrano, ressortissant colombien en situation migratoire irrégulière et père de deux enfants belges, cela voulait dire que les autorités belges ne pouvaient lui refuser ni un droit de séjour dérivé ni un permis de travail, étant donné que de tels refus « [auraient eu] pour conséquence que lesdits enfants, citoyens de l'Union, se [verraient] obligés de quitter le territoire de l'Union pour accompagner leurs parents »,[16] les privant ainsi de « la jouissance effective de l'essentiel des droits conférés par leur statut de citoyen de l'Union ». Le fait que ces deux enfants étaient nés en Belgique et n'avaient jamais exercé leur droit à la libre circulation n'était pas une raison suffisante pour exclure l'application de l'Article 20 TFUE.

Il ressort de l'arrêt Ruiz Zambrano que l'existence d'un élément transfrontalier n'est pas toujours une condition préalable et nécessaire à l'application des dispositions du traité relatives à la citoyenneté de l'Union. Cet arrêt a donc confirmé la nouvelle approche dont la portée sera, par la suite, clarifiée par la Cour dans les affaires McCarthy, Dereci et Iida.

Dans l'affaire McCarthy, la Cour a été interrogée sur le point de savoir si l'Article 20 TFUE était applicable à une situation telle que celle de Mme McCarthy, une citoyenne de l'Union qui n'avait jamais fait usage de son droit à la libre circulation, qui avait toujours séjourné dans un État membre dont elle possédait la nationalité, en l'occurrence le Royaume-Uni, et qui jouissait, par ailleurs, de la nationalité d'un autre État membre, en l'occurrence l'Irlande. Dans le litige au principal, Mme McCarthy et son mari, ressortissant jamaïcain en situation migratoire irrégulière, avaient demandé au Secretary of State une autorisation de séjour et un titre de séjour conformément au droit de l'Union, en tant que, respectivement, citoyenne de l'Union et conjoint d'une citoyenne de l'Union. Le Secretary of State a toutefois rejeté leur demande au motif que Mme McCarthy n'était pas une personne subvenant à ses besoins, mais dépendait de l'assistance sociale. Mme McCarthy a alors attaqué cette décision devant les juridictions anglaises, en faisant valoir qu'une telle décision était incompatible avec l'Article 20 TFUE.

---

de l'article 3 de la directive 2004/38, intitulé "Bénéficiaires", celle-ci s'applique à tout citoyen de l'Union qui "se rend ou séjourne dans un État membre autre que celui dont il a la nationalité, ainsi qu'aux membres de sa famille". Dès lors, ladite directive ne trouve pas à s'appliquer dans une situation telle que celle en cause au principal ».

16 Ruiz Zambrano, *supra*, note 2, point 44.

Ayant constaté que la directive 2004/38 n'était pas applicable dans le cas d'espèce,[17] la Cour a dit pour droit que « la situation d'un citoyen de l'Union qui, telle Mme McCarthy, n'a pas fait usage du droit de libre circulation ne saurait, de ce seul fait, être assimilée à une situation purement interne ».[18] « Cependant », a-t-elle jugé au point 49 de l'arrêt, « aucun élément de la situation de Mme McCarthy, telle que décrite par la juridiction de renvoi, ne fait apparaître que la mesure nationale en cause au principal aurait pour effet de la *priver* de la jouissance effective de l'essentiel des droits attachés à son statut de citoyenne de l'Union ou *d'entraver* l'exercice de son droit de circuler et de séjourner librement sur le territoire des États membres, conformément à l'Article 21 TFUE ».[19]

En effet, contrairement à ce qui caractérisait l'affaire ayant donné lieu à l'arrêt Ruiz Zambrano, Mme McCarthy, en tant que ressortissante du Royaume-Uni, bénéficiait d'un droit inconditionnel de séjour dans ledit État membre et, partant, la décision attaquée ne l'obligeait aucunement à quitter le territoire de l'Union.[20] De plus, la Cour a également distingué la situation de Mme McCarthy de celle ayant donné lieu à l'arrêt Garcia Avello.[21] En se référant à cet arrêt, la Cour a rappelé que « l'application de la réglementation d'un État membre à [des citoyens de l'Union,] ressortissants de cet État membre ayant également la nationalité d'un autre État membre[,] avait pour effet que ces citoyens de l'Union portaient des noms de famille différents au regard des deux systèmes juridiques concernés et que cette situation était de nature à engendrer, pour eux, de sérieux inconvénients d'ordre tant professionnel que privé, résultant, notamment, des difficultés à bénéficier dans un État membre dont ils ont la nationalité des effets juridiques d'actes ou de documents établis sous le nom reconnu dans l'autre État membre dont ils possèdent également la nationalité ».[22] Ainsi, ce n'était pas la double nationalité des citoyens de l'Union concernés qui créait un lien de rattachement avec le droit de l'Union, mais le fait que la diversité des noms patronymiques « était de nature à engendrer pour lesdits citoyens

17 McCarthy, *supra*, note 3, point 34. S'agissant de la directive 2004/38, la Cour a jugé que ladite directive « concernant les conditions d'exercice du droit de circuler et de séjourner librement sur le territoire des États membres, ne saurait avoir vocation à s'appliquer à un citoyen de l'Union qui jouit d'un droit de séjour inconditionnel en raison du fait qu'il séjourne dans l'État membre de sa nationalité ».

18 *Ibid.*, point 46.

19 C'est nous qui soulignons.

20 *Ibid.*, point 50.

21 Garcia Avello, *supra*, note 1.

22 McCarthy, *supra*, note 3, point 51.

de l'Union des inconvénients sérieux qui constituaient une entrave à la libre circulation ».[23]

Il ressort de l'arrêt McCarthy que les Articles 20 TFUE et 21 TFUE sont applicables dès lors que la mesure nationale en cause au principal a pour effet soit « de priver les citoyens de l'Union de la jouissance effective de l'essentiel [de leur droit à la libre circulation] » (ci-après l'« effet de privation »), comme c'était le cas dans l'affaire Ruiz Zambrano, soit d'entraver l'exercice dudit droit, comme c'était le cas dans l'affaire Garcia Avello.[24] À la différence des mesures nationales produisant le premier type d'effet, celles entravant l'exercice du droit à la libre circulation ne relèvent du champ d'application des Articles 20 TFUE et 21 TFUE que s'il existe un élément transfrontalier. Autrement dit, l'analyse d'une mesure nationale ayant pour effet d'entraver le droit à la libre circulation s'insère dans la ligne jurisprudentielle classique des libertés fondamentales. De plus, ainsi que la Cour l'a souligné à plusieurs reprises et le rappellera dans l'affaire Iida, bien qu'une entrave puisse être potentielle, elle ne saurait être purement hypothétique.

Par ailleurs, afin de déterminer si une mesure nationale a pour effet d'entraver le droit à la libre circulation, il suffit que celle-ci engendre pour le citoyen de l'Union concerné de « sérieux inconvénients ». En revanche, s'agissant de mesures nationales ayant pour effet « de priver [le citoyen de l'Union concerné] de la jouissance effective de l'essentiel [de son droit à la libre circulation] », celles-ci doivent produire plus que de « sérieux inconvénients » : elles doivent mettre le citoyen de l'Union concerné dans l'impossibilité d'exercer son droit à la libre circulation.

Ce dernier aspect de l'arrêt McCarthy a été mis en exergue par la Cour dans l'affaire ayant donné lieu à l'arrêt Dereci. Ladite affaire présente deux points en commun avec l'affaire Ruiz Zambrano. En premier lieu, de même que M. Ruiz Zambrano, M. Dereci était un ressortissant d'un État tiers, en l'occurrence de la Turquie, en situation migratoire irrégulière. En second lieu, tout comme les enfants de M. Ruiz Zambrano, ceux de M. Dereci étaient des citoyens de l'Union demeurant dans l'État membre dont ils possédaient la nationalité, en l'occurrence l'Autriche, mais qui n'avaient jamais fait usage de leur droit à la libre circulation. Toutefois, à la différence des enfants de M. Ruiz Zambrano, ceux de M. Dereci ne dépendaient pas de leur père pour leur subsistance, étant donné que lesdits enfants étaient à charge de leur mère, ressortissante autrichienne.

---

23 *Ibid.*, point 52.

24 Voir, en ce sens, Adam, S., et Van Elsuwege, P., « Citizenship rights and the federal balance between the European Union and its Member States : Comment on *Dereci* », *European Law Review*, 2012, p. 176.

À cet égard, la Cour a clarifié le critère relatif à la privation de l'essentiel des droits conférés par le statut de citoyen de l'Union énoncé au point 42 de l'arrêt Ruiz Zambrano, en jugeant que ledit critère « se réfère à des situations caractérisées par la circonstance que le citoyen de l'Union se voit obligé, en fait, de quitter le territoire non seulement de l'État membre dont il est ressortissant, mais également de l'Union pris dans son ensemble ».[25] La Cour a également précisé que ledit critère ne doit pas prendre en compte l'impact négatif que l'expulsion d'un ressortissant d'un État tiers, membre de la famille d'un citoyen de l'Union, pourrait avoir sur la vie économique et familiale dudit citoyen.[26] « Cela ne préjuge certes pas », a-t-elle jugé, « la question de savoir si, sur d'autres bases, notamment en vertu du droit relatif à la protection de la vie familiale, un droit de séjour ne saurait être refusé. Cette question doit cependant être abordée dans le cadre des dispositions relatives à la protection des droits fondamentaux et en fonction de leur applicabilité respective »,[27] à savoir dans le cadre de l'Article 51 de la charte.

Finalement, l'affaire ayant donné lieu à l'arrêt Iida concernait un ressortissant japonais qui, à la différence de la situation migratoire de MM. Ruiz Zambrano, McCarthy et Dereci, avait obtenu un droit de séjour en Allemagne en raison de son activité rémunérée. M. Iida était le père d'une mineure, ressortissante allemande, qui habitait avec son épouse en Autriche. Les époux Iida exerçaient en commun l'autorité parentale sur leur fille. Toutefois, étant donné que la prorogation de son droit de séjour était discrétionnaire, M. Iida avait demandé une carte de séjour sur le fondement de la directive 2004/38 au motif qu'il était l'ascendant d'une citoyenne mineure de l'Union. Sa demande a cependant été rejetée par les autorités allemandes au motif qu'il ne pouvait pas prétendre à une telle carte en se fondant sur le droit de l'Union. Il a attaqué la décision devant une juridiction allemande qui a alors demandé à la Cour si une décision telle que celle en cause au principal était compatible avec les dispositions du traité FUE concernant la citoyenneté de l'Union.

Tout d'abord, ayant constaté que M. Iida avait résidé légalement depuis plus de cinq ans en Allemagne et semblait disposer de ressources économiques suffisantes pour subvenir à ses besoins et avait une assurance maladie, la Cour a jugé qu'il pouvait bénéficier du statut de résident de longue durée au sens de la directive 2003/1999.[28] Elle a

25 Dereci, *supra*, note 4, point 66.

26 *Ibid.*, point 68.

27 *Ibid.*, point 69.

28 Directive 2003/109/CE du Conseil du 25 novembre 2003 relative au statut des ressortissants de pays tiers résidents de longue durée, *JO* L 16 du 23 janvier 2004, p. 44.

estimé en revanche qu'il ne relevait pas du champ d'application de la directive 2004/38, au motif qu'il n'était pas à charge de sa fille et qu'il n'avait pas rejoint son épouse en Autriche. S'agissant des Articles 20 TFUE et 21 TFUE, la Cour a constaté que « l'absence d'un droit de séjour au titre du droit de l'Union [n'avait pas] dissuadé sa fille ou son épouse d'exercer leur droit de libre circulation en déménageant en Autriche ».[29] Elle a également relevé que M. Iida ne risquait pas d'être expulsé du territoire allemand, étant donné qu'il, « d'une part, [disposait] d'un droit de séjour conformément au droit national jusqu'au 2 novembre 2012, de prime abord prorogeable, selon le gouvernement allemand, et, d'autre part, [pouvait], en principe, se voir accorder le statut de résident de longue durée au sens de la directive 2003/109 ».[30] Ainsi, elle a jugé qu'« il ne saurait être valablement soutenu que la décision en cause dans le litige au principal [risquait] de priver la fille ou l'épouse de M. Iida de la jouissance effective de l'essentiel des droits attachés à leur statut de citoyen de l'Union ou d'entraver l'exercice de leur droit de circuler et de séjourner librement sur le territoire des États membres ».[31]

Par ailleurs, en se référant à son arrêt Kremzow,[32] la Cour a également rappelé que l'exercice purement hypothétique du droit à la libre circulation ne constitue par un lien de rattachement suffisant avec le droit de l'Union. De même, des perspectives purement hypothétiques d'entrave audit droit ne relèvent pas du champ d'application des dispositions du traité FUE concernant la citoyenneté de l'Union.[33] Il va de soi qu'un tel rappel est sans préjudice des entraves « potentielles » qui, ainsi qu'il ressort d'affaires telles que l'affaire Carpenter,[34] relèvent du champ d'application des Articles 20 TFUE et 21 TFUE.

2. La citoyenneté de l'Union européenne et les droits fondamentaux

A. Les traités laissent-ils de la place à la théorie de l'incorporation « à l'européenne » ?

Dans l'affaire Ruiz Zambrano, la juridiction de renvoi a demandé, par sa troisième question, si les droits fondamentaux, notamment les

---

29 Iida, *supra*, note 5, point 74.

30 *Ibid.*, point 75.

31 *Ibid.*, point 76.

32 Arrêt du 29 mai 1997, *Kremzow*, C-299/95, Rec. p. I-2629, point 16.

33 Iida, *supra*, note 5, point 77.

34 Arrêt du 11 juillet 2002, Carpenter, C-60/00, Rec. p. I-6279, point 39.

Articles 21, 24 et 34 de la charte, devaient être pris en compte afin de déterminer la compatibilité de la mesure nationale en cause avec les dispositions du traité concernant la citoyenneté de l'Union. Il est possible d'interpréter cette question comme une invitation à étendre le champ *ratione materiae* des dispositions de la citoyenneté au-delà des droits qui sont énumérés à l'Article 20, paragraphe 2, TFUE.

Si la Cour avait répondu par l'affirmative, les droits fondamentaux de l'Union auraient été « incorporés » au statut de citoyen de l'Union. Ainsi, le système de protection des droits fondamentaux prévu par les traités aurait servi comme un « catalyseur fédéral », dès lors que ces droits auraient été appliqués de manière autonome, à savoir indépendamment de la question de savoir si la mesure nationale en cause affecte « le droit de circuler et de séjourner librement sur le territoire des États membres » du citoyen concerné. Pour que la mesure nationale relève du champ d'application de l'Article 20 TFUE, il aurait suffi que cette mesure porte atteinte, par exemple, au droit au respect de la vie privée et familiale du citoyen de l'Union concerné.

À cet égard, des leçons importantes peuvent être tirées de l'expérience constitutionnelle des États-Unis où le *Bill of Rights* de la Constitution fédérale a fonctionné en tant que force centripète qui protège les individus contre l'ingérence des pouvoirs publics, qu'ils soient fédéraux ou étatiques.[35] En particulier, la *Privileges or Immunities Clause* et la *Due Process Clause* du XIVe Amendment ont servi comme passerelles pour l'« incorporation » du *Bill of Rights* dans cet Amendement afin de le rendre ainsi applicable aux États fédérés.[36] Selon certains auteurs, l'Article 20 TFUE pourrait, de la même manière, servir de base à une théorie de l'incorporation « à l'européenne »,[37] dès lors que cette dispo-

---

35 Le « *Bill of Rights* » (Ier au Xe Amendements à la Constitution) a été conçu, à l'origine, pour limiter les pouvoirs de l'État fédéral, mais pas ceux des États fédérés. Cela tient au fait que la majorité des pères de la Constitution fédérale croyaient que l'application du « *Bill of Rights* » aux États fédérés donnerait lieu à « un effet de levier » bénéficiant à l'État fédéral qui, sous prétexte de protéger les droits fondamentaux, augmenterait ses compétences au-delà des limites prévues par la Constitution. Voir Chemerinsky, E., *Constitutional Law*, 4e éd, New York, Kluwer, 2011. Pour un examen de droit comparé portant sur les États-Unis et l'Union européenne en matière de protection des droits fondamentaux, voir Knook, A., « The Court, the Charter, and the vertical division of powers in the European Union », *Common Market Law Review*, 2005, p. 367.

36 La « *Privileges or Immunities Clause* » ainsi que la « *Due Process Clause* » sont rédigées dans les termes suivants : « No State shall make or enforce any law which shall abridge the privileges or immunities of citizens of the United States ; nor shall any State deprive any person of life, liberty, or property, without due process of law ; nor deny to any person within its jurisdiction the equal protection of the laws. »

37 S'agissant de l'application de la doctrine américaine de l'incorporation dans un contexte européen, voir van den Brink, M.J., « EU Citizenship and EU Fundamental

sition du traité prévoit que « [l]es citoyens de l'Union jouissent des droits et sont soumis aux devoirs prévus par les traités », tout en énumérant, de manière non exhaustive, ces droits. Le raisonnement consiste donc à dire que le statut de citoyen de l'Union comprend plus de droits que ceux exposés aux Articles 21 à 24 TFUE, de sorte que, en suivant l'exemple de la Cour suprême des États-Unis, la Cour devrait s'appuyer sur l'Article 20 TFUE en vue d'attacher les droits fondamentaux à ce statut.

Une telle théorie de l'incorporation « à l'européenne », lue à la lumière de l'arrêt Ruiz Zambrano, dans lequel la Cour a jugé que, indépendamment de l'existence d'un élément transfrontalier, « l'Article 20 TFUE s'oppose à des mesures nationales ayant pour effet de priver les citoyens de l'Union de la jouissance effective de l'essentiel des droits conférés par leur statut de citoyen de l'Union », signifierait que les droits fondamentaux consacrés par la charte pourraient être invoqués dans des situations purement internes, instaurant ainsi un système de protection des droits fondamentaux similaire à ceux prévus par les constitutions nationales et la Convention européenne des droits de l'homme (la « CEDH »).

À notre avis, un tel résultat serait incompatible avec le principe d'attribution, dès lors qu'il aurait pour effet d'affecter la répartition verticale des compétences entre l'Union et les États membres.[38] Il faut rappeler, à cet égard, que le principe d'attribution s'applique d'une manière tant positive que négative. D'un côté, il limite les domaines dans lesquels l'action de l'Union peut être engagée.[39] De l'autre, il garantit que l'Union ne vide pas de leur substance les compétences retenues par les États membres.[40] En conséquence, si toutes les mesures nationales, indépendamment de leur lien matériel avec le droit de

---

Rights : Taking EU Citizenship Rights Seriously ? », *Legal Issues of Economic Integration*, 2012, p. 273, pp. 287-288 (qui plaide pour suivre l'exemple de la Cour suprême des États-Unis, tout en permettant aux États membres d'opter pour un niveau de protection des droits fondamentaux plus élevé).

38 Voir Van Elsuwege, P., « Shifting the Boundaries ? European Union Citizenship and the Scope of Application of EU Law – Case n° C-34/09, Gerardo Ruiz Zambrano v. Office national de l'emploi », *Legal Issues of Economic Integration*, 2011, p. 263, p. 267 (qui soutient qu'une telle proposition suggère une révolution copernicienne dans le système juridique et politique de l'Union, comparable à l'impact de l'affaire *Gitlow v New York* sur le droit constitutionnel des États-Unis).

39 Voir l'article 5, paragraphe 2, TUE : « En vertu du principe d'attribution, l'Union n'agit que dans les limites des compétences que les États membres lui ont attribuées dans les traités pour atteindre les objectifs que ces traités établissent. Toute compétence non attribuée à l'Union dans les traités appartient aux États membres. »

40 Voir l'article 4, paragraphe 1, TUE : « Conformément à l'article 5, toute compétence non attribuée à l'Union dans les traités appartient aux États membres ».

l'Union, devaient être examinées sur leur conformité à la charte, celle-ci deviendrait applicable au-delà des limites des compétences attribuées à l'Union.[41]

De plus, l'incorporation des droits fondamentaux dans le statut de citoyen de l'Union ne saurait être effectuée par la voie jurisprudentielle, étant donné que l'Article 25, paragraphe 2, TFUE dispose que « sans préjudice des autres dispositions des traités, le Conseil, statuant à l'unanimité conformément à une procédure législative spéciale, et après approbation du Parlement européen, peut arrêter des dispositions tendant à compléter les droits énumérés à l'Article 20, paragraphe 2, [TFUE]. Ces dispositions entrent en vigueur après leur approbation par les États membres, conformément à leurs règles constitutionnelles respectives ». Il s'ensuit que l'Article 25, paragraphe 2, TFUE consacre clairement une double « garantie politique du fédéralisme ».[42] D'une part, il protège l'ensemble des États membres, puisque l'unanimité est exigée au sein du Conseil. D'autre part, il protège les parlements nationaux et même les peuples de l'Europe, si le consentement de ces derniers est requis par la constitution nationale en cause. De plus, l'Article 25, paragraphe 2, TFUE s'applique « sans préjudice des autres dispositions des traités », notamment de l'Article 6, paragraphe 1, TUE qui prévoit que « [l]es dispositions de la charte n'étendent en aucune manière les compétences de l'Union telles que définies dans les traités ».

Enfin, et surtout, la théorie de l'incorporation serait incompatible avec les objectifs visés par les auteurs des traités. En particulier, elle irait à l'encontre du fait que, conformément à l'Article 4, paragraphe 2, TUE, l'Union s'engage à respecter l'identité nationale des États membres, les dispositions constitutionnelles nationales faisant partie intégrante de cette dernière.[43]

---

41 van den Brink, M.J., *supra*, note 37, p. 283, estime cependant que ce n'est pas la charte mais le statut de citoyen de l'Union qui modifierait le champ d'application du droit de l'Union. Selon cet auteur, dans la mesure où le statut de citoyen de l'Union modifierait le champ d'application du droit de l'Union, les droits fondamentaux pourraient toujours être appliqués à des situations qui relèvent dudit statut. Toutefois, à notre avis, cet argument est circulaire étant donné que c'est justement en ayant recours à la charte que les nouveaux droits attachés au statut de citoyen de l'Union seraient créés, ce qui étendrait le champ d'application du droit de l'Union.

42 Notion empruntée à Wechsler, H., « The Political Safeguards of Federalism : The Role of the States in the Composition and Selection of the National Government », *Columbia Law Review*, 1954, p. 543.

43 Voir arrêt du 22 décembre 2010, *Sayn-Wittgenstein*, C-208/09, Rec. p. I-13693.

B. La Cour et l'Article 51 de la charte

Puisque, dans l'affaire Ruiz Zambrano, l'Article 20 TFUE s'opposait à la mesure nationale en cause, la Cour n'a pas dû répondre à la question délicate du respect des droits fondamentaux des personnes concernées. Ensuite, dans l'affaire McCarthy, la Cour n'a pas pris en considération les droits fondamentaux de Mme McCarthy pour déterminer l'existence ou l'absence de « l'effet de privation ». De manière implicite, la Cour a considéré que l'impact négatif qu'aurait l'expulsion de son mari sur la vie privée et familiale de Mme McCarthy n'était pas décisif afin d'établir si cette expulsion avait pour effet de la priver de la jouissance effective de l'essentiel des droits conférés par son statut de citoyen de l'Union.[44] En revanche, dans l'affaire Dereci, elle s'est penchée, de manière directe, sur cette question.

Après avoir affirmé que la mesure nationale en cause avait un « effet de privation » lorsque « le citoyen de l'Union se voit obligé, en fait, de quitter le territoire non seulement de l'État membre dont il est ressortissant, mais également de l'Union pris dans son ensemble »,[45] la Cour a jugé que l'impact, sur la vie familiale ou le bien-être économique d'un citoyen de l'Union, de l'expulsion des membres de sa famille, qui ne disposent pas de la nationalité d'un État membre, « ne suffit pas en soi pour considérer que le citoyen de l'[Union concerné] serait contraint de quitter le territoire de l'[Union] si un tel droit n'est pas accordé ».[46] Autrement dit, les droits fondamentaux ne doivent pas être pris en compte afin de déterminer l'existence ou l'absence de « l'effet de privation ». Ces droits ne sont donc pas pertinents aux fins de déterminer le champ d'application des dispositions du traité relatives à la citoyenneté de l'Union dans des situations telles que celles de M. Ruiz Zambrano, Mme McCarthy ou M. Dereci. Sinon, la Cour s'appuierait sur les droits fondamentaux pour étendre l'application matérielle du droit de l'Union au-delà des compétences conférées à l'Union, ce qui irait à l'encontre des Articles 6, paragraphe 1, TUE et 51, paragraphe 2, de la charte.

En effet, en ce qui concerne les mesures nationales, la charte s'applique uniquement lorsque les « États membres […] mettent en œuvre le droit de l'Union ». Cette expression couvre toutes les situations dans lesquelles les États membres remplissent une obligation

---

44 McCarthy, *supra*, note 3, point 49.

45 Dereci, *supra*, note 4, point 66.

46 *Id.*, point 68.

concrète découlant pour eux du droit de l'Union.[47] À la lumière de la jurisprudence de la Cour, il est possible de distinguer deux types d'obligations que le droit de l'Union impose aux États membres, à savoir (1) les obligations qui requièrent que l'État membre agisse (ainsi que l'illustrent les affaires ayant donné lieu aux arrêts Wachauf et Karlsson),[48] et (2) les obligations auxquelles les États membres doivent se conformer dès lors qu'ils dérogent au droit de l'Union (ainsi que l'illustre l'affaire ayant donné lieu à l'arrêt ERT).[49] En revanche, lorsque le droit de l'Union n'impose aucune obligation concrète à un État membre, la charte ne s'applique pas (ainsi que l'illustre l'affaire ayant donné lieu à l'arrêt Annibaldi).[50]

À cet égard, comme les mesures nationales en cause dans les affaires McCarthy et Dereci n'ont pas privé Mme McCarthy ni les enfants de M. Dereci de la « jouissance effective des droits conférés par leur statut de citoyen de l'Union »,[51] les autorités du Royaume-Uni et de l'Autriche, en prenant les mesures nationales contestées, ne remplissaient aucune obligation concrète découlant du droit de l'Union. La compatibilité de ces mesures avec les droits fondamentaux protégés par la charte ne pouvait donc pas être examinée par la Cour.

Il découle ainsi de l'arrêt Dereci que les droits fondamentaux reconnus par la charte, tels que le droit au respect de la vie privée et familiale d'une personne, ne définissent pas le champ d'application des dispositions du TFUE relatives à la citoyenneté de l'Union. Cet arrêt respecte strictement l'Article 52, paragraphe 2, de la charte qui dispose que « [l]es droits reconnus par la présente charte qui font l'objet de dispositions dans les traités s'exercent dans les conditions et limites définies par ceux-ci ».[52] À cet égard, les explications relatives à l'Article 52, paragraphe 2, de la charte,[53] qui font mention expresse des droits « qui découlent de la citoyenneté de l'Union », établissent que « ces droits

---

47 Voir, en ce sens, Lenaerts, K., « The Court of Justice of the European Union and the Protection of Fundamental Rights », *Polish Yearbook of International Law*, 2011, p. 79 *et seq.*

48 Voir arrêts du 13 juillet 1989, *Wachauf*, 5/88, Rec. p. 2609, et du 13 avril 2000, *Karlsson e.a.*, C-292/97, Rec. p. I-2737.

49 Voir arrêt du 18 juin 1991, ERT, C-260/89, Rec. p. I-2925.

50 Voir arrêt du 18 décembre 1997, *Annibaldi*, C-309/96, Rec. p. I-7493.

51 Ruiz Zambrano, *supra*, note 2, point 42.

52 Voir Hinarejos, A., « Citizenship of the EU : clarifying "genuine enjoyment of the substance" of citizenship rights », *Cambridge Law Journal*, 2012, p. 279 *et seq.*, qui a noté qu'une interprétation plus large aurait des effets dramatiques sur l'équilibre des pouvoirs entre l'Union et les États membres.

53 Voir les explications relatives à la charte des droits fondamentaux, *JO* C 303 du 14 février 2007, p. 17 (ci-après les « explications relatives à la charte »).

restent soumis aux conditions et limites applicables au droit de l'Union sur lequel ils sont fondés et qui sont prévues dans les traités ». En d'autres termes, la charte ne vise ni à étendre les droits attachés au statut de citoyen de l'Union ni à créer de nouveaux droits.

Il s'ensuit que ce n'est qu'une fois établi que la mesure nationale en cause produit un « effet de privation » au sens de l'arrêt Ruiz Zambrano, que cette mesure peut être examinée à la lumière de la charte. En revanche, si ladite mesure ne produit pas un tel effet, elle ne relève pas du champ d'application matériel du droit de l'Union. La question de savoir si une mesure nationale est compatible avec les droits fondamentaux tels que protégés par la charte doit donc être examinée en aval de la constatation selon laquelle cette mesure rentre dans le champ d'application matériel du droit de l'Union. Si tel est le cas, toute justification avancée par l'État membre sera appréciée à l'aune de sa compatibilité avec les droits fondamentaux protégés par la charte. À notre avis, cette analyse en « deux étapes », qui a été effectuée par la Cour dans l'arrêt Dereci, est respectueuse de la jurisprudence antérieure, notamment de l'arrêt ERT, dans lequel la Cour a jugé que « lorsqu'un État membre invoque [un objectif légitime reconnu par le droit de l'Union] pour justifier une réglementation qui est de nature à entraver l'exercice de la libre prestation des services, cette justification, prévue par le droit [de l'Union], doit être interprétée à la lumière des principes généraux du droit et notamment des droits fondamentaux ».[54]

Sur ce point, le scénario suivant inspiré par les faits de l'affaire Ruiz Zambrano fournit un exemple. Un État membre « A » décide d'expulser deux ressortissants d'un État tiers qui sont les parents d'un citoyen de l'Union, qui, lui, est un enfant en bas âge, citoyen de l'État « A » et n'a jamais exercé son droit à la libre circulation. Les autorités de l'État membre « A » font valoir que la décision d'expulsion est fondée sur des considérations d'ordre public. Comme dans l'affaire Ruiz Zambrano, il est clair que la mesure nationale en cause produit un « effet de privation » : afin de suivre ses parents dont il est entièrement dépendant, le citoyen de l'Union est obligé de quitter le territoire de l'Union dans son ensemble. Toutefois, contrairement aux faits dans l'affaire Ruiz Zambrano, l'État membre « A » avance que la décision d'expulsion est justifiée par des considérations d'ordre public. À la lumière de l'arrêt Rottmann,[55] il apparaît que la mesure produisant un « effet de privation » peut être justifiée dès lors que l'objectif qu'elle poursuit est reconnu comme légitime par l'ordre juridique de l'Union et qu'elle est conforme au principe de proportionnalité. C'est dans le contexte de

[54] ERT, *supra*, note 49, point 43.

[55] Rottmann, *supra*, note 9.

l'application de ce principe que les droits fondamentaux protégés par la charte jouent un rôle important. La juridiction nationale, en coopération avec la Cour, doit déterminer si la mesure nationale en cause comporte des limitations à l'exercice des droits fondamentaux des citoyens de l'Union concernés, et si tel est le cas, si ces limitations sont compatibles avec l'Article 52, paragraphe 1, de la charte.

Par ailleurs, s'il est certes vrai que, en l'absence d'un élément transfrontalier et d'une mesure nationale produisant un « effet de privation », il n'est pas possible d'examiner la compatibilité de ladite mesure avec la charte, cela ne signifie toutefois pas que les droits fondamentaux des personnes concernées sont dépourvus de toute protection. Ainsi que la Cour l'a clairement affirmé, dans de tels cas, il incombe à la juridiction nationale et, le cas échéant, à la Cour européenne des droits de l'homme (la « Cour EDH ») de veiller à ce que les autorités publiques respectent les droits fondamentaux contenus dans les constitutions nationales et dans la CEDH.[56] Il ressort ainsi de l'arrêt Dereci que le système de protection des droits fondamentaux découlant des traités doit être appréhendé à la lumière du « pluralisme constitutionnel ». La Cour ne vise pas à devenir l'unique et suprême garant des droits fondamentaux. La protection juridictionnelle des droits fondamentaux constitue un rôle partagé par différents acteurs qui doivent interagir dans le respect des compétences respectives. Tout comme les juridictions nationales doivent sanctionner le respect de la charte dès lors que les États membres « mettent en œuvre le droit de l'Union », la Cour doit éviter d'empiéter sur les compétences des juridictions nationales et, le cas échéant, de la Cour EDH lorsque les États membres ne mettent pas en œuvre le droit de l'Union et agissent donc au regard des dispositions protégeant les droits fondamentaux contenues dans leurs constitutions nationales et dans la CEDH.

4. Conclusion

Les arrêts de la Cour dans les affaires Rottmann, Ruiz Zambrano, McCarthy, Dereci et Iida font ressortir que les dispositions du traité relatives à la citoyenneté de l'Union peuvent être invoquées même en l'absence d'un élément transfrontalier. Cela constitue un développement jurisprudentiel positif qui met en évidence l'importance constitutionnelle de la citoyenneté de l'Union. Les libertés fondamentales cessent d'être le seul point de repère pour l'interprétation et l'application des dispositions du traité concernant la citoyenneté de l'Union. Conçue comme « le statut fondamental des ressortissants des États membres »,[57]

[56] Dereci, *supra*, note 4, points 72 et 73.

[57] Voir, par exemple, Garcia Avello, *supra*, note 1, point 21.

la citoyenneté de l'Union est désormais devenue un « concept autonome ».

Toutefois, afin de ne pas bouleverser la répartition verticale des compétences envisagée par les auteurs des traités, la Cour a limité la nouvelle jurisprudence concernant les « mesures nationales ayant pour effet de priver les citoyens de l'Union de la jouissance effective de l'essentiel des droits conférés par leur statut de citoyen de l'Union ».[58] À la lumière de l'arrêt Dereci, cela signifie que l'Article 20 TFUE s'applique uniquement « à des situations caractérisées par la circonstance que le citoyen de l'Union se voit obligé, en fait, de quitter le territoire non seulement de l'État membre dont il est ressortissant, mais également de l'Union pris dans son ensemble ».[59] Il s'ensuit que cette nouvelle jurisprudence ne s'applique que dans des situations extrêmes, à savoir lorsque le citoyen de l'Union est obligé de quitter le territoire de l'Union dans son ensemble.

Afin d'établir la présence, ou non, d'un « effet de privation », il découle de l'arrêt Dereci que les droits fondamentaux protégés dans la charte ne doivent pas être pris en considération comme tels, et ce en conformité avec les Articles 51 et 52 de celle-ci. De toute évidence, cela ne signifie pas que les droits fondamentaux du citoyen de l'Union concerné sont laissés sans protection. Au contraire, ainsi que le confirme l'arrêt Dereci, il faut faire confiance aux systèmes de protection des droits fondamentaux garantis par les ordres constitutionnels des États membres et par la CEDH dès lors que les États membres ne mettent pas en œuvre le droit de l'Union. En effet, de la même manière que les juridictions nationales ont confié à la Cour le soin de protéger les droits fondamentaux dès lors que le droit de l'Union s'applique, cette dernière fait confiance aux juridictions nationales et à la Cour EDH dans l'hypothèse inverse. Loin d'avoir abandonné son rôle de protecteur des droits fondamentaux au sein de l'ordre juridique de l'Union, la Cour a, avec l'arrêt Dereci, démontré que le dialogue inter-juridictionnel au sein d'un système à plusieurs niveaux de gouvernance peut uniquement avoir lieu s'il y a confiance entre les acteurs qui en font partie.

---

58 Ruiz Zambrano, *supra*, note 2, point 42.

59 Dereci, *supra*, note 4, point 66.

La relation ambiguë de la Cour européenne des droits de l'homme avec le droit international humanitaire

Yves SANDOZ

Ancien professeur de droit international humanitaire à l'Académie de droit international humanitaire et de droits humains de Genève à l'Université de Fribourg

Le droit international humanitaire et le droit international des droits de l'homme sont deux branches distinctes du droit international, mais elles ont à l'évidence des points communs étant, comme il l'a été dit, « par excellence le domaine d'élection de l'éthique dans le droit ».[1] On comprend dès lors mal qu'il puisse y avoir des frictions entre ces deux branches. La relation entre elles est pourtant délicate car, partant d'un point de vue différent, elles se recoupent parfois et peuvent ainsi donner lieu à des conflits de normes.

Sans aller au fond de problèmes qui sont complexes et ont fait l'objet de nombreuses réflexions, nous rappellerons d'abord brièvement l'origine du droit international humanitaire et du droit international des droits de l'homme en tant que branches du droit international (1) avant d'examiner les principaux points qui peuvent faire problème dans leur relation sur un plan général (2) et d'examiner ensuite les liens du droit international humanitaire avec la Convention européenne des droits de l'homme et la manière dont celui-ci est traité par la Cour européenne des droits de l'homme (3). La brièveté de cet Article ne nous permettra pas de nous arrêter sur les nombreux arrêts qui touchent à ces liens mais nous essaierons d'en tirer les principales lignes de force. Nous terminerons par quelques réflexions plus générales inspirées par ce qui précède (4).

---

[1] Guellali, A., « La convergence entre les droits de l'homme et droit humanitaire dans la jurisprudence du Tribunal pénal international pour l'ex-Yougoslavie », *Revue de droit international de sciences diplomatiques et politiques*, Lausanne, vol. I 83, n° 3, septembre-décembre 2005, p. 291.

1. Origine du droit international humanitaire et des droits de l'homme en tant que branches du droit international

C'est depuis le milieu du XIXe siècle que les États ont adopté des conventions multilatérales ouvertes, à vocation universelle, fixant des règles que l'on souhaitait voir appliquer par l'ensemble de la « communauté internationale » (c'est-à-dire, dans la perspective de cette époque, des États « civilisés » comme on les appelait alors). Et ces Conventions visaient d'abord, pour la plupart, à assurer une meilleure protection aux victimes de la guerre et à fixer certaines limites à l'usage de la force, soit le droit de la guerre (dans sa signification de règles applicables dans la guerre, ou « jus in bello »), que l'on appelle aujourd'hui droit international humanitaire. Les droits de l'homme, quant à eux, sont le produit d'une confrontation entre les citoyens et leur souverain. Ils ont fait leur nid dans les Constitutions nationales et sont longtemps restés un problème interne de chaque État. Le droit international humanitaire fixait donc essentiellement des obligations aux États dans leurs rapports avec les autres, les droits de l'homme restaient une affaire interne.[2] Il ne pouvait donc pas y avoir de frictions car il n'y avait pas de contact.

Ce n'est qu'après la Seconde Guerre mondiale que s'est opéré un rapprochement, avec l'adoption d'une part de la Déclaration universelle des droits de l'homme, en 1948 ; d'autre part d'une disposition des Conventions de Genève reconnaissant l'application des règles essentielles du droit international humanitaire lors des conflits armés non internationaux, en 1949. À partir de la première, les États allaient se donner un droit de regard toujours plus aigu dans les autres États sur le respect de normes des droits de l'homme qu'ils avaient formulées en commun ; en adoptant la seconde, les États faisaient aussi du droit international humanitaire une question interne.

Comme souvent, c'est en réaction à des événements tragiques – les abominations de la Seconde Guerre mondiale et des guerres civiles sans merci, comme la guerre d'Espagne – que ces développements positifs ont pu voir le jour : la politique d'extermination du régime nazi, quand elle fut pleinement mise en lumière, a causé un choc si profond sur les peuples qu'elle a ébranlé le sacro-saint principe de la souveraineté nationale, amenant les États à reconnaître que l'on ne pouvait plus, au nom du respect de celle-ci, laisser sans réagir des Gouvernements commettre les pires horreurs contre leurs propres citoyens. L'on a donc

[2] De très nombreux ouvrages traitent de ces questions et nous renonçons à sélectionner ici les principaux d'entre eux. On mentionnera toutefois, pour une vue succincte de la question, le court article de Kolb, R., « Aperçu de l'histoire de la Déclaration universelle des droits de l'homme et des Conventions de Genève », *Revue internationale de la Croix-Rouge*, n° 831, septembre 1998, pp. 437-448.

commencé, timidement, à se soucier de la « qualité » des États, en tant que membres de la communauté internationale. Ayant fait tomber ce tabou et gardant à l'esprit les excès sanglants de récents conflits internes, on a pu, dans la foulée, introduire aussi l'Article 3 commun aux Conventions de Genève, qui fixent certains principes et règles minimales qui doivent être respectés même dans les conflits armés non internationaux. La cloison entre ces deux branches du droit s'est ainsi fissurée. Avec les Conventions régionales des droits de l'homme, qui fixent à leurs États membres des obligations allant au-delà des obligations universelles, on a ensuite introduit un nouveau développement, mais aussi une nouvelle complication dans la relation.

2. La relation des droits de l'homme avec le droit international humanitaire sur un plan général

A. Relation du droit international humanitaire et des droits de l'homme avec le droit international général

Cette question s'inscrit dans la problématique plus large de la fragmentation du droit international, liée à l'important développement de celui-ci. Plusieurs régimes ayant non seulement leurs propres règles, mais également leurs propres systèmes de mise en œuvre, de contrôle, d'arbitrage ou de sanctions se sont développés. La multiplication de ces sous-systèmes a justement conduit les internationalistes à s'inquiéter de la cohérence globale du droit international. D'un système pyramidal, on est passé à une multiplication de sous-systèmes qui se côtoient et sont quasi indépendants, tout en ayant tout de même des points de contact et sans être non plus totalement déconnectés des règles générales du droit international.[3] On parle de « régimes autonomes » (« self-contained »), tout en admettant qu'on ne saurait les concevoir comme totalement autonomes. Comme le droit international humanitaire, le droit international des droits de l'homme fait partie de ces régimes à l'autonomie relative. Il faut constater d'ailleurs que le droit international humanitaire est lui-même fragmenté, chacun des Pactes internationaux, et également les Conventions régionales, ayant son propre système de contrôle. Il convient de relever, en outre, qu'une distinction doit être faite entre les règles primaires du droit international et les règles secondaires, le problème concernant « la primauté des règles secondaires spéciales des

[3] À ce sujet, cf. i.a., Simma, B. et Pulkowski, D., « Of Planet and the Universe : Self-contained Regimes in International Law », *The European Journal of International Law*, vol. 17, n° 3, pp. 483-529, p. 484.

sous-systèmes sur les règles secondaires du droit international ».[4] Nous n'allons pas nous arrêter ici sur la relation de chacun de ces sous-systèmes avec le droit international général.[5] Il faut toutefois noter que la relation du droit international humanitaire avec le droit international général est plus complexe car il ne s'agit pas seulement d'un sous-système qu'il convient d'intégrer harmonieusement dans le cadre général du droit international, mais d'un système qui s'inscrit – partiellement en tout cas – en marge de ce droit : pour les conflits armés internationaux, en effet, il ne devient applicable que quand le droit international est transgressé puisque celui-ci, depuis l'entrée en vigueur de la Charte des Nations unies, ne tolère plus la guerre entre les États et sanctionne l'État agresseur. Or cet agresseur devient pourtant un sujet de droit international humanitaire, sur un pied d'égalité, dans ce système marginal, avec l'État agressé. C'est donc quand coule le navire du droit international général, entraîné par la perte de l'un de ses principaux fondements, la coexistence pacifique entre les États, que l'on jette la bouée du droit international humanitaire pour essayer de sauver quelques normes minimales dans des situations où la force armée a remplacé le dialogue, la négociation, l'arbitrage ou la solution judiciaire. Certes, le droit international humanitaire ne se substitue pas à toute autre obligation internationale des États en conflit. Son respect n'absout pas l'État agresseur qui reste sujet à sanctions de la part de la communauté internationale pour ce seul fait. Et la guerre ne délie pas les États en conflit de toute autre obligation que celles imposées par le droit international humanitaire : de nombreuses obligations découlant de traités internationaux multilatéraux, régionaux ou universels, de normes internationales coutumières ou d'engagements régionaux ou bilatéraux, restent en vigueur. La Commission du droit international en a d'ailleurs fait le recensement dans un projet d'Articles qu'elle a accepté et vient de transmettre à l'Assemblée générale de l'Organisation des Nations unies.[6] Il n'en reste pas moins que le droit international humanitaire a ses propres exigences et possède un système de contrôle spécifique, qui fonctionne avec une certaine autonomie aussi longtemps que perdure le conflit armé.

---

4 Cf. Hafner, G., « Les risques que pose la fragmentation du droit international », Rapport préliminaire présenté à l'Assemblée générale des Nations unies lors de sa 55e session, Doc. A/55/10, pp. 314-315.

5 À ce sujet, cf. notamment Caflisch, L. et Cançado Trindade, A., « Les Conventions américaine et européenne des droits de l'homme et le droit international général », RGDIP, Tome 108/2004/1, pp. 5-62.

6 Voir le Projet d'articles sur les effets des conflits armés sur les traités et conventions y relatifs, texte adopté par la Commission du droit international à sa 63e session, en 2011, et soumis à l'Assemblée générale dans le cadre du rapport sur les travaux de ladite session. Document ONU A/66/10.

Il s'agit de noter, toutefois, que c'est pour les conflits armés internationaux que le droit international humanitaire occupe cette place très particulière dans le système des relations régies par le droit international. Les conflits armés non internationaux ressortent en effet encore, hormis les normes du droit international humanitaire (et, aujourd'hui, du droit international pénal),[7] du seul domaine de la souveraineté nationale et ne concernent donc pas le droit international. Dès lors, le droit international humanitaire n'est pas, dans ces situations, un droit par défaut, applicable seulement en cas de violation du droit international. La communauté internationale reste en effet neutre en ce qui concerne le conflit, le droit international ne se prononçant pas sur la légitimité ou non de la lutte armée qui se déroule sur le territoire d'un seul État. Il laisse à celui-ci le soin de réprimer les actes commis contre le Gouvernement mais n'exclut pas non plus qu'il y ait de justes motifs de se soulever contre celui-ci, voire de prendre les armes dans des cas extrêmes, qu'il s'agisse de guerres de libération, comme on les a appelées à l'époque coloniale, ou de soulèvement contre des régimes dictatoriaux, comme on vient de le voir en Lybie, en Tunisie ou en Égypte. Cette « non-ingérence » s'explique par le fait que, sur le plan universel, la communauté des États n'a pas de bien hautes exigences quant à la légitimité démocratique des Gouvernements et ne saurait donc donner forcément tort à ceux qui s'opposent à l'un ou l'autre d'entre eux. L'approche peut évidemment être différente dans un cadre, comme celui de l'Union européenne, qui a des règles et un système de contrôle beaucoup plus stricts quant au caractère démocratique des États membres et des exigences plus élevées quant au respect des droits de l'homme.

Or ce sont les conflits armés non internationaux qui sont de loin, aujourd'hui, les plus nombreux et c'est bien dans le cadre de ces conflits, hormis la question de l'occupation qui relève du droit des conflits armés internationaux, que se pose de la manière la plus aiguë la question de la relation entre les sous-systèmes du droit international des droits de l'homme et du droit international humanitaire.

B. Relations du droit international humanitaire avec les droits de l'homme

Dans le cadre global, le Pacte international relatif aux droits civils et politiques, dont l'application intégrale en temps de conflit armé aurait entraîné une contradiction entre diverses de ses dispositions et le droit

---

7 Avec la reconnaissance que des crimes de guerre peuvent aussi être commis lors de conflits armés non internationaux et l'introduction de ces crimes dans le statut de la Cour pénale internationale.

international humanitaire, a prévu de possibles dérogations dans le cas « où un danger public exceptionnel menace l'existence de la nation ». Les conflits armés, y compris non internationaux, peuvent sans aucun doute être considérés comme présentant un tel danger. De ce fait, il n'y a pas *a priori* de conflits de normes avec le droit international humanitaire : d'une part, les restrictions tolérées par ce droit concernent certains droits de l'homme auxquels le Pacte accepte qu'il soit dérogé en situations exceptionnelles ; d'autre part le droit international humanitaire proscrit lui aussi les activités qui violeraient des droits de l'homme auxquels le Pacte n'accepte aucune dérogation. Mais c'est dans l'interprétation des normes et la mise en œuvre qu'il peut y avoir divergence. En principe, le droit international humanitaire s'applique automatiquement et intégralement dès qu'éclate un conflit armé alors que le bien-fondé des dérogations prévues par le droit international des droits de l'homme doit être justifié même dans les situations, y compris les conflits armés, qui permettent de telles dérogations.

Il n'y a pas, par ailleurs, parfaite concordance entre l'applicabilité du droit international humanitaire, soit l'existence avérée d'un conflit armé, et la possibilité de déroger à certains droits de l'homme, les situations dans lesquelles « un danger exceptionnel menace l'existence de la nation » ne se limitant pas aux conflits armés. Il existe donc dans le système un point faible, celui des situations dans lesquelles les États peuvent déroger à plusieurs droits de l'homme sans encore être obligés d'appliquer le droit international humanitaire. C'est ce point faible qui a été identifié, notamment, par le professeur Meron.[8] Elle a incité des internationalistes à chercher à renforcer la protection des individus dans ce type de situations. Leur travail a surtout mis en lumière l'ensemble des textes internationaux qui restaient applicables, démontrant que la protection juridique était plus développée que l'on ne pouvait le craindre. Encore faut-il connaître les règles pour les respecter et la déclaration qu'ils ont adoptée avait le double but de rappeler celles-ci et de permettre à la communauté internationale – États et société civile – d'être mieux à même de veiller à leur respect.[9]

Mais l'existence d'un conflit armé – en l'occurrence non international – n'a pas seulement pour effet d'imposer de nouvelles obligations à

---

8 Cf. Meron, T., *Human Rights in international strife : their international protection*, Cambridge, Grotius Pubications, 1987.

9 Cette Déclaration des règles humanitaires minimales d'humanité, qui, selon son article 1, s'applique « dans tous les cas, y compris les situations internes de violence, de conflit ethnique, religieux ou national, de troubles, de tension ou de danger public exceptionnel », a été discutée à la Sous-Commission de la lutte contre les mesures discriminatoires et de protection des minorités, qui l'a transmise à la Commission des droits de l'homme. Cf. Document E/CN.4/1995/116 du 31.1.1995.

l'État concerné. Deux autres conséquences majeures découlent de cette situation. D'abord, elle autorise le Gouvernement à utiliser des méthodes et des moyens de guerre, c'est-à-dire à faire un usage de la force armée allant bien au-delà de ce qui est autorisé pour lutter contre la criminalité en temps de paix, et même en cas d'émeutes ou autres situations de troubles intérieurs. Ensuite, elle donne naissance à une entité juridique nouvelle, inhérente au système du droit international humanitaire (mais limitée à celui-ci). La partie dissidente d'un conflit armé non international est titulaire de droits et d'obligations. C'était une petite révolution, acceptée par les États sous la pression des horreurs commises dans ces situations. Ils s'y sont donc résignés, mais nom sans réticence, craignant aussi bien l'érosion de leur souveraineté nationale que la reconnaissance internationale qui pourrait être donnée à leurs opposants.

L'idée de deux parties titulaires des mêmes droits et obligations dès lors qu'une confrontation armée atteint un haut niveau d'intensité entre un Gouvernement et un groupe armé organisé, n'était pourtant pas nouvelle. Emer de Vattel l'avait, notamment, déjà clairement exprimée. À la question de savoir « si le Souverain doit observer les lois ordinaires de la guerre envers des sujets rebelles, qui ont pris ouvertement les armes contre lui », il répond positivement dans les cas d'oppression manifeste et quand le conflit s'aggrave et devient une guerre civile, qui donne « naissance dans la nation à deux partis indépendants, qui se regardent comme ennemis et ne reconnaissent aucun Juge commun ». Il faut donc assimiler les « partis dans une guerre civile aux États en guerre », l'un et l'autre devant respecter les lois de la guerre.[10] Les États-Unis ont *de facto* mis en œuvre cette doctrine dans la guerre de Sécession, le président Lincoln ayant fait recenser de manière très détaillée les règles applicables dans les guerres par un grand juriste de l'époque avant de les faire appliquer dans ce conflit, pourtant interne.[11] Sur le plan théorique, l'on a parlé de « reconnaissance de belligérance »

---

10 Cf. de Vattel, E., *Le Droit des gens ou Principes du Droit naturel*, Neuchâtel, 1758, Édition de Carnegie Institution, 1916, Livre III, Chap. XVIII, pp. 238-244. Là-dessus, voir aussi Siotis, J., *Le droit de la guerre et les conflits armés d'un caractère non international*, Librairie générale de droit et de jurisprudence, Paris, 1958, pp. 55-59. Et Kolb, R., « La validité du modèle de Vattel après 1945 », dans Y. Sandoz (ed.), *Réflexions sur l'impact, le rayonnement et l'actualité du « Droit des Gens » d'Emer de Vattel*, Bruylant, 2010, pp. 137-175, p. 163.

11 Il s'agit des « Instructions pour le comportement des armées des États-Unis d'Amérique en campagne » proclamée par le président Lincoln en tant qu'Ordre général n° 100 le 24 avril 1863, qui avaient été préparées pas Francis Lieber et sont souvent citée comme « le Code Lieber ». Elles sont notamment reproduites dans Schindler, D. et Toman, J., *Droit des Conflits armés, Recueil des conventions, résolutions et autres documents*, Genève, CICR/Institut Henry-Dunant, 1996, pp. 3-22.

et les conditions de celle-ci ont été clarifiées par le prestigieux Institut du droit international à sa session de 1900.[12] Ouverte au Gouvernement d'un État engagé dans une guerre civile comme aux autres États – qui s'imposent alors d'adopter une attitude de neutralité entre la partie gouvernementale et la partie dissidente – la reconnaissance de belligérance reste toutefois facultative. Même si les conditions fixées à la partie rebelle pour que l'on puisse parler de conflits armés sont remplies, le Gouvernement garde la faculté de procéder à une reconnaissance de belligérance, le respect de sa souveraineté excluant qu'on ne la lui impose. Et, de fait, elle a très peu été utilisée dans la pratique[13] et l'on peut même dire qu'elle est aujourd'hui tombée en désuétude.

L'élément fondamentalement nouveau apporté en 1949 par les Conventions de Genève réside précisément dans l'application automatique du droit international humanitaire aux conflits armés non internationaux. Mais, nous l'avons relevé, les États n'ont pas accepté cette nouveauté sans réticence et ils ont tenté d'en minimiser les effets : d'abord ce n'est pas tout le droit international humanitaire mais seulement les règles et principes essentiels, tels que décrits dans l'Article 3 commun aux quatre Conventions, qui sont applicables dans ce type de conflits. Les parties sont encouragées à s'accorder sur une application plus étendue des Conventions, mais cela reste de leur bon vouloir. Ensuite, il est précisé que l'application des dispositions de l'Article 3 « n'aura pas d'effet sur le statut des parties concernées ».[14] C'est là l'expression du grand souci des États que le droit international humanitaire ne devienne pas un cheval de Troie utilisé par les Rebelles pour se profiler sur la scène internationale. On ne peut toutefois bien sûr pas dénier à ceux-ci une certaine personnalité juridique internationale puisque des obligations leur sont imposées par les Conventions de Genève mais, par la disposition ci-dessus relevée, les États ont tenu à souligner qu'il s'agissait d'une personnalité restreinte, strictement limitée au cadre du droit international humanitaire et qu'elle ne donnait aucun titre à la partie dissidente pour s'en prévaloir dans d'autres domaines. Enfin, ils ont exclu les conflits armés non internationaux du principal système de contrôle sur place développé par les Conventions de Genève, celui des Puissances protectrices, soit de représentants d'États neutres déployés dans chacune des Parties en conflits afin de veiller à la bonne application des Conventions. Les États ne supportaient en effet pas l'idée d'être amenés à désigner d'un commun accord avec une partie dissidente les

[12] Cf. Annuaire de l'Institut de droit international, sessions de 1897 à 1904, pp. 333ss. Voir aussi Siotis, *supra*, note 7, en particulier pp. 108ss.

[13] Pour un historique de la question, cf. notamment Siotis, *supra*, note 7, en particulier la Deuxième partie, pp. 51-132.

[14] Article 3 commun des Conventions de Genève de 1949, dernier alinéa.

représentants d'États neutres qui se seraient alors déployés tant dans la partie contrôlée par le Gouvernement que dans celle contrôlée par celle-ci.

Tous ces éléments étant rappelés, on ne peut pas éluder la question de la relation entre les obligations imposées par le droit international humanitaire d'une part, par le droit international des droits de l'homme, de l'autre. Il reste vrai que les droits de l'homme sont essentiellement liés au temps de paix (et que l'on peut même considérer leur respect comme l'une des conditions d'une paix véritable) ; et que le droit international humanitaire est exclusivement réservé au temps de guerre. Comme leur substance se recoupe, l'on a même pu se demander si le second se substituait au premier en cas de conflit armé, en tout cas international. Israël, notamment, a encore défendu ce point de vue en ce qui concerne les territoires occupés devant la Cour internationale de justice en 2004,[15] mais contre l'avis de la quasi-totalité de la communauté internationale et cette *opinio juris* a été clairement rejetée par la Cour internationale de justice.[16] L'on peut donc considérer cette question comme réglée : il y a bien cohabitation des deux corps de droit en cas de conflit armé. L'on doit dès lors affronter la question d'un éventuel conflit de normes, à laquelle la Cour internationale de justice a également donné une réponse claire, au moins en ce qui concerne le droit à la vie : « En principe, le droit de ne pas être arbitrairement privé de la vie vaut aussi pendant les hostilités. C'est toutefois, en pareil cas, à la *lex specialis* applicable, à savoir le droit applicable dans les conflits armés, conçu pour régir la conduite des hostilités, qu'il appartient de déterminer ce qui constitue une privation arbitraire de la vie ».[17] Rappelons que le principe de la *lex specialis* exprime l'idée, comme l'explicite son énoncé complet (à savoir « *lex specialis derogat legi generali* »), qu'en cas de conflit avec des normes du droit international général, ce sont celles de la *lex specialis* qui prévalent. Ici encore, Vattel avait déjà très clairement exprimé l'idée : « De deux lois, ou de deux Conventions, toutes choses d'ailleurs égales, on doit préférer celle qui est la moins générale, et qui approche le plus de l'affaire dont il s'agit. Parce que ce qui est spécial souffre moins d'exceptions que ce qui est général : il est

---

15 Cf. l'Avis consultatif de la Cour internationale de justice sur les conséquences de l'édification d'un mur dans le territoire palestinien occupé, du 9 juillet 2004, § 102, Recueil 2004 des Arrêts, Avis consultatifs et Ordonnances de la Cour internationale de justice, p. 177.

16 *Ibid.*, § 105, pp. 177-178.

17 Cf. Avis consultatif sur la licéité de la menace ou de l'emploi d'armes nucléaires, du 8 juillet 1996, §25, Recueil 1996 des Arrêts, Avis consultatifs et Ordonnances de la Cour internationale de justice, p. 240.

ordonné plus précisément, et il paraît qu'on l'a voulu plus fortement ».[18] Un siècle avant lui, Grotius, notamment, avait d'ailleurs également défendu ce point de vue sans ambiguïté.[19] En l'occurrence, il ne s'agit pas de la substitution d'une norme par une autre, mais de l'interprétation de la norme d'un traité qui doit être faite à la lumière de celle donnée par un autre traité, considéré comme « *lex specialis* ».

Plusieurs points restent néanmoins à éclaircir. Le premier est celui de la portée de cet *orbiter dictum* de la Cour internationale de justice. En effet, l'on n'a pas reconnu à la Cour internationale de justice le pouvoir de trancher les différends qui pourraient survenir sur des points de principe entre les différentes instances judiciaires internationales, permanentes ou *ad hoc.*[20] Le rôle et les compétences des Cours régionales, qui veillent à l'application de Conventions qui, certes, ne peuvent pas aller en deçà des obligations internationales impératives des États membres, mais peuvent étendre celles-ci ; et la signification du principe de la *lex specialis* dans la relation entre un texte à portée universelle et un texte régional posent également des questions autant de principes que de pratiques. Ces questions sont liées en premier lieu à l'analyse de la situation dans laquelle sont commises certaines actions, car c'est de cette situation que dépendent l'applicabilité du droit international humanitaire et, donc, l'existence d'éventuels conflits de normes. Le caractère « spécial » de certaines normes régionales par rapport aux normes internationales impératives du droit international des droits de l'homme doit par ailleurs être mis dans la balance avec le caractère « spécial » du droit international humanitaire en relation avec le droit international des droits de l'homme. Tout cela est donc assez compliqué et ne peut guère s'éclaircir qu'à travers des cas concrets. Sans approfondir l'ensemble de ces questions, nous allons chercher à relever les principales d'entre elles, essentiellement à la lumière de la jurisprudence de la Cour européenne des droits de l'homme.

3. Relation du droit international humanitaire avec la Convention européenne des droits de l'homme

En ce qui concerne le droit international humanitaire en tant que *lex specialis* dans son rapport avec la Convention européenne des droits de l'homme, on rencontre deux types d'objections.

---

18 de Vattel, *supra*, note 7, Liv. II, Ch. XVII, §316.

19 Cf. Grotius, H., *De jure belli ac pacis, libri tres*, 1653, Liber II, Caput XVI, § XXIX.

20 Sur cette question de la relation entre les différentes juridictions internationales, universelles, régionales ou *ad hoc*, et sur une éventuelle hiérarchisation de celles-ci, cf. notamment : Delas, O., Côté, R., Crépeau, F. et Leuprecht, P. (eds.), *Les juridictions internationales : complémentarité ou concurrence ?*, Bruylant, 2005.

La première tend à relativiser la porte de *l'orbiter dictum* de la Cour internationale de justice sans le remettre vraiment en cause, avec une analyse fouillée de la signification de la maxime et de son implication. La Cour elle-même relève que « certains droits peuvent relever exclusivement du droit international humanitaire ; d'autres peuvent relever exclusivement des droits de l'homme ; d'autres enfin peuvent relever à la fois de ces deux branches du droit international ».[21] La question de la *lex specialis* ne se pose donc que dans ce dernier cas. Or même dans celui-ci, selon ces auteurs, « on ne peut affirmer que le droit international humanitaire constitue toujours la *lex specialis* ».[22] En réalité, il s'agit plutôt de distinguer les cas où des éléments des droits de l'homme peuvent éclairer l'application du droit international humanitaire, qui, dans le domaine de la détention par exemple, n'est pas aussi précis que les droits de l'homme. Mais il peut alors paraître abusif de parler de l'application des droits de l'homme en tant que *lex specialis* qui prévaudrait sur le droit international humanitaire car il n'y a pas dans ces cas de contradictions avec celui-ci.[23]

En revanche, si une « *lex posterior* » du droit international général ou du droit international des droits de l'homme n'a pas automatiquement prévalence sur le droit international humanitaire, il peut y avoir des exceptions où l'on peut considérer que c'est le cas : d'une part quand une norme s'impose en tant que *jus cogens*, d'autre part quand une nouvelle norme est reconnue par les États qui l'adoptent comme applicable et tout temps, y compris donc lors de conflits armés. On peut donner comme exemple pour le premier cas le principe du non-refoulement, qui devrait exclure le rapatriement à la fin des hostilités de prisonniers de guerre qui courent des risques avérés de persécution à leur retour, alors que la 3e Convention de Genève ne prévoit pas cette exception.[24] Et pour le second cas le Protocole n° 6 de la Convention européenne des droits de l'homme concernant l'abolition de la peine de mort, du 28 avril 1983.[25]

---

21 Avis consultatif du 9 juillet 2004, *supra*, note 12, §106.

22 Cf. Sassoli, M., « Le droit international humanitaire, une *lex specialis* par rapport aux droits humains ? », *Études en l'honneur du professeur Giorgio Malinverni : les droits de l'homme et la constitution*, Auer, A., Flückiger, A. et Hotelier, M. (eds.), Genève, Zurich, Bâle, Schulthess, 2007, pp. 375-395, p. 395.

23 Au moins en apparence car on pourrait considérer, dans certains cas, que « le silence » du droit international humanitaire est qualifié et qu'il serait donc abusif de prétendre qu'il laisse le champ ouvert à toutes les normes du droit international des droits de l'homme. Nous ne traiterons toutefois pas de cette question dans le présent article.

24 Cf. Article 118 de la IIIe Convention de Genève et Sassoli, *supra*, note 22, p. 392.

25 Certes, le Pacte n'exclut pas totalement la peine de mort, qui peut être prévue dans la législation d'un État pour des actes « commis en temps de guerre ou de danger immi-

La seconde objection revient à contester plus radicalement la compétence de la Cour internationale de justice pour imposer ses vues en ce qui concerne l'interprétation à donner à la Convention européenne des droits de l'homme et rejette l'idée que le droit international humanitaire prévaut dans les situations de conflit armé dans lequel la Convention européenne est applicable. Les tenants de cette thèse[26] s'appuient sur le fait que la Cour européenne n'a pas la compétence d'interpréter le droit international humanitaire ; que les deux régimes, selon eux, sont incompatibles sur certains points ; que si la Cour « peut examiner *proprio motu* si une dérogation satisfait aux exigences de compatibilité avec les autres obligations juridiques internationales, elle ne saurait se plier aux exigences du droit international humanitaire » ; et que l'on ne peut pas simplement transposer la relation entre deux conventions internationales à une confrontation opérée « entre les dispositions d'une convention internationale et celles d'une convention régionale ».[27]

La jurisprudence de la Cour européenne des droits de l'homme (y compris les décisions de la Commission européenne quand elle fonctionnait) est restée assez peu fournie au début pour deux raisons.

La première réside dans le libellé de l'Article 15. Cet Article permet des dérogations à la Convention « en cas de guerre ou en cas d'autres dangers publics menaçant la vie de la nation ». Cette formulation n'est pas heureuse. D'abord elle utilise le mot « guerre » sans autre précision, alors que le droit international humanitaire, dans les Conventions de Genève, a préféré l'expression « conflit armé ». Comme il y a des conflits armés internationaux et des conflits armés non internationaux, il n'est pas évident de savoir ce que recouvre exactement le mot guerre. Il semble que son introduction avait été demandée par le Royaume-Uni, qui obtint gain de cause en « ayant fait valoir la nécessité de mesures d'exception notamment en cas de guerre civile ».[28] Cela n'empêche toutefois pas certains auteurs de penser que « dans le contexte de l'Article 15, la guerre s'analyse… en un conflit armé interétatique présentant une

---

nent de guerre ». Mais cet État ne peut alors pas simplement se référer au droit international humanitaire, qui pose certaines restrictions mais n'exclut pas la peine de mort. Il doit expressément prévoir une telle exception dans sa législation nationale.

26 Parmi lesquels cf. i.a. Kot, J.P., « Le droit humanitaire devant les juridictions internationales de protection des droits de l'homme : propos autour des arrêts *Issaieva, Youssoupova et Bazaieva c. Russie* et *Issaieva c. Russie* de la Cour européenne des droits de l'homme », *L'Observateur des Nations unies*, Revue de l'Association Française pour les Nations unies, Section Aix-en-Provence, n° 19, Automne-Hiver 2005, pp. 101-122.

27 Cf. Kot, *supra*, note 26, pp. 112ss.

28 Cf. Tavernier, P., « Article 15 », dans L.E. Pettiti, E. Decaux et P-H. Imbert, *Convention européenne des droits de l'homme, Commentaire article par article*, Paris, Economica, 1995, pp. 489-503, p. 490.

certaine intensité ».[29] Ensuite, comme l'on met sur un même pied la guerre et un « autre danger public menaçant la vie de la nation », les États peuvent justifier leurs dérogations à la Convention européenne des droits de l'homme sans invoquer l'existence d'un conflit armé et, donc, l'applicabilité du droit international humanitaire. Et c'est ainsi qu'ils ont procédé dans un premier temps. On pouvait d'ailleurs espérer que, dans le cadre européen, on n'aurait plus à évoquer les conflits armés, le respect des impératifs de démocratie et de droits de l'homme sur lesquels est fondé le statut du Conseil de l'Europe devant couper l'herbe sous les pieds à toute contestation de la légitimité des Gouvernements. La réalité est toutefois plus complexe et les contrôles moins serrés dans le cadre large du Conseil de l'Europe qu'au sein de l'Union européenne.

La deuxième raison vient du fait que c'est l'État qui l'applique qui doit invoquer la clause dérogatoire, avec seulement l'obligation *d'informer* la Cour européenne des droits de l'homme. La Cour ne va donc pas se prononcer sur l'existence d'un conflit armé à moins que celle-ci ne soit invoquée comme une raison valable de déroger à certains des articles de la Convention européenne des droits de l'homme, ne se posant pas spontanément la question de la coexistence des obligations découlant du droit international humanitaire et de la Convention. Or comme la dérogation peut aussi se produire sans qu'il n'y ait de conflit armé, en vertu d'un « autre danger public menaçant la vie de la nation », il peut arriver que le Gouvernement concerné préfère ne pas invoquer le droit international humanitaire même s'il y a objectivement conflit armé. Et cela sans que la Cour européenne des droits de l'homme ne réagisse, son rôle n'étant pas de qualifier les situations mais d'évaluer le bien-fondé des dérogations.

Ces dernières années, la Cour européenne des droits de l'homme a néanmoins été amenée à se pencher à plusieurs reprises sur des situations de conflits armés non internationaux et l'on voit apparaître d'autres problèmes de compatibilité. Avec l'application du droit international humanitaire, on bascule dans un nouveau système qui a ses propres règles, notamment quant à l'usage de la force. Le but général d'un conflit armé est de vaincre l'ennemi à travers l'affaiblissement des forces armées de l'ennemi. C'est une donnée générale pour toute la durée du conflit. Or même si toute attaque doit respecter un certain nombre de règles, concernant les armes et les méthodes utilisées ainsi que la protection des personnes et biens civils, l'on peut attaquer des personnes ou biens militaires de l'ennemi de manière moins restrictive que ce que ne semble autoriser la Convention européenne des droits de

29 Ergec, R., *Les droits de l'homme à l'épreuve des circonstances exceptionnelles*, Bruxelles, Bruylant, 1990, § 182.

l'homme, qui ne permet des dérogations, même en cas de guerre, que « dans la stricte mesure où la situation l'exige ». Il est douteux que l'on puisse se borner à évoquer une situation de conflit armé de manière générale en réponse à cette restriction et l'on constate bien, au contraire, que la Cour examine la légitimité des dérogations en évaluant chaque attaque pour elle-même.

La Cour se borne à juger le comportement du Gouvernement.[30] Si celui-ci est empêché d'agir dans une partie du territoire, elle va donc se demander s'il a tout mis en œuvre pour remplir ses devoirs de protection à l'égard de la population qui s'y trouve et c'est sur les « obligations positives » de celui-ci à cet égard qu'elle va s'arrêter. Elle a d'ailleurs considérablement renforcé cette idée d'obligations positives dans sa jurisprudence récente,[31] dans la ligne du « devoir de protéger » dont on a beaucoup débattu dans le cadre de l'Organisation des Nations unies.[32] En ce sens, elle a insisté sur le devoir du Gouvernement de protéger la population contre les effets des hostilités, allant jusqu'à la prise en compte dans sa planification des effets sur la population des réactions des forces rebelles à ses attaques ;[33] et au devoir de minimiser autant que possible non seulement les dommages incidents des attaques sur les personnes et biens civils, mais également les pertes chez les combattants rebelles.[34] Elle a également souligné l'obligation de protéger et d'assister les personnes déplacées ;[35] et l'importance de la prévention des risques que représentent pour la population les restes de guerre, notamment les mines et d'autres engins explosifs, qu'ils aient été placés ou utilisés par les forces gouvernementales ou les forces rebelles.[36] La Cour

30 Sur un plan général, la question de la responsabilité de la partie dissidente d'un conflit armé non international pour le respect des droits de l'homme est une question encore non résolue. À ce sujet, cf. notamment Zegveld, L., *Accountability of Armed Opposition Groups in International Law*, Cabridge university press, 2002 et Clapham, A., *Human Rights Obligations of Non-State Actors*, Oxford university press, 2006.

31 À ce sujet, cf. notamment Krähenmann, S., « Positive obligations in human rights law during armed conflicts » dans R. Kolb et G. Gaggioli (eds.), *Research Handbook on Human Rights and Humanitarian Law*, Cheltenham (UK) and Northampton (USA), Edward Elgar Publishing, chapter 9 (à paraître).

32 Cf. notamment le *Document du sommet mondial 2005*, Doc. ONU A/60/L.1 et le *Rapport du Secrétaire général de l'ONU sur la responsabilité de protéger* du 12.1.2009, Doc. ONU A/63/677.

33 Cf. i.a. l'affaire Ergi c. Turquie, Jugement du 28.7.1998.

34 Cf. i.a. les affaires Esmukhambetov et autres c. Russie, jugement du 29.3.2011 et Kerimova et autres contre Russie, jugement du 3.5.2011.

35 Cf. i.a. l'affaire Dogan et autres c. Turquie, Jugement du 29.6.2004.

36 Cf. i.a. les affaires Pasa et Ekran Erol c. Turquie, jugement du 12.12.2006 et Amaç et Okkan c. Turquie, jugement du 20.11.2007.

a également mis l'accent sur le « devoir de rendre compte », notamment en ce qui concerne les personnes disparues.[37] En revanche, elle ne va pas évaluer le comportement, ni la responsabilité, de la partie dissidente. La question que se posera la Cour par rapport à des exactions commises par celle-ci est de savoir si le Gouvernement a fait ce que l'on pouvait raisonnablement attendre de lui, s'il a exercé son devoir de « diligence due ».[38] Elle scrute toutefois avec une attention plus grande la responsabilité du Gouvernement à l'égard du comportement de forces paramilitaires, en fonction des liens qui peuvent exister entre celles-ci et le Gouvernement et du laxisme de celui-ci, voire de ses incitations explicites ou occultes.

Mais ce ne sont donc que les organes de contrôle du droit international humanitaire, peu développés dans les situations de conflits armés non internationaux – soit essentiellement l'ensemble des États à travers l'obligation peu précise de « faire respecter le droit international humanitaire » en toutes circonstances que leur imposent les Conventions de Genève ;[39] et le Comité international de la Croix-Rouge sur la base du droit d'initiative qui lui est aussi reconnu dans les conflits armés non internationaux[40] – qui vont se pencher sur le comportement des parties dissidentes. Et c'est le Comité international de la Croix-Rouge qui va rechercher le dialogue avec celles-ci sur leurs obligations en ce domaine, ce qu'il réussit à faire dans la plupart des cas. Une Organisation non gouvernementale a par ailleurs pris l'initiative de réunir divers groupes armés en vue de les associer au développement de normes humanitaires et de suivre la mise en œuvre de celles-ci,[41] avec l'idée que c'était en impliquant ainsi ces groupes que l'on avait la meilleure chance de les voir respecter le droit international humanitaire.

Il est clair que la Cour européenne des droits de l'homme, quant à elle, n'a de relations qu'avec les États. Mais cette approche unilatérale

37 Cf. i.a. l'affaire Imakayeva c. Russie, jugement du 9.11.2006.

38 Cf. i.a. l'affaire Osman c. Royaume-Uni, jugement de la Grande chambre du 28.10.1998.

39 Au sujet de laquelle cf. notamment Condorelli, L. et Boisson-de-Chazournes, L., « Quelques remarques à propos de l'obligation de "faire respecter" le droit international humanitaire "en toutes circonstances" », *Études et essais sur le droit international humanitaire et sur les principes de la Croix-Rouge en l'honneur de Jean Pictet*, C. Swinarski (ed.), Leiden, CICR/Martinus, Nijhoff, 1984, pp. 17-36 ; et « Common article 1 of the Geneva Conventions revisisted : Protecting collective interests », *Revue internationale de la Croix-Rouge*, n° 837, mars 2000, pp. 67-86.

40 Sur le contenu de ce droit, cf. notamment Sandoz, Y., « Le droit d'initiative du Comité international de la Croix-Rouge », *German Yearbook of International Law*, vol. 22, 1979, pp. 352-373.

41 « L'appel de Genève », organisation basée à Genève et dont les activités sont décrites sur son site internet : www.genevacall.org/.

est en porte-à-faux avec l'idée du droit international humanitaire qui tend à mettre, en ce qui concerne les droits et obligations qui émanent de lui, les deux parties à un conflit sur un pied d'égalité. Cela se manifeste notamment dans le domaine de la détention. Le droit international humanitaire lui-même a précisé, dans le cadre du Protocole additionnel II de 1977, les garanties de traitement dont doivent bénéficier toutes les personnes « privées de liberté pour des motifs en relation avec le conflit armé ».[42] Mais cela laisse ouvertes de nombreuses questions qui ne sont pas clairement résolues. Dans les conflits armés, l'on connaît l'internement des combattants ennemis, qui ont le statut de prisonniers de guerre et bénéficient de nombreux droits pendant leur détention, mais peuvent être retenus sans jugement jusqu'à la fin des hostilités. Est-il admissible de procéder ainsi dans les conflits armés non internationaux ? La Convention européenne des droits de l'homme pose à son Article 5 des conditions strictes en ce qui concerne la privation de liberté, qui contredirait cette interprétation du droit international humanitaire, à moins d'inclure les conflits armés non internationaux dans la clause de l'Article 15. Mais même si l'on considère les conflits armés non internationaux comme des « guerres » au sens de cet Article, il est douteux qu'un internement d'une durée indéterminée soit compatible avec l'exigence de ne maintenir les dérogations que « dans la stricte mesure où la situation l'exige ». Or l'Article 3 commun des Conventions de Genève demande aux parties en conflit de s'efforcer « de mettre en vigueur par voie d'accords spéciaux tout ou partie des autres dispositions » de chacune des Conventions. Selon cette disposition, les parties en conflit devraient donc s'efforcer de donner le statut de prisonnier de guerre aux soldats capturés. Or ce statut, quoique très protecteur pendant la détention, permet de priver de liberté sans jugement les soldats ennemis jusqu'à la fin des hostilités.

Un autre problème, dont l'origine est à rechercher dans le droit international humanitaire lui-même, provient du fait que ni l'Article 3 commun des Conventions de Genève ni leur Protocole additionnel II n'interdisent au Gouvernement de punir un combattant ennemi capturé lors d'un conflit armé non international pour le seul fait de sa rébellion, même s'il n'a pas commis de violation du droit international humanitaire. S'il condamne ce combattant dans un tel cas, ce que les droits de l'homme ne proscrivent évidemment pas, le Gouvernement doit veiller à ce que toutes les garanties judiciaires soient respectées. Mais quelle va être alors l'attitude de la partie dissidente ? Ne risque-t-elle pas de condamner elle aussi les combattants gouvernementaux capturés pour le seul fait de leur engagement auprès de celui-ci, dont elles contesteront la

42 Article 5, par. 1 du Protocole additionnel II de 1977.

légitimité ? Certes, cette ambiguïté a été instillée dans le droit international humanitaire par des Gouvernements qui ne pouvaient s'engager à renoncer à leur droit de punir, de peur de faire la part trop belle à ceux qui veulent renverser les autorités en place par la force. Il est donc peu probable que cela puisse changer. En revanche, on regrettera que le Protocole 6 de la Convention européenne des droits de l'homme ait précisément laissé entre-ouverte la porte de la peine de mort pendant les guerres (avec le doute sur l'interprétation qu'il faut donner à cette notion). Car c'est précisément lors des conflits armés non internationaux qu'il serait essentiel d'interdire la peine de mort, ou pour le moins de geler toute condamnation à mort, car on voit bien le cercle vicieux qu'enclencherait l'exécution de combattants ennemis dans le cadre de tels conflits.

Reste à savoir si une partie dissidente à un conflit armé non international est en mesure de respecter les garanties judiciaires fondamentales en cas de procès pénal. Sur cette question non plus, on ne peut attendre des éclaircissements de la part de la Cour européenne des droits de l'homme, puisque, comme on l'a vu, elle n'a pas compétence à l'égard de la partie dissidente d'un conflit armé non international. Il est toutefois important de souligner qu'un respect imparfait des garanties judiciaires par la partie dissidente ne saurait en aucun cas servir d'excuse à la Partie gouvernementale pour d'éventuels manquements de sa part dans ce domaine. Il est clair que ni le droit international humanitaire ni le droit international des droits de l'homme ne tolèrent ce type d'excuses. Par ailleurs, les questions liées à la compétence professionnelle minimale et à l'indépendance d'une autorité judiciaire qui serait mise sur pied par la partie dissidente restent ouvertes, étant entendu que l'on ne peut pas faire totalement abstraction des circonstances. Dans un autre domaine, l'égalité des combattants devant le droit international humanitaire n'empêche pas une partie au conflit d'avoir des armes dont l'autre ne dispose pas et c'est en fonction des moyens à disposition qu'il faut évaluer les actes des uns et des autres.

La question du droit applicable n'est, elle non plus, pas clarifiée. Pour les infractions de droit commun qui se produiraient dans le territoire contrôlé par une partie dissidente et pour les questions de procédure, on peut penser que le droit national devrait rester la référence, mais il n'est pas exclu que certains aspects de ce droit soient liés avec la lutte armée et, de ce fait, soient inacceptables pour la partie dissidente. Pourrait-elle alors préparer et adopter des lois nouvelles ou révisées ? La question est loin d'être résolue et il est bien difficile de le faire abstraitement. Concrètement, c'est surtout sur le traitement des prisonniers (respect de l'intégrité et de la dignité, nourriture, assistance médicale, logement salubre, contacts avec la famille, etc.), ainsi que sur l'exclusion de toute exécution capitale que l'on peut et doit mettre l'accent auprès de la partie dissidente. Il est rare en effet qu'elle soit à même de garantir une justice indépendante de qualité, plus encore qu'elle puisse s'engager dans un processus législatif avec la sérénité et les compétences voulues.

4. Remarques finales

On constate à quel point la question de la relation entre l'application du droit international humanitaire et celle du droit international des droits de l'homme reste délicate. La Cour internationale de justice a été confrontée à la question à de multiples reprises, de même que les organes des droits de l'homme, que ce soit, sur le plan mondial, le Conseil des droits de l'homme (et la Commission des droits de l'homme qui l'a précédé) et les organes de contrôle et de recours des Pactes des Nations unies (Comité des droits de l'homme et Comité des droits économiques, sociaux et culturels) ; et, sur le plan régional, la Cour européenne des droits de l'homme, la Cour interaméricaine des droits de l'homme (et la Commission) et la Cour africaine des droits de l'homme et des peuples. À cela s'ajoutent de nombreux cas traités par les Cours pénales internationales. Une très riche jurisprudence s'est donc développée, de manière évolutive. Mais elle n'est ni coordonnée, ni toujours cohérente.[43]

Il n'est pas aisé de prétendre en tirer une leçon. On sent bien la tension qui existe entre la philosophie première du droit international humanitaire et celle des droits de l'homme. La notion de « nécessité militaire » imprègne la première, avec l'idée que dans une situation de guerre, c'est l'intérêt national qui prime et que tout ce qui est nécessaire pour gagner la guerre peut (et doit) être mis en œuvre. C'est d'abord et

---

[43] Le traitement du droit international humanitaire par ces différentes juridictions a fait l'objet de nombreuses publications. Citons i.a. : Chétail, V., « On contribution of the ICJ to International Humanitarian Law », *Revue internationale de la Croix-Rouge*, n° 850, juin 2003, pp. 235-268 ; Quéguiner, J.F., « Dix ans après la création du Tribunal pénal international pour l'ex-Yougoslavie : évaluation de la contribution de sa jurisprudence au droit international humanitaire », *ibid.*, pp. 271-310 ; Cerna, C.M., « The History of the Inter-American System's Jurisprudence as Regards Situations of Armed Conflicts », *International Humanitarian Legal Studies*, vol. 2, 2011, Leiden, Martinus Nijhoff, pp. 3-52 ; Sassoli, M., « La Cour européenne des droits de l'homme et les conflits armés », *Human Rights, Democracy and the Rule of Law*, in S. Breitenmoser *et al.* (eds.), Zurich, Dike, 2007 ; Droege, C. and Arimatsu, L., « The European Convention on Human Rights and International Humanitarian Law : Conference Report », *Yearbook of International Humanitarian Law*, The Hague, Asser, 2009, pp. 435-449 ; Gaggioli, G. et Kolb, R., « A Right to Life in Armed Conflicts ? The contribution of the European Court of Human Rights », *Israel Yearbook of Human Rights*, vol. 37, 2007 ; Doswald-Beck, L., *Human Rights in Times of Conflict and Terrorism*, Oxford University Press, 2011.

surtout la violence inutile, les « maux superflus » que veut éviter le droit international humanitaire. Il est ensuite allé un peu plus loin en interdisant de manière absolue certains moyens et méthodes, comme la prise d'otages, la torture, la perfidie, l'utilisation d'armes indiscriminées ou particulièrement cruelles et l'affamement de la population, indépendamment de « l'utilité » que l'on pouvait trouver à ces méthodes ou moyens ; et en introduisant le principe de proportionnalité, qui proscrit même des attaques utiles du point de vue militaire si l'avantage qu'on en attend est inférieur à la gravité des dommages incidents qu'elles risquent de provoquer à des personnes ou biens civils. Mais l'idée que, dans une situation de guerre, la priorité absolue est de gagner celle-ci reste très présente. Les droits de l'homme, quant à eux, restent avant tout soucieux d'éviter les abus que les Gouvernements peuvent commettre sur ceux qui dépendent d'eux et ne tolèrent des dérogations, même lors de conflits armés, qu'avec circonspection et de strictes exigences.

Ces deux logiques ne se sont pas encore totalement réconciliées, d'autant plus que les deux domaines doivent faire face à des évolutions qui peuvent les remettre en cause. La « guerre à la terreur » est notamment un concept qui a créé beaucoup de confusion car l'expression fait penser à une application du droit international humanitaire alors qu'il ne l'est que si les éléments constituants d'un conflit armé sont remplis, soit s'il y a réellement des forces armées qui s'affrontent ou en cas d'intervention militaire dans un État sans l'accord de celui-ci. Plus généralement, les attentats terroristes à résonnance mondiale et les réactions provoquées par ceux-ci ont aussi ébranlé certains aspects des droits de l'homme avec la remise en cause de principes qui paraissaient intangibles et définitivement acquis, telle l'interdiction de la torture ou des détentions secrètes. L'absence d'arbitre reconnu pour qualifier les situations augmente également la confusion. Si, par exemple, une situation de conflit armé non international n'est pas reconnue comme telle par un État partie à la Convention européenne des droits de l'homme, le dialogue de celui-ci avec la Cour européenne des droits de l'homme risque d'être en porte-à-faux avec celui que le Comité international de la Croix-Rouge entretiendra avec ce même État. La Cour européenne des droits de l'homme, en effet, s'en tient aux dires de l'État puisque le conflit est en fait un argument pour justifier des dérogations à la Convention européenne des droits de l'homme ; alors que pour le Comité international de la Croix-Rouge le conflit armé est un point de départ « objectif » qui lui permet d'évoquer le droit international humanitaire. Les analyses de la Cour européenne des droits de l'homme et du Comité international de la Croix-Rouge risquent donc d'être contradictoires et de miner ainsi la crédibilité des conclusions que l'une et l'autre en tirent pour leur dialogue avec l'État concerné.

Parmi les nombreux points qui méritent encore éclaircissements, nous relèverons tout particulièrement la définition du conflit armé non international. Faut-il ne prendre que les critères d'intensité des affrontements et d'organisation de la partie dissidente ou faut-il également tenir compte de la volonté de celle-ci d'appliquer le droit international humanitaire. Le risque, en tenant compte de ce critère subjectif, est de voir les gouvernements nier l'applicabilité du droit international humanitaire sous le seul prétexte que leurs adversaires sont des « bandits » ou des « terroristes ». Mais ne tenir aucun compte de ce critère revient à donner à des organisations criminelles très organisées et disposant de moyens considérables, y compris des armes lourdes, un statut de partie au conflit qui implique, comme on l'a vu, une certaine « neutralité » à leur égard de la part de la communauté internationale, difficilement envisageable dans la lutte contre la grande criminalité. Cela d'autant plus que les activités criminelles de ces groupes débordent généralement des frontières nationales. La manière d'organiser la lutte dans ces situations et les normes internationales qui sont applicables méritent indéniablement un dialogue approfondi au sein de la communauté internationale.

Il faut noter, enfin, le développement heureux de la justice pénale internationale qui, à travers la reconnaissance que des crimes de guerre peuvent se produire dans des conflits armés non internationaux, a permis de pénétrer dans le champ, encore mal défriché, de la responsabilité des groupes armés à l'égard de la population qui se trouve dans un territoire sur lequel ils ont une maîtrise totale ou partielle. Il faut éviter, néanmoins, que ce développement ne devienne une source supplémentaire de confusion, dans la mesure où une poursuite pénale individuelle dans ce cadre implique aussi une analyse de la situation.

Il reste donc important que les États qui ont une responsabilité particulière de maintenir la paix dans le monde, en particulier les membres du Conseil de sécurité ; les gardiens du droit international en général ; les (nombreux) gardiens du droit international des droits de l'homme ; les gardiens du droit international humanitaire ; et les juges des juridictions pénales internationales ne fonctionnent pas dans des bulles étanches mais se connaissent les uns les autres, se comprennent, dialoguent et recherchent ensemble les meilleures solutions possibles. Un gros effort reste à faire. Les juges – et c'est particulièrement vrai à la Cour européenne des droits de l'homme – sont aujourd'hui submergés et n'ont pas le temps de prendre le recul suffisant et de dialoguer avec les autres acteurs de la scène internationale. Il est donc indispensable de donner à tous ces acteurs des moyens et un soutien suffisants pour qu'ils puissent prendre un peu de recul dans l'accomplissement de leurs nobles tâches.

En amont, il est essentiel que les jeunes gens qui seront appelés à remplir des fonctions dans ces domaines aient une connaissance de l'ensemble d'entre eux, une bonne compréhension de leur complémentarité et le sens du dialogue. En introduisant le droit international humanitaire dans le Collège d'Europe, dans lequel il a par ailleurs si bien su préserver et développer la qualité de l'enseignement et la culture du dialogue, Paul Demaret a fait franchir au Collège un pas dans cette direction. L'Europe, en dépit de ses tourments actuels, doit garder la vocation d'être à l'avant-garde dans tous ces domaines, dont l'objectif suprême est un monde pacifié et respectueux des droits de l'homme, cette « utopie nécessaire » du XXIe siècle.

III

Aspects institutionnels de l'intégration européenne/Institutional Aspects of European Integration

Une vue outre-atlantique de la Cour et de sa Jurisprudence

George A. BERMANN

Jean Monnet Professor of European Union Law, Columbia Law School, New York; professeur affilié, Ecole de droit, Institut des sciences politiques (Sciences po) (Paris)

No court in the world has attracted as much attention in legal academic literature in the United States as the European Court of Justice (ECJ).[1] Given the prominence of European Union law in the world of comparative and international law, this probably comes as no surprise. One can perhaps sum it up this way, with no disrespect intended: the Court of Justice looks to the American jurist's eyes as something like the U.S. Supreme Court's "younger sibling" or "distant relative". The ECJ shares with the Supreme Court the common mission of protecting the integrity of the legal order at whose judicial summit it sits.

The fact remains that the two courts perform this basic function in quite different ways. Of course, those differences – like all differences between courts across national boundaries – reflect the distinctive legal cultures of which the two courts are, respectively, a part. But there is one pervasive and utterly crucial difference that deserves emphasis. Unlike the Supreme Court, the ECJ is impelled by a perfectly understandable attachment to certain more or less programmatic goals that we can describe globally as "the European project".

I. A Force for Legal Integration

One must not of course exaggerate the differences. To begin with the institution itself, the ECJ – not unlike the Supreme Court – has played a

1 Mauro Cappelletti, Monica Seccombe & Joseph Weiler, *Integration Through Law: Europe and the American Federal Experience*, Berlin, New York, Walter de Gruyter, 1986; Eric Stein, "Lawyers, Judges and the Making of a Transnational Constitution", *American Journal of International Law*, Vol. 75, p. 1, 1981; George A. Bermann, "Taking Subsidiarity Seriously", *Columbia Law Review*, Vol. 94, p. 331, 1994.

positively fundamental role in the construction of the legal and political entity of which it forms a part. It is very difficult, if not impossible, to imagine the European Union presenting itself today as it does without the contribution that the ECJ has made to that enterprise. Both courts have powerfully pursued the goal of legal integration, and both have managed to lend that undertaking a legitimacy among constituent states and a citizenry that were not necessarily, at the outset, so very committed to that endeavor.[2] In both the American and European polities, the initial resistance stemmed mainly from state and local interests that saw their power and influence subject to considerable risk.[3]

But although the ECJ and the Supreme Court as a general matter may be situated similarly *vis-à-vis* the states that constitute, respectively, the European Union and the United States, the Supreme Court finds itself the object of much fiercer political critiques emanating from sources that have not to the same extent made the ECJ their target. Supreme Court case law is thus severely contested by two other constituencies: on the one hand, the other branches of the federal government and, on the other hand, a variety of social, economic and political interests. The former tend to regard the Supreme Court as something of a menace to the principle of the separation of powers; the latter feel from time to time disfavored by the position taken by the Court on social, economic and political issues.

2. The Personalization of Justice

This last remark leads directly to another important point of comparison between the two courts. The Supreme Court has consciously adopted a certain number of procedures and practices that contribute importantly to the political visibility of its role in American public life, and in consequence to the very social, economic and political critiques to which it has been subject. I refer to procedures and practices of the Supreme Court that the ECJ has knowingly not followed. For American observers, among the most remarkable features of the judgments of the Luxembourg court is their relative brevity, their depersonalized character and, of course, the absence of dissenting and concurring opinions.[4] If the drafting style of ECJ judgments does not lend itself to a great deal of

---

2 Gary Born, "A new generation of international adjudication", *Duke Law Journal*, 2012, pp. 777, 817; Lawrence Baum, *The Supreme Court* 20, 10th ed., Washington D.C., CQ Press, 2010.

3 Born, *supra*, note 2, p. 818; Baum, *supra*, note 2.

4 Vlad Perju, "Reason and Authority in the European Court of Justice", *Virginia Journal of International Law*, Vol. 49, p. 307, 2009; Paul Craig & Gráinne de Burca, *EU Law: Text, Cases & Materials*, Oxford, 2011, 3rd ed., p. 63.

transparency and candor, it at least has the merit of being concise (or relatively so) and better distanced from polemics of a political character.

3. The Mission of the Court

To a certain extent, the features that I have identified as distinguishing the Court of Justice from the Supreme Court stem from a profound difference between their missions, as viewed by the courts themselves. It is not to be overlooked that in the United States, the Supreme Court represents the highest echelon of the federal judicial power, and accordingly bears in some measure responsibility for the administration of justice throughout the country. In this respect, it is no different from the supreme (or constitutional) court of any other country. As much as the Supreme Court would like to, and does, concentrate on questions of a constitutional nature, it is ultimately fully responsible for any and all questions arising from federal law under the U.S. constitutional system or implicating the functioning of the judicial power in the U.S. The Court pursues law's most general objective, viz. seeing to it that members of society can live and work in a climate of dependable social order, marked by the rule of law.

As the highest court (alongside the European Court of Human Rights) in the European legal order, the ECJ has a much less expansive and significantly more precise mission. Far from bearing responsibility for safeguarding the integrity of judicial administration in Europe (a responsibility belonging more properly to the national judiciaries and, more particularly to the supreme and constitutional courts of the Member States), it rightly devotes itself to the realization of the objectives of the European Union, whatever they may at any particular time happen to be.[5] The European Union's objectives have of course evolved over the years. If construction of the internal market has for a long time been the EU's preponderant objective, it has come to be joined by more and more sectoral objectives such as protection of the environment or of consumers or investors. At just about any moment, the Court of Justice finds itself implicated in the accomplishment of various objectives flowing from the European treaties. To this extent, the ECJ acts in a far more programmatic fashion than does the U.S. Supreme Court whose decisions are of course nevertheless infused with political considerations.

5 Karen Davies, *Understanding European Union Law*, New York, Routledge, 2011, 4th ed., p. 44.

4. Access to the Court

The special role that the Court of Justice performs within the European Union is reflected in the very means of access to the Court. Two of the important avenues that lead to the Court directly reinforce the Court's special mission. On the one hand, the Court enjoys competence to determine, at the behest of the Commission, whether a Member State has or has not failed in its obligations under EU law and, in aggravated circumstances, to impose on a State for that reason a financial sanction.[6] The very existence of this mechanism reveals the strong engagement of the Court of Justice in the accomplishment of European Union objectives.

But more common and perhaps also more useful in the Court's pursuit of an ever more effective enforcement of EU law are the judgments that the ECJ renders in reply to preliminary questions that are put to it by Member State courts.[7] By definition, when the Court renders a judgment which interprets an Article of the Treaty or of secondary legislation, or determines its validity, and when the Court sends the matter back to the referring national judge for decision in conformity with the judgment of the Court, it participates directly in the implementation of EU law at the national level.

5. The Burden of Cases on the Court

The Court of Justice's special role is also reflected in the very large number of cases that it decides, especially by comparison with the U.S. Supreme Court. The latter enjoys the totally discretionary power to determine the cases that it will hear and judge. In fact, in recent years it has accepted to decide only around 85 cases annually. This means of course not only that the Court freely establishes its own judicial agenda, but also that many divergences in the doctrine of the federal courts of appeal are left intact and unresolved.[8] Even if these divergences relate to the correct interpretation of federal legislation, they can endure over a long period.

By contrast, the Court of Justice has the possibility of putting an end to all jurisprudential discrepancies among national courts, at least in so far as the correct interpretation of European texts is concerned. One can even fairly say that the Court feels an obligation to do precisely that.

---

6 Articles 258, 260 TFUE; see Craig & de Burca, *supra*, note 4, pp. 417-422.

7 Article 19 par. 3 let. b) TUE; Article 267 TFUE; see Craig & de Burca, *supra*, note 4, pp. 442-482.

8 Baum, *supra*, note 2.

The case law burden on the ECJ is all the heavier inasmuch as it decides vastly more cases in the first instance than the U.S. Supreme Court.[9]

6. An Independent Judge

In order to contribute appropriately and effectively to the construction of Europe, the judges of the Court of Justice must possess total independence from the Member States, in practice no less than in theory. An American observer would be surprised to learn that judges of the ECJ are named by the Member States themselves and that they have terms in office that the governments of the Member States may or may not renew, as they please.[10] He or she would be impressed by the capacity of the Court – and more importantly of its individual members – to nevertheless distance themselves, *de facto* as well as *de jure*, from the interests of the Member States to which they owe their nomination.

7. A Constitutional Court

The preceding discussion deals only with more or less purely institutional aspects of the ECJ, and many more could be added. But a comparison between the two courts also has a substantive dimension that merits attention.

To the extent that over the decades the ECJ has developed its classic case law, illustrated by judgments such as *van Gend en Loos*,[11] *Costa v. ENEL*,[12] or *Simmenthal*,[13] it has followed a path rather similar to the one that Chief Justice John Marshall travelled in the *grands arrêts constitutionnels* of the first decades of that Court's existence.[14] The contribution of the two courts to the consolidation of their respective legal regimes was altogether fundamental to the future development of the two legal systems themselves. The parallelism is perfectly evident.

---

9 George A. Berman, Roger J. Goebel, William J. Davey & Eleanor M. Fox, *Cases and materials on European Union Law*, St. Paul, American Casebook Series, 2011, 3rd ed., p. 63.

10 Bermann, Goebel, Davey & Fox, *supra*, note 9.

11 *NV Algemene Transport- en Expeditie Onderneming van Gend & Loos c. Administration fiscale néerlandaise*, 5.2.1963, affaire C-26/62, *Rec.* 00003.

12 *Flaminio Costa c. E.N.E.L.*, 15.7.1964, affaire C-6/64, *Rec.* 01141.

13 *Administration des finances de l'État c. Société anonyme Simmenthal*, Judgment of 9 March 1978, Case C-106/77, *ECR* 00629.

14 Kenneth Jost, *The Supreme Court A to Z*, Washington, CQ Press, 2007, 4th ed., p. 289.

8. A Demanding Court

But in many respects, the ECJ has gone much further in this direction. Two lines of the Court's case law should suffice to demonstrate how much bolder and more assertive the ECJ has been than the U.S. Supreme Court. One may as well start with the ECJ's ample case law on the question of whether Member States have provided adequate remedies by which persons may assert the rights that they derive from EU law. The ECJ demands that all procedural advantages of which parties may avail themselves in Member State courts under Member State law must be equally available to them in those courts law for comparable rights under EU law. This is the so-called "principle of equivalence".[15] This move would seem to be altogether reasonable and, frankly, not radically different from the position that U.S. courts would take under comparable circumstances.[16]

More remarkable from an American point of view is the ECJ's case law on the so-called "principle of effectiveness", according to which the national judge must in any case (that is to say, even if the principle of equivalence is respected), make available to parties remedies that are adequate for enabling them to assert the rights that EU law gives them and for ensuring the efficacy of this law.[17] In this way, the ECJ has managed to require the courts of the Member States to provide parties who are invoking their EU law rights remedies that are adequate for this purpose, even if these remedies do not already exist in national law and indeed even if they are inconsistent with existing national procedural norms.[18]

The second highly remarkable line of cases that is noteworthy in this regard stems from the ECJ's *Francovich* decision.[19] This judgment is scarcely even imaginable in the U.S. The imposition of liability in damages on Member States based on their violation of obligations derived from European law would almost certainly be considered as exorbitant if transferred to the American scene. Several reasons explain this reaction, including the silence of the European treaties (or, in the U.S., of the Constitution) on a so fundamental question and the poten-

---

15 Bermann, Goebel, Davey & Fox, *supra*, note 9, p. 351.

16 Jost, *supra*, note 14, p. 417.

17 Anthony Arnull, *The European Union and its Court of Justice*, Oxford, New York, Oxford EC Law Library, 2006, 2nd ed., p. 330.

18 See e.g. *Dilexport Srl c. Amministrazione delle Finanze dello Stato*, judgment of 9 February 1999, Case C-343/96, *ECR* I-00579.

19 *Andrea Francovich et Danila Bonifaci et al. c. République italienne*, Judgment of 10 November 1991, Case C-6/90, *ECR* I-05357.

tially excessive liability that such condemnation in damages could have on the American states under case law of this kind.[20]

9. A Teleological Methodology

The interpretation of legislative texts constitutes one of the Court of Justice's most important tasks, just as it is for the Supreme Court. In this regard, both courts profess to appreciate the great importance of the legislative text itself and, if necessary, also their legislative history. Both courts are highly attuned to the presumed intentions of the legislature. Still, one simply cannot read and compare the judgments of the Supreme Court and of the Court of Justice without observing the major role that teleological interpretation plays under the practices of the ECJ as compared to the U.S. Supreme Court.[21] I doubt that these differences may be attributed entirely to differences in legal culture between Europe and the U.S. Here figures importantly the ECJ's commitment to the fundamental objectives of EU law as outlined in the previous sections.

10. The Court's Contribution to European Policy

It is perfectly to be expected that, on the level of substance, European and American law would resemble one another much more prominently in some domains than in others. It is in any event often difficult to draw a comparison on the basis of the content of the law in a specific domain, since both the legislative texts and the underlying policies in the two jurisdictions are often themselves, frankly, quite different. Under these circumstances it would therefore be misleading to attribute to the courts of one system or another specific policy preferences. For example, European instruments may establish a higher level of protection of consumers than their American counterparts. Under these circumstances, the higher level of protection of consumers in Europe that results owes rather little to judicial policymaking and much more to the policies of legislators and regulators.

But assuredly, there are domains of law in which legislative texts play a reduced role, thus leaving room for the Court of Justice and the Supreme Court alike to develop their own policies, if only under the appearance of statutory interpretation. Here courts enjoy an appreciably greater freedom to advance the fundamental principles and policies of their respective systems, as they see them. Competition law offers the

---

20 Daniel J. Meltzer, "Member State Liability in Europe and the United States", *International Journal of Constitutional Law*, 2006, pp. 39-83; voir l'arrêt de la Cour Suprême dans l'affaire *Alden v. Maine*, 527 U.S. 706, 1999.

21 Bermann, Goebel, Davey & Fox, *supra*, note 9, p. 534.

most paradigmatic example, thanks to the laconic phrasing of the key legislative texts in this area of the law. As a result, the Court of Justice, on the one hand, and the Supreme Court, on the other, have elaborated jurisprudential preferences that are distinctly different from one another.[22]

11. The Judicial Role in Market Integration

The differences in practice of the two courts are most revealing when the courts confront the question of whether and how far to give direct effect to the norms that prohibit barriers to trade within the internal market. In an area such as this one, the policies that the Court of Justice pursues are perhaps less dictated by the European legislator than by the Treaty text itself. When it pursues them, the ECJ is fully cognizant of the immense importance of the internal market for the construction of Europe.[23] A comparative analysis of the respective case law of the two courts plainly reveals the greater degree of engagement of the ECJ in the deliberate construction of an internal market. The ECJ makes use in this regard of general legal notions that are originally of its own creation, such as the principle of proportionality, the requirement of mutual recognition, and the principles of equivalence and effectiveness that were raised earlier, so as to produce effects that are much more market-integrating than those resulting from the constitutional case law of the Supreme Court, even under the so-called "dormant" or "negative" commerce clause."[24]

12. The Highest Courts and Comparative Law

The coexistence of elements that are both common and non-common as between the two high courts opens up highly fertile terrain for contemporary comparative law. All the various objectives of comparative law stand to benefit from a transatlantic judicial comparison. These include law reform, legal harmonization and unification, inter-jurisdictional cooperation, the application of foreign law by courts, and above all a better understanding of one's own law and of law in gen-

---

22 Eleanor Fox, *Competition Law of the European Union in Comparative Perspective, Cases and Materials*, St. Paul, American Casebook Series, 2009.

23 Arnull, *supra*, note 17, pp. 438-441; Thomas G. Papadoulos, *EU Law and the Harmonization of Takeovers in the Internal Market*, Austin, Boston, Chicago, New York, The Netherlands, Wolters Kluwer Law & Business, 2010, p. 151.

24 Donald H. Regan, "The Supreme Court and State Protectionism: Making Sense of the Dormant Commerce Clause", *Michigan Law Review*, 1986, Vol. 84, p. 1091; David G. Savage, *The Supreme Court and the Powers of the American Government*, Washington D.C., CQ Press, 2009, 2nd ed., p. 95.

eral.[25] Both the ECJ and the Supreme Court occupy a central place in the inquiries that a comparison between American and European law inspires. The importance of the two Courts thus resides not only in the role and functions they perform, and the way they perform them, but also in the vast case law that each of them produces.

25 Daniela Caruso, "The European Union 20 Years after Maastricht: Transatlantic Perspectives Symposium Articles", *Tulane Journal of International and Competition Law*, 2011, Vol. 20, pp. 175, 178.

Agences décentralisées : vers un statut unifié ?

Approche commune du Parlement européen, du Conseil de l'Union européenne et de la Commission européenne sur les agences décentralisées

Françoise COMTE[1]

Chef de secteur à la Direction générale Affaires intérieures de la Commission européenne

1. Introduction

Le 13 juin 2012, la Commission européenne publiait un communiqué de presse relatif à l'adoption d'une approche commune relative aux agences décentralisées par les institutions du triangle institutionnel de l'Union européenne, Parlement européen, Conseil de l'Union européenne et Commission européenne.[2] La Commission se réjouit d'une « *avancée décisive* » grâce à cet accord.

Cet accord scelle une étape importante d'une longue marche institutionnelle vers un statut unifié des agences décentralisées. Cette contribution se propose d'étudier succinctement comment les institutions en sont arrivées à adopter cette approche commune (2.), le contenu et les éléments caractéristiques généraux du texte (3.) et enfin quelles seraient les conséquences à envisager pour les institutions et les agences (4.).

---

1 Les opinions exprimées par l'auteur le sont à titre personnel et ne peuvent être attribuées à l'institution à laquelle elle appartient. Cet article est finalisé à la date du 15 novembre 2012.

2 Communiqué de presse IP/12/604, http://europa.eu/rapid/press-release_IP-12-604_fr.htm.

2. Vers l'adoption d'une approche commune

La création de la première agence décentralisée remonte aux années 1975, avec la création du CEDEFOP, Centre européen pour le développement de la formation professionnelle. Ensuite, de nombreuses autres agences ont été créées. Ces agences sont désormais au nombre de 31, elles ont leur siège dans des États membres et travaillent dans des domaines très variés de l'activité de l'Union européenne. Les plus jeunes agences européennes ont été créées dans le cadre de la réponse à apporter au niveau européen à la crise économique et financière de 2008, afin de renforcer le système européen de surveillance financière (Autorité bancaire européenne, Autorité européenne des assurances et des pensions professionnelles et Autorité européenne des marchés financiers). Dans le domaine des affaires intérieures, deux agences ont récemment été établies (Bureau européen d'appui en matière d'asile et Agence européenne pour la gestion opérationnelle des systèmes d'information à grande échelle au sein de l'espace de liberté, de sécurité et de justice – SIS/VIS/EURODAC), dites « agence IT ».

Un certain nombre de traits communs unissent les agences décentralisées. Une telle agence à la personnalité juridique, est une entité institutionnelle indépendante par rapport aux institutions européennes (elle est gérée par des organes de direction autonomes : conseil d'administration et directeur), est créée par le législateur par l'adoption d'un règlement, participe à la régulation d'un secteur de l'activité européenne et est chargée d'une mission de service public.

Cependant, en dehors de ces éléments généraux, les règles horizontales présidant au fonctionnement au sens large de ces agences, et concernant en particulier des aspects aussi importants que leur création, leur structure, leur fonctionnement, leur évaluation et leur contrôle ne sont pas unifiées. Ces agences appartiennent au même monde institutionnel et pourtant leur caractéristique principale est finalement qu'elles ne répondent à aucun schéma institutionnel directeur, aucun statut général et cohérent. Chacune d'entre elles a été créée au cas par cas, pour répondre à des besoins sectoriels. Les règles relatives par exemple à la composition du conseil d'administration et à son mandat, à la nomination et au mandat du directeur, sont différentes d'un règlement fondateur à l'autre. Chaque agence est donc une créature institutionnelle spécifique.[3]

---

[3] Certains parlent de « *zoo administratif* ». Voir Jan Werner, Tobias Bach, Julia Fleischer, Thurid Hustedt, « Best practice in governance of agencies – A comparative study in view of identifying best practice for governing agencies carrying activities on behalf of the European Union » (Parlement européen, 2008).

La réflexion en vue d'unifier les règles applicables aux agences s'est donc engagée rapidement. S'il est naturel que le mandat sectoriel diffère d'une agence à l'autre, le mode de fonctionnement de ces entités du paysage institutionnel européen, devenues de plus en plus nombreuses au fil du temps, devrait répondre à des règles horizontales semblables, sinon harmonisées. Il en va de la légitimité même des agences. Ceci a été renforcé par le fait que le Traité de Lisbonne a formellement reconnu l'existence des agences en droit primaire en consacrant en particulier leur soumission au contrôle juridictionnel de la Cour de justice de l'Union européenne.[4] Cependant, le Traité de Lisbonne ne donne aucune indication quant à la définition d'une agence ou à son fonctionnement. Il se contente d'entériner leur existence et de les soumettre à l'ordre juridique européen.

Lors de la préparation par la Commission européenne du livre blanc relatif à la gouvernance en 2001,[5] le sujet avait déjà suscité un vif débat.[6] La Commission avait ensuite adopté en 2002 une Communication relative à « l'encadrement des agences européennes de régulation ».[7] Cette Communication tentait de poser quelques éléments de définition de la notion d'agence de régulation et de lancer quelques pistes en vue d'une approche cohérente en termes institutionnels pour la création et le fonctionnement de ces agences, sur la base de critères à définir et applicables à toute création d'une agence de l'Union. Cette Communication avait reçu un accueil favorable de la part du Parlement européen[8] et, quoiqu'en des termes plus mesurés, également du Conseil.[9]

La Commission s'était alors, suite à ces signes positifs de la part du co-législateur, engagée dans un exercice titanesque de recensement et de mise à plat des règles et critères applicables de façon générale aux agences de régulation futures lors de leur création et durant leur fonctionnement. Ceci avait donné lieu en 2005 à l'adoption par la Commission du projet d'accord interinstitutionnel pour un encadrement des agences de régulation.[10] Ce projet ambitieux avait permis à la Commis-

---

4 Articles 230, 232 et 234 TFUE.

5 Voir rapport du groupe de travail 3a du Livre Blanc sur la gouvernance : « Établissement d'un cadre pour les agences de régulation à vocation décisionnelle – Mieux exercer les responsabilités exécutives », 2001. Voir aussi rapport « The role of specialised Agencies in decentralising EU Governance », Michelle Everson, Giandomenico Majone, Les Metcalfe et Adriaan Schout, 1999.

6 Com(2001)428 Final, 25/07/2001.

7 Com(2002)718 Final, 11/12/2002.

8 Résolution du Parlement européen (JO C 92/E/119 du 16/04/2004).

9 Conclusions du Conseil de l'UE, juin 2004, document 10442/04 INST 174 JUR 285.

10 Com(2005)59 Final, 22/02/2005.

sion de proposer – pour la première fois dans l'histoire des agences de régulation – une définition de la notion d'agence ainsi que des missions dont celle-ci peut être investie, et à clarifier un certain nombre de règles horizontales relatives à la création, la structure, le fonctionnement, l'évaluation et le contrôle des agences européennes de régulation.[11] Ce projet avait reçu un accueil positif de la part du Parlement européen, qui y avait vu une avancée institutionnelle majeure.[12] Par contre, le Conseil n'avait pas souhaité débattre du projet et avait freiné toute velléité de la part de la Commission pour avancer dans une négociation de fond sur le projet.[13] Il est probable que le Conseil, entre autres raisons, ait préféré ne se lier en rien pour mener librement les négociations sectorielles sur les propositions d'agences en discussion à l'époque.

Prenant acte de l'échec des négociations sur le projet d'accord interinstitutionnel, la Commission, dans une communication de mars 2008, a fait une nouvelle tentative pour assainir la discussion sur les agences européennes et relancer le débat sur des bases nouvelles en invitant le Conseil et le Parlement européen à se joindre à elle dans le cadre d'un dialogue renouvelé sur la place des agences européennes dans la gouvernance européenne.[14] Pour ce faire, la Commission proposait la création d'un groupe de travail interinstitutionnel qui serait chargé de réfléchir et définir « *les règles de base applicables à toutes les agences compte tenu des enjeux auxquels elles ont à faire face* ».

Ce groupe interinstitutionnel a été créé le 10 mars 2009.[15] Une courte déclaration commune était alors adoptée et indiquait laconiquement

> Le Parlement européen, le Conseil de l'Union européenne et la Commission européenne sont convenus de lancer un dialogue interinstitutionnel sur les agences de régulation en vue d'évaluer la situation existante, et plus particulièrement la cohérence, l'efficacité, la responsabilité et la transparence de ces agences, et de trouver un terrain d'entente sur les moyens d'améliorer leurs travaux. Les trois institutions ont reconnu le rôle important des agences de régulation dans la mise en œuvre des politiques de l'Union européenne et la nécessité d'en faire en l'occurrence un outil plus efficace. Le groupe de

---

[11] Pour un commentaire éclairé du projet d'accord interinstitutionnel, voir Manuel Szapiro, « The Framework for European Regulatory Agencies : a Balance between Accountability and Autonomy », 3rd European Consortium for Political Research (ECPR), 2005, conference Budapest, 8-11 September 2005.

[12] Résolution PE, 01/12/2005, P6 TA(2005)0460.

[13] Question orale avec débat au Parlement européen, QO 0093/05 du 12/10/2005.

[14] Pour un commentaire de la Communication de 2008 COM(2008)135 final, voir Françoise Comte, « Agences européennes : Relance d'une réflexion interinstitutionnelle européenne ? », *Revue du Droit de l'Union européenne*, vol. 3, 2008, pp. 461-506.

[15] IP/09/413, 18/03/2009, http://europa.eu/rapid/press-release_IP-09-413_fr.htm.

travail interinstitutionnel abordera un certain nombre de questions essentielles soulevées par les institutions participantes, notamment le rôle et la place des agences dans le paysage institutionnel de l'Union européenne, la création, la structure et le fonctionnement de ces agences, ainsi que les questions de leur financement, de leur budget, de leur surveillance et de leur gestion.

Les travaux du groupe ont été peu transparents.[16] Ils ont consisté en la préparation de 34 « fiches » recensant l'ensemble des questions relatives aux agences. Ces fiches sont des documents d'analyse et suivent toutes une même structure, décrivent la situation de fait existante, les problèmes, et enfin élaborent les solutions possibles et leur mise en œuvre. C'est la Commission européenne qui s'est chargée du secrétariat du groupe et a fourni un travail important de préparation de ces fiches. Si la partie factuelle a été relativement facile à établir, les autres parties des fiches ont donné lieu à d'intenses discussions. Sur le plan de la méthode de travail, de nombreuses réunions interinstitutionnelles à niveau technique ainsi qu'à niveau politique ont eu lieu.

3. Approche commune : quelques éléments caractéristiques

A. Caractères généraux

Le texte adopté par les trois institutions[17] est divisé en deux parties : une « déclaration commune » suivie d'une annexe dénommée « approche commune ». La déclaration commune est un court texte d'à peine deux pages, de nature générale. L'approche commune, document plus long et plus détaillé, décrit quelques règles destinées à gouverner la création et le fonctionnement des agences. Le texte adopté par les institutions est un instrument non prévu par le Traité de Lisbonne, de nature purement politique, et marque la volonté des institutions parties prenantes d'avoir une vision commune pour les agences décentralisées. Ceci peut être considéré comme une avancée institutionnelle majeure. En effet, c'est la première fois dans l'histoire de l'Union que les institutions parviennent à un accord sur un texte commun dans le domaine des agences décentralisées.

À y regarder cependant de plus près, le texte contient des éléments amenant à considérer le texte sous un autre angle et probablement avec

---

16 Voir Françoise Comte, « 2008 Commission Communication "European Agencies – the Way Forward" : What is the follow-up since then ? », *Review of European Administrative Law*, 1/2010, vol. 3, n° 1, pp. 65-110. Les fiches sont maintenant publiées sur le site Europa de la Commission européenne sous http://europa.eu/agencies/regulatory_agencies_bodies/index_en.htm.

17 Document du Conseil 11450/12 du 18/06/2012.

moins d'enthousiasme. La déclaration commune insiste en effet sans ambiguïté sur deux éléments majeurs : d'une part, les trois institutions précisent clairement le *caractère juridiquement non contraignant* de l'approche commune et d'autre part indiquent que l'approche commune sera prise en compte dans le cadre de décisions futures relatives aux agences, sur la base d'une *analyse au cas par cas*.

Ces deux éléments, caractère juridiquement non contraignant et analyse au cas par cas, ont probablement été la condition pour que le Conseil accepte de participer aux discussions. En effet, lors des négociations sur le projet d'accord interinstitutionnel en 2005-2006, l'une des raisons pour lesquelles le Conseil refusait d'examiner le texte était justement la nature juridique du projet, qui pouvait être considéré comme ayant une valeur juridique contraignante. Or le Conseil, dans les négociations relatives aux agences, veut pouvoir décider librement et adapter le texte du règlement fondateur sur la base de considérations sectorielles. Les exigences de nature horizontale sont généralement mal accueillies, et considérées comme un carcan mal adapté aux exigences du secteur en cause.

Par ailleurs, l'une des raisons pour lesquelles le travail en vue d'une approche commune avait été lancé était précisément le fait que les agences ne répondent à aucun schéma directeur ni aucune vision d'ensemble, chaque règlement d'agence étant négocié au cas par cas. On peut donc considérer qu'il y a une contradiction interne au texte, qui prône une approche commune tout en proclamant la nécessité de ne se lier en rien et de continuer à travailler sur une base sectorielle en ignorant si nécessaire les considérations horizontales nécessaires au bon fonctionnement de l'agence. Ceci laisse mal augurer de la volonté réellement harmonisatrice du texte.

Enfin, ni la déclaration commune ni son annexe, l'approche commune, ne posent une définition de l'agence décentralisée. L'agence reste donc une créature institutionnelle indifférenciée, non définie, ni en droit primaire ni en droit secondaire, ni même dans un texte de nature politique. Il est probable qu'une telle définition s'est révélée comme un point de conflit trop important pour permettre aux institutions de se mettre d'accord sur un texte commun. La question a donc été éludée et les discussions se sont concentrées sur quelques règles de fonctionnement des agences.

B. Éléments généraux de contenu

L'approche commune, texte annexé à la déclaration commune, parvient cependant à poser quelques règles générales sur un certain nombre d'éléments horizontaux relatifs aux agences. C'est un tour de force compte tenu des positions contradictoires des parties prenantes à la négociation. Cela montre que les institutions ont tout de même voulu donner un signal fort sur le sujet.

Il est intéressant de noter que le texte couvre l'ensemble des questions relatives à la création, la vie et la disparition des agences. Les questions relatives à la création des agences, à leur structure et à leur gouvernance, à leur mode de fonctionnement, et aux contrôles exercés sur les agences sont abordées.

Le caractère limité de cette contribution ne permet pas de passer en revue l'ensemble des règles posées par l'approche commune. Un certain nombre d'éléments majeurs sont mis en exergue ci-dessous.

I. Création des agences

Le texte pose un certain nombre d'éléments relatifs à la création des agences. Il confirme la nécessité de disposer d'une analyse d'impact pour fonder la création d'une agence sur des éléments factuels permettant au co-législateur de prendre une décision éclairée. Dans la communication de 2008, la Commission avait annoncé une méthodologie spécifique en matière d'analyse d'impact pour les agences décentralisées. Ceci pourrait être très approprié compte tenu des difficultés inhérentes à l'exercice, une analyse d'impact pour la création d'une agence devant couvrir à la fois des éléments institutionnels (structure de l'agence) et sectoriels (mandat de l'agence).

Le texte insiste également sur la nécessité pour tous les règlements d'agence de contenir une clause de révision du règlement ou une clause prévoyant la fin des activités de l'agence. La clause de révision était déjà généralement incluse dans les règlements fondateurs, qui prévoient très souvent une révision du règlement fondateur après évaluation de l'agence. La clause de fin de vie de l'agence est rare. Une seule agence décentralisée a été fermée dans l'histoire de ces agences, l'agence européenne pour la reconstruction (Balkans).

II. Fusion des agences

Le texte de l'approche commune traite, avec un certain luxe de détails, la question de la fusion entre agences, si celle-ci s'avérait nécessaire. Une petite ou une moyenne agence pourrait alors être fusionnée avec une autre agence au mandat proche ou complémentaire afin d'optimiser l'efficacité des deux structures réunies.

La question n'est pas nouvelle. Par exemple, dans l'analyse d'impact visant à la création du Bureau européen d'appui en matière d'asile (EASO), la question avait été étudiée de façon approfondie pour savoir si le bureau devait être créé dans le cadre d'une autre agence pouvant être considérée comme ayant un mandat proche, FRONTEX (Agence européenne pour la gestion de la coopération opérationnelle aux frontières extérieures, chargée de la protection des frontières européennes) et EUROPOL (Office européen de police, chargé d'améliorer la coopération policière entre États membres). Ces options avaient été écartées compte tenu notamment de la spécificité du mandat d'EASO par rapport à EUROPOL et du possible conflit d'intérêts entre FRONTEX et EASO (protection des frontières/protection des personnes bénéficiant d'une protection internationale).[18]

Deux exemples possibles d'une telle opération de fusion sont cités de façon récurrente depuis des années dans les discussions européennes, la fusion de l'agence CEPOL (Collège européen de police), chargée de la formation des polices européennes, avec EUROPOL (Office européen de police), chargé d'améliorer la coopération policière entre États membres pour lutter contre le terrorisme, le trafic illicite de drogues et les autres formes graves de la criminalité organisée internationale. L'autre exemple souvent cité est celui d'une fusion du CEDEFOP (Centre européen pour le développement de la formation professionnelle) avec l'ETF (Fondation européenne pour la formation) dont les mandats sont parfois considérés comme complémentaires (le CEDEFOP concentre ses activités de formation dans l'Union, l'ETF exerce son mandat dans des pays tiers). On pourrait également envisager la réunion des deux agences opérant dans le domaine des droits de l'homme, l'agence des droits fondamentaux de l'Union européenne (FRA) avec l'Institut européen pour l'égalité entre les hommes et les femmes (EIGE).

C'est le Parlement européen, par le biais de sa puissante commission budgétaire, qui demande de façon récurrente que les possibilités de fusion entre agences soient étudiées. Celle-ci considère souvent que les agences représentent un budget conséquent et que des économies d'échelles pourraient être réalisées en fusionnant des agences et notamment leurs services horizontaux. Il reste à voir comment une telle fusion d'organismes existants pourrait s'organiser en pratique. De nombreuses questions seraient à régler, de toute nature, juridiques, techniques et politiques. Le problème juridique majeur serait d'éviter que l'agence fusionnée, celle qui disparaît, soit phagocytée par l'agence hôte. La question se pose par exemple pour la représentation dans le conseil d'administration des intérêts de l'agence qui disparaît, celle de la préservation de son budget en tant que ligne budgétaire autonome, le transfert du mandat de l'agence fusionnée vers celui de son agence hôte. Des problèmes pratiques tels que la fermeture d'un site et la réinstalla-

---

[18] Voir Françoise Comte : « A New Agency is born in the European Union : The European Asylum Support Office », *European Journal of Migration and Law*, vol. 12, 2010, pp. 373-405.

tion/le transfert du personnel sur le site hôte (dans un autre pays) seraient à résoudre. Enfin, en termes politiques, dans le cas où certaines agences ont par exemple été créées sur demande des États membres, sont bien évaluées ou ont une image forte de leur activité dans les États membres, il n'est pas certain que de telles opérations seraient bien reçues au Conseil.

III. Siège des agences

L'approche commune traite de la nécessité pour l'État hôte de recevoir dans les meilleures conditions possibles l'agence qui va être créée. L'État hôte doit respecter un certain nombre de critères objectifs, par exemple l'accessibilité du site, l'existence d'écoles appropriées pour les enfants du personnel et un accès facilité au marché du travail, à la sécurité sociale et aux soins médicaux pour les enfants et les conjoints des agents. Ces éléments sont importants pour rendre l'agence attractive pour du personnel plurilingue de haut niveau et très spécialisé, qui doit accepter dans certains cas de s'expatrier dans des sites européens excentrés ou difficiles d'accès.

L'approche commune demande également que les agences concluent un accord de siège avec leur pays hôte. On peut noter que certaines agences ne disposent toujours pas d'un accord de siège, par exemple FRONTEX qui a de grandes difficultés à conclure un accord de siège avec la Pologne et Varsovie, ville où elle est située. L'approche commune indique que la Commission pourrait proposer un texte modèle, pouvant servir de base pour des accords futurs de siège. Il faudra voir si l'approche commune peut servir de base pour de jeunes agences en train de conclure leur accord de siège. Un exemple particulièrement frappant est celui de l'Agence IT. Cette agence aura son cœur administratif à Tallin en Estonie, son cœur technique (systèmes informatiques) à Strasbourg en France et son système de back-up en Autriche. Il sera intéressant de comparer les accords de siège à conclure avec les trois États pour savoir si les conditions offertes à l'agence sont favorables et comparables.

IV. Conseils d'administration

Le texte de l'approche commune est rédigé de façon très intéressante quant à la composition du conseil d'administration de l'agence. Il apparaît que la pleine participation des États membres et de la Commission – avec droit de vote – doit être assurée dans le conseil d'administration. C'est un pas en avant clair pour la Commission, dont le rôle au sein du conseil d'administration d'une agence est expressément reconnu, en ce qui concerne la « *supervision de la gestion administrative, opérationnelle et budgétaire de l'agence* ». Ceci devrait permettre de mettre fin à des anomalies dans des agences héritées des procédures et pratiques de troisième pilier, par exemple CEPOL, dans le conseil d'administration de laquelle la Commission n'est pas représentée (pas de droit de vote).

En ce qui concerne le Parlement européen, sa représentation sera possible dans le cas où cela se révélera approprié. De la même façon, un certain nombre de représentants de groupes d'intérêts pourra être prévu, si approprié.

Il est souvent considéré qu'il est peu souhaitable que le Parlement européen soit représenté dans le conseil d'administration d'une agence. En effet, le membre du Parlement européen est confronté à un conflit d'intérêts. Il vote le budget de l'agence en tant que membre de son conseil d'administration et il vote la décharge du même budget en tant que membre du Parlement européen. C'est pourquoi souvent, dans les quelques cas où le Parlement est représenté dans un conseil d'administration d'une agence, le représentant du Parlement est nommé en tant qu'expert. La formule de l'approche commune entérine cette solution : pas de représentation d'une façon générale pour le Parlement dans un conseil d'administration.

V. Nomination du directeur

La formule de compromis endossée par les parties prenantes reprend la formule la plus usitée en ce qui concerne la nomination du directeur : préparation par la Commission d'une « *short-list* » et choix sur cette *short-list* d'un candidat par le conseil d'administration. C'est le conseil d'administration qui nomme le directeur. Le texte élude cependant l'une des questions chères au Parlement européen : celle de sa participation dans le processus de nomination du directeur de l'agence. Dans des règlements récents, comme ceux d'EASO ou de l'agence IT, sur le modèle initié par l'ENISA (Agence européenne chargée de la sécurité des réseaux et de l'information), le Parlement européen a obtenu le droit de procéder à une audition du candidat directeur retenu par le conseil d'administration. Cela lui donne un droit de regard sur le futur directeur. Dans le cas (qui ne s'est jamais produit) où le Parlement européen donnerait un avis négatif sur le candidat présenté par le conseil d'administration, celui-ci devrait en tenir compte, bien que l'avis n'ait pas de valeur juridique contraignante. En effet, nommer un directeur contre l'avis du Parlement européen pourrait préparer des conflits lors des auditions du directeur devant le Parlement, en particulier durant la décharge budgétaire.

VI. Fonctionnement et contrôle des agences

Le cadre limité de cet Article ne permet pas d'aborder ces questions. Les règles posées par l'approche commune constituent globalement une consolidation et une confirmation des règles applicables en la matière dans les règlements fondateurs récents d'agences nouvellement créées. Ces règles avaient été consolidées par la Commission dans le projet d'accord interinstitutionnel de 2005 et étaient systématiquement reprises par la Commission dans ses propositions (révision ou création d'agences) depuis 2005. Ces règles se retrouvent en grande partie dans l'approche commune.

VII. Système d'alerte

L'approche commune comporte une nouveauté institutionnelle. Elle confère à la Commission une responsabilité spécifique en lui demandant de déclencher un « *système d'alerte* » dans le cas où celle-ci a des raisons sérieuses de penser que le conseil d'administration d'une agence est sur le point de prendre des décisions qui sont en contradiction avec le mandat de l'agence, sont susceptibles de violer le droit de l'Union européenne ou sont en contradiction manifeste avec les objectifs de la politique européenne.

Dans ces cas, le représentant de la Commission au conseil d'administration de l'agence doit soulever formellement la question et demander à celui-ci de s'abstenir d'adopter la décision litigieuse. Dans le cas où le conseil d'administration (dans lequel la Commission est en minorité) passe outre, la Commission informe formellement le Parlement européen et le Conseil, afin de permettre au triangle institutionnel de réagir. La Commission peut demander au conseil d'administration de s'abstenir d'adopter la décision en cause tant que les représentants des institutions discutent de la question.

Il faudra voir comment la Commission fera usage de ce nouveau droit. Pour l'instant, la procédure, sur le plan technique, n'est pas définie précisément. Par ailleurs, l'usage de cette possibilité pour la Commission ne pourra s'envisager que dans des cas gravissimes de violation du droit par le conseil d'administration. La menace d'user de ce droit sera sans doute tout aussi efficace que l'usage lui-même.

Cette nouvelle procédure donne des responsabilités particulières à la Commission, qui peut être considérée comme investie de ce nouveau droit en tant que gardienne des Traités et de l'ordre juridique européen au nom de toutes les institutions européennes.

4. Approche commune : conséquences institutionnelles

Les institutions et les agences seront responsables de la bonne mise en œuvre de l'approche commune. Voyons brièvement comment les choses se présentent.

A. Pour le Conseil

Le Conseil s'engage à tenir compte de l'approche commune dans les négociations futures portant sur la création ou la révision d'agences. Compte tenu du fait que le texte n'a pas de valeur juridique contraignante et sera mis en œuvre au cas par cas, il faudra voir si la pratique décisionnelle du Conseil évolue de façon décisive suite à l'adoption de l'approche commune.

Les éléments relatifs à l'accord de siège et à l'accueil sur son territoire d'une nouvelle agence pourront servir utilement à l'avenir de cadre de référence. Il faudra voir en pratique si ces éléments améliorent la situation et permettent aux nouvelles agences de s'installer plus facilement et plus rapidement, par exemple en évitant des difficultés dans la négociation des accords de siège et en évitant des situations transitoires coûteuses et difficiles (bâtiments provisoires par exemple).

B. Pour le Parlement

Le Parlement s'engage à tenir compte de l'approche commune dans les négociations futures portant sur la création ou la révision d'agences. Le Parlement soutenait la Commission lorsqu'elle a adopté le projet d'accord interinstitutionnel en 2005. En ce sens, il est probable que le Parlement aura à cœur de mettre en œuvre les règles de l'approche commune.

Cependant, il est à remarquer que le Parlement ne paraît pas être le grand gagnant des négociations sur l'approche commune. On peut considérer que les règles en matière de contrôle des agences, qui consolident les règles déjà applicables, lui apportent satisfaction en particulier en tant qu'autorité budgétaire. Cependant, ses revendications en matière institutionnelle – participation au conseil d'administration et participation au processus de nomination du directeur – n'ont pas été entendues. Le fait que l'approche commune sera mise en œuvre au cas par cas et la formulation habile du texte, qui évite de se prononcer sur ces points et les laissent donc ouverts, lui permettra, comme par le passé, de négocier dans le cadre de chaque règlement et notamment sa participation à la nomination du directeur.

C. Pour les agences

Les agences doivent mettre en œuvre l'approche commune. Un certain nombre d'éléments les concernent directement, par exemple l'obligation de prévoir des stratégies pluriannuelles et de lier strictement leur planification d'activités à une planification de leurs ressources (budget et personnel). Ceci correspond clairement aux préoccupations de l'autorité budgétaire, Conseil et Parlement, qui en temps de crise, ne veulent pas voir déraper les budgets des agences. La question des conflits d'intérêts, qui a fait récemment l'objet de critiques de la Cour des Comptes et du Parlement (dans le cadre de la décharge), est également abordée dans l'approche commune, pour que les agences y travaillent de concert avec la Commission.

D. Pour la Commission

C'est sur la Commission que pèse la plus lourde responsabilité de mise en œuvre de l'approche commune. La Commission a annoncé qu'elle produirait rapidement, pour fin 2012, une feuille de route visant à la mise en œuvre de l'approche commune. Il faudra voir si la Commission saisit cette occasion pour conserver l'impulsion politique donnée par l'adoption de l'approche commune, tout en donnant des éléments précis techniques de mise en œuvre. Ce sera de toute évidence pour la Commission un exercice d'équilibre difficile à trouver.

La Commission se trouve également investie de la responsabilité du déclenchement du système d'alerte, si nécessaire. Ceci constitue un renforcement de son rôle dans la gestion et le contrôle des agences, en tant que gardienne des Traités.

5. Conclusion

L'approche commune constitue un grand espoir pour ceux qui pensent que les agences doivent désormais répondre à des règles unifiées dans le paysage institutionnel européen. Les règles horizontales de fonctionnement des agences contenues dans l'approche commune constituent en très grande partie une consolidation des règles déjà connues et mises en œuvre, en particulier depuis le projet d'accord interinstitutionnel qui avait permis de les mettre à plat de façon synthétique et coordonnée.

C'est la pratique institutionnelle qui montrera si l'approche commune donne des résultats. La responsabilité de la Commission est immense à cet égard. La Commission a indiqué qu'elle ne procédera pas à une révision en bloc des règlements fondateurs d'agence sur la base de l'approche commune. L'harmonisation des règles horizontales de fonctionnement dans les règlements fondateurs devra donc se faire petit à petit et au fur et à mesure, soit lors d'une proposition en vue de la création d'une nouvelle agence, soit lors de la révision d'un règlement existant, par exemple après évaluation de l'agence. C'est la Commission en premier lieu qui devra faire preuve de fermeté durant les négociations – par nature sectorielles – pour ne pas céder sur les questions institutionnelles horizontales majeures afin de faire prévaloir les règles de l'approche commune.

La souveraineté dans l'Union européenne et dans ses États membres

Retour sur une question qui divise

Vlad CONSTANTINESCO

Professeur émérite de l'Université de Strasbourg

Ces quelques lignes[1] entendent honorer Paul Demaret, dont l'engagement en faveur d'une éducation européenne[2] de qualité ne s'est pas démenti tout au long des diverses fonctions qu'il a occupées tant à l'université de Liège qu'au Collège d'Europe. Directeur du Département juridique, puis recteur du Collège d'Europe, il a œuvré sans cesse dans le souci de développer l'institution dont il avait la charge, sans jamais renoncer à l'idéal de qualité, qui est devenu la marque de fabrique du Collège, que ce soit sur le campus de Bruges ou sur celui de Natolin. En hommage au collègue et à l'ami, je veux revenir sur une question de fond toujours posée, jamais résolue, peut-être même insoluble, voire impossible à résoudre. Il me semble que le moment actuel est propice pour reprendre ce débat ancien, qui remonte aux origines de la construction européenne : la question de la souveraineté dans l'Union européenne.[3] Il me reste à solliciter d'emblée l'indulgence de Paul Demaret, auquel ces lignes n'apprendront sans doute pas grand-chose ! Qu'il sache que c'est avec admiration et amitié que je les lui dédie.

Partons d'un constat : les évolutions nationales et européennes en cours, comme l'ample crise économique qui continue à se développer,

---

1 Compte tenu du cadre limité de cette contribution, l'appareil de notes infra-paginales sera réduit à l'essentiel.

2 Au Collège d'Europe, c'est bien d'une éducation européenne qu'il s'agit et pas seulement d'une instruction portant sur les questions européennes. À propos d'*Éducation européenne*, c'est aussi le titre d'un livre de Romain Gary paru en 1945 et d'où j'extrais cette citation : « Le patriotisme, c'est l'amour des siens, le nationalisme, c'est la haine des autres. »

3 Cf. Florence Chaltiel, *La souveraineté de l'État et l'Union européenne, l'exemple français, Recherches sur la souveraineté de l'État membre*, Paris, LGDJ, 2000.

obligent, à notre avis, et plus que par le passé, à interroger la notion de *souveraineté*. On s'aperçoit que le terme ou l'adjectif est aujourd'hui accolé à de multiples signifiants, ce qui atteste peut-être de la mutation de la notion, en tout cas d'une certaine plasticité, alors que les juristes tout au moins, ont tendance à la considérer comme immuable et définitive.

Ne parle-t-on pas couramment, aujourd'hui, de *dettes souveraines*, à propos desquelles on évoque même l'hypothèse de *faillites souveraines* ? La possibilité pour un État de ne pas rembourser ses dettes serait-elle alors une marque de souveraineté ? Par ailleurs, n'évoque-t-on pas la *souveraineté de l'État sur ses ressources naturelles* ? S'agit-il d'une notion nouvelle, ou de l'actualisation de la capacité reconnue par certaines constitutions à l'État de contrôler, au nom de l'intérêt de la collectivité, les ressources qui présentent un intérêt pour le bien-être de sa population ?[4] Ne réfléchit-on pas à la *divisibilité de la souveraineté* voire à son *irréductibilité* ?[5]

Beaucoup considèrent que l'imbrication actuelle des dépendances mutuelles de toutes sortes entre les États – causée par la généralisation du principe de libre circulation et par l'instantanéité des communications – prive cette notion de toute réalité, même si les États continuent, à tort peut-être, de s'en prévaloir : plutôt que de la *souveraineté des États*, ne conviendrait-il pas de parler de la *souveraineté des marchés financiers*, ou de celle des *agences de notation* ? En d'autres termes, la *souveraineté de l'État* serait, aujourd'hui, une notion obsolète et dépassée, car elle ne correspondrait plus aux circonstances historiques qui l'ont vue naître et prospérer. D'autres entités, sans doute illicites, – comme les mafias, par exemple – seraient sans doute plus souveraines que bon nombre d'États !

Ces différents qualificatifs et usages mettent en cause les définitions traditionnelles de la souveraineté comme puissance suprême, irrésistible, inaliénable, indivisible, ou encore comme *compétence de la compétence*.[6]

---

4 À l'instar de ce que dispose le Préambule de la Constitution française du 27 octobre 1946 : « Tout bien, toute entreprise, dont l'exploitation a ou acquiert les caractères d'un service public national ou d'un monopole de fait, doit devenir la propriété de la collectivité ».

5 Il y a plus de 50 ans, déjà, Charles Chaumont lui consacrait une étude remarquée : « Recherche du contenu irréductible de la souveraineté internationale de l'État » dans *Hommage d'une génération de juristes au président Basdevant*, Paris, Pedone, 1960, p. 114.

6 La formule est éloquente, comme tout oxymore, mais sans doute contradictoire et donc peu exacte, si l'on admet que la notion de compétence ne peut être que limitée…

Il s'agit, dans un premier temps, de chercher la manière dont la notion de souveraineté a été affectée par l'existence de l'Union européenne (1), avant d'examiner les mutations territoriales et de population que pourraient connaître certains États membres, ce qui conduirait également à reconsidérer la notion de souveraineté (2).

1. Souveraineté et Union européenne

L'Union européenne a depuis longtemps fait la preuve de son originalité en déroutant les notions et qualifications que la doctrine a tenté de lui appliquer pour la caractériser. Ainsi, si chacun s'accorde à considérer que l'Union européenne est une organisation internationale, fondée sur une série de traités internationaux, chacun reconnaît aussi qu'il ne s'agit sans doute pas d'une organisation internationale comme les autres… Mais c'est la mesure et la portée qu'il convient d'assigner à ce *sui generis* qui sont évidemment difficiles à apprécier ! La formule la plus courante consiste alors à dire que l'Union européenne est probablement davantage qu'une simple organisation internationale, mais sans doute moins qu'un État. Est-on plus avancé ?

C'est pour mieux préciser la nature juridique de l'Union que fut proposée la distinction entre *organisations internationales de coopération*, et *organisations internationales d'intégration.*

Dans la première catégorie, sont regroupées l'essentiel des organisations internationales aujourd'hui existantes : c'est par une coopération entre États membres qu'ensemble ces États atteignent les objectifs qu'ils ont assignés à l'organisation. Les États demeurent identiques à eux-mêmes du début jusqu'à la fin du processus de coopération, qui se déploie de façon linéaire et qui est régi par la règle de l'unanimité.

Au contraire, les États engagés dans un processus d'intégration ont accepté à l'avance de voir leurs structures se modifier profondément. Des pans entiers de leur législation subiront l'influence de décisions prises à la majorité, leurs administrations, y compris leurs juridictions, fonctionneront dans un autre cadre en dépendant de décisions prises au-delà des seules autorités étatiques. Le processus d'intégration est finalisé et il interfère verticalement dans les structures internes de l'État, qui n'est plus le même à la fin de ce processus que ce qu'il était au début. Comment ne pas traduire cela par le constat selon lequel les organisations d'intégration érodent la souveraineté de leurs États membres, jusqu'à la faire asymptotiquement disparaître ? Autre constat, qui relativise la distinction entre ces deux catégories d'organisations internationales : la catégorie d'organisation d'intégration semble faite sur mesure pour l'Union européenne. On ne voit pas, aujourd'hui, d'autre organisation internationale qu'elle qui puisse partager ces caractères.

Dès lors, l'on se trouve devant une nouvelle manifestation du *sui generis*, peu satisfaisant pour l'esprit !

Il reste que la question de la souveraineté est débattue depuis les origines de la construction européenne, dans son versant communautaire. L'adjectif *supranational* n'avait-il pas été jadis forgé pour qualifier la situation de la CECA et de sa Haute-Autorité, ainsi que le proposait Robert Schuman ? :

> L'institution supranationale, telle que notre Communauté, représentée par la Haute Autorité, ne possède pas les caractéristiques d'un État ; mais elle détient et exerce certains pouvoirs souverains.[7]

Depuis cette époque, l'évolution de l'Union européenne a confirmé que, dans des domaines aussi décisifs, par exemple, que la monnaie – et pour les États de la zone Euro – l'Union exerçait bien des « *pouvoirs souverains* », sans qu'elle devienne pour autant souveraine, et sans que les États membres cessent de l'être…

Les termes de *supranationalité* ou de *supranational* ne sont cependant plus guère utilisés, probablement à cause de leur caractère de notion sur mesure ou *sui generis*, mais les réalités qu'ils recouvrent trouvent davantage à s'inscrire dans l'opposition entre *Confédération d'États (Staatenbund)* et *État fédéral (Bundestaat)*. L'Union européenne pourrait présenter alors une nature composite : certains de ses éléments relèvent indiscutablement de la *Confédération d'États*, par exemple, le droit de retrait d'un État membre tel qu'il est consacré par le Traité de Lisbonne (Article 14 TUE) évoque le droit de sécession propre aux Confédérations d'États, tandis qu'au contraire des notions comme la *primauté* du droit de l'Union, l'*invocabilité* de certaines de ses dispositions devant un juge national, l'existence d'une monnaie unique pour les États faisant partie de la zone Euro relèvent plutôt de traits qui caractérisent l'*État fédéral*.

On peut aussi, comme le propose Olivier Beaud,[8] à la suite des analyses de Carl Schmitt, considérer que l'Union devrait plutôt relever de la *Fédération*, catégorie juridique en soi, différente par sa substance et par sa nature de celle de l'État, et qui, échappant ainsi à l'« *étaticité* », verrait suspendue, en son sein, la question de la souveraineté. Séduisante vision, irénique, et qui dépasserait la dichotomie ancienne *Confédération d'États/État fédéral*, elle-même liée aux conditions historiques du XIXe siècle et aux conceptualisations américaine, helvétique et

---

7 Robert Schuman, préface à l'ouvrage de Paul Reuter : *La Communauté européenne du charbon et de l'acier*, Paris, LGDJ, 1953, p. 7.

8 On songe essentiellement aux travaux d'Olivier Beaud, et notamment à son maître-ouvrage : *Théorie de la Fédération*, Paris, PUF, Coll. Léviathan, 2007.

allemande. Le succès de la formule de Jacques Delors, selon laquelle l'Union européenne serait une *Fédération d'États-nations*, quelle que soit son imprécision voire son ambiguïté, s'explique aisément parce qu'elle vient donner à la catégorie de *Fédération* une illustration actuelle et une incarnation contemporaine, mais aussi parce qu'elle permet de faire l'économie de la question de la souveraineté – sujet sensible s'il en est – mais qui se trouve, grâce au recours à la notion de *Fédération*, écarté d'emblée des débats.

Certains estiment que la réalité actuelle de l'Union pourrait préfigurer déjà celle d'une *Fédération*, la *Fédération* n'étant ni un *État fédéral*, ni une *Confédération d'États*. La *Fédération* serait une forme politique spécifique, sans véritable précédent historique, qui – loin de chercher à localiser la souveraineté à l'échelon fédéral (*État fédéral*) ou à l'échelon des États fédérés (*Confédération d'États*) – mettrait entre parenthèses la *question de la souveraineté*, celle-ci étant en quelque sorte « suspendue » entre le tout et ses parties.[9] Ces analyses, quelles que soient leur richesse et leur profondeur, ne se heurtent-elles pas au constat qu'elles supposent d'avance résolue – mais par prétérition – la question de la *souveraineté* ?

Plus exacte semble cependant la formule d'Alan Dashwood, évoquant, à propos de l'Union européenne, « *a constitutional order of sovereign States* »,[10] qui a aussi l'avantage de ne pas se prononcer sur la catégorie juridique à laquelle appartiendrait ce *constitutional order*.

Ces différentes interrogations et qualifications trouvent à s'illustrer dans le débat politique qui, à la faveur de la crise, commence à s'engager au sein de l'Union européenne. Ainsi, les récentes propositions du président Barroso,[11] appelant à une *Union politique* qui prendrait la forme d'une *fédération d'États-nations*,[12] pour laquelle il faudra un nouveau traité, relancent inévitablement le débat sur la souveraineté en Europe.

Pour autant, on peut se demander si la notion de *souveraineté*, jadis une notion-clé du droit constitutionnel et de la théorie de l'État, forgée en effet dans le contexte historique de l'avènement de cette forme

---

9 À rapprocher de l'idée de *souveraineté duale*, chaque ordre étant souverain dans sa sphère.

10 Alan Dashwood *in* Wyatt & Dashwood's *European Union Law*, 4th edition, 2000, p. 151. C'est aussi le titre du *Liber Amicorum* qui lui fut offert par ses collègues : Anthony Arnull, Catherine Barnard, Michael Dougan and Eleanor Spaventa (eds.), *A Constitutional Order of States ? Essays in EU Law in Honour of Alan Dashwood*, London, Hart Publishing, 2011.

11 Discours sur l'état de l'Union, prononcé devant le Parlement européen, le 12 septembre 2012.

12 On sait que la formule est de Jacques Delors.

politique spécifique, et liée à cette époque, est encore aujourd'hui une notion pertinente pour saisir les profonds phénomènes qui se déroulent tant à l'intérieur des États membres que dans leurs relations avec l'Union européenne. Si le signifiant de la notion de souveraineté est resté le même, son signifié a certainement évolué depuis ses origines. Il s'agit donc de savoir si l'on parle, aujourd'hui, de la même chose que jadis.

En deux mots, l'évolution qui s'est produite depuis le XVIe siècle a fait passer la souveraineté du statut de puissance irrésistible, indivisible et inaliénable au statut de titre de légitimité fondant l'exercice de la puissance d'État.

Si la notion de *souveraineté* a pu subir, depuis ses origines, une aussi profonde transformation, c'est notamment parce que la *souveraineté* se trouve liée, depuis la Révolution française, au principe démocratique et à son exercice. La *souveraineté démocratique* a remplacé la *souveraineté de droit divin.* Parallèlement, la *souveraineté*, entendue comme une *quantité de pouvoir* a évolué pour devenir une *qualité de pouvoir*, à savoir un titre de légitimité à exercer le pouvoir, voire à le déléguer.[13]

Dans l'ordre interne, la *souveraineté démocratique* désignera alors le titre légitime à exercer le pouvoir, le souverain étant aujourd'hui le peuple, le *demos*, ce qui oblige d'abord à l'identifier et à le délimiter, et donc à dégager les procédures adéquates pour le faire. En ce qui concerne l'Union européenne, la formule nouvelle[14] de l'Article 14 § 2 TUE selon laquelle : « Le Parlement européen est composé de représentants des citoyens de l'Union » renvoie-t-elle à un *peuple européen* qui serait la résultante de l'addition des citoyens de l'Union européenne ? Il est certainement difficile de constater aujourd'hui l'existence d'un véritable « corps politique européen » composé de l'ensemble des citoyens de l'Union européenne… L'impression serait plutôt l'inverse : celle – composite – d'une addition de peuples nationaux.

Faute de pouvoir aujourd'hui constater facilement l'existence d'un peuple européen, au sens de « corps politique », une autre piste s'offre, celle de rechercher quel pourrait être le *pouvoir constituant* au sein de l'Union européenne. Il s'agit, bien sûr, du *pouvoir originaire*, de celui

---

[13] Cf. Michael Neumann, *Democracy, Sovereignty and the European Union*, C. Hurst & C° Publishers Ltd., 1996, p. 13 : « (…) if sovereignty is regarded as a *quantity* of powers, the transfer of some forms of legal competences may be seen as *reducing* the power of the state. If, however, it is seen as a definitional attribute to statehood, there is no necessary reason to assume that the transfer of certain legal competences reduces overall state power – it may even increase it if it brings other gains » (italiques de l'auteur).

[14] La version précédente indiquait que le Parlement européen représentait les peuples des États membres, ce qui est assez différent…

qui dispose, par principe, de la *compétence de la compétence*. L'identification du ou des titulaires de ce pouvoir souverain, sa localisation, ne sont pas choses simples, car le droit originaire de l'Union européenne – les traités constitutifs – ne prévoit que des procédures mettant en œuvre la *compétence constituante*, c'est-à-dire le *pouvoir constituant dérivé*... Il faut donc que les juristes fassent preuve d'imagination.

Une récente recherche aborde cette question avec talent.[15] Après avoir constaté que la méthode fonctionnaliste a délibérément écarté le recours à un pouvoir constituant européen en fondant le droit originaire sur la compétence conventionnelle des États fondateurs, cette recherche estime que s'il s'agit de construire *de lege ferenda* un pouvoir constituant européen, celui-ci ne peut être trouvé que dans la conjonction de la volonté des peuples des États membres mais aussi dans la volonté de préserver les *droits fondamentaux des États*, au sein du futur ordre constitutionnel européen.

La doctrine s'est aussi tournée vers la remise en cause des caractéristiques traditionnelles et jugées essentielles de la souveraineté, telles que les légistes de la Couronne les avaient jadis dépeintes. Parmi elles, et au premier chef, l'*indivisibilité* et l'*inaliénabilité* de la souveraineté. L'intégration européenne a conduit à des analyses qui relativisent ces deux caractéristiques, pour ne pas dire qu'elles les contredisent.

Une première manifestation de cette remise en cause peut être trouvée dans l'analyse de la répartition des compétences entre l'Union et ses États membres, qui débouche sur le constat de la *divisibilité de la souveraineté* étatique : l'État membre garde des sphères où il demeure souverain, tandis que l'Union exerce, comme déjà constaté, des pouvoirs souverains. Se met ainsi en place une *souveraineté duale*, chaque ordre étant souverain dans sa sphère, ce qui permet d'expliquer pourquoi, dans la sphère des compétences – exclusives – de l'Union, la primauté de son droit s'impose sur toute norme contraire du droit national, qui ne pourrait intervenir qu'à tort dans cette même sphère – comme issue d'un pouvoir incompétent.

La remise par les États membres de certaines de leurs compétences à l'Union met au jour un autre phénomène qui intéresse l'indivisibilité de la souveraineté. D'abord, on a distingué, notamment dans la jurisprudence du Conseil constitutionnel, l'*attribution de compétences* de leur *transfert*. Puis on a opposé le *transfert de compétences* (jugé conforme à la constitution) au *transfert des conditions essentielles d'exercice de la souveraineté nationale* (jugé contraire à la constitution, et nécessitant, de ce fait, une révision de la constitution pour lever l'objection). Au

15 Il s'agit de la thèse de Gaëlle Marti : *Le pouvoir constituant européen*, Bruxelles, Bruylant, 2012.

détour de ces périphrases, comment ne pas constater que l'idée même de l'indivisibilité de la souveraineté est atteinte ?

En considérant que la *souveraineté* ne peut se comprendre que comme un *faisceau de compétences*, n'en accepte-t-on pas par là une sorte de démembrement, contradictoire avec la conception indivisible de la notion, mais commode pour comprendre que malgré leur importance, les compétences de l'Union ne sont que des *compétences d'attribution*, tandis que les États membres, investis de la *compétence de droit commun*, témoignent, par là, qu'ils restent titulaires de la *souveraineté ?*[16] Il resterait aussi à savoir à partir de quel niveau de transfert ou de quel volume d'attribution de compétences à l'Union les États membres cesseraient de pouvoir se revendiquer comme souverains ? C'est tout le problème philosophique du passage de la quantité à la qualité, déjà évoqué par le fameux *paradoxe sorite.*[17]

2. Souveraineté et État membre

La doctrine des *droits fondamentaux des États*[18] peut être considérée comme la version moderne de la souveraineté, s'agissant de l'État membre de l'Union. Celui-ci se trouve doté, par le droit originaire de l'Union, de certains droits parmi lesquels on retiendra tout spécialement le droit de chaque État membre à préserver son *identité nationale*, en la rendant opposable aux actes de l'Union, comme l'indique l'Article 4 § 2 TUE :

> 2. L'Union respecte l'égalité des États membres devant les traités ainsi que leur identité nationale, inhérente à leurs structures fondamentales politiques et constitutionnelles, y compris en ce qui concerne l'autonomie locale et régionale. Elle respecte les fonctions essentielles de l'État, notamment celles qui ont pour objet d'assurer son intégrité territoriale, de maintenir l'ordre public et de sauvegarder la sécurité nationale. En particulier, la sécurité nationale reste de la seule responsabilité de chaque État membre.

Parmi les divers éléments de cette *identité nationale*, ceux qui présentent un caractère constitutionnel sont certainement parmi les plus

---

16 Le droit de se retirer de l'Union, reconnu expressément par le traité de Lisbonne aux États membres, témoigne bien que l'Union européenne relève de la catégorie de la *Confédération d'États*, et confirme que les États membres demeurent souverains.

17 Ou « paradoxe du tas » (du grec *soros* = tas) : combien de grains faut-il pour former un tas ? L'auteur de ce paradoxe serait Eubulide de Milet (IVe siècle av. J.-C.). Le paradoxe a été « revisité » par Hegel dans *L'Encyclopédie des sciences philosophiques*, 1817, aux § 107-111.

18 Voir par exemple, Jean-Denis Mouton : « Vers la reconnaissance des droits fondamentaux des États dans le système communautaire », dans *Les dynamiques du droit européen en début de siècle : Études en l'honneur de Jean-Claude Gautron*, Paris, Pedone, 2004, p. 463.

importants, ce qui autorise parfois à parler du droit de l'État membre à invoquer son *identité constitutionnelle nationale.* La question demeure de savoir comment les identifier parmi toutes les dispositions de la constitution nationale au sens formel du terme. Il me semble pouvoir suggérer que présentent un caractère identitaire national les dispositions que la constitution de l'État membre reconnaît comme non susceptibles de révision. Il y a, dans la plupart des constitutions des États membres – tout au moins de ceux qui possèdent une constitution écrite et rigide – des dispositions que la constitution elle-même rend non révisables. Le souci d'assurer une permanence de dispositions jugées essentielles autant que fondamentales par le pouvoir constituant originaire révèle qu'elles appartiennent bien au *noyau dur* de la constitution, et qu'avec leurs semblables, elles configurent bien l'identité nationale de l'État.

Mais d'autres phénomènes interrogent aussi la souveraineté en Europe : les perspectives de démembrement à l'œuvre dans certains États de l'Union européenne. Sans remonter à la partition de l'ex-Yougoslavie ou à celle de la Tchécoslovaquie, dont le contexte particulier était sans doute lié à la chute du mur de Berlin et à la dissolution de « l'empire » soviétique, comment ne pas être attentif à des signes plus récents d'amorce d'une fragmentation d'États souverains ?

Trois cas pourraient être en particulier évoqués : l'*Écosse*[19] et le prochain référendum qui doit décider de son indépendance vis-à-vis du *Royaume-Uni*, la *Catalogne* et sa revendication ancienne d'indépendance à l'égard de l'*Espagne*, enfin, la cohabitation tendue entre *Flandre* et *Wallonie* qui pourrait conduire à un éclatement de la *Belgique.*[20]

Bien entendu, chacune de ces hypothèses est bien différente des autres, mais il n'empêche que ces différents cas, si on les relie au droit de l'Union européenne, présentent des similitudes notables. Plus exactement, ces hypothèses conduiront le droit de l'Union à résoudre des questions nouvelles et sans doute inédites, que l'on se contentera d'indiquer sommairement et davantage sur un mode interrogatif.[21]

---

19 Cf. *Discussion Paper de Arno Engel et Roderick Parkes : Accomodating an independant Scotland : how a British-style constitution for the EU could secure Scotland's future, Brussels, European Policy Center, 24 October 2012.*

20 Ces hypothèses ne sont pas les seules : outre la revendication d'une *Padanie* indépendante en Italie, et celle d'un *Pays basque* indépendant, à cheval sur la France et l'Espagne, et l'indépendance du *Kosovo*, d'autres régions d'Europe pourraient être le siège de ces mouvements de fragmentation.

21 Le cas du Groenland est souvent cité à titre de précédent. Territoire danois devenu autonome en 1979, autonomie confirmée en 2008 et 2009, il possède le statut de PTOM – Pays et territoire d'outre-mer –. À noter que les transferts publics du Danemark vers le Groenland représenteraient 40 % du budget groenlandais, ce qui suffit

– Le droit de retrait d'un État membre de l'Union est désormais reconnu depuis le traité de Lisbonne. Ses modalités figurent à l'Article 14 TUE. La question est de savoir si ce droit est invocable et applicable à la situation présentée par l'accès à l'indépendance d'une partie du territoire d'un État membre. À première vue, on est tenté de dire que les deux situations n'ont rien de comparable, et que par conséquent elles n'ont pas à être assimilées. Le droit de l'Union peut-il trouver à s'appliquer au cas où une région se sépare d'un État ? L'organisation constitutionnelle d'un État membre – y compris les modalités internes relatives à l'autonomie ou à l'indépendance de certaines parties de son territoire – ne relève-t-elle pas de l'identité nationale, telle que la définit l'Article 4 § 2 TUE ? Les conditions auxquelles les droits nationaux pourraient, si tel était leur choix, subordonner l'accès à l'indépendance – et donc à la souveraineté – d'une partie de leur territoire et de leur population, relèvent de leur compétence nationale.

– Supposons maintenant qu'après avoir respecté la procédure établie par le droit national apparaisse un nouvel État. Quelle sera sa situation vis-à-vis de l'Union européenne ? Ce nouvel État devient-il un État tiers par rapport à l'Union européenne ? L'État nouveau, si telle est sa volonté, devrait-il se porter candidat à l'adhésion à l'Union européenne et commencer à négocier les termes de son adhésion ? Quel effet produirait l'insertion, dans sa déclaration d'indépendance, d'une manifestation de volonté de sa part, indiquant qu'il est lié par l'ensemble des obligations découlant du droit de l'Union telles qu'assumées par l'État prédécesseur ? Jusqu'à quel point les règles concernant la succession d'États pourraient-elles jouer ici ? Et l'État membre antérieur pourrait-il s'opposer à l'ouverture de nouvelles négociations avec le nouvel État issu d'un démembrement de son territoire ? Qui plus est, l'État dont ce nouvel État s'est séparé pourrait-il s'opposer à son adhésion, l'adhésion reposant sur le consentement unanime des États membres de l'Union ?

– Au-delà de ces questions pratiques qu'il faudra bien résoudre au fur et à mesure du développement des situations concrètes, demeurent deux interrogations. N'y a-t-il pas un risque, si ces mouvements séparatistes gagnaient du terrain – car le risque d'une contagion sécessionniste existe bien – à aboutir à une « balkanisation » de l'Union européenne, nouveau facteur d'affaiblissement de celle-ci ? Que deviendrait le *principe d'intangibilité des frontières issues de la Deuxième Guerre mondiale*, consacré par les accords d'Helsinki (1977) ? À l'inverse, une application renouvelée du principe des nationalités ne conduirait-elle

---

avec les autres données, notamment constitutionnelles, à faire de cet exemple davantage un cas particulier qu'un précédent. (Source : http://ec.europa.eu/europeaid/where/octs_and_greenland/countries/greenland_fr.htm).

pas à cette *Europe des régions*, chère à Denis de Rougemont,[22] conséquence logique de ce mouvement de tenaille qui, vidant l'État-nation par le haut (Europe) et par le bas (autonomie régionale), aboutirait à une nouvelle cartographie de l'Europe politique ?

Si la notion de *souveraineté* perdure au XXIe siècle, et peut encore conserver quelque utilité alors qu'elle est issue d'un autre âge, c'est parce qu'elle s'est transformée. S'il s'agit aujourd'hui d'un titre de légitimité à exercer le pouvoir, et si l'Union est bien un « pouvoir public », alors il est temps de définir le fondement de sa légitimité en termes de souveraineté constituante.

Certes, le débat amorcé en 2004 et 2005 a échoué, peut-être parce qu'il était prématuré, et les perspectives constituantes et constitutionnelles semblent s'être évanouies : toute la symbolique constitutionnelle (devise, drapeau, hymne) a disparu du traité de Lisbonne, en dépit des regrets exprimés par un grand nombre d'États[23] dans la déclaration n° 52 annexée à ce même traité… Pour autant, peut-on se contenter de rester dans la seule logique d'une intégration fonctionnelle, replâtrée, de révision en révision, par des réformes institutionnelles, non négligeables certes en termes de légitimité et d'efficacité pour les initiés, mais qui ne suffisent pas à ancrer de manière durable la légitimité du projet européen dans les opinions publiques nationales ? Le peu de visibilité de ce projet, l'absence de pédagogie qui l'entoure sont autant de facteurs de désamour envers l'Union européenne, désamour que ne parvient pas à combler l'attribution du prix Nobel qui lui a été faite…

Les cultures politiques nationales forment encore le prisme obligé à travers lequel les évènements qui affectent l'Union européenne sont perçus et pensés dans chaque État. Une culture politique européenne fait encore largement défaut, de même qu'une information de masse qui soit honnête et impartiale, sans compter la méconnaissance réciproque des peuples européens les uns par rapport aux autres. Faute d'*espace public européen*, il semble alors périlleux d'éveiller les nationalismes et les populismes en proposant un projet européen en termes de souveraineté. Mais en attendant, le refus de poser la question de la souveraineté constituante et constituée abandonne cette souveraineté à des acteurs qui ne sont ni légitimes ni responsables, mais puissants : banques, agences de notations, marchés financiers, qui peuvent décider du sort des peuples

---

22 Encore que Denis de Rougemont privilégiait une conception fonctionnelle des régions davantage qu'une conception strictement territoriale.

23 Autriche, Belgique, Bulgarie, Allemagne, Grèce, Espagne, Italie, Chypre, Lituanie, Luxembourg, Hongrie, Malte, Portugal, Roumanie, Slovénie, Slovaquie. Intéressant aussi de voir quels sont les États membres qui n'ont pas signé cette déclaration…

d'Europe sans que ceux-ci aient véritablement voix au chapitre ! Que vive la souveraineté démocratique européenne !

The Role of the Presidency of the Council of the EU after Lisbon

A Legal Appraisal

Jenő CZUCZAI[1]

Legal Adviser in the Legal Service of the Council of the EU

1. Introduction

It was in October 1998 that I first met with Professor Demaret at our traditional annual Law Faculty meeting in Bruges, having received an invitation to teach at the College of Europe in 1997. I was still very young (only 31 years old), but Prof. Demaret welcomed me in the College with sincere pleasure and said to me: "*For me what counts is not the age, but the talent and the quality of the knowledge*." My predecessor was Professor Martonyi in the College, who as Foreign Minister of Hungary invited me in late 2010 to help him as Legal Adviser (seconded Council official) in conducting the first ever Hungarian Presidency of the EU Council during the first half of 2011. This six months' period of the Presidency in Budapest gave me a unique opportunity to see the concrete and real changes in the role and the main functions of the EU Presidency after Lisbon. This contribution, therefore, tries to give a short summary of all my post-Lisbon experiences concerning the new role of the EU Council Presidency in office, of course, only from a legal point of view, but at the same time thus paying my tribute to Rector Demaret.

The first part of this contribution deals with a brief historical introduction on the legal and procedural context of the EU rotating Presiden-

1 This contribution is to a large extent based on my CLEER Guest Lecture on "*The experiences of the Hungarian Presidency of the EU Council-a legal assessment*", delivered on 27 October 2011 in The Hague at the Asser Institute, but it has been further developed and made more general in terms of its content. All views and opinions, expressed in this contribution is purely those of the Author, and do not constitute an official position neither of the Council of the EU nor of its Legal Service.

cy until Lisbon; the second addresses the role and the main functions of the Presidency after the entry into force of the Lisbon Treaty with special emphasis on the changes and the novelties; the third part gives a general overview concerning each of the main functions like e.g. (i) the Presidency as negotiator under the ordinary legislative procedure; (ii) the remaining role for the Presidency under CFSP after Lisbon (including its role still left in relation to the external representation of the EU after Lisbon); (iii) the Presidency as chairing the General Affairs Council meetings, which is the new Council formation responsible *inter alia* for the preparation of all the meetings of the European Council etc.; (iv) the Presidency's main tasks in the broader context of the Council – Parliament relationship (so-called "inter-institutional" issues); finally I will try to draw some concluding remarks, based on my experiences since 1st December 2009.

My starting hypothesis is that I don't agree with those, who are of the view, that after Lisbon the role of the rotating Presidencies has weakened. On the contrary, in my opinion, it has been even strengthened, but it is true that in terms of its nature as well as in its context, its role has clearly changed, its focuses have been switched rather to its role as negotiator on behalf of the Council with the EP as well as to the political representation function of the Council *vis-à-vis* other institutions, especially with regard to the European Parliament and the European Council.

2. A Brief Historical Introduction on the Legal and Procedural Context of the EU Rotating Presidency until Lisbon

The role of every Presidency in office in the successful working of the Council of the EU is crucial, although, beyond any doubt, it is changing over the time, and, of course, in the context of the changes in the founding Treaties. The classical role of every Council Presidency, however, is even today is that the Presidency should be an "honest broker" and should be neutral as well as a good facilitator, especially concerning those dossiers, which are of primary significance for the EU (and to certain extent for the Presidency's own priorities as well). This changing character of the Presidency role on the other hand has become more and more significant after the entry into force of the Lisbon Treaty, since the new Treaties substantially changed the Presidency functions. In order to understand these changes, we have to see first of all in a nutshell what was the related legal framework under the Nice Treaty:

A. Based on ex Article 18 TEU and ex Articles 302-304 TEC (external representation):

– The Presidency represented the Union in matters coming within the CFSP;

– The Presidency was responsible for the implementation of decisions, taken under ex Title V TEU, in that capacity it expressed the position of the EU in international organizations and international conferences. The Presidency could be assisted in these tasks if need be by the next Member State to hold the Presidency;

– Though it was the Commission, which ensured maintenance of all appropriate relations with the organs of the UN and its specialised agencies, with all the international organizations (e.g. Council of Europe, OECD, etc.), since the Commission, representing the Community, had typically an observer status in these bodies, nonetheless if an EU statement was related also to the CFSP issues, then it was the Presidency, which on behalf of the EU and its Member States, in practice read out the concerned part of the statement.

B. Based on ex Article 21 TEU (relationship with the EP):

– The Presidency had to consult the EP on the main aspects and basic choices of the CFSP. It ensured that the views of the EP were duly taken into account and that the EP was regularly informed about the development of the EU CFSP.

C. Based on ex Article 24 TEU (international Treaty-making process)

– The Presidency was practically the negotiator of the so-called CFSP – related agreements, and on its recommendations the Council concluded those agreements.[2]

D. Based on ex Article 251 TEC (co-decision procedure)[3]

– The Presidency represented the Council in the legislative deliberations with the EP. It is to be noted, however, that co-decision was not the general rule before Lisbon and ex Article 251(1) TEC made it absolutely clear that only "*Where reference is made in this Treaty to this*

2 It should be noted that ex Article 38 TEU extended the powers of the rotating Presidency in this respect to the former JHA areas as well. On the other hand, pursuant to ex Article 300(1) TEC, it was the Commission, who represented the Community in international negotiations if matters fell under the Community competences ("The Council shall authorize the Commission to open negotiations…The Commission shall conduct these negotiations…within the framework of such directives as the Council may issue to it.").

3 *Mutatis mutandis*, the same applied to the cooperation procedure (ex Article 252 TEC).

Article for the adoption of an act, the following procedure shall apply..." (emphasis added).[4]

E. Based on ex Articles 203 and 207(3) TEC (the office of President of the Council)

– The Office of President was held in turn by each Member State in the Council for a period of 6 months in the order, decided by the Council unanimously;

– The Presidency represented the Council externally and in inter-institutional matters in accordance with the Rules of Procedure of the Council.

3. The Role and the Main Functions of the Presidency after the Entry into Force of the Lisbon Treaty with Special Emphasis on the Changes and the Novelties

Within the page-limit of this contribution, the currently in force legal framework can be summarised as follows:

1. The Council exercises jointly with the EP legislative and budgetary functions and it carries out policy-making and coordinating functions (Article 16(1) TEU);

2. The Council meets in different configurations, which are, in principle, presided by the six-monthly Presidency, held by the Member States' representatives on the basis of rotation (Article 16(9) TEU, Article 236 TFEU);[5]

---

4 As regards the concrete co-decision policy fields and the role of the rotating Presidency before Lisbon, see in more details, Piris, J.-C., *The Constitution for Europe – A Legal Analysis*, CUP, 2006, pp. 105-107, pp. 168-169, and Annex II pp. 207-210. Similarly see Jacqué, J.-P., *Droit institutionnel de l'Union européenne*, Dalloz, 2010, 6th ed., pp. 299 *et seq.* and pp. 415 *et seq.*

5 It should be mentioned that one of the main novelty of the Lisbon Treaty is about the introduction of the so-called "Trio Presidency system". In this respect Article 1(4) of the Council Rules of Procedure provides that: "The Presidency of the Council, with the exception of the Foreign Affairs configuration, *shall be held by pre-established groups of three Member States for a period of 18 months*. The groups shall be made up on a basis of equal rotation among the Member States, taking into account their diversity and geographical balance within the Union. *Each member of the group shall in turn chair for a six-month period* all configurations of the Council, with the exception of the Foreign Affairs configuration. The other members of the group shall assist the Chair in all its responsibilities on the basis of a common programme. The members of the team may decide alternative arrangements among themselves." (emphasis added). The Trio Presidency provides better continuity among the participating Presidencies, which is extremely important, for example, concerning the negotiations with the EP on very sensitive and difficult legislative files as well as more flexibility as regards replacement facilities when there is lack of expertise or other constraints of human resources with regard to a specific policy area in the Presidency

3. The rotating Presidency is exercised in accordance with the European Council Decision No. 2009/881/EU;[6] It should be stressed that the newly established General Affairs Council is chaired by the rotating Presidency as well as all the sector-specific Council configurations (except the Foreign Affairs Council). The General Affairs Council has a special status, since it prepares all the meetings of the European Council, it provides horizontal coordination between the different Council configurations, it deals with enlargement, budget-related issues, cohesion policy and all the institutional and administrative questions.[7]

4. The High Representative of the EU for CFSP represents the EU in matters falling under the CFSP except if the diplomatic level requires that the President of the European Council represents the EU in a given international event (Article 15(6) 2nd subparagraph and 27(2) TEU);[8]

5. The Council meeting in its Foreign Affairs configuration (FAC) is presided by the High Representative of the EU for CFSP (Articles 18(3) and 27(1) TEU), who may, however, where necessary, ask to be replaced by the Member of the FAC holding the rotating Presidency (Article 2(5) of the Council Rules of Procedure).[9] It should be added, therefore, that the Trade[10] and in practice also the Development formation of the FAC is chaired even after Lisbon by the rotating Presidency in office.

6. Concerning the Council Working Groups and high level Committees (hereinafter: Council preparatory bodies), as a general rule,

---

staff etc. See further in more details: Articles 2(6)-(7), 3(1), 8(3), 20(2), and Article 26 1st subparagraph of the Council Rules of Procedure.

6 See European Council Decision No. 2009/881/EU of 1 December 2009 on the exercise of the Presidency of the Council, OJ L 315, 2 December 2009, p. 50, adopted in accordance with Declaration (No. 9), annexed to the Final Act of the Lisbon Treaty.

7 See in more details Council Rules of Procedure Article 2. See also Decision of the Council (General Affairs) No. 2009/878/EU of 1 December 2009 establishing *the list of Council configurations* in addition to those referred to in the second and third subparagraphs of Article 16(6) TEU, as amended by the European Council Decision 2010/594/EU of 16 September 2010, OJ L 263, 6 October 2010, p. 12.

8 See in this respect Howorth, J., "The 'New faces' of Lisbon: Assessing the Performance of Catherine Ashton and Herman van Rompuy on the Global Stage", *European Foreign Affairs Review*, No. 16, 2011, pp. 303-323.

9 See Council Decision No. 2009/937/EU of 1 December 2009 adopting the Council's Rules of Procedure, OJ L 325, 11 November 2009, p. 35. See also Article 26 2nd subparagraph in terms of the replacement of the HR for CFSP when appearing before the EP. It is to be noted, however, that the PSC shall be chaired by a representative of the HR for CFSP (Article 19(4) 2nd subparagraph).

10 See footnote (1) to Article 2(5) of the Council Rules of Procedure.

they are chaired by the Presidency in office[11] with some exceptions (e.g. as a rule preparatory bodies of the FAC, preparatory bodies with a fixed chair either elected or given by the GSC (e.g. Military Committee, EFC, Security Committee, etc.).[12]

The most important changes, therefore, – as compared to the Nice Treaty situation – can be summarised as follows:

A. Areas, in which the Presidency lost powers after Lisbon

1. The Presidency is not a negotiator anymore for international agreements, to be concluded by the EU, though one in principle cannot exclude its possible involvement somehow in the working of a so-called "EU negotiating Team", if legally justified. (Article 218(3) TFEU);

2. The Presidency cannot represent the EU in international fora in CFSP/CDSP-related fields as a general rule, but there are exemptions (for example, when the EU has not even an observer status in an international organization or when there is no EU diplomatic representation in a third country at all etc.);[13]

3. The Presidency cannot represent the EU in matters falling under the competence of the European Council, since the European Council has now its own permanent President, therefore, it is not anymore the rotating Presidency in office, which holds the chairmanship of the European Council;[14]

4. The role of the Presidency's diplomatic representations in third countries and at international organizations has also been drastically reduced because of the establishment of the EEAS and of the fact that by today the Union Delegations took over the representation tasks of the EU in this context (Article 221 TFEU).

---

11 See in particular Article 19(4)-(6) of the Council Rules of Procedure.

12 See in more details Council Decision No. 2009/908/EU of 1 December 2009 laying down measures for the implementation of the European Council Decision on the exercise of the Presidency of the Council, and on the chairmanship of preparatory bodies of the Council, OJ L 322, 9 December 2009, p. 28.

13 See "EU diplomatic representation in third countries-first half of 2012", Council doc. 18975/1/11, REV 1, dated 11 January 2012. Updates may be found at http://eeas.europa.eu/delegations/web_en.htm.

14 See European Council Decision No. 2009/882/EU adopting its Rules of Procedure, OJ L 315, 2 December 2009, p. 51, in particular Articles 2(1), Article 5, and Article 14. However, Article 2(4) of this Rules of Procedures should be also recalled, pursuant to which under certain circumstances "the member of the European Council representing the Member State holding the six-monthly Presidency of the Council" can replace the President of the European Council.

B. Areas, Where the Presidency Kept or even increased its Powers after Lisbon

1. The enhanced and increased role of the Presidency as the *negotiator*, on behalf of the Council, with the European Parliament under the so-called ordinary legislative procedure. At the outset, it should be stressed that after Lisbon the ordinary legislative procedure (the former co-decision procedure) became the main rule and, therefore, not just applied when specifically so defined in the Treaties! (Article 289(1)-(3) TFEU). Moreover, it was extended to areas where it either never existed before or just was used in a very limited or different context[15] like, for instance, to the Common Agriculture and Fishery Policy (Article 43(2) TFEU), to the Common Commercial Policy (Article 207(2) TFEU), or to the Economic, social and territorial cohesion policy (Articles 174-178 TFEU), not speaking about the former Justice and Home Affairs areas (Part III/Title V. TFEU).[16] This increased number of policy areas and the evolving complexity of the related legislative files falling now also under the co-decision procedure has substantially increased the responsibilities and the concrete tasks of the rotating Presidency in office after Lisbon.[17]

2. The *remaining important role for the Presidency in office under EU CFSP*, in particular in replacing the EU High Representative for Foreign Affairs and Security Policy, at her request, in contacts with third partners (e.g. at Association Council meetings or Partnership and Cooperation Council meetings or for example at the ACP Ministerial Summit etc.) in her capacity as President of the Foreign Affairs Council and because of the fact that the High Representative has no deputies according to the Lisbon Treaty.[18] It continues to be also an important legal and practical question for every Presidency of the Council in office to assess on a case by case basis whether or not there has still remained any role for the rotating Presidency in terms of the *EU exter-*

---

15 For example, before Lisbon the assent of the EP was required to legislate on the general provisions in the field of Structural Funds.

16 See in more details the changes in the Lisbon Treaty for the co-decision procedure, Piris, J.-C., *The Lisbon Treaty-A Legal and Political Analysis*, CUP, 2010, pp. 205-212, pp. 255-261, and Appendix 4 on pp. 365-368.

17 See, for example, the relevant statistic from the former Hungarian Presidency period: "The most important results of the Hungarian Presidency", Budapest, 2011, Ministry of Foreign Affairs, www.mfa.gov.hu/.../hu/Hirek/20110701_EU_elnokseg_eredmenyei.htm, in particular from pp. 31 *et seq*.

18 For illustrative purposes, under the former Hungarian Presidency, for example, the High Representative was replaced by the Hungarian Foreign Minister or his Parliamentary State Secretary more than 20 times at Ministerial level meetings, held with third countries or in international fora.

nal representation after Lisbon (notably what concerns the areas falling under either *shared competences* or exclusive Member States' competences)?[19]

3. The role of the Presidency in office *vis-à-vis* the other EU institutions, especially the contacts and the cooperation between the *President of the General Affairs Council and the President of the European Council* after Lisbon – which, from a legal point of view, is also a new dimension, brought about by the Lisbon Treaty and which, for sure, engages very much each Presidency in office;

4. Finally we should mention the increased workload for the Presidencies concerning the inter-institutional relationship with the European Parliament,[20] where the number of unresolved problems after the entry into force of the Lisbon Treaty seems still to be significant. These issues shall also be somehow managed and that is always one of the main tasks for every rotating Presidency in office (in addition to the normal Presidency's representation tasks of the Council in the different instances of the EP).

4. A Broad Practical Overview concerning each of the Main Functions of the Post-Lisbon Council Presidency's Role

A. The Presidency as Negotiator under the Ordinary Legislative Procedure

Based on practice so far, what can be stated is that one of the most time-consuming job for the Presidency in office is to reach a general approach or at least a partial general approach concerning the pending legislative files in the Council as well as to deblock, for example, a legislative file, frozen already for a long time, by finding good compromise solutions (for example on a horizontal issue, which was in 2011 the so-called correlation table question etc.) or by working out different options, finally being acceptable for the Council as possible way out of difficult pending dossiers.[21]

---

19 See "EU Statements in multilateral organisations-General Arrangements" in Council doc. 15855/11, dated 21 October 2011.

20 See Article 26 of the Council Rules of Procedure.

21 A good example, though not in connection with the ordinary legislative procedure, but for this Presidency creativity from the former Hungarian Presidency period is the last stage of the negotiation process of the Croatian Accession Treaty (which was closed down in political terms on 30 June 2011) and especially the creative legal drafting solutions on the so-called "pre-accession safeguard clause" as well as on the enhanced pre-accession monitoring tools and pre-accession information exchange and consultation procedures, see the Documents concerning the accession of the Re-

For the negotiator role of the Presidency, the statistics of the former Hungarian Presidency[22] might be of illustrative nature:

– Hungary handled all in all, during its Presidency, cc. 200 dossiers in the Council, out of which 16 general approaches (or political agreement) were reached,[23] cc. 40 ordinary legislative files were successfully closed (including also important ones like, for example, the new Comitology Regulation,[24] the so-called Citizens's initiative Regulation,[25] or the Regulation on the Passengers' rights in bus transportation,[26] etc.). The former Hungarian Presidency also processed 6 special legislative files and close to 40 Treaty-making acts as well as more than 60 Council conclusions were adopted during those 6 months.[27]

---

public of Croatia to the EU, OJ L 112, 24 April 2012, in particular Article 3(5) of the Accession Treaty (p. 14), Article 36 of the Act of Accession (p. 31) and Annexes VII-IX (pp. 88-91), and the Exchange of Letters in the Final Act between the EU and the Republic of Croatia on an information and consultation procedure for the adoption of certain decisions and other measures to be taken during the period preceding the accession (pp. 108-110).

22 For a comparison and in order to see better the changing character in the working of the rotating Presidency after Lisbon, see for example the Czech Presidency' main tasks in the first half of 2009, Chaltiel, F., "D'une présidence à une autre…La présidence tchèque et ses enjeux à mi-parcours", *Revue du Marché commun et de l'Union européenne*, No. 528, mai 2009, pp. 284-297. Similarly, see still from the last two years' perspective Heywood, P.M., "Spain's EU Presidency: Ambitions beyond capacity?", *JCMS*, 2011, Vol. 49, Blackwell, pp. 77-89 as well as Drieskens, E., "Ceci n'est pas une présidence: The 2010 Belgian Presidency of the EU", *JCMS*, 2011, Vol. 49, Blackwell, pp. 91-102.

23 It should be noted that in the majority of the cases the most difficult task for the Presidency is not about conducting negotiations with the EP and reaching a final compromise, but rather to reach general (or partial general) approaches (or finally a political agreement) on the given legislative file among the Member States within the Council! The best example for this from the former Hungarian Presidency period is the so-called "six-pack" legislative package on economic governance, in which case reaching the general approaches in the Council already by mid March 2011 / after cc. half a year of the submission of the Commission proposals/ substantially contributed to the relatively quick adoption of the concerned six legislative acts, see the special edition of the OJ, OJ L 306, 23 November 2011.

24 See Regulation (EU) No. 182/2011 of the European Parliament and of the Council of 16 February 2011 laying down the rules and general principles concerning mechanisms for control by Member States of the Commission's exercise of implementing powers, OJ L 55, 28 February 2011, p. 13.

25 See Regulation (EU) No. 211/2011 of the European Parliament and of the Council of 16 February 2011 on the citizens' initiative, OJ L 65, 11 March 2011, p. 1.

26 See Regulation (EU) No. 181/2011 of the European Parliament and of the Council of 16 February 2011 concerning the rights of passengers in bus and coach transport and amending Regulation (EC) No. 2006/2004, OJ L 55, 28 February 2011, p. 1.

27 See in more details the results of the former Hungarian Presidency, *supra*, note 17, pp. 40 *et seq.*

– what concerns the ordinary legislative procedures (Article 294 TFEU), Hungary was engaged in 34 dossiers under the first-reading process (including, for example, such important ones as the Directive on the consumers' rights[28] or the Directive dealing with preventing and combating trafficking in human beings,[29] etc.). Under the second reading stage 7 dossiers were treated by the former HU Presidency (e.g. the so-called Euro-vignette Directive,[30] etc.). Finally, there was one conciliation dossier, which unfortunately was not adopted despite all efforts of the former Hungarian Presidency concerning the draft novel food Regulation.

The above statistics, in my view, clearly show the significant switch what concerns the role of the Presidency from the area of international representation of the EU or negotiating international agreements etc., towards the practical facilitation of the more and more evolving legislative function of the Council after Lisbon.

B. The Remaining Role for the Presidency under CFSP after Lisbon (including its Role still left in Relation to the External Representation of the EU after Lisbon)?

In practical terms, an unexpectedly huge workload has still been left for the Presidency concerning the replacement needs of the High Representative of the EU for CFSP due to the fact that she has no deputies according to the Lisbon Treaty. This means replacing her, where necessary, in chairing the FAC meetings, or at her request replacing her, in her capacity as President of FAC,[31] at ministerial level international summits or conferences, or in the context of ministerial level structured dialogues with third countries. Normally, this means no problem for the Presidency in office, because the COREPER II meetings, where the

---

28 See Directive 2011/83/EU of the European Parliament and of the Council of 25 October 2011, OJ L 304, 22 November 2011, p. 64.

29 See Directive 2011/36/EU of the European Parliament and of the Council of 5 April 2011, OJ L 101, 15 April 2011, p. 1.

30 See Directive 2011/76/EU of the European Parliament and of the Council of 27 September 2011 amending Directive 1999/62/EC on the charging of heavy goods vehicles for the use of certain infrastructures, OJ L 269, 14 October 2011, p. 1.

31 It is to be recalled that pursuant to Article 17(1) TEU: "The Commission shall ensure the Union's external representation *with the exception of CFSP* and other cases, provided for in the Treaties." (emphasis added). Argumentum a contrario, in CFSP fields the Commission cannot undertake the external representation of the EU. See in more details Van Vooren, B. and Wessel, R.A., "External representation and the EAAS: selected legal challenges" in S. Blockmans and R.A. Wessel (eds.), "Principles and practices of EU external representation", *CLEER Working Papers*, 2012, No. 5, pp. 59-82.

CFSP/CDSP dossiers are also examined and processed, are chaired by the rotating Presidency.

But, there are other practical needs as well, when, even after Lisbon, the role of the rotating Presidency has remained indispensable in external representation of the EU. For example, it is still the Presidency, which represents the EU in third countries, where there are no Union Delegations (e.g. in Iran, or until end 2011 this was the case also in Libya,[32] and in some other countries).[33] Similarly, this might be the case within certain international organizations (e.g. UN, WHO, UNESCO, etc.) in matters falling either under exclusive Member States' competence or shared competences and if so decided in the given sensitive policy areas.[34]

C. *The Presidency as Chairing the General Affairs Council (GAC) Meetings, which is a New Council Configuration after Lisbon*

One of the novelties, introduced by the Lisbon Treaty, is that it divided the former GAERC and established two Council configurations instead, namely the FAC and the GAC (Article 16(6) TEU).

The GAC is chaired by the rotating Presidency. The huge workload relating to the GAC can be seen from its main functions:

– the GAC shall prepare and ensure the follow up to meetings of the European Council in liaison with the President of the European Council and of the Commission.[35]

---

32 It is to be noted that, like every Presidency, Hungary had to handle also in the first half of 2011 *a lot of so-called unexpected dossiers*, e.g. see what happened in North Africa in 2011, in particular in Libya, where there was no Union delegation, which could represent the EU during the civil war etc., therefore, it was the Hungarian Embassy in Tripoli, which took over this function partly in its capacity as the diplomatic representation of the rotating Presidency of the Council on the ground, partly at the request of the High Representative of the EU for CFSP.

33 See *supra*, note 13.

34 See "General arrangements on EU Statements in multilateral organizations", adopted by COREPER in October 2011, Council doc. 15855/11 as well as the EEAS Guidelines for EU cooperation in third countries, dated 7 November 2011, ref.: Ares(2011)1195341. Similarly, see still as a detailed analysis from the practice in this context, Serrano de Haro, P.A., "Participation of the EU in the work of the UN: General Assembly Resolution 65/276", *CLEER Working Paper*, 2012, No. 4.

35 See Article 16(6) TEU 2nd sub-paragraph and Article 2(2) and Article 3 of the European Council Rules of Procedure. A good example for the mutual respect of each other's sphere of responsibilities and thus for the smooth cooperation between the rotating Presidency in office and the President of the European Council from the former Hungarian Presidency period can be seen in the quick adoption of the European Council Decision of 25 March 2011 amending Article 136 of the Treaty on the

– the GAC provides the coordination among the activities of all the other sector-specific Council configurations. The GAC deals with all the institutional issues (e.g. the reform package of the CJEU), or the cohesion policy issues, the budget-related questions (including the MFF discussions), or with the adoption of EU strategies (e.g. the Danube Macro-regional Strategy or the Roma EU Framework Strategy, etc.).[36]

– finally, the President of the GAC reports on the Council activities to the European Council.[37]

D. *The Presidency's Main Tasks in the Broader Context of the Council-Parliament Relationship (so-called "Inter-Institutional" Issues)*

It is generally believed that the European Parliament is the biggest winner of the Lisbon Treaty, since its powers have increased substantially after 1st December 2009. On the other hand, in inter-institutional context, these increased powers of the EP have caused also a lot of tensions, especially between the Council and the EP. In this contribution, due to the length-limitation, I can only present a short skeleton of the different aspects of the issues prevailing between the Council and the EP, the solution of which, however, is always the main job of the rotating Presidency after Lisbon alongside with its classical tasks of representing the Council in matters relating to it (other than those falling under the competence of the FAC) at the plenary sessions of the EP as well as before the different EP Committees during the Presidency period.

The main problem areas could be summarised briefly as follows:

– The so-called "Comitology" issue, namely how to deal with delegated acts after Lisbon (Article 290 TFEU). This problem was solved under the HU Presidency on 3 March 2011 by adopting the so-called "Common Understanding on delegated acts".[38]

– The so-called "Correlation Tables" issue, which related to the obligation of the Member States to prepare for the Commission a detailed report on how the EU Directives were practically transposed into their respective national legal orders (on an Article by Article basis). The Commission and the EP insisted on keeping this obligation in the post-

---

Functioning of the EU with regard to a stability mechanism for Member States whose currency is the euro, OJ L 91, 6 April 2011, p. 1.

36 It should be noted that both very important EU Strategies were adopted by the GAC under the former Hungarian Presidency during the first half of 2011.

37 See Article 4(1) 2nd subparagraph of the European Council Rules of Procedure.

38 See Council doc 8753/1/11 REV 1 (including legal drafting templates).

Lisbon legislative acts too, while the Member States wanted to soften it. Finally, a compromise was found under the Polish Presidency in the second half of 2011 by virtue of adopting two inter-institutional political declarations and a standard recital, but not having anymore a direct legislative obligation on the Member States to do "correlation tables".

– Another main set of issues relates to the implementation of new Article 218 TFEU (the EU international Treaty-making procedural code) in so far what concerns the prerogatives of the EP therein. In this respect, one major problem lies in the interpretation difficulties of the new Article 218(10) TFEU,[39] which provides that the EP shall be immediately and fully informed at all stages of the EU Treaty-making procedure. But, this very broad obligation on the Council raises a number of questions, for example: what is to be meant by "immediately", "fully" or "at all stages" in Article 218(10) TFEU?,[40] then the issue of the access by the MEPs to the classified information of the Council, since, for example, the negotiating directives, issued by the Council to the Commission in relation to the negotiation process of an international agreement, are in practice always classified; or the open issue about whether the verb of "shall be informed" can extend to cover also any sort of participation of the MEPs in the concrete negotiation process? etc. It is good to report that the last two issues have been in the meantime solved with the impressive contributions of the last four Presidencies in office and by concluding an Inter-institutional Agreement with the EP on the access by the MEPs to the Council classified information.[41]

– A joint success of the former Hungarian and Polish Presidencies was about the elaboration of the concrete modalities of how the EP could be informally involved in the MFF process via informal debrief-

39 It is to be noted that under the new Article 218(10) TFEU the EP's powers have been substantially increased since the corresponding pre-Lisbon provision had only provided that: "The EP shall be immediately and fully informed of any decision under this paragraph concerning the provisional application or the suspension of agreements, or the establishment of the Community position in a body set up by an agreement." (ex Article 300(2) 3rd subparagraph), whereas today the Council obligation is in place "at all stages" whatever this expression means. Moreover, the new Article 218(10) now applies to all the international agreements, aimed at being concluded by the EU, whereas in the pre-Lisbon period, as already mentioned above, the EP had no role at all with regard to certain type of agreements (e.g. based on ex Article 24 TEU or on ex Article 38 TEU, or on ex Article 133 TEC, etc.).

40 In this respect, there is already a pending case before the Court, see Case C-658/11 *European Parliament v Council*, which, when decided upon, hopefully will give us a clearer guidance on Article 218(10) TFEU.

41 See Council doc. 8436/1/12.

ings, to be given by the President of the GAC to the EP before and after the GAC meetings dealing with this topic.

– There are other still pending dossiers, for the future Presidencies, with which they have to deal with, for example, the draft Regulation on the EP's right to inquiry, the Council annual discharge issue, or the signing of the act establishing the EU annual budget (namely whether it is legally sufficient if this act is signed only by the President of the EP or the President of the Council should also sign it?) etc., but entering into the details of all these prevailing issues would go already beyond the scope of this contribution.

5. Conclusions

To sum it up, on the one hand one may conclude that the main and classical role of the Presidency in office has remained unchanged even after Lisbon: namely that the Presidency should be *a honest broker, and should be neutral*, which means that, during the 6 months period, every Presidency is primarily focusing on the fulfilment of the priorities of their respective Presidency programmes (but, after Lisbon, already by paying close attention to the so-called 18 months Trio Presidencies' programmes as well) and not pursuing purely national interests. On the other hand, in my view, after Lisbon, the Presidency's role has been even strengthened, but it is true that in terms of its nature as well as in its content, its role has clearly changed, its main focuses have been switched undoubtedly to its key function as the negotiator on behalf of the Council with the EP under the ordinary legislative procedures as well as to its political representation function of the Council *vis-à-vis* other institutions, especially as concerns the European Parliament and the European Council.

Faut-il souhaiter l'« européanisation » des élections nationales ?

L'exemple des élections présidentielles françaises

Renaud DEHOUSSE

Centre d'études européennes, Sciences Po, Paris

Dans son analyse de l'impact de la construction européenne sur les systèmes partisans nationaux, Peter Mair dresse le constat d'un décalage entre les responsabilités effectives de l'Europe et de ses États membres, d'une part, et les thèmes qui sont au cœur de la compétition électorale à ces deux niveaux, d'autre part. Les grandes décisions sur l'orientation et l'ampleur du processus d'intégration continuent à tenir une place centrale dans les élections européennes, alors que le Parlement européen, en dépit de ses revendications récurrentes, n'a qu'une faible influence sur ces questions. À l'inverse, les élections nationales continuent à être dominées par un affrontement sur des enjeux politiques « nationaux », bien que ceux-ci soient très largement déterminés par les choix arrêtés au niveau européen. En d'autres termes, chaque arène tend à se concentrer sur des questions qui devraient plutôt être abordées à un autre niveau. De cette inadéquation découle un double déficit : les enjeux de politique publique sont trop largement absents au moment des élections européennes, tandis que le débat sur l'avenir de l'Europe est généralement escamoté au niveau national, bien que c'est à cette occasion que sont choisis ceux qui prendront les décisions décisives sur ces questions. De la sorte, les choix des électeurs finissent par n'avoir qu'un impact limité sur les décisions qui sont prises à ces deux niveaux.[1]

Un des intérêts de l'élection présidentielle française de 2012 tient précisément à ce que l'on semble s'être éloigné sur plusieurs points du modèle défini par Mair. Plusieurs des thèmes majeurs de la campagne

---

1 « The Limited Impact of Europe on National Party Systems », in Klaus H. Goetz and Simon Hix (eds.), *Europeanised Politics ? European Integration and National Political Systems*, Portland, OR Frank Cass, 2000, pp. 27-51.

avaient des ramifications européennes évidentes, ce qui a conduit les principaux candidats à définir certains aspects essentiels de la politique qu'ils entendaient suivre *au niveau européen* s'ils étaient élus et à indiquer les alliances qu'ils entendaient rechercher au sein de l'Union. La campagne a du reste été largement suivie dans les autres pays membres, plusieurs chefs de gouvernement allant jusqu'à indiquer leur préférence pour un des candidats en lice. Les considérations liées à différents aspects de la construction européenne semblent également avoir pesé sur le choix de différentes catégories d'électeurs. Cette européanisation du débat et du vote a inévitablement transformé la nature de l'exercice électoral, qui est devenu un moment important de la vie politique *européenne.* S'il est encore trop tôt pour apprécier les conséquences de l'élection de François Hollande au niveau européen, il n'en est pas moins manifeste qu'elle a contribué à un changement de cap. Il reste bien sûr à voir si la transformation des règles du jeu électoral à laquelle on a assisté constitue avant tout un phénomène singulier lié au contexte de crise dans lequel il intervenait, ou si elle annonce une mutation en profondeur de la compétition partisane dans le cadre européen.

1. Qu'est-ce qu'un débat européen ?[2]

Pour bien cadrer notre propos, une précision d'ordre sémantique est nécessaire. Qu'entend-on exactement par des enjeux « européens » ? La réponse la plus immédiate à cette question inclut un ensemble de thèmes relativement abstraits : parler d'Europe signifie indiquer la place que l'on accorde à l'intégration européenne, la façon dont on considère que le système politique européen devrait être organisé, les tâches qu'il devrait assumer, les rapports qu'il devrait entretenir avec les sociétés nationales, etc. Si l'on s'en tient à cette acception relativement simple, on peut relever que l'Europe occupe généralement une place appréciable, mais jamais la première, dans la campagne des candidats à la présidentielle. Dominique Labbé et Denis Molière ont publié de nombreuses analyses lexicométriques de la campagne présidentielle,[3] mesurant notamment le poids de chaque thème (en pourcentage de mots) dans le corpus constitué par l'ensemble des communiqués et discours des principaux candidats. Le tableau 1 reprend les 5 principaux thèmes utilisés par les différents candidats. Il en ressort que dans une palette

---

[2] L'analyse qui suit est tirée de Renaud Dehousse et Angela Tacéa, « L'Europa nelle elezioni presidenziali », in Riccardo Brizzi (dir.), *La Francia di Hollande*, Bologne, Il Milino, 2013 (à paraître).

[3] Ces analyses ont été publiées sur le site du réseau TriElec, https://sites.google.com/a/iepg.fr/trielec/.

nécessairement très vaste, puisqu'il faut parler à de nombreuses catégories sociales, l'Europe figure généralement en bonne place (que ce soit pour en dire du bien ou du mal !).

Tableau 1. Les principaux thèmes de la campagne présidentielle

Candidats	Thèmes	%
François Bayrou	Économie	6,02
	Éducation	3,83
	Déficit	4,27
	Allemagne	4,33
	Europe	**3,93**
François Hollande	Économie	6,42
	Éducation	5,37
	Emploi-Chômage	4,44
	Europe	**4,27**
	Déficit	3,83
Marine Le Pen	Économie	6,47
	Europe	**6,04**
	Nation	4,27
	Immigration	3,89
	Argent	3,84
Nicolas Sarkozy	Économie	7,9
	Entreprise	6,59
	Crise	6,53
	Chômage	6,09
	Europe	**5,72**

Source : Dominique Labbé et Denis Monière, *Radioscopie 10, La dernière ligne droite, Annexes*, https://docs.google.com/viewer?a=v&pid=sites&srcid=aWVwZy5mcnx0cml lbGVjfGd4OjFmYjNhY2MxNjQ1MTM4MmY

On constate également que l'importance relative accordée à l'Europe par chaque candidat varie. Pour Marine Le Pen, qui a fait de la dénonciation de perte de la souveraineté nationale un de ses principaux chevaux de bataille, avant même le fonds de commerce classique que constituent pour le Front national l'immigration et l'insécurité, c'est un des principaux thèmes de campagne avec 6 %. En revanche, l'Europe n'arrive qu'en cinquième position dans la campagne du premier tour du président sortant, Nicolas Sarkozy, ou de son principal rival, François Hollande. On retrouve là une caractéristique des campagnes pour les élections européennes, dans lesquelles ce sont souvent les opposants à la construction européenne qui abordent le plus directement les questions relatives à ses finalités.

Mais après plus d'un demi-siècle d'intégration, la nature même du thème européen a évolué. Si l'Union européenne est bien loin de fournir la matière à 80 % de la législation nationale, comme on l'affirme trop souvent,[4] elle n'en est pas moins devenue un acteur incontournable dans de nombreux domaines. Les responsables politiques nationaux savent que la marge de manœuvre dont ils peuvent disposer peut être amoindrie, voire réduite à néant, par des décisions prises à Bruxelles. Ils ont généralement tendance à occulter ce phénomène, qui peut atténuer le prestige des fonctions auxquelles ils aspirent, contribuant ainsi largement à un déficit de lisibilité de l'action publique – nationale et européenne.[5] Dans le cas qui nous intéresse, toutefois, ce phénomène d'escamotage était rendu plus difficile par le contexte de crise dans lequel se déroulait la campagne. Alors que les réunions de la dernière chance se multipliaient pour tenter d'apporter une réponse à la crise de la dette souveraine et aux menaces qu'elles faisaient peser sur l'avenir de l'Euro, il était difficile pour François Hollande de parler de relance aux classes défavorisées sans tenir compte des contraintes que faisaient peser sur la France les nouveaux instruments de gouvernance économique mis en place par la législation communautaire et par le « pacte budgétaire » au cours des mois qui précèdent. De la même façon, Nicolas Sarkozy, qui avait choisi de mettre l'accent sur le thème des frontières pour répondre au besoin de protection qu'il sentait chez les Français, ne pouvait pas feindre d'ignorer que la liberté de circulation joue un rôle central dans le projet européen tel qu'il a été défini. Lorsqu'ils abordent ces questions de politique publique, les candidats sont immanquablement appelés à se positionner par rapport à l'action de l'Europe, que ce soit pour dire la façon dont ils répondront à ses injonctions ou les choix qu'ils entendent défendre à Bruxelles. Le « discours européen » en est ainsi transformé : il ne s'agit plus seulement de se prononcer de façon générale sur l'organisation idéale du continent, mais aussi d'indiquer la façon dont on entend gérer le rapport à l'Europe dans une série de domaines.

Examinée dans cette optique, la campagne présidentielle de 2012 prend un tour nettement plus européen. Parmi les discours de campagne de François Bayrou, par exemple, aux 4 % consacrés à l'Europe *stricto*

---

4 Sylvain Brouard, Olivier Costa, Thomas König (dir.), *The Europeanization of Domestic Legislatures. The Empirical Implications of the Delors Myth in Nine Countries*, New York, Springer, 2012.

5 Vivien Schmidt, *Democracy in Europe : The EU and National Polities*, Oxford, Oxford University Press, 2006.

sensu évoquée plus haut, peuvent ainsi être ajoutés les références à l'Allemagne (4 %), à la Grèce (3 %) ou au déficit public (5 %), portant ainsi les thématiques européennes *lato sensu* à 16 %. De même, pour les raisons qui viennent d'être indiquées, il ne paraît pas abusif de considérer que les thèmes comme la crise (7 %), la finance (4 %) et l'immigration (2 %) chez Nicolas Sarkozy, ou l'économie (7 %), le déficit (4 %) chez François Hollande, comportent une dimension européenne importante. Si l'on accepte ce genre de regroupement, on voit ainsi les thèmes liés – directement ou indirectement – à l'Europe passer au premier rang des sujets de la campagne. Certes, celle-ci en comportait bien d'autres, comme le montrent bien les études citées, mais ces données suffisent pour mettre à mal l'idée d'un débat dont les enjeux européens auraient été complètement absents.

L'Européanisation de la campagne a aussi pris la forme d'interventions plus marquées que par le passé de responsables politiques des autres pays membres de l'Union. En début de campagne, à l'occasion d'un conseil des ministres franco-allemand à Paris, la chancelière allemande a apporté publiquement son soutien au candidat Nicolas Sarkozy, alors même que celui-ci ne s'était pas encore déclaré, allant même jusqu'à critiquer les velléités de renégociation du « pacte budgétaire » de son adversaire socialiste au cours d'un entretien télévisé conjoint. La possibilité de meetings communs a été un moment évoquée, avant d'être abandonnée au lendemain du meeting de Villepinte, qui marquait une radicalisation de la campagne du président sortant, avec l'évocation d'une possibilité de « sortie des accords de Schengen » (voir ci-dessous). Le Premier ministre britannique David Cameron a également pris position dans le même sens, et l'idée d'un accord des principaux dirigeants conservateurs européens pour ne pas recevoir le candidat socialiste a été évoquée par la presse.[6] Dans les jours qui suivaient, François Hollande, souvent raillé pour son manque d'expérience et de réseaux internationaux, a tenu à s'afficher en compagnie de responsables des partis socialistes européens à l'occasion d'une réunion consacrée au volet européen de son programme. Le poids électoral de ces manifestations de solidarité est incertain, mais la volonté d'afficher de façon symbolique la dimension européenne du choix proposé aux électeurs français était, elle, claire de part et d'autre.

---

6 Veit Medick, « Merkel Forges Anti-Hollande Alliance in Europe », *Der Spiegel Online*, 5 mars 2012, http://www.spiegel.de/international/europe/meddling-in-france-merkel-forges-anti-hollande-alliance-in-europe-a-819297.html.

2. Des logiques d'opposition

S'il a beaucoup été question d'Europe au cours de la campagne, cet objet aux contours flous a souvent été abordé d'une façon qui mettait en évidence l'opposition des candidats à ce qui se fait à Bruxelles. On peut toutefois distinguer différentes logiques d'opposition.[7]

La première est radicale et frontale : ce que l'on rejette, c'est l'idée même d'une construction politique de l'Europe, avec son corollaire, des cessions de souveraineté. Durant la campagne, cette attitude a été le fait du candidat souverainiste Nicolas Dupont-Aignan, qui a choisi pour son parti un nom qui résume bien l'essentiel de son programme : Debout la République ! Mais elle a surtout été reprise, avec un réel succès, par la candidate du Front national Marine Le Pen qui s'érigeant en candidate du *peuple* français – une des expressions fétiches de son argumentaire[8] – a fait de la dénonciation de l'Europe et de la mondialisation un des thèmes majeurs de sa campagne, annonçant son intention de renoncer à l'Euro et de quitter l'Union européenne en cas de victoire.[9]

Une deuxième ligne d'opposition, moins directe celle-là, concerne non plus le projet européen, auquel on adhère ou que l'on choisit d'accepter, mais les choix politiques de l'Union européenne. C'est sur cette ligne que l'on trouve le candidat de la gauche radicale Jean-Luc Mélenchon, qui sans parler de retrait, n'en énonçait pas moins une série d'objectifs qu'il savait peu susceptibles de recueillir l'aval des partenaires européens de France, comme l'abrogation du traité de Lisbonne ou la mise sous tutelle de la banque centrale, annonçant qu'il n'appliquerait pas les décisions européennes incompatibles avec son programme. Qu'un candidat radical s'affiche sur cette ligne n'avait pas de quoi surprendre ; en revanche, la nouveauté de la campagne a été de voir les représentants des partis de gouvernement s'inscrire dans le même registre. Sans aller aussi loin que son ancien camarade de parti,[10] le principal candidat de l'opposition, François Hollande, a adopté un discours très critique sur la façon dont la crise de l'Euro avait été gérée. Mais la véritable surprise est venue du président sortant, Nicolas Sarkozy, qui a choisi lui aussi une tonalité très critique à son discours, attitude

7 Peter Mair, « Political Opposition *and the* European Union », *Government and Opposition*, 2007, vol. 42, n° 1, pp. 1-17.

8 Dominque Labbé et Denis Monière, « La dernière ligne droite, La campagne électorale du 8 au 21 avril », *Radioscopie*, n° 10, 30 avril 2012, http://www.trielec2012.fr/.

9 Son programme prévoit d'« initier une renégociation des traités pour rompre avec la construction européenne dogmatique en total échec » ; http://www.marinelepen2012.fr/le-projet/politique-etrangere/europe/.

10 Jean-Luc Mélenchon a été élu dans les rangs du parti socialiste jusqu'en 2008.

quelque peu singulière pour quelqu'un qui a revendiqué tout au long de son quinquennat un rôle de pilote de la politique européenne.[11]

À quelques jours d'intervalle, en mars, l'un et l'autre ont choisi de consacrer une partie substantielle de leur communication à leur vision de l'Europe. Nicolas Sarkozy a ouvert le feu dans un meeting organisé à Villepinte, qui se voulait le véritable lancement de sa campagne ; François Hollande a répliqué dans les jours qui suivaient au cours d'une réunion avec plusieurs responsables socialistes européens. Si la teneur de leur propos était différente, la symétrie de leurs argumentations respectives n'en est pas moins remarquable. L'un et l'autre ont choisi d'exposer leurs ambitions pour la France, mais aussi pour l'Europe, Nicolas Sarkozy allant même jusqu'à s'adresser aux électeurs européens :

> Je veux le dire à tous les Français. Mais je veux le dire aussi à tous les Européens.
>
> Si nous voulons préserver notre mode de vie. Si nous voulons préserver notre modèle de civilisation. (...) Alors l'Europe ne doit pas être une menace, mais une protection.[12]

Ce thème de l'Europe-protection, qui lui est cher, le conduit à un éloge remarqué des frontières, rempart de l'Europe contre l'immigration indésirée et contre la concurrence internationale déloyale. Mais le thème est décliné dans une tonalité d'opposition résolue à l'Europe telle qu'elle s'est construite jusqu'alors. La « droitisation » tant remarquée de la campagne trouve ici des accents euro sceptiques :

> L'Europe ne peut pas être la seule région du monde à si mal faire respecter ses frontières, à si peu défendre ses intérêts, à tant ignorer les angoisses de ses citoyens.
>
> Une Europe qui ne défendrait pas ses frontières, ses intérêts, ses citoyens, qui ne penserait qu'au consommateur, jamais au producteur, qui oublierait que derrière le consommateur il y a le travailleur, cette Europe serait condamnée parce qu'elle serait la cause de trop de tensions, de trop de souffrances...

De son côté, François Hollande choisit de concentrer ses critiques sur les questions économiques, revendiquant clairement un lien entre l'agenda national et l'agenda européen :

---

11 Sur les ambiguïtés de la politique européenne de Nicolas Sarkozy, voir Renaud Dehousse, « Nicolas Sarkozy l'Européen », in J. de Maillard et Yves Surel (dir.), *Les politiques publiques sous Sarkozy*, Paris, Presses de Sciences Po, 2012, pp. 153-166.

12 http://www.u-m-p.org/sites/default/files/fichiers_joints/articles/11_03_discours_villepinte.pdf.

> Quand je défends ici en France l'emploi, la croissance, la solidarité, la justice fiscale, je sers aussi les intérêts de l'Europe qui attend la croissance, l'emploi, la justice et la solidarité.

Là aussi, l'analyse commence par une critique de l'orientation actuelle de l'Europe :

> … perçue comme impuissante face aux forces du marché, obsédée même par la dérégulation, incapable de résister à la mondialisation libérale. C'est cette Europe que je ne veux plus. C'est cette Europe que je veux réorienter.

Tout en reconnaissant la nécessité de la discipline budgétaire pour faire face à la crise de la dette souveraine, François Hollande dénonce la ligne d'austérité envisagée par le « traité budgétaire » signé quelques semaines auparavant sous la pression de l'Allemagne :

> il n'y aura pas de retour à l'équilibre si le traité (…) n'est qu'un traité de disciplines, de sanctions qui deviendront vite des austérités pour tous les peuples. (…) Personne ne peut imaginer que si la croissance n'est pas là, les objectifs posés par ce pacte, par ce traité, pourront être atteints. Même les agences de notation, même les marchés le savent et s'inquiètent face à la menace de récession…[13]

En clair, chacun semble avoir concentré le tir sur des thèmes inspirés par les préoccupations de son cœur de cible électoral : immigration et sécurité pour la droite, chômage et pouvoir d'achat pour la gauche.[14]

Dans un cas comme dans l'autre, la critique s'accompagnait d'indications quant à l'action que les candidats entreprendront à l'échelle européenne en cas de victoire. Du côté de Nicolas Sarkozy, une réforme des « accords de Schengen » destinée à en renforcer la discipline, assortie en cas d'échec des négociations d'une menace de sortie unilatérale de la France qui a choqué de nombreux responsables européens. François Hollande, lui, réitère sa volonté de renégocier le traité budgétaire afin d'y adjoindre de nouveaux objectifs – croissance et emploi – pour lesquels seront mobilisés des financements supplémentaires. En clair, le programme de gouvernement que l'un et l'autre esquissent ne se limite pas à leur action à l'Élysée : le mandat qu'ils demandent à leurs électeurs vise également à infléchir l'action de l'Europe,[15] avec en prime

---

13 http://www.jean-jaures.org/content/download/16559/161450/file/Discours_Hollande.pdf.

14 Viviane Le Hay, « Les thèmes importants dans le choix électoral au second tour de la présidentielle 2012 », https://sites.google.com/a/iepg.fr/trielec/resultats-analyses/enquetes-pre-electorales/vague-t2/lesthemesimportantsdanslechoixelectoralausecondtourdelapresidentielle2012, 10 mai 2012.

15 La demande est explicite dans le cas de François Hollande : « J'ai donc demandé un mandat au peuple français. S'il fait le choix de me porter à la présidence de la Répu-

quelques indications quant à la méthode qu'ils entendent suivre à Bruxelles – résolument intergouvernementale pour Sarkozy ; plus ouverte à une approche communautaire pour Hollande, qui égratigne au passage le comportement du tandem « Merkozy », peu soucieux de la sensibilité de ses partenaires.[16]

Figure 1. Attitude de l'opinion à l'égard de l'Europe au début de la campagne

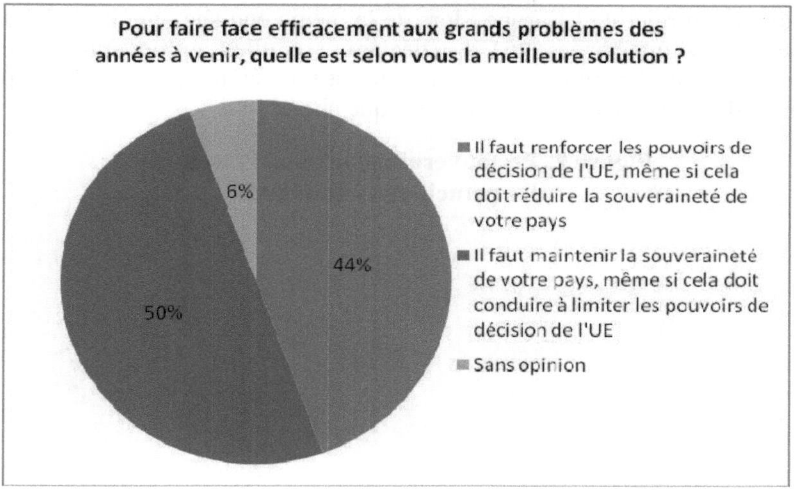

Source : enquête TNS Sofres – TriElec vague 3, Contexte politique à 5 mois de l'élection présidentielle, décembre 2011

Comment expliquer que tous les candidats, à des degrés divers, aient choisi de s'inscrire dans une ligne d'opposition ? Si les motifs de mécontentement varient, tous semblent avoir partagé un même constat : il y a plus de voix à gagner en critiquant l'Europe qu'en la soutenant. Cette remarque convergence s'explique sans doute par l'état de l'opinion au moment de la campagne. On sait en effet depuis l'échec du referendum sur le traité constitutionnel que l'Europe est avant tout source de craintes.[17] Confrontée de surcroît à une crise économique et financière

blique, j'aurai alors le devoir, l'obligation de renégocier ce traité parce que le peuple français en aura souverainement décidé. »

[16] « La France et l'Allemagne ne peuvent pas penser diriger à elles seules l'Europe. L'Europe est la responsabilité commune de la France et de l'Allemagne. L'Europe n'est pas la propriété commune de la France et de l'Allemagne. »

[17] Renaud Dehousse, *La fin de l'Europe*, Paris, Flammarion, 2005 ; Sylvain Brouard, Emiliano Grossman et Nicolas Sauger, *Les Français contre l'Europe : les sens du référendum du 29 mai 2005.*

sans précédent, l'opinion paraissait avant tout soucieuse de préserver les acquis. Ainsi, interrogées sur ce qu'il conviendrait de faire pour répondre aux grands défis du moment au moment même d'un Conseil européen présenté comme décisif pour l'avenir de l'Euro et de l'annonce du nouveau « traité budgétaire », une majorité de personnes indiquaient préférer voir préserver la souveraineté nationale plutôt que de renforcer les pouvoirs de l'Union européenne (figure 1).

La domination du souverainisme ne doit toutefois pas être lue comme un rejet de l'Europe : lors de la même enquête, une majorité de personnes interrogées (51 %) déclarait qu'elles éprouveraient des regrets si la disparition de l'Union européenne était annoncée, le sentiment de soulagement ne l'emportant que chez 21 %.

Figure 2. Le souverainisme dans l'électorat des principaux candidats

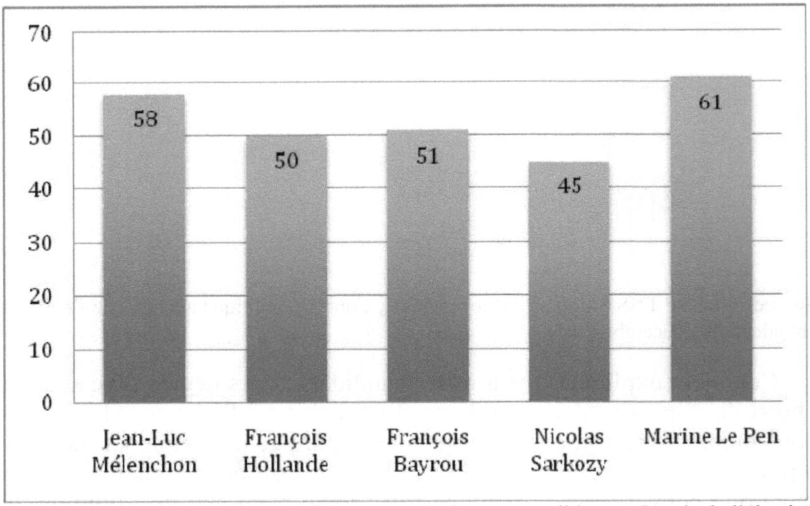

Source : enquête TNS Sofres – TriElec vague 3, Contexte politique à 5 mois de l'élection présidentielle, décembre 2011[18]

Le système électoral a sans doute contribué à une certaine radicalisation des candidats des « partis de gouvernement ». Dans un système majoritaire comme celui de l'élection présidentielle, les candidats doivent généralement ratisser au-delà de leur camp au second tour pour

18 La question était : « Pour faire face efficacement aux grands problèmes des années à venir, quelle est selon vous la meilleure solution. » Deux réponses étaient proposées : maintenir la souveraineté, même si cela doit conduire à limiter les pouvoirs de l'UE, ou renforcer les pouvoirs de l'UE.

pouvoir l'emporter. Or une des particularités du scrutin de 2012 tenait à ce que les réservoirs de voix potentiels des deux principaux candidats – les électeurs du Front national pour Nicolas Sarkozy ; ceux du Front de gauche pour François Hollande – se montraient beaucoup plus frileux que leurs propres électeurs à l'égard de nouveaux transferts de pouvoir à l'Union européenne.

La figure 2 illustre bien cet effet de tenaille : si les sympathisants des deux principaux candidats se montrent (un peu) plus favorables au renforcement des pouvoirs européens que la moyenne des Français, le souverainisme frôle les 58 % parmi les sympathisants de Jean-Luc Mélenchon et atteint 61 % chez ceux de Marine Le Pen. Dans ces conditions, il n'est guère surprenant que la campagne des deux principaux candidats ait pris une tonalité d'opposition à la ligne politique européenne.

3. L'Europe dans les logiques de vote

Quelle influence cette « européanisation » de la campagne a-t-elle eue sur le choix des électeurs ? La réponse doit se faire en plusieurs temps.

Tableau 2. Les thèmes qui ont pesé sur le choix électoral aux premier et second tours de la présidentielle de 2012

	22 avril 2012 (T1)	6 mai 2012 (T2)
La lutte contre le chômage	49	49
La réduction de la dette et des déficits »	31	35
L'amélioration de l'école et l'enseignement	30	32
L'amélioration du pouvoir d'achat	26	30
Le financement du système de protection sociale (retraites, santé, etc.)	25	28
La lutte contre les inégalités et les injustices	24	23
La lutte contre la pauvreté	19	18
La politique fiscale, les impôts et les taxes	16	15
La lutte contre l'insécurité	14	16
La lutte contre l'immigration clandestine	13	18
La protection de l'environnement	11	7
La situation internationale	9	9
L'intégration des minorités dans la société française	4	6

Source : enquête TNS Sofres – TriElec Jour du Vote T1 et T2

Interrogés sur les thèmes qui leur ont paru les plus importants, rares sont les Français qui évoquent spontanément les questions européennes : dans l'enquête post-électorale CEE, ils n'atteignent même pas

1 %. Cependant, lorsqu'on les invite à choisir entre quatre thèmes – nucléaire, immigration, réduction du nombre de fonctionnaires et pouvoirs de l'Europe – c'est de loin ce dernier qui récolte le plus de suffrages (43 %, contre 27 à l'immigration), en particulier parmi les électeurs de François Hollande, parmi lesquels il atteint 48 %.[19] Les thèmes qui ont influencé le choix des électeurs semblent avant tout d'ordre économique et social, comme le montre le tableau 2.

Cependant, l'observation qui a été faite plus haut vaut également à ce niveau : l'Europe se cache souvent derrière bien d'autres sujets. Au cours de sa campagne, le nouveau président avait explicitement lié l'action de l'Union européenne aux deux premiers thèmes évoqués dans ce tableau – l'emploi et la réduction de la dette. Nicolas Sarkozy en avait fait de même avec l'immigration et l'insécurité. Si l'on adopte cette lecture large de la thématique européenne, elle semble bel et bien avoir retenu l'attention d'un grand nombre d'électeurs.

Quel a été son poids sur le résultat ? Les enquêtes post-électorales dressent le tableau d'un électorat inquiet, qui voit son identité menacée (65 % trouvent qu'il y a trop d'immigrés en France), et se montre pessimiste pour l'avenir. Dans ce contexte, l'Europe est souvent associée à des changements redoutés : 67 % des personnes interrogées craignent qu'elle ne soit source d'une réduction de la protection sociale en France ; 53 % qu'elle n'ait un impact négatif sur l'identité nationale et la culture.[20] La campagne électorale, dominée comme on l'a vu par des tonalités négatives, n'a pas contribué à apaiser ces craintes. Comme le montre la figure 3, les Français en sont sortis moins enclins à accepter les transferts de souveraineté. L'écart entre les partisans d'un renforcement de l'Europe et ceux d'un maintien de la souveraineté, qui était de 14 points en décembre 2011, atteignait 32 points le soir du vote, sans que l'on puisse dire ce que ce résultat doit à la rhétorique des candidats et à l'aggravation de la crise de l'Euro.

---

19 Source : Enquête post-électorale CEE.

20 *Ibid.*

Figure 3. Progression du souverainisme

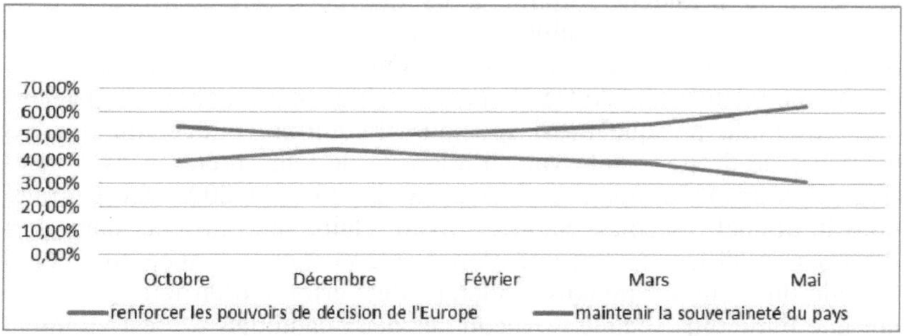

Sources : enquête TNS Sofres – TriElec vagues 2 à 5 pour les valeurs d'octobre à mars ; enquête post-électorale du CEVIPOF pour mai

Comme on l'a dit plus haut, cette évolution ne doit cependant pas être interprétée comme un rejet pur et simple de l'Europe, une nette majorité de personnes interrogées continuant tout au long de la période à indiquer qu'elle regretterait de voir celle-ci disparaître. Néanmoins, dans un tel contexte, on ne peut guère s'étonner de ce que près d'un tiers des suffrages exprimés au premier tour se soient portés sur des candidats porteurs, à des degrés très divers, d'un discours très critique à l'égard de l'intégration européenne (Marine Le Pen, Jean-Luc Mélenchon et Nicolas Dupont-Aignan, Philippe Poutou et Nathalie Arthaud). Pour générale qu'elle soit, la montée du souverainisme n'a pas eu le même impact sur l'électorat des différents candidats. L'opposition à l'Europe semble avoir été une des principales motivations du vote Le Pen.[21] Le discours de Villepinte de Nicolas Sarkozy a également été suivi d'une hausse marquée du souverainisme parmi ses sympathisants, où il est passé de 47 en février à 60 % en mars.[22] À l'évidence, au durcissement de son discours a répondu une radicalisation de son électorat.

L'électorat de François Hollande reflète bien les préoccupations d'une bonne partie de la gauche française à l'égard de la construction européenne. S'il reste (de peu : 59 %, contre 52 % pour les électeurs de Nicolas Sarkozy) majoritairement convaincu que la France a bénéficié de son appartenance à l'Union européenne, il n'en voit pas moins celle-ci comme une source de menaces pour le niveau de protection sociale des Français (73 % contre 59 % chez les électeurs de Nicolas Sarkozy). En revanche, il adhère moins à l'idée d'une perte d'identité culturelle

21 Nonna Mayer, « From Jean-Marie to Marine Le Pen. Electoral Change on the Far Right », à paraître dans *Parliamentary Affairs*, 2012.

22 Source : enquête TNS Sofres – TriElec vagues 4 à 5.

(43 %), et se montre moins critique à l'égard de l'immigration que les électeurs du président sortant : alors que ceux-ci étaient 82 % à se déclarer tout à fait ou plutôt d'accord avec l'idée qu'il y a trop d'immigrants en France, la proportion tombe à 45 % parmi les électeurs de François Hollande. Autre élément notable, ceux-ci se montrent dans leur ensemble presque aussi soucieux d'équilibre budgétaire que les électeurs de droite : seule varie l'intensité de leurs préférences respectives. Évoquant la fracture causée par le vote de 2005 sur le traité constitutionnel, Nicolas Sarkozy avait clairement affiché dans son discours de Villepinte son intention de réconcilier la France du « non » et celle du « oui ». François Hollande s'est efforcé d'en faire de même sur une ligne plus sociale.[23] Aucun des deux candidats n'y est vraiment parvenu, 56 % des partisans du « oui » choisissant d'apporter leur voix au président sortant le soir du 6 mai, tandis que plus des deux tiers de partisans du « non » se portaient sur François Hollande.[24]

4. Conclusion

Si l'on a pu parler d'une Europe « invisible mais omniprésente » lors de l'élection présidentielle de 2002,[25] il n'en allait pas de même en 2012. Dans une période dominée par la crise, où la prégnance des choix européens était incontestable, il devenait difficile de les escamoter. Cette incontestable européanisation du scrutin s'est accompagnée d'un développement des logiques d'opposition. Conscients du climat morose dans lequel intervenait l'élection, les candidats ont dans leur ensemble coulé leur discours dans une rhétorique d'opposition plus ou moins forte à l'Europe, chacun s'efforçant de parler aux craintes dominantes parmi des électeurs. Ce discours a porté. À une réticence de principe à l'intégration s'ajoutent aujourd'hui deux formes de résistance à l'Europe : une variante de gauche, soucieuse avant tout de la préservation des acquis sociaux et une variante de droite, pour laquelle priment les considérations liées à l'identité nationale.

La victoire de François Hollande a ouvert la porte à une série d'interrogations. En politique intérieure, la marge de manœuvre dont il dispose est étroite : porté à l'Élysée par une majorité consciente du poids de l'Europe sur les politiques publiques, mais plus soucieux de préservation des acquis que de changement, il aura du mal à ne pas décevoir. La tâche ne sera guère plus aisée au niveau européen, où à la

23 Enquête post-électorale CEE.

24 Source : enquête TNS Sofres – TriElec Jour du Vote T2.

25 Céline Belot et Bruno Cautrès, « L'Europe, invisible mais omniprésente », in Bruno Cautrès et Nonna Mayer (dir.), *Le Nouveau Désordre électoral : les leçons du 21 avril 2002*, Paris, Presses de Sciences Po, 2004, pp. 119-141.

demande de l'Allemagne et des autres pays du Nord, la gouvernance par les règles a été durcie. Durant sa campagne, le nouveau président avait clairement inscrit son combat politique dans une logique d'alternance à l'échelle européenne : « si le mouvement se lève en France, il sera irréversible dans toute l'Europe, en Allemagne d'abord, en Italie ensuite », déclarait-il en mars,[26] évoquant les échéances électorales de 2013. Le Conseil européen qui a suivi son élection a d'ailleurs été marqué par un infléchissement de la ligne économique européenne, avec l'adoption d'un programme de croissance destiné à tempérer les effets de la crise. D'aucuns ont évoqué à ce propos le remplacement de l'axe « Merkozy » par une « alliance latine ».[27] Sans doute est-ce là aller un peu vite en besogne ; car la décision à l'échelle européenne est avant tout affaire de consensus. Toutefois on voit clairement poindre l'idée d'un lien entre la compétition politique, qui intervient avant tout à l'échelle nationale, et les choix en matière de politiques, souvent déterminés de façon plus ou moins directe au niveau européen. Il reste toutefois à voir si le phénomène qui s'est fait jour à l'occasion de l'élection présidentielle française tient avant tout au contexte de crise dans laquelle celle-ci intervenait, ou s'il indique un changement structurel qui pourrait concerner d'autres pays. Dans ce dernier cas, nous devrions nous interroger sur les effets de cette européanisation sur le système politique de l'Union européenne. Aborder ouvertement les questions européennes à l'occasion des scrutins nationaux peut certes contribuer à la qualité de la démocratie en clarifiant les enjeux des campagnes. Mais si, faute de pouvoir infléchir de façon radicale les choix politiques qui se font à l'échelle européenne, chacun des candidats choisit de s'en tenir à une logique d'opposition à Bruxelles, les forces centrifuges qui seront libérées à cette occasion pourraient contribuer à rendre plus ardu encore le gouvernement de l'Europe.

---

26 Discours de Paris, 17 mars 2012.

27 Massimo Franco, « Una nuova guerra di religione », *Corriere della Sera*, 5 septembre 2012.

L'évolution du contrôle parlementaire de l'exécutif dans le droit de l'Union européenne

Gregorio GARZÓN CLARIANA

Professeur de droit international public à l'Université autonome de Barcelone ; Chaire Jean Monnet ad personam *de droit de l'Union européenne*

1. Introduction

Seule mission confiée à l'Assemblée par le Traité de Paris,[1] le contrôle de l'activité de l'exécutif est resté un aspect essentiel du rôle du Parlement européen malgré l'expansion progressive de ses autres prérogatives.[2] Il a même connu un grand développement, qui l'a rapproché des procédures de contrôle parlementaire traditionnelles dans les États membres de l'Union européenne.[3]

Cette évolution sera présentée ici en plaçant les principaux aspects du contrôle exercé en perspective historique,[4] et en les regardant sous l'angle de la légitimité démocratique de l'Union.[5] Il ne sera question que

---

1 « L'Assemblée, composée de représentants des peuples des États réunis dans la Communauté, exerce les pouvoirs de contrôle qui lui sont attribués par le présent traité » (Article 20 du Traité CECA).

2 Les considérations qui suivent s'inspirent de l'enseignement de l'auteur au Collège d'Europe dans le cadre du séminaire intensif sur le rôle institutionnel du Parlement européen qu'il a animé jusqu'à 2011.

3 Cf. e.g. Jacqué, J.P., *Droit institutionnel de l'Union européenne*, 6e éd., Paris, Dalloz, 2010, pp. 602 ss. ; Rideau, J., *Droit institutionnel de l'Union européenne*, 6e éd., Paris, LGDJ, 2010, pp. 801 ss.

4 Il ne sera pas question du contrôle exercé par les Parlements des États membres, compte tenu qu'il vise plutôt l'activité du législateur de l'Union suivant les dispositions des Protocoles 1 et 2.

5 La présente contribution fait partie des activités de recherche prévues par le projet « Démocratie et droit dans les institutions européennes » de la Chaire Jean Monnet *ad personam* de l'auteur.

du contrôle de l'exécutif : seront ainsi exclues des activités qui ne rentrent pas dans la notion habituelle de contrôle,[6] comme les études ou la codécision du Parlement européen dans les procédures législatives ou budgétaires, et également le contrôle par le Parlement de la bonne gestion financière des institutions, organes u organismes de l'Union[7] quelle que soit la nature de leurs fonctions, sauf dans la mesure où il est devenu un aspect significatif de ses relations avec l'exécutif.

2. Les procédures de contrôle

A. Le rôle des membres

L'Article 23 du Traité CECA prévoyait déjà que la Haute Autorité était tenue de répondre « aux questions qui lui [seraient] posées par l'Assemblée *et par ses membres* »[8] et cette disposition a été reprise sans modification par l'Article 140 du Traité CEE. En ce qui concerne la pratique, on relèvera que le Conseil s'est engagé dès 1962 de répondre aux questions des parlementaires[9] et aussi qu'en 1973 on a ajouté aux séances plénières une « heure des questions » s'inspirant de la tradition britannique.[10] D'autres heures des questions, avec une structure différente, ont été rajoutées en application des dispositions de l'Accord-cadre de 2010 avec la Commission européenne ;[11] en outre, les commissions parlementaires donnent aux parlementaires l'occasion de poser des questions, notamment à des fonctionnaires de la Commission.[12]

L'importance des questions dans la vie du Parlement paraît indéniable, et elles ont servi pour pallier à la pénurie des instruments de contrôle à sa disposition avant le Traité sur l'Union européenne. Mais

6 Cf. *e.g.* Garzón Clariana, G., « El control internacional. Contribución al estudio de los controles jurídicos », *Revista Española de derecho Internacional*, vol. 35, 1983, pp. 9 ss.

7 Voir, par exemple, les décisions de décharge et les résolutions y afférentes, publiées au *JO* L 286 du 17 octobre 2012.

8 Italique ajouté.

9 Cf. *e.g.* Jacqué, *supra*, p. 603.

10 C'est pour cette raison qu'on a parlé de « confluence de traditions parlementaires » dans les dispositions sur les questions au Règlement du Parlement : voir notamment Allúe Buiza, A., « Evolución del control del Parlamento Europeo », in A. Elvira Perales et M.D. González Ayala (coord.), *Nuevos retos del control parlamentario : comunidades autónomas y Unión Europea*, Valencia, Tirant lo Blanch, 2002, pp. 211 ss. ; p. 223.

11 Accord-cadre sur les relations entre le Parlement européen et la Commission européenne, point 46, *JO* L 304 du 20 novembre 2010, p. 47.

12 Cf. R. Corbett, F. Jacobs et M. Shackleton, *The European Parliament*, 8e éd., London, John Harper, 2011, p. 320.

on peut se demander si, sous un angle juridique, ces questions constituent des exemples de l'exercice du contrôle du Parlement, ou plutôt un préalable. On rappellera, à cet égard, que la jurisprudence du Tribunal (de Première Instance) a distingué nettement les droits des députés en ce qui concerne leurs questions, des prérogatives du Parlement en tant que tel ;[13] et aussi que les réponses aux questions, si elles donnent certes des informations utiles pour les travaux parlementaires, ne débouchent pas toujours sur une appréciation institutionnelle du Parlement.

B. Le contrôle ex parte

Le droit de pétition a été présent dès le début dans le Règlement de l'Assemblée,[14] mais il a fallu attendre le Traité de Maastricht pour le voir entrer dans les Traités, en même temps que le droit de s'adresser au médiateur européen. On a vu dans ces droits l'expression d'un « *contrôle citoyen* »,[15] et il est vrai qu'ils font désormais partie des droits de citoyenneté reconnus par la Charte des droits fondamentaux (arts. 43 et 44 de la Charte).

On peut classer l'examen des pétitions parmi les procédures de contrôle parlementaire,[16] *a fortiori* au vu des dispositions pertinentes du Règlement du Parlement.[17] En ce qui concerne le médiateur, on a relevé « *la nature hybride de son statut et son rôle* »[18] du fait que, malgré ses liens multiples avec le Parlement européen, il (ou elle) est tenu d'exercer ses fonctions en pleine indépendance.[19] En tout cas, les rapports soumis par le médiateur en application de son Statut donnent au Parlement des éléments précieux pour son propre contrôle.[20]

---

13 Ordonnance du 17 janvier 2002, affaire T-236/00 *Stauner et al. /Parlement européen et Commission européenne, Rec.* p. II-135.

14 Cf. Kovar, R. et Simon, D., « La citoyenneté européenne », *Cahiers de droit européen*, vol. IX, 1993, pp. 285 ss. ; p. 300.

15 Cf. Molina del Pozo, C.F. et Degiorgis de Pirro, P.E., *El control parlamentario de las políticas comunitarias*, Barcelona, Cálamo, 2004, p. 46.

16 Voir dans ce sens, Jacqué, *supra*, p. 606.

17 Article 202 du Règlement du Parlement, 7e législature, éd. octobre 2012.

18 Magnette, P., « The European Ombudsman : Protecting Citizen's Rights and Strengthening Parliamentary Scrutiny », in N. Diamandouros *et al.*, *The European Ombudsman-Origins, Establishment, Evolution*, Luxembourg, OPEC, 2005, pp. 106 ss. ; p. 106.

19 Cf. Gosalbo Bono, R., « Médiateur », *Répertoire de droit communautaire*, Paris, Dalloz, juin 1995, p. 3.

20 Article 3 du Statut du médiateur, *JO* L 113 du 4 mai 1994 p. 15. Voir aussi Rideau, *supra*, p. 807.

C. Les commissions temporelles

Après les premières élections par suffrage universel direct le Parlement européen a établi des commissions temporelles, dont certaines avaient une mission d'enquête,[21] s'écartant ainsi de l'approche consistant à confier des tâches de détermination des faits à des membres des commissions permanentes, qui avait été retenue par l'Assemblée commune de la CECA.[22]

Le Traité de Maastricht a consacré les commissions temporaires d'enquête, tout en contraignant le Parlement à rechercher l'approbation du Conseil et de la Commission sur la réglementation des modalités d'exercice de son propre droit d'enquête, condition qui demeure d'ailleurs toujours applicable suivant l'Article 226 du Traité sur le Fonctionnement de l'Union européenne.

C'est aux seules commissions temporaires d'enquête qu'il appartient, en règle générale, d'examiner « *des allégations d'infraction ou de mauvaise administration dans l'application du droit de l'Union* » qui seraient le fait des institutions ou organes de l'Union, des administrations publiques des États membres ou de personnes agissant sur leur mandat.[23] Le Parlement peut établir d'autres commissions temporaires (les « commissions spéciales » visées à l'Article 184 de son Règlement intérieur), entre autres pour des missions de *fact finding* ou de suivi, mais elles ne semblent pas habilitées à porter des appréciations d'ordre juridique et ne bénéficient pas des facilités accordées aux commissions d'enquête.

Dans la pratique, les commissions temporaires d'enquête du Parlement européen ont connu un vrai succès, particulièrement visible dans le cas de la commission sur l'Encéphalopathie spongiforme bovine (ESB)[24] qui a facilité, entre autres, une modification de la base juridique applicable au domaine de la santé publique, visant à attribuer à l'Union la compétence pour légiférer afin de faire face aux enjeux communs de sécurité.[25] Ceci étant, c'est seulement trois commissions qui ont été

---

21 Cf. Corbett, Jacobs et Shackleton, *supra*, pp. 331-333.

22 Résolution du 2 décembre 1954, texte reproduit dans Parlement européen, Direction générale de la Présidence, *Vers un Parlement unique – l'influence de l'Assemblée commune de la CECA sur les Traités de Rome*, Parlement européen 2007, pp. 163-166.

23 Décision du Parlement européen, du Conseil et de la Commission du 6 mars 1995 portant modalités d'exercice du droit d'enquête du Parlement européen, *JO* L 78 du 6 avril 1995 p. 1.

24 Cf. Blanquet, M., « Le contrôle parlementaire européen et la crise de la vache folle », *Revue du Marché commun*, 1998, pp. 457 ss.

25 Voir l'actuel Article 168 TFUE.

constituées jusqu'ici, et on a pu constater des limites dans ses pouvoirs, notamment en ce qui concerne l'audition de témoins, qui ont amené à une initiative législative du Parlement visant à améliorer les modalités d'exercice du droit d'enquête.[26]

D. Les commissions permanentes

Certaines commissions permanentes ont acquis un rôle particulier dans l'exercice du contrôle parlementaire résultant de l'évolution du droit dans leurs domaines respectifs d'activité. C'est le cas, bien sûr, de la commission compétente pour les pétitions, mais aussi, notamment de la commission de contrôle budgétaire et de la commission des affaires juridiques.

Relevant, à l'origine, de la seule compétence du Conseil, la décharge à la Commission sur l'exécution du budget est donnée, depuis les modifications des Traités de 1975, par le Parlement européen sur recommandation du Conseil. Le contrôle sur les dépenses a été ensuite renforcé par le Traité de Maastricht, surtout grâce aux devoirs de la Commission de soumettre au Parlement, « *à la demande de ce dernier, toute information nécessaire* », et de mettre « *tout en œuvre* » pour donner suite aux observations du Parlement.[27] C'est dans cet environnement favorable qu'on a développé une pratique de la décharge comme une décision reflétant une appréciation de la gestion budgétaire, distincte de la clôture des comptes, ce qui à son tour a amené à accepter la possibilité d'un refus de la décharge,[28] devenue une épée de Damoclès pour la Commission européenne.[29] Dans ces conditions, même un report de la décharge risque d'avoir des conséquences sérieuses, comme l'illustre la démission collective de la Commission Santer en 1999.[30]

---

26 Rapport de la commission d'affaires constitutionnelles du 14 octobre 2011, A7-0352/2011 (Rapporteur David Martin). Adoption en plénière le 25 mai 2012.

27 Article 206 du Traité CE modifié par l'Article G.74 du Traité de Maastricht (actuel Article 319 TFUE). La doctrine avait anticipé, à l'époque, que ces modifications allaient provoquer des « tensions » entre le Parlement européen et la Commission : cf. Peláez Marón, J.M., « El control parlamentario según el Tratado de la Unión », *Cuestiones actuales de Derecho comunitario europeo*, vol. 3, 1995, pp. 161 ss. ; p. 172.

28 Cf. Graf, R. et Theato, D., *Das Europaische Parlement und der Haushalt der Europäischen Gemeinschaften*, Baden-Baden, Nomos, 1994, p. 132 ; Bieber, R., commentaire à l'Article 206 in H. Groeben, J. Thiesing, C.-D. Ehlermann, *et al.*, *Kommentar zum EU-/EG-Vertrag*, Baden-Baden, Nomos, 1997.

29 Règlement du Parlement *supra*, arts. 76-78 et Annexe VI.

30 Cf. Priestley, J., *Six Battles that Shaped Europe's Parliament*, London, John Harper, 2008, pp. 144-202 ; Viñas, A., *Al servicio de Europa*, Madrid, Complutense, 2004, pp. 321-414.

Il est de tradition que la commission des affaires juridiques examine, toutes les années, les mesures prises par la Commission dans le contrôle de l'application par les États membres du droit de l'Union ; en outre, elle est censée rendre son avis sur la participation du Parlement dans des affaires devant la Cour de justice.[31]

Pour le reste, suite aux améliorations introduites par le Traité de Lisbonne sur le régime applicable aux actes non législatifs, c'est pratiquement toutes les commissions permanentes qui contribuent désormais au contrôle, en ce qui concerne les actes délégués et les projets de mesures d'exécution des actes législatifs adoptés suivant la procédure législative ordinaire.[32]

3. Les activités contrôlées

A. L'activité de la Commission européenne

Bien qu'elle semble relever du domaine des sanctions plutôt que de celui du contrôle, la censure de la Commission, prévue dès l'origine dans les traités, constitue, même si elle est assortie d'une procédure qui la rend peu probable dans la pratique,[33] un élément particulièrement révélateur de l'esprit dans lequel on a conçu la mission de la Commission et le contrôle que le Parlement doit exercer sur son activité. Cette approche reste toujours d'actualité et a trouvé un prolongement dans les dispositions, plus récentes, associant le Parlement à la nomination du président de la Commission et du Collège des commissaires d'une manière toujours plus intense, dont les potentialités ont été pleinement exploitées grâce aux procédures prévues au Règlement du Parlement.

Le contrôle parlementaire de l'activité de la Commission doit respecter les principes juridiques de l'équilibre institutionnel et de la collégialité et l'indépendance de la Commission. La collégialité implique, entre autres, que le Parlement ne peut pas décider la destitution des membres individuels de la Commission, mais ne s'oppose pas, en

---

31 Article 128 du Règlement du Parlement. On rappellera que, suite au Traité de Nice, le Parlement est pleinement entré dans la catégorie des requérants privilégiés pour ce qui est des recours en annulation.

32 Voir arts. 290 et 291 TFUE ; Règlement 182/2011 du Parlement européen et du Conseil établissant les règles et principes généraux relatifs aux modalités de contrôle par les États membres de l'exercice des compétences d'exécution de la Commissión, Article 11, *JO* L 55 du 28 février 2011 p. 13 ; Règlement intérieur du Parlement, articles 87 bis et 88.

33 Cf. *e.g.* Allué Buiza, A., « Evolución de la función de control del Parlamento europeo », in Elvira Perales, A. et González Ayala, M.D., *Nuevos retos del control parlamentario : comunidades autónomas y Unión Europea*, Valencia, Tirant lo Blanch, 2002, pp. 211 ss. ; p. 220.

l'état actuel des Traités, à la fin du mandat d'un(e) commissaire sur demande du président de la Commission.[34] Le Parlement peut prendre l'initiative d'une telle demande, et dans ce cas le président de la Commission aura le choix entre donner suite ou expliquer les motifs de son refus.[35]

Le principe de l'indépendance de la Commission, d'une importance essentielle, n'est pas incompatible avec la mise en place de procédés et bonnes pratiques en vue d'une coopération plus structurée avec le Parlement, y compris par des accords interinstitutionnels ; mais le Conseil y a vu traditionnellement des risques qui l'ont amené à réserver sa position. En ce qui concerne la doctrine, si le « partenariat spécial » mis en œuvre par l'Accord-cadre de 2010 a été parfois mal reçu, c'est en raison d'un prétendu affaiblissement à terme du rôle institutionnel de la Commission, plutôt que par des considérations proprement juridiques.[36]

B. Les activités du Conseil et du Conseil européen

La doctrine juridique a souvent souligné les limites du contrôle du Parlement européen sur l'activité du Conseil de l'Union, et l'a parfois expliqué par la composition intergouvernementale de cette institution, dont les membres « tirent leur légitimité du soutien qui leur est accordé par les Parlements nationaux ».[37] Le Parlement n'est pas dépourvu, certes, de pouvoirs de contrôle sur les actes du Conseil : il peut désormais former des recours devant la Cour de justice visant à faire vérifier leur légalité,[38] et aussi contrôler la bonne gestion financière du Conseil par la procédure de décharge.[39] Mais ces procédures, également présentes en ce qui concerne les autres Institutions de l'Union, ne sont pas l'équivalent du régime du contrôle de l'exécutif dans les traditions constitutionnelles communes aux États membres.

On peut se demander, toutefois, si le Conseil est vraiment un exécutif. En effet, malgré la théorie du « *dual executive* » provenant de la

34 Article 17. para. 6 TUE.

35 Point 5 de l'Accord-cadre du 20 octobre 2010, *supra.*

36 Cf. Note éditoriale : « Dispatch from the Euro Titanic : And the Orchestra Played On », *European Journal of International Law*, vol. 29, 2010, pp. 805 ss.

37 Jacqué, *supra*, p. 602. Cet argument ne paraît pas entièrement convaincant du moment que les Protocoles 1 et 2 ont instauré des contrôles sur l'activité du Conseil, s'ajoutant à ceux déjà existants sur l'activité de ses membres considérés *uti singuli.*

38 On rappellera que, suite aux modifications introduites par le Traité de Nice, le Parlement a la légitimation active dans les recours en annulation, dans les mêmes conditions que les États membres, le Conseil et la Commission.

39 Voir, par exemple, la Décision et la Résolution du Parlement du 10 mai 2012, *JO* L 286 du 17 octobre 2012 pp. 22 ss.

science politique,[40] force est de constater que suite aux dispositions du Traité de Lisbonne, portant notamment sur le Haut Représentant et sur les actes non législatifs, le Conseil paraît désormais relever du pouvoir législatif, plutôt que de l'exécutif.[41] Par conséquent, il est douteux que les limites au contrôle de l'activité du Conseil doivent être regardées comme une anomalie inhérente au stade actuel de l'intégration européenne, ou comme un aspect du « déficit démocratique ».

On peut également douter que le Conseil européen, devenu l'une des Institutions européennes en vertu du Traité de Lisbonne, soit l'équivalent du Gouvernement dans les États, mais la question du contrôle parlementaire de ce Conseil mériterait une analyse plus poussée.

C. L'activité de la Banque centrale européenne

En ce qui concerne la Banque centrale européenne, elle exerce incontestablement une activité exécutive, mais le contrôle parlementaire de l'activité de la Banque a été conçu en fonction des particularités de son statut,[42] visant, comme l'a relevé la jurisprudence de la Cour de justice, à la protéger d'influences externes et surtout de toutes pressions politiques.[43] Même si la raison d'être de ces dispositions semble avoir été, plutôt de mettre la Banque à l'abri des éventuelles ingérences des gouvernements des États membres, elles n'ont pas épargné le Parlement européen. Ainsi, la participation du Parlement dans la nomination des membres du directoire de la Banque n'est pas, malgré les dispositions de son Règlement intérieur,[44] le même que dans le cas des membres de la Commission, et on ne trouve pas une procédure qui ressemble à une motion de censure. C'est dans ces conditions que le Parlement s'est efforcé d'obtenir de la Banque, au moins davantage d'informations et de publicité sur ses travaux et ses décisions.[45]

Plus récemment le Parlement européen s'est prononcé pour un renforcement de la légitimité démocratique et de son propre rôle dans la

---

[40] Cf. Hix, S. et Hoyland, B., *The Political System of the European Union*, 3e éd., Palgrave Macmillan, 2011, pp. 23 ss.

[41] Voir, dans le même sens, Corbett, Jacobs et Shackleton, *supra*, p. 317.

[42] Cf. *e.g.* Zilioli, C. et Selmayr, M., « Recent Developments in the Law of the European Central Bank », *Yearbook of European Law*, 2006, pp. 1 ss.

[43] Arrêt du 10 juillet 2003, Affaire C-11/00, *Commission/Banque centrale*, *Recueil* p. I-07147.

[44] Article 109 du Règlement du Parlement.

[45] Cf. Magnette, P., Contrôler l'Europe – pouvoirs et responsabilité dans l'Union européenne, Bruxelles, Éditions de l'Université, 2003, pp. 53 ss.

gouvernance de l'UEM.[46] Il semblerait cohérent de procéder à un réexamen du contrôle de la Banque dans ce contexte.

D. Les activités des organismes de l'Union européenne

La création de nombreux organismes avec une personnalité juridique et un budget propres[47] pour l'externalisation de tâches relevant de la Commission constitue une caractéristique de l'évolution de l'exercice de la fonction exécutive dans le système institutionnel de l'Union européenne. Si dans les années 1980 du siècle dernier on connaissait la fondation pour la formation professionnelle de Berlin et la fondation pour la qualité de la vie et du travail de Dublin, maintenant on ne décompte pas moins de trente-quatre Agences « de régulation », auxquelles il faut encore ajouter trois Agences dans le domaine de la PESC, et six Agences « exécutives » pour la mise en œuvre de programmes européens.

On a soutenu, dans la doctrine, que la prolifération des Agences aurait provoqué une fragmentation des fonctions exécutives, au détriment du contrôle du Parlement européen.[48] Il n'est pas possible de vérifier ici cette thèse par un examen fouillé des nombreux actes législatifs portant création d'organismes de l'Union ou de la pratique suivie par le Parlement et ses commissions en vue de contrôler leur activité, mais la diversité de formules et le manque d'orientations communes qui ont présidé à l'établissement de ces organismes, déjà été critiquée par le Parlement,[49] se projette inévitablement dans ses relations avec eux.[50] D'ailleurs, si le Parlement a été souvent admis à participer dans la nomination des membres du conseil d'administration des organismes, par contre il a été exclu de la nomination du directeur exécutif, suivant l'approche traditionnellement retenue par le Conseil.[51] Dans ces condi-

---

46 Résolution du 20 novembre 2012, paragraphe 9 du dispositif.

47 La généralisation du mot « organismes » pour désigner les Fondations, Agences et Offices autonomes soumis au droit de l'Union procède des travaux du « groupe Piris » chargé de réviser les textes issus de la Convention européenne.

48 Cf. Laurent, S., « Les agences communautaires, facteur d'incohérence institutionnelle ? – De la nécessité d'un renforcement du contrôle parlementaire des agences », in Michel, V. (ed.), *Le Droit, les Institutions et les politiques face à l'impératif de la cohérence*, Strasbourg, 2009, pp. 107 ss. ; pp. 129-130.

49 Résolution du Parlement du 13 janvier 2004 sur l'encadrement des agences de régulation européennes, *JO* C 92E p. 119.

50 Voir, par exemple, l'article 126 du Règlement du Parlement visant les demandes adressées à des agences « *dans les cas où le Parlement a le droit de soumettre une demande à une agence* » (italique ajouté).

51 Le Règlement 168/2007 du Conseil portant création de l'Agence des droits fondamentaux de l'Union européenne (*JO* L 53 du 22 février 2007) associe le Parlement « à la sélection des candidats proposés aux fonctions de directeur » à titre exception-

tions, on a dû se contenter de prévoir que les candidats au poste « *devraient* se présenter aux auditions des commissions parlementaires ».[52]

Le Parlement a essayé de renforcer son contrôle sur les organismes de l'Union, notamment dans l'exercice de ses pouvoirs de contrôle budgétaire et par les dispositions de son Règlement intérieur, mais aussi par l'intermédiaire de la Commission, dont les services demeurent apparemment les principaux interlocuteurs des agences.[53] À l'avenir, on pourra parvenir à une situation plus satisfaisante grâce à la déclaration et approche communes sur les agences de régulation approuvées par le Parlement, le Conseil et la Commission le 13 juin 2012, suite aux travaux d'un groupe interservices établi en 2009.[54] Mais la mise en œuvre complète de ce texte devra attendre des modifications législatives des actes instituant les différents organismes.

E. Les activités des administrations des États membres

On a parfois l'impression, en parcourant les incursions dans le domaine du droit de l'Union d'auteurs mieux familiarisés avec d'autres disciplines juridiques, l'impression qu'ils éprouvent des difficultés à accepter la réalité du contrôle par le Parlement des activités des exécutifs étatiques, comme s'il s'agissait plutôt d'un principe théorique, qui devrait se heurter forcément à des obstacles sérieux au moment de sa mise en œuvre.[55] Mais cette perception résulte d'un *a priori* qui ne paraît pas conforté par l'examen de la pratique, où l'on trouve même des exemples allant dans le sens contraire.[56]

La soumission des actes des administrations étatiques au contrôle du Parlement européen est une conséquence de la décentralisation des fonctions exécutives dans le système institutionnel de l'Union euro-

---

nel et en précisant : « *sans que cela constitue un précédent pour les autres agences* » (considérant n° 23).

52 Accord-cadre *supra*, point 23 (italique ajouté).

53 C'est du moins l'une des conclusions d'une étude empirique fondée sur des entretiens avec des *senior officials* de ces organismes : cf. Egeberg, M. et Trondal, J., *EU-level Agencies : New executive centre formation or vehicles for national control ?*, ARENA Online Working Paper n° 12, Oslo, novembre 2010.

54 Cf. Bernard E., « Accord sur les Agences européennes : la montagne accouche d'une souris », *Revue du Droit de l'Union européenne*, 2012, pp. 399 ss. ; pp. 421-429.

55 Cf. *e.g.* : Rosado Iglesias, G., « La función de control del Parlamento Europeo », in Elvira Perales, A. et González Ayala, M.D., *Nuevos retos del control parlamentario*, *supra*, pp. 231 ss. ; pp. 261-262.

56 C'est ainsi, par exemple, que certaines commissions temporaires constituées avant le Traité de Maastricht ont bénéficié des témoignages de fonctionnaires nationaux, avec l'autorisation des États membres, qui n'étaient pourtant pas obligés à l'accorder ou à coopérer avec ces commissions : voir Corbett, Jacobs et Schakleton, *supra*, p. 332.

péenne, pratiquement dépourvu d'une administration périphérique.[57] C'est pourquoi elle est expressément visée dans le cas des commissions temporaires d'enquête,[58] avec des conséquences précises telle que le droit d'inviter un État membre à désigner un ministre pour participer aux travaux de la commission.[59] C'est aussi la pratique courante et non contestée sur l'exercice du droit de pétition, où l'examen de la pétition amène souvent à des « missions d'information » sur le territoire de l'État membre visée. Un autre exemple pourrait être le droit d'initiative du Parlement européen dans le domaine de la constatation d'un risque clair de violation grave par un État membre de valeurs fondamentales de l'Union,[60] qui présuppose l'exercice d'un contrôle du respect de ces valeurs.

Il est évident, pour le reste, que le contrôle du Parlement européen sur l'activité des exécutifs des États membres ne s'apparente pas au régime de la responsabilité politique des Gouvernements des États membres devant leurs Parlements respectifs, de la même manière que la Commission européenne ou les organismes de l'Union n'ont pas à répondre de leur activité exécutive devant les Parlements des États membres. La gouvernance multiniveau ne saurait être confondue avec une fusion des niveaux.

4. Conclusions

Le contrôle parlementaire de l'exécutif présente, dans le système institutionnel de l'Union européenne, des caractéristiques particulières, liées à la double décentralisation géographique et fonctionnelle de l'activité exécutive et à la conception de l'indépendance de la Banque centrale européenne retenue par les Traités. Les prérogatives du Parlement européen semblent, dans ce domaine, plus réduites que celles de parlements des États membres, même s'il s'agit parfois de limites contingentes, susceptibles de modification par la voie législative ; certaines réformes législatives sont d'ailleurs déjà en cours.

57 Il y a quelques exceptions, comme les Représentations ou les Bureaux de la Commission ou du Parlement, établies dans le cadre de leur politique d'information.

58 Le mandat des commissions sur l'EEB et sur la crise d'Equitable Life Insurance comprennait expréssement l'examen des activités des autorités des États membres impliqués : voir Décision du Parlement européen du 17 juillet 1996, paragraphe 3, JO C 239 du 17 août 1996, p. 1 ; Décision du 7 juillet 2006, art. 2 premier tiret, JO L 186 du 7 juillet 2006, p. 58.

59 Arts. 2 et 3 de la décision du 6 mars 1995, *supra*.

60 Article 7 para. 1 TUE.

Si le Parlement européen a été marqué jusqu'aux années 1990 du siècle dernier, par une culture du contrôle parfois jugée « négative »,[61] le passage à la culture de la coresponsabilité ne l'a pas amené à oublier l'importance capitale du contrôle parlementaire, comme le montrent, par exemple, les dispositions de l'accord-cadre sur les relations entre le Parlement et la Commission européenne de 2010, ou plus récemment les travaux pour améliorer les moyens à la disposition des commissions temporaires d'enquête.

Il paraît difficile de partager la thèse suivant laquelle « *les mécanismes de contrôle démocratique de l'Union européenne... sont ceux hérités de la CECA, avec toutefois quelques améliorations* ».[62] Ce serait trop sous-estimer l'effet combiné des modifications des Traités, inspirées des traditions constitutionnelles communes des États membres, et des accords et bonnes pratiques qui ont vu le jour dans le cadre de la coopération loyale entre les institutions ou du pouvoir d'auto-organisation du Parlement européen. Ceux qui, après avoir parcouru ces pages, voudront se référer à la doctrine des années 1980 pourront mesurer toute l'ampleur de cette transformation.[63]

Finalement, on pourrait se demander si des progrès substantiels dans ce domaine, comme dans d'autres, pourront encore être accomplis sans des réformes du régime électoral et des partis politiques européens, susceptibles d'organiser la vie parlementaire en fonction d'une dialectique majorité/opposition. Mais cela, c'est déjà une autre histoire.

---

61 Cf. Allué, *supra*, p. 211.

62 Levrat, N., *La construction européenne est-elle démocratique ?*, Paris, La Documentation Française, 2012, p. 59.

63 Cf. Chauchat, M., *Le contrôle politique du Parlement européen sur les exécutifs communautaires*, Paris, LGDJ, 1989.

La Cour de justice face à l'article 51 de la Charte des droits fondamentaux

Timidité ou perspectives d'ouverture

Jean Paul JACQUÉ

Professeur émérite à l'Université de Strasbourg ;
Directeur général honoraire au Conseil de l'Union européenne

Le recteur Demaret a non seulement assuré pendant les années de son mandat la prééminence du Collège dans le champ des études européennes. Il a également contribué de manière exceptionnelle depuis de longues années au développement de la recherche en droit de l'Union, ce dont toute la Communauté universitaire lui est reconnaissante. C'est une bien pauvre manière de lui exprimer celle-ci, mais c'est la seule à la disposition de l'auteur, que de lui dédier une étude sur un thème qui suscite aujourd'hui l'intérêt de la doctrine. En effet, la question du champ d'application[1] de la Charte a été constamment présente lors des travaux qui ont conduit à l'adoption de celle-ci, puis à sa révision dans le cadre du traité de Lisbonne et enfin lors de la révision du traité lui-même. Un grand nombre d'États membres de l'Union redoutaient en effet les interférences entre le système de protection des droits fondamentaux propre à l'Union et leur propre système national. Plus encore, ils redoutaient que la reconnaissance de certains droits ou principes par la Charte n'ait comme conséquence de leur imposer le respect de ceux-ci sous le contrôle de la Cour de justice dans des domaines qui relevaient de leur compétence propre. C'était la grande crainte du

1 Pour deux études récentes de la question, voir le rapport au XXVe Congrès FIDE 2012 de Clemens Ladenburger, « The interaction between the Charter of Fundamental Rights, The European Convention of Human Rights and National Constitutions », Tartu University Press, vol. 1 ; Voir aussi Paul Craig, *The Lisbon Treaty, Law, Politics, and Treaty Reform*, Oxford University Press, 2010, pp. 193 et ss. ; Koen Lenaerts, Exploring the Limits of the EU Charter of Fundamental Rights, *European Constitutional Law Review*, 2012, pp. 375-405; Alan Rosas, The Applicability of the EU Charter of Fundamental Rights at National Level, *European Yearbook on Human Rights*, 2013, pp. 97-112.

Royaume-Uni en matière de droits sociaux qui finit par conduire à l'adoption du protocole sur l'application de la Charte à la Pologne et au Royaume-Uni. En dehors du cas des droits sociaux, la Pologne, l'Irlande ou la République tchèque redoutaient, à tort vraisemblablement, que certains droits classiques en matière de mariage, de droit à la vie privée et familiale ou de propriété ne heurtent certains de leurs intérêts ou de leurs valeurs. Certes la plupart de ces droits étaient déjà protégés par la Convention européenne des droits de l'homme et placés sous le contrôle de la Cour de Strasbourg. Mais il existe une grande différence entre un arrêt déclaratoire de la Cour européenne des droits de l'homme et une constatation de manquement ou un jugement de renvoi préjudiciel à Luxembourg. Dans le premier cas, l'exécution de l'arrêt est placée sous le contrôle du Comité des ministres du Conseil de l'Europe et ne produit pas d'effet immédiat en droit interne. Dans le second, il est revêtu de la primauté du droit de l'Union et s'impose aux juridictions nationales. Le dernier motif d'inquiétude des États résidait à leurs yeux dans le risque que la reconnaissance de certains droits ne conduise à une extension des compétences de l'Union.[2]

Finalement, l'acceptation de l'insertion de droits qui, aux yeux de certains États membres, était sans rapport avec les compétences de la Communauté se fit au prix de la précision dans l'article 51, paragraphe 2, de la Charte que celle-ci n'étendait, ni ne modifiait les compétences et les tâches de l'Union. Lors de l'inclusion de la Charte dans le traité, certains États ont craint que le simple fait pour un État d'adopter une législation interne dans un domaine couvert par un droit garanti par la Charte ne conduise à considérer que cette législation constituait une

2 Sur ce point, ils auraient pu être rassurés par l'avis 2/94 rendu à propos de l'adhésion de la Communauté européenne à la Convention européenne des droits de l'homme. Dans cette affaire, la Cour souligne clairement la différence entre l'obligation de respecter les droits fondamentaux et la compétence pour légiférer en ce domaine, la première n'ayant aucun effet sur la seconde. Dans l'affaire Laval, la Cour est encore plus directe. L'interdiction posée par l'article CE de légiférer sur le droit de grève n'interdit pas à l'Union d'apprécier celui-ci au regard de la liberté d'établissement et de vérifier si l'obligation de respecter celui-ci peut constituer une restriction légitime à l'exercice de cette liberté : « … la circonstance que l'article 137 CE ne s'applique ni au droit de grève ni au droit de lock-out n'est pas de nature à soustraire une action collective telle que celle en cause au principal au domaine de la libre prestation des services, etc. Si le droit de mener une action collective doit donc être reconnu en tant que droit fondamental faisant partie intégrante des principes généraux du droit communautaire dont la Cour assure le respect, il n'en demeure pas moins que son exercice peut être soumis à certaines restrictions. … À cet égard, la Cour a déjà jugé que la protection des droits fondamentaux constitue un intérêt légitime de nature à justifier, en principe, une restriction aux obligations imposées par le droit communautaire, même en vertu d'une liberté fondamentale garantie par le traité », Arrêt du 18 décembre 2007, aff. C-341/05.

mise en œuvre du droit de l'Union et tombe de ce fait dans le champ d'application du droit de l'Union. La formule fut reproduite également à l'article 6 TUE. Ce n'est pas parce que la Charte impose le respect du droit de grève dans le cadre du droit de l'Union que toute législation nationale sur la question tomberait *ipso facto* dans le champ d'application de ce droit. D'où l'ajout à l'article 52 de la formule selon laquelle la Charte : « n'étend pas le champ d'application du droit de l'Union au-delà des compétences de l'Union ». Cette précision est reprise dans la déclaration n° 1 à l'acte final du traité de Lisbonne. Enfin, pour couronner le tout, l'exclusion de la création de nouvelles compétences sur la base de la Charte est inscrite à l'article 6 TUE.

Dans ce contexte, la question du champ d'application de la Charte se pose essentiellement à l'égard des États membres (1), l'application de la Charte aux institutions, organes et organismes de l'Union ne soulevant guère de problème. Mais ceci ne suffit pas à épuiser les difficultés. Une fois réglée la question du champ d'application *ratione materiae* de la Charte, reste à savoir si celle-ci est uniquement applicable dans les rapports entre États et particuliers ou bien si elle peut être invoquée également horizontalement dans les rapports entre personnes privées (2).

1. Les États membres et la mise en œuvre du droit de l'Union

La question du champ d'application de la Charte a donné lieu à de difficiles discussions au sein de la Convention entre partisans d'une approche large et tenants d'une position plus restrictive. Comme souvent, le résultat, retranscrit à l'article 51, paragraphe 1 de la Charte, est un compromis. La formule initialement proposée selon laquelle les États membres devaient respecter la Charte dans le champ d'application du droit de l'Union a été écartée au profit d'une formulation beaucoup plus restrictive faisant référence « uniquement » à la mise en œuvre du droit de l'Union. Mais d'un autre côté, il a été admis qu'une interprétation plus ouverte figurerait dans les explications que le TUE a élevé au rang d'instrument privilégié d'interprétation de la Charte : « En ce qui concerne, les États membres, il résulte sans ambiguïté de la jurisprudence de la Cour que l'obligation de respecter les droits fondamentaux définis dans le cadre de l'Union ne s'impose aux États membres que lorsqu'ils agissent dans le champ d'application du droit de l'Union (arrêt du 13 juillet 1989, *Wachauf*, aff. 5/88, *Rec*. 1989, p. 2609 ; arrêt du 18 juin 1991, *ERT*, *Rec*. 1991, p. I-2925 ; arrêt du 18 décembre 1997, aff. C-309/96 *Annibaldi*, *Rec*. 1997, p. I-7493) ». Dans ces conditions, il revenait à la Cour de justice de se prononcer sur l'interprétation à donner à l'article 51 à la lumière des explications. L'utilisation dans cet article de l'adverbe « uniquement » invitait à une démarche prudente tout comme les divers avertissements relatifs au respect des compétences de l'Union. Mais les explications proposaient une interprétation plus ouverte.

A. La continuité dans l'application des jurisprudences Wachauf et ERT

1. Le plus petit commun dénominateur est la référence à l'arrêt *Wachauf*. La Charte est bien entendu applicable lorsque l'État met en œuvre le droit de l'Union en appliquant un règlement ou en transposant une directive. Dans ce cas, l'État agit en quelque sorte comme un agent décentralisé de l'Union et est pleinement soumis au respect du droit de l'Union, y inclus la Charte. Sur ce point, la jurisprudence de la Cour à propos de la Charte est identique à celle qui avait été développée auparavant. Ainsi, dans l'affaire *J. McB. contre L. E.* qui concerne le droit de garde des enfants et met en cause l'interprétation d'un règlement communautaire, la Cour prend en compte les dispositions de la Charte, même pour des faits antérieurs au traité de Lisbonne.[3] Après avoir rappelé les limitations imposées par l'article 51, la Cour estime qu'

> il convient de tenir compte de la charte aux seules fins de l'interprétation du règlement n° 2201/2003, sans procéder à une appréciation du droit national en tant que tel. Il s'agit plus particulièrement de vérifier si les dispositions de la charte s'opposent à l'interprétation de ce règlement exposée au point 44 du présent arrêt, compte tenu notamment du renvoi au droit national que cette interprétation implique.[4]

De la même manière, à propos de l'application de la directive sur le commerce électronique, la Cour constate que le juge national ne peut ordonner à un fournisseur d'accès de filtrer tous les accès pour protéger la propriété intellectuelle garantie par la Charte parce que ce droit doit être mis en balance avec la liberté d'entreprendre également garantie par la Charte.[5] Ainsi également, la balance entre les droits fondamentaux et

---

3 Il est vrai que la motivation de l'acte faisait référence au respect de la Charte.

4 Arrêt du 21 octobre 2010, aff. C-400/10 PPU ; voir plus clairement dans l'affaire *Kamberaj* : « Il s'ensuit que, en déterminant les mesures de sécurité sociale, d'aide sociale et de protection sociale définies par leur législation nationale et soumises au principe d'égalité de traitement consacré à l'article 11, paragraphe 1, sous d), de la directive 2003/109, les États membres doivent respecter les droits et observer les principes prévus par la Charte, notamment ceux énoncés à l'article 34 de celle-ci. Aux termes du paragraphe 3 de ce dernier article, afin de lutter contre l'exclusion sociale et la pauvreté, l'Union, et donc les États membres lorsqu'ils mettent en œuvre le droit de cette dernière, reconnaît et respecte le droit à une aide sociale et à une aide au logement destinées à assurer une existence digne à tous ceux qui ne disposent pas de ressources suffisantes, selon les modalités établies par le droit de l'Union et les législations et pratiques nationales ». Arrêt du 24 décembre 2012, aff. C-571/10.

5 Arrêt du 24 novembre 2011, *Scarlett*, aff. C-70/10.

les intérêts en présence doit être prise en considération lors de la transposition d'une directive. C'est la raison pour laquelle un État ne peut, à cette occasion, prévoir une limitation supplémentaire au traitement de données à caractère personnel lorsque l'intéressé n'a pas donné son consentement, en l'espèce que les données figurent déjà dans des bases de données publiques. En effet, la pondération entre l'intérêt légitime du traitement et la protection des données personnelles et de la vie privée mentionnée aux articles 7 et 8 de la Charte doit être effectuée par l'État au cas par cas et non d'une manière globale dans le cadre de l'acte de transposition.[6]

Dans le cadre de cette analyse du champ d'application, la Cour semble avoir une vision large du concept de responsabilité des États membres. De même qu'en ce qui concerne l'effet direct des directives, l'invocabilité ne joue pas seulement à l'égard des autorités centrales, mais peut découler du comportement de toutes les entités étatiques ou contrôlées par l'État, le concept d'État dans la mise en œuvre du droit de l'Union s'étend à d'autres entités que l'État au sens strict. Il en va ainsi lorsqu'une directive autorise sa mise en œuvre par les partenaires sociaux. Dans cette hypothèse, le non-respect de la Charte par ces derniers peut être invoqué et l'on reste dans le cadre de la mise en œuvre. Comme le déclare la Cour à propos d'une convention collective relative à la mise en œuvre de la directive 2000/78 instituant un cadre général pour la lutte contre la discrimination notamment sur la base de l'âge :

> La Cour a déjà jugé que les partenaires sociaux ne constituent pas des entités de droit public… Cette considération n'empêche cependant pas les États membres d'autoriser, par des règles d'habilitation, les partenaires sociaux à adopter des mesures, au sens de l'article 2, paragraphe 5, de la directive 2000/78, dans les domaines visés à cette disposition qui relèvent des accords collectifs. Ces règles d'habilitation doivent être suffisamment précises afin de garantir que lesdites mesures respectent les exigences énoncées audit article 2, paragraphe 5.[7]

Dans ce cas, le droit à la négociation collective visé à l'article 28 de la Charte ne peut s'opposer à la mise en œuvre du droit de l'Union par les partenaires sociaux.

Il advient parfois que certains actes de l'Union offrent aux États membres des options pour la mise en œuvre ou leur laissent une certaine marge d'appréciation. Est-on alors encore dans le cadre de la mise en œuvre du droit de l'Union ou s'agit-il de mesures nationales qui échap-

---

6 Arrêt du 24 novembre 2011, *ASNEF*, aff. C-468/10.

7 Arrêt du 13 septembre 2011, *Prigge et autres*, aff. C-447/09 ; voir aussi arrêt du 8 septembre 2011, *Hennigs*, aff. C-297/10.

pent au contrôle au titre de la Charte ? La réponse a été rapidement apportée par la Cour dans l'affaire *N.S.*[8] Était en cause le règlement Dublin II qui prévoit le renvoi des demandeurs d'asile dans le premier État d'entrée dans l'Union et, plus particulièrement, le paragraphe 2 de l'article 3 du règlement qui, par dérogation, autorise discrétionnairement, un État à examiner lui-même la demande d'asile. Un afghan menacé au Royaume-Uni de renvoi en Grèce contestait la décision de renvoi au motif qu'il serait soumis en Grèce à un traitement contraire aux droits fondamentaux.[9] Un des problèmes posé par l'affaire était de savoir si l'option laissée au Royaume-Uni par le règlement entrait dans le cadre de la mise en œuvre du droit de l'Union et était donc soumise au respect de la Charte. La réponse de la Cour est sans équivoque : « Ces éléments confortent l'interprétation selon laquelle le pouvoir d'appréciation conféré aux États membres par l'article 3, paragraphe 2, du règlement n° 343/2003 fait partie des mécanismes de détermination de l'État membre responsable d'une demande d'asile prévus par ledit règlement et, dès lors, ne constitue qu'un élément du système européen commun d'asile. Partant, un État membre qui exerce ce pouvoir d'appréciation doit être considéré comme mettant en œuvre le droit de l'Union au sens de l'article 51, paragraphe 1, de la charte ». Le Royaume-Uni était donc dans l'obligation d'examiner lui-même la demande d'asile pour des raisons tirées du respect de l'article 4 de la Charte. Le pouvoir d'appréciation laissé aux États membres par un acte de l'Union entre bien dans le cadre de la mise en œuvre du droit de l'Union.

Ceci n'implique pas que la Cour ait une vision extensive de la mise en œuvre. Cette dernière notion doit être conciliée avec l'étendue de la préemption exercée par l'acte en cause. Ainsi, dans l'affaire C-483/09, était en cause une décision d'éloignement provisoire du domicile d'une victime de mauvais traitements de la part de son conjoint, alors même que la victime n'avait pas été entendue sur le prononcé de cette décision. Les conjoints ayant repris la vie commune au lendemain de la sentence, l'époux fut sanctionné pénalement pour avoir violé la décision d'éloignement. L'article 7 de la Charte consacrant le respect de la vie privée et familiale s'opposait-il à cette sanction alors même que les deux conjoints étaient d'accord pour reprendre la vie commune ? Le lien avec le droit de l'Union était la décision-cadre 2001/220 relative aux droits des victimes. La Cour constate que si la participation à la procédure relève de la décision-cadre, il n'en va pas de même du droit pénal

---

[8] Arrêt du 21 novembre 2011, aff. jointes C-411/10 et C-493/10.

[9] La Cour européenne des droits de l'homme avait non seulement condamné la Grèce dans une affaire similaire pour violation de l'article 3 de la Convention, mais également la Belgique pour avoir renvoyé le requérant en Grèce en application du règlement Dublin II, arrêt du 21 janvier 2011, requête n° 30696/09.

matériel et de la fixation des peines, ce qui exclut le recours à la Charte : « Enfin, il convient de constater que l'obligation, en tant que telle, de prononcer une mesure d'éloignement conformément au droit matériel en cause au principal ne relève pas du champ d'application de la décision-cadre et, par suite, elle ne saurait, en tout état de cause, être appréciée à la lumière des dispositions de la Charte des droits fondamentaux de l'Union européenne ».[10]

2. Si la Cour tire pleinement les conséquences de la jurisprudence Wachauf quant à la mise en œuvre du droit de l'Union, il en va de même en ce qui concerne la jurisprudence *ERT*. Lorsque l'État déroge au droit de l'Union, il doit le faire en conformité avec la Charte. Sur ce point encore, la Cour suit quant au champ d'application de la Charte la solution retenue en ce qui concerne les principes généraux du droit. On en trouve une première trace dans la jurisprudence *Sayn-Wittgenstein* lorsque la Cour indique que « L'ordre juridique de l'Union tend indéniablement à assurer le respect du principe d'égalité en tant que principe général du droit. Ce principe est également consacré à l'article 20 de la charte des droits fondamentaux. Il ne fait donc pas de doute que l'objectif de respecter le principe d'égalité est compatible avec le droit de l'Union ».[11] Une entrave à la libre circulation des personnes peut donc être justifiée pour des raisons tirées notamment du respect de la Charte. C'est le même raisonnement qui est tenu dans l'affaire *Malgozata Runevic-Wardyn* à propos du refus des autorités lituaniennes de respecter la graphie polonaise dans les actes d'état civil. Ce refus peut constituer une entrave à la liberté de circulation et de séjour d'une citoyenne de l'Union européenne qui a déjà exercé ces libertés. Pour apprécier la validité de cette entrave, il convient de prendre en considération tant l'article 7 de la Charte sur la vie privée et l'article 22 sur le respect de la diversité culturelle par la préservation de la langue invoquée par le gouvernement au titre de la protection de l'identité nationale. Aussi la Cour considère-t-elle que la balance d'intérêts entre ces deux droits doit être effectuée par le juge national : « S'il est établi que le refus de modification du nom de famille commun au couple de citoyens de l'Union en cause au principal provoque de sérieux inconvénients d'ordre administratif, professionnel et privé à leur égard et/ou à l'égard de leur famille, il appartiendra à la juridiction de renvoi de déterminer si un tel refus respecte un juste équilibre entre les intérêts en présence, à savoir, d'une part, le droit des requérants au principal au respect de leur vie privée et familiale ainsi que, d'autre part, la protec-

[10] Arrêt du 15 septembre 2011, *Magatte Geye*.

[11] Arrêt du 22 décembre 2010, aff. C-208/09.

tion légitime par l'État membre concerné de sa langue officielle nationale et de ses traditions ».[12]

B. De la prudence initiale face à une interprétation extensive à un retour à la théorie du champ d'application

1. Au-delà de l'application des jurisprudences *Wachauf* et *ERT*, existerait-il un troisième cas de figure qui irait au-delà de la mise en œuvre du droit de l'Union entendue strictement ? La Charte pourrait-elle être applicable dans tout le champ d'application du droit de l'Union au-delà des cas précités ? Il était difficile de donner une réponse définitive dans la mesure où la Cour faisait preuve d'une certaine prudence, compte tenu du texte même de la Charte lequel exprime la très forte réticence des États membres à l'encontre d'une extension du champ d'application de la Charte. Une démarche extensive aurait pu en effet conduire à soumettre à la Charte des situations qui relevaient essentiellement du droit interne et n'avaient qu'un lien ténu avec le droit de l'Union. Cela aurait été méconnaître le principe de subsidiarité mentionné dans le préambule de celle-ci et substituer la Charte aux protections offertes par le droit national et la Convention européenne des droits de l'homme. Dans l'arrêt *Dereci* qui met le point final aux doutes exprimés à propos des arrêts *Ruiz Zambrano*[13] et *Mc Carthy*,[14] la grande chambre de la Cour semble s'inspirer de ce principe lorsqu'elle rappelle au juge national que si l'affaire ne peut être jugée sous l'angle de la Charte, il lui revient d'appliquer la Convention européenne des droits de l'homme : « … les dispositions de la charte s'adressent … aux États membres uniquement lorsqu'ils mettent en œuvre le droit de l'Union … la charte n'étend pas le champ d'application du droit de l'Union au-delà des compétences de l'Union, ni ne crée aucune compétence ni aucune tâche nouvelle pour l'Union et ne modifie pas les compétences et les tâches définies dans les traités. Ainsi, la Cour est appelée à interpréter, à la lumière de la charte, le droit de l'Union dans les limites des compétences attribuées à celle-ci … si la juridiction de renvoi considère … que la situation des requérants au principal relève du droit de l'Union, elle devra examiner si le refus du droit de séjour de ces derniers porte atteinte au droit au respect de la vie privée et familiale prévu à l'article 7 de la charte. En revanche, si elle considère que ladite situation ne relève pas du champ d'application du droit de l'Union, elle devra faire un tel examen à la lumière de l'article 8, paragraphe 1, de la CEDH ».[15] Entre

---

12 Arrêt du 12 mai 2011, aff. C-391/09.

13 Arrêt du 8 mars 2011, aff. C-34/09.

14 Arrêt du 5 mai 2011, aff. C-434/09.

15 Arrêt du 15 novembre 2011, aff. C-256/11.

parenthèses, il est surprenant que la détermination du champ d'application du droit de l'Union soit laissée à l'appréciation des juridictions nationales. Mais, pour revenir à la question, ne pourrait-on dire cependant que, dès lors qu'il existe un lien substantiel avec le champ d'application, la Charte pourrait être invocable. C'est la situation actuelle pour la protection des données parce qu'elle est mentionnée tant dans la Charte que dans l'article 18 TFUE qui indique expressément que celle-ci joue dans le champ d'application du droit de l'Union.

2. Il est des cas dans lesquels la Cour a appliqué de manière extensive certains droits ancrés dans le traité. C'est le cas pour les discriminations fondées sur la nationalité et c'est aussi le cas pour la citoyenneté dans la jurisprudence *Ruiz Zambrano*. Mais il s'agissait d'hypothèses spécifiques qui visaient à protéger un élément central de l'Union européenne dont l'application ne devait pas être étendue au-delà de ces situations. Dans l'affaire *Dereci*, il apparaît clairement que l'objet de la Cour était moins de protéger les droits fondamentaux que la citoyenneté en elle-même : « En tant que ressortissants d'un État membre, les membres de la famille des requérants au principal jouissent du statut de citoyen de l'Union en vertu de l'article 20, paragraphe 1, TFUE et peuvent donc se prévaloir, y compris à l'égard de l'État membre dont ils ont la nationalité, des droits afférents à un tel statut (voir arrêt *McCarthy*, *supra*, point 48). Sur ce fondement, la Cour a jugé que l'article 20 TFUE s'oppose à des mesures nationales qui ont pour effet de priver les citoyens de l'Union de la jouissance effective de l'essentiel des droits conférés par ce statut (voir arrêt *Ruiz Zambrano*, *supra*, point 42) ». Cette considération ne s'étend pas à l'ensemble des droits. La doctrine a tenté de manière intéressante de soutenir que des violations manifestes des droits fondamentaux dans un État membre portaient atteinte à des éléments essentiels de la citoyenneté et ont appelé la Cour de justice à étendre sa jurisprudence au-delà de l'article 51 pour couvrir éventuellement des situations internes.[16] Mais il est peu probable qu'une telle évolution se dessine rapidement tant la Cour semble réservée à l'idée de toute incorporation de la Charte dans le droit national au-delà de ce que prévoient les traités.

On trouve trace de la réserve de la Cour dans l'arrêt *Iida* du 8 novembre 2012.[17] Il concerne la situation très spécifique d'un ressortissant d'un pays tiers qui séjournait légalement en Allemagne et aurait pu obtenir un permis de séjour de longue durée dans cet État au titre du

---

16 Von Bogdandy, Kottmann, Anpöhler, Dickchen, Hentrei et Smrkolj, « Reverse Solange, Protecting the essence of fundamental rights against EU Member States », *Common Market Law Review*, 2012, pp. 489-519.

17 Affaire C-40/11.

droit de l'Union. Il avait cependant retiré une demande faite à ce titre pour lui substituer une demande en qualité de membre de la famille d'un citoyen de l'Union. Mais son épouse et sa fille s'étaient établies en Autriche. En application du droit de l'Union, le requérant ne pouvait obtenir un titre de séjour que dans l'État où demeurait sa famille et non dans l'État d'origine de celle-ci. Le droit de l'Union n'était donc pas applicable en l'espèce, mais la situation n'était pas dépourvue de tout lien avec celui-ci. Or les dispositions allemandes relatives au droit de séjour d'un citoyen de l'Union invoquées par le requérant visaient bien à mettre en œuvre le droit de l'Union, mais, n'étant pas applicables en l'espèce, la situation de ce dernier ne présentait aucun lien de rattachement avec le droit de l'Union. La Cour n'exclut pas totalement l'application de la Charte lorsqu'existe un lien de rattachement, mais celui-ci doit être substantiel. À cet égard, elle reprend les termes de la jurisprudence *Annibaldi* :

> Afin de déterminer si le refus des autorités allemandes d'accorder à M. Iida la « carte de séjour de membre de la famille d'un citoyen de l'Union » relève de la mise en œuvre du droit de l'Union au sens de l'article 51 de la Charte, il y a lieu de vérifier, parmi d'autres éléments, si la réglementation nationale en cause a pour but de mettre en œuvre une disposition du droit de l'Union, le caractère de cette réglementation et si celle-ci poursuit des objectifs autres que ceux couverts par le droit de l'Union, même si elle est susceptible d'affecter indirectement ce dernier, ainsi que s'il existe une réglementation du droit de l'Union spécifique en la matière ou susceptible de l'affecter.[18]

Le simple fait qu'une réglementation nationale puisse indirectement affecter un particulier n'était donc pas suffisant pour entraîner l'application de la Charte.

3. Cependant l'arrêt Iida manifeste une certaine ouverture qui devait se concrétiser dans l'affaire *Akerberg Fransson*.[19] En l'espèce était en cause l'application du principe *non bis in idem* au cumul de sanctions administratives et pénales. Indépendamment du fond de l'affaire, la question essentielle était celle de l'application de la Charte à une situation dans laquelle le droit de l'Union se limitait à imposer à l'État « l'obligation de prendre toutes les mesures législatives et administratives propres à garantir la perception de l'intégralité de la TVA due sur son territoire et à lutter contre la fraude ». Le lien entre cette obligation et la nature des sanctions adoptées par l'État membre était-il suffisant

18 Arrêt du 18 décembre 1997, aff. C-309/96, points 21 à 23 cité dans les explications de la Charte ce que n'indique pas la Cour.

19 Arrêt du 26 février 2013, aff. C-617/10, rendu contre l'avis de la Commission et les Conclusions de l'Avocat général.

pour entraîner l'application de la Charte. Pour la Cour, la réponse est positive au prix d'une interprétation plus extensive qu'auparavant du champ d'application de la Charte en s'écartant de la formule restrictive du texte de l'article 51 pour promouvoir la référence au champ d'application du droit de l'Union et non plus à sa mise en œuvre.[20] S'appuyant sur les explications à l'article 51, la Cour estime qu'il ne peut exister de situation relevant du droit de l'Union dans laquelle la Charte ne saurait s'appliquer. Cet arrêt semble ainsi clore une période de self-restraint judiciaire et aligner sa jurisprudence sur la Charte sur celle qui prévalait lorsque les droits fondamentaux étaient protégés au titre de principes généraux du droit. La difficulté réside maintenant dans la définition du champ d'application du droit de l'Union et comme il a été signalé dans l'affaire *Iida* de l'étroitesse du lien entre la situation en cause et le droit de l'Union. Il ne suffit qu'existe une règle de droit de

---

20 La solution retenue dans l'arrêt *Fransson* n'est pas inédite, elle apparaissait déjà dans l'arrêt *Vinkov* du 7 juin 2012, C-27/11 : « Dès lors, dans le cadre d'un renvoi préjudiciel au titre de l'article 267 TFUE, lorsqu'une réglementation nationale entre dans le champ d'application du droit de l'Union, la Cour doit fournir tous les éléments d'interprétation nécessaires à l'appréciation par la juridiction nationale de la conformité de cette réglementation avec les droits fondamentaux, tels qu'ils résultent en particulier de la Charte ». Cependant, dans l'affaire *Fransson*, la Cour développe une position de principe argumentée : En effet, il résulte, en substance, de la jurisprudence constante de la Cour que les droits fondamentaux garantis dans l'ordre juridique de l'Union ont vocation à être appliqués dans toutes les situations régies par le droit de l'Union, mais pas en dehors de telles situations. C'est dans cette mesure que la Cour a déjà rappelé qu'elle ne peut apprécier, au regard de la Charte, une réglementation nationale qui ne se situe pas dans le cadre du droit de l'Union. En revanche, dès lors qu'une telle réglementation entre dans le champ d'application de ce droit, la Cour, saisie à titre préjudiciel, doit fournir tous les éléments d'interprétation nécessaires à l'appréciation, par la juridiction nationale, de la conformité de cette réglementation avec les droits fondamentaux dont elle assure le respect … Cette définition du champ d'application des droits fondamentaux de l'Union est corroborée par les explications relatives à l'article 51 de la Charte, lesquelles, conformément à l'article 6, paragraphe 1, troisième alinéa, TUE et à l'article 52, paragraphe 7, de la Charte, doivent être prises en considération en vue de son interprétation (voir, en ce sens, arrêt du 22 décembre 2010, *DEB*, C-279/09, *Rec.* p. I-13849, point 32). Selon lesdites explications, l'obligation de respecter les droits fondamentaux définis dans le cadre de l'Union ne s'impose aux États membres que lorsqu'ils agissent dans le champ d'application du droit de l'Union ». Les droits fondamentaux garantis par la Charte devant, par conséquent, être respectés lorsqu'une réglementation nationale entre dans le champ d'application du droit de l'Union, il ne saurait exister de cas de figure qui relèvent ainsi du droit de l'Union sans que lesdits droits fondamentaux trouvent à s'appliquer. L'applicabilité du droit de l'Union implique celle des droits fondamentaux garantis par la Charte. Lorsque, en revanche, une situation juridique ne relève pas du champ d'application du droit de l'Union, la Cour n'est pas compétente pour en connaître et les dispositions éventuellement invoquées de la Charte ne sauraient, à elles seules, fonder cette compétence (voir, en ce sens, ordonnance du 12 juillet 2012, *Currà e.a.*, C-466/11, non encore publiée au Recueil, point 26).

l'Union, mais il faut également que cette règle soit directement relevante dans le cas en question. D'ailleurs, la Cour a fréquemment relevé par ordonnance l'absence de lien entre le droit de l'Union et le droit en cause évitant une application pas trop extensive de la Charte (voir par exemple, ordonnances du 14 décembre 2011 dans les affaires C-434/11, C-462/11 et C-484/11).

4. Dans certains cas spécifiques, la Cour semblait déjà avoir une vision large de la mise en œuvre. Ainsi, dans l'affaire DEB, en ce qui concerne le droit à un recours effectif, elle reproduit sa jurisprudence classique en y ajoutant une référence à la Charte établissant un lien entre la mise en œuvre par les États membres du droit de l'Union et leur obligation d'assurer l'application effective de celui-ci. Le raisonnement de la Cour se fait en trois étapes. Tout d'abord, le principe d'effectivité impose un accès effectif à la justice afin de permettre la sauvegarde des droits que les justiciables tirent du droit de l'Union. Ce principe est un principe général du droit consacré par une longue jurisprudence. Mais, après l'entrée en vigueur du traité de Lisbonne, il convient de tenir compte de la Charte et notamment de son article 47 qui consacre le droit à une protection juridictionnelle effective ainsi que le droit à une aide juridictionnelle si celle-ci est nécessaire à une protection effective. Certes la Cour faisait référence à l'article 51 qui limite le champ d'application de la Charte à la mise en œuvre par les États membres, mais, au fond, elle utilisait le champ d'application d'un principe général du droit pour l'appliquer à la Charte dans un cas où l'on n'est pas en présence d'une mise en œuvre directe d'une norme de l'Union, mais plus simplement d'une application d'une norme nationale générale à un litige qui porte sur le droit de l'Union. Ceci fait, elle utilise le droit à l'aide judiciaire contenu dans la Charte alors que celui-ci ne résultait pas à l'évidence du principe général. Elle conclut ainsi : « Eu égard à ces éléments, il convient de reformuler la question posée en ce sens qu'elle porte sur l'interprétation du principe de protection juridictionnelle effective, tel que consacré par l'article 47 de la charte, afin de vérifier si, dans le contexte d'une procédure d'action en responsabilité de l'État introduite au titre du droit de l'Union, cette disposition s'oppose à ce qu'une réglementation nationale subordonne l'exercice de l'action en justice au paiement d'une avance sur frais et prévoie que l'aide judiciaire ne peut pas être accordée à une personne morale alors même que cette dernière n'est pas en mesure de faire cette avance ».[21] Les États membres ne s'attendaient vraisemblablement pas à une telle extension du concept de mise en œuvre et à ce jeu entre les principes généraux et la Charte. Mais la question touchait un domaine très sen-

[21] Arrêt du 22 décembre 2010, *DEB*, aff. C-279/09.

sible, celui de la protection juridictionnelle des particuliers qui est une des conditions indispensables de la mise en œuvre correcte du droit de l'Union.

En conclusion, sur ce point, la Cour de justice a adopté dans un premier temps une démarche prudente et respectueuse de la lettre des traités, mais elle n'a pu échapper à l'exigence de maintenir une cohérence entre sa jurisprudence antérieure au traité de Lisbonne sur les principes généraux du droit et celle relative à l'article 51 de la Charte. Il n'existait aucune raison de traiter différemment le champ d'application d'un droit fondamental selon qu'il résultait d'un principe général du droit ou de la Charte. Il n'était pas possible non plus de soutenir que la Charte avait réduit le champ d'application des droits fondamentaux dans l'Union.

2. L'application horizontale de la Charte

1. La question de l'application des dispositions relatives aux droits fondamentaux dans le cadre de litiges entre personnes privées n'est pas spécifique au droit de l'Union et la réponse varie selon les interprétations données par les cours constitutionnelles nationales aux différentes constitutions. La Cour constitutionnelle allemande a admis dès 1958 un effet horizontal indirect dans la célèbre affaire *Lüth/Harland*.[22] Les constitutions espagnole et portugaise prévoient que les droits fondamentaux doivent être également appliqués aux personnes privées. La Cour européenne des droits de l'homme a également admis un effet horizontal indirect.[23] Il n'est donc pas surprenant que la question puisse être également posée en ce qui concerne la Charte.[24] Elle doit être examinée en tenant compte du fait que la Charte ne s'impose aux États que dans la mise en œuvre du droit de l'Union ce qui réduit les possibilités d'effet horizontal. La Charte ne pourra donc être invoquée dans un litige entre particuliers sans aucune connexion avec le droit de l'Union.

A. Tous les droits ne sont pas susceptibles de produire un effet horizontal

1. Tous les droits contenus dans la Charte ne sont pas soumis au même régime. Ainsi l'article 24 paraît répondre lui-même à la question lorsqu'il indique que l'intérêt supérieur de l'enfant doit être pris en

22 Arrêt du 15 janvier 1958, BverfGE t. 7, pp. 198-230.

23 Arrêt du 26 mars 1985, *X et Y c. Pays-Bas*.

24 Voir par exemple, Danwitz et Paraschas, « A fresh start for the Charter, Fundamental questions on the application of the Charter », *Fordham International Law Journal*, 2012, à paraître.

compte dans tous les actes relatifs aux enfants « qu'ils soient accomplis par des autorités publiques ou des institutions privées ». À l'inverse, d'autres droits ne semblent pas présenter les conditions requises de précision et d'inconditionnalité pour produire un effet direct. Certains droits sociaux font référence à des mesures de mise en œuvre nationales. Il est donc nécessaire de vérifier au cas par cas si leur précision est telle qu'ils peuvent être invoqués en l'absence de toute mesure de mise en œuvre, faute de quoi la Cour de justice se substituerait au législateur. Ainsi, l'article 33 sur la conciliation de la vie privée et professionnelle crée un droit au congé de maternité payé, mais il ne fixe pas les conditions de mise en œuvre. Il peut être difficile à la Cour, en l'absence de législation de l'Union, de se prononcer sur les modalités de ce droit tant qu'elles ne remettent pas en cause l'existence du droit lui-même. C'est le cas plus généralement des principes contenus dans la Charte puisque, selon l'article 52, paragraphe 5, les principes doivent faire l'objet d'une mise en œuvre au niveau de l'Union et ne peuvent être invoqués devant le juge que pour le contrôle de légalité des actes de mise en œuvre. Par contre, la prohibition de la discrimination sur la base de l'âge ou du sexe dans le cadre des conditions de travail est suffisamment précise et inconditionnelle pour pouvoir produire un effet horizontal comme l'indiquent les arrêts *Mangold*[25] et *Kücükdeveci*[26] pour l'âge ou l'arrêt *Defrenne II*[27] pour les conditions de travail.

3. Quelles sont les indications que l'on peut trouver dans la Charte à cet égard ? Il ne fait aucun doute que les droits fondamentaux peuvent produire un effet direct vertical en ce sens qu'ils peuvent être invoqués devant un juge national à l'encontre d'un acte national mettant en œuvre le droit de l'Union. S'agissant de l'effet horizontal, une lecture stricte du texte de la Charte semble l'exclure puisque l'article 51, paragraphe 1, précise que la Charte s'adresse aux institutions, organes et organismes de l'Union ainsi qu'aux États membres. Les personnes privées sont donc exclues. Comme le note l'avocat général, Mme Verica Trstenjak, cette interprétation est confirmée par le fait que les particuliers n'ont pas à leur disposition la réserve légale prévue pour les limitations aux droits fondamentaux puisque les droits fondamentaux ne peuvent être limités que par la loi.[28] Ce dernier argument n'est guère convainquant. Outre le fait qu'il n'a jamais empêché les juridictions constitutionnelles de reconnaître un effet horizontal, la question n'est pas celle de la limitation des droits, mais celle de la violation de la Charte par un

25 Arrêt du 22 novembre 2005, aff. C-144/04.

26 Arrêt du 19 janvier 2010, aff. C-555/07.

27 Arrêt du 8 avril 1976, aff. 43/75.

28 Conclusions sous Dominguez, aff. C-282/10.

particulier au détriment d'un autre particulier. Dans cette affaire était en cause le droit au congé payé annuel dans un litige entre un salarié et son employeur. Si l'avocat général a examiné de manière détaillée la question de l'effet horizontal du droit au congé payé, soit en tant que droit garanti par la Charte, soit en tant que principe général du droit, la Cour a soigneusement évité de traiter le problème et a limité son examen au problème de l'effet direct de la directive.[29] Elle ne pourra le faire indéfiniment puisque la Cour de cassation française l'a saisie directement de la question.[30]

B. Une question qui reste encore ouverte

1. En fait, les auteurs de la Charte ont laissé la question ouverte et la rédaction de l'article 51 n'avait pas pour objet d'exclure tout effet horizontal. Mais, surtout, doit-on considérer que, bien que la Charte ait la même valeur que les traités, ses dispositions doivent avoir un régime différent de celle des traités en ce qui concerne l'effet horizontal ? De la même manière, doit-on accorder un traitement différent aux droits garantis par la Charte et aux principes généraux du droit dans la mesure où certains principes généraux du droit produiraient un effet horizontal ? Dès lors qu'un principe général du droit serait repris dans la

---

29 Arrêt du 24 janvier 2012.

30 11 avril 2012, arrêt n° 1040 FS-P+B+R dans laquelle la Cour de cassation semble prendre clairement position en faveur de l'effet horizontal : « Attendu qu'il est de jurisprudence constante que les droits fondamentaux de l'Union européenne peuvent être invoqués dans un litige entre particuliers aux fins de vérifier le respect par les institutions de l'Union et les États membres, lorsqu'ils mettent en œuvre le droit de l'Union, de ces mêmes droits fondamentaux ; que les articles 51 et 52 de la Charte ne comportent aucune limitation de l'invocation des dispositions de la Charte, que celles-ci contiennent des principes ou des droits, aux litiges de nature horizontale, pas plus que les Explications ad article 51 et ad article 52, lesquelles sont dûment prises en considération par les juridictions de l'Union et des États membres en application de l'article 52 §7 de la Charte ; … qu'aux termes de l'article 53 de la Charte, aucune disposition de la Charte ne doit être interprétée comme limitant ou portant atteinte aux droits de l'homme et aux libertés fondamentales reconnus notamment par la Convention européenne de sauvegarde des droits de l'Homme et des libertés fondamentales ; Attendu qu'il résulte de la jurisprudence de la Cour de justice que les principes généraux du droit tels que précisés par une directive de l'Union européenne peuvent être invoqués dans un litige entre particuliers (CJCE, 22 novembre 2005, *Mangold*, aff. C-144/04 ; CJUE, 19 janvier 2010, *Kücükdeveci*, aff. C-555/07) ; … RENVOIE à la Cour de justice de l'Union européenne les questions suivantes : 1/ le droit fondamental relatif à l'information et à la consultation des travailleurs, reconnu par l'article 27 de la Charte des droits fondamentaux de l'Union européenne, tel que précisé par les dispositions de la Directive 2002/14/CE du Parlement européen et du Conseil, du 11 mars 2002, établissant un cadre général relatif à l'information et à la consultation des travailleurs dans la Communauté européenne, peut-il être invoqué dans un litige entre particuliers aux fins de vérifier la conformité d'une mesure nationale de transposition de la directive ? »

Charte, devrait-on être contraint de continuer à le traiter en qualité de principe général lorsqu'une question relative à l'effet direct est en cause afin de préserver l'effet horizontal ? La cohérence du système juridique de l'Union exigerait qu'une démarche unique soit adoptée dans tous ces cas.

2. La Cour a admis sans difficulté en matière de droit social que la Charte pouvait être invoquée dans les rapports entre un particulier et une organisation syndicale dotée de prérogatives de puissance publique.[31] En outre, sans qu'il s'agisse d'un effet horizontal au sens propre du terme, la Charte peut être invoquée lorsqu'il s'agit de l'interprétation d'un acte de l'Union dans des relations entre particuliers et les règles de l'interprétation conforme trouvent application dans ce cadre. Il semble également possible d'invoquer la Charte afin de justifier une entrave à une liberté fondamentale comme dans l'affaire *Viking* où le droit de grève était utilisé pour justifier une atteinte à la liberté d'établissement.[32]

3. Il est également intéressant de noter que dans l'affaire *Scarlett extended*, la Cour fait référence à la Charte dans un litige qui oppose cette société à la Société des auteurs compositeurs belges (Sabam), qui est une société coopérative de droit privé, tout en faisant également référence au droit dérivé.[33] Mais la prudence de la Cour qui s'est refusée, dans l'arrêt *Dominguez*, à interpréter l'article 51 quant à l'effet horizontal, laisse la question ouverte pour le moment. La logique du droit de l'Union devrait l'amener à harmoniser sur ce point sa vision avec celle qu'elle a patiemment construite dans d'autres domaines, notamment en matière de discrimination. Ceci n'implique pas une réponse uniforme sur l'effet direct et, dans tous les cas, l'analyse doit être menée droit par droit. Dans ce cas, la Cour, à l'instar de certaines juridictions nationales, serait amenée à faire jouer la protection des droits fondamentaux pour venir à l'aide d'une partie plus faible dans un litige entre particuliers. Certes, cette arme doit être maniée avec prudence. En l'absence de mesures de mise en œuvre, la réponse de la Cour anticipe une éventuelle action législative et sa réponse enferme le législateur dans un corset qui méconnaît sa capacité d'action. Mais cette éventuelle préemption législative n'a pas empêché la Cour de développer sa jurisprudence dans le domaine du marché intérieur ou dans celui des soins de santé.

---

[31] Voir les espèces citées *supra*, note 7.

[32] Arrêt du 11 décembre 2007, aff. C-438/05.

[33] Arrêt du 24 novembre 2011, aff. C-70/10.

Conclusion

L'utilisation de la Charte par la Cour n'en est qu'à ses débuts et la prudence de la Cour est compréhensible compte tenu des craintes manifestées par les États membres et traduites, tant dans la Charte elle-même que dans l'article 6 du TUE. Cependant, il convient de noter que cette prudence n'a pas interdit à la Cour de donner du protocole britannique et polonais sur la Charte l'interprétation que commandait la raison.[34] Mais, par nature, la démarche de la Cour ne peut être que casuistique dans un domaine où il n'est pas toujours possible de prévoir à long terme les conséquences d'une décision de principe. Il convient aussi de ne pas entretenir les illusions de ceux qui ont vu dans la Charte un moyen d'assurer une protection des droits fondamentaux au-delà même du champ d'application du droit de l'Union.[35] Dans une Union où les États respectent les valeurs inscrites à l'article 2 du TUE, la protection des droits fondamentaux dans le cadre du domaine d'application du droit national est assurée par les juridictions nationales, auxquelles la Cour ne saurait se substituer pas plus qu'elle ne saurait prendre à cet égard la place de la Cour européenne des droits de l'homme. Aussi, pour être encore incertaines, les limites du champ d'application de la

---

34 Arrêt du 21 novembre 2011, *N.S.*, aff. jointes C-411/10 et C-493/10 : « Il ressort du libellé de cette disposition que, comme l'a relevé Mme l'avocat général notamment aux points 169 et 170 de ses conclusions dans l'affaire C-411/10, le protocole n° 30 ne remet pas en question l'applicabilité de la charte au Royaume-Uni ou en Pologne, ce qui est conforté par les considérants dudit protocole. Ainsi, selon le troisième considérant du protocole (n° 30), l'article 6 TUE dispose que la charte doit être appliquée et interprétée par les juridictions de la République de Pologne et du Royaume-Uni en stricte conformité avec les explications visées à cet article. Par ailleurs, selon le sixième considérant dudit protocole, la charte réaffirme les droits, les libertés et les principes reconnus dans l'Union et les rend plus visibles, sans toutefois créer de nouveaux droits ou principes. Dans ces conditions, l'article 1er, paragraphe 1, du protocole (n° 30) explicite l'article 51 de la charte, relatif au champ d'application de cette dernière, et n'a pas pour objet d'exonérer la République de Pologne et le Royaume-Uni de l'obligation de respecter les dispositions de la charte, ni d'empêcher une juridiction de l'un de ces États membres de veiller au respect de ces dispositions ».

35 Ainsi, après avoir développé au début de son mandat, une vision extrêmement large, la vice-présidente de la Commission, madame Viviane Reding adopte aujourd'hui une conception plus orthodoxe : « *Whether we choose a broader or a narrower interpretation of Article 51 of the Charter, this does not change the principle : the Charter first and foremost applies to the EU institutions and to their actions. It does not replace national constitutions, but merely complements them. Citizens thus have to get used to the fact that they are faced with a two-layered system of fundamental rights protection : the national system of fundamental rights that normally protects them and the EU Charter of Fundamental Rights that comes into operation only when an action by an EU institution is involved* ». Discours à l'ouverture du congrès de la FIDE en 2012.

Charte existent. Elles seront progressivement précisées au fil des cas examinés à Luxembourg.

La Cour de justice et les sources externes du droit de l'Union européenne

Les liaisons équivoques

Rostane MEHDI

Professeur à l'Université d'Aix-Marseille ; Centre d'étude de recherches internationales et communautaires (CERIC/UMR « Droit comparé – Droit international – Droit européen » 7318)

On sait la place que l'étude du droit des relations extérieures de l'Union occupe dans l'œuvre de Paul Demaret.[1] Aussi est-ce dans ce registre que j'inscrirai ma contribution à l'hommage amical qui lui est ici rendu.

Est-il encore besoin de souligner que l'Union n'est pas coupée du contexte international dans lequel elle se développe ? Elle nourrit sans ambages l'intention d'y assumer le rôle d'un acteur pesant effectivement sur les destinées du monde et entendant ainsi être active sur les dossiers globaux qui engagent le devenir de celui-ci. Partie aux accords de l'OMC, admise à participer aux travaux de l'Organisation des Nations unies,[2] l'Union affiche également une remarquable « ambition environnementale et le souhait d'affirmer son leadership dans la construction d'un régime international sur le changement climatique ».[3] Il serait sans doute laborieux et inutilement dispendieux des pages qui

1 Demaret, P. (ed.), *Relations extérieures de la Communauté européenne et marché intérieur : aspects juridiques et fonctionnels*, Collège d'Europe, n° 45, 1986, p. 233 ; Cameron, J., Demaret, P. & Geradin, D. (eds.), *Trade and environment : the search for balance*, London, Cameron May, 1995, 2 vol.

2 Résolution adoptée par l'Assemblée générale des Nations unies, 65/276, *Participation de l'Union européenne aux travaux de l'Organisation des Nations unies*, 10 mai 2011.

3 Maljean-Dubois, S. & Wemaëre, M., *La diplomatie climatique, Les enjeux d'un régime international du climat*, Paris, Pedone, 2010, p. 261.

nous sont imparties d'égrener les nombreux domaines dans lesquels l'Union déploie son action externe.[4]

Je me contenterai de rappeler, à ce stade, que l'Union démontre une capacité à mobiliser le droit international qui n'est guère différente de celle des États eux-mêmes. L'existence d'un sentiment d'obligation assez commun chez l'ensemble des sujets, conduit ceux-ci à se référer au droit international en tant que besoin. À l'instar des États, l'Union en tient dûment compte pour définir ses positions. Elle le fait alternativement ou cumulativement pour s'y conformer, s'y soustraire, se défendre d'éventuelles accusations de manquements ou encore suggérer une adaptation des règles existantes voire l'adoption de règles nouvelles. En ce sens, le droit international apparaît à la fois comme un instrument et un obstacle de la politique étrangère.[5] Il est conçu comme un vecteur utile lorsque son application scrupuleuse permet de protéger les intérêts essentiels de l'Union qui veillera naturellement à en renforcer l'autorité y compris d'ailleurs en facilitant l'intégration des normes dont il est porteur dans son ordre juridique. À l'inverse, perçu comme une menace dès lors que ses prescriptions vont (ou semblent aller) à l'encontre des intérêts fondamentaux de l'Union, le droit international peut susciter chez cette dernière une attitude de repli.

M'abstenant de brosser un tableau d'ensemble, je m'en tiendrai donc à l'étude du rôle déterminant que la Cour a joué dans la définition des principes devant présider aux relations entre l'ordre juridique de l'Union (dont on sait qu'elle a élevé les murs porteurs) et l'ordre juridique international. Pour connaître des relations extérieures de la Communauté,[6] la Cour devait s'adosser à de solides bases de compétences.[7] Elle a ainsi dynamisé au moyen d'une lecture constructive de ses propres prérogatives la procédure consultative. La Cour a ainsi considéré qu'en se référant à un « accord », l'Article 228 § 1 CEE (devenu 300 § 6 CE puis 218 § 11 TFUE) entendait utiliser ce terme dans un sens général, pour désigner tout engagement pris par des sujets de droit

4 Fenet, A. (dir.), *Droit des relations extérieures de l'Union européenne*, Litec, LexisNexis, 2006, p. 396.

5 Selon la formule de M. Virally, « Panorama du droit international contemporain », *Recueil des Cours de l'Academie de Droit International*, 1983, 183, p. 30.

6 Que l'on me pardonne cette expression surannée mais j'évoque ici un temps où l'Union était encore dans les limbes.

7 Boulouis, J., « La jurisprudence de la Cour de justice des Communautés européennes relative aux relations extérieures des Communautés », *Recueil des Cours de l'Academie de Droit International*, vol. 160, 1978, p. 344.

international et ayant force obligatoire.[8] Dans le fil de son avis 1/75,[9] elle s'en est toujours tenue à une perception large et dénuée de tout formalisme. De même, elle a considéré que la demande d'avis pouvait, au-delà de la compatibilité de l'accord envisagé avec le traité, porter également sur le choix de la base juridique de l'acte de conclusion.[10] Jouant d'une ambiguïté mise en évidence par la doctrine,[11] le Conseil opérait une distinction entre, d'une part, l'accord proprement dit, acte établissant des relations entre sujets du droit international et définissant des engagements susceptibles d'être incompatibles avec le traité, et, d'autre part, la décision interne par laquelle la Communauté achève la phase de conclusion. Pour le Conseil seul l'accord *stricto sensu* aurait été, par son objet, de nature à relever de la procédure de l'Article 300, § 6, CE (218 § 11 TFUE). Relevant d'une autre logique, le choix de la base juridique de l'acte de conclusion ne pouvait être accessible qu'à un recours en annulation. Une éventuelle censure ne mettrait pas en péril les relations extérieures de la Communauté, dans la mesure où les institutions devraient, comme le leur commande l'Article 233 CE (266 TFUE), adopter une décision fondée sur les dispositions appropriées, tandis que la Cour pourrait faire application, par analogie, de l'Article 231 alinéa 2 CE (264 TFUE). En refusant de souscrire à une analyse aussi byzantine, la Cour a confirmé une vision compréhensive de sa compétence consultative. Ses avis peuvent être, en effet, recueillis sur « toute question susceptible d'être soumise à l'appréciation judiciaire pour autant que ces questions seraient de nature à provoquer des doutes quant à la validité matérielle et formelle de l'accord au regard du traité ».[12]

Par ailleurs la Cour a apporté une réponse positive à la question, longtemps controversée, de savoir si elle pouvait connaître des relations extérieures à d'autres titres. Aussi, a-t-elle accepté, non sans risque, d'exercer un contrôle *a posteriori* (quoiqu'indirect) sur la conformité des accords externes (*lato sensu*) avec les exigences de l'ordre juridique de l'Union. On voit ainsi se dessiner les contours d'une cosmogonie juridique. Le juge de Luxembourg est porteur d'une vision de l'ordre juridique dont il doit assurer l'intégrité. Il est à la fois un passeur du

---

8 Avis du 24 mars 1995, 2/92, Compétence de la Communauté ou de l'une de ses institutions pour participer à la troisième décision révisée du Conseil de l'OCDE relative au traitement national, *Rec.* p. I-521.

9 CJCE, avis du 11 novembre 1975, aff. 1/75, *Rec.* p. 1355.

10 *Ibid.*

11 Sur ce point voir Rideau, J., « L'article 228 », in V. Constantinesco, R. Kovar, D. Simon (ed.), *Traité instituant la CEE. Commentaire article par article*, Paris, Economica, 1992.

12 Avis du 15 novembre 1994, aff. 1/94, *Rec.* p. I-5267.

droit international et le protecteur d'un ordre juridique de l'Union que menaceraient des normes externes éventuellement corruptrices. Aux figures de Jupiter, Hercule et Hermès,[13] de la célèbre trilogie ostienne, sans doute convient-il d'ajouter celle de Janus. En ce sens, le juge de Luxembourg s'est attaché à assurer la perméabilité de l'ordre juridique de l'Union aux impératifs du droit international, à penser des formes maîtrisées d'invocabilité de celui-ci (1) tout en œuvrant à une « dualisation » implicite des rapports de systèmes (2). En cela, il a tissé entre ceux-ci des liaisons que je qualifierais, faute de mieux, d'équivoques.

1. La perméabilité de l'ordre juridique de l'Union au droit international

Sujet dérivé, l'Union européenne se fond dans un environnement juridique à la création duquel elle n'a pas initialement contribué mais qui s'impose à elle.[14] Son action, autant que celle des États membres (du moins lorsque l'on situe dans le champ d'influence du droit de l'Union) est soumise au droit international pris dans toutes ses dimensions. La jurisprudence de la Cour a clarifié les modalités d'insertion et d'invocabilité des normes de droit international spécial et général dans le système des sources du droit de l'Union.

A. Les normes internationales sources d'obligations pour l'Union et ses États membres

On déduit généralement de l'Article 216, paragraphe 2, TFUE que lorsqu'ils sont régulièrement conclus, les accords constituent, dès leur entrée en vigueur, des normes que les institutions et les États membres doivent respecter.[15] La Cour a, du reste, développé une jurisprudence visant à renforcer la prégnance des engagements internationaux puisqu'elle admet que l'Union peut être liée par des règles conventionnelles auxquelles elle a souscrit ou pour lesquelles elle s'est substituée à ses États par l'effet d'un transfert intégral de compétences.[16]

Le droit de l'Union postule, à cet égard, une forme de monisme sans doute tempéré. Il est vrai qu'il n'existe, en ce domaine, que peu de modèles purs et parfaits. L'acte de conclusion sans lequel l'engagement

---

13 Voir en ce sens, Ost, F., « Jupiter, Hercule, Hermès : trois modèles du juge », in F. Ost, *Dire le droit, faire justice*, Bruxelles, Bruylant, 2007, pp. 32-60.

14 Fenet, *supra*, note 4, p. 117.

15 Sur l'ensemble de cette question, Neframi, E., « Accords internationaux – Statut des accords internationaux dans l'ordre juridique de l'UE », *JurisClasseur Europe Traité*, Fasc. 192-2, 2011.

16 CJCE, 15 décembre 1971, *International fruit company*, aff. jointes 51/71 à 54/71, *Rec.* p. 1107.

ne peut déployer effectivement la plénitude de ses effets, sur un plan interne, n'a pas pour conséquence d'en transformer la nature. Conservant son essence, l'accord s'impose aux institutions et aux États en sa qualité de norme internationale qui n'a nullement besoin d'être « reçue » pour être obligatoire. Dit autrement, les obligations posées par un traité ou une convention s'enracinent matériellement dans un terreau exclusivement international. En revanche, si l'accord est classiquement assimilé, par la Cour, à un acte des institutions ce n'est qu'aux fins de fonder la compétence de contrôle qu'elle peut être amenée à exercer lorsqu'elle est saisie d'un renvoi préjudiciel ou d'un recours contentieux. Pour autant, il est difficile de ne pas déceler dans le fait pour le juge d'accorder à l'acte de conclusion une telle densité juridique l'indice de sa volonté de donner parfois prise à un contrôle permettant, le cas échéant, de préserver efficacement l'intégrité des fondements mêmes du droit de l'Union (*infra*).

Les accords conclus par l'Union (seule ou avec ses États membres)[17] s'insèrent dans son ordre juridique à un rang inférieur à celui du droit primaire (auquel sont assimilés les principes généraux du droit) mais leur assurant une prévalence sur les actes de droit dérivé. Dans cette perspective, et sous réserve d'en admettre l'invocabilité, le juge appréhendera ces accords comme des paramètres de légalité, c'est-à-dire des normes étalonnant la rectitude juridique des actes déférés à son examen. Sur cette base, la Cour ou le Tribunal peuvent accueillir une action visant à contrôler directement ou par la voie de l'exception[18] la validité d'un acte ou d'un comportement imputable aux institutions (recours en annulation,[19] en carence[20] ou en indemnité) ou aux autorités nationales. Ainsi, lorsqu'ils manquent aux obligations résultant pour eux d'engagements liant l'Union et ses États membres, ceux-ci s'exposent à un risque contentieux polymorphe.[21] On relève, sur ce point, que la Cour n'a pas hésité à constater le manquement de la France aux dispositions d'un accord mixte (la Convention de Barcelone pour la protection de la mer

---

17 Neframi explicite les conditions d'affirmation du statut européen des accords mixtes dans l'ordre juridique de l'Union, *supra*, note 15, par. 17 et s.

18 La Cour s'est reconnue compétente pour statuer à titre préjudiciel sur l'interprétation des accords conclus par la Communauté, cela afin d'en garantir l'application uniforme dans l'ordre juridique communautaire (CJCE, 30 avril 1974, *Haegeman*, aff. 181/73, *Rec.* p. 00449).

19 CJCE, 10 mars 1992, *NMB c. Commission*, aff. C-188/88, *Rec.* p. I-1689.

20 Trib. UE, 6 septembre 2011, *M. Mugraby c. Conseil et Commission*, aff. T-292/09, non encore publié.

21 Ils s'exposent non seulement à un recours en constatation de manquement mais aussi à un recours devant les tribunaux internes aux fins de faire établir l'illégalité de leurs actes et en réparer les conséquences éventuellement dommageables.

méditerranée contre la pollution) alors même que les rejets en cause n'avaient pas fait l'objet d'une réglementation communautaire spécifique mais que cette question s'inscrivait dans un « domaine largement couvert par le droit communautaire ».[22]

Les compétences de l'Union doivent donc être exercées dans le respect du droit international[23] y compris lorsque celui-ci est de nature coutumière.[24] C'est ainsi que la Cour a jugé, par exemple, que « les règles du droit coutumier international portant sur la cessation et la suspension des relations conventionnelles en raison d'un changement fondamental de circonstances lient les institutions de la Communauté et font partie de l'ordre juridique communautaire ». Saisie d'un recours visant à faire établir l'irrégularité des conditions d'extinction de l'accord liant la Communauté à la Yougoslavie, elle a indiqué que pour être légales les mesures prises par le Conseil devaient respecter les deux conditions cumulatives formulées par le droit international coutumier tel que codifié par la Convention de Vienne. Elle a, de la même manière, admis l'opposabilité aux institutions du principe de droit coutumier international selon lequel chaque État dispose d'une souveraineté complète et exclusive sur son propre espace aérien.[25]

B. Une invocabilité à géométrie variable

La Cour a développé une conception de l'invocabilité des accords internationaux qui dépend de conditions plus restrictives que celles communément exigées. Elle assume ici le rôle d'un « gate-keeper »[26] ne reconnaissant aux sources externes qu'une invocabilité à éclipse c'est-à-dire variant en fonction de l'idée qu'elle se fait de la défense des intérêts de l'Union.

Certes, une règle posée par une convention internationale peut produire des effets directs lorsqu'« eu égard à ses termes ainsi qu'à l'objet et à la nature de l'accord, elle comporte une obligation claire et précise, qui n'est subordonnée, dans son exécution et ses effets, à l'intervention

---

22 CJCE, 7 octobre 2004, *Commission c. République française* (étang de Berre), aff. C-239/03, *Rec.* p. I-09325.

23 CJCE, 24 novembre 1992, *Poulsen et Diva navigation*, aff. C-286/90, *Rec.*, p. I-6019, pt. 19.

24 CJCE, 16 juin 1998, *A. Racke GmbH & Co. c/ Hauptzollamt Mainz*, aff. C-162/96, *Rec.* p. I-3655.

25 CJUE, 21 décembre 2011, *Air transport association of America et autres*, aff. C-366/10, non encore publié ; Simon, D., « Droit international conventionnel et coutumier : l'invocabilité au cœur de la lecture juridictionnelle des rapports de systèmes (à propos de l'arrêt Air Transport) », *Europe*, mars 2012, étude 3.

26 Selon l'expression de F. Snyder, « The Gatekeepers: The European Courts and WTO Law », *Common Market Law Review*, 2003, 40, issue 2, p. 313.

d'aucun acte ultérieur ».[27] Elle a d'ailleurs reconnu, sans difficulté, un effet direct à de nombreuses dispositions notamment d'accords d'association et de libre-échange.[28] Elle reconnaît la même propriété aux actes décisoires des organes de gestion de certains accords[29] dès lors qu'ils établissent « un principe précis et inconditionnel, suffisamment opérationnel pour être appliqué par un juge national et, dès lors, susceptible de régir la situation juridique des particuliers ».[30]

Ce faisant, elle favorise incontestablement l'imprégnation de l'ordre juridique de l'Union par le droit international. Il est, toutefois, plus frappant de noter que la Cour a développé une jurisprudence subordonnant de manière ambiguë l'invocabilité de certains accords internationaux à la capacité de leurs dispositions à produire un effet direct[31] établissant par là même entre les deux notions une relation causale inédite. C'est ainsi qu'elle a jugé que dépourvue d'effet direct, la Convention de *Montego Bay* ne peut constituer une norme par rapport à laquelle le contrôle de la légalité d'une directive peut être envisagé.[32] Mais, c'est probablement à l'égard des règles définies par le GATT que la Cour s'est montrée la plus circonspecte en leur refusant avec constance la valeur d'éléments du contrôle de la légalité des actes communautaires. Dans son arrêt *International fruit company*,[33] tout en confirmant sa compétence pour vérifier les motifs d'invalidité tirés du droit international, la haute juridiction a conditionné l'exercice de ses prérogatives préjudicielles au fait que la « disposition [invoquée] soit de nature à engendrer pour les justiciables de la Communauté le droit de s'en prévaloir en justice ». Or, tel n'était pas, selon elle, le cas des stipulations du GATT compte tenu, d'une part, de leur grande souplesse qui ménage de multiples possibilités de dérogations et, d'autre part, de

---

27 CJCE, 30 septembre 1987, *Demirel*, aff. 12/86, *Rec.* p. 3719 ; CJCE, 12 avril 2005, *Simutenkov*, aff. C-265/03, *Rec.* p. I-2579 ; CJCE, 13 décembre 2007, *Asda Stores*, aff. C-372/06, *Rec.* p. I-11223.

28 Par ex. pour l'accord CE-Pologne CJCE, 21 septembre 2001, *Gloszczuk*, aff. C-63/99, *Rec*, p. 1-6369 ; ou pour l'accord d'association avec le Royaume du Maroc, CJCE, ord., 13 juin 2006, *Echouikh*, aff. C-336/05, *Rec.* p. I-05223.

29 CJCE, 20 septembre 1990, *Sevince*, aff. C-192/89, *Rec.* p. I-3461.

30 CJUE, 19 juillet 2012, *Natthaya Dülger*, aff. C-451/11, non encore publié.

31 Par ex. CJCE, 10 janvier 2006, *International Air Transport Association*, aff. C-344/04, *Rec.* p. I-00403.

32 CJCE, 3 juin 2008, *International Association of Independent Tanker Owners [Intertanko] e.a.*, aff. C-308/06, spéc. par. 59 à 65, *Rec.* p. I-04057 ; voir également CJUE, 8 mars 2011, *Lesoochranárske zoskupenie VLK c. Ministerstvo životného prostredia Slovenskej republiky*, aff. C-240/09, non encore publié, décision dans laquelle la Cour estime que l'article 9, paragraphe 3, de la convention d'Aarhus est dépourvu d'effet direct en droit de l'Union).

33 CJCE, 12 décembre 1972, aff. jointes 21/72 à 24/72, *Rec.*, p. 1219.

l'incomplétude du système de règlement des différends. Ces réserves initiales l'ont conduite à décliner sa compétence pour interpréter, à titre préjudiciel, les règles du GATT.[34] Partant des mêmes prémisses, la Cour s'est prononcée en faveur d'une compétence limitée du juge de l'Union, considérant que les caractéristiques des règles du GATT non seulement impliquent « qu'un justiciable de la Communauté ne peut s'en prévaloir en justice afin de contester la légalité d'un acte communautaire mais s'oppose également à ce que la Cour prenne en considération les dispositions de l'accord général pour apprécier la légalité d'un règlement dans le cadre d'un recours introduit par un État membre au titre de l'Article 173, premier alinéa, du traité ».[35] Elle a toutefois admis, dans la ligne de décisions antérieures,[36] qu'elle pouvait exercer un tel contrôle dans deux situations, « l'hypothèse où la Communauté a entendu donner exécution à une obligation particulière assumée dans le cadre du GATT ou dans celle où l'acte communautaire renvoie expressément à des dispositions précises de l'accord général ».

La Cour a confirmé que ces solutions s'étendaient aux accords de Marrakech et aux accords qui y sont annexés.[37] Concluant dans l'affaire *Portugal c. Conseil*, l'avocat général A. Saggio soulignait que la jurisprudence de la Cour suscite la perplexité plus qu'elle ne clarifie un débat pour le moins délicat. Pour que les accords du GATT, ou aujourd'hui de l'OMC, constituent un « paramètre » de la légalité des actes des institutions, on exige inexplicablement que les justiciables soient en mesure de se prévaloir en justice de leurs dispositions. On ne voit pas en quoi le contrôle de validité d'un acte d'une institution dont on pense qu'il contrevient à une règle (européenne ou internationale) de rang supérieur devrait être subordonné à l'applicabilité directe des normes de référence. Aussi, invitait-il la Cour à dissocier l'effet obligatoire des accords en cause de leur pleine applicabilité directe estimant qu'une « une règle issue d'une convention internationale, en raison de son caractère clair précis et inconditionnel, peut en principe être un

---

34 CJCE, 16 mars 1983, *SIOT*, aff. 266/81, *Rec.* p. 731 ; également CJCE, 12 décembre 1995, *Chiquita italia*, aff. C-469/93, *Rec.* p I-4753. Elle a néanmoins accepté d'interpréter l'article 50 du TRIPs, CJCE, 16 juin 1998, *Hermès International*, aff. C-53/96, *Rec.* p. I-3603, pt. 29.

35 CJCE, 5 octobre 1994, *Allemagne c. Conseil*, aff. C-280/93, *Rec.* p. I-4973.

36 CJCE, 22 juin 1989, *Fediol*, aff. 70/87, *Rec.* p. 1781 ; CJCE, 7 mai 1991, *Nakajima*, aff. C-69/89, *Rec.* p. I-2069.

37 CJCE, 23 novembre 1999, *Portugal c. Conseil*, aff. C-149/96, *Rec.* p. I-8395 sur cette question, Eeckhout, P., « The domestic legal status of the WTO agreement : interconnecting legal system », *Common Market Law Review*, vol. 34, n° 1, 1997, p. 11 ; Laget-Annamayer, A., « Le statut des accords OMC dans l'ordre juridique communautaire : en attendant la consécration de l'invocabilité », *Revue trimestrielle de droit européen*, 2006, p. 249.

critère du contrôle de la légalité des actes communautaires. Cela n'implique pas au regard du droit communautaire en la matière qu'une règle dotée de ces caractéristiques confère nécessairement aux particuliers la position de sujets habilités à agir en justice. Pour que ce dernier effet se réalise dans l'ordre juridique communautaire (…) il faut qu'il résulte du contexte général de l'accord que ses règles sont invocables en justice par les particuliers ». C'est pourquoi l'avocat général était « d'avis qu'une règle issue d'une convention internationale [pouvait] éventuellement ne pas être d'application directe sans que cela justifie qu'on lui dénie tout effet obligatoire à l'égard des institutions communautaires et par conséquent, la fonction de paramètre communautaire de la légalité ». Limiter la compétence du juge communautaire, en ce qui concerne l'interprétation et l'application des règles du GATT-OMC, aux hypothèses envisagées par les arrêts *Fédiol* et *Nakajima* revient de surcroît à subordonner la mise en œuvre de ces normes à la condition que l'ordre juridique de l'Union ait été adapté à l'accord international au moyen d'un acte d'exécution ou de « transposition ». La Cour a, en effet, développé une appréhension particulièrement restrictive de ces deux exceptions, précisant ainsi que la mise en œuvre de la jurisprudence *Nakajima* suppose que l'acte attaqué « assure spécifiquement la transposition en droit communautaire de prescriptions issues des accords de l'OMC ».[38] Ce faisant, l'Union ne doit pas seulement manifester une intention de se conformer à une règle mais bien démontrer sa volonté de lui donner exécution. Or, une telle exigence va très au-delà de ce que paraît impliquer l'Article 216 § 2 TFUE.

La Cour a dénoué l'affaire C-149/96 par un raisonnement très classique. Au-delà de leurs différences, elle estime que les accords GATT et OMC réservent une place également importante aux négociations entre les parties. Elle juge ici que « dans ces conditions, imposer aux organes juridictionnels l'obligation d'écarter l'application des règles de droit interne qui seraient incompatibles avec les accords OMC aurait pour conséquence de priver les organes législatifs ou exécutifs des parties contractantes de la possibilité (…) de trouver, fût-ce à titre temporaire, des solutions négociées ».[39]

La Cour s'attache à souligner la singularité des accords GATT-OMC, rappelant qu'ils se fondent clairement sur le principe de négociations entreprises sur une base de réciprocité et d'avantages mutuels. Constatant que pour nombre des partenaires les plus importants de l'Union, les accords OMC ne peuvent, compte tenu de leur objet et de leur but, constituer des normes de référence pour un contrôle de la

---

38 TPI, 3 février 2005, *Chiquita Brands*, aff. T-19/01, *Rec.* p. II-00315.

39 Pt. 40.

légalité de leur droit interne, la Cour juge qu'il est impératif de prévenir un déséquilibre dans l'application des règles de l'OMC.[40] En fait, elle se refuse, par la promotion hâtive d'une juridictionnalisation des différends, à priver les organes législatifs ou exécutifs de l'Union de la marge de manœuvre dont jouissent les organes similaires des partenaires commerciaux de cette dernière. Elle prend ainsi la mesure d'un système qui érige en priorité la nécessité de parvenir à un « juste équilibre » tant qu'existe un espace de négociation. Ce faisant, elle vulnérabilise les opérateurs ou les États membres qui souhaiteraient obtenir du juge qu'il stigmatise les décisions par lesquelles l'Union refuserait, en dépit des conclusions contraires de l'ORD, par exemple, l'importation d'une marchandise. Ainsi, la Cour choisit d'assurer (par son *self restrain*) aux institutions la marge de liberté dont elles ont besoin pour préserver au mieux les intérêts de l'Union dans les conflits l'opposant à certains de ses concurrents. En n'enfermant pas ces institutions dans le carcan excessivement rigide du seul règlement judiciaire, elle leur ouvre la perspective, politiquement très opportune, de se soustraire autant que nécessaire aux rigueurs de la discipline qu'implique l'OMC afin d'amener, le cas échéant, ses adversaires à composer.[41]

2. La « dualisation » des rapports de systèmes

L'Union est une entité résolument engagée sur la voie de la constitutionnalisation, processus qui ne peut lui-même rester sans conséquence sur le statut des sources externes de son droit. Le monisme qui semble être au fondement des relations que l'ordre juridique de l'Union entretient avec le droit international a, on l'a déjà vu, très largement été tempéré par l'effet d'une jurisprudence contrôlant précautionneusement les modalités d'insertion et d'invocation des normes externes. Il y a là un mouvement de repli, une véritable « dualisation », que renforce une double évolution de l'ordre juridique de l'Union : sa constitutionnalisation et sa « fondamentalisation » subséquente.

A. Les limites « constitutionnelles » au pouvoir de négociation

En le jetant aux orties, les rédacteurs du Traité de Lisbonne ont sans doute entendu signifier aux adversaires comme aux partisans du TECE

[40] Pt. 45.

[41] La Cour et le Tribunal ont, par la suite, confirmé que pas plus que les accords OMC eux-mêmes (TPI, 11 janvier 2002, *Biret international c. Conseil*, aff. T-174/00, *Rec.* p. II-17, sp. pt. 67), les décisions de l'ORD les appliquant ne sont, en principe, invocable (TPI, 20 mars 2001, *Cordis c. Commission*, aff. T-18/99, *Rec.* p. II-913 ; *Chiquita Brands*, *supra*, note 38 ; CJCE, 1er mars 2005, *Léon Van Parys NV*, aff. C-377/02, *Rec.* p. I-01465).

que c'en était fait d'un processus de constitutionnalisation que d'aucuns se plaisaient à décrire comme irréversible. Ce faisant, ils prétendaient dissiper les craintes qui conduisirent parfois les opinions à basculer dans une irrationalité débridée.[42] Il est vrai que les non-dits, les arguments de nécessité, les approximations terminologiques, les décalages entre prescription juridique et pratique politique autant que l'incapacité à saisir le sens des concepts structurant une entreprise complexe ont durablement ruiné une « certaine idée » de la construction européenne. Il n'est pourtant pas certain que les États soient effectivement parvenus (le voulaient-ils seulement) à inverser le sens de l'histoire. Le changement de paradigme, compris comme un « déplacement de l'imaginaire », un « basculement du centre de gravité de la représentation dominante »,[43] n'est peut-être qu'apparent tant la prégnance du constitutionnalisme reste évidente.

On sait le rôle que la Cour a joué, depuis l'origine, dans la constitutionnalisation de l'ordre juridique de l'Union. Bien plus que la promotion d'une terminologie de facture constitutionnelle, elle a assuré le développement d'un ordre juridique uniforme, autonome et primant les ordres juridiques nationaux et internationaux.

Jamais par son raisonnement la Cour n'a nié l'essence originellement conventionnelle des traités communautaires. Elle a, en revanche, souligné le fait qu'ils apparaissent bien comme le socle constitutionnel d'une organisation politique et juridique inédite, qui est « suprême dans sa sphère de compétence, sous réserve de respecter les procédures institutionnelles qui s'imposent à elle ».[44] Sous son impulsion on est donc rapidement passé d'une perception « internationaliste » des traités à une vision explicitement « constitutionnaliste » qui n'a cessé depuis lors d'être affirmée. C'est ainsi que la haute juridiction a considéré, sans équivoque, que « la Communauté économique européenne est une Communauté de droit en ce que ni ses États membres ni ses institutions n'échappent au contrôle de la conformité de leurs actes à la charte constitutionnelle de base qu'est le traité ».[45] Or, la Cour s'attache à préserver l'intégrité des valeurs qui étayent juridiquement ce système.

---

42 Sur ce point, Ziller, J., « Le processus des ratifications du traité établissant une constitution pour l'Europe et la période de réflexion », *EUI Working papers*, Law n° 2006/29, sp. p. 21 et s.

43 Delmas-Marty, M., « La tragédie des trois C », préface in M. Doat, J. Le Goff, P. Pedrot, *Droit et complexité – Pour une nouvelle intelligence du droit vivant*, Presses Université de Rennes, 2007, p. 10.

44 Lenaerts, K., *Le juge et la Constitution aux États-Unis d'Amérique et dans l'ordre juridique communautaire*, Bruxelles, Bruylant, 1988, p. 253.

45 CJCE, 23 avril 1986, *Parti écologiste « Les Verts »*, aff. 294/83, *Rec.* p. 01339.

Aussi, a-t-elle signifié aux États membres et aux institutions en charge du *Treaty Making Power* que leur pouvoir de négociation était strictement limité par l'existence d'un bloc de normes insusceptibles d'être amendées. Contrastant avec un acquis législatif adaptable au gré des évolutions ressenties comme nécessaires, cet acquis prééminent est supérieur en ce qu'il renvoie à des éléments fondamentalement structurants pour l'Union et à des règles dont la méconnaissance hypothéquerait l'unité, l'identité et même le devenir du projet européen. Telle est la raison pour laquelle, la Cour a jugé que le projet d'accord créant un système unifié de règlement des litiges en matière de brevets était en l'état inacceptable. En effet, il conduisait à la mise en place d'une juridiction internationale appelée à interpréter et à appliquer non seulement les dispositions dudit accord, mais également des dispositions du droit de l'Union.[46]

En outre, la Cour a constaté que prévoyant un mécanisme préjudiciel réservant la faculté de renvoi préjudiciel à la « Juridiction du brevet européen et du brevet communautaire », l'accord priverait les juridictions nationales d'une prérogative que leur confère le droit de l'Union et déstabiliserait le système de coopération directe entre celles-ci et la Cour. Or, les fonctions attribuées, respectivement, aux juridictions nationales et à la Cour apparaissent essentielles à la sauvegarde de la nature même du droit de l'Union. Si la perspective d'une révision offre, en principe, de larges possibilités de modification aux États membres, ceux-ci ne doivent en aucun cas perdre de vue que cet exercice est enfermé dans certaines limites formelles et matérielles. C'est précisément cette entrave au pouvoir des États membres que la Cour a voulu mettre en évidence dans son célèbre avis 1/91.[47] En effet, soucieuse de faire échec à une tentative de contournement conduite au moyen d'une révision du traité, la Cour avait indiqué que toute décision portant sur l'agencement de la structure judiciaire devrait préserver l'indépendance, et *a fortiori* l'existence, des instances juridictionnelles et l'autorité de leurs arrêts, sous peine de porter atteinte aux bases mêmes de l'ordre juridique communautaire. Ce faisant, elle éclairait d'un jour nouveau ces « fondements de la Communauté » en les plaçant hors d'atteinte du pouvoir constituant.

---

[46] CJUE, Avis 1/09 du 8 mars 2011, *Juridiction du Brevet européen et du brevet communautaire*.

[47] CJCE, Avis 1/91 du 14 décembre 1991, *Projet d'accord entre la CE et les pays de l'AELE portant création de l'Espace économique européen*, *Rec.* p. I-6079.

B. *Les effets liés à la « fondamentalisation » de l'ordre juridique de l'Union*

Véritable pionnière,[48] la Cour a initié un mouvement de subjectivisation de l'ordre juridique se traduisant par un renforcement constant des exigences en matière de protection des droits de l'homme.[49] Fût-elle perfectible, cette dimension de la construction européenne est celle qui en signe le plus clairement l'essence constitutionnelle. Or, c'est précisément au point de contact le plus délicat entre l'ordre juridique de l'Union et l'ordre juridique international que la Cour a manifesté avec le plus de fermeté sa volonté de protéger les acquis d'une Union de droit. Étendant le champ de sa propre compétence à des domaines qui y échappaient traditionnellement,[50] la Cour a choisi, avec l'arrêt *Kadi*,[51] de définir le fondement autant que le cadre de son contrôle par référence aux seules exigences de l'ordre juridique de l'Union. Aussi, le contrôle de la validité d'un acte de l'Union au regard des droits fondamentaux est-il l'expression d'une garantie constitutionnelle découlant du traité en tant que système juridique autonome et prévalent.[52] Les obligations résultant d'un « accord international » ne peuvent en aucune circonstance affecter les « principes constitutionnels du traité CE, au nombre desquels figure le principe selon lequel tous les actes communautaires doivent respecter les droits fondamentaux ».[53] Ni les États membres ni les institutions ne peuvent, lorsqu'ils adoptent des actes visant à l'exécution d'une résolution du Conseil de sécurité, s'affranchir du

48 Kovar, R., « La contribution de la Cour de justice à l'édification de l'ordre juridique communautaire », *Receuil de l'Académie de droit européen*, 1993, vol. IV, Tome 1 ; Fernandez Esteban, M.L., *The rule of law in the european constitution*, Kluwer law international, 1999.

49 Rideau, J. (dir.), *Les droits fondamentaux dans l'Union européenne, dans le sillage de la Constitution européenne*, Bruylant, 2009, p. 489.

50 Voir la remarquable thèse de G. Bachoué-Pédrouzo, « Le contrôle juridictionnel de la coopération intergouvernementale dans l'Union européenne – Contribution au processus de juridictionnalisation de l'Union », soutenue à Bayonne le 21 novembre 2012.

51 CJCE, 3 septembre 2008, *Kadi c. Conseil et Commission*, aff. C-402/05 P, *Rec.* p. I-06351 ; notre étude Labayle, H. & Mehdi, R., « Le contrôle juridictionnel de la lutte contre le terrorisme : les "blacks lists" de l'Union dans le prétoire de la Cour de justice », *Revue trimestrielle de Droit Européen*, 2009, pp. 231-265 ; également Jacqué, J.-P., « Primauté du droit international versus protection des droits fondamentaux, à propos de l'arrêt Kadi de la Cour de justice des Communautés européennes », *Revue Trimestrielle de Droit Européen*, 2009 ; Tridimas, T. et Guttierrez-Fons, J., « EU Law, international law and economic sanctions against terrorism : the judiciary in distress ? », *Fordham International Law Journal*, 2009, p. 901.

52 Pt. 316.

53 Pt. 285.

respect des droits de l'homme dont on sait qu'il constitue une condition essentielle de la légalité des actes. Aucune des dispositions des traités ne saurait être comprise comme « autorisant une dérogation aux principes de la liberté, de la démocratie ainsi que du respect des droits de l'homme et des libertés fondamentales consacrés à l'Article 6, paragraphe 1, UE en tant que fondement de l'Union ».[54]

La Cour va plus loin en tenant pour impossible l'idée même d'un conflit résultant d'allégeances contradictoires, respect dû au droit international ou soumission aux impératifs de l'ordre constitutionnel de l'Union. En effet, elle juge dans la plus pure tradition dualiste, que la censure d'un acte d'exécution d'une résolution pour violation d'une norme supérieure relevant de l'ordre juridique communautaire n'impliquerait pas une remise en cause de la primauté de cette résolution au plan du droit international.[55] Le juge de Luxembourg inscrit ainsi son contrôle dans un univers largement hermétique, estimant que la validité de l'acte déféré à son examen ne peut s'apprécier ici qu'à l'aune de l'ordre juridique dans lequel il a été posé. Dit autrement, bien que nécessaire à la mise en œuvre de la norme internationale la mesure attaquée ne peut être placée dans un rapport de validation au regard de cette dernière. Soucieuse de sauvegarder les droits fondamentaux tels qu'ils ont été conçus par l'Union, la Cour n'hésite pas à s'engager dans une « dualisation » des rapports de systèmes.

En toute logique, au regard des prémisses du raisonnement retenu, elle refuse de considérer que l'immunité accordée, pour des raisons inhérentes à la séparation des ordres juridiques, aux résolutions du Conseil de sécurité s'étendrait par translation aux actes que l'Union adopte pour leur exécution. Par l'effet d'une assimilation aux actes conventionnels, Charte des Nations unies comprise,[56] les résolutions du Conseil de sécurité sont réduites à une primauté « sur le plan international » dont on comprend qu'elle n'a pas d'autre vocation que d'élever un mur de protection. Préoccupée de garantir la primauté sans faille du droit de l'Union tout en en assurant sa complète autonomie, la Cour pose abruptement la question de l'opposabilité d'un droit « interne » au jeu de sujétions internationales auxquelles l'Union et ses États membres ont librement consenti. Fut-il justifié par des raisons légitimes, cet unilatéralisme fragilise l'ensemble de l'édifice en ouvrant une brèche dans laquelle pourraient s'engager des sujets moins vertueux dans le seul but de s'affranchir d'obligations résultant de la combinaison des Articles 25 et 103 de la Charte. En s'opposant pour des motifs de fond,

---

[54] Pt. 303.

[55] Pt. 288.

[56] Pt. 307.

à l'application d'un accord externe ou ici d'une résolution, elle ouvre en premier lieu la voie à une éventuelle mise en cause de la responsabilité internationale de l'Union.[57] Il y a sans doute quelque artifice à distinguer ici la résolution proprement dite de la décision interne d'exécution pour en déduire qu'une annulation de cette dernière n'aurait de conséquences que dans la sphère de l'Union. Dans la ligne d'une jurisprudence continue,[58] la Cour perd donc de vue délibérément les exigences d'une « loi » structurellement impérative d'une société internationale ordonnée dont l'Union est partie intégrante. Au-delà, la Cour ne tient aucun compte du caractère universel du système de sécurité collective et passe par pertes et profits la responsabilité principale que la Charte confie au Conseil de sécurité. Arguant d'un impératif catégorique, la protection d'un système de valeur reposant pour l'essentiel sur le respect dû aux droits fondamentaux, la jurisprudence *Kadi* met en cause la verticalité des rapports entre l'ordre universel et les ordres régionaux ou nationaux tels qu'ils avaient été conçus par les rédacteurs de la Charte.

Quoi qu'il en soit, l'arrêt *Kadi* exprime même maladroitement le souci de trouver un équilibre entre la protection des droits fondamentaux tels qu'ils sont garantis, de manière convergente, par le droit de l'Union, les constitutions nationales et la Convention européenne des droits de l'homme et les nécessités du combat mené, à l'échelle internationale, pour la sécurité. La Cour a, récemment encore, confirmé sa volonté d'assumer, à titre principal, la fonction de gardienne des valeurs de l'Union face aux dérives pouvant affecter l'action contre le terrorisme, en retenant une lecture du traité neutralisant le Parlement européen.[59] Cette solution est-elle rassurante, quand on connaît la manière

---

57 Conclusions M. Maduro Poiares, pt. 39.

58 Voir par exemple, CJCE, 10 mars 1998, *République fédérale d'Allemagne soutenue Royaume de Belgique c. Conseil de l'Union*, aff. C-122/95, *Rec.* p. I-973. La Cour est allée plus loin en vérifiant indirectement la conformité substantielle d'un accord externe, en vigueur, aux prescriptions matérielles des Traités communautaires. En l'espèce, l'Allemagne avait introduit un recours contre la décision 94/800/CE du Conseil relative à la conclusion d'un accord-cadre mettant fin à la « guerre de la banane » qui opposait depuis de nombreuses années la Communauté à plusieurs républiques latino-américaines. Aussi, la Cour a-t-elle annulé certaines des dispositions de cette décision au motif que l'arrangement conclu par le Conseil violait le principe de non-discrimination. On peut également évoquer l'arrêt du 30 mai 2006, *Parlement c. Conseil*, aff. C-317/04, *Rec.* p. I-04721. Comme le souligne l'avocat général Maduro Poiares, « toutes ces affaires ont en commun le fait que, bien que la Cour ait pris grand soin de respecter les obligations qui incombent à la Communauté en vertu du droit international, elle cherche, avant tout, à préserver le cadre constitutionnel créé par le traité », § 24.

59 CJUE, 19 juillet 2012, *Parlement européen c. Conseil*, aff. C-130/10, non encore publié ; Bachoué-Pedrouzo, G., « Le rattachement de la lutte contre le terrorisme à la

dont la Cour a su développer un discours sur la protection juridictionnelle qui tient à bien des égards de la figure de style ? Tentée de préserver la quiétude des institutions en charge de la conduite de la politique étrangère, par un contrôle sur le fond au mieux minimaliste, la Cour accrédite sans doute les thèses selon lesquelles sa grille d'analyse serait ici plus politique que strictement juridique. Ce faisant, ne vient-elle pas rappeler que l'Union est probablement un acteur de la vie internationale répondant aux mêmes stimuli que les autres. La conception qu'elle a forgée non seulement du statut des sources externes mais plus largement des rapports de systèmes atteste que le droit de l'Union est avec le droit international, probablement pour longtemps encore, dans une « uneasy relationship ».[60]

PESC ou comment la Cour de justice déroule son fil d'Ariane… », http://www.gdr-elsj.eu/.

60 Cameron, Demaret & Geradin, *supra*, note 1, p. 277.

La Pologne en acteur majeur de l'UE, le test de la présidence[1]

Georges MINK

Directeur de Recherche émérite à l'ISP-CNRS ;
directeur d'études au Collège d'Europe (campus de Natolin)

Le chemin parcouru par la Pologne jusqu'à la présidence de l'UE au deuxième semestre 2011 pourrait être décrit par une anecdote. À l'occasion du referendum sur le traité de Maastricht en 1992, Laurent Fabius, à cette époque ne représentant pas encore le camp « noniste », invite Adam Michnik, célèbre dissident, prisonnier du régime communiste, un des intellectuels polonais le plus emblématique de la nouvelle démocratie, déjà rédacteur en chef de Gazeta Wyborcza, à soutenir l'intégration européenne, dans la ville dont il est maire, Grand-Quevilly. Avoir une telle personnalité à ce moment-là dans sa circonscription n'était pas dénoué d'intérêt électoraliste. À l'époque l'élargissement est encore loin et Laurent Fabius interroge Adam Michnik : vous les Polonais voulez vous vraiment l'Europe ? Michnik, avec son célèbre bégaiement, répond « je préfère être l'arrière-garde de l'Europe que l'avant-garde de l'Asie ».[2] Aujourd'hui la Pologne est au cœur de l'Europe. Et le même Adam Michnik dit « la présence dans l'Union a apporté à la Pologne des résultats exclusivement positifs. Son sauvetage et son renforcement sont de notre intérêt bien compris ».[3]

Pour faire le bilan de la présidence polonaise, la démarche la plus logique serait de comparer les présidences comparables. En deuxième lieu il faut examiner les quelques points forts de la présidence polonaise tels qu'ils sont énoncés par les brochures de marketing polonais. Enfin, nous présenterons les résultats d'un sondage qualitatif « artisanal »

---

1 Ce texte s'inspire de l'exposé fait dans le cadre d'une conférence internationale qui s'est tenue à Varsovie, le 5 décembre 2011 sous les auspices du Centre franco-autrichien pour le rapprochement en Europe, de l'Institut frrançais des relations internationales, intitulée « La Présidence polonaise de l'Europe : chances et défis ».

2 Souvenir personnel.

3 *Gazeta Wyborcza*, 15 décembre 2011.

effectué sur une population cible. Elle est constituée des Alumnis polonais du Collège d'Europe, les deux campus confondus. Une évidence s'impose : la présidence polonaise fut victime du contexte international, des révolutions arabes à la généralisation de la crise de l'eurozone, et malgré ou en raison de cela, comme l'aura dit un observateur polonais averti, elle aura été certes « silencieuse, mais efficace ».

1. Comparer le comparable...

Avec la Pologne c'est déjà la 4e fois qu'un pays anciennement communiste aura exercé la présidence tournante de l'UE : il y a eu d'abord la Slovénie en 2008, puis la République tchèque en 2009, puis la Hongrie en 2010. Une comparaison s'impose mais elle est difficile dans la mesure où on s'aperçoit que chaque cas doit être pondéré par deux variables indépendantes de la bonne volonté : les turbulences de la scène politique interne et les effets de contexte.

Si la présidence slovène a été réussie, c'est entre autres parce que la Slovénie a été étroitement insérée dans la troïka avec l'Allemagne et le Portugal pour réussir la signature du traité de Lisbonne par les États membres ; la mauvaise surprise est venue du *non* irlandais. Mais elle a réussi pratiquement toutes ses priorités qu'il serait trop fastidieux d'énumérer ici.

Les présidences tchèque et hongroise illustrent bien le fait que les priorités les plus ambitieuses peuvent être contrariées par les facteurs imprévisibles. Succédant à la France, la République tchèque n'a pas su « sortir de l'ombre de la France » comme l'a noté Tony Barber, le correspondant de Financial Times. Il a rappelé le phénomène « Sarkozy », « sans cesse entre deux avions, un jour à Berlin, le lendemain à Bruxelles, Londres ou Moscou ». Mais il y avait aussi le contexte international difficile avec l'intervention israélienne à Gaza et le conflit gazier entre Moscou et Kiev. Pourtant la République tchèque a su réagir et, en plus, elle a réussi la déclaration sur le Partenariat oriental, grâce au lobbying polono-suédois. Mais elle a été victime d'une crise gouvernementale interne, avec en prime l'image eurosceptique de son président Vaclav Klaus, puis de la mésaventure « bunga bunga » du Premier ministre Mirek Topolanek.[4] Quant à la présidence hongroise le double discours de son Premier ministre Victor Orban, a recouvert les véritables avancées. Personne n'a oublié l'attaque de l'eurodéputé, Daniel Cohn Bendit, au Parlement européen, à propos du projet de la constitution hongroise, contre Victor Orban et la réponse de ce dernier « La

---

[4] Une photo du premier ministre tchèque dénudé, prise à la résidence de Sylvio Berlusconi a circulé très largement dans les tabloïdes.

Hongrie n'est pas subordonnée à Bruxelles, Bruxelles n'est pas le centre de commandement de la Hongrie ». Tout au long de cette présidence, le débat sur les entorses à la démocratie a caché les réalisations de la présidence. Rien de tel pour la Pologne. Au plan interne la situation était confortable : les eurosceptiques étaient marginalisés, l'exécutif et le pouvoir législatif agissaient en harmonie, unis par une conviction eurofile, tandis que l'opinion publique polonaise manifestait un taux record de soutien à l'intégration, le plus élevé dans toute l'Union. De plus la Pologne présentait un bilan économique positif dans un environnement en crise. Paradoxalement, ce fut cette variable extérieure de la crise généralisée qui a contrarié la flamboyance annoncée de cette présidence. La crise de l'eurozone a quelque peu voilé les actions polonaises. Pourtant, il s'est agi d'un parcours sans faute d'une présidence aussi riche que dynamique.

2. Alors que gagne la Pologne à avoir présidé l'Union ?

Elle a d'abord gagné la bataille de l'image. On se souvient de l'effet catastrophique de l'œuvre Entropa du sculpteur tchèque Cerny représentant les pays européens avec des clichés, sinon vexatoires, du moins simplistes : La France = la grève, l'Allemagne = la croix gammée, La Bulgarie = les WC à la turque.

La Pologne a su créer un emblème d'un symbolisme fortement communautaire, solidariste et paneuropéen. Imitation du sigle de Solidarnosc qui a symbolisé le mouvement antitotalitaire syndicale des années 1980 qui a ébranlé le système communiste, réalisé par le même artiste, Jerzy Janiszewski, qui a créé cet emblème célèbre, le message qu'il contenait voulait tout dire, la tradition et la modernité, la solidarité et l'association des couleurs nationales. On parlera à Bruxelles d'une « communication décomplexée ». Dans la foulée la Pologne achève la construction de sa nouvelle représentation permanente auprès de l'UE présentée comme « la meilleure carte de visite de la Pologne en Europe ». Enfin, un effort particulier a été fait pour renforcer la collaboration avec le secteur associatif polonais, un des remèdes les plus efficaces au déficit démocratique de l'Europe.

La Pologne a aussi produit une imposante promotion de sa culture. Il suffit de dire que sous la férule de l'Institut Adam Mickiewicz[5] 1 400 événements culturels ont été organisés : près de 1 000 en Pologne, environ 400 dans les capitales d'autres pays : Berlin, Paris, Bruxelles, Kiev, Londres, Madrid, Pékin, Tokyo, Moscou et même Minsk. Le bilan

[5] Institution en charge du rayonnement culturel de la Pologne à l'étranger, à l'instar de l'Institut Goethe, ou de l'Institut Cervantès ou encore de British Council.

de l'ensemble des réalisations des priorités polonaises doit beaucoup au volontarisme de 3 priorités de la présidence polonaise :

- intégration européenne comme source de croissance
- une Europe plus sûre
- une Europe bénéficiant de l'ouverture

3. À l'écoute des acteurs de la présidence

Il y a une autre façon de répondre à la question du bilan de cette présidence que de mettre en surbrillance les brochures de marketing polonais. J'ai décidé de faire ce que je sais faire le mieux : un peu de sociologie d'opinion. Pour cela je me suis tourné vers l'Association des alumnis du Collège d'Europe, plus exactement sa section polonaise. C'est une population avertie des questions européennes. Les alumnis du Collège ont été pour la plupart des observateurs directs de la fabrication et de la réalisation des politiques de la Présidence polonaise du Conseil. Sans être représentatifs leur proximité avec l'action européenne et ses institutions donne un poids illustratif à leurs propos. Je leur ai donc posé la question des gains polonais. J'ai reçu 9 réponses et j'ai sélectionné les propos les plus significatifs. Les représentations de cette présidence permettent de nuancer le point de vue gouvernemental. J'ai décidé par conséquent de préserver l'anonymat de mes interlocuteurs.

Entretien n° 1 « le Pessimiste »

À mon avis la présidence ne nous a rien apporté. Dans l'UE pendant la présidence il est difficile de jouer ses propres intérêts. (...) Au plus la présidence permet de dicter l'agenda mais dans notre cas l'agenda nous a été imposé par la crise dans la zone euro et là nous n'avons rien à dire (...)

la tentative de déplacer l'attention de l'Europe des pays du Sud (Maghreb, Égypte) vers ceux de l'Est s'est terminée par un fiasco (...)

Cependant visuellement c'était pas mal, c'est là que le bilan est positif (...)

Entretien n° 2 « modérément Satisfait »

(...) d'un point de vue d'un fonctionnaire parlementaire je peux dire qu'il y a de nombreux éléments positifs que la Présidence nous a apportés. Notamment dans quatre domaines : à la classe politique, aux fonctionnaires, la marque de fabrique « Pologne », enfin, aux Polonais.

À la classe politique, notamment aux parlementaires polonais la présidence a offert l'opportunité d'une socialisation et des échanges intensifs avec des parlementaires étrangers. Certains de députés polonais présidaient des réunions ce qui était un rôle tout à fait nouveau à une telle échelle.

Mais il était difficile de mobiliser les députés et la plupart n'ont pas saisi cette chance pour apprendre ou perfectionner leurs connaissances linguistiques. Les réunions étaient traduites en polonais.

Quant aux fonctionnaires ils ont amélioré leur connaissance des mécanismes européens. Cette période a permis de sélectionner des fonctionnaires selon leurs aptitudes et leur volonté de se mobiliser. Lorsqu'il s'agira de diminuer les effectifs de la fonction publique en raison de la crise il sera ainsi plus facile de décider qui doit être licencié ...

La mise en valeur de l'image de la Pologne a été positive, notamment grâce à des cadeaux gadgets qui étaient très populaires dans les rangs des députés.

Au niveau national le fait à souligner est que les Polonais ont pu voir que la Pologne joue un rôle important, que nous n'appartenons plus à cette Europe de la deuxième vitesse (...).

Entretien n° 3 « Plutôt satisfait »

La Pologne est observée par les plus importants médias du monde, la fréquence des articles qui nous sont consacrés a augmenté. C'est donc un bénéfice en termes de visibilité de notre pays (...). Nous sommes apparus comme un partenaire prévisible, stable et responsable. Mais la présidence tournante a perdu en importance depuis le Traité de Lisbonne. (...) De plus nous ne faisions pas partie de la zone euro ce qui ne nous permettait pas de participer à toutes les réunions. (...)

C'est une amère coïncidence qu'en raison de la crise l'attention a été détournée de nos objectifs comme par exemple celui du partenariat oriental.

Un autre aspect positif a été la formation d'une armée de fonctionnaires.

Entretien n° 4 « Observateur lucide et satisfait »

Au plan intérieur : amélioration de l'efficacité de l'administration d'État, preuve de la capacité de coordonner le travail administratif de 27 pays comme preuve de la solidité mais aussi de la plasticité de l'administration polonaise. Au plan extérieur, la présidence a contribué à améliorer la réputation de notre pays dans l'UE comme un État efficace, sérieux et dynamique. Cela peut par un effet de feed-back influencer positivement notre politique (...)

Entretien n° 5 « Entièrement satisfait »

184 jours de la présidence ont permis de diffuser un message communicationnel en direction d'un groupe de décideurs et de formateurs d'opinion sur la qualité du label « Pologne ». Environ 30 000 fonctionnaires ont visité la Pologne, de centaines de journalistes et des artistes. (...) Pour résumer : notre image de marque s'est renforcée dans le monde ; les stéréotypes sur notre pays ont été contrés et notre image est devenue plus positive ; notre pays a démontré sa capacité de jouer le rôle de leader et de partenaire responsable ; nous avons promu nos régions et nos villes ; notre administration a fait des grands progrès dans l'européanisation ; notre culture a été largement promue à travers le monde ; promotion de notre design a renforcé l'idée d'un pays créatif possédant un fort capital intellectuel (...)

Entretien n° 6 « Très négatif »

La Pologne n'a rien gagné. Dans le domaine parlementaire qui est le mien les réunions étaient stériles et formelles. (...) Le fait de donner à la Belarus les données bancaires d'un opposant cela a été suicidaire, surtout dans le contexte de la promotion du partenariat oriental. Mais c'est intrinsèque à toute Présidence ; qui se souvient de celle de l'Espagne ou de République tchèque ? Il faut réformer le système des compétences institutionnelles, notamment du rôle de la présidence tournante.

Entretien n° 7 « observateur avisé » a travaillé au sein du secrétariat général des présidences française puis belge, enfin polonaise

Il me semble que le gain majeur pour les Polonais impliqués dans l'organisation des événements fut la nécessité de parfaire la coordination interministérielle et interinstitutionnelle avec les délégations invitées. Le bénéfice pour l'ensemble des personnels statutaires ou occasionnels a été d'apprendre les pratiques d'action déjà mises en place par leurs homologues européens. Mais malgré ces 6 mois d'européanisation intense nous souffrons du retard technique, de l'incompréhension des procédures ou des sous-effectifs du centre de coordination victime d'une surcharge de travail. (...) Mais ces faiblesses n'ont pas été ressenties par les invités étrangers ou les acteurs externes. (...)

Entretien n° 8 « Satisfait »

La présidence a permis de montrer à nos partenaires européens l'excellente préparation de notre administration, le professionnalisme de nos fonctionnaires, le niveau élevé de connaissance de la thématique européenne. Dommage que ces ressources et ce professionnalisme des Polonais ne sont pas encore assez admis à Bruxelles.

Entretien n° 9 « réaliste »

Peu importe les bénéfices ou les imperfections. La question est de savoir si la Pologne a bien accompli la mission qui est assignée à un État appelé à présider l'UE. La réponse est positive ; (...) On ne peut répondre à cette question qu'en connaissance du calendrier réalisé et du déroulement des initiatives, seuls ceux qui l'ont vécu de l'intérieur peuvent donner la réponse. (...) Le plus important est que la présidence s'est déroulée calmement, sans affaires ni scandales ni controverses majeurs, pourtant dans un contexte extrêmement tendu de la crise. Ainsi donc la Pologne a gagné la réputation d'un partenaire fiable et sérieux (...).

En guise de récapitulatif : le test est plutôt positif.

La Présidence polonaise a permis surtout de faire avancer en Pologne même les processus de l'européanisation de l'administration polonaise mais aussi de diffuser une image positive du pays en levant au passage certains stéréotypes négatifs. Plusieurs des objectifs de la Présidence ont été réalisés comme la rédaction du traité d'adhésion de la Croatie. D'autres, comme l'élargissement de la zone Schengen à la Bulgarie et à la Roumanie, n'ont pu être atteints. La Pologne n'a pu lever l'obstacle à l'accord d'association avec l'Ukraine, Julia Timochenko restant emprisonnée. Si le bilan est largement positif, toutefois jusqu'au 28 novembre cette Présidence a été silencieuse, étouffée médiatiquement par les événements environnants. Puis soudainement, à Berlin, comme un coup de tonnerre a retenti le discours du ministre polonais des Affaires étrangères Radoslaw Sikorski. Par sa qualité de proposition, par le courage de son expression, par sa conviction européaniste, il peut être rangé dans la série des grands textes comme ceux de jadis sous la plume de Karl Lamers et Wolfgang Schaüble, de Joschka Fisher ou de Jürgen Habermas. Ce n'est pas ici le lieu de le commenter. On peut observer seulement que la Pologne a rejoint par la série des prises de position récentes comme celle de Donald Tusk ou de Michal Dowgielewicz, à quelques jours de la fin de la Présidence et du Sommet européen, le petit nombre des pays membres qui se distinguent par leur acharnement à affirmer le credo pro-européen, par l'originalité de leurs propositions et la volonté de contribuer à son sauvetage par l'approfondissement. La rentabilité du discours du ministre polonais des Affaires étrangères peut se mesurer par le débat déclenché en Allemagne et aussi paradoxalement par le silence assourdissant en France car il fallait attendre plusieurs jours pour que ce discours soit mentionné dans la presse. De ce côté-là, la Pologne a aussi gagné quelque chose car il ne se trouve plus personne en France pour dire que les Polonais (propos de Jacques Chirac adressés aux nouveaux membres de l'UE ayant soutenu l'intervention américaine en Irak) ont perdu une occasion de se taire.

EU Treaty Reforms as "Canalisers" of EU Policies

Enabling and Impeding Effects in the Justice and Home Affairs Domain

Jörg MONAR

Director, European Political and Administrative Studies Department, College of Europe

1. Introduction

Being neither a state nor an international organisation in the traditional sense, the European construction which has evolved from the 1950 Schuman Plan keeps defying any simple categorisation. Yet, whatever it may be categorised as there can be no question about the main means by which it has been created and progressively developed: Treaty law. Looking at the range of well established EU policy fields today – from the Internal Market over Economic and Monetary and the Area of Freedom, Security and Justice to the Common Foreign and Security Policy –, at the array of institutions and agencies and also at major instruments such as the budget and the continuous flow of secondary legislation it is sometimes easy to overlook that all of what constitutes the European Union of today has ultimately been conditioned by its original founding treaties, their various reforms and current successors. It is through the instrument of Treaty law that the Member States have created, developed and expanded this European construction, making it in the words of former Commission President Walter Hallstein in the first place a "creation of the law".[1]

Yet, however fundamental, the law of the EC and EU Treaties has never fitted perfectly well the dynamic development of EU policy domains: Treaty law can define policy objectives and competences,

---

1 "*Schöpfung des Rechts*". Walter Hallstein, *Die Europäische Gemeinschaft*, Düsseldorf, Econ Verlag, 1979, 5th ed., p. 53.

instruments and procedures to achieve them, but it does so always only on the basis of specific political comprises negotiated between the Member States at a given moment in history. It then codifies both the political ambitions of the Member States as "masters of the Treaties" and their limitations as well as the tensions and contradictions prevalent at the time of the negotiations. Subsequent dynamics of political evolution can fit relatively well within the policy potential opened up by the Treaties, but they also can relatively quickly run against the limitations of this potential and expose the inherent contradictions within the Treaties itself – which may then sooner or later necessitate further reform.

On may compare the EU Treaties – and their successive reforms – to river canalisation works: Each Treaty or Treaty reform tries to define a canal for the expected stream of policy developments with the aim of controlling both its flow volume and direction. It therefore always has a policy enabling dimension. Yet, due to a variety of political factors, the flow may exceed the capacity of the canal bed and banks provided or be at variance with the direction the Treaties' canalisation efforts have tried to impose, in which case the flow may be impeded or even dammed up with a potential risk that it breaks out of the designed canalisation works. Also possible is that the Treaties provide for a broad canal but at the same time for so many safeguards not generate too much of a policy stream that the canal remains largely empty, putting into question the effectiveness of the canalisation works from a different perspective. In all of those scenarios a redesign of the canal works, i.e. Treaty reforms, may become desirable.

This contribution in honour of a colleague who has like few others enlightened our understanding of the enabling and constraining effects of European law tries to shed some light on the potential and limitations of EU Treaty reforms in enabling and constraining policy developments in the domain of justice and home affairs (JHA). This domain can be regarded as a particularly interesting field of inquiry in this context, not only because it has been – in the form of the "Area of freedom, security and justice" (AFSJ) one of the fastest expanding EU policy domains since the Treaty of Amsterdam reforms of 1999, but also because it has been the object of major reforms in the three of last four completed Treaty reform rounds.[2]

[2] Those of the Maastricht, Amsterdam and Lisbon Treaties, as the Treaty of Nice – which entered into force in 2003 – was in the JHA domain essentially limited to the acceleration of the passage to co-decision in the fields of asylum, immigration and visa policy already envisaged by the Treaty of Amsterdam and the creation of a legal base for Eurojust.

2. The Treaty of Maastricht: A Wide Canal for a Trickle of Policy Developments

Before the Treaty of Maastricht cooperation between the Member States in the JHA domain was marked by an extreme degree of fragmentation and complexity: All Member States participated in the law enforcement cooperation mechanisms of TREVI established back in 1975, but these were of a rather loose intergovernmental nature, involving no legal and permanent institutional basis and taking place entirely outside of the existing EC Treaty framework. The Schengen countries cooperated since 1985 on a more solid legal and institutional basis on all "compensatory" JHA matters related to their objective of abolishing controls on persons at internal borders, but they involved at the time only a minority of the Member States and were relegated to an involuntary exile outside of the EC Treaty because of the opposition of the UK and other countries to their core objective. Since the formal launch on the Internal Market Programme with its progressive reduction of border checks on transports of goods and liberalisation of other cross-border economic transactions JHA issues had also appeared on the EC agenda because of the associated internal security and migration management risks, but in the absence of any explicit powers for the EC to deal with the JHA the EC Member States had limited their action to the setting-up of several coordination groups such as the *Ad Hoc Group on Immigration* and the *"Rhodes" Coordinators' Group on Free Movement*. Apart from the inevitable problems of overlap between the different frameworks and groups, the effectiveness of this early JHA cooperation was severely impaired by the absence of any real common action potential within the existing EC Treaty framework. In the months preceding the 1990/91 Maastricht IGC a critical mass of Member States emerged which felt that this state of affairs was not any longer adequate to the common challenges in this domain: Not only was the completion of the Internal Market necessitating some "hard" compensatory legal measures rather than only loose coordination of national measures, but the dismantling of the former "iron curtain" borders as a result of the revolutionary transformation in Central and Eastern Europe were seen adding to the already existing challenges in the fields of migration, border management and fight against cross-border crime. Unsurprisingly the Schengen countries formed the core of that critical mass, but within this core it was Germany in particular, which became the protagonist of bringing JHA cooperation into the Treaty reform as – with reunification completed in 1990 – it found itself in charge of an even longer stretch of the newly opened Eastern borders and rapidly increasing asylum and immigration challenges. On the other hand, several other Member States, amongst which mainly the UK, opposed any "communitarisation" of the JHA domain and clearly wanted to avoid a sudden surge of common policy-making in such sensitive domains as law enforcement, justice and migration management.[3] The IGC result reflected, inevitably, these lines of tension.

The Maastricht Treaty – to return to our image of Treaties as canalisation works – not only created for the first time ever a bed for EU policy development in the JHA domain but it also did so also on a very broad scale. In the case of asylum and judicial cooperation in civil and criminal matters (Article K.1(1), (6) and (7) TEU) the entire fields were opened up for cooperation without any restrictive definition. Even in the sensitive fields of immigration policy and police cooperation (Articles K.1(3) and (9) TEU – where specific matters instead of the entire field were identified as being of "common interest" – the new provisions covered the most substantive issues such as family reunion, access to employment and combating unauthorized immigration in the field of immigration and all forms of serious international crime in the field of police cooperation. However – due to the above mentioned concerns of some Member States – the new Treaty not only created this bed carefully separated from the main (EC) stream of policy-making in the form of Title VI TEU (the "third pillar") but also failed to give any more specific direction to the potential new flow of policy-making by not defining any objectives[4] (on which there had been no consensus during the IGC). It also failed to define adequate legislative instruments – as instead of the traditional EC legal instruments CFSP-type "joint positions" and "joint actions" of uncertain legal effects as well as national ratification subjected "conventions" were provided for by Article K.3(2) TEU[5] – and, finally, provided maximum protection to individual national interests by subjecting the entire domain to unanimity and a non-exclusive right of initiative of the Commission.

In retrospect the JHA domain in the Treaty of Maastricht appears as an excellent example for the both enabling and impeding effects of EU Treaty reforms.

On the one hand there can be no doubt that the Treaty of Maastricht pushed the gate towards JHA cooperation within the EU framework wide open and thus crucially prepared the ground for what is now a

---

3 On the positions adopted by the Member States during the Maastricht negotiations see Richard Corbett, *The Treaty of Maastricht. From Conception to Ratification*, Harlow, Longman, 1993, pp. 48-49.

4 Article K.1 TEU only defined JHA matters as "matters of common interest".

5 On the shortcomings of the available instruments under the Maastricht Title VI TEU see Steve Peers, *EU Justice and Home Affairs Law*, Oxford, Oxford University Press, 2011, 3rd ed., pp. 14-15.

fundamental EU Treaty objective – the creation of the AFSJ – and one of the EU's main policy-making domains. It did so not only through the aforementioned very wide ranging inclusion of JHA fields in the newly established cooperation under Title VI TEU but also by firmly integrating the loose intergovernmental cooperation structures and mechanisms of TREVI and the various "coordinators" groups set up in relation with the JHA issues arising out of the completion of the Internal Market within the institutional framework of the EU. The JHA Council and its groups took the place of all of these structures and the Commission – although with a non-exclusive right of initiative – became for the first time fully "associated" with Member States' JHA cooperation (Article K.4(2) TEU). As regards the EU JHA domain the Treaty of Maastricht will stand in history as the Treaty which for the first time enabled the EU as an actor in this domain – and subsequent reforms of the Treaty have clearly benefitted from and built on this original enabling step.

Yet the impeding effects the Maastricht Treaty has had through its aforementioned lack of objectives, adequate instruments and decision-making constraints are no less obvious. It resulted in reducing the stream of policies which might have flown through the widely opened canal in the light of the many JHA challenges of the 1990s and the preparedness of a range of Member State for substantial action to a mere trickle. By the time the Maastricht "third pillar" was fundamentally transformed by the Amsterdam Treaty reform of 1999 it had barely gone beyond the establishment of Europol (with a still rather limited mandate) and a few rather basic common denominator compromises regarding common principles in the fields of asylum and immigration and the fight against organised crime and drug trafficking.[6] In addition, most of the texts adopted were of non-binding nature, and most of them were replaced by much more advanced instruments after the Amsterdam reforms. While not all of the poor record of the Maastricht "third pillar" can be attributed to limitations of the Treaty framework – major political disagreements between Member States over common objectives and action significantly added to the limited use which was made of the already limited possibilities provided by the Treaty – the latter was clearly marked by a huge discrepancy between the vast new field of policy-making brought within the EU framework and the means to fill it with substance.

With the canal of JHA cooperation within the EU opened broad and wide by Maastricht but safeguards and construction errors largely preventing the streams of policy developments from entering it – to

6 See Wenceslas de Lobkowicz, *L'Europe de la sécurité intérieure. Une élaboration par étapes*, Paris, La documentation Française, 2002, pp. 64-87.

return to our image – the latter were both dammed up and forced to find alternative ways. The damming up effect can be taken from the fact that after the Amsterdam reforms had lifted many of the impeding factors there was from 1999 onwards well into the next decade a significant surge of policy-making in the JHA domain with an ambitious strategic programme adopted by the European Council – the Tampere Programme –, a stream of Commission proposals and over a hundred texts adopted by the JHA Council that very year. It was almost as if a retaining dam had been broken and a huge policy backlog had to be caught up with. The effect of the policy development pressures finding alternative ways can also be traced back as the development of what today is EU JHA *acquis* developed during the 1990s much faster within the context of the Schengen group (which had agreed in 1990 on the important Convention Implementing the Schengen Agreement) than within the EU "third pillar" context. Would the Schengen countries have seen a possibility to develop part of the measures necessary for their objectives within the EU framework they would surely have gladly done so as their intention was always to see the whole of Schengen rather sooner than later integrated into the EU framework. But with the EU "third pillar" proving to be a not very propitious framework for JHA policy progress they had no real alternative than to continue to develop all JHA measures necessary to their system within the framework of the Schengen agreements.

3. The Treaty of Amsterdam: Two Canals for a Variable Policy Flow

By providing for a huge tension between the policy enabling opening up of the JHA domain for cooperation within the EU on the one hand and the major policy impeding factors in terms of lack of defined objectives, adequate instruments and effective decision-making capabilities on the other, the Treaty of Maastricht had the surely unintended consequence of providing itself a very strong case for the need of a further major Treaty reform in this domain. Already by 1995 both the Reflection Group and the European Commission concluded on the inadequacy of the Maastricht "third pillar" in terms of substantive policy development.[7] Although the dissatisfaction about the (non-)functioning of the JHA "pillar" generated considerable pressure for a

[7] See in particular Council of the European Union: Progress Report from the Chairman of the Reflection Group on the 1996 Intergovernmental Conference 1995. SN 509/1/95 REV 1 (REFLEX 10). Brussels: Council of the European Union 1995, p. 24, and Commission of the European Communities: Report on the Operation of the Treaty on European Union. SEC(95)731 final. Brussels, Commission of the European Communities 1995, p. 6.

comprehensive reform during the 1996/97 Intergovernmental Conference – with the by now much larger Schengen group at the core of this pressure – the major overhaul eventually provided for by the Treaty of Amsterdam became only possible, almost at the last minute, after the freshly elected UK Labour Government lifted the until then prevailing British vetoes on all crucial issues – and at the price of the "opt-outs" granted to the UK, Ireland – and on different grounds – to Denmark.

The Treaty of Amsterdam reforms in the JHA domain were clearly led by a forceful policy enabling rationale which found a major reflection already into the elevation of this domain – in the form of the "Area of freedom, security and justice" to one of the fundamental EU Treaty objectives listed in Article 2 TEU. Remedying the previous absence of any precise objectives the Amsterdam Treaty almost went to the other extreme by defining a host of detailed objectives – and corresponding EC/EU competences – for each of the main JHA policy fields from asylum and immigration over border control to judicial cooperation in civil and criminal matters to police cooperation (Articles 61-63 and 65 TEC and 29-31 TEU). In that way it narrowed the canal bed (in the sense of our image) by replacing the wide fields opened by the very vaguely defined JHA "matters of common interest" of the Maastricht Treaty by fairly specific measures to be taken. Yet at the same time the Treaty also gave a much stronger direction to the intended policy developments, adding to the likely policy pressure by setting a five year deadline for achieving a number of objectives in the fields of border controls, asylum and immigration (Articles 62 and 63 TEC). The stronger policy development pressure provided for in these latter fields was partially due to the integration of the Schengen system into the EU as the Schengen group – which at the time of the entry into force of the new Treaty included all Member States except Ireland and UK – had a special interest in progress in these fields which were in many respects directly related to the abolition of controls on persons at internal borders. The integration of Schengen itself was another major change of the JHA policy framework generated by the Amsterdam Treaty as it brought the existing Schengen policy stream – which had had to find an outlet outside of the Treaties – into the JHA main stream within the EU, adding considerably to the dynamic and volume of the latter. Amongst the impeding elements removed by Amsterdam, the replacement of the Maastricht Treaty JHA instruments by more appropriate legislative instruments (the EC legal instruments in the fields of asylum, immigration borders and civil a justice cooperation and "decisions" and "framework decisions" in those of criminal justice and police cooperation) were of particular importance as was a move from unanimity to qualified majority voting, immediately in the field of visa policy and potentially after five years for all other matters of asylum, immigration and border control policy (Article 67 TEU).[8]

However, the Treaty of Amsterdam's strong policy enabling rationale for the new AFSJ came in conjunction with a number of partially new impeding elements which reflected the concerns of several Member States – and not only those of the "opt-out" countries – about the most sovereignty and politically sensitive fields covered by the AFSJ. The primary reflection of this was the only partial communitarisation agreed upon during the final stage of the IGC which resulted in the fields of asylum, immigration, border controls and civil justice cooperation being transferred from the old EU "third pillar" to new Title IV TEC. Only judicial cooperation in criminal matters and police cooperation – the most sensitive fields from most of the governments' point of view – remained within the more intergovernmental context of the reformed Title VI TEU. This resulted in a major legal divide introduced into the newly created AFSJ, and this legal divide actually opened up two different "canals" for AFSJ policy developments: One for the fields of Title IV TEC in which objectives were linked (at least partially) to deadlines, where "Community" legal instruments and principles where fully applicable and where there was at least an initial opening towards qualified majority voting, and another one for the fields of Title VI TEU where objectives were less substantial, not linked to deadlines, where legislative instruments of more limited legal effect were applicable[9] and where decision-making remained within the firm grip of unanimity. Criminal justice cooperation under Title VI TEU had to cope with an additional impediment by the fact that the Treaty of Amsterdam did not create any legal basis for measures in the field of criminal procedural law. This void can be explained, again, by some Member States' concerns about a potential criminal law harmonisation surge, but it created an obvious tension especially with the intended progress on the mutual recognition of judicial decisions in criminal matters for which certain common minimum procedural standards were crucial from the mutual trust perspective.

---

8 For a more detailed analysis of the Amsterdam reforms in the JHA domain see Bernd Meyring, "Die Reform der Bereiche Justiz und Inneres durch den Amsterdamer Vertrag", *Europarecht*, Vol. 34, 1999, pp. 309-324, and Jörg Monar, "Justice and Home Affairs in the Treaty of Amsterdam: Reform at the Price of Fragmentation", *European Law Review*, Vol. 23, 1998, pp. 320-335.

9 Article 34(2)(b) and (c) TEU explicitly ruled out any direct effect of Title VI TEU "framework decisions" and "decisions". However, in its judgement on the "Pupino" case the Court of Justice later deprived this restriction of much of its substance by declaring the principle of conforming interpretation also fully applicable to "framework decisions" as part of the Member States' duty of loyal cooperation (Case C-105/03 (Criminal proceedings against Maria Pupino) [2005] ECR I-5285).

The canal architects of the Amsterdam IGC (to stay within our picture) had thus created two separate canals for JHA policy developments with one providing distinctly more impediments than the other although both were intended to serve the same objective, that "to maintain and develop" the Union as an AFSJ (Article 2 TEU). While crucial for securing the Amsterdam compromise on the AFSJ this divide generated its own problems of political and legal coherence of the AFSJ which necessitated – for instance in the field of the fight against illegal immigration – the adoption of parallel legislative acts under both Title IV TEC and Title VI TEU and also complicated international negotiations on JHA matters because of the different legal personalities and procedures of the EC and the EU.

Nevertheless, at least in the first few years, the strong political momentum generated by the JHA backlog accumulated during the Maastricht period, the final integration of the Schengen group and the political will of the Heads of State or Government – as it became clear during the Tampere European Council of October 1999 – to use the potential of the newly created AFSJ in response to common challenges and a more active role of the Commission in the period of Commissioner Antonio Vitorino ensured a quit extensive use of the enabling potential created by the Amsterdam Treaty through both "channels". During the five year period of the Tampere Programme until 2004 the "communitarised" fields of Title IV TEC saw the adoption, in spite of many weaknesses, of most of the "first phase" legislation of what today is called the "Common European Asylum System" (CEAS), the completion of the Common (Schengen) visa policy, the putting into place of at least some foundation stones for a common approach to immigration (such as Directives 2003/86/EC on family reunification and 2003/109/EC on a long-term residence status), the progressive move towards a more active common management of external border challenges since the Seville European Council of 2002 (which prepared the establishment of Frontex in 2005) and in the civil justice domain the adoption of the Brussels I and Brussels II Regulations.[10] The aforementioned impeding elements codified under Title VI TEU contributed to a slightly slower post-Amsterdam start in the fields of police and judicial cooperation in criminal matters, with only one instrument of substantive law – Framework Decision 2001/500/JHA on money-laundering – being adopted during the first 30 months after the entry into force. Yet even in these fields the general political momentum resulted in a host of new initiatives – one leading to the establishment of Eurojust in 2002 –, and what

10 Regulations (EC) 1347/2000 (Brussels II), 44/2001 (Brussels I) and 2201/2003 (Brussels II bis).

may be initially compared to a brook turned for some time into a rather forceful stream after the 9/11 terrorist attacks generated unprecedented political will and pressure to strengthen the Union's defences on the criminal justice and law enforcement side. This additional momentum went far beyond the by EU standards extraordinarily rapid adoption with a few months of the Framework Decisions on combating terrorism (2002/475/JHA) and on the European Arrest Warrant (2002/584/JHA), driving forward during the rest of the Tampere period also other measures of mutual recognition and substantive harmonisation in the criminal law field as well a strengthening of Europol.[11]

In terms of the enabling and impeding potential of EU Treaty reforms in the JHA domain in the post-Amsterdam Tampere period has shown that Treaty provisions (and their revision) are indeed crucial enablers of policy developments. In the case of the newly created AFSJ the Amsterdam reforms "unlocked" to a considerable extent a considerable policy-making potential in the JHA domain which had remained largely dammed up during the Maastricht period and provided much more adequate canals for transforming the political potential in eventual policy results. The EU's response to the 9/11 challenges is particularly obvious case in point in this context: It is highly doubtful whether without the 1999 Amsterdam reforms and their reinforced JHA objectives, competences and instruments the EU could have adopted instruments like the aforementioned 2002 Framework Decisions on combating terrorism and on the European Arrest Warrant. But if the crucial enabling role of the Treaty reforms is thus beyond doubt, the post-Amsterdam period has also shown that the policy development potential provided by the Treaties' enabling provisions remains fundamentally dependent on political factors to be turned into actual policy streams. The significant post-Amsterdam JHA policy developments in the context of the AFSJ were to a considerable extent driven by political factors such as the relatively strong political consensus reached during the Tampere European Council and – later – the political pressure resulting from the 9/11 attacks. The same could be observed in the later stages of the post-Amsterdam period in the reverse sense: When the high-tide of political momentum generated by Tampere and the 9/11 factor receded around 2003/4 the policy JHA streams also slowed down, especially in the fields of police and judicial cooperation in criminal matters, but also in those of asylum and immigration. The Treaties enabling role can thus be regarded as a clearly fundamental and necessary condition for major

---

11 For a fairly comprehensive analysis of the policy acceleration impact of the 9/11 attacks see Pierre Berthelet, "L'impact des événements du 11 septembre sur la création de l'espace de liberté, de sécurité, et de justice", in *Cultures & Conflits*, No. 46, 2002, pp. 30-63.

EU policy developments, but not a sufficient condition as the later require a significant political momentum in addition.

The post-Amsterdam period also offers additional insights into the impact of the impeding factors built into the Treaties: While the Title VI TEU ("third pillar") canal had clearly been vested with more impeding factors than its Title IV TEC ("first pillar") counterpart the less extensive objectives and competences and the rigid unanimity requirement did not impede the massive surges of criminal justice and police cooperation policies after the 9/11 attacks, showing that Treaty conditioned impeding factors are of a much lower impact if the political momentum in favour of rapid progress is forceful enough. To use our canal image: If the policy/water pressure is strong enough the canal can be filled to capacity with any impeding elements submerged by the flows. However, there has also been evidence for the converse effect: By the time of the 2005-2010 Hague Programme for the AFSJ much of the post-9/11 high policy tide had ebbed away, with the result that the above mentioned impeding factors of the Title VI TEU framework regained in importance, leading to lengthy negotiations with weak least common denominator outcomes, such as in the case of the many limitations of the 2008 European Evidence Warrant (Framework Decision 2008/978/JHA). Our canal image can be applied here as well: If the policy flow fed by political momentum falls far enough the impeding factors come to the surface again like shoals at ebb tide which become an obstacle to navigation.

It is also interesting to recall that the strong re-emergence of the impeding factors in the Title VI TEU after the ebbing away of the 9/11 effect generated enough dissatisfaction amongst some Member States to generate a brief "spill-out" from the canal. Frustrated by the lack of progress with major law enforcement cooperation measures in the context of Title VI TEU a group of seven Member States concluded on 27 May 2005 the Prüm Convention on the stepping up of cross-border cooperation, particularly in combating terrorism, cross-border crime and illegal migration[12] which, inter alia, implemented the principle of availability of DNA files and fingerprinting data to cross-border law enforcement searches. Although much of the content of the Prüm Convention – which was quickly signed by a range of other Member States – was subsequently incorporated into equivalent EU legislation (mainly through the 2008 "Prüm Decisions")[13] this highlighted the persisting

12 Council of the European Union: Prüm Convention, document 10900/05, 7 July 2005.

13 Council Decisions 2008/615/JHA and 2008/616/JHA.

risk[14] of a JHA policy stream finding an outlet outside of the framework of the Treaties if too much impeded by the existing "canals".

4. The Treaty of Lisbon: A Merged Canal ready for more Political Momentum

After the Treaty of Amsterdam, the Treaty of Lisbon reforms in the AFSJ domain – which entered into force in December 2009 – could only be much more modest in terms of their enabling dimension. Amsterdam had already largely pre-empted the field in terms of objectives for the AFSJ – many of which remained only partially fulfilled when the Lisbon Treaty entered into force –, and in terms of instruments and decision-making capacity the Amsterdam Treaty had clearly provided an infinitely better framework for policy progress than its predecessor. However, while a new major "enabling" expansion of objectives and competences was clearly not needed, there were a number of impeding factors which were already identified and addressed during the 2002/2003 negotiations on the Draft Constitutional Treaty within the European Convention and led to reforms which made their way over the (failed) Constitutional Treaty into the Lisbon Treaty, bought, again, at the price of extended "opt-outs" granted to the UK, Ireland and Denmark.

One of those impediments was the "pillar divide" of the AFSJ between Title IV TEC and Title VI TEU which had added countless complications for JHA decision-making and coherence. It has been removed by the merger of former Title IV TEC and Title VI TEU in the new Title V of Part Three of the TFEU which effectively "communitarised" the former "third pillar" fields from the point of view of legal instruments and framework. As regards the latter, the hitherto unrestricted rule of the unanimity requirement has been removed with qualified majority voting now being the standard procedure on AFSJ matters, although with some exceptions – such as for the establishment of the European Public Prosecutor's Office under Article 86 TFEU. The gap/impediment in the field of criminal procedural law has also been addressed by a new corresponding EU competence under Article 82(2)

14 What is clearly a risk from the perspective of the legal and policy coherence of the EU may obviously be regarded as a chance by those arguing that Member States wishing to move ahead in certain policy fields should not be unduly obstructed as long as this serves defined EU objectives. Yet the full consequences of such a partial breaking out from the framework provided by the Treaties are often difficult to predict at the time – and there was certainly a lot of political uncertainty and tension initially surrounding the Prüm initiative (see Daniela Kietz, Andreas Maurer, "Der Vertrag von Prüm: Vertiefungs- und Fragmentierungstendenzen in der Justiz- und Innenpolitik der EU", *Integration*, Vol. 29, 2006, pp. 201-212).

TFEU, and several of the Amsterdam objectives have been adjusted by codifying elements which over the last decade have become part of the political *acquis*, such as the "integrated management of external borders" (Article 77(1)(c) TFEU) and the "common European asylum system" (Article 78(2) TFEU). The Lisbon reforms have also addressed the question of the legitimacy of AFSJ policies which had become more and more important because of the post-Amsterdam expansion of policies and could have turned into a major impediment. This has been addressed by the generalisation – with only very few exceptions – of co-decision by the European Parliament on all AFSJ legislative acts, the removal of the remaining restrictions on judicial control by the Court of Justice and, last but not least, the codification of the Charter of Fundamental Rights as part of the binding EU Treaty framework which – because of the particular sensitivity of many AFSJ fields from the fundamental rights perspective – can be regarded as particularly relevant for the EU JHA domain.[15]

While it is certainly too early to form a comprehensive judgement about the effects of the Lisbon "canalisation works" in the JHA domain one can observe so far a continuous policy flow in the various fields which, however, is at times rather slow (especially in sensitive fields such legal immigration)[16] and comes no way near the dynamic of the early post-Amsterdam years. This can be regarded as being due to the lack of a stronger political momentum rather than to a lack of sufficient enabling conditions or to major impeding elements in the reformed Treaties. With much of the more consensual ground of JHA policy-making already covered during the Amsterdam period, further progress on many JHA issues now often touches much more sensitive questions of domestic politics, legal traditions and national sovereignty (such as in the fields of legal immigration and criminal procedural law). Many Member States therefore tend to be more cautious or outright reluctant, and the Eurozone crisis has surely cast a shadow over the political dynamics of the EU's development well beyond the EMU context. After the Lisbon reforms the Treaty "canalisation" works for the AFSJ seem quite adequate to meet currently defined Treaty objectives, so that the main factor of further policy evolution will be the variable (and unpredictable) flow of political momentum.

---

15 For a more detailed analysis of the Lisbon reforms in the JHA domain, see Francisco Javier Donaire Villa, "El espacio de libertad, seguridad y justicia tras el Tratado de Lisboa: entre supranacionalidad e integracion diferenciada", *Revista española de Derecho Europeo*, No. 35, 2010, pp. 337-364.

16 See Jörg Monar, "Justice and Home Affairs", *Journal of Common Market Studies*, Annual Review, Vol. 50, 2012, pp. 116-131.

5. Conclusions

Our look at the enabling and impeding impact of EU Treaty reforms in the JHA domain, although necessarily sketchy because of the limited space, suggests three conclusions with regard to the role of Treaty reforms in "canalising" policy developments.

Firstly, the Treaties (and their reform when needed) are absolutely crucial as enablers of EU policies. Without the putting into place of a first "canal" by the Treaty of Maastricht and without – in a certain sense – the opening of the floodgates by the Treaty of Amsterdam in terms of objectives and competences there would simply be no AFSJ domain worth the name today, although political momentum determines much of the extent to which the enabling conditions are used for actual policy development.

Secondly, the Treaties can provide for so many policy impeding factors that they can either neutralise much of the general enabling provisions (as happened in the case of the Treaty of Maastricht) or considerably slow down significant policy evolutions (as happened in the case of the Title VI TEU fields in the later post-Amsterdam period). However, the impact of the impeding factors can vary considerably in function of the political momentum/pressure at the given time, with a strong political momentum able to overcome the impeding factors at least to some extent (as happened with the Title VI TEU fields during the post-9/11 political momentum), and a weak political momentum, vice versa, rendering the impeding factors much more powerful obstacles.

Thirdly, if the policy development canal(s) defined by the Treaties are unable to accommodate a strong political momentum/pressure by volume or direction there can be a risk the policy stream "spilling outside" of the Treaty framework and finding alternative ways, although this will then only involve part of the Member States (as it happened in the case of the Schengen system and the Prüm Convention).

The "canal architects" at work during the IGCs therefore bear much responsibility for what may be possible or not possible in terms of later substantive policy evolution – in the JHA domain as well as other EU policy fields. However, once a policy domain has been brought into the Treaties, their impact as enablers of policy developments tends to be more fundamental and far-reaching than their impact as impeders – which should be taken as a positive sign for the integration process and a, hopefully encouraging, signal to future reformers of the Treaties.

Ode an die Freu(n)de

The European Commission as *Amicus Curiae* before European and National Courts

Piet VAN NUFFEL[1]

Member of the Legal Service of the European Commission; Professor in European Law, KU Leuven

Since the 2003 reform of the system of enforcement of the EU competition rules, the Commission has the right to intervene before national courts as *amicus curiae*.[2] That is a quite novel situation, as the Commission used to stand for national courts only when bringing an action in law on behalf of the European Union (EU) or defending the EU in a lawsuit.[3] It does not mean that the Commission is not used to assist courts as an independent adviser. On the contrary, the Commission has been performing that role ever since the beginning of the European Communities by submitting observations to the European Court of Justice (ECJ) in preliminary ruling proceedings. The Commission has also intervened as *amicus curiae* before the European Court of Human Rights[4] and before courts in third countries, in particular in the United States.[5] The aim of this contribution is to analyse to what extent the Commission's right to intervene before national and European courts

1 All views expressed are personal and cannot be ascribed to the European Commission.

2 Article 15(3) of Council Regulation (EC) No. 1/2003 of 16 December 2002 on the implementation of the rules on competition laid down in Articles 81 and 82 of the Treaty [2003] OJ L1/1.

3 E.g., actions brought against taxes imposed in violation of the EU's tax immunity, see Case 199/05 *European Community* [2006] ECR I-10485, or to claim damages incurred as a result of an infringement of competition rules, see C-199/11 *Otis and Others*, nyr (Judgment of 6 November 2012).

4 E.g., European Court of Human Rights, Judgment of 30 June 2005 in *Bosphorus v Ireland*, No. 45036/98.

5 E.g., the Commission's briefs before the US Supreme Court in *Sosa v Alvarez-Machain* (2004) and in *Esther Kiobel v Royal Dutch Petroleum Co. and Others* (2012).

corresponds to the role that is generally ascribed to an *amicus curiae*. The focus will be on the two situations where EU law expressly allows the Commission to intervene in pending proceedings: the interventions before national courts in competition cases and the interventions before the ECJ in preliminary ruling proceedings. Is the Commission as guardian of the Treaties well placed to perform such role, or, in other words, can the *amicus Unionis* perform the function of *amicus curiae*? This contribution is dedicated to Rector Demaret, a true *amicus* of European integration.

1. Introducing the Institution of *Amicus Curiae* in European Union Law

In her doctoral thesis on the institution of the *amicus curiae* Menétrey explains that its origins are apparently not to be found in Roman law but rather in medieval English law.[6] Since judges at that time were generally no professional jurists, they were allowed to call upon lawyers to inform them about specific statutes or precedents that the parties to the case did not indicate in their pleadings.[7] English courts also looked for advice when a party was not entitled to representation, which was most notably the case for suspects of certain serious crimes. Here the *amicus curiae* had to ensure that this person's interest was taken into account.[8] Menétrey cites several contemporaneous definitions and descriptions of the *amicus curiae*, which all have at least two main characteristics in common.[9] On the one hand, they refer to an intervention in a pending case by a person or entity that is not a party to the case but authorised or invited to intervene. On the other hand, the aim of the intervention is to submit information related to the subject matter of the case and purporting to enlighten the court's judgment.

First, it is essential that the *amicus curiae* is not a party to the lawsuit. Its *raison d'être* is precisely to assist the court with arguments or views that may not have been presented by the parties. The *amicus curia* does not necessarily side with one of the litigating parties and certainly does not intervene to defend any proper right in the lawsuit. Its intervention is generally motivated by concerns that go beyond the concrete interest of the parties.

---

6 S. Menétrey, *L'amicus curiae, vers un principe commun de droit procédural?*, Dalloz, 2010, pp. 22-24.

7 *Ibid.*, 24.

8 *Ibid.*, 25.

9 *Ibid.*, 3-4.

Second, the *amicus curiae* purports to bring to the court's attention views or arguments deemed worthwhile to be taken into account. It may raise arguments on behalf of parties which are not represented in the case or present other considerations of general interest. This does not exclude that the interests defended may coincide with those of one the parties. Indeed, the fact that the *amicus curiae* has no proper right to defend in the lawsuit does not mean that it may not choose side.

In European Union law, the function that comes nearest to the *amicus curiae* is the role of the Advocate General at the ECJ, who is called upon to "make, in open court, reasoned submissions on cases which, in accordance with the [ECJ Statute], require his involvement" while "acting with complete impartiality and independence".[10] A more recent expression of *amicus curiae* intervention in EU law is the abovementioned right of the Commission to submit observations to national courts in competition matters. This intervention is clearly different from that of the Advocate General as the Commission's institutional role is not primarily that of an independent adviser, but rather one of formulating legislative proposals, implementing legislation and enforcing EU law. The Commission's right to intervene before national courts may thus trigger questions as regards the impact of its intervention on the parties to the proceedings and about the *rationale* for granting such right to the Commission. Similar questions may however be asked with respect to the right that the Commission enjoys since long to submit observations before the ECJ in preliminary ruling proceedings. It seems appropriate to first discuss this older form of intervention in court proceedings and then compare it to the more recent *amicus curiae* right.

2. Is the Commission a Real *Amicus Curiae* in Preliminary Ruling Proceedings?

A. Submitting Observations in Preliminary Reference Cases

The Commission systematically intervenes in all preliminary reference cases by submitting written observations and, where an oral hearing is organised, by intervening orally. Pursuant to Article 23 of the ECJ Statute, the Court's Registry notifies all references for a preliminary ruling to the Commission, which is then to lodge its written observations within a period of two months.

It follows from the ECJ Statute that the Commission and the Member States are "entitled" to submit written observations in preliminary

---

10 Article 252 TFEU. See Borgsmidt, K., "The Advocate General at the European Court of Justice: A Comparative Study", *European Law Review*, 1988, pp. 106-119.

ruling proceedings. The ECJ sees the right of intervention as an essential element of these proceedings. This can be deduced from the ECJ's case law on the necessity for national courts to define the factual and legal context of the questions they are asking.[11] When applying this requirement, the ECJ commonly explains that the information provided by national courts in their references "must not only enable the Court to reply usefully but also give the governments of the Member States and other interested parties the opportunity to submit observations".[12] The Court sees it as its "duty to ensure that that opportunity is safeguarded, bearing in mind that, by virtue of the abovementioned provision, only the decisions making references are notified to the interested parties".[13]

The ECJ's Statute and Rules of Procedure lay down the formalities to be followed when submitting observations. Like the Member States, the Commission can be represented by members of its staff acting as "agents", who may be assisted by a lawyer or other adviser.[14] Members of the Commission's Legal Service represent the Commission in all court proceedings, hence also before the ECJ, where they may be assisted in certain cases by an external lawyer.

In those cases where the ECJ organises a hearing, the Commission will also intervene orally. That hearing is the only occasion for the parties to the main proceedings, the Member States and the Commission to respond to each other's written observations. Parties or Member States that did not submit written observations may still decide to submit their observations orally at the hearing.[15] In so far as a hearing is organised, the parties to the main proceedings thus have the right to reply to the Commission's observations. In that respect, the Commission's intervention in preliminary ruling procedures derogates less to the principle of contradictory proceedings than, for instance, the Opinion delivered by the Advocate General. There is indeed no right for the parties to the main proceedings to submit comments on the Advocate General's Opinion.[16] Likewise, there is no right to respond to the Com-

---

11 See, e.g., Joined Cases 141/81 to 143/81 *Holdijk and Others* [1982] ECR 1299, paragraph 6; Case C-176/96 *Lehtonen and Castors Braine* [2000] ECR I-2681, paragraph 23. These requirements have since 1 November 2012 been integrated in the ECJ Rules of Procedure, Article 94.

12 See, e.g., Case C-176/96 *Lehtonen and Castors Braine* [2000] ECR I-2681, paragraph 23; Case C-506/04 *Wilson* [2006] ECR I-8613, paragraph 39.

13 *Ibid.*

14 ECJ Statute, Article 19.

15 ECJ Rules of Procedure, Article 96(2).

16 See Order of the Court of Justice in Case C-17/98 *Emesa Sugar (Free Zone) and Aruba* [2000] ECR I-665, paras. 10-18. Whereas that situation has been criticised for

mission's submissions when there is no hearing, for example where the ECJ decides to rule by reasoned order or considers that it has sufficient information to rule without holding a hearing.[17]

B. The Contribution of the Commission's Submissions to the Judicial Debate

It is telling that the Commission enjoys before the ECJ the same procedural rights as the parties to the main proceedings. The preliminary ruling procedure is indeed conceived not as a continuation of the national procedure but as a dialogue between courts,[18] in the context of which both the parties to the main proceedings and the interveners are invited to inform the ECJ on the interpretation that should be given to the relevant provisions of EU law rather than to exchange arguments.[19] This may explain why the procedure does not necessarily provide the parties to the main proceedings with a right to respond to the Commission's observations. The Commission's right to intervene can be assessed from two perspectives: one is the perspective of the parties to the main proceedings; the other is that of the Court, or rather of the legal system as a whole.

First, for the parties to the main proceedings, it is clear that the possibility of having the Commission and the Member States intervene before the ECJ interferes with the autonomy that they may enjoy in the context of the national proceedings, at least in civil cases. Once a case has been referred to Luxembourg, the parties to the main proceedings are indeed no longer master of the scope of their legal dispute and have no control over the legal arguments that may be produced. The only aspects of the dispute over which they preserve some degree of "control" are, on the one hand, the factual background of the dispute, for which the ECJ starts from the description given by the national court and, on the other hand, the interpretation of national law, for which the ECJ will equally defer to the national court. As far as the discussion on EU law is concerned, the parties have no control over the content of the debate. The ECJ does not hesitate to respond to a preliminary reference on the basis of EU law provisions that the national court did not men-

---

not respecting the safeguards flowing from Article 6 of the European Convention on Human Rights, the European Court of Human Rights did not see any problem as parties have the right to ask for the oral procedure to be re-opened: decision of 20 January 2009 in *PO Kokkelvisserij v The Netherlands*, No. 13645/05.

17 ECJ Rules of Procedure, Articles 76(2) and 99.

18 See Joined Cases 28/62, 29/62 and 30/62 *Da Costa and Others* [1963] ECR 31, at 38; Case C-2/06 *Kempter* [2008] ECR I-411, paragraphs 41-42.

19 See the Order in Case C-73/07 *Satakunnan Markkinapörssi Oy and Satamedia Oy* [2007] ECR I-7075, paragraph 11.

tion or by pronouncing on issues that were not touched upon in the national court's reference. In many instances this is the result of the Commission (or the Member States) having brought up issues that had not been discussed in the main proceedings.[20] In such cases, it is of course essential for the parties to the main proceedings to have the possibility to respond to the Commission's submissions.

Whether or not the parties to the main proceedings are pleased with the Commission's submissions depends on their position in the case. In some cases, the Commission cannot avoid siding with one of the parties to the main proceedings. The Commission may have submitted legislative initiatives in a field, adopted guidelines or communications or even have taken action against Member States or – in the field of competition – against undertakings on similar issues as the ones brought up in the preliminary reference.

Seen from the angle of the ECJ, the Commission's submissions are certainly a valuable source of information that complements the more "partisan" views of the parties to the main proceedings with a viewpoint that places the concrete dispute in the larger context of EU law and policies. The Commission's submissions certainly also facilitate the work of the Advocate General, who after having heard the parties to the main proceedings and the interveners will present his or her own view on the issues. What distinguishes the Commission's submissions from the Opinion of the Advocate General is not only that they come earlier in the proceedings, but also that they express the institution's policy line whereas the Advocate General presents a purely personal view. The fact that the Commission may defend its own policy line does not however diminish the *amicus curiae* character of its submissions.[21] The Commission indeed will not defend a view for the sole purpose of assisting one of the parties to the main proceedings: its views are always based on general considerations of law and policy that go beyond the interest of the parties involved in the main proceedings.

The possibility for the Commission (and the Member States) to intervene in preliminary ruling proceedings clearly demonstrates how the role of the ECJ in these proceedings is understood to be more that of a "law maker" than that of a court settling disputes between opposing parties. Inviting other entities than the parties to submit their views on the questions raised by the national court implicitly confirms that the Court's ruling will not only be decisive for the dispute in the main proceedings but also contribute to the development of the law to be applied in all other situations caught by the relevant legal provisions.

---

20 See, e.g., Case C-437/09 *AG2R Prévoyance*, [2011], ECR I-973, paragraphs 23-27.

21 See also S. Menétrey, *supra*, note 6, p. 143.

This begs the question why it has been the Commission that – together with the Member States – has been given the right to submit observations in preliminary reference cases. The answer is probably to be found in the pivotal role that the Treaty makers wished to grant to both the Commission and the Member States in the development of the EU legal order. The same entities indeed have the right to challenge the legality of any binding EU act by introducing an action for annulment without having to prove any specific interest.[22] As far as the Commission is concerned, the right to submit observations in preliminary ruling proceedings also corresponds to its task as "guardian of the Treaties" to ensure the correct application of EU law within the Member States. Conferring the right to intervene on both the Commission and the Member States might have been chosen as a method to ensure that the Court would be enlightened by submissions that reflect both the general Union interest and the more particular interests of the Member States' governments.

3. The Commission's Intervention as "Amicus Curiae" before National Courts in the Area of Competition Law

A. Submitting Observations on Competition Issues before National Courts

In the field of competition law, it has since long been accepted that the principle of sincere cooperation implies that the Commission is obliged to provide national courts with all information they need to have EU law enforced.[23] This form of cooperation has been codified in Article 15(1) of Regulation No. 1/2003, which entitles national courts in proceedings for the application of Articles 101 or 102 TFEU to ask the Commission either to transmit information in its possession or to give its opinion on competition issues. At the same time, national competition authorities (NCAs) and the Commission have been given the right to intervene as *amici curiae* by submitting written observations in cases before the national courts (Article 15(3) Regulation No. 1/2003). These observations differ from "opinions" issued by the Commission under Article 15(1) of Regulation No. 1/2003 since such opinions are made only in response to a specific request from a national court, whereas the

22 See Van Nuffel, P., "What's in a Member State? Central and Decentralized Authorities before the Community Courts", *Common Market Law Review*, 2001, pp. 874-875.

23 Order in Case C-2/88 IMM *Zwartveld and Others* [1990] ECR I-3365, paragraph 18; Case C-234/89 *Delimitis* [1991] ECR I-935, paragraph 53; Case C-344/98 *Masterfoods and HB* [2000] ECR I-11369, paragraph 56.

Commission usually submits observations under Article 15(3) on its own initiative. So far, the Commission has made a selective use of this possibility to intervene as *amicus curiae*, with around ten interventions between 2006[24] and 2012.[25] Most of them are published on the website of the Commission's Directorate General for Competition.[26]

Article 15 of Regulation No. 1/2003 seems to have been written in the understanding that such *amicus curiae* interventions would be triggered by the Commission's own systematic analysis of the national court's application of Articles 101 or 102 TFEU. Article 15(2) indeed requires the Member States to inform the Commission of any judgment deciding on the application of Articles 101 or 102 TFEU. In practice, however, the Commission is not systematically informed of all relevant cases and mostly hears about important cases from NCAs or the press.[27] Moreover, Article 15(3) of Regulation No. 1/2003 is not meant to have the Commission systematically intervene whenever there is a risk of inconsistent application of the EU competition rules. That would indeed be contrary to the spirit of the 2003 reform that introduced a system of decentralised enforcement of EU competition rules, in which responsibility for supervising compliance with Articles 101 and 102 TFEU is vested primarily in the national courts and the NCAs in order to enable the Commission to concentrate on investigating the most serious infringements.

Article 15(3) of Regulation No. 1/2003 establishes a clear "right" for the Commission to submit written observations before national courts provided that these observations concern the coherent application of Articles 101 and 102 TFEU. Thus, the Commission's power to intervene was disputed before a Dutch court where the Commission wished to submit observations in a case concerning the tax deductibility of a fine imposed by it on a German undertaking, who had passed it on in part to a Dutch subsidiary (anonymised as "X BV"). The Dutch tax authorities did not allow X BV to deduct the fine, which led to a dispute before the Amsterdam Court of Appeal. The undertaking contested the Commission's right to intervene in that litigation as it concerned the

24 Observations submitted to the Paris Court of Appeal in *Garage Gremeau*.

25 See the observations submitted in 2009 to the Paris Court of Appeal in *Pierre Fabre Dermo-Cosmétique* and to the Amsterdam Court of Appeal in *X BV*; in 2010 to the Irish High Court in *BIDS*; to the Slovak Supreme Court in *Cargo Slovakia* and to the Dutch Supreme Court in *X BV*; in 2011 to the French Supreme Court in *France Télécom e.a.*, to the UK High Court in *National Grid* and to the Austrian Supreme Court in *Schenker* and in 2012 to the Belgian Constitutional Court in *Tessenderlo Chemie*.

26 http://ec.europa.eu/competition/court/antitrust_amicus_curiae.html (accessed on July 2013).

27 E.g. Case C-429/07 *X BV* [2009] ECR I-4833, paragraph 16.

application of Dutch tax law and not Articles 101 or 102 TFEU. The Amsterdam Court asked the ECJ for a preliminary ruling. For the ECJ there was no doubt that the Commission could rely on Article 15(3) of Regulation No. 1/2003 in this case as any decision allowing the tax deductibility of the Commission's fines "is capable of impairing the effectiveness of those penalties and therefore might compromise the coherent application of Articles [101 or 102 TFEU]".[28] Whereas the ECJ thus made a broad reading of the scope for intervention under Regulation No. 1/2003, it is clear that the Commission cannot bring up whatever issue of EU law before the national court.

Regulation No. 1/2003 does not lay down a procedural framework within which the Commission's observations are to be submitted.[29] The Regulation only foresees the Commission's right to request the national court to transmit or ensure the transmission to it of any documents necessary for the assessment of the case.[30] The Commission's intervention is thus governed by the procedural rules and practices of the national court. These rules and practices must however respect the general principles of EU law. In line with the ECJ's case law, they cannot make the submission of the Commission's observations more difficult than the submission of observations in court proceedings where equivalent national law is applied and cannot make the submission of such observations excessively difficult or practically impossible.[31]

In accordance with these principles, the Commission is to respect the relevant national procedural rules as far as they do not constitute an undue obstacle to its right to submit observations. In that respect, account must be taken of the other party's procedural rights and the importance for the parties of having their case decided within a reasonable period of time. Accordingly, one can expect the Commission to accept the national court's case as it finds it at the moment of its intervention. In practice, the Commission's services will inform the national court of their intention to intervene, after which the court may invite the Commission to submit its written observations within a given period of time. According to Article 15(3) of Regulation No. 1/2003, the Commission has the right to submit written observations but needs the permission of the national court to also make oral observations. The

---

28 *Ibid.*, paragraphs 37 and 38.

29 Commission Notice on the cooperation between the Commission and the courts of the EU Member States in the application of Articles 81 and 82 EC, OJ 2004 C101/54 (hereinafter "Cooperation Notice"), point 34.

30 Regulation No. 1/2003, Article 15(3), second subparagraph.

31 Case 33/76 *Rewe* [1976] ECR 1989, paragraph 5, and Case 45/76 *Comet* [1976] ECR 2043, paragraphs 13-16.

Commission usually does not request to be heard orally, but where an oral hearing is organised, it will generally be represented.

B. The Contribution of the Commission's Submissions to the Judicial Debate

The Commission's intervention pursuant to Article 15(3) of Regulation No. 1/2003 has a clear objective, namely to ensure the coherent application of Articles 101 and 102 TFEU. In the first place, the Commission's intervention aims at ensuring consistency in the application of the EU competition rules throughout the Member States. It follows from the ECJ's Judgment in *X BV* that the Commission can submit observations to ensure not only the uniform application of the competition rules but also the effectiveness of their enforcement. It is not the purpose of the Commission's intervention to consider the merits of the case pending before the national court. In its Notice on the cooperation with national courts the Commission announced that it would rather provide the national court with a legal or economic analysis of the relevant facts underlying the case.[32] In practice, it often limits itself to a presentation of the legal framework, with references to the relevant case law, decisional practice and guidelines and, if need be, some further orientations on the way these provisions should be applied in a case such as the one pending before the national court. Both as to their form and contents, the Commission's observations under Article 15(3) of Regulation No. 1/2003 therefore do not differ greatly from observations submitted before the ECJ. Most of the Commission's interventions occur before national courts of appeal or supreme courts reviewing the decision taken at a lower instance.[33] The Commission can then take from the lower court's judgment the issues on which it specifically wishes to make observations.

In order to assess the *amicus curiae* character of the Commission's observations, it is again necessary to analyse not only the usefulness of the Commission's intervention for the national court but also the impact of the intervention on the position of the parties to the proceedings.

As regards its relationship with the other parties, the Commission stresses that its intervention is part of its duty to defend the public interest and not intended to serve the private interests of any of the parties to the proceedings.[34] The Commission will not therefore hear any of the parties about its assistance to the national court. In practice,

32 Cooperation Notice, point 32.

33 The only exception so far being the intervention in *National Grid*.

34 Cooperation Notice, point 19.

however, it occurs that the Commission has been informed about the case by one of the parties, in particular where the national court reviews the decision of a NCA. In that situation, the Commission endeavours to be transparent on its previous contacts with that party.[35]

Nevertheless, even though the Commission commits to remaining "neutral" and "objective" in its intervention before the national court, its views in a given case may correspond more to one party's views than to another's. In cases where the Commission intervenes to have the effectiveness of competition law enforcement preserved, it is even likely that its intervention will take the side of the public authorities enforcing the competition rules as opposed to the interests of the undertakings held to infringe those rules. It is therefore important to ensure that the intervention at least does not impair the other parties' procedural rights, such as the right to respond to the Commission's observations. Whereas Regulation No. 1/2003 itself does not regulate the parties' procedural rights before the national court, Member States clearly have to implement its provisions in full respect of the parties' fundamental rights,[36] which includes the right to fair trial. National provisions implementing Article 15(3) of Regulation should therefore provide for the parties' right to respond to the Commission's observations.[37]

Second, from the point of view of the national courts, the Commission's right to submit observations undoubtedly provides them with a useful source of information. For its part, the Commission usually stresses in its observations that these are not binding and that only the ECJ can issue a binding interpretation of the provisions of EU law via the preliminary ruling procedure. In two cases, the Commission's observations have prompted the national court to refer questions to the ECJ.[38]

The Commission's selective use of the right to submit observations under Regulation No. 1/2003 and its insistence on the last word on the interpretation of EU law remaining with the ECJ suggest that the purpose of these *amicus curiae* observations may be more to direct national courts in their resolution of a specific case rather than to assist the courts in the development of EU competition law. In this respect, inter-

35 *Ibid.*

36 *Ibid.*, point 35(a).

37 See European Court on Human Rights, *Vermeulen v Belgium*, Reports 1996-I, p. 234, § 33; *Van Orshoven v. Belgium*, Reports 1997-III, p. 1051, § 41; *Kress v France*, 7 June 2001, No. 39594/98, § 74.

38 See Case C-439/09 *Pierre Fabre Dermo-Cosmétique*, nyr (Judgment of 13 October 2011) and Case C-681/11 *Schenker & Co and Others*, nyr (Judgment of 18 June 2013). A somewhat different situation occurred in *X BV*, where the court's referral to the ECJ concerned the very right of the Commission to intervene.

ventions under Regulation No. 1/2003 would then differ from interventions in preliminary ruling proceedings, where, as discussed above, the Commission's systematic involvement purports to assist the ECJ in its uniform interpretation of EU law. The *amicus curiae* interventions under Regulation No. 1/2003 are a clear sector-specific instrument for the Commission in an area where competition authorities and courts are together responsible for the enforcement of the same rules and interventions by the competition authorities before the national courts are a means to ensure consistency in the application of these rules.

4. Conclusive Remarks

The Commission is clearly privileged to have been granted the right to intervene in any preliminary ruling proceedings and, more recently, in national proceedings where competition matters are at stake. In the first situation, the Commission's right to intervene is justified by its pivotal role in ensuring the correct application of EU law. In the second case, its intervention serves the more specific aim to ensure the coherent application of EU competition rules. Without doubt, such interventions serve to "enlighten" the courts in a manner that is typical for *amicus curiae* interventions.

As any *amicus curiae* intervention, the Commission's submissions in either situation inevitably have an impact on the parties to the proceedings, whose position may or may not be supported by the Commission's views. In this respect, the importance has been stressed of enabling the parties to react to the Commission's submissions. As far as the ECJ is concerned, the parties can respond to the Commission's observations in those cases only where an oral hearing is organised. Still, the proceedings in preliminary reference cases are not autonomous and parties may eventually claim respect of their procedural rights before the national courts, like in national proceedings where the Commission intervenes under Regulation No. 1/2003.

IV

Marché intérieur et politiques d'accompagnement/ Internal Market and Related Policies

Good Law or not Good Law

Les avatars de la jurisprudence *Keck* et *Mithouard*

Frédérique BERROD

Professeure à l'IEP, Université de Strasbourg ;
directrice de la Fédération de recherche
L'Europe en mutation FR UdS/CNRS 3241

Sortie nord de Strasbourg, prendre l'autoroute en direction de Paris. Le lecteur attentif des arrêts de la Cour de justice de l'UE peut apercevoir, dans le paysage industriel aux alentours immédiats de l'autoroute, la matérialisation de deux jurisprudences fondatrices du droit de l'Union européenne. La Brasserie du Pêcheur apparaît d'abord, laquelle est à l'origine de l'établissement, par la Cour de justice, du principe de la responsabilité de l'État législateur en cas de violation du droit de l'Union.[1] À quelques encablures, se dégage sur l'horizon la grande surface dans laquelle messieurs Keck et Mithouard avaient autorisé la revente à perte de café et de picon bière, amenant la Cour à opérer un revirement de la jurisprudence concernant le critère de qualification d'une réglementation étatique en une mesure d'effet équivalant à une restriction quantitative.[2]

Au-delà de l'anecdote, l'actualité jurisprudentielle amène à se demander si la solution dégagée il y a presque 20 ans dans l'arrêt *Keck* est toujours pertinente. Il faut rappeler en deux mots que, dans cet arrêt, la Cour établit un système de présomption qui distingue entre les mesures afférentes aux produits, présumées entravantes en application de la logique *Cassis de Dijon* (point 15) et certaines modalités de vente,

1 Arrêt de la Cour du 26 mars 1995, *Brasserie du Pêcheur*, aff. C-46 et 48/93, Rec. p. I-1131. Cette affaire traite par ailleurs des conséquences contentieuses de l'incompatibilité de la loi allemande de pureté de la bière avec l'actuel article 34 TFUE, constatée par la Cour dans son arrêt du 12 mars 1987, *Commission c. Allemagne*, aff. 178/84, Rec. p. 1227.

2 Arrêt du 24 novembre 1993, *Keck et Mithouard*, aff. C-267 et 268/91, Rec. p. I-6097.

présumées non entravantes, dès lors qu'elles sont indistinctement applicables et affectent de la même manière, en droit comme en fait, la commercialisation des produits nationaux et importés (point 16).

Simple et aisément compréhensible, cette approche duale des mesures d'effet équivalent par leur objet et pas par leurs effets avait pour principal objectif de désengorger les services des juges de l'Union, submergés – à les en croire – par l'afflux des contentieux dans lesquels les entreprises contestaient toute forme de réglementation commerciale au regard de l'actuel Article 34 TFUE.[3] Mettant en place un système de présomption, la jurisprudence *Keck* redonnait aux États la liberté de principe de réglementer les modalités de vente[4] et facilitait le travail de qualification des juges nationaux.

On ne fait pourtant pas une bonne jurisprudence avec ces bons sentiments et l'arrêt *Keck* est certainement à ce jour l'arrêt le plus violemment commenté.[5] La question qui est posée est celle de l'opportunité et de la pérennité de cette approche duale des points 15 et 16. Se pose plus globalement la question du critère de la mesure d'effet équivalent. On peut se demander, au fil de la jurisprudence post-Keck, quel est le critère qui permet de considérer qu'une modalité de vente constitue une mesure d'effet équivalent interdite par l'Article 34 TFUE.

La jurisprudence de la Cour de justice de l'Union européenne a tenté de répondre à ces questions et, ce faisant, a incontestablement révélé l'efficacité de la jurisprudence *Keck*.[6] L'Article 34 TFUE ne permet plus concrètement de contester toute réglementation étatique, mais permet de concentrer le contrôle sur les mesures qui sont les plus entravantes parce

---

3 Ce que l'on déduit implicitement du point 14 de l'arrêt *Keck*.

4 Compétence partagée au titre de l'article 4, paragraphe 2 a) TFUE. La compétence partagée permet, selon l'article 2 TFUE, à l'Union comme aux États de légiférer. Ces derniers doivent néanmoins se conformer à l'harmonisation de l'Union quand elle existe.

5 L'auteure de ces lignes se souvient des discussions passionnées soulevées par l'arrêt Keck au moment où elle était assistante du professeur Demaret au département d'études juridiques du Collège d'Europe, des conférences très critiques données à l'époque par le professeur Mattera et de l'échange encore très vif entre ce dernier et le professeur Kovar dans une conférence donnée à Strasbourg en décembre 2008 sur le principe de reconnaissance mutuelle. Voir aussi, par exemple, A. Mattera, « De l'arrêt Dassonville à l'arrêt Keck : l'obscure clarté d'une jurisprudence riche en principes novateurs et en contradictions », *Revue du Marché Unique Européen*, 1994, p. 117 ; R. Kovar, « Dassonville, Keck et les autres : de la mesure avant toute chose », *Revue trimestrielle de droit européen*, 2006, p. 213 ; F. Picod, « La nouvelle approche de la Cour de justice en matière d'entraves aux échanges », *Revue trimestrielle de droit européen*, 1998, p. 169 ; S. Weatherill, « After Keck : some thoughts on how to clarify the clarification », *Common Market Law Review*, 1996, p. 885.

6 Dans ce sens, voir l'analyse de R. Kovar, *supra*.

qu'elles empêchent en droit ou en fait la vente, sur le marché national, de produits légalement fabriqués dans un État membre.[7] Il faut aussi reconnaître que l'approche de la Cour dans cette affaire fut source d'interrogation : la distinction entre le point 15 et le point 16 est moins simple qu'elle n'y paraît. Les États ont enfin profité de l'arrêt *Keck* pour éviter de se poser la question de l'euro-compatibilité de leurs lois nationales.

La keckophonie[8] ambiante à la Cour de justice était peut-être à bout de souffle et la juridiction a senti un avis de vent contraire. C'est pourquoi elle a posé, en 2009, la question très directement à l'ensemble des États membres et à la Commission, en rouvrant la procédure orale dans l'affaire *Commission contre Italie* dite *remorques italiennes*[9] et en les invitant à répondre à la question suivante :

> Dans quelle mesure et sous quelles conditions les dispositions nationales qui régissent non pas les caractéristiques d'un produit mais son utilisation, et qui sont indistinctement applicables aux produits nationaux et importés, doivent-elles être considérées comme des mesures d'effet équivalant à des restrictions quantitatives ?

L'avocat général Yves Bot répond très clairement à la question dans les deuxièmes conclusions de cette affaire, en plaidant pour une nouvelle conception de la mesure d'effet équivalent dans cette hypothèse et dans cette hypothèse seulement – qui comprend des réglementations nationales qui régissent les conditions d'utilisation des produits. Il estime que de telles réglementations, dès lors qu'elles entravent l'accès au marché national, sont à considérer comme des mesures d'effet équivalent interdites par l'Article 34 TFUE.[10]

À cet égard, la réponse de la Cour de justice est beaucoup moins claire. Elle conclut que

> il ressort d'une jurisprudence également constante que l'Article 28 CE reflète l'obligation de respecter les principes de non-discrimination et de reconnaissance mutuelle des produits légalement fabriqués et commercialisés

---

7 Voir les explications données par l'avocat général Tesauro, dans ses conclusions dans l'affaire *Hünermund*, arrêt de la Cour du 15 décembre 1993, aff. C-292/92, Rec. p. I-6787, spéc. p. I-6800 et suiv.

8 Expression empruntée à Anne Rigaux, « Symphonie déconcertante ou Keckophonie. À propos des dissonances de l'arrêt Morellato, CJCE, 18 sept. 2003, aff. C-416/00 », Europe, novembre 2003, chron. n° 13.

9 Arrêt de la Cour du 10 février 2009, *Commission c. Italie*, aff. C-110/05, Rec. p. I-519. Premières conclusions de l'avocat général Léger rendues le 5 octobre 2006.

10 Point 137 des deuxièmes conclusions de l'avocat général Bot, rendues le 8 juillet 2008.

> dans d'autres États membres, ainsi que celle d'assurer aux produits communautaires un libre accès aux marchés nationaux,[11]

sans discuter au fond la pertinence de la jurisprudence *Keck*.

Cette apparente continuité signifie-t-elle que l'arrêt *Keck* est *still good law*, au prix d'une lecture recentrée sur le critère de l'accès au marché ? Ou est-ce que la Cour enterre discrètement la jurisprudence *Keck* ?

L'analyse de cette évolution jurisprudentielle conduit à constater un dépassement progressif de l'arrêt *Keck* (1) et, au final, son *aggiornamento* (2).

1. Le dépassement progressif de l'arrêt *Keck*

La jurisprudence *Cassis de Dijon* a permis aux institutions de l'Union de contrôler des mesures qui, même en étant indistinctement applicables, sont constitutives d'une entrave pour le commerce entre les États membres.[12] Ce contrôle plus poussé de l'entrave est compensé par la possibilité, pour les États, d'invoquer des exigences impératives d'intérêt général, en plus des motifs énumérés limitativement par l'Article 36 TFUE, pour justifier leur mesure d'effet équivalent. Les institutions de l'Union, dont la Cour de justice, peuvent alors vérifier la proportionnalité de la mesure, par rapport à la protection de l'exigence impérative mise en avant par les États. Cette approche présentait l'avantage de contraindre les États à devoir justifier de la proportionnalité de leur réglementation, mais risquait – notable désavantage – de remettre en cause, sur le fond, leur compétence de réglementer leur marché national.[13] En effet, toute réglementation commerciale devait être justifiée, sans que la Cour mesure toujours son effet d'entrave et refuse de considérer que seules les entraves substantielles doivent être justifiées.[14]

L'arrêt *Keck* a permis de recentrer le critère de la mesure d'effet équivalent en évitant de considérer que toute réglementation, du simple fait qu'elle empêche ou prescrit tel ou tel comportement, est une entrave

[11] Point 34.

[12] Arrêt de la Cour du 20 février 1979, *Rewe-Zentral*, dit « *Cassis de Dijon* », 120/78, Rec. p. 649.

[13] Voir dans ce sens les conclusions de l'avocat général Bot, deuxièmes conclusions dans l'affaire *remorques italiennes*, points 75 et 94.

[14] On peut rappeler que la Cour avait refusé l'application de la théorie *de minimis* pour l'application des règles de libre circulation, défendue par l'avocat général Jacobs dans ses conclusions, arrêt de la Cour du 9 février 1995, *Leclerc-Siplec*, aff. C-412/93, Rec. p. I-179.

au commerce entre les États membres.[15] Si les mesures nationales afférentes aux conditions que le produit doit remplir sont présumées entravantes, les modalités de vente sont quant à elles présumées non entravantes.

La distinction entre produits et modalités de vente repose sur l'expérience pratique du contrôle des mesures des États à l'aune de l'Article 34 TFUE, en 1993. Il apparaissait clairement que le fait, pour un opérateur économique, de devoir transformer un produit ou de le réemballer se révélait indubitablement plus coûteux et entravant pour le commerce entre les États que le simple fait de ne pas pouvoir utiliser un canal de distribution ou de devoir adapter une campagne de publicité, ou encore de ne pas revendre à perte. Dans cette dernière hypothèse, il est clair que la législation nationale peut aboutir, certes, à diminuer le volume des ventes,[16] mais sans empêcher ou rendre excessivement difficile, en principe, la commercialisation du produit sur le marché national. Cette apparente simplicité s'est en réalité avérée trompeuse. L'affaire *remorques italiennes* a été l'occasion de poser, pour la première fois de front, la question de la pertinence de l'approche duale de l'arrêt *Keck* (A).

Si l'on met en perspective toutes les réglementations qui se trouvent en réalité à la frontière des points 15 et 16, on voit que la Cour passe d'une application mécanique de l'arrêt *Keck* à une lecture combinée des points 16 et 17, mettant à jour le critère de l'accès au marché (B).

A. *Une distinction finalement simpliste entre produits et modalités de vente*

À première vue, la distinction opérée par l'arrêt *Keck* est simple : les mesures afférentes aux produits sont celles qui concernent notamment leur dénomination, leur forme, leurs dimensions, leur poids, leur composition, leur présentation, leur étiquetage ou leur conditionnement. Les modalités de vente sont, en principe, les règles qui n'entrent pas dans le champ du point 15. À bien lire la Cour, ces deux catégories sont mutuellement exclusives et épuisent les « figures » juridiques que peuvent prendre les différentes réglementations étatiques de nature commerciale.

---

15 Voir par exemple ces conséquences à partir de l'arrêt de la Cour du 29 juin 1995, *Commission c. Grèce* dit lait pour nourrissons, aff. C-391/92, Rec. p. I-1642 ; l'application du point 16 évite toute discussion sur les justifications puisqu'il n'y a pas d'entrave à la libre circulation des marchandises. Raisonner autrement revient, il faut le souligner, à considérer la diversité des législations comme étant, par nature, un désavantage commercial.

16 Voir l'arrêt *Keck*, point 13.

La réalité est vite devenue plus complexe. Comment classer les règles relatives à des conditions de fabrication[17] ou à l'utilisation d'un produit,[18] comment qualifier une publicité qui figure sur l'emballage du produit ?[19] Ces questions ont dans un premier temps été ignorées par la Cour,[20] puis elle va tenter d'appliquer le précédent de l'arrêt *Keck*, tout en en soulignant certaines spécificités.

Par exemple, dans l'arrêt *Alfa Vita*,[21] la Cour évite la question, en expliquant maladroitement que :

> Il est constant que la caractéristique principale des produits « *bake-off* » est d'être livrés, dans les points de vente, après que les étapes importantes de préparation desdits produits ont été achevées. [...] Dans ces conditions, exiger des vendeurs de produits « *bake-off* » de se mettre en conformité avec l'ensemble des prescriptions applicables à une boulangerie traditionnelle, [...], ne tient pas compte de la spécificité de ces produits et engendre des coûts supplémentaires rendant ainsi plus difficile la commercialisation desdits produits. Cette réglementation constitue donc un obstacle à l'importation qui ne peut être considérée comme établissant une modalité de vente au sens de l'arrêt Keck.[22]

Est-ce à dire que la réglementation nationale n'est pas une modalité de vente puisque la Cour conclut qu'elle ne l'est pas au sens de l'arrêt *Keck* ? Elle peut aussi vouloir dire que c'est une modalité de vente qui ne bénéficie pas de la présomption de non-entrave posée par le point 16, puisqu'elle « constitue un obstacle à l'importation ». Il est difficile de savoir si la Cour se rattache artificiellement au point 16 ou si elle fait évoluer cette jurisprudence eu égard à la spécificité de l'affaire sous examen.

Il est en tout état de cause démontré par l'ensemble de la jurisprudence qu'il existe une zone grise, non couverte par la distinction point 15/point 16. Tout consiste donc à savoir s'il faut abandonner la

---

17 Arrêt de la Cour du 18 septembre 2003, *Morellato*, aff. C-416/00, Rec. p. I-9357.

18 Voir les conclusions de l'avocat général Léger dans l'affaire *remorques italiennes*.

19 Arrêt de la Cour du 6 juillet 1995, *Mars*, aff. C-470/93, Rec. p. I-1923.

20 Ainsi, dans l'affaire *Morellato*, la Cour dévoie la qualification de modalité de vente, en l'appliquant à une exigence de conditionnement du produit, qui devrait, logiquement, tomber dans le point 15 de l'arrêt *Keck*. Anne Rigaux, dans son commentaire *supra*, conclut que « la dichotomie artificiellement introduite depuis une dizaine d'années dans la jurisprudence relative au contrôle par la Cour des réglementations nationales relatives aux produits et celles relatives aux modalités de vente n'est évidemment pas l'instrument de simplification adéquate, et il est clair que bon nombre de réglementations se réduisent difficilement à l'un ou l'autre des cas de figure ».

21 Arrêt de la Cour du 14 septembre 2006, *Alfa Vita Vassilopoulos*, aff. C-158/04, Rec. p. I-8156.

22 Point 19.

distinction opérée par l'arrêt *Keck* ou admettre des hypothèses dans lesquelles cette distinction ne s'applique pas.[23]

Les atermoiements des institutions révèlent ici que la catégorie des modalités de vente n'est pas aussi cohérente qu'il y paraissait dans une première analyse. Toute réglementation ne pouvant pas *per se* être considérée comme entravant la libre circulation des marchandises, il faut bien déterminer un critère de qualification de son effet entravant.

B. Le pivot du raisonnement : le critère du libre accès au marché

Pour ce faire, on peut relire l'arrêt *Keck* pour tenter d'élucider le fondement de la distinction entre les mesures afférentes aux produits et les modalités de vente. Dans le cadre du point 15, les mesures afférentes aux produits sont présumées entravantes, en application de la jurisprudence *Cassis de Dijon*. Dans ce dernier arrêt, la réglementation allemande des alcools rendait en effet impossible la commercialisation de Cassis de Dijon sur le marché allemand.

Si on combine ce constat avec la directive 70/50,[24] il apparaît que les mesures interdites par l'Article 34 TFUE sont les mesures distinctement applicables qui subordonnent l'accès au marché national à une condition discriminatoire ou plus difficile à satisfaire pour les produits importés.[25] Mais on déduit aussi de l'affaire *Cassis de Dijon* que peuvent être interdites les mesures indistinctement applicables qui ont un effet anormal sur le commerce entre les États membres,[26] c'est-à-dire rendent impossible ou trop difficile l'accès des importations au marché national. L'arrêt *Cassis de Dijon* donne l'occasion à la Cour de justice de donner une signification juridique à la condition des « effets restrictifs sur la libre circulation des marchandises qui dépassent le cadre des effets propres d'une réglementation commerciale » de l'Article 3 de la directive 70/50. Cet effet anormal est matérialisé par une réglementation indistinctement applicable qui empêche l'accès des produits importés au marché national, sans pouvoir être justifiée par la protection proportionnée d'une exigence impérative. En cela, le point de l'arrêt 15 de l'arrêt *Keck* est bien fondé sur le critère de l'accès au marché, qui est présumé

---

23 Voir l'avocat général Poiares Maduro dans l'affaire *Alfa Vita* et les conclusions de l'avocat général Bot dans l'affaire *remorques italiennes*, point 81 en particulier.

24 Directive de la Commission du 22 décembre 1969, fondée sur les dispositions de l'article 33, paragraphe 7, portant suppression des mesures d'effet équivalant à des restrictions quantitatives à l'importation non visées par d'autres dispositions prises en vertu du traité CEE, JOCE du 19 janvier 1970, n° L 13, p. 29.

25 Considérants 4 et 5 de la directive 70/50.

26 Article 3 de la directive 70/50.

trop entravé par toutes les mesures étatiques qui conditionnent la forme, la dimension, le poids, la composition, la présentation, l'identification et le conditionnement des produits.[27]

Dans l'application « mécaniste » de la jurisprudence *Cassis de Dijon*, qui caractérise la jurisprudence des années 1980, la Cour va peu à peu « oublier » de caractériser l'entrave à l'accès au marché pour exiger directement que les États membres prouvent la proportionnalité de leurs mesures commerciales à la protection d'objectifs d'intérêt général.[28] C'est en ce sens qu'il faut comprendre les « dérapages » de la Cour dans les affaires sur l'interdiction du travail du dimanche par exemple.[29]

L'arrêt *Keck* a pour ambition de mettre fin à cette utilisation invasive de l'Article 34 TFUE. Il permet de comprendre que les modalités de vente indistinctement applicables affectent, en principe, de la même manière, en droit comme en fait, la commercialisation des produits nationaux et importés (point 16).

> En effet, dès lors que ces conditions sont remplies, l'application de réglementations de ce type à la vente de produits en provenance d'un autre État membre et répondant aux règles édictées par cet État n'est pas de nature à empêcher leur accès au marché ou à le gêner davantage qu'elle ne gêne celui des produits nationaux (point 17).[30]

La lecture combinée des points 16 et 17 permet de conclure que, pour les modalités de vente, la présomption est celle de la non-entrave et que cette présomption repose sur le fait que ce type de mesure n'empêche pas, en principe, l'accès des importations au marché national. Le critère de qualification d'une mesure étatique en mesure d'effet équivalent interdite par l'Article 34 TFUE est donc bien, au moins implicitement, celui du libre accès au marché national.

En ce sens, comme le dit la Cour de justice dans l'affaire *remorques italiennes*,[31]

---

27 Liste de l'article 3 de la directive 70/50, reprise presque mot pour mot par le point 15 de l'arrêt *Keck*.

28 Voir la démonstration de l'avocat général Tesauro dans ses conclusions de l'affaire *Hünermund*.

29 Arrêt de la Cour du 23 novembre 1989, *Torfaen*, aff. C-145/88, Rec. p. I-3851, du 28 février 1991, *Conforama*, aff. C-312/89, Rec. p. I-997 et du 16 décembre 1992, *Council of the city of Stroke-on-Trent*, aff. C-169/91, Rec. p. I-6635.

30 Voir en ce sens la lecture de la Cour dans l'arrêt du 2 décembre 2010, *Ker Optika*, aff. C-108/09, point 51.

31 Voir la critique de A. Rigaux sur ce cas test : « La déception vient finalement du caractère flottant et inutilement complexe des formules employées par la Cour pour qualifier l'atteinte à la libre circulation. Alors qu'il avait pourtant semblé que le critère de la mesure d'effet équivalent se structurait de manière de plus en plus nette dans un certain nombre d'arrêts antérieurs autour de la notion d'accès au marché et

il ressort d'une jurisprudence également constante que l'Article 28 CE reflète l'obligation [...] d'assurer aux produits communautaires un libre accès aux marchés nationaux (voir, en ce sens, arrêts du 14 juillet 1983, Sandoz, 174/82, Rec. p. 2445, point 26 ; du 20 février 1979, Rewe-Zentral, dit « Cassis de Dijon », 120/78, Rec. p. 649, points 6, 14 et 15, ainsi que Keck et Mithouard, précité, points 16 et 17).[32]

La jurisprudence citée par la Cour est présentée comme « constante » mais, en réalité, a connu des variations d'interprétation notables ! Il n'en demeure pas moins qu'il suffit en fait de bien relire l'arrêt *Keck* pour tracer, comme on vient de le faire, la formalisation du principe de la liberté d'accès au marché. La jurisprudence *Keck* serait donc *still good law*. La jurisprudence *remorques italiennes* montre juste que la distinction des points 15 et 16 est trop simpliste, ce qui autorise la Cour à s'en départir, dans certaines hypothèses, sans créer, à proprement parler, d'exception à la logique qui sous-tend le système de présomption des points 15 et 16, lu en combinaison avec le point 17.[33] La Cour peut ainsi procéder au simple *aggiornamento* de la jurisprudence *Keck*.

2. L'aggiornamento de la jurisprudence Keck

La question que l'on doit à présent poser est celle de savoir si l'on a encore besoin de l'arrêt *Keck*, à partir du moment où l'on consacre le critère, implicite ou explicite, de l'accès au marché pour définir la mesure d'effet équivalent. La Cour avait posé cette question, pour les mesures étatiques relatives aux modalités d'utilisation des produits, lors de la réouverture de la procédure orale dans l'affaire *remorques italiennes*. L'avocat général Bot avait estimé peu opportun de revenir sur la jurisprudence *Keck* mais nécessaire de la dépasser dans le cadre des

---

d'affectation "en fait" de cet accès (pour une illustration récente, et pourtant à propos des mesures d'effet équivalent à l'exportation, V. CJCE, 16 déc. 2008, aff. C-205/07, Lodewijk Gysbrechts et Santurel Inter BVBA : Europe 2009, comm. 77, obs. A. Rigaux. – V. aussi, autour de la formule d'"affectation différente" des produits importés, CJCE, 11 déc. 2008, aff. C-524/07, Commission c/ Autriche : Europe 2009, comm. 75, obs. A. Rigaux), et alors que l'avocat général optait clairement pour une analyse fondée sur ce critère unique, les formulations retenues par la Cour dans la présente affaire sont malencontreusement plus contournées », in « Réouverture de la procédure orale dans l'examen de l'interdiction absolue d'utiliser des remorques attelées à un motocycle en Italie : un cas "test" pour l'abandon de la jurisprudence Keck et la consécration d'un critère refédéré de la mesure d'effet équivalent ? », Europe, 2009, comm. 158.

32 Remarquer le système de citation choisi par la Cour, qui veut démontrer la continuité de la jurisprudence.

33 Sur ces problématiques, voir les stimulantes réflexions présentées dans « L'entrave dans le droit du marché intérieur », (sous la dir. de) L. Azoulai, Collection Droit de l'UE, Bruylant, 2011.

mesures relatives aux conditions d'utilisation des produits, qui matérialisent une nouvelle forme de règles étatiques qui n'appartiennent ni au point 15, ni au point 16 de l'arrêt *Keck*, alors même qu'elles « peuvent constituer un obstacle sérieux aux échanges entre les États membres ».[34]

La Cour, plus prudente, s'attache à promouvoir clairement le principe de liberté d'accès au marché, mais s'emploie à le faire découler d'une « jurisprudence constante » depuis l'arrêt *Dassonville* jusqu'à l'arrêt *Keck*. Ce qui apparaît ensuite est une référence à l'affaire *remorques italiennes*, sans référence formelle à l'arrêt *Keck*.

Est-ce à dire que l'arrêt *Keck* est abandonné (A) ? En tout état de cause cette approche clarifiée des mesures d'effet équivalent contribue à mettre à jour des principes fondamentaux du marché intérieur (B).

A. L'abandon du point 16 de la jurisprudence Keck

À ce jour, la Cour de justice n'est pas formellement revenue sur la jurisprudence *Keck*. On peut observer néanmoins que, depuis 2010, la Cour s'appuie sur les jurisprudences *Dassonville*,[35] *remorques italiennes* et *Ker Optika*, sans plus de référence explicite à l'arrêt *Keck*. Cela n'est pas nécessairement le signe de l'abandon de cette dernière jurisprudence, étant donné que la Cour privilégie aujourd'hui la référence aux derniers arrêts pertinents, lesquels renvoient à la jurisprudence *Keck* ; mais pourquoi alors s'obstiner à mentionner l'arrêt *Dassonville ?*

Ce qui est plus certain, c'est que la Cour s'appuie systématiquement sur le principe de la liberté d'accès au marché pour qualifier une mesure de mesure d'effet équivalent : ainsi,

> relève également de la […] notion [de mesure d'effet équivalent] toute autre mesure qui entrave l'accès au marché d'un État membre des produits originaires d'autres États membres.[36]

En ce sens, il y a continuité avec l'arrêt *Keck* et plus globalement avec la jurisprudence depuis l'arrêt *Dassonville*.

La jurisprudence a donc bien opéré une clarification du critère de la mesure d'effet équivalent, en optant pour un critère simple et lisible, celui de l'entrave à l'accès au marché. Elle permet de mieux cerner le sens de l'intégration des marchés nationaux en un marché intérieur : le but est de dévaloriser les frontières[37] pour assurer la fluidité des

---

34 Point 92 des deuxièmes conclusions de l'affaire *remorques italiennes*.

35 Arrêt de la Cour du 11 juillet 1974, aff. 8/74, Rec. p. 836.

36 Point 50 de l'arrêt *Ker Optika*.

37 Expression de Robert Schuman, voir aussi notre édito sur le site internet de la Fédération de recherche L'Europe en mutation, Unistra/CNRS 3241 et du CEIE EA

échanges commerciaux, c'est-à-dire de décloisonner les marchés, sans pour autant mettre en cause la compétence – et la légitimité – des États membres de réglementer leurs marchés nationaux, en promoteurs et protecteurs de l'intérêt général.[38] Le marché intérieur n'a pas pour vocation, dans ce contexte, d'assurer une rente de situation aux opérateurs économiques mais constitue le moyen de promouvoir l'accès aux marchés nationaux ; aux opérateurs économiques d'agir pour assurer un surcroît de développement à leur activité économique.

Cette mise à jour était aussi conceptuellement indispensable, afin de pallier les défauts de la jurisprudence *Keck*. La jurisprudence avait en effet montré que la distinction entre les points 15 et 16 était simpliste, et qu'il était difficile de s'accorder sur le critère de la modalité de vente entravante et donc qualifiable de mesure d'effet équivalent, sauf à être justifiée par des exigences impératives ou la justification expresse de l'Article 36 TFUE.[39]

Il y a pourtant bien une rupture dans la jurisprudence, qui autorise à penser que l'arrêt *Keck* est historiquement daté. Suite à l'affaire *remorques italiennes*, on peut en effet observer que la Cour de justice ne passe plus par l'analyse de l'objet de la mesure et privilégie une analyse de l'entrave à l'accès au marché, pour en déterminer au fond le caractère substantiel.

Dans l'affaire *remorques italiennes* il est vrai que la mesure italienne rentrait difficilement dans la distinction produit/modalités de vente des points 15 et 16 de l'arrêt *Keck*. Mais ce n'était pas le cas de l'affaire *Ker Optika*, dans laquelle la mesure hongroise qui consiste à interdire la vente de lentilles de contact par internet est, sans conteste, une modalité de vente. La Cour de justice ne la qualifie pas comme telle, contrairement à l'avocat général Mengozzi. Ce dernier se fonde sur le point 16 de l'arrêt *Keck* pour analyser dans quelle mesure la mesure hongroise affecte de la même manière, en droit comme en fait, la commercialisation des lentilles de contact importées et hongroises. D'où il conclut

> qu'il [me] semble que les conditions exigées par le droit hongrois pour la commercialisation des lentilles de contact affectent plus lourdement la

---

3994, à l'adresse : http://ceie.unistra.fr/editorial/edito/?tx_ttnews%5Btt_news%5D=5538&cHash=c9f62afcf50e3a6899b4f5b8edbe050c.

38 Voir notre contribution, « Intérêt général des États membres et droit de l'Union : inéluctable opposition ou fructueuses interactions ? », in Réformes des Finances publiques et Modernisation de l'Administration, Mélanges Herzog, Economica, 2011, p. 43.

39 On a pu croire qu'il s'agissait de la discrimination, puis la Cour a rappelé les deux conditions du point 16, soit la non-discrimination et le fait que la mesure nationale pèse de la même manière sur les produits nationaux et importés, en rappelant le point 17 de façon non systématique.

> commercialisation des produits en provenance d'autres États membres, ne serait-ce que parce qu'elles contraignent les opérateurs des autres États membres à ouvrir, en Hongrie, un magasin spécialisé, commerce dont le caractère contraignant et onéreux [...] est manifeste.[40]

La Cour de justice ne cherche même pas à entrer dans ce moule du raisonnement du point 16 de l'arrêt *Keck*. Elle ignore en fait ce point, pour n'étudier que le critère de l'accès au marché, sans même prendre la peine de qualifier la mesure de modalité de vente, ce qui était pourtant le cas en l'espèce.[41] Cela lui permet d'élargir cette catégorie du point 16 ;[42] cette démarche est constante depuis. Par exemple, dans l'affaire *Elenka*, la Cour estime que la mesure italienne qui impose un marquage CE spécifique,

> bien qu'applicable sans distinction, interdit la commercialisation en Italie des produits de construction litigieux, commercialisés légalement dans d'autres États membres. Dans ces conditions, l'obligation de marquage CE doit être considérée comme ayant un effet équivalant à une restriction quantitative à l'importation au sens de l'Article 34 TFUE et constitue, dès lors une entrave à la libre circulation des marchandises,[43]

laquelle peut être justifiée par une exigence impérative ou l'un des motifs énumérés par l'Article 36 TFUE.

Si le point 16 de l'arrêt *Keck* est indubitablement corrigé par la jurisprudence récente, la présomption du point 15 n'est pas pour autant abandonnée. Depuis l'arrêt *Ker Optika*, la Cour reformule sa jurisprudence pour établir une présomption d'entrave pour les mesures

> ayant pour objet ou pour effet de traiter moins favorablement des marchandises en provenance d'autres États membres, de même que des règles relatives aux conditions auxquelles doivent répondre ces dernières, même si ces dernières sont indistinctement applicables à tous les produits.[44]

Les mesures qui établissent une discrimination ou celles du point 15 de l'arrêt *Keck* sont donc en principe des mesures d'effet équivalent, alors que toutes les autres mesures ne le sont que si, et seulement si, elles entravent l'accès au marché des produits des autres États membres.

Dans l'affaire *ANETT*, la Cour commence ainsi par constater que la mesure espagnole qui interdit aux détaillants de tabac d'importer directement ces produits à partir d'autres États membres n'établit pas de

---

40 Voir ses conclusions points 64 et 65.

41 Voir point 51 de l'arrêt *Ker Optika*.

42 Voir point 49 de l'arrêt *Ker Optika*.

43 Points 24 et 25 de l'arrêt de la Cour du 18 octobre 2012, *Elenka*. aff. C-385/10.

44 Point 48 de l'arrêt *Ker Optika*, repris par exemple au point 33 de l'arrêt de la Cour du 26 avril 2012, *ANETT*, aff. C-456/10.

discrimination et qu'elle ne porte pas sur les conditions auxquelles doivent répondre les tabacs,[45] pour constater que « cela étant, encore faut-il examiner si cette mesure n'entrave pas l'accès au marché espagnol des tabacs originaires d'autres États membres »,[46] ce qui est d'ailleurs le cas en l'espèce.

En dehors de la présomption, il importe donc de vérifier l'entrave à l'accès au marché, c'est-à-dire établir la démonstration que la mesure étatique litigieuse rend impossible ou excessivement difficile l'accès au marché national, conformément au point 17 de l'arrêt *Keck*. On peut noter que cette solution n'est pas éloignée de la troisième voie, proposée en son temps par l'une des chambres de la Cour.[47] Elle est cependant plus claire car ce qui constitue le critère de la mesure d'effet équivalent c'est l'entrave substantielle à l'accès au marché et pas son effet « trop aléatoire et trop indirect » sur le commerce entre les États membres.

Cette mise à jour des principes qui gouvernent l'application de l'Article 34 TFUE a le double mérite de préserver la continuité de la jurisprudence, tout en clarifiant le critère de l'entrave au commerce, renforçant, de ce fait, la cohérence de l'approche des institutions de l'Union, en permettant de dégager les principes fondamentaux du marché intérieur.

B. *La formalisation des principes fondamentaux du marché intérieur*

La Cour prend soin dans sa jurisprudence, depuis 2010, d'inscrire l'Article 34 TFUE dans la logique plus globale du fonctionnement du marché intérieur. Cette disposition

> reflète l'obligation de respecter les principes de non-discrimination et de reconnaissance mutuelle des produits légalement fabriqués et commercialisés dans d'autres États membres ainsi que celle d'assurer aux produits de l'Union un libre accès aux marchés nationaux.[48]

L'Article 34 TFUE doit donc être interprété comme une *lex specialis* du marché intérieur. Le fait de consacrer le libre accès au marché comme critère de la mesure d'effet équivalent interdite est, en ce sens, un supplément de cohérence, en ce qu'il permet de réunifier la conception des libertés économiques dans le marché intérieur.

---

[45] Point 36.

[46] Point 37.

[47] Arrêt de la Cour du 5 octobre 1995, Centro Servici Spediporto, aff. C-96/94, Rec. p. I-2883 et le commentaire de Denys Simon, Europe, 1995, comm. 426.

[48] Arrêt *Ker Optika*, point 48.

Si la jurisprudence *Keck* a montré son utilité pour la libre circulation des marchandises, il faut rappeler que la distinction entre produit et modalité de vente n'a jamais trouvé d'équivalent dans les autres libertés de circulation. En revanche, la liberté d'établissement suppose, par exemple, que soient interdites « toutes les mesures qui interdisent, gênent ou rendent moins attrayant l'exercice de cette liberté ».[49] Les mesures visées sont celles qui rendent excessivement difficile l'accès au marché d'accueil de l'activité économique, sans que la Cour ne soit à même de garantir par le jeu des libertés de circulation, un droit à pouvoir exercer, de la même manière et en tout lieu, une activité économique.

En posant le principe de la liberté d'accès aux marchés nationaux, la Cour dégage au fond le sens de l'interdiction des mesures d'effet équivalent, en abandonnant, au final, une conception « dérégulatrice » des règles du marché intérieur. Ce qui est à présent plus clair, dans la détermination du champ de l'article de 34 TFUE, c'est que

> les ressortissants communautaires ne sauraient tirer de cette disposition un droit absolu à la liberté économique ou commerciale. En effet, les dispositions du traité sur la libre circulation des marchandises ont pour objet de garantir le décloisonnement des marchés nationaux, en offrant aux producteurs et aux consommateurs la possibilité de jouir pleinement des bénéfices d'un marché intérieur communautaire, non de favoriser une dérégulation généralisée des économies nationales.[50]

Tirant pleinement parti du parallélisme entre les libertés de circulation, la Cour peut concevoir le principe de la liberté d'accès au marché en cohérence avec deux autres principes. Tout d'abord le principe de non-discrimination, qui innerve l'ensemble du marché intérieur. Sur ce point, il est clair que la Cour conduit les États à réguler leurs marchés nationaux dans le sens de la protection de l'intérêt général par des mesures non discriminatoires. La discrimination doit par principe être prohibée. On peut d'ailleurs s'étonner que la Cour manque, sur ce point, de constance dans sa jurisprudence, puisqu'on peut observer, dans certains cas, qu'elle accepte de justifier une mesure, pourtant discriminatoire, par une raison d'intérêt général,[51] raison qu'elle semblait pourtant avoir réservée à la justification des seules mesures indistinctement applicables depuis l'arrêt *Cassis de Dijon*. Au-delà de ce constat de

---

[49] Arrêt de la Cour du 30 novembre 1995, *Gebhard*, aff. C-55/94, Rec. p. I-4165, point 37.

[50] Voir les conclusions de l'avocat général Poiares Maduro dans l'affaire *Alfa Vita*, point 37.

[51] Voir par exemple, dans le champ de la liberté d'établissement, arrêt de la Cour du 1er décembre 2011, *Commission c. Hongrie*, aff. C-253/09, point 69.

circonstances, il est clair que les États membres de l'Union européenne voient légitimer par la Cour de justice leur compétence de principe à réglementer leur marché national pour des raisons impérieuses d'intérêt général. Ce faisant, ils sont contraints, en tant qu'ils sont États membres, de tenir compte des effets transnationaux de leurs règles nationales. La frontière ne doit plus être la « ligne bleue » du législateur ; il doit œuvrer à raison de l'intérêt général national, sans plus penser que le produit – ou l'étranger – représente, au sein de l'Union, un quelconque danger. La non-discrimination est le fondement de la confiance qui doit présider aux relations interétatiques au sein de l'espace du marché intérieur. Passer de la défiance à la confiance est, on en convient, le germe fécond de l'Union et le cœur du processus – à cet égard authentiquement révolutionnaire – de l'intégration « à l'européenne ».

Le dernier principe évoqué par la Cour comme principe fondateur du marché intérieur est le principe de reconnaissance mutuelle. Ce principe est en effet la colonne vertébrale de l'intégration, en ce qu'il pose en principe la libre circulation, sous condition d'équivalence de la protection de l'intérêt général. Il suppose que les États partent du principe de la confiance dans les législations et les contrôles des autorités nationales des autres États membres. La Cour procède par ce biais à une ouverture douce des droits nationaux qu'elle connecte aux droits des autres États membres,[52] tout en protégeant une réelle diversité des approches nationales.[53]

Le principe de reconnaissance mutuelle vient en réalité compléter le principe de liberté d'accès, en le rendant effectif. Ce n'est en effet que si un produit légalement fabriqué ou commercialisé dans un État membre peut être vendu sur le marché d'un autre État membre qu'il a accès au marché. Cet accès n'est cependant pas inconditionnel, puisque l'État d'accueil dispose en la matière d'un droit de regard, pour garantir l'effectivité des règles nationales garantissant l'intérêt général, dans le sens du règlement « reconnaissance mutuelle ».[54] Les États doivent donc, dès la conception de leurs règles nationales, reconnaître la pertinence d'autres approches et techniques nationales et les prendre en compte pour déterminer leurs propres choix.[55] En ce sens, la reconnaissance mutuelle convie les États à une approche de droits comparés, sans

52 L'une des plus belles illustrations de ce phénomène se trouve dans l'affaire *Garcia Avello*, arrêt du 2 octobre 2003, aff. C-148/02, Rec. p. I-11613.

53 Voir l'arrêt de la Cour du 11 septembre 2008, *Commission c. Allemagne* dit *approvisionnement des hôpitaux en médicaments*, aff. C-141/07, Rec. p. I-6935.

54 Règlement du 9 juillet 2008, n° 764/2008, du Parlement et du Conseil, JOUE du 13 août 2008, n° L 218, p. 21.

55 Article 2 du règlement reconnaissance mutuelle.

pour autant sacrifier leurs conceptions singulières. Les principes fondateurs du marché intérieur sont, dans cette perspective, le reflet de l'Union dans la diversité.[56]

[56] Devise de l'Union que l'on trouvait dans le traité établissant une constitution pour l'Europe, qui a malheureusement disparu dans le traité de Lisbonne.

Quelques remarques sur la proposition de règlement relatif au statut de la fondation européenne[1]

Miguel GARDEÑES SANTIAGO

Profesor Titular de droit international privé, Universitat Autònoma de Barcelona

1. Avant-propos

Au milieu des années 1990, le Master d'Études européennes de l'Université Autonome de Barcelone s'est bénéficié des excellents enseignements du dédicataire de cet hommage, et c'est dans ce contexte que j'ai eu l'occasion de le rencontrer. À l'époque j'ai eu le privilège de l'assister à son cours magistral sur les aspects externes du droit du marché intérieur, un cours qui suscitait toujours un vif intérêt chez les étudiants, et qui m'avait profondément marqué. Les conversations et échanges de ces jours m'ont apporté des nouvelles perspectives sur le droit de l'Union, et aussi l'occasion de découvrir la grande qualité humaine et scientifique du professeur Demaret, sa sagesse et ses vastes connaissances. Je garde aussi un très bon souvenir de l'aimable invitation du professeur Demaret à participer à un projet éditorial particulièrement intéressant, l'ouvrage *Regionalism and Multilateralism After the Uruguay Round. Convergence, Divergence and Interaction*,[2] et je dois le remercier aussi de m'avoir ouvert les portes du Collège d'Europe, au

---

1 Ce travail a été réalisé dans le cadre du projet de recherche « *Interacción entre la autonomía de la voluntad y la protección de los intereses generales en la regulación de la actividad internacional de las sociedades* », financé par la Subdirección General de Proyectos de Investigación du Ministère de la Science et de l'Innovation de l'Espagne. La référence du projet est DER2009-09039 (subprogramme JURI), et l'investigateur principal est le professeur Rafael Arenas García. Date du commencement du projet : 1er janvier 2010 ; date de finalisation : 31 décembre 2012.

2 Édité par P. Demaret, J.-F. Bellis et G. García Jiménez, Bruxelles, Institut d'Études juridiques européennes « Fernand Dehouse », *European Interunivesity Press (EIP)*, 1997.

sein duquel j'ai eu l'occasion de rencontrer des très chers collègues et amis, et de partager une expérience unique dans un contexte authentiquement européen. Même si modeste, ce travail veut témoigner ma gratitude et admiration pour Paul Demaret.

Nous avons choisi le sujet du statut de la fondation européenne parce que, dans le contexte européen, le droit des fondations ouvre des nouveaux chemins à explorer : les activités à travers l'Union d'entités poursuivant des finalités d'utilité publique déborderaient le cadre classique du marché intérieur, et la toute récente publication, le 8 février 2012, du projet de règlement relatif au statut de la Fondation européenne (ci-après, FE)[3] invite à réfléchir sur certains éléments essentiels de cette initiative. Ainsi, après avoir rappelé les antécédents et motifs de la proposition (2), nous analyserons les questions relatives à la détermination de la finalité d'utilité publique justifiant la création d'une FE (3) et celles relatives à la détermination de la dimension transnationale des activités de celle-ci (4). Nous finirons avec quelques considérations finales (5).

2. Les antécédents et motifs de la proposition

Les analyses qui ont précédé la présentation du projet de règlement[4] indiquent que les activités des fondations d'intérêt général à l'échelle de l'Union européenne doivent faire face à des difficultés dérivées de la nécessité d'agir dans un contexte de pluralité de systèmes légaux natio-

3 COM(2012)35 final ; voir l'avis du Comité économique et social européen (ci-après CESE) sur cette proposition, du 18 septembre 2012 (rapporteur Ms Hellam, INT/645) ; voir aussi l'avis de l'*European Foundation Centre* (EFC), *Preliminary Legal Analysis of the European Commission Proposal for a Council Regulation on the Statute for a European Foundation*, juin 2012, http://www.efc.be/. En ce qui concerne le régime juridique des fondations au regard du droit de l'Union, et concrètement sur le *statu quo* antérieur à la présentation de la proposition de règlement, Font i Mas, M., *El dret internacional privat de fundacions en el procés d'integració europea*, thèse doctorale, Universitat de Barcelona, 2008 (http://hdl.handle.net/10803/1404), spécialement pp. 439-639) ; voir aussi le nouveau travail de cet auteur « Las fundaciones en el Derectio de la Unión Europea », in J.J. Forner Delaygua, C. González Beilfuss, R. Vitras i Farré (eds.), *Entre Bruselas y La Haya. Estudios sobre la unificación internacional y regional del Derectio internacional privado. Liber amicorum Alegria Borrás*, Madrid, Marcial Pons, 2013, pp. 389-404. Ce travail contient une intéressante analyse de la proposition de règlement de 2012. Nous n'avons pu incorporer ce travail que dans la phase de correction des épreuves, après avoir remis notre contribution à l'éditeur.

4 Voir, en particulier, l'étude de faisabilité élaborée par l'Université de Heidelberg et le Max Planck Institute for Comparative and International Private Law (*Feasibility Study on a European Foundation Statute. Final Report*, 2009 ; http://ec.europa.eu/internal_market/company/eufoundation/index_fr.htm ; voir, dans le même site internet, les réponses reçues au questionnaire sur la création éventuelle d'un statut de la fondation européenne.

naux. À notre avis, ces difficultés peuvent se résumer en quatre aspects essentiels : tout d'abord, se poserait le problème de la reconnaissance de la personnalité et de la capacité juridique des fondations dans les États autres que celui où elles ont été créées. À vrai dire, aujourd'hui ce problème de base ne serait pas le plus important, étant donné la tendance, répandue en droit comparé, de reconnaître l'existence des personnes juridiques légalement créées conformément à un droit étranger. Cependant, dans les États suivant le modèle du « siège réel » (*Sitztheorie*), cette reconnaissance pourrait être niée si la fondation s'était constituée selon la loi d'un État autre que celui où elle aurait son siège réel ou établissement principal.[5] S'agissant des fondations, dans un bon nombre d'États l'élément de supervision publique de ses activités est plus accentué que dans d'autres personnes morales, et cela pourrait expliquer que, même des États qui ne suivraient pas le modèle du siège réel de manière générale, exigeraient aux fondations exerçant leurs principales activités sur leur territoire de se constituer conformément à leurs lois.[6]

La deuxième série de difficultés dériverait des obligations imposées aux fondations étrangères par les lois des États où elles déploient leurs activités. Ici on devrait mentionner des exigences telles que l'obligation de s'enregistrer ou d'établir une délégation ou établissement permanent. Bref, il s'agirait des obligations imposées par les autorités locales lorsque la fondation d'un autre État membre exerce des activités de manière régulière ou habituelle sur leur territoire. Même si ces obligations peuvent se justifier, l'obligation de s'accommoder aux exigences de chacun des États où elles agissent peut augmenter les coûts de fonctionnement des entités.[7]

Troisièmement, une difficulté considérable est celle du régime fiscal, étant donné que traditionnellement les législations des États réservaient

---

5 Voir, à cet égard, Arenas García, R., *Registro mercantil y Derecho del comercio internacional*, Madrid, Centro de Estudios Registrales, 2000, pp. 134-152.

6 Tel serait le cas du système espagnol : l'article 6.1 de la Loi 50/2002, du 26 décembre, oblige les fondations exerçant leurs principales activités en Espagne à établir leur domicile aussi en Espagne, ce qui implicitement revient à exiger qu'elles se constituent conformément au droit espagnol. Cette obligation viserait à garantir l'impérativité du droit espagnol des fondations dans tous les cas où la fondation exercerait ses principales activités en Espagne ; autrement dit, dans ces cas le fondateur ne pourrait pas contourner l'application des normes impératives du droit de fondations espagnol moyennant la constitution de la fondation selon une loi étrangère (voir, à cet égard, notre travail « Las fundaciones en el contexto internacional », in Beneyto Pérez, J.M. (dir.) et Rincón García Loygorri, A. (coord.), *Tratado de fundaciones*, Barcelona, Bosch, 2007, vol. 2, pp. 1171-1175).

7 Sur ces coûts, Salole, G., « Why is the European Foundation Statute Needed ? », *International Journal of Not-for-Profit Law*, vol. 11, n° 1, November 2008, pp. 77-78.

le traitement fiscal privilégié aux seules fondations nationales ou aux fondations établies ou exerçant leurs activités d'intérêt général sur leur territoire. Ainsi, les différences de traitement fiscal étaient devenues l'un des plus importants obstacles à l'internationalisation des activités philanthropiques.[8] Cependant, il faut dire que dans les dernières années la jurisprudence de la Cour de justice a ouvert une importante brèche dans cet état de choses, en reconnaissant, sur le fondement des dispositions du Traité sur la libre circulation de capitaux, le droit des entités d'utilité publique des autres États membres à jouir d'un traitement fiscal équivalent à celui des entités nationales similaires. Ainsi, dans l'arrêt *Walter Stauffer* du 14 septembre 2006,[9] la Cour a condamné la loi allemande exonérant de l'impôt sur les sociétés les revenus locatifs perçus sur son territoire par une fondation d'intérêt général, mais refusant cette exonération au cas où la fondation serait établie dans un autre État membre. Dans l'arrêt *Persche*, du 27 janvier 2009,[10] il s'agissait d'un contribuable résident en Allemagne qui demandait une déduction de son impôt sur le revenu pour un don qu'il avait fait à un établissement de bienfaisance situé au Portugal. La Cour a jugé que le droit de l'Union s'opposerait à une législation nationale accordant le bénéfice de cette déduction fiscale pour les dons effectués à des organismes reconnus d'intérêt général établis sur le territoire national, sans possibilité aucune pour le contribuable de démontrer qu'un don versé à un organisme établi dans un autre État membre satisfait aux conditions imposées par la législation nationale pour l'octroi d'un tel bénéfice ; c'est-à-dire, lorsqu'un organisme reconnu d'intérêt général dans un État membre remplirait les conditions imposées à cette fin par la législation d'un autre État membre, de sorte qu'il serait susceptible d'être reconnu d'intérêt général dans ce dernier État membre, les autorités de ce dernier État ne sauraient refuser à cet organisme le droit à l'égalité de traitement pour la seule raison qu'il ne serait pas établi sur leur territoire. Dans l'arrêt *Missionswerk*, du 10 février 2011,[11] la Cour a condamné la législation belge qui réservait la possibilité de bénéficier du taux réduit de l'impôt de succession aux organismes sans but lucratif ayant leur siège d'opération en Belgique ou dans l'État où le *de cujus* aurait eu sa résidence ou lieu de travail. Finalement, l'arrêt Commission c. Autriche,

---

8 Voir, par exemple, Gallop, B., « Cross-border Issues facing Foundations and their Donors », in A. Schlüter, V. Then et P. Walkenhorst (eds.), *Foundations in Europe. Society, Management and Law*, London, The Directory of Social Change, 2001, pp. 746-795 ; voir aussi Salole, G., *ibid.*, p. 78.

9 Affaire C-384/06.

10 Affaire C-318/07.

11 Affaire C-25/10.

du 16 juin 2011[12] condamne la législation nationale autorisant la déduction fiscale des dons en faveur des institutions chargées d'activités de recherche et d'enseignement exclusivement lorsque ces institutions étaient établies en Autriche.[13]

Finalement, un obstacle important à la mobilité transnationale des fondations est le manque de prévision de certaines opérations dans les lois nationales, comme par exemple le transfert de siège vers un autre État membre ou la fusion de fondations soumises à des lois nationales différentes, parce que les lois des États ne s'occuperaient de ce genre d'opérations que dans un contexte purement national. En conséquence, un instrument de droit supranational serait le véhicule approprié pour réglementer ces opérations dans l'espace européen.

3. La finalité d'utilité publique

Pour surmonter les difficultés mentionnées, une forme juridique paneuropéenne, dont la personnalité juridique et le statut *non-profit* seraient reconnus dans tous les États membres, paraît une solution appropriée. Depuis une dizaine d'années, cet instrument a été réclamé surtout par le secteur des fondations. La proposition de règlement de 2012 a été précédée par deux modèles ou projets de statut de la FE, bien sûr non officiels, élaborés l'un par le *European Foundation Centre* (ci-après « projet EFC »),[14] et l'autre par la Fondation Bertelsmann (ci-après « projet Bertelsmann »).[15] Ces deux projets et puis la proposition de règlement réservent le statut de Fondation européenne aux seules entités

---

12 Affaire C-10/10.

13 À cet égard, voir Heidenbauer, S., *Charity Crossing Borders. The Fundamental Freedom's Influence on Charity and Donor Taxation in Europe*, Wolters Kluwer, 2011. Comme S. Hemels l'a souligné, la jurisprudence antérieure a choisi l'approche du *host country control* en matière fiscale, c'est-à-dire, les États membres ne sont pas tenus de se reconnaître mutuellement le statut d'utilité publique octroyé dans l'État d'origine de l'entité, mais ils doivent appliquer les bénéfices fiscaux établis par leur législation aux entités non résidentes, pourvu que celles-ci remplissent les conditions prévues par cette législation, sauf la condition de résidence (« The European Foundation Proposal : an Effective, Efficient and Feasible Solution for Tax Issues Related to Cross Border Charitable Giving and Fundraising ? », (27 avril 2012) SSRN : http://dx.doi.org/10.2139/ssrn.2046993, p. 6).

14 *European Foundation Centre Proposal for a Regulation on a European Statute for Foundations*, Bruxelles, 2005, dernière modification nov. 2010 (http://www.efc.be).

15 Projet réalisé par cette fondation en coopération avec la *Compagnia di San Paolo* (Torino) et la ZEIT-Stiftung Ebeling und Gerd Bucerius (Hamburg) ; on peut trouver le projet, assorti d'un commentaire très détaillé, à K.J. Hopt, W.R. Walz, T. von Hippel et V. Then (eds.), *The European Foundation. A New Legal Approach*, Gütersloh, Bertelsmann Stiftung, 2006. Sur les principales différences entre les deux projets, Font i Mas, M., *El dret… supra*, note 3, pp. 606-608.

constituées pour un objectif d'utilité publique. En effet, la FE devrait poursuivre un « *objectif d'utilité publique* » (Article 5.1), et elle devrait servir l'intérêt général « *au sens large* » (Article 5.2),[16] et ceci impliquerait que la catégorie des bénéficiaires potentiels devrait être établie de manière suffisamment ouverte. En conséquence, une fondation ayant une catégorie « fermée » de bénéficiaires – tel serait clairement le cas d'une fondation de famille ou d'intérêt privé – ne pourrait pas prendre la forme d'une FE.[17] De même, les fondations conçues pour bénéficier exclusivement aux membres d'un groupe privé ou fermé, tels que les membres d'un club ou d'une compagnie, ne pourraient être considérées comme bénéficiant au public en général.[18] Par contre, le cercle des bénéficiaires pourrait être restreint ou même très limité, pourvu que le critère de délimitation soit ouvert.[19] En outre, la vérification de l'intérêt public impliquerait, de manière implicite, un contrôle d'ordre public, en ce sens qu'on ne pourrait pas admettre les critères de détermination (ou d'exclusion) des bénéficiaires qui se baseraient sur des critères de distinction inacceptables.[20] Bien sûr, il serait aussi contraire à l'ordre public de poursuivre des objectifs illégaux, ou d'utiliser des moyens illicites pour achever les objectifs visés.[21]

La liste d'objectifs d'intérêt public retenue par l'Article 5.2, même si elle est très large,[22] a un caractère exhaustif.[23] Cette décision peut

---

16 Cependant cette expression n'est pas dépourvue d'ambiguïté. À notre avis, la version anglaise du texte (*"serve the public interest at large"*) est plus précise.

17 Voir, en ce sens, EFC, commentaire à l'article 2 du projet EFC, pp. 27-28. L'on pourrait déduire des articles 5 et 32.3 du projet de règlement que les fondations « mixtes », c'est-à-dire celles poursuivant en partie des intérêts d'utilité publique et en partie des intérêts privés, ne pourraient prendre non plus la forme d'une FE. Ce genre de fondations seraient relativement courantes dans certains pays, comme l'Allemagne et l'Autriche (*Feasability Study...*, *supra*, note 4, pp. 28-29).

18 Voir, en ce sens, les intéressants commentaires de Fries, R. à l'Article 1.2 du projet Berlelsmann (K.J. Hopt *et al.*, *supra*, note 15, pp. 78-83).

19 Selon Fries, R., tel pourrait être le cas, par exemple, d'une fondation en faveur des personnes souffrant d'une maladie rare (*ibid.*, p. 80).

20 Selon Fries, R., tel serait le cas, par exemple, si le critère pour déterminer les bénéficiaires potentiels était la couleur de la peau (*ibid.*, pp. 81-82).

21 Tel serait le cas, par exemple, si on envisageait de poursuivre des objectifs tels que le progrès de la science ou de la médecine moyennant des formes d'expérimentation interdites avec des êtres humains.

22 Pourtant, il faut souligner que les objectifs de nature religieuse ne sont pas inclus dans la liste de l'article 5, et cela pourrait s'expliquer par les problèmes spécifiques, et souvent délicats, suscités par les organisations religieuses (à cet égard, Fries, R., *supra*, note 18, pp. 79-80 et 82 ; voir aussi la vision critique de Hemels, S., *supra*, note 13, p. 13). La politique en général est aussi exclue de la liste. Cependant, en ce qui concerne les fondations liées à des partis politiques, voir le règlement 1524/2007, du 18 décembre 2007, modifiant le règlement 2004/2003, relatif au statut et au financement des partis politiques au niveau européen (JOUE L 343, du 27 décembre

s'expliquer parce que le projet de règlement contient aussi des dispositions octroyant un traitement fiscal favorable aux FE (chapitre VIII, Articles 49 à 51), et donc on peut imaginer que les États souhaiteraient une détermination précise des finalités concrètes justifiant un tel traitement fiscal.[24] Finalement, l'on doit dire qu'un élément additionnel de protection de l'intérêt général est que le projet analysé exige que les actifs de la fondation soient « *irrévocablement affectés* » à l'un des objectifs de la liste de l'Article 5.2, ce qui équivaut à interdire la possibilité de réversion des biens au fondateur, ou à sa famille par exemple.[25] Cette interdiction s'appliquerait même si la fondation n'est pas constituée pour une durée illimitée, mais pour une période de temps limité, ce qui serait permis par l'Article 12.2.

4. La dimension transnationale des activités

Sans aucun doute, le projet de la FE a été conçu comme un moyen de favoriser l'activité transnationale des fondations d'utilité publique ou, plus généralement, la philanthropie au niveau paneuropéen, en facilitant les donations ou subventions. Par conséquent, la question de savoir si le futur règlement doit établir des critères pour déterminer le caractère « transnational » ou « européen » de la fondation, et le cas échéant lesquels, est tout à fait pertinente. À cet égard, on peut observer une approche très différente dans les deux projets ayant précédé l'adoption de la proposition de règlement : le projet EFC établissait que la FE devait être active au moins dans deux États membres (Article 1.4), et qu'elle devait servir l'intérêt général au niveau européen ou international (Article 2.1.a), tandis que le projet Bertelsmann établissait que les FE pouvaient servir les objectifs d'utilité publique « *at domestic and/or international level* » (Article 1.2), ce qui indiquait clairement qu'une

---

2007), qui introduit la figure de la « fondation politique au niveau européen », conçue comme une entité affiliée à un parti politique au niveau européen (sur ces fondations, Font i Mas, M., *El dret... supra*, note 3, pp. 604-606).

23 En revanche, les projets EFC (Article 2) et Bertelsmann (Article 1.2) contenaient des listes ouvertes.

24 Ainsi, par exemple, dans le projet Bertelsmann la liste de finalités est ouverte dans la partie de droit privé, tandis qu'elle est fermée dans la partie de droit fiscal, l'une des raisons étant que l'octroi d'un pouvoir discrétionnaire aux autorités fiscales dans ce domaine pourrait être problématique (voir le commentaire de Walz, W.R., von Hippel, T. et Fries, R. à l'article 1 de la partie fiscale, *supra*, note 15, pp. 290-295).

25 À cet égard, l'Article 19.1.l) prévoit que les statuts doivent établir la répartition des actifs nets après la liquidation de la fondation, et l'article 44.2 prévoit que, en cas de liquidation, les actifs restant après le remboursement des créanciers doivent être transférés à une autre entité d'utilité publique ayant un objectif similaire ou bien ils doivent être affectés à la réalisation d'objectifs d'utilité publique aussi proches que possible de ceux pour lesquels la FE aurait été créée.

activité transfrontalière n'était pas requise. Les arguments avancés pour justifier cette dernière option ne sont pas dépourvus de pertinence. Premièrement, on a indiqué que l'un des principaux objectifs de la proposition est de favoriser les donations à l'échelle européenne, et cet objectif intéresserait toutes les fondations en Europe, pas seulement celles ayant une dimension « européenne » et, deuxièmement, la définition de cette dimension poserait des questions difficiles à résoudre.[26] En outre, si on devait exiger des activités dans plus d'un État, se poserait la question de quel serait le minimum d'activités requis, ou bien si l'activité de collecte des fonds suffirait à cet égard.[27]

Certainement, l'élection d'une de ces deux options est une question de décision politique et, à notre avis, la question essentielle est la suivante : si on admet la création d'une FE sans nécessité d'activités transnationales (disons un FE purement « domestique ») cela revient à octroyer au statut de la FE un domaine d'application potentiellement très étendu. À vrai dire, cela équivaudrait à créer dans chaque État un régime légal additionnel au droit national de fondations, de telle sorte que la FE deviendrait une figure légale concurrente de la fondation reconnue par les lois de l'État, parce que les éventuels fondateurs pourraient choisir entre l'une ou l'autre, sans avoir à justifier des conditions spécifiques pour créer une FE. Par contre, l'exigence de dimension transnationale serait une option plus respectueuse des droits nationaux de fondations : si on exige cette dimension transnationale, la FE ne devient pas un « concurrent » des fondations nationales, mais une option ouverte aux fondateurs seulement dans la mesure où ils envisageraient d'entreprendre des activités au-delà des frontières. Pour ces raisons, l'exigence de dimension transnationale permet de sauvegarder l'impérativité des droits nationaux de fondations dans leur domaine d'application naturel. Par exemple, on peut comprendre que le législateur espagnol envisage de soumettre à son droit toutes les fondations exerçant ses activités principales en Espagne (et, *a fortiori*, celles ayant des activités uniquement en Espagne).[28] Dans ce cas, l'obligation de constituer la fondation selon les règles du droit espagnol est le moyen pour garantir l'impérativité du droit espagnol de fondations à l'égard des entités ayant leurs activités principales ou uniques en Espagne. En

---

26 En ce sens, par exemple, on a indiqué qu'une fondation ayant pour but de conserver un bâtiment d'intérêt culturel devrait être acceptée comme fondation européenne, indépendamment de la question de si dans un tel cas cet objectif devrait être considéré « national » ou « européen », ce qui serait d'ailleurs une controverse artificielle (commentaire à l'Article 1.1 de Hopt, K.J. et von Hippel, T., *supra*, note 15, pp. 62-63).

27 Hopt, K.J. et von Hippel, T., *ibid.*, p. 63.

28 Article 6.1 de la Loi 50/2002, *supra*.

revanche, si on admettait qu'on puisse constituer une FE en Espagne pour faire des activités seulement en Espagne, l'impérativité du droit espagnol serait mise en question, parce qu'il pourrait être facilement éludé par les fondateurs, qui auraient toujours l'option de créer une FE.

Cela dit, on peut se poser la question de savoir comment déterminer la dimension transnationale d'une fondation ; à notre avis, il y aurait essentiellement deux critères possibles (mais l'un n'exclurait pas nécessairement l'autre) : le premier se baserait sur la « nature » de l'activité, tandis que le deuxième serait focalisé sur l'étendue géographique des activités envisagées. Du point de vue du premier des critères indiqués, l'on pourrait considérer qu'il y aurait une dimension « européenne », même si l'entité agit seulement dans un État, si elle avait pour finalité, par exemple, de promouvoir des études sur l'histoire de l'Europe. L'inconvénient de ce critère est qu'il oblige à une appréciation discrétionnaire au cas par cas des finalités envisagées, sans qu'il soit toujours facile de déterminer si le but en question serait plutôt d'intérêt national ou européen. En revanche, le critère basé sur la localisation des activités dans plus d'un État serait plus facile à déterminer, et donc plus sûr.

La proposition présentée par la Commission exige que la FE ait une « dimension transnationale », et celle-ci est déterminée par le fait de « *mener des activités ou avoir pour objectif statutaire de mener des activités dans deux États membres au moins* » (Article 6).[29] Pour les raisons précédemment expliquées, nous sommes d'avis que le critère choisi est approprié, parce qu'il établit de manière suffisamment claire les cas dans lesquels on peut constituer une FE. D'ailleurs, la condition d'exercer des activités dans plusieurs États ne devrait pas être comprise comme impliquant la nécessité d'avoir des établissements dans plus d'un État. L'Article 10.1 dispose que la FE aura la pleine capacité juridique dans tous les États membres, et qu'elle jouira de toute une série de droits nécessaires pour exercer ses activités. Plus spécifiquement, cette disposition octroie à la FE « *le droit d'établissement dans tout État membre* » lorsque « *cela est nécessaire à l'exercice de ses activités* », mais cet établissement ne devrait pas être considéré comme une condition préalable à l'exercice de l'activité.[30] D'autre part, nous croyons

29 La FE aurait aussi la possibilité de mener des activités dans tout pays tiers, sauf restrictions prévues par ses statuts (Article 10.3).

30 À vrai dire, la consécration d'une « libre prestation de services » pour les FE à travers d'un acte de droit dérivé serait utile, parce que aujourd'hui les fondations « non marchandes » (exclues, donc du domaine de l'Article 54 TFUE), ne seraient pas des titulaires « actifs » de la libre prestation de services, mais seulement des bénéficiaires « passifs », en tant que possibles récepteurs de services. En outre, tel que Font i Mas, M. l'a souligné, la directive générale sur les services dans le marché intérieur (directive 2006/123/CE) aurait exclu de son domaine d'application les services

qu'il serait convenable d'interpréter la réalisation d'activités dans plus d'un État avec une certaine souplesse. Par exemple, une institution académique accueillant habituellement des étudiants de plusieurs États, ou organisant des programmes transnationaux d'échange d'étudiants, pourrait être considérée comme ayant une activité transnationale. Un cas pouvant susciter des doutes serait celui des entités ayant une activité d'utilité publique dans un État et réalisant des activités de collecte de fonds dans d'autres États. L'on peut se demander si la simple collecte de fonds pourrait être considérée une « activité » dans un autre État.[31] À notre avis, il faudrait distinguer diverses situations. Imaginons, par exemple, une FE crée en Allemagne par des ressortissants italiens originaires de la ville de Firenze, mais qui résident en Allemagne, ayant pour but de soutenir la conservation d'un monument historique de cette belle ville. Dans un tel cas, nous croyons qu'on devrait admettre que la fondation en question a des activités dans les deux États.[32] En revanche, un cas différent serait celui des fondations ayant une activité purement locale – par exemple, la même fondation de l'exemple antérieur, mais créée en Italie par des résidents de la ville de Firenze – et qui inclurait dans ses statuts la volonté d'obtenir des fonds à travers des collectes dans d'autres États membres. Dans ce dernier cas, nous croyons qu'on ne devrait pas considérer que la fondation a des activités dans plus d'un État, et la raison est simple : il suffirait aux fondateurs d'inclure dans les statuts une déclaration générique de la volonté d'obtenir des recettes dans d'autres États membres pour qu'une fondation avec une dimension purement locale puisse se former comme une FE, ce qui à notre avis serait excessif et constituerait un moyen facile de contourner le droit national applicable.

Finalement, l'on doit dire que, même si nous partageons la décision du projet analysé d'exiger pour les FE une dimension transnationale, nous sommes d'avis que cette condition n'est pas suffisamment assurée par le texte de la Commission, qui donc présente certaines faiblesses à cet égard. La première est que l'Article 6 indique que cette dimension

---

d'intérêt général qui ne seraient pas offerts dans le cadre des activités marchandes (*El dret... supra*, note 3, pp. 638-639, 648).

31 L'avis de l'EFC sur la proposition de règlement, du juin 2012, se prononcerait en faveur d'une interprétation large du concept d'activités ; cependant, il indique que le texte de l'article 6 n'est pas suffisamment clair à cet égard (*supra*, note 3, commentaire à l'Article 6, p. 4).

32 À cet égard, nous sommes de l'avis que, dans le contexte de la FE, on devrait abandonner la vision restrictive selon laquelle les activités d'intérêt public devraient nécessairement se réaliser sur le territoire de l'État ayant reconnu la fondation. Cette vision « localiste » ne serait pas appropriée dans le contexte d'un nouvel instrument juridique ayant pour but de promouvoir les initiatives solidaires à l'échelle européenne.

transnationale doit être vérifiée au moment de l'enregistrement de la FE. Nous croyons que cette condition devrait être vérifiée aussi après l'enregistrement, dans le cadre de la supervision courante des activités de l'entité.[33] En outre, il serait aussi convenable d'inclure à l'Article 19, sur le contenu minimal des statuts, l'obligation de mentionner dans ceux-ci le domaine territorial d'activités envisagé. La dernière question qui se poserait à cet égard est celle de la conséquence juridique du fait de ne pas exercer des activités effectives dans au moins deux États membres. Tel que le texte de la proposition est rédigé, on devrait chercher la réponse dans les mécanismes généraux prévus par le règlement pour garantir que la FE agisse conformément à ses buts (obligations de fournir un rapport annuel d'activité et de rendre comptes, mécanismes de surveillance par les autorités compétentes…). C'est-à-dire, qu'il n'y a pas dans la proposition de règlement une disposition concrète sur les conséquences d'enfreindre la condition d'entreprendre des activités à une échelle transnationale, et nous croyons qu'il serait convenable de considérer la possibilité d'inclure celle-ci.

Notre proposition serait la suivante : au chapitre sur la dissolution de la FE, la proposition de règlement prévoit la possibilité de dissolution par transformation en une entité d'utilité publique régie par le droit de l'État membre dans lequel elle aurait son siège (Articles 41 et 42). Bien sûr, cette transformation serait volontaire, et elle devrait être sollicitée par le conseil d'administration de la FE à l'autorité compétente de l'État du siège. Alors, ce que nous proposons est d'utiliser ce mécanisme de transformation en une entité de droit national dans les cas d'absence d'activité transnationale, mais avec la différence que cette fois la transformation serait obligatoire, et non plus volontaire. Ce mécanisme pourrait être prévu de la façon suivante : si au terme d'une certaine période de temps (par exemple, deux années), l'autorité compétente constate que la FE n'a pas réalisé des activités dans au moins deux États membres, elle devrait concéder un nouveau délai de deux ans à la FE pour, soit commencer effectivement ces activités, soit solliciter la transformation de la FE en une entité d'utilité publique soumise au droit national. Si, au bout de ces deux années supplémentaires, la FE n'a pas entrepris les démarches nécessaires pour se conformer à une de ces deux possibilités, alors on pourrait prévoir la possibilité pour l'autorité de surveillance compétente de promouvoir la transformation forcée de la FE en une entité soumise au droit national. Nous croyons qu'il s'agit d'une solution suffisamment souple qui offre un remède *ex post* aux cas

---

[33] En ce sens, par exemple, l'avis du CESE sur le projet de règlement, du 18 septembre 2012 (point 3.7.a) se prononce clairement en faveur d'exiger l'élément transnational au-delà du moment du registre, pendant la vie de la fondation (*supra*, note 3, pp. 4-5).

où la figure de la FE aurait été utilisée sans justification, sans préjudice, bien sûr, de la possibilité d'appliquer d'autres mesures plus sévères en cas de fraude ou mauvaise gestion.

5. Considérations finales

La proposition de règlement avancée par la Commission présente d'autres éléments d'intérêt. Cependant, l'espace limité dont nous disposons ne nous permet pas de les analyser ici en détail. Pourtant, il convient de les mentionner, même de manière très succincte. Premièrement, la proposition inclut aussi un volet fiscal (Articles 49-51), clairement inspiré par la jurisprudence établie dans les affaires *Stauffer*, *Persche*, *Missionswerk* et *Commission vs. Autriche*, auparavant analysées. Il ne s'agit pas vraiment d'une harmonisation des normes fiscales des États à l'égard des fondations, mais plutôt de la proclamation du principe d'application aux FE, dans chaque État membre, du même régime fiscal que celui appliqué aux fondations d'utilité publique nationales, tout en respectant la compétence des États pour réglementer les régimes fiscaux en question. À notre avis, la différence la plus significative avec le *statu quo* jurisprudentiel actuel est que l'Article 49.3 établirait l'équivalence entre la FE et les entités d'utilité publique nationales, et donc l'intéressé serait dispensé de prouver cette équivalence au cas par cas. Ce principe d'égalité de traitement s'appliquerait aussi à l'égard de la fiscalité des donations en faveur des FE (Article 50) et du traitement fiscal des bénéficiaires de la FE (Article 51).[34] Nous sommes de l'avis que ces dispositions fiscales sont d'une importance majeure, et qu'un statut de la FE assorti d'un *label* fiscal assurant, dans chaque État membre, un traitement comparable à celui des fondations nationales serait sans doute un élément très attractif pour les éventuels fondateurs. Si finalement le législateur n'acceptait pas le volet fiscal de la proposition, l'on

[34] Cependant, comme S. Hemels l'a souligné, ce principe d'équivalence en matière fiscale ne s'appliquerait pas à l'égard de tous les tributs frappant la FE et les donateurs, mais seulement à l'égard des tributs mentionnés dans les articles 49 et 50 (*supra*, note 13, p. 17). En outre, même si le principe d'égalité de traitement qu'on vient d'exposer est une solution simple en apparence, on ne devrait pas exclure certaines difficultés dans son application. À notre avis tel serait le cas des États où il y a plus d'un régime fiscal applicable aux entités d'utilité publique, auquel cas on pourrait avoir des doutes sur le régime à appliquer. En Espagne, par exemple, il y a un régime privilégié pour les fondations en général et puis un régime spécialement privilégié pour les fondations remplissant certaines conditions supplémentaires, établi par la Loi 49/2002, du 23 décembre, sur le régime fiscal des entités sans but lucratif et les incitations fiscales au mécénat (sur ce régime, spécialement en ce qui concerne les donations en faveur des entités bénéficiaires de cette loi, Sánchez Huete, M.A., « Las entidades beneficiarias del mecenazgo. Reflexiones sobre la justificación de un régimen privilegiado », *Nueva Fiscalidad*, 10-2005, novembre de 2005).

peut se demander si l'acceptation du statut de la FE par les milieux intéressés serait la même.

En outre, nous voudrions souligner ce qui, à notre avis, constitue deux faiblesses importantes de la proposition de règlement, qui peuvent mettre en question sa faisabilité et même sa crédibilité. La première est qu'elle n'établit pas le niveau ou pourcentage minimum de revenu à dépenser pour les finalités d'utilité publique, ni le niveau maximum de dépenses d'administration, ni les limites à la rémunération des membres du conseil d'administration et d'autres personnes impliquées dans la gestion de l'entité. Cette omission ouvre la porte à des éventuels abus, sous la forme de rémunérations ou dépenses de gestion excessives, au détriment de l'intérêt public. Nous croyons, donc, qu'il est indispensable que la proposition réglemente ces questions de manière uniforme pour tous les États membres, sans rémission aux différentes lois nationales. Cela devient particulièrement indispensable si finalement le statut de la FE comporte un traitement fiscal bénévole dans tous les États membres, afin d'éviter tout risque de détournement fiscal.[35]

La deuxième faiblesse se rapporte au système de surveillance. La proposition de règlement prévoit des obligations de coopération entre les registres nationaux (Article 22.1), entre les autorités de surveillance des différents États (Article 47), et aussi avec les autorités fiscales (48), et ces dispositions doivent être bienvenues. Cependant, le système présente des lacunes. La responsabilité principale incombe à l'autorité de l'État d'enregistrement de la FE (Article 45), qui aurait la compétence pour prendre les mesures nécessaires. Même si ce principe du *home country control* nous paraît approprié, nous croyons qu'on ne devrait pas arriver à laisser « désarmées » les autorités des autres États, et notamment de ceux où la FE exercerait des activités. D'après le texte de la proposition, ces autorités auraient seulement la capacité de demander aux autorités de l'État du siège d'enquêter sur la FE en cas de soupçon d'infraction, et l'autorité de l'État du siège serait tenue d'informer les autorités de l'autre État des résultats de l'enquête et des mesures prises (Article 47.3). Ce dispositif est insuffisant. On devrait prévoir aussi l'éventualité où l'autorité de l'État d'origine de la FE ne remplirait pas ses devoirs de surveillance de manière satisfaisante, et dans ce cas prévoir, même à titre subsidiaire, la possibilité pour les autorités des autres États membres d'enquêter et de prendre les mesures nécessaires. D'ailleurs, le devoir d'informer les autorités fiscales dès qu'une enquête est commencée ne devrait pas être prévu seulement au profit des autorités de l'État du siège social de la FE (Article 48), mais

---

35 Voir, à cet égard, Hemels, S., *supra*, note 13, pp. 10, 16-20.

aussi en faveur des autorités fiscales des autres États affectés par les activités de la fondation, des donateurs ou des bénéficiaires.[36]

Pour finir, nous voudrions suggérer certaines possibles modifications à la proposition :

– En ce qui concerne la coopération entre autorités de surveillance, nous croyons qu'on devrait étudier la possibilité d'étendre cette coopération au-delà du domaine strict des FE ; c'est-à-dire, d'étendre cette coopération à l'égard du reste des fondations. Ceci permettrait une meilleure surveillance des activités transnationales de toutes les fondations, y compris celles ne prenant pas la forme d'une FE.

– La rédaction de l'Article 3 (dispositions applicables aux FE) pourrait être clarifiée. L'Article 3.2 établit l'application du droit des États membres aux questions non régies par le règlement « *et/ou les statuts des FE* ». Cette rédaction pourrait donner l'impression que les États ne seraient autorisés à adopter à l'égard des FE que des normes à caractère dispositif, parce que les normes des États ne s'appliqueraient que dans la mesure ou la question ne serait pas régie par les statuts de la FE. Nous sommes d'avis qu'on devrait accepter la possibilité pour les États d'adopter des normes impératives à l'égard des FE, et non seulement des normes à caractère dispositif auxquelles pourraient déroger les statuts.

– Quant à la capacité juridique et à la possibilité pour la FE d'exercer des activités économiques (Articles 10 et 11), et afin de préserver le patrimoine de la FE, l'on pourrait songer à la possibilité d'indiquer que la FE seulement aurait la possibilité de participer dans des personnes juridiques à responsabilité limitée. Au cas où la FE recevrait une participation dans une société dans laquelle les associés seraient tenus de répondre personnellement des dettes sociales, la FE devrait vendre cette participation, sauf si la société en question se transforme en une société à responsabilité limitée.

– Afin de mieux assurer le respect de la condition de dimension transnationale des activités, l'on pourrait inclure, dans la disposition sur le contenu minimal des statuts (Article 19), l'obligation d'indiquer de manière expresse le domaine territorial des activités envisagées. De la version actuelle du texte, on peut interpréter que la détermination de ce domaine pourrait se faire, même de façon implicite, en relation avec la définition des objectifs de l'entité (Articles 6 et 19.1.d). Toutefois, nous croyons que l'obligation d'inclure une indication expresse pourrait être un moyen de contrôle *ex ante* relativement sûr et simple.

---

36 Sur les lacunes du système de surveillance prévu, et sur les risques de détournement fiscal qui peuvent se produire, voir Hemels, S., *supra*, note 13, pp. 15-20.

– L'Article 25 établit que seules les FE peuvent utiliser l'abréviation « FE ». Toutefois, par voie d'exception, il prévoit que les entités enregistrées dans un État membre avant la date d'entrée en vigueur du règlement, et dont la dénomination contiendrait « FE » ou serait suivie de cette abréviation, ne seraient pas tenues de modifier leur dénomination ou cette abréviation. Même si on peut comprendre les raisons de cette exception, il est évident que dans ce cas il y aurait un possible risque de confusion, parce que dans les cas visés par cette exception il s'agirait nécessairement d'entités soumises au droit d'un État. Nous croyons, donc, que pour éviter ce risque au moins il serait opportun de prévoir que, dans un tel cas, l'entité en question puisse conserver sa dénomination, mais en y ajoutant une mention indiquant le type d'entité juridique dont il s'agit et le droit national selon lequel elle s'est constituée, c'est-à-dire, sa loi personnelle. Pour les mêmes raisons, nous croyons qu'on devrait adopter des précautions similaires s'agissant de l'utilisation de l'adjectif « européenne » pour les fondations autres que les FE.[37]

Pour conclure, l'on peut constater que le projet du statut de la FE fait suite à toute une série d'initiatives qui ont eu lieu depuis une dizaine d'années. Même si des vues sceptiques ont douté de la réelle nécessité d'un tel statut, il semble que le secteur des fondations lui donnerait son support. Sous réserve du contenu définitif du texte, au cas où il serait finalement approuvé, nous sommes de l'avis que la FE peut constituer un instrument utile pour faciliter tant les activités transnationales des fondations comme pour la mobilisation des fonds pour des finalités d'utilité publique. À l'heure actuelle, le système juridique de l'UE garantit aux entreprises les avantages de la mobilité transnationale de manière très large. Nous croyons que le moment d'étendre ces mêmes avantages au secteur *non-profit* est arrivé. Étant donné les limitations du traité – et surtout le fait que l'Article 54 TFUE exclut de son domaine d'application les personnes juridiques sans but lucratif[38] – l'adoption d'un instrument de droit dérivé applicable aux fondations d'utilité publique, indépendamment du fait qu'elles s'engagent ou non dans des activités marchandes, doit être saluée. Cependant, les importantes faiblesses du projet actuel – notamment l'absence de régulation du niveau minimum de revenu à employer pour la finalité d'utilité publique, ainsi que la limitation des rémunérations et dépenses de gestion, et les la-

37 Sur le risque de confusion du fait de l'utilisation de l'adjectif « européenne » par les fondations nationales, Font i Mas, M. (*El dret... supra*, note 3, p. 624).

38 Même si on accepte que cette exclusion se réfère seulement aux entités ne participant pas au marché et que, par conséquent, l'article 54 TFUE s'appliquerait aux fondations réalisant des actes de commerce, même si les bénéfices sont affectés à leur objectif d'utilité publique.

cunes du système de coopération d'autorités et supervision – compromettent la viabilité du projet de statut FE. Espérons que des solutions satisfaisantes soient trouvées pendant la procédure législative et que le statut de la FE puisse voir le jour.

Third-Country Goods in the Internal Market

Some Issues

Laurence W. GORMLEY

Professor of European Law & Jean Monnet Professor, University of Groningen; Barrister

1. Introduction

Paul Demaret has been an inspiring and devoted servant of the College of Europe for many years, and his distinguished Rectorship has seen significant expansion of the College's activities. I first encountered his work when writing my doctorate thesis: his book on *Patents, Territorial Restrictions and EEC Law*[1] was a major contribution to the literature on intellectual property rights in what is now EU law. Our paths crossed for the first time when we both served – he was President – on a *concours* jury recruiting lawyers for the Commission. Under his leadership we avoided pitfalls and maintained the integrity of the process. Later, under his Rectorship, I have enjoyed the privilege of teaching excellent students in the Department of Legal Studies at the College of Europe, which is one of the real pleasures of academic life.

2. The Approach to Third-Country Goods

The treatment of third-country goods in EU law is a subject of not inconsiderable practical importance. Yet the published version (at least) of the Treaty on the Functioning of the European Union (TFEU) initially got it wrong through what was obviously a clerical error[2] that has

1 Weinheim, 1978.

2 Which was pointed out in Gormley, L.W., "Some Problems of the Customs Union and the Internal Market", in N. Nic Shuibhne & L.W. Gormley (eds.), *From Single Market to Economic Union, Essays in Memory of John A Usher*, Oxford, Oxford University Press, 2012, pp. 87-88.

now been rectified.[3] By virtue of Article 28(2) TFEU the free movement of goods provisions extend to products coming from third countries which are in free circulation in Member States. Article 29 TFEU provides that such products are considered to be in free circulation in a Member State if the import formalities have been complied with and any customs duties or charges having equivalent effect which are payable have been levied in that Member State, and if they have not benefited from a total or partial drawback of such duties or charges. Although the Treaty requires not only completion of formalities but also that duties or charges payable actually be levied, it does not actually require them to have been paid: the Customs Code permits release of the goods when the customs debt has been paid, guaranteed, or deferred.[4] Drawback of duties means in effect repayment or reduction of the import duties or charges concerned, but it does not refer to suspension or reduction granted by EU legislation, as the amount paid takes account of the suspension or reduction, nor does it refer to overpayments.

On the basis of Article 28(2) TFEU the rule is that once they are in free circulation, products coming from third countries are treated on all fours with products originating in the European Union. This was emphasized by the Court of Justice in 1975 in Case 41/76 *Criel, née Donckerwolcke et al. v Procureur de la République, Lille et al.* in the following terms:

> It appears from Article [28] that, as regards free circulation of goods within the Community, products entitled to "free circulation" are definitively and wholly assimilated to products originating in Member States.
>
> The result of this assimilation is that the provisions of Article [34] concerning the elimination of quantitative restrictions and all measures having equivalent effect are applicable without distinction to products originating in the community and to those which were put into free circulation in any one of the Member States, irrespective of the actual origin of these products.[5]

---

3 See Art. 28(2) TFEU OJ 2012 L 326/47 at 60 (as to the earlier version, see *OJ* 2010 C83/47 at 60).

4 See Regulation 2913/92, OJ 1992 L 302/1, latest consolidated version at http://eur-lex.europa.eu/LexUriServ/LexUriServ.do?uri=CONSLEG:1992R2913:20070101:EN:PDF. This is because of the general rule that where the acceptance of a customs declaration gives rise to a customs debt, the goods covered by that declaration must not be released for free circulation until the customs debt has been paid (except in the case of temporary importation with partial relief) or secured, see Regulation 2913/92, Art. 74(1). If payment is deferred it must be secured: Art. 225. Hence Art. 74 makes no express reference to deferment (as to which, see Arts. 224-228). See further, Gormley, L.W., *EU Law of Free Movement of Goods and Customs Union and Customs Union*, Oxford, Oxford University Press, 2009, pp. 145-148.

5 1976, ECR 1921 at 1933 (paras. 17 & 18).

Other examples of this approach can be seen in Case 288/83 *Commission v Ireland*[6] and in Case 119/78 *SA des grandes distilleries Peureux v Directeur des Services fiscaux de la Haute-Saône et du territoire de Belfort.*[7] In the latter judgment the Court stated that

> "the prohibition of measures having an effect equivalent to quantitative restrictions in intra-Community trade has the same scope as regards products imported from another Member State after being in free circulation there as for those originating in the same Member State."[8]

The relevance of this last statement in the discussion about the mutual acceptance of goods is discussed below. Consistent with this approach, in relation to internal taxation on imports, the expression "products of other Member States" in Article 110 TFEU is interpreted to include third-country products imported from other Member States.[9]

The major deviation from this principle of assimilation concerns industrial and commercial property rights, so that third country products bearing a trade mark applied in a third country and imported into the European Union by a person other than the mark holder in the Union without the latter's consent, do not benefit from free movement rights throughout the Union.[10] But there is an additional problem to which Oliver has rightly drawn attention,[11] namely the rather strange situation of bananas imported from the Canary Islands into Spain: Article 4(2)(a) of Protocol 2 to the Act of Spanish and Portuguese Accession[12] provided that bananas imported from the Canary Islands were to be exempt from customs duties on release into free circulation in the rest of Spain (apart

6 1985, ECR 1761.

7 1979, ECR 975.

8 *Ibid.* at 986 (para. 26).

9 Case 193/85, *Cooperativa Co-Frutta Srl v Amministrazione delle Finanze dello Stato*, 1987, ECR 2085 at 2111-2113 (paras. 24-29); Case C-130/92, *OTO SpA v Ministeo delle Finanze*, 1994, ECR I-3281 at 3299 (para. 16); Case C-284/96, *Tabouillot v Directeur des Services Fiscaux de Meurthe-et-Moselle*, 1997, ECR I-7471 at 7491 (para. 23), confirming the view advanced in 52 *Halsbury's Laws of England*, London, Butterworths, 1986, 4th ed., para. 20.07.

10 This approach, originally in Case 51/75, *EMI Records Ltd v CBS United Kingdom Ltd*, 1976, ECR 811 and in the parallel German and Danish cases, demonstrates that the exhaustion of rights doctrine does not apply in such circumstances, see e.g. Case C-355/96, *Silhouette International Schmied GmbH & Co KG v Hartlauer Handelsgesellschaft mbH*, 1998, ECR I-4799; Case C-173/98, *Sebago Incet et al. v G-B Unie SA*, 1999, ECR I-4103; Joined Cases C-414-416/99, *Zino Davidoff et al. v A & G Imports Ltd et al.*, 1999, ECR I-8691. See, further, Directive 2008/95, OJ 1995 L 299/25, Art. 7.

11 Oliver, P. (ed.), *Oliver on Free Movement of Goods in the European Union*, Oxford, Hart, 2009, 5th ed., pp. 26-27.

12 OJ 1985 L302/1 at 400-403.

from Cueta and Melilla) and bananas imported under those arrangements were deemed not to be in free circulation in Spain for the purposes of what is now Article 29 TFEU when they were reconsigned to another Member State. Although the Canary Islands are now within the customs territory of the Union,[13] so that goods from the Canary Islands are no longer assimilated to third country goods, Article 10(3) of that regulation provides that the provisions of the Protocol continue to apply in respect of bananas, Article 10(2) providing for the expiry of the Protocol for other products. Given that there has for many years been a common organization of the market for bananas within the European Union,[14] the reason for the continued existence of Article 4(2)(a) of the Protocol is something of a mystery, and it is submitted that the better view that it is otiose but should still be formally repealed. Finally, it is worth recalling that it is no longer possible for the Member States to refuse Union treatment to goods coming from third countries imported from other Member States;[15] since the abolition of border controls on the movement of goods between Member States with the completion of the internal market on 1 January 1993, refusal of Union treatment had in any event lost its practical importance.[16]

3. Mutual Acceptance and Third-Country Goods

The concept of the mutual acceptance of goods is celebrated by EU lawyers and by traders throughout the European Union. Its most renowned association is of course with thoughts of Kir or Kir royale, and thus of Cassis de Dijon. But the judgment in *Cassis de Dijon*[17] contained

13 This was effected by Regulation 1911/91, OJ 1991 L 171/1, last amended by Regulation 1105/2001, OJ 2001 L 151/1; see now, Regulation 2913/92 (as consolidated, note 4), Art. 3(1).

14 See now Regulation 1234/2007, OJ 2007 L 299/1 (as amended on myriad occasions). Regulation 1234/2007 repealed the old Regulation 404/93, OJ 1993 L 47/1, which originally established the common organization of the market in bananas; the penultimate recital to the latter expressly takes account of the social, economic, cultural and environmental importance of banana-growing in the Canary Islands.

15 Article 134 EC was not taken over into the TFEU. In a previous version as Article 115 EC its use had declined significantly, and its demise is wholly unlamented.

16 The former EEC Treaty Art. 115 ought to have been repealed by the Single European Act (OJ 1986 L 169/1), but that provision (which became Art. 115 EC) was actually strengthened by the amendments made at Maastricht (Treaty on European Union, OJ 1992 C 191/1); it most certainly ought to have been repealed along with other otiose provisions by the Treaty of Amsterdam (OJ 1997 C 340/1) but, endowed, it appeared, with the quality of survivorship, it then became Art. 134 EC and also survived the Treaty of Nice (OJ 2001 C 80/1) unscathed.

17 Case 120/78, *Rewe-Zentral AG v Bundesmonopolverwaltung für Branntwein*, 1979, ECR 649.

an apparently exclusive statement that the Court has never formally rectified.[18] The famous statement

> There is therefore no valid reason why, provided that they have been lawfully produced and marketed in one of the Member States, alcoholic beverages should not be introduced into any other Member State.

In its reference to "lawfully produced and marketed" the Court failed to take account of third country products lawfully marketed in a Member State. Technically there was no need to do so, because the facts solely concerned the marketing in Germany of Cassis de Dijon produced in France. Yet it clearly cannot have been the intention of the Court to limit mutual acceptance of goods so as to exclude third country products lawfully marketed in a Member State. This view is reinforced by the observation on assimilation cited earlier from the judgment in Case 119/78 *Peureux*, which was handed down shortly after the judgment in *Cassis de Dijon.* Relatively recently, in Case C-88/07 *Commission v Spain*[19] the Court found that

> The mere existence of legislation or of a practice in a Member State applicable without distinction to domestic and imported products is likely to deter traders from importing into that Member State goods lawfully produced or marketed in another Member State and therefore has the effect of restricting the free movement of goods.[20]

On the basis of *Peureux* and *Commission v Spain* it is submitted that any suggestion that the mutual acceptance of goods should be limited to goods lawfully produced and marketed in a Member State is wholly misguided.

It is clear, though, that third country goods imported into a Member State to be marketed there must satisfy the lawful requirements applicable in that Member State; those may be requirements implementing EU legislation, or they may be unilateral measures, depending on the intensity of such legislation (the extent to which it occupies the field) and whether there is EU legislation involved at all. Such products may not necessarily have to comply with domestic requirements of the country in which they are produced. Some third country products may be placed in free circulation in a Member State without being marketed there; they would not then benefit from the mutual acceptance presumption as such,

18 The other "mistake" in *Cassis de Dijon* was including the protection of public health in the list of mandatory requirements, although that has now been rectified, see Gormley, L.W. in A. Arnull *et al.* (eds.), *Continuity and Change in EU Law, Essays in Honour of Sir Francis Jacobs*, Oxford, Oxford University Press, 2008, p. 189 and p. 193.

19 2009, ECR I-1353 at 1402.

20 *Ibid.* at 1402 (para. 108).

but would still benefit from the principle of free movement and could only be refused entry into the market of another Member State if refusal could be justified under EU law. Third country goods imported into, for example, the Netherlands but moving under suspensive arrangements to Germany, and being placed in free circulation there, would have to satisfy the relevant rules applicable in Germany, as first marketing would take place there.

4. Third Country Goods and Public Procurement

In pursuance of its obligations under Article III of the Agreement on Government Procurement[21] (the GPA) no less favourable treatment is offered to the products, services and suppliers offering products, services and supplies from other Parties to the GPA than that afforded to domestic products, services and suppliers; and than that accorded to products, services and suppliers of any other Party. Moreover, EU entities may not treat a locally-established supplier less favourably than another locally-established supplier on the basis of degree of foreign affiliation or ownership. Nor may EU entities discriminate against locally-established suppliers on the basis of the country of production of the good or service being supplied, provided that the country of production is a Party to the GPA. These obligations in the plurilateral context are reflected in Article 5 of Directive 2004/18 on public procurement[22] and in Article 12 of Directive 2004/17 on utilities procurement.[23]

Where no multilateral or bilateral agreement for comparable or effective access exists, Article 58(2) of Directive 2004/17 permits contracting entities to reject tender where the products involved are more than 50% of non-EU origin.[24] Subject to this provision, where two or more tenders are equivalent in the light of the contract award criteria, preference is to be given to those tenders which may not be rejected, i.e. those where the products involved are more than 50% of EU origin, and those tenders from countries covered by access arrangements. The prices of those tenders are considered equivalent for these purposes if the price difference does not exceed 3%.[25] For these purposes too, third

---

21 OJ 1994 L 336/273.

22 OJ 2004 L 134/14 (as amended).

23 OJ 2004 L 134/1 (as amended). A number of agreements concluded by the EU also have implications for procurement, such as those with Chile, CARIFORUM, Korea, Mexico, Switzerland, and Annex XVI (as amended) to the EEA Agreement also embraces procurement provisions.

24 Software is treated as a product.

25 Directive 2004/17, Art 58(3). However, preference will not be given where this would oblige the contracting entity to acquire equipment having technical character-

country products are treated (albeit to a limited extent) in a disadvantageous manner.

Not infrequently politicians or activists seek to express their disapproval of practices in third countries, or to encourage the production of goods under better conditions. Procurement policies tend to be the vehicle they tend to use to give expression to these ideas, although they may also seek to have national measures adopted which would prevent the marketing on their territory of goods that do not satisfy the conditions the politicians or activists are seeking to promote. Those latter steps can sometimes give rise to calls for retaliation, and even to international trade disputes, although it may be thought that EU-level action or pressure might have a better chance of promoting changes in practices elsewhere than pious local expressions of self-importance.

Social and environmental conditions in particular are not infrequently invoked in the procurement context, and indeed are important issues for bargaining in the discussion of the Commission's proposals for a new procurement regime, just as they were important in the discussions leading to the adoption of the 2004 procurement package.[26] The Court of Justice has had the opportunity to respond to the use of fair trade requirements in Case C-368/10 *Commission v Netherlands*, often referred to as the *EKO & Max Havelaar* judgment.[27] This case involved the procurement of the supply, installation and maintenance of dispensing machines for hot drinks, and the supply of tea, coffee and other ingredients: questions of sustainable purchases and socially responsible business were high on the agenda. While the use of products bearing the EKO and/or the Max Havelaar label was not as such compulsory, such products would be favourably weighted in the assessment of the most economically advantageous tender. The EKO label was awarded to products which were made up of at least 95% of ingredients of organic agricultural production; the Max Havelaar label was intended to promote the marketing of fair trade products and certified that the products in respect of which it was granted were purchased at a fair price and under fair conditions from organisations made up of small-scale producers in developing countries. The grant of that label is based on compliance with four criteria: the price must cover all the costs; it must contain a premium compared to the market price; production must be subject to pre-financing and the importer must have long-term trading relation-

istics different from those of existing equipment, resulting in incompatibility, technical difficulties in operation and maintenance, or disproportionate costs (*ibid.*).

26 See, generally, Arrowsmith, S. & Kunzlik, P. (eds.), *Social and Environmental Policies in EC Procurement Law*, Cambridge, Cambridge University Press, 2009 and McCrudden, C., *Buying Social Justice*, Oxford, Oxford University Press, 2007.

27 2012 ECR I-nyr, 10 May 2012.

ships with the producers. The Fairtrade Labelling Organization audits and certifies compliance with these requirements.

The Court found that by requiring, in the contract documents, that certain products to be supplied were to bear a specific eco-label, the contracting authority had acted in breach of Article 23(6) of Directive 2004/18. Thus contracting authorities are free to use the detailed specifications defined by that eco-label, but not to prescribe the label as such. The Court also set its face against the unbridled use of social policies to determine or heavily influence the outcome of procurement exercises: it found that there had to be a sufficient link between the award criteria and the subject-matter of the contract concerned. The criteria for the grant of the Max Havelaar label were found by the Court not to correspond to the definition of the concept of technical specification in paragraph 1(b) of Annex VI to Directive 2004/18, as that definition applies exclusively to the characteristics of the products themselves, their manufacture, packaging or use, and not to the conditions under which the supplier acquired them from the manufacturer. However, the Court found that compliance with those criteria did fall under the concept of "conditions for performance of contracts" within the meaning of Article 26 of the directive. That provision permits the conditions governing the performance of a contract in particular to refer to social considerations. Hence a requirement that the tea and coffee to be supplied had to come from small-scale producers in developing countries, subject to trading conditions favourable to them, fell within those considerations. While the lawfulness of such a requirement fell to be examined in the light of Article 26, the Commission referred to that provision only at a very late stage, so the Court ruled its submissions on that point inadmissible.

The Court expressly accepted that contracting authorities were authorized to choose award criteria based on considerations of a social nature, which could concern the persons using or receiving the works, supplies or services which are the object of the contract, but also other persons.

In order to assess the validity of the claim that there was an insufficient link between the award criterion at issue and the subject-matter of the contract, the Court looked at the criteria underlying the EKO and Max Havelaar. It had little difficulty in concluding that organic agriculture and fair trade amounted to social and environmental characteristics for the purposes of Article 53(1)(a) of Directive 2004/18. Organic production promotes environmental protection, through inter alia significant restrictions on the use of fertilizers and pesticides; as for fair trade, the criteria applied for the authorization to use the Max Havelaar label promoted the interests of small-scale producers in developing countries while maintaining trading relations with them which took into account the actual need of those producers, and not only the dictates of the market.

Moreover, the contract concerned in particular the supply of coffee, tea and the other ingredients required for the manufacture of the drinks available in the dispensers. The award criterion was actually drafted so narrowly that it covered only the ingredients to be supplied in the framework of that contract; it had no any bearing on the general purchasing policy of the tenderers. The Court was able to conclude on that ground that the criteria related to products the supply of which constituted part of the subject-matter of that contract. Given that there was no requirement that an award criterion relate to an intrinsic characteristic of a product, there was nothing, in principle, to preclude such a criterion from referring to the fact that the product concerned was of fair trade origin. For these reasons the Court concluded that the award criterion at issue was indeed linked – as required by Article 53(1)(a) of Directive 2004/18 – to the subject-matter of the contract concerned.

The Court then turned to examine the requirement of the possession of specific labels in its award criterion, which would be rewarded in the assessment weighting, noting that Article 23(3)(b) of Directive 2004/18 provided that the specifications had to be sufficiently precise to allow tenderers to determine the subject-matter of the contract and to allow contracting authorities to award the contract. Article 23(6) of the directive authorized the contracting authorities to have recourse to the criteria underlying an eco-label in order to establish certain characteristics of a product, but not to make an eco-label a technical specification, use of such a label being allowed only in order to create a presumption that the products bearing that label comply with the characteristics thus defined, expressly subject to any other appropriate means of proof being allowed. Labelitis as it were, was thus impermissible.

Finally, the Court turned to the criteria of sustainable purchasing and socially responsible business, noting that this was wholly unconnected to the factors on which a contracting authority could evaluate and assess the technical and professional abilities of the tenderers; it was indeed permissible to establish minimum capacity levels that tenderers had to satisfy in order for their tender to be considered, but those levels had to be fixed by reference to the factors listed in Article 48 of the directive, concerning technical and professional ability. Demanding explanations of how a tenderer satisfied the criteria of sustainable purchasing and socially responsible business and contributed to improving the sustainability of the coffee market and to environmentally, socially and economically responsible coffee production' did not fall within those factors.

From this judgment it is clear that the Court is unwilling to let social and environmental considerations be used as a cover for all sorts of preferential policies in relation to procurement. In respect of procurement not covered by the directives, it is submitted that such policies would merely have to comply with the normal case-law on the free movement of goods, workers, establishment, services, and capital and payments. However, the indications which the Court has given in the context of the procurement directives will form useful guidelines outside that field, when looking at the necessity, appropriateness, and proportionality of national measures which it is sought to justify on these or similar grounds. The writing is clearly on the wall for abuse, and in any event, given that the Court has a good track record in sniffing out indirect or disguised discrimination,[28] attempts to keep third-country good out on spurious grounds will most likely be treated with the ignominy they deserve.

It is also worth recalling the problem with widespread use of social and environmental criteria, namely that they increase the opportunities for corruption, for favouring pet projects or hobbies of local or national politicians, or of entrenched administrations where the civil or local government service is too cosily involved with political interests. Thus the unstated, but certainly recognized menace should not be forgotten or consigned to the list of details with which politicians are too uninterested to be bored with.

5. Concluding Observations

The above discussion demonstrates that for third-country goods all is not quite what it might seem on reading the TFEU. Yet the situation of third country goods within the EU is not really an unhappy one. Legitimate channels of trade find the procedures relatively straightforward; those involved in illegitimate trade find them rather less so,[29] and the parallel importer of goods from outside the EU is certainly not the darling of EU law, as the intellectual property cases demonstrate. In relation to attempts to promote the pursuit of social and environmental policies in third countries, the Court has been strict in what it will accept; this approach is to be commended as upholding the rule that the

[28] E.g. Case 61/77, *Commission v Ireland*, 1977, ECR 417 (disguised discrimination through apparently objective conditions for fishing vessels); Case 207/83, *Commission v United Kingdom*, 1985, ECR 1201 (apparently non-discriminatory rule found in reality a measure disadvantaging imports).

[29] As to counterfeit goods, see Gormley, *supra*, note 2, pp. 92-98. The European Parliament has in first reading proposed a considerable toughening of the Commission's proposals for new legislation in this field, see EP Document TA-2012-272, and the debate on Monday 2 July 2012.

freedoms and the principles behind EU legislation must be interpreted widely, and exceptions must be construed strictly. It also strikes a blow against the temptation to indulge in mere hobbyism and gesture politics. These issues are still live issues in the debates on the revision of the EU's procurement regime that are presently underway. They have also featured in the renegotiation of the GPA.[30] There is no doubt that these and other issues will remain live for some time to come. Sufficient food for thought for further research!

30 See, Arrowsmith, S. & Anderson, R.D. (eds.), *The WTO Regime on Government Procurement: Challenge and reform*, Cambridge, Cambridge University Press, 2011, especially the contributions by P. Trepte, A. Davies, J. Linarelli & P. Bolton & G. Quinot. As to the revised GPA (not yet in force), see WTO Document GPA/113 of 2 April 2012.

Des marchés publics à la délivrance des authorisations

Spill-over all over?

Vassilis HATZOPOULOS

Professeur à l'université Démocrite de Thrace (Grèce),
Maître de Conférence honoraire à l'université de Nottingham (RU)

Authorisation requirements imposed by Member States constitute restrictions to free movement. Yet, they represent an effective means of regulating and monitoring sensitive economic activities. Hence, EU law does tolerate, and occasionally encourage, the imposition of authorization requirements by Member States. In order, however, to make sure that fundamental EU freedoms do not suffer as a consequence, EU law progressively frames the conditions, both procedural and substantial, under which authorisations are being delivered by national authorities. To this end, the rules and principles applicable in the field of public procurement serve as strong guidelines.

Que l'exigence d'une autorisation pour l'exercice d'une activité économique constitue une restriction tantôt à la libre prestation de services, tantôt à la liberté d'établissement, ne fait aucun doute. En effet, si une autorisation est requise dans un État d'accueil pour la poursuite d'une activité, tout opérateur économique qui ne dispose pas de cette autorisation est, d'emblée, exclu du marché concerné. Ainsi, à partir du moment où l'on accepte que les règles sur le marché intérieur puissent être enfreintes par des mesures non discriminatoires, il ne fait aucun doute que les systèmes nationaux de délivrance d'autorisations, même indistinctement applicables, constituent *prima facie* des restrictions. Ceci a été reconnu par la Cour de justice de l'UE (ci-dessous : la Cour, la CJUE) dès sa jurisprudence fondatrice en matière de liberté d'établissement et de libre prestation de services,[1] et constamment confirmée depuis.[2]

Pour contourner les obstacles à la libre circulation ainsi créés, le législateur européen a dû inventer des techniques selon lesquelles les autorisations délivrées par un État membre seraient reconnues par tous les autres États. Dans certains cas, le législateur a procédé par une harmonisation préalable étendue, se gageant ainsi de la confiance mutuelle entre États ; c'est la technique qui a été largement suivie en matière de transport. Dans d'autres domaines, tels les services financiers, le législateur a procédé par des « passeports » européens, fondés sur une harmonisation minimale des conditions de fonds propres, de consolidation des recettes, de publicité, etc.[3] Du fait de la complexité accrue des transactions financières et de failles qui ont nourri la crise de 2008, ce système « décentralisé » a évolué vers une harmonisation poussée, soumise toutefois au contrôle d'une autorité de surveillance européenne.[4] Dans d'autres domaines, comme les services audiovisuels et électroniques, le législateur s'est contenté de « clauses de marché intérieur », fondées sur une harmonisation vraiment marginale.[5] La reconnaissance « gérée » des autorisations a aussi été au cœur de la législation européenne des industries de réseaux.[6]

En l'absence de législation secondaire, en revanche, il est difficile de se débarrasser des systèmes nationaux d'autorisation, puisqu'ils peuvent être justifiés par des raisons objectives (1.A). Si le principe de recon-

---

1 V. déjà CJUE, 4 décembre 1986, aff. 205/84, *Commission c. Allemagne (assurances), Rec.* p. 3755, att. 42 *et seq.*

2 V. toute la jurisprudence discutée ci-dessous.

3 Pour les passeports v. Lomincka, E., « The Home Country Control Principle in the Financial Services Directives and the Case Law », in M., Andenas and W.H. Roth (eds.), *Services and Free Movement in EU Law*, Oxford, Oxford University Press, 2002, pp. 295-319 ; et bien avant Hatzopoulos, V., *Le principe communautaire d'équivalence et de reconnaissance mutuelle dans la libre prestation de services*, Athènes/Bruxelles, Sakkoulas/Bruylant, 1999, pp. 414-449.

4 Spécialement depuis l'adoption de la MiFiD, Directive du PE et du Conseil 2004/39/CE pour les marchés et les instruments financiers (2004) OJ L145/1 ; la MiFiD elle-même a été modifiée par les directives 2006/31/CE (2006) JOCE L114/60, 2007/44/CE (2007) JOCE L247/1, 2008/10/CE (2008) JOCE L76/33, 2009/65/CE (2009) JOUE L 302/32 et 2010/78 (2010) JOUE L 331/120.

5 Directive du Conseil 89/552/CEE (1989) JOCE L298/23, modifiée par la directive du PE et du Conseil 97/36/EC (1997) JOCE L202/60 et par la directive 2007/65/CE (2007) JOCE L332/27 ; directive du PE et du Conseil 1999/93/EC sur la signature électronique (2000) JOCE L13/12 ; directive du PE et du Conseil 2000/31/CE sur le commerce électronique (2000) JOCE L178/1.

6 V. en particulier la directive 2002/20/EC du PE et du Conseil relative aux autorisations pour les réseaux et services de communications électroniques (Directive autorisations) (2002) JOCE L 108/21.

naissance mutuelle peut, dans la grande majorité des cas, aider les professionnels à accéder aux marchés des autres États membres, celui-ci est complètement inopérant lorsque les États divergent fondamentalement quant à la façon dont ils conçoivent l'activité en question (1.B). Il est en conséquence nécessaire d'encadrer non seulement les procédures de délivrance des autorisations nationales (2.A), mais aussi la manière dont toute décision négative est contrôlée (2.B). Ainsi, peut-on dire que si le droit de l'UE est inadéquat pour écarter les systèmes nationaux d'autorisations (1), il est parfaitement à même de les encadrer au profit du marché intérieur (2).

1. L'inadéquation du droit de l'UE pour écarter les systèmes nationaux d'autorisations

A. Les raisons justifiant les systèmes nationaux d'autorisation

En l'absence d'harmonisation à l'échelle de l'UE, il revient aux États membres de réglementer les différentes activités économiques, le cas échéant, en imposant des systèmes d'autorisation. Aussi restrictifs soient-ils, les systèmes d'autorisation ne sont pas, pour autant, prohibés. Si la « Directive Services », le seul instrument horizontal qui traite de l'abolition des restrictions à la libre prestation de service, n'exige pas l'abolition des régimes d'autorisation, elle demande, en revanche, qu'ils soient justifiés par des raisons objectives et qu'ils répondent à des conditions procédurales strictes.[7] Dans leur effort de justifier les systèmes d'autorisation en place, les États membres ont invoqué une multitude des raisons trouvant toutes leur source d'inspiration dans la jurisprudence de la Cour.[8] Quatre raisons peuvent y être décelées, pour justifier la mise en place et/ou le maintien des systèmes d'autorisation.

I. La prestation de services d'intérêt économique général (SIEG)

Sous la pression de la théorie économique dominante qui veut moins d'état, renforcée par la crise économique qui diminue les ressources étatiques, les SIEGs sont de plus en plus offerts par des opérateurs

---

7 Directive du PE et du Conseil 2006/123/CE relative aux services dans le marché intérieur (2006) JOCE L 376/36.

8 V. le récent « paquet services » présenté par la Commission en juin 2012 et consistant d'une Communication COM(2012)261 final, trois longs Documents de Travail de la Commission, trois notes d'information ainsi que 27 rapports nationaux préparés pour la Commission par Milieu Ltd ; pour tous ces documents v. http://ec.europa.eu/internal_market/services/services-dir/implementation_report-fr.htm, lien actif au 20/08/13.

privés ou par le secteur tertiaire.[9] L'Article 106(2) TFUE prévoit expressément une exception aux règles du traité en faveur des entreprises chargées de l'accomplissement d'une mission d'intérêt général et/ou jouissant de droits exclusifs ou spéciaux. Il est vrai que la liberté des États d'accorder des droits exclusifs/spéciaux n'est pas illimitée, puisque ces droits ne devraient ni entraîner des discriminations sur la base de nationalité entre les destinataires de services, ni rendre la prestation de services plus difficile dans l'hypothèse où elle opère à travers les frontières.[10]

Selon la jurisprudence traditionnelle en la matière, l'État doit charger un ou plusieurs opérateur(s) par un acte d'autorité publique.[11] Or, la mise en place d'un système d'autorisation, délivré selon des critères objectifs et entraînant, à la charge du titulaire, des obligations spécifiques, constitue bien un acte d'autorité publique. Ceci a été jugé de manière claire par le Tribunal dans *BUPA* concernant la délivrance de plusieurs autorisations dans le domaine de l'assurance santé.[12] La Cour semble partager cette même analyse, puisque dans *ASM Brescia*, elle accepte que des autorisations déjà délivrées, y compris en violation du droit de l'UE, puissent être prolongées si elles sont justifiées par le principe de sécurité juridique et par les exigences liées au service public (de distribution des carburants, en l'occurrence).[13]

II. La distribution des ressources rares

L'indulgence de la Cour dans l'affaire susmentionnée devrait être contrastée avec l'affaire *Centro Europa 7*, où la Cour a condamné l'Italie pour avoir manqué à son obligation de prendre les mesures nécessaires pour que les entreprises de télévision ayant obtenu une autorisation (en application de la « Directive Autorisations »),[14] puissent avoir accès aux fréquences correspondantes. Cette affaire enjambe la prestation d'un service économique d'intérêt général (des émissions télévisuelles) et la gestion des ressources rares (les fréquences radio). Le fait que les conditions de délivrance d'autorisation soient prévues par un

---

9 Pour l'apport du secteur tertiaire v. Busschaert, G., « Revisiting the Fundamentals of Internal Market Law : Civil Society as a Third Sector between the State and the Market », *European Business Law Review*, 2011, pp. 725-739.

10 Pour une expression récente de ces deux limitations v. CJUE 31 janvier 2008, aff. C-380/05, *Centro Europa 7 Srl*, *Rec.* I-349, att. 78-79.

11 CJUE, 14 juillet 1971, aff. 10/71, *Port de Mertert*, *Rec.* 723 ; cette même condition a été reprise dans les communications successives de la Commission sur l'application de la jurisprudence *Altmark.*

12 CJUE, 12 février 2008, aff. T-289/03, *BUPA*, *Rec.* II-81, att. 182-183.

13 CJUE, 17 juillet 2008, aff. C-347/06, *ASM Brescia SpA*, *Rec.* I-5641, att. 71.

14 *Supra*, note 5.

texte de droit dérivé explique la fermeté avec laquelle la Cour a condamné l'Italie dans cette affaire. Outre les textes sectoriels, l'exigence d'une procédure transparente de délivrance d'autorisation portant sur des ressources rares découle de manière horizontale par la Directive Services (Article 12(1)).[15] Ainsi, tantôt dans la jurisprudence tantôt dans la législation secondaire, la solution demeure qu'en présence de ressources rares un système d'autorisation n'est pas simplement toléré, il est requis.

III. La protection de l'ordre, de la santé et de la sécurité publique

La règle de l'Article 12(1) de la Directive Services émane directement du jugement de la Cour dans l'affaire *Placanica*, où la Cour avait jugé, qu'afin de remédier à l'attribution d'autorisations en violation des exigences du marché intérieur, l'Italie devait distribuer des nouvelles autorisations ou révoquer et redistribuer les autorisations existantes, par « une mise en concours ».[16] À une différence près : dans *Placanica* le nombre limité d'autorisations n'était pas dû à la rareté naturelle et/ou technique des ressources correspondantes, mais à une limitation artificielle, liée à un choix politique. Ce choix, lui-même, était dicté par la volonté de protéger l'ordre et la sécurité publics. La Cour reconnaît, en effet, qu'« un système de concessions peut, dans ces circonstances, constituer un mécanisme efficace permettant de contrôler les opérateurs actifs dans le secteur des jeux de hasard, dans le but de prévenir l'exploitation de ces activités à des fins criminelles ou frauduleuses ».[17] De même, dans les affaires concernant les jeux et les paris, la Cour admet que les régimes d'autorisation, les droits exclusifs et les autres mesures restrictives mises en place par les États membres sont essentiellement justifiés par le respect des objectifs liés à l'ordre et la sécurité publics.[18]

---

15 V. pour le contenu de cette disposition et ses rapports avec la jurisprudence *Placanica*, v. Hatzopoulos, V., « Que reste-t-il de la Directive Services », 2008, *Cahiers de Droit Européen*, pp. 43, 299-358, 333-334.

16 *Placanica*, att. 63.

17 *Ibid.*, att. 57.

18 Pour une présentation d'ensemble de la jurisprudence en question v. Bernard, E., « La Cour de justice précise les règles du jeu », *Europe*, 2010, Étude 12 ; Sibony, A.-L. et Robin-Olivier, S., « Les jeux en ligne et le marché intérieur : Les effets des libertés d'établissement et de prestation de services sur les politiques nationales et les stratégies d'entreprises », in Guignot et Behar-Touchais (dir.), *Les Jeux en Ligne*, Paris, La Documentation française, à paraître en 2013 ; Van den Bogaert, M. and Cuyvers, A., « Money for Nothing : The case law of the EU Court of Justice on the regulation of gambling », *Common Market Law Review*, 2011, vol. 48, pp. 1175-

Un tel régime d'autorisation, dicté par des raisons liées à l'ordre et à la sécurité publics, doit cependant, pour être proportionnel, répondre à deux conditions : a) faire partie d'un ensemble de mesures qui poursuivent le même objectif et b) être évalué par les autorités publiques quant à son efficacité.[19] Par cette dernière exigence, les autorisations justifiées par l'ordre et la sécurité publics se rapprochent de celles justifiées par la prestation de SGEI.

IV. La protection de quelque raison impérieuse d'intérêt général

La Cour reconnaît régulièrement, dans sa jurisprudence concernant le marché intérieur, que des raisons impérieuses d'intérêt général peuvent justifier un régime d'autorisation.[20] De même, et de manière tout aussi significative, la Directive Services admet clairement que des raisons impérieuses puissent justifier la mise en place d'autorisations (Article 9(1)).

Cette position pourrait toutefois être remise en question par la Cour elle-même, si elle maintenait sa jurisprudence classique au terme de laquelle les raisons impérieuses ne peuvent justifier que des mesures non discriminatoires.[21] En effet, par une jurisprudence audacieuse, la Cour tend à qualifier de discriminatoires les systèmes d'autorisations, notamment lorsque les acteurs déjà autorisés l'ont été en violation du droit de l'UE et sont essentiellement des nationaux de l'État d'accueil. Si l'élément de discrimination était latent déjà dans les affaires des assurances de 1986,[22] c'est dans *Placanica*, et encore plus dans *Costa et*

1213 ; Hörnle, « Online Gambling in the European Union : a Tug of War without a Winner ? », *Yearbook of European Law*, 2011, vol. 30, pp. 255-297.

19 Pour une analyse des exigences de cohérence et de systématicité v. Mathisen, G., « Consistency and Coherence as Conditions for Justification of Member State Measures Restricting Free Movement », *Common Market Law Review*, 2010, vol. 47, pp. 1021-1048 ; pour une analyse quelque peu différente, v. Hatzopoulos, V. *Regulating Services in the EU*, Oxford, Oxford University Press, 2012, pp. 176-178.

20 V. par exemple CJUE 8 septembre 2010, aff. jtes C-316/07, 358/07, 359/07, 360/07, 409/07, 410/07, *Markus Stoss e.a.*, *Rec.* p. I-8069.

21 Il est vrai que la Cour n'est pas infaillible dans l'application de cette règle, mais la tendance lourde dans sa jurisprudence va dans ce sens ; pour une discussion des différents chefs de justification aux restrictions au marché intérieur et de leurs différences v Hatzopoulos, V., « La justification des atteintes aux libertés de circulation : cadre méthodologique et spécificités matérielles », in A. Dubout & A. Lemaire (eds.), *L'unicité des libertés fondamentales du traité*, Bruxelles, Bruylant/Larcier, à paraître) ; see also Hatzopoulos, V., *Regulating Services*, *supra*, pp. 146-179.

22 Parmi une série d'affaires de la même date v. CJUE, 4 décembre 1986, aff. 205/84, *Commission c Allemagne (assurances)*, *Rec.* p. 3755.

Cifone que la Cour se rend plus explicite à cet égard.[23] C'est pour remédier à la discrimination ainsi opérée que le gouvernement italien devait révoquer et redistribuer les concessions de jeux dans *Placanica*. Dans *Costa et Cifone*, la Cour se rend plus explicite en utilisant, à deux reprises, les mots « égalité de traitement » et « discrimination » afin de condamner le nouveau système d'autorisations mis en place par l'Italie : tout en n'introduisant aucune discrimination entre les nouveaux concurrents, il renforcerait la protection des opérateurs déjà en place. *Costa et Cifone* vient compléter, voire requalifier, la jurisprudence récente de la Cour en matière de restrictions géographiques, notamment dans les affaires *Attanasio Group*, concernant les stations de service en Italie et *Commission c. Espagne* et l'implantation des grandes surfaces.[24] Si dans ces affaires antérieures, la Cour avait identifié des restrictions à « l'accès au marché », dans *Costa et Cifone*, elle raisonne expressément en termes de discrimination. Si cette tendance jurisprudentielle devait se confirmer, elle pourrait remettre en cause l'idée selon laquelle des raisons impérieuses d'intérêt général peuvent justifier la mise en place des systèmes d'autorisations.

B. Les circonstances excluant complètement le jeu de la reconnaissance mutuelle

Il a été brièvement mentionné, en introduction, qu'afin de contourner les restrictions résultant des systèmes nationaux d'autorisations, le législateur européen a mis en place des systèmes sectoriels de reconnaissance mutuelle appuyés, selon le cas préalable, un degré d'harmonisation.[25] Le fait, cependant, que la Directive Services n'ait pu être adoptée qu'une fois le principe du pays d'origine évincé, fait qu'aucune obligation générale et horizontale n'existe pour la reconnaissance mutuelle d'autorisations délivrées dans les autres États membres.

Dans les domaines où la reconnaissance mutuelle d'autorisations délivrées par un État membre est « gérée » par quelque texte du droit

23 CJUE, 6 mars 2007, aff. jtes C-338/04, C-359/04 et C-360/04, *Placanica e.a.*, *Rec.* p. I-1891 ; CJUE, 16 février 2012, aff. jtes, C-72/10 et C-77/10, *Costa et Cifone*, n.e.p.

24 CJUE, 11 mars 2010, aff. C-384/08, *Attanasio Group*, nep ; CJUE, 24 mars 2011, aff. C-400/08, *Commission v Spain (centres commerciaux)*, Rec. I-2055.

25 Sur les différentes variantes de reconnaissance mutuelle et le rôle joué par l'harmonisation v. Hatzopoulos, V., *Le principe communautaire d'équivalence et de reconnaissance mutuelle dans la libre prestation de services*, Athènes/Bruxelles, Sakkoulas/Bruylant, 1999 ; et pour une évaluation plus brève et plus mise à jour par le même auteur, « Le principe de reconnaissance mutuelle dans la libre prestation de services », *Cahiers de Droit Européen*, 2010, pp. 47-93 ; v. aussi Nicolaidis, K., « Trusting the Poles ? Constructing Europe through mutual recognition », *Journal of European Public Policy*, 2007, vol. 15, pp. 682-698.

dérivé, la Cour y attache une grande importance même si ce texte ne procède qu'à une harmonisation minimale. Ainsi, dans l'arrêt *Mesopotamia*, qui mettait en cause l'activité en Allemagne de deux chaînes de télévision autorisées au Danemark par application de la « Directive TV sans frontières », la Cour, tout en accueillant l'argument allemand concernant l'ordre et la sécurité publics, n'a pas admis l'interruption de leurs émissions.[26]

Dans les domaines, où, au contraire, toute législation secondaire fait défaut, la Cour suit une approche plus ambivalente : alors que dans la grande majorité de cas, elle met les autorités nationales sous pression pour qu'elles reconnaissent tous les éléments menant à l'autorisation (à l'exclusion de l'autorisation elle-même),[27] dans d'autres circonstances – plutôt exceptionnelles – elle exclut entièrement le jeu de la reconnaissance mutuelle et tolère le partitionnement correspondant du marché intérieur.

Il en a été ainsi dans le domaine sensible des jeux et des paris. La contamination vers d'autres domaines tout aussi sensibles ne saurait, cependant, être exclue. Cette tendance restrictive du principe de la reconnaissance mutuelle a trouvé sa première expression dans l'affaire *Liga Portuguesa* qui concernait le droit exclusif concédé en faveur d'un seul opérateur contrôlé par l'État. La Cour considéra qu'en l'absence d'harmonisation, « le seul fait » qu'un opérateur était autorisé par un autre État membre où il était soumis à des contrôles « *ne saurait être considéré comme une garantie suffisante de protection des consommateurs nationaux* ».[28] L'idée ainsi exprimée est surprenante à, au moins, deux égards. D'une part, elle inverse la présomption instaurée par les arrêts fondateurs du marché intérieur, d'après laquelle un bien ou un

---

26 Elle a, en revanche, permis aux autorités allemandes d'imposer des restrictions aux activités « collatérales » de ces mêmes chaînes, telles l'organisation des concerts, d'actions de sympathie, etc. en faveur du groupe terroriste kurde PKK ; v. CJUE, 22 septembre 2011, aff. jtes, C-244 et 245/10, *Mesopotamia Broadcast and Roj*, nep.

27 Pour l'analyse de la jurisprudence correspondante v. Hatzopoulos (2010) dans l'avant-dernière note ; indicative du niveau d'exigence que la Cour impose aux autorités d'États membres est l'attendu suivant de l'arrêt CJUE, 18 novembre 2010, aff. C-458/08, *Commission v Portugal (construction)*, *Rec.* p. I-11599, att. 100 où la Cour s'exprime de la manière suivante : « La Cour a ainsi notamment jugé qu'un régime national d'autorisation irait au-delà de ce qui est nécessaire au cas où les exigences auxquelles la délivrance de l'autorisation se trouve subordonnée feraient double emploi avec les justifications et les garanties équivalentes exigées dans l'État membre d'établissement, en en déduisant notamment l'obligation pour l'État membre d'accueil de tenir compte des contrôles et des vérifications déjà effectués dans l'État membre d'établissement ».

28 CJUE, 8 septembre 2009, aff. C-42/07, *Liga Portuguesa de Futebol et Bwin*, *Rec.* p. I-7633, att. 69.

service autorisé dans un État membre est présumé adéquat pour le marché de tout autre État membre.[29] L'utilisation, dans l'arrêt discuté, de l'expression « seul fait » ne fait que souligner le détachement de la Cour par rapport à ce qui a été, jusqu'à présent, le fait générateur et la pierre angulaire de tout le système de reconnaissance mutuelle. D'autre part, si la Cour dit bien que cette nouvelle approche s'applique en l'absence d'harmonisation, elle ne précise pas pour autant le degré d'harmonisation requis pour éviter cette approche réductrice : si l'harmonisation complète exclut (par hypothèse) le jeu de la reconnaissance mutuelle, tout comme l'absence de toute harmonisation (selon la jurisprudence discutée), le domaine de la reconnaissance mutuelle se trouve réduit à une zone grise mal définie entre les deux extrêmes.

Dans ces conditions, où les États membres retrouvent leur liberté entière d'imposer des régimes d'autorisation, il est plus que jamais nécessaire d'encadrer les procédures nationales de délivrance par ces mêmes autorisations.

2. La capacité du droit de l'UE pour encadrer les systèmes nationaux d'autorisation

A. *Encadrement pour la délivrance de l'autorisation – et application du «* soft law *» de la Commission ?*

En vertu d'une jurisprudence qui date déjà de plus de quinze ans, la Cour exige que toute procédure nationale d'autorisation réponde à trois critères : a) qu'elle opère selon des critères objectifs, non discriminatoires et connus à l'avance, b) qu'elle soit conclue dans des délais raisonnables et c) qu'elle soit soumise à un contrôle (de préférence) juridictionnel.[30]

Dans le domaine de la libre prestation de services, en particulier, la Cour tient, s'agissant d'une autorisation purement formelle, à ce qu'elle « *ne doit ni retarder ni compliquer l'exercice du droit ... de fournir ses services* ».[31] De plus, si les conditions pour la délivrance d'une autorisa-

29 CJUE, 3 décembre 1974, aff. 33/74, *Van Binsbergen*, *Rec.* p. 1299 ; CJUE, 20 février 1979, aff. 120/78, *Rewe-Zentral AG v Bundesmonopolverwaltung für Branntwein (Cassis de Dijon)*, *Rec.* 649.

30 V. par ex. les arrêts sur la mobilité des patients, notamment CJUE, 12 juillet 2001, aff. C-157/99, *Smits et Peerbooms*, *Rec.* p. I-5473, att. 90 ; pour un rappel de ces conditions v. CJUE, 3 juin 2010, aff. C-203/08, *Sporting Exchange*, *Rec.* p. I-4695, att. 50 où il est mis au clair, contrairement à des arrêts précédents plus laxistes, que le recours contre le refus de délivrance des autorisations devrait être de nature juridictionnelle.

31 CJUE, 30 octobre 2000, aff. C-58/98, *Corsten*, *Rec.* p. I-7919, att. 47 ; et CJUE, 11 décembre 2003, aff. C-215/01, *Schnitzer*, *Rec.* p. I-14847, att. 36.

tion dans l'État d'origine sont similaires à celles de l'État d'accueil, « *une éventuelle exigence d'inscription au registre des métiers de l'État membre d'accueil ne peut être autre qu'automatique, elle ne peut ni constituer une condition préalable à la prestation de services, ni conduire à des frais administratifs pour le prestataire concerné* ».[32]

Ces mêmes exigences ont été entérinées dans la Directive Services. En effet, l'Article 9(2) prévoit que les critères doivent être objectifs, connus à l'avance, etc. ; 9(3) que des exigences similaires de délivrance devraient faire l'objet de reconnaissance mutuelle dans les différents États ; 9(5) que l'autorisation devrait être délivrée dans des délais raisonnables ; et 9(6) que toute décision négative « *doit être dûment motivée et doit pouvoir faire l'objet d'un recours devant les tribunaux ou autres instances de recours* ». Par ailleurs, l'Article 13 intitulé « Procédures d'autorisation » prescrit avec détail les conditions que doivent remplir les procédures d'autorisation. En vertu de la règle énoncée aux paragraphes (3) et (4) de cet Article, les autorités nationales sont tenues de répondre dans un délai prévu à l'avance, faute de quoi, l'autorisation « est considérée comme octroyée ». Cette règle, qui renverse la présomption classique du droit administratif continental, selon laquelle « le silence vaut refus », pourrait révolutionner le fonctionnement des administrations publiques.[33]

À cette première série d'exigences qui tend à encadrer la discrétion des autorités nationales et à offrir des garanties procédurales minimales aux agents économiques, s'ajoute une deuxième, bien plus exigeante. Commençant par *Placanica*, se rendant plus explicite dans *Sporting Exchange* et *Engelmann*[34] et se concrétisant davantage dans *Costa et Cifone*, la Cour établit un véritable régime pour la délivrance des autorisations par les autorités nationales ; régime calqué sur celui applicable en matière de marchés publics et de concessions, puisque, selon les termes de la Cour « *le fait que la délivrance d'autorisations d'exploiter des établissements de jeux n'équivaudrait pas à des contrats de concession de services ne saurait, à lui seul, justifier que les exigences qui découlent de l'Article 49 CE [56 TFUE], notamment le principe d'égalité de traitement et l'obligation de transparence, soient méconnues* ».[35] À l'instar de ce qui se passe avec les contrats de concession, des partenariats publics-privés, des marchés publics ne dépassant pas les

---

32 V. p. ex *Schnitzer*, att. 37.

33 La question de savoir si une obligation de délivrance tacite résultait directement des dispositions du traité, en dehors du champ d'application de la Directive Services, a été discutée par la Cour et par son AG dans l'affaire des *Centres Commerciaux Espagnols*, *supra*, note 24, où la Cour a conclu par la négative.

34 CJUE, 9 septembre 2010, aff. C-64/08, *Engelmann*, *Rec*. p. I-8219.

35 *Sporting Exchange*, att. 46 et, dans des termes identiques, *Engelmann*, att. 52.

seuils des directives pertinentes, etc.,[36] « *sans nécessairement impliquer une obligation de procéder à un appel d'offres, ladite obligation de transparence ... impose à l'autorité concédante de garantir, en faveur de tout soumissionnaire potentiel, un degré de publicité adéquat permettant une ouverture de la concession à la concurrence ainsi que le contrôle de l'impartialité des procédures d'attribution* ».[37] Une telle obligation n'existe que lorsque la concession ou l'autorisation en question présente un intérêt pour des opérateurs établis dans d'autres États membres.

De sorte que la « révolution » inaugurée par la Cour, il y a plus de dix ans, dans le domaine des marchés publics, consistant en l'imposition d'un principe de transparence chaque fois où l'État est appelé à choisir un co-contractant (notamment par des contrats de concessions, des partenariats privés/publics, et des marchés publics au-dessous des seuils) est, à présent, étendu pour couvrir les procédures de délivrance d'autorisations. De la même manière qu'en matière d'autorisations, la jurisprudence en question s'applique uniquement dans des situations présentant, du moins potentiellement, un intérêt transfrontalier.[38]

Cette jurisprudence « transparence » a poussé la Commission à publier une Communication interprétative « relative au droit communautaire applicable aux passations des marchés non soumises ou partiellement soumises aux directives "marchés publics" » (connue aussi sous le nom Communication *de minimis*).[39] Elle a aussi publié deux Communications sur les contrats de concessions et les partenariats privés/publics (PPPs),[40] lesquelles ont, à la suite d'une large consultation, abouti à la proposition d'un nouveau « paquet marchés publics » par lequel la

36 Pour la reconnaissance progressive des exigences découlant du principe de non-discrimination et d'égalité de traitement en matière des marchés publics non couverts par les directives, concessions, etc. v. les arrêts CJUE, 7 décembre 2000, aff. C-324/98, *Telaustria Verlags*, *Rec.* p. I-10745 ; CJUE, 27 octobre 2005, aff. C-234/03, *Contse et al.*, *Rec.* p. I-9315 ; CJUE, 13 octobre 2005, aff. C-458/03, *Parking Brixen*, *Rec.* p. I-8585 ; ainsi que les textes de la Commission cités ci-dessous note 40.

37 *Costa et Cifone*, att. 55.

38 See *Costa et Cifone* para. 55 ; l'exigence d'un intérêt transfrontalier a été rendue explicite dans l'affaire CJUE 13 novembre 2007, aff. C-507/03, *Commission v Ireland (An Post)*, *Rec.* p. I-9777 et davantage détaillé dans CJUE, 15 mai 2008, aff. jtes, C-147-148/06, *SECAP SpA and Santorso*, *Rec.* p. I-3565, att. 24.

39 OJ (2006) C179/2.

40 Communications de la Commission COM(2005)569 final et C (2007) 6661 (2008) OJ C 91/4, sur les partenariats publics-privés et les concessions.

Commission entend modifier les directives en place et adopter une nouvelle directive en matière de concessions.[41]

Ainsi, on pourrait avancer l'idée selon laquelle les règles et principes mis en avant par la Commission dans ces textes de « *soft law* » pour matérialiser le principe de transparence en matière des marchés publics, sont également transposables et applicables en matière de délivrance d'autorisations. Cette proposition serait d'autant plus sensée qu'elle aboutirait à compléter la règle de l'Article 12(1) de la Directive Services : si ladite disposition du droit dérivé exige que le principe de transparence soit respecté lors de la délivrance d'autorisations limitées par des raisons techniques et/ou naturelles, la transposition des règles de « *soft law* » décrites ci-dessus rendrait ces mêmes principes de rigueur dans toute autre procédure d'autorisation.[42]

B. Pour le contrôle juridictionnel des décisions négatives – vers la transposition de la « Directive Recours » en matière d'autorisations

Bien que l'existence d'un contrôle juridictionnel des décisions négatives constitue une exigence classique de la jurisprudence de la Cour, la Cour en a renforcé substantiellement la portée dans ses arrêts les plus récents. Selon elle, le principe de transparence exige que toute décision de retrait ou de rejet d'une autorisation et/ou imposant des sanctions pécuniaires devrait être « *fondée sur un jugement ayant autorité de chose jugée et concernant un délit suffisamment grave* »[43] et que « *l'exclusion d'opérateurs du marché pourrait être considérée comme proportionnée seulement à condition de prévoir un recours en justice efficace ainsi qu'un dédommagement du préjudice subi* ».[44]

Il résulte de la première partie précitée, qu'en subordonnant l'exécution d'une mesure administrative à la délivrance d'un jugement revêtu de l'autorité de la chose jugée, la Cour remet en question la présomption de base du droit administratif, celle de la légalité des actes et, en corollaire, l'absence d'effet suspensif des recours administratifs et/ou judiciaires. Dans la deuxième partie précitée, la Cour va au-delà de la

[41] V. COM(2011)897 final du 20 décembre 2011 ; pour l'ensemble de ces propositions v. http://ec.europa.eu/commission_2010-2014/barnier/headlines/news/2011/12/2011 1220_fr.htm#.

[42] Directive 123/2006, Article 12(1) ; pour une brève présentation de cette disposition et ses rapports avec la jurisprudence *Placanica* v. Hatzopoulos, V., « Que reste-t-il de la Directive Services », *Cahiers de Droit Européen*, 2008, vol. 43, pp. 299-358, 333-334.

[43] *Costa et Cifone*, att. 81.

[44] *Ibid.*

simple exigence d'un recours hiérarchique, non seulement en exigeant un recours juridictionnel, mais en précisant de plus celui-ci doit être effectif. Ainsi la Cour semble stigmatiser des règles procédurales nationales imposant des périodes de prescription trop courtes ou limitant le montant du dédommagement exigible en cas de violation du droit de l'Union.

Deux observations s'imposent. D'abord, il devient évident que si la jurisprudence ci-dessus devait se maintenir, elle affecterait de manière profonde la manière dont la justice serait rendue dans les États membres. L'autonomie procédurale des États serait ainsi sacrifiée à l'autel de l'effet utile et de l'efficacité du droit de l'Union. Aussi choquante que cette idée puisse paraître, elle n'est pour autant pas inopportune : l'expérience montre que l'autonomie *procédurale* est source de divergences *substantielles* dans l'application du droit de l'Union, si bien que la Cour, en tant que Cour constitutionnelle de l'UE, devrait tôt ou tard réviser le contenu et l'étendue de cette autonomie.

Ensuite, on ne peut manquer de faire le parallèle entre la jurisprudence discutée ci-dessus et la Directive Recours en matière des marchés publics.[45] En effet, ladite directive institue des délais précis pendant lesquels la procédure de passation est suspendue pour permettre aux soumissionnaires d'introduire utilement leurs recours ; elle prévoit en outre, la possibilité d'obtenir des dommages-intérêts substantiels au cas où l'on serait illégalement évincé du marché. Le parallèle est d'autant plus frappant que dans *Costa et Cifone* le plaignant, considérant que la procédure de délivrance d'autorisations était entachée d'un vice, n'y avait pas participé. Une des particularités de la Directive Recours est qu'elle peut être invoquée par toute partie intéressée par le marché, même si elle n'a pas participé à la procédure.[46]

Ainsi la boucle est-elle bouclée et la transposition, aux procédures nationales de délivrance des autorisations, des principes découlant du droit des marchés publics, est-elle complétée. S'appuyant sur une obligation de transparence et de publicité adéquate, la Cour n'hésite pas à prescrire tout un régime pour la délivrance d'autorisations, voire à empiéter sur l'autonomie procédurale des États membres afin d'assurer l'effet utile du droit de l'Union.

Conclusion

La jurisprudence récente de la Cour, en matière d'autorisations, fait plus que pousser aux extrêmes l'encadrement procédural des pratiques

---

45 Directive du PE et du Conseil 2007/66/CE (2007) JOCE L 335/31.

46 V. par ex. C.J. 12 février 2004, aff. C-230/02, *Grossmann*, *Rec.* p. I-1829.

nationales. En effet, si la logique de cette jurisprudence était poursuivie, l'encadrement des autorités nationales cesserait d'être purement procédural pour devenir substantiel ; ceci à deux titres.

En premier lieu, le fait que la Cour qualifie de discriminatoires les régimes d'autorisation, dès lors qu'ils privilégient les opérateurs déjà en place, marque un saut logique : la Cour ne limite pas son contrôle à la simple procédure d'autorisation, mais l'étend au-delà, aux conditions effectives d'exercice de l'activité en cause. En effet, la Cour retient que le principe de non-discrimination serait violé par « *le fait même que les opérateurs existants aient pu commencer leur activité quelques années plus tôt que les opérateurs illégalement exclus, et ainsi pu s'établir sur le marché avec une certaine renommée et une clientèle fidélisée* ».[47] De la sorte, un principe procédural se transforme en condition substantielle, de même qu'un objectif de marché intérieur (égalité d'accès à l'activité économique) se transforme en finalité du droit de la concurrence (concurrence non faussée de manière artificielle).

En second lieu, en exigeant que les conditions pour le refus et/ou la révocation d'une autorisation devaient être « *formulées de manière claire, précise et univoque* »,[48] et en laissant inapplicable toute réglementation qui n'y satisfait pas, la Cour s'érige en juge de la qualité de la réglementation nationale. Ceci, en combinaison avec le principe classique selon lequel les instruments administratifs non contraignants ne se prêtent pas à l'application correcte du droit de l'Union, pourrait affecter, de manière profonde la manière dont opèrent les administrations nationales, surtout dans les États du sud de l'Europe où les « circulaires » règnent.

Le principe de non-discrimination et de transparence, inventé par la Cour pour compléter le cadre réglementaire de la passation des marchés publics, se trouve transposé en matière de délivrance d'autorisations, un domaine où l'Union n'a pas légiféré de manière horizontale. Ce même principe prend de la chaire et se concrétise, pas seulement sur le plan procédural, mais aussi sur le plan matériel. En effet, l'application de ce principe en matière d'autorisations n'a pas pour seul résultat d'offrir des garanties aux opérateurs concernés, mais, en même temps, il se répercute sur l'organisation des marchés correspondants. De manière plus étonnante encore, ce même principe affecte la manière dont sont organisées l'administration et la justice nationales : *spill over all over* ?

[47] *Costa et Cifone*, att. 53.

[48] *Ibid.*, att. 78.

Le développement de l'abus de droit en matière fiscale

Philippe MARCHESSOU

Professeur à l'Université de Strasbourg

Le prononcé, le 29 mars 2012, par la CJUE d'un arrêt *3M*,[1] dans lequel elle pose en principe l'interdiction de l'abus de droit, rappelle le chemin parcouru par ce concept dans le droit fiscal européen, mais aussi ses implications. À l'origine, l'abus de droit n'est pas fiscal, il naît comme concept à propos du droit de propriété et amène le juge à rechercher les mobiles qui ont animé le titulaire d'un droit afin de déterminer s'il usait de ce dernier dans un but légitime ou avec l'intention de nuire à autrui, auquel cas l'utilisation dévoyée d'un droit est constitutive d'un abus de droit. La jurisprudence du juge civil français a depuis longtemps stigmatisé ce comportement, depuis la fausse cheminée édifiée dans l'affaire *Doerr* pour gêner un voisin[2] jusqu'aux poteaux agressifs édifiés par l'irascible voisin de l'usine de construction de dirigeables de la société Clément-Bayard.[3]

L'extension à la matière fiscale viendra en France par une loi de 1941.[4] Le texte, substantiellement réécrit depuis 2009,[5] prévoit que l'administration est en droit d'écarter, comme ne lui étant pas opposables, les actes constitutifs d'un abus de droit,

– soit que ces actes présentent un caractère fictif ;

– soit que ces actes, recherchant le bénéfice d'une application littérale des textes ou de décisions à l'encontre des objectifs poursuivis par leurs auteurs, n'aient pu être inspirés par aucun autre motif que celui

---

1 CJUE, 4e ch., 29 mars 2012, aff. C-417/10, *3M Italia*, non encore publié.

2 CA Colmar, 2 mai 1855, D. 1856, 2, p. 9.

3 Cass., req., 3 août 1915, DP 1917, 1, p. 79.

4 Codifiée à l'Article L 64 du Livre des procédures fiscales.

5 Article 35 de la loi de finances rectificative pour 2008, n° 2008-1443 du 30 décembre 2008, JO du 31.

d'éluder ou d'atténuer les charges fiscales normalement applicables à la situation ou aux activités réelles de l'intéressé.

L'abus de droit semble être entré dans la jurisprudence de la Cour de justice avec l'arrêt *Grundig-Consten*, qui relève que « le système communautaire [...] n'admet pas l'emploi abusif des droits découlant de l'un ou l'autre droit national des marques, pour mettre en échec l'application du droit communautaire des ententes ».[6] Si son champ d'application est devenu large,[7] la place qu'il a prise en matière fiscale est singulière. Son apparition dans la jurisprudence paraît avoir été provoquée par les États membres en réplique à l'imagination des contribuables (1), et son développement entraîne des implications discutables (2).

1. Une apparition provoquée par les États membres en réplique à l'imagination des contribuables

Le système juridique de l'Union est un système en construction. Sur le territoire des États membres, les administrations fiscales se sont trouvées confrontées aux comportements de contribuables qui développent une planification fiscale agressive et usent pour ce faire des potentialités que leur offre chacune des grandes libertés du Traité. Sollicitée d'intervenir pour réguler ces conflits en définissant l'exacte portée desdites libertés, la Cour de justice a appliqué l'abus de droit à la matière fiscale. Elle l'a fait pour la première fois, de manière éclatante, dans un secteur plutôt inattendu, celui de la TVA (A). Elle l'a fait de manière plus classique dans le domaine de la fiscalité directe (B).

A. L'apparition solennelle de l'abus de droit en matière de TVA

C'est à l'occasion de l'arrêt *Halifax*[8] que la Grande Chambre est venue consacrer le poids de l'abus de droit en matière fiscale. Cette affirmation est apparue d'autant plus significative qu'elle est intervenue là où on ne l'attendait pas, c'est-à-dire pour un impôt réel qui prend en compte la nature et le déroulement des opérations, sans se préoccuper intrinsèquement de considérations personnelles relatives à l'opérateur et à ses motivations. La Cour y fait œuvre de clarté en traçant d'abord le cadre général de son intervention. L'acteur de cette petite révolution est le gouvernement du Royaume-Uni, qui a pallié la carence de sa législation nationale en instrumentalisant la Cour, proclamant au passage que « *Le principe d'abus de droit est un principe général du droit commu-*

---

6 CJCE, 13 juillet 1966, aff. 56 et 58/64, *Grundig-Consten*, 1966, Rec. p. 00429.

7 Pour une application récente en matière de libre circulation des travailleurs, cf. CJUE, 2e ch., 21 juillet 2011, aff. C-186/10, *Toural Oguz*, 2011, Rec. p. I-06957.

8 CJCE, 21 février 2006, aff. C-255/02, *Halifax*, 2006, Rec. p. I-01609.

nautaire ».[9] La Cour affirme ainsi que le montage sophistiqué réalisé par le Groupement constitué par Halifax pour obtenir la déduction de la TVA afférente à l'édification de ses centres d'appel s'analysait comme constitutif d'un abus de droit. Tout d'abord, les justiciables ne sauraient frauduleusement ou abusivement se prévaloir des normes communautaires.[10] La lutte contre la fraude, l'évasion fiscale et les abus éventuels constituent un objectif reconnu et encouragé par la sixième directive.[11]

Certes, le contribuable à la TVA est libre de choisir la voie la moins imposée,[12] et ce n'est que dans l'hypothèse où les opérations en cause ont pour but « essentiel » l'obtention d'un avantage fiscal, que l'abus de droit est constitué.[13] La délimitation du concept est claire, à ceci près que le but essentiel semble signifier une sorte d'intention de l'opérateur majoritairement tournée vers la volonté d'obtenir un avantage indu mais pas une dédication exclusive.

La filiation de cette jurisprudence est plus incertaine puisque, selon les chambres de la Cour, le niveau d'exigence varie. La 2e et la 7e chambres se situent dans le droit fil de l'arrêt *Halifax* en se bornant à exiger un but « essentiel », respectivement dans les arrêts *Part Service*[14] et *Tanoarch*,[15] tandis que la 3e chambre, dans l'arrêt *Ampliscientifica*[16] exige de l'administration qu'elle apporte la preuve de la volonté « exclusive » d'obtenir un avantage fiscal. Cette divergence entre chambres semble s'analyser comme le fruit d'une démarche encore peu assurée.

B. La confirmation de l'abus de droit dans le domaine de la fiscalité directe

Le mouvement développé par la Cour intervient dans un domaine apparemment plus naturel pour déceler les abus de droit, dans la mesure où l'équation personnelle du contribuable joue dans le processus d'assujettissement et, corrélativement, permet de déceler plus facilement que pour un impôt réel si la situation relève de l'abus de droit. Ceci étant, l'imposition directe relève de la compétence des États, il est par conséquent naturel que la Cour ait éprouvé quelque réticence à intervenir dans un domaine traité par la législation de la majorité des États

9 Point 63.

10 Point 68.

11 Point 71.

12 Point 74.

13 Points 75, 81 et 86.

14 CJCE, 21 février 2008, aff. C-425/06, *Part Service*, 2008, Rec. p. I-00897, point 62.

15 CJCE, 27 octobre 2011, aff. C-504/10, *Tanoarch*, non encore publié, point 52.

16 CJCE, 22 mai 2008, aff. C-162/07, *Ampliscientifica*, 2008, Rec. p. I-04019, point 30.

membres. Dans l'arrêt *Cadbury*,[17] un dispositif anti-abus de droit est confronté à la liberté d'établissement.

La législation britannique des sociétés étrangères contrôlées[18] qui réintègre, dans le résultat du groupe imposable au Royaume-Uni, le résultat d'une filiale implantée dans un paradis fiscal[19] est-elle ou non attentatoire à la liberté d'établissement (qui prohibe les discriminations tant à l'entrée qu'à la sortie), lorsqu'elle est appliquée aux deux filiales irlandaises d'une multinationale britannique. Ce dispositif national a été édicté pour lutter contre les montages abusifs, et la Cour le valide en tant qu'il a pour ambition de neutraliser les schémas qui ne répondent pas de manière positive au test du mobile, lequel comporte deux conditions cumulatives dont le contribuable doit montrer la matérialité. D'une part, le contribuable britannique doit démontrer que la diminution de l'impôt dû n'était pas l'objectif principal ou l'un des objectifs principaux de l'opération ; d'autre part, la société résidente doit démontrer que la raison principale ou l'une des raisons principales de l'existence de cette société étrangère n'était pas l'obtention d'une diminution de l'impôt dû au Royaume-Uni par la voie d'un détournement de bénéfices. Autrement dit, la lutte contre l'abus de droit justifie suffisamment la validité d'un dispositif pourtant attentatoire dans une certaine mesure à la liberté d'établissement.

La Cour prend soin d'insérer cette décision dans un contexte général marqué à la fois par la prohibition de la référence abusive aux normes communautaires pour se soustraire à la législation nationale,[20] mais aussi par le souci d'assurer sa pleine efficacité à la liberté d'établissement, y compris lorsque le contribuable en use dans le but de bénéficier d'une législation plus avantageuse, y compris fiscale.[21]

La jurisprudence rendue est peu abondante,[22] sans doute parce que pour ces impôts non harmonisés existent des dispositifs nationaux de répression de l'abus de droit. Ainsi, l'arrêt *3M*[23] prend soin de préciser « *qu'il n'existe en droit de l'Union aucun principe général duquel découlerait une obligation pour les États membres de lutter contre les*

---

17 CJCE, 12 septembre 2006, aff. C-196/04, *Cadbury*, 2006, Rec. p. I-07995.

18 *SEC* ou *CFC*, *Controled Foreign Companies*.

19 C'est-à-dire pratiquant une imposition inférieure d'au moins 75 % à l'imposition normalement applicable au Royaume-Uni.

20 Point 35 de l'arrêt.

21 Points 36 à 38 de l'arrêt, qui citent notamment les arrêts *Centros*, CJCE, 9 mars 1999, aff. C-212/97, 1999, Rec. p. I-01459 et *Inspire Art*, CJCE, 30 septembre 2003, aff. C-167/01, 2003, Rec. p. I-10155.

22 CJCE, 5 juillet 2007, aff. C-321/05, *Kofoed*, 2007, Rec. p. I-05795.

23 *3M Italia*, *supra*, note 1.

pratiques abusives dans le domaine de la fiscalité directe... et que le droit de l'Union n'est pas en jeu».[24] La démarche de la Cour vaut également pour une fusion d'entreprises qui a pour résultat de prévenir le prélèvement des droits de mutation.[25]

Ce développement entraîne des implications variées et discutables.

2. Le développement du concept d'abus de droit en matière fiscale entraîne des implications variées et discutables

L'admission par la Cour du concept d'abus de droit correspond à un moment de sa politique jurisprudentielle. Les premières décennies de son intervention en matière fiscale – singulièrement en matière de fiscalité directe – ont été des années d'évangélisation, au cours desquelles elle a donné une solennité particulière à l'affirmation des grandes libertés du Traité. Cette période, amorcée à compter de 1982,[26] se montre peu tolérante avec les dispositifs nationaux qui contreviennent à ces libertés, hors quelques rares exceptions.[27]

Sans qu'il soit possible de dater avec précision le moment de l'évolution,[28] la jurisprudence de la Cour s'infléchit dans le sens d'une consolidation. Sans renier la période précédente, elle prête dorénavant une oreille plus attentive aux revendications des États membres, lesquels font valoir la nécessité de tolérer la survivance de dispositions nationales qui portent à une liberté du Traité une atteinte mesurée et juste adaptée au nom d'une raison impérieuse d'intérêt général à la portée plus essentielle. La tonalité est beaucoup plus systématique à compter des années 2005 ; c'est dans ce contexte que surgit la prohibition de l'abus de droit parce que les États ont su montrer à la Cour que l'application indifférenciée des libertés du Traité pouvait conduire à l'éclosion d'effets d'aubaine constitutifs d'un abus d'invocation de ces libertés.

Deux séries d'implications résultent de ce qu'il faut bien appeler un tournant de la jurisprudence, qui se révèlent d'ailleurs comme les deux facettes de ce tournant :

---

24 Point 32.

25 CJUE, 1re ch., 20 mai 2010, aff. C-352/08, *Modehuis A. Zwijnenburg BV*, 2010, Rec. p. I-04303.

26 CJCE, 5 mai 1982, aff. 15/81, *Gaston Schul*, 1982, Rec. p. 01409 ; CJCE, 28 janvier 1986, aff. 270/83, *Commission c/ France*, 1986, Rec. p. 00273 ; CJCE, 8 mai 1990, aff. 175/88, *Biehl*, 1990, Rec. p. I-01779.

27 CJCE, 28 janvier 1992, aff. C-204/90, *Bachmann*, 1992, Rec. p. I-00249 et C-300/90, *Commission c/ Belgique*, 1992, Rec. p. I-00305.

28 Peut-être l'arrêt *Marks & Spencer*, CJCE, 13 décembre 2005, aff. C-446/03, 2005, Rec. p. I-10837.

– c'est d'abord la plasticité du concept d'abus de droit (A) ;

– c'est ensuite l'amoindrissement de la sécurité juridique qui en résulte (B).

A. La plasticité du concept d'abus de droit

La référence à la sculpture vient de ce que la réflexion se loge à deux niveaux. Le premier, le plus évident et le plus important, tient à la nécessité pour un État de droit de châtier les surdoués de la fiscalité pour leur péché,[29] puisque leur habileté s'analyse comme un dévoiement de la norme. Le principe de la répression n'est pas contestable, il est l'expression d'un système juridique sophistiqué dont le fonctionnement ne saurait être cantonné à une vision exclusivement formelle des normes.

Le second niveau est plus épineux car il s'agit de la qualification retenue pour tracer la frontière entre l'usage adéquat de la norme et l'usage prohibé. Dans l'espace juridique français, c'est longtemps le caractère exclusivement fiscal du schéma retenu qui permettait de le qualifier d'abus de droit puisque ce schéma n'avait été édifié que dans le seul but d'échapper à l'imposition normalement due.[30] La législation française a intégré, depuis 2008, les apports de la jurisprudence du Conseil d'État qui suivent une trajectoire semblable à celle de la Cour de justice. Or, celle-ci donne l'impression, soit d'hésiter sur l'ampleur qu'il lui faut conférer au concept lui-même, soit de décider de lui conférer une plasticité importante dans le dessein de permettre aux administrations fiscales des États membres de réagir aux manifestations futures de l'imagination développée par les contribuables pour asservir les textes communautaires à leur désir d'optimisation fiscale. À ce jour, cette jurisprudence hésite entre le but « exclusivement » fiscal[31] qu'elle utilise parfois, et le but « essentiellement » fiscal[32] qu'elle emploie davantage. Entre une motivation unique qu'il est difficile à l'administration de déceler dans la vie des affaires contemporaines et une motivation principale qui pose une présomption à laquelle le contribuable ne pourra échapper qu'en apportant la preuve contraire, la marge est substantielle. Elle est génératrice d'incertitude et amoindrit la sécurité juridique.

---

29 L'expression est de Maurice Cozian ; notamment M. Cozian et F. Deboissy, Précis de fiscalité des entreprises, 35e éd., 2011, p. 742.

30 Article L 64 du Livre des procédures fiscales, dans sa rédaction antérieure à 2008.

31 Cf. arrêt *Ampliscientifica*, *supra*, note 16.

32 Outre *Halifax*, *supra*, note 8, les arrêts *Part Service*, *supra*, note 14, et *Tanoarch*, *supra*, note 15.

B. L'amoindrissement de la sécurité juridique provoqué par le développement de l'abus de droit dans la jurisprudence de la Cour

Débusquer l'abus de droit pour disqualifier au regard du droit fiscal le schéma juridique adopté par le contribuable nécessite de rechercher les motifs qui ont conduit ce contribuable à adopter un tel schéma. Le risque de dérive d'une telle démarche, l'atteinte portée à la liberté d'entreprendre du contribuable constituent des écueils potentiels. Le bien-fondé de la démarche du juge est de considérer que l'essence d'un régime juridique réside dans un rapport harmonieux et cohérent entre le droit positif et l'intention du législateur, rapport que ne respecte pas le comportement abusif puisque ce dernier privilégie mal à propos la lettre des textes. Ceci étant, en remontant aux principes généraux qui sous-tendent toute la jurisprudence de la Cour, il apparaît que le danger d'arbitraire n'est peut-être pas aussi important que le donnerait à penser l'emploi de l'adverbe « essentiellement ». La Cour a bien conscience du risque d'altération de la sécurité juridique. Ainsi, dans l'arrêt *Halifax*, elle prend le soin de rappeler que

> la législation communautaire doit également être certaine et son application prévisible pour les justiciables. Cet impératif de sécurité juridique s'impose avec une rigueur particulière lorsqu'il s'agit d'une réglementation susceptible de comporter des charges financières, afin de permettre aux intéressés de connaître avec exactitude l'étendue des obligations qu'elle leur impose.[33]

Dans cette même décision, elle insiste également sur l'importance du droit à déduction[34] qui ne peut être limité que d'une manière exceptionnelle en cas de fraude ou d'abus. De manière plus profonde, toute sa jurisprudence est guidée dans ce domaine par une logique économique. La répression de l'abus de droit risque de léser de manière privilégiée la liberté d'établissement,[35] or celle-ci a exclusivement une dimension économique. La Cour l'avait précisé de manière lapidaire dès l'arrêt *Werner*[36] et dans des situations sur la marge, elle préférera le concept de citoyenneté européenne.[37] Or, dans ce cadre économique, c'est la réalité des flux, l'absence de caractère artificiel des montages et l'authenticité de la structure qui permettront de déterminer avec un degré d'approximation raisonnable si le contribuable a commis ou non un abus de droit.

---

33 Point 72 de l'arrêt.

34 Points 83 et 84.

35 Ce peut être également le cas pour les directives, par exemple la directive 90/434 « fusions », cf. l'arrêt *Modehuis A. Zwijnenburg BV*, *supra*, note 25.

36 CJCE, 26 janvier 1993, aff. C-112/91, *Werner*, 1993, Rec. p. I-00429.

37 CJCE, 9 novembre 2006, aff. C-520/04, *Turpeinen*, 2006, Rec. p. I-10685.

La Cour agit donc dans un cadre qui n'est pas nouveau, elle est aidée pour s'éloigner du risque de l'arbitraire par la démarche de la Commission qui, en 2007, a demandé un alignement des règles anti-abus des États membres sur les exigences du droit communautaire, en demandant à ceux-ci de ne viser que les montages purement artificiels, c'est-à-dire les situations caractérisées par l'absence d'implantation véritable ou, plus généralement, de justifications commerciales.[38] Le souci de ne pas entraver la création de richesse et, plus simplement, le développement des entreprises donne aussi aux États le souci de pacifier leur terrain d'action en développant la pratique des rescrits, qui offre le double mérite d'obliger l'administration fiscale à s'engager, mais aussi le contribuable à soumettre sa solution pour examen préalable.

Ainsi, l'abus de droit rénové devient essentiellement un facteur de dissuasion, ce qui est le meilleur de son rôle. La balance entre administration fiscale et contribuables est alors bien tracée, et le rôle du juge moins écrasant.

---

[38] Comm. CE, communiqué du 10 décembre 2007, IP/07/1878.

The Legal Readjustment of the European Economic and Monetary Union

Peter-Christian MÜLLER-GRAFF

Professor Dr. Dr.h.c.mult.; Direktor des Instituts für deutsches und europäisches Gesellschafts- und Wirtschaftsrecht der Universität Heidelberg

The legal readjustment of the Economic and Monetary Union (EMU) is the main recent challenge for economic legal policy in the European Union, but it also touches the idea of national statehood and sovereignty.[1] It concerns nothing less than a core element of the economic and public order: the guarantee of an internally and externally stable currency in a politically defined economic area. This is challenging enough for a single state currency. For a transnational common currency of at present seventeen states, which are independent in matters of economic and budgetary policies and economically heterogeneous, this is a Herculean task in terms of politics and economics. Without a firm and reliable legal framework, it seems to be impossible. The categorical implications of the legal readjustment in view of the political and economic context shall be analysed in three steps: first, the relevant primary law of the European Union in May 2010 when the budget crisis of several Member States reached the political emergency level (1) which, second, has provoked new legal constructions since then (2) and third demands a readjustment in matters of legal rules and state policy (3).

1 This text is based on a lecture on the role of law in the European Economic and Monetary Union given by the author at Cornell University Law School on 13 September 2012. The author is grateful for the privilege of participating in the work of the College of Europe as member of the "Corps enseignant" in Bruges and Natolin over the years.

1. The Relevant Primary Law of the European Union at the Outbreak of the Budget Crisis in May 2010

The relevant primary law of the European Union at the outbreak of the crisis turned out to be neither firm nor reliable for the concept of an EMU without excessive national sovereign debts and without the necessity of transnational budget aid of whatever source and technical kind (by states, the ECB or other institutions of the Union). It was not reliable in view of ensuring budget discipline because of its weakness in terms of prevention and its generous treatment of transgressions (A). And it was not firm against politically discretionary transnational budget aids because of legal ambiguities in important areas (B).

A. *Unreliability in View of Budget Discipline and Coordination of Economic Policies*

The unreliable aspects of primary law in view of budget discipline and economic policy stem from the intergovernmental nature of the economic union.

I. Weak Supranational Traits

It is well known that the supranational traits of the economic union are *weak*. They exist only to a limited degree as in the procedure of support in emergencies (Article 122 TFEU) and in the competences of the Union for a more precise definition of certain technical terms in Articles 123 to 125 TFEU. Aside from these provisions supranational elements only partly exist in the two regular pre-emptive procedures of economic stabilisation, namely in the coordination of economic policies of Member States and in the supervision of their budget policies. In addition to that, the protocol on the excessive debt deficit procedure can be replaced by appropriate provisions of the Council in accordance with a special legislative procedure. However, this allows also the mitigation of discipline as practised in order to fit excessive budget deficits of France and Germany in 2005. The jurisdiction of the ECJ is available only in part, in particular for actions of annulment (Article 263 TFEU) against measures of EU institutions, herein the ECB included.

II. Intergovernmental Approach

In its basic *intergovernmental* approach, the law of the economic union reflects the hesitation of the Member States against a strong European regime that governs their economic and budgetary politics. When politically agreeing upon the EMU in 1992 this scheme was probably unavoidable, but as predicted by many economists it contained a potential conflict with the ambition of a monetary union. The language of the

Treaty uses the classic diplomatic formula that the Member States consider their economic policy "as a matter of common interest" and coordinate it in the Council. Therefore, the tools of recommendations, advisory opinions, as well as reports, conclusions, supervisions, overall evaluations, briefings, warnings, publications and requests are dominant in the rules on the procedures of coordination and supervision. The explicit exclusion of the jurisdiction of the ECJ regarding actions against Member States for not fulfilling the obligations in budget policy (Article 126 par. 10 TFEU) follows this soft legal scheme.

B. Lacks of Clarity in View of Transnational Budget Aids

Besides this unreliability in the prevention of budget turbulences primary law is also weak in view of political demands for transnational budget aids. This weakness derives from certain lacks of clarity of formulation. Three provisions demonstrate this situation.

I. Prohibition of Assuming Commitments (Article 125 TFEU)

The extent of the prohibition of the EU and its member-states to assume the commitments of another member-state (Article 125 TFEU) is particularly controversial. This norm, which is often imprecisely labelled as "bail-out prohibition" by economists and politicians, is on a closer inspection less watertight than a conceptually rigid prohibition of any kind of transnational budgetary aid or support. The wording only allows two conclusions: there is no legal liability for the debts of (another) member-state and there is a prohibition of assuming commitments in relation to third parties (e.g. taking over the debt, entering into the debt, giving direct guarantees and sureties to creditors).

No explicit mention is made, however, of a general prohibition of voluntary assistance between the parties, as happened with the decision to aid Greece from 7 May 2010 and the creation of the European Financial Stability Facility (EFSF) from May 10, 2010, and their respective implementation, and as now formalized by the European Stability Mechanism (ESM). In so far only two reservations can be found in primary law: the EU itself may only provide financial support under the strict conditions of a narrowly defined emergency (Article 122 TFEU), and neither the European Central Bank nor the national central banks may *directly* purchase debt instruments of a member-state. These provisions follow the concept of pre-emptively furthering the fulfilment of the duty of the member-states and of avoiding excessive public deficit (Article 126 TFEU). However, whether – in the case of budget troubles of a Member State – Article 125 TFEU also contains a prohibition of *voluntary* transnational budget aids in order to avoid serious problems for the common currency is fervently disputed. It cannot be overlooked that such a rigid prohibition would contradict the overall Treaty objective of a stable monetary union. It would mean to regard the Euro-countries as being bound to surrender their own currency to the whims of capital investors. Such a far-reaching abdication of sovereignty can hardly be considered to be behind the rules agreed upon in Maastricht. It is another (and political) issue whether it is wise to provide aids to Member States which have neglected their obligation to avoid excessive sovereign deficits.

II. The Emergency Clause (Article 122 TFEU)

The range of emergencies which allow financial assistance according to Article 122 TFEU may also appear ambiguous. The regulation of the European Council from 11 May 2010 (establishing the European Finance Stabilising Mechanism EFSM), which had been triggered by the difficulties of Greece, was based on it. However, according to its wording, Article 122 paragraph 2 TFEU only concerns the situation that a Member State is seriously threatened with severe difficulties caused by natural disasters or exceptional occurrences beyond its control. A country's difficulty in raising credit on the capital market as a result of a debt policy which is disproportionate to its sources of potential revenue is neither an extraordinary event in terms of economic history nor is its occurrence beyond the country's control. Another assessment may be reasonable for the very first and unclear situation in May 2010, but certainly not for future occurrences of this kind. Insane political life patterns are not a natural disaster, but a human and social failure. The core of the problem is not the market (nor dubious rating agencies) but careless budgetary policy and those political patterns of life that support it.

III. "Direct" and "Indirect" Purchase of Debt Instruments by the ECB (Article 123 TFEU)

The prohibition of the "direct" purchase of debt instruments by the European Central Bank and national central banks is clearly formulated (Article 123 TFEU). But the formulation invites to circumventions, if the "indirect" acquisition (open-market policy) is considered to be allowed in any case. A central ratio of the distinction is the assumption that government bonds purchased on the primary market have successfully passed the private investors' risk assessment. This ratio of the distinction between prohibiting the financing of national debt by the ECB and allowing the purchase (and the use) of debt instruments which were taken by investors in the first place is blurred if the first purchaser of government bonds of troubled countries takes no risks, because before his purchase the ECB had announced its willingness to buy such debt instruments afterwards.

2. Moving Prerequisites of the EMU into New Legal Territory and Categories since 2010

Against this background the measures taken by the Union and their members and by the Euro countries since May 2010 are – from a legal point of view – an expression of a groping and searching departure into new territory without having already found a satisfying overall form. The chosen legal categories are very different: first help for Greece the EFSM, the EFSF, the ECB measures, the expanded EFSF, the so called "Six-pack", the so called "Haircut" of creditors, as well as the start of a simplified revision procedure of the TFEU (i.e. the addition of a third paragraph to Article 136 TFEU) and the ESM, as well as most recently a fiscal compact. They form a conglomerate of four different legal categories: EU law, trans-national law outside EU law, private law and national law.

A. European Union Law

It is most noteworthy that the readjustment of the law of the EMU, which has been attempted since May 2010, only partly starts from the EU law itself. It partly does so on disputed ground. Five steps have been taken.

I. EFSM

The first step taken in EU law was the establishment of the EFSM, which had been initiated in order to grant financial support. In addition to the boundaries of the legal basis (Article 122 para. 2 TFEU), as shown before, its use for authorizing the European Commission to raise credits in the name of the EU also appears dubious in view of the Treaty's imperative that the budget of the Union shall be wholly financed from own resources (Article 311 para. 1 TFEU). Article 122 TFEU is no good as a permanent solution for measures of transnational budget aids. These are also exposed to fundamental political objections, that they contradict the projected goal of an economic and monetary union on the basis of full budget autonomy and responsibility of every Member State *without* any transnational or European aid – notwithstanding specific project programmes.

II. Treaty Amendment

These political objections can be met with a legally clarifying (although in terms of conceptual change politically fundamental) amendment of the TFEU. The simplified revision procedure (Article 48 para. 6 TEU) was already triggered with the decision of the European Council of 25 March 2011 to add a third paragraph to Article 136 TFEU – which is solely applicable for the Euro states – with the following text: "The

Member States whose currency is the Euro may establish a stability mechanism to be activated if indispensable to safeguard the stability of the Euro area as a whole. The granting of any required financial assistance under the mechanism will be made subject to strict conditionality." This addition needs the consent of all Member States of the EU, not only the Euro members. The creation of a "mechanism" outside EU law is not explicitly mentioned in the wording of this planned amendment. But if it enters into force, EU law paradoxically implicitly opens the door for an exit from EU law to other transnational legal devices. The amendment itself does not transgress the limits of Article 48 para. 6 TEU since this revision does not increase the competences conferred on the Union in the Treaties.

III. Purchases of Government Bonds by the ECB

The use of the open market policy powers of the ECB since 2010 in order to support Euro states with budget problems could be found to operate in a grey *area* of primary law. If the purchase of government bonds of certain Member States on the so called secondary market (in other words from primary investors such as banks) is announced by the ECB in advance, i.e. before they are issued by an ailing State, then it can not be said that they have already "undergone market evaluation" in form of the first purchase by an investor. Applying the open market policy in this way means bypassing the prohibition of direct acquisition of national debt instruments by the ECB.

IV. "Sixpack"

The six legal acts for the strengthening of pre-emptive procedures which came into effect on 12 December 2011 (five regulations and one directive, the so-called "*Sixpack*"), partly stand on disputed ground concerning the legal competence of the Union. They are not concerned with trans-national budget aids for states which are already in trouble, but with a focus on the coordination of economic policy and budget supervision in the interest of economic convergence and budgetary discipline: on the one hand for all States of the Union (in particular: supervision procedures, acceleration of the excessive deficit procedure, avoidance and adjustment of macroeconomic imbalances, demands for the frameworks of budgetary policy), and on the other hand specifically for the Euro countries (in particular: effective implementation of the supervision of budgetary policy and adjustment of excessive macroeconomic imbalances). It seems doubtful that every measure of intensification contained therein is covered by the respectively chosen bases of authorisation under primary law according to Articles 121, 126 and 136 TFEU (in particular the presumption of acceptance of a decision recommended by the Commission if the Council does not reject it within a certain time limit).

V. Revision of Coordination and Supervision Procedures

The attempt of an intensification of pre-emptive procedures secured under primary law failed on 9 December 2011 due to the British attitude. Therefore the possibilities of a readjustment of EU primary law are blocked, as long as Britain does not reconsider its position or leaves the EU under Article 50 TEU.

B. Transnational Law outside EU Law

The option to choose a transnational path that lies – in terms of legal category – outside EU law in order to readjust the economic union between the Euro countries appears well nigh inevitable. Remarkably this happened already before the efforts to activate EU law. This implies a risky experiment and is not unknown since Schengen, but it seems more daring, to promote this main goal of the EU by means outside EU law. Until now already several steps of readjustment leap in this legal category.

I. First Aid for Greece

The aforementioned decision of help for Greece of 7 May 2010 marks the beginning of this *innovation*. It is an *intergovernmental* declaration of the heads of state and government of the Euro-area. On 8 May 2010, this led to an agreement about a loan facility for 80 billion €, which were incorporated into an overall package of 110 billion €, which has been made in cooperation with the IMF.

II. EFSF

Despite the objections deriving from the overall concept of a EMU without transnational budget aid, the next step towards the autonomisation of the law of the Euro-countries outside EU law followed already on 10 May 2010. As an expansion to the rescue package, which was completed on the next day (together with the mentioned EFSM under EU law), there was another intergovernmental decision by the representatives of the Euro states about an EFSF. It contains the commitment "to provide assistance through a Special Purpose Vehicle that is guaranteed [...] by participating Member States [...] and that will expire after three years, up to 400 billion €, in accordance with their share in the paid-up capital of the European Central Bank." This decision was also quickly implemented and the creative power of private law was explicitly used to this purpose. The expanded EFSF also follows this legal track. With it the guaranteed volume was increased to about 780 billion € and the forms of action were expanded.

III. Against this, the ESM, which entered into force on 26 September 2012, changes the legal background. Instead of an intergovernmental decision and a contract between the Euro-countries under private law, it is based on an independent Treaty under international law, which establishes an independent international financial institution of the Euro countries with an approved capital fund of 700 billion €. It places the autonomisation of the Euro countries in their mutual (but factually most probably one-sided North-South) budgetary assistance on the level of a new international organisation. However, this cannot release them from their duties under EU law, in particular not from the commitment to rules of the internal market. If the ESM were to give out assistance to banks that would distort competition, the participating Member States would be liable for this and would have to be subjected to the aid-monitoring rules of Article 107 TFEU.

IV. Fiscal Compact

The decision by 26 of the 27 heads of state and government of 9 December 2011, about a fiscal compact, extends the path outside of EU law to the two pre-emptive procedures concerning economic and budgetary policy (including the non-Eurozone member-states except Britain). This would not be necessary if the plan were possible to be realised as an Enhanced Cooperation, in the sense of Article 20 TEU, under the umbrella of the EU. However, there might exist limits of authority, depending on the mechanisms envisaged (see below at C). A consolidation of the economic union outside of EU law does not (against sporadic voices) in itself contravene primary law. The method may be surprising, but no single Member State is prohibited from being stricter in its budgetary and economic discipline than prescribed in EU law, nor is a subset of Member States prohibited from promising such a stricter discipline mutually among themselves (sort of "self-help group"). The Member States interested in the creation of the fiscal compact as concluded on 1 March 2012 are not prohibited to do this under the condition that they comply with EU law.

C. Private Law

The category of private law also plays a role in the readjustment of the economic union since May 2010.

I. Implementation of the EFSF

In this context it was first used for the implementation of the EFSF through the establishment of a *société anonyme* in Luxemburg on

17 June 2010 for the purpose of granting "stability aids" to Euro countries. Instead of a Treaty under international law, a private framework contract was agreed on between the Euro countries as shareholders of the EFSF and the *société anonyme*. This contract explicitly contains the rules concerning the granting of loans and the consequences of guarantees and is subject to a national (strangely enough, English) law and its interpretation. Whether this solution or one under international law is preferable will only be seen by a comparison between the (short-term) EFSF and (long-term) ESM. The jurisdiction that was agreed on also follows *the private* law model. For conflicts between one or more Euro countries and the EFSF, the exclusive jurisdiction of the courts of Luxemburg has been agreed upon. For conflicts between the Euro countries alone, the ECJ has been agreed upon as sole instance under an arbitration clause. This is not impossible under EU law due to the ECJ's powers of arbitration under the conditions of Article 273 TFEU, since a conflict between Euro countries in the context of the EFSF, because of its purpose to stabilise the economic and monetary union, can be considered to be "a dispute between Member-States which relates to the subject matter of the Treaties".

II. "Haircut"

The use of private law in the so-called "Haircut"-procedure (debt-cut) as applied in the case of Greece seems preferable to a sovereign order. The "autonomous" waiver of demands of the creditors avoids the problem of expropriation. However, the deterrent effect for future bond investors is tremendous. It is therefore understandable that the waiver was called as a "unique exception" in the declaration from 9 December 2011. Against this, a very reasonable mechanism lays in the future use of collective action *clauses* in all government bonds issued by Euro states. This technique had been determined on 25 March 2011 by the European Council and confirmed by the heads of government of the Euro states on 9 December 2011. It concerns new indebtedness, is able to sharpen the risk assessment of creditors and can lessen the states' readiness and factual possibility to incur new debts in the light of expected risk premiums, if the pretended "open market policy" of the ECB does not thwart these efforts.

D. National Legitimizing Law

In the case of any new trans-national law outside the secondary law of the EU, the readjustment requires legitimising laws of the participating states. For Germany, this has happened through respective acts for the decision to aid Greece, for the EFSF, for the expanded EFSF, for the ESM, for the amendment of Article 136 TFEU and for the Fiscal Compact. In this respect, national constitutional law has to provide the decisive criteria norms. All the mentioned assent acts – as predicted – have passed this test before the Federal Constitutional Court of Germany. At the same time, its Lisbon judgement and its first decision on budgetary aid point to boundaries of future international obligations which could be overcome only by enacting a new constitution. They also point to an *ultra vires* control on behalf of the Federal Constitutional Court for EU-measures. This *ultra vires* reservation of control contains, in principle, a potential danger for the European community of law. However, in reality, it is somewhat diffused through the so called Honeywell decision of 2011, insofar as the Federal Constitutional Court for the first time hinted at its willingness to refer such a question of interpretation of a competence provision of the EU to the ECJ, although without acknowledging its duty to follow its judgement.

3. Perspectives of Readjustment in View of Legal Categories

The perspectives of the readjustment as they can be recognised at the moment are therefore still mixed, but need conceptual orientation in terms of legal categories.

A. Multi-Dimensionality

The presently visible path of legal readjustment is multi-dimensional in terms of legal categories. The bisection into special Euro-states' law and EU law with possible overlap in its content is intensified. Besides this, the projected special law for the Euro countries looks for attachment to the institutions of the EU for the ESM (and for the special law of the "fiscal compact"). The connection to the jurisdiction of the ECJ in matters of arbitration in the EFSF is also established for the ESM. The partial use of the work of other institutions and bodies of the EU (Commission, ECB and EIB) "by assignment" in the EFSF is again found in the ESM (e.g.: after the end of an aid programme supervision shall be through the Commission and the Council in line with the procedure of coordination of economic policy). In the fiscal compact, statements and recommendations of the Commission are to be starting-points for tougher measures in deficit proceedings between the signatories. This is possible without changing the EU-Treaty only if the Commission is not supposed to take on any additional tasks.

B. Conceptual Perspectives

In this situation, conceptual orientation is necessary also in matters of legal categories.

I. Union Law as the Straight Way

The silver bullet is certainly to proceed as far as possible under EU law. This is already evident from the fact that the establishment of an economic and monetary union is one of the explicitly mentioned four main operative goals of the EU. The organisation and safeguarding of these objectives (in a way appropriate to counter challenges of political hazards through pre-emptively proactive measures, as well as through compensating aid measures) will find the range of proven supranational institutions, decision-making procedures, forms of measures and redress mechanisms in EU law. The *reinvention* of equivalent supra-nationality outside of EU law is, in principle, a superfluous task. But supranationalisation of the economic union must develop adequate substantive devices. In the interests of a stable EMU, the preventative budgetary self-responsibility of Member States and the limitation of financial aid to situations of dire necessity for the stability of the Euro area as a whole must not be relinquished. The necessity is obvious to develop the pre-emptive systems of warnings and sanctions into more effective and automatic mechanisms to reduce, at least for the Euro states, the scope of political negotiations and discretion. Some of this can already be found in the "Sixpack" and is to be applied in the fiscal compact. At the same time, jurisdiction for infringement proceedings in budget supervision procedures should be given to the ECJ. If the possibility of a separate withdrawal from the monetary union should be envisaged, it should made contingent on the assent of the other Euro countries. Such a rule demands a change of the Treaty, but would avoid the need for a separate change of Treaty for an *actus contrarius* in an individual case of an accepted withdrawal.

II. Enhanced Cooperation

Since such changes to the TFEU seem to be impossible at the moment (due to the British veto), the second-best way to supranationalise the economic union appears to be an Enhanced Cooperation in the sense of Article 20 TEU. This has the advantage of a legitimate usage of the EU's institutions by a (minimum) subset of Member States. However, it only allows actions within the existing competences of the EU. Insofar as this requirement is not met by new measures of the preventative and compensatory readjustment, this path is not available. On the other side, a protocol agreed upon and ratified by all EU states which follows the model of the former protocol concerning social policy, would be conceivable. This became necessary in Maastricht due to Britain's resistance against an amendment to the Treaty and allowed a subset of Member States (at that time eleven out of twelve) the use of institutions, processes and bodies for special powers which had only been agreed on between this subset of Member States in the context of a social policy Treaty concluded outside of Community law.

III. Coherent Combination

In the context of the current political conditions the readjustment is therefore to be achieved by a coherent combination of EU law and transnational law outside EU law. While new primary EU law requires the ratification by all Member States of the EU, special transnational law can be used for further measures by a subset of Member States. It does not have to avoid creating its own supra-nationality.

Irrespective of the division of labour between both legal categories, an overall concept for the stabilising readjustment of the EMU will have to be composed from a bundle of several elements and principles of content. The most important of these are: the individual responsibility of every Member State towards an enduringly solid economic and budgetary policy; the availability of internal market compatible incentives for the capacity to successfully compete in the "real" economy; the protection against dubious patterns of financial transactions; the realisation of effective preventative procedures of coordination of economic policies and of supervision of national budget policies; the reduction of politically discretionary decisions in the procedure of supervision of national budget policies; the use of flexible instruments of private law on the bond market (such as collective action clauses); the strict legal framing of transnational budget aid (reduction to exceptional situations; limitation to the reason to stabilise the common currency; conditionality; transparency).

IV. Finally, a *clearly-defined system of legal protection* is preferable to a complex system of dispute settlement. To give the authority to make decisions in the last instance in questions of transnational law of the economic union outside EU law (or in questions of EU law) to the courts of Member States would not be felicitous. Therefore full jurisdiction should be given to the ECJ as the judicative authority of resolving conflicts both within the EU law of the EMU as within special transnational law (in this case as a compulsory court of arbitration).

4. The Role of Law in the Readjustment of the Economic and Monetary Union

A last remark concerns the role of law in the readjustment of the EMU in general. It is reasonable not to overestimate the effectiveness of legal norms in questions of economic, budgetary and monetary policy. Convictions, political intentions and determination cannot be replaced by the mere existence of ideal norms of behaviour according to an agreement. On the other hand, the effectiveness of these norms should not be underestimated either. Insofar as rules are an expression and reservoir of experience of practical reason, they are not only publicly embarrassing for divergent policies and dubious excuses for indebtedness, they can also cause those who are responsible for public debt policy to lose their reputation, their influence and their office. Above all, legal standards are able to quietly and continuously develop their force for an enduring civilized society and polity. In accordance with the values of the Union (Article 2 TEU) this is, above all, the objective of the transnational European Union.

The Past, Present and Future of Brussels I

Peter ARNT NIELSEN*

Professor, Copenhagen Business School

1. Brussels I

In 1968, the Member States of the EEC concluded the Brussels Convention on Jurisdiction and the Recognition and Enforcement of Judgments in Civil and Commercial Matters (the Convention).[1] It worked well for almost 30 years. From 1998-2000, the Convention underwent a major revision, and it was transformed into a Regulation (*Brussels I*).[2] Ten years later, in 2010-2012, *Brussels I* was revised thoroughly under the recast procedure and adopted on 12 December 2012.[3]

Brussels I is a cornerstone within civil cooperation. It has created free movement of judgments in the EU and harmonised the rules of international jurisdiction where the defendant is domiciled in a Member State. The Member States apply their national rules of international jurisdiction where the defendant is domiciled in a non-Member State, and they apply national law in respect of recognition and enforcement

---

* Member of the Danish delegations on the revision of the Convention (1998-1999), the adoption of *Brussels I* (1999-2000), and the recast negotiations (2010-2012).

1 Convention of 27 September 1968.

2 Regulation 44/2001 of 22 December 2000 on Jurisdiction and the Recognition and Enforcement of Judgments in Civil and Commercial Matters. For the 1998-2000 Revision, see Nielsen, P.A., *Liber Professorum College of Europe 1973/74-2003/04*, 2005, pp. 241-261.

3 O.J. 2012 L 351/1. For the 2010-2012 negotiations, see Nielsen, P.A., *Liber Amicorum Ole Lando*, 2012, pp. 257-276, and Nielsen, P.A., *Common Market Law Review*, 2013, pp. 503-528.

of judgments from such States. *Brussels I* is in force in all Member States, including the United Kingdom, Ireland and Denmark.[4]

In the following, the most important issues that were dealt with during the negotiations in 1998-2000 and 2010-2012 are discussed. First, however, a brief description of the structural framework for the instruments and the rules of negotiation in 1998-2000 and 2010-12, that differed fundamentally, will be given.

A. The Convention

The purpose of the Convention was to create free movement of judgments in civil and commercial matters in the then EEC. The intention was to draft a "simple" convention providing uniform provisions on recognition and enforcement of judgments only. However, the result became a "double" convention providing also for uniform provisions on jurisdiction. This type of instrument was preferred for two reasons. First, uniform provisions on jurisdiction facilitate recognition and enforcement of judgments, because courts recognizing and enforcing judgments from other Contracting States are generally not permitted to review the rules of jurisdiction applied by the court of origin. Second, uniform provisions on jurisdiction in the Contracting States eliminate the risk of forum shopping, and make it more transparent where proceedings can be brought in the Contracting States.[5]

The Convention was a great success.[6] One reason was that the European Court of Justice (the ECJ) was granted competence to rule on the interpretation of it. And the ECJ handed down more than 130 judgments on the Convention, clarifying a number of issues. Furthermore, the ECJ developed principles of interpretation of the Convention that also apply to *Brussels I*, since they have been codified in the recitals of *Brussels I.*[7] So far, the ECJ has delivered roughly 50 judgments on the interpretation of the Regulation. In brief, the principles of interpretation are:

1) Concepts are to be interpreted in a uniform manner in order to ensure uniform and efficient application of the Regulation (uniformity),

2) The provisions on jurisdiction shall be predictable (predictability),

---

4 The UK and Ireland opted in to *Brussels I.* It also applies to Denmark due to a convention between the EU and Denmark. See also Nielsen, P.A., *IPRax*, 2007, pp. 506-509.

5 Explanatory Report by P. Jenard, 1979, Danish version, OJ C59/7-8 (JENARD).

6 The EFTA States wanted an instrument similar to the Brussels Convention. Thus, in 1988, the EFTA and EEC Member States signed the Lugano Convention of 16 September 1988. The old Lugano Convention was superseded by the new Convention of 30 October 2007 with the same content as *Brussels I.*

7 Especially Recitals 11, 12 and 16-18. See also Case C-103/05, *Reisch.*

3) The provisions on jurisdiction are founded on the need for the efficient conduct of proceedings in respect of the taking of evidence (procedural proximity),

4) The Regulation shall be interpreted in such a way as to increase recognition and enforcement of judgments (free movement of judgments), and

5) Proceedings shall be based on adversarial hearings (due process).

The Convention underwent minor revisions in 1978, 1986 and 1989 in connection with adhesion of new States. During the 1990s, it became evident that the instrument was in need of revision. So, in 1998, the Contracting States to the Convention and the identical Lugano Convention between the EFTA States and the EU States set up a working group to carry out a thorough revision. The group worked intensively for 18 months, and it presented a proposal for reform only days before the Amsterdam Treaty entered into force on 1 May 1999.[8] The group negotiated under the principle of unanimity. This principle is generally advantageous because all efforts are made to reach compromises acceptable to all delegations. Nevertheless, the principle also made it possible for a minority of States, or even one State, to block progress, which all other states agreed on.

B. The Regulation

Due to the institutional changes of the EU on 1 May 1999, the Member States decided to implement the agreed amendments of the Convention by transforming it into a Regulation. Thus, in September 1999, the Commission tabled a Proposal for a *Brussels I* Regulation.[9] It was adopted in 2000 and entered into force on 1 March 2002.

C. The Recast

Generally, the application of *Brussels I* proved satisfactory. However, during 2004-2009, the Commission conducted surveys of the application of it. First, a team of professors made an extensive report on the application of *Brussels I* (*the Heidelberg Report*) and suggested proposals for improvements.[10] Second, a professor made a study on residual jurisdiction.[11] Third, *Groupe européen de droit international privé*

8 *Brussels I*, Recital 5.

9 Commission Proposal of 28 December 1999 for a Regulation on Jurisdiction and the Recognition and Enforcement of Judgments in Civil and Commercial Matters, 1999, OJ C376/1.

10 Hess, B., Pfeiffer, T. and Schlosser, P., "Study JLS/C4/2005/03", Report on the Application of Regulation Brussels I, September 2007.

11 Nuyts, A., "Study on Residual Jurisdiction", General Report, 3 September 2007.

(GEDIP) proposed amendments to *Brussels I* in order to apply it to "External Situations"; cases where the defendant is domiciled in a non-Member State, and where the judgment originates from such a State.[12] In 2009 the Commission adopted a Green Paper on the review of *Brussels I*.[13] On 26 January 2011, it tabled a proposal for a review of the Regulation ("*the Proposal*").[14] *The Proposal* was backed up by an impact analysis.[15]

The overall objective of *the Proposal* was to abolish the exequatur procedure.[16] The working party on *Brussels I* worked for nearly two years under the recast procedure. This procedure means that only issues that have been taken up by the Commission in *the Proposal* can be reviewed. Issues not addressed by the Commission could only be discussed if the Commission agreed to that, or, if all Member States supported the initiative. The recasted *Brussels I* will be applicable from 10 January 2015.

2. Domicile and Seat

The general rule in the Convention and *Brussels I* is Article 2, according to which "persons domiciled in a Contracting/Member State shall, whatever their nationality, be sued in the courts of that State." Thus, the definition of domicile is crucial.

Under the Convention, Article 52, the determination of domicile for natural persons is left to national law. This solution was agreed in 1968, because most States preferred their national concepts to a uniform concept, and because there was a fear of getting different interpretations of a possible uniform concept. In 1968, the drafters of the Convention also discussed the possibility of using habitual residence, but the idea was rejected mainly because of difficulties with the interpretation of "habitual."[17]

---

12 Gedip, *IPRax*, 2009, pp. 283-284.

13 The Green Paper on the review of Council Regulation (EC) No. 44/2000 on Jurisdiction and the Recognition and Enforcement of Judgments in Civil and Commercial Matters, COM(2009)175 final.

14 Proposal for a Regulation of the European Parliament and of the Council on Jurisdiction and the Recognition and Enforcement of Judgments in Civil and Commercial Matters of 14 December 2010, COM(2010)748 final/2.

15 Study on Data Collection and Impact Analysis Certain Aspects of a Possible Revision of Council Regulation No. 44/2001 on Jurisdiction and the Recognition and Enforcement of Judgments in Civil and Commercial Matters, Centre for Strategy & Evaluation Services (CSES), 2010, The Impact Assessment.

16 The Proposal, p. 3. The Programme was adopted at the meeting of the European Council held in Stockholm on 10 and 11 December 2009.

17 Jenard, *supra*, note 5, pp. 15-16.

After 30 years of European integration in the field of civil procedural law, this state of affairs seemed clearly unsatisfactory to the 1998-1999 working group. The group wanted to apply habitual residence as a uniform concept, since the concept is used as a connecting factor in a number of Hague conventions adopted by all or most of the negotiating States, and it is applied in the Rome Convention on the Law Applicable to Contractual Obligation.[18] Finally, it is the decisive connecting factor in the Regulation on Jurisdiction and the Recognition and Enforcement of Judgments in Matrimonial Matters and in Matters of Parental Responsibility for Children of both Spouses (*Brussels II*) negotiated by all EU Member States during 1998-2000 and unanimously adopted in 2000.[19] The proposal to use habitual residence was accepted by the vast majority of negotiating States. However, a few States successfully opposed it.

Ten years later, the Commission did not pursue the question; *the Proposal* for the recast of *Brussels I* was silent on the issue. However, one Member State proposed that habitual residence should replace the national concepts of domicile, but as the Commission did not support this proposal and a couple of Member States were against it, the question could not be pursued further during the recast negotiations. In conclusion, national law still governs the concept of domicile for natural persons, and in principle, European courts apply 28 different concepts, which is paradoxical.

The Convention treated legal persons differently from natural persons. Under the Convention, a legal persons domicile is substituted by seat, and in order to determine the seat, a court according to Article 53 "shall apply its own rules of private international law". The solution therefore lies not in national law, but in private international law. Open to different sophisticated interpretations, this provision was adopted in 1968, because the drafters of the Convention did not want to interfere with the then on-going harmonization of company law. Furthermore, it seemed that the various national laws were quite different as to where a legal person should have its seat for procedural purposes.[20] In this context, some States preferred the statutory seat, others the central administration or the principal place of business.

In spite of the failure to harmonize domicile for natural persons, the 1998-1999 working group agreed on a new solution for legal persons. According to *Brussels I*, Article 60, "a legal person has, for the purposes of the Regulation, its domicile at the place where it has its statutory seat,

18 Convention of 19 June 1980 on the Law Applicable to Contractual Obligations.

19 See Article 3 (1) and Article 8 of Council Regulation 1347 of 29 May 2000.

20 Jenard, *supra*, note 5, p. 57.

or central administration, or principal place of business, so the claimant was given a choice in cases where a legal person has set up its organisation in such a way that the statutory seat, the central administration and/or the principal place of business are not in the same State. Naturally, this may lead to forum shopping, but this is only possible because the defendant decided to organise its business in this way. Therefore it seems reasonable to let the organisational structure have procedural consequences. Furthermore, with this new concept of seat, the legal person will be unable to hide behind any corporate structure of its choice. As far as the claimant is concerned, he can base his strategic decision on where to institute proceedings on a number of relevant considerations, such as the location of evidence and the defendant's assets. The concept of seat adopted in Article 60 is a uniform concept, see Recital 11, and it is "copied" from the Treaty, Article 54.

3. Contract Jurisdiction

One of the most controversial provisions of the Convention was Article 5(1).[21] According to that provision, a party domiciled in a Contracting State "may also be sued in another Contracting State in matters relating to a contract, in the courts for the place of performance of the obligation in question." The provision entails a complicated application of choice of law and substantive contract law in order to determine the proper alternative place to bring proceedings in contractual matters. First, the obligation in question has to be determined. Second, the law applicable to the contract has to be determined. Third, the place of performance of the obligation in question must be determined under that law.

Article 5(1) of the Convention shall ensure that jurisdiction is granted to the place of performance of the obligation that forms the basis of the claimant's claim. This *forum solutionis* approach is founded on the reasonable rationale that this place has a strong connection with the dispute regarding the taking of evidence. Another guiding principle was that the provision would limit the risk of creating a multiplicity of forums.[22]

In spite of the good intentions, Article 5(1) turned out to be a stepping-stone for forum shopping; it has certainly not been difficult for sophisticated counsels to find an obligation to be performed in the claimant's country. As such, the provision became a *forum actoris* rule in stark contrast to the general rule of jurisdiction in Article 2.

---

21 See Pålsson, L., *Festskrift til Ole Lando*, 1997, pp. 259-282.

22 Jenard, *supra*, note 5, pp. 22-24.

Article 5(1) has given rise to a number of rulings from the ECJ. The most significant issues have been how to determine the obligation in question, which obligation should be decisive where a number of obligations are involved, the application of the provision where the obligation is not to do something, and whether the provision should be interpreted as providing a uniform place of performance.[23] It is also evident that Article 5(1) applies to payment obligations under the contract, even if the relevant evidence is situated in a State other than the one in which payment is to be effected. In such cases, the provision works as a creditor-friendly tool. This interpretation has been justified by the ECJ due to the need for predictability in contractual matters, even if this is in conflict with the principle of procedural proximity.[24]

During the 1998-1999 negotiations, one of the most important goals was to find a better solution for contract jurisdiction. The working group examined a number of proposals. The most popular proposal – inspired by Article 4(2) of the Rome Convention – was to allocate contract jurisdiction to the State where the characteristic obligation of the contract is or was to be performed. Under this proposal, the claimant cannot choose between different obligations, so the proposal would eliminate sophisticated possibilities for forum shopping in contractual matters. However, a substantial disadvantage of the proposal emerges in the case of sale of goods where the place of delivery is at the seller's domicile, even if the goods under the contract have been shipped to the buyer and upon arrival appear not to be in conformity with the contract. Here, the principle of procedural proximity would favour jurisdiction at the buyer's domicile as the factual place of delivery. Although a large majority of the negotiating States preferred this proposal, it was not adopted, because some States had strong preferences for the original provision. It was also proposed to introduce an exception for payment obligations in order to put an end to creditor jurisdiction. Although acceptable to many delegations, the proposal was not adopted, because some delegations were strongly in favour of creditor jurisdiction.

Having examined these different proposals for reform, the working group had to come up with a compromise acceptable to all delegations. It became clear that the only possible way forward was to combine the most popular proposal with the existing provision. The compromise appears in *Brussels I,* Article 5(1). This provision is divided into 3 subparagraphs: (a), (b) and (c). The starting point is the "old" provision of the Convention. However, according to subparagraph (b), for the

23 Case 12/76, *Tessili*, Case 266/85, *Shenavai*, Case C-420/97, *Leathertex*, Case C-256/00, *Besix*, and Case C-440/97, *Groupe Concorde*.

24 Case C-288/92, *Custom Made Commercial*, para. 16-21.

purpose of this provision and unless otherwise agreed, the place of performance of the obligation in question shall be in case of the sale of goods, the place in a Member State where, under the contract, the goods were delivered or should have been delivered. In the case of the provision of services, the place of performance of the obligation in question shall be the place in a Member State where, under the contract, the services were provided or should have been provided. This new provision allocates contract jurisdiction to the place of performance of the characteristic obligation of the contract in case of sale of goods and provision of services. Consequently, it is a concession to States favouring the characteristic obligation as the connecting factor. However, the solution is restricted to these two types of contracts. As far as other contracts are concerned, the "old" *forum solutionis* still applies, and that is a concession to States in favour of the old provision.

The new provision eliminates creditor jurisdiction for contracts for sale of goods and for provision of services. In theses cases, the claimant can no longer choose the obligation in question. Thus, the former sophisticated possibilities for forum shopping have been eliminated. On the other hand, it is clear that all existing problems with the former provision still exist in respect of contracts other than contracts for the sale of goods and contracts for the provision of services.

The new provision has improved matters, but it is likely to provoke more case law from the ECJ. For instance, how is the line between subparagraphs (a) and (b) to be drawn? Is the place of delivery of goods and the place for provision of services uniform concepts or still based on the applicable national law?[25] The understanding of the working group was that the latter interpretation was the right one. However, recent case law from the ECJ has clarified many of these questions and introduced uniform concepts for the place of delivery of goods and provision of services in Article 5(1)(b), but maintained the old case law in respect of the general rule in Article 5(1)(a).[26]

4. E-commerce and Consumers

During the 1998-2000 negotiations, the question was raised whether the Convention's provisions on consumer contracts covered contracts concluded over the internet. It was obvious to the working group that this would and should be the case, provided the conditions for applying Article 13(1)(3) of the Convention were fulfilled. Article 13 is based on

[25] See Takahashi, K., *European Law Review*, 2002, pp. 530-550, for criticism.

[26] Case C-533/07, *Falco*, Case C-386/05, *Color Drack*, Case C-204/08, *Rehder*, Case C-19/09, *Wood Floor*, Case C-381/08, *Car Trim*, and Case C-87/10, *Electrosteel.*

the principle that the commercial party is targeting the consumer in the consumer's country.

For the sake of clarity, the working group decided to redraft the provision to send the signal that e-commerce is covered. Thus, *Brussels I*, Article 15(1)(c) provides that the consumer is protected, if "the contract has been concluded with a person who pursues commercial or professional activities in the Member State of the consumer's domicile or, by any means directs such activities to that Member State or to several Member States including that Member State and the contract falls within the scope of such activities." To some extent, the provision is inspired by American case law concerning e-commerce.

Certain parts of the e-commerce sector were against procedural consumer protection due to the risk of being sued in the consumer's State. However, consumer protection, also in international litigation, has a long tradition in the EU. Furthermore, in e-commerce, it is highly unlikely that a commercial party will institute proceedings against a consumer, because in most cases a commercial party receives payment electronically before performing his obligations under the contract. Thus, a dispute is only likely to occur, if the seller does not deliver the goods or delivers defective goods. Finally, advanced consumer protection in respect of e-commerce improves consumer confidence in e-commerce, and thus increases the business potential. As expected by the working group, the concept of "directing commercial activities" to the consumer's State needed to be elaborated in case law.[27]

Finally, during the 2010-2012 negotiations it was agreed that Article 16 shall apply regardless of the domicile of the commercial party, thus replacing national law for cases where the commercial party is domiciled in a non-Member State.

5. Employment Contracts

The 1998-2000 working group agreed on improving the procedural protection of employees. First, in the Convention the provisions on employment contracts were placed in different parts of it, so in *Brussels I* they are placed together in Section 5. This emphasizes that employees, like consumers, are weak parties in need of the same procedural advantages that consumers have. Second, the provisions have been improved in that the employer can no longer bring proceedings against the employee in the Member State where the employee habitually carried out his work. Consequently, proceedings against the employee

[27] Case C-585/08, *Pammer*.

can only be brought in the Member State where the employee is domiciled, see *Brussels I*, Article 20(1).

Since the protection of the employee got upgraded at the level of jurisdiction, it would have seemed a natural consequence to ensure for employees the same level of protection that consumers enjoy in respect of recognition and enforcement. Under the Convention, a judgment should be denied recognition and enforcement, if the court of origin disregarded the provisions on jurisdiction protecting the consumer, see Article 28(1). During the 1998-2000 negotiations a proposal to that effect was tabled, but the working group rejected it. However, the question was raised again during the recast in 2010-2012, and accepted. Consequently, according to *Brussels I*, Article 48(e), a judgment shall be refused if the court of origin took jurisdiction in conflict with Sections 3, 4 and 5 of Chapter II to the extent the injured party, the beneficiary of the insurance contract, the consumer or the employee was the defendant.

6. Choice of Court Agreements and *Lis Pendens*

A controversial issue is the relationship between choice of court agreements and *lis pendens* under *Brussels I*, Articles 23 and 27. According to Article 23, choice of court agreement must be respected, while Article 27 prevents parallel proceedings between the same parties in different Member States from continuing. Article 27 provides that any other court than the one first seized, shall of its motion stay its proceedings until such time as the jurisdiction of the court first seized is established. Where the jurisdiction of the court first seized is established, any other court than the court first seized shall decline jurisdiction in favour of that court. Case law in Britain clearly suggested that choice of court agreements had priority over the *lis pendens* provision.[28]

During the 1998-2000 negotiations a proposal was tabled giving a court designated in an exclusive choice of court agreement exclusive jurisdiction to determine the validity of the agreement. The proposal also contained the suggestion that judgments delivered in disrespect of an exclusive jurisdiction clause should be denied recognition and enforcement. The proposal was based on commercial needs and, reasonable. On the other hand, as the Convention is founded on mutual trust, the proposal could be regarded as going against that principle. Ultimately, the proposal was not accepted.

---

[28] Continental Bank NA v Aekos Compania Naviera SA, 1994, Weekly Law Reports I-588.

Subsequently, in 2003, the ECJ in the well-known, but criticized Gasser case endorsed the view that the *lis pendens* rule also applies in respect of choice of court agreements.[29] A contract had been concluded between an Austrian (Gasser) and an Italian party (Misat). The contract provided, inter alia, that the Austrian courts should have exclusive jurisdiction to determine any dispute between the parties. However, Misat instituted proceedings against Gasser in Italy claiming that the exclusive choice of court agreement was invalid. Subsequently, Gasser instituted proceedings in Austria relying on the choice of court agreement. Before the Austrian court, Misat claimed that it should stay its proceedings until such time as the Italian court had decided whether the choice of court agreement were invalid, and, in the affirmative, whether the court had jurisdiction. The ECJ ruled that the Austrian court should stay its proceedings and wait for the decision of the Italian court on its jurisdiction. The Court referred to the fact that the proceedings in Italy were instituted first. However, due to the inefficiency of the Italian court system, it would probably take years for the Italian court to reach a decision on its jurisdiction. Meanwhile, proceedings in other Member States should be put on hold due to the *lis pendens* provision.

The Gasser judgment has created "Italian Torpedoes"; a party can obtain de facto immunity from court proceedings in the Member States of the EU for years, provided that this party manages to institute proceedings first in Italy.[30] This is an unacceptable situation, especially where the parties have entered into a choice of court agreement. Consequently, during the recast negotiations in 2010-2012, the Commission wanted to address the problem and improve the efficiency of choice of court agreements where a litigant would be acting in bad faith to delay the resolution of the dispute in the agreed forum by first seizing a non-competent court.[31]

The Commission proposed a provision inspired by Article 5(1) of the Hague Choice of Court Convention from 2005 ensuring a coherent approach within the EU and at the international level were the EU to decide to conclude the Hague Convention in the future, *the Proposal*, Article 32(2):[32]

---

29 Case C-116/02, *Gasser*. For criticism, see Hartley, T., *Mélanges en l'honneur de Paul Lagarde*, 2005, pp. 322-335, and Fentiman, R., *Common Market Law Review*, 2005, pp. 241-259.

30 Italian Torpedoes were invented by Franzosi, M., *European Intellectual Property Review*, 1997, p. 382. See also *The Heidelberg Report*, p. 159 and pp. 194-201.

31 The Proposal, p. 3.

32 The Proposal, p. 8. Convention of 30 June 2005 on Choice of Court Agreements, Article 5. The convention has been signed by the US and the EU and ratified by Mexico.

> Where an agreement referred to in paragraph 1 confers exclusive jurisdiction to a court or the courts of a Member State, the courts of other Member States shall have no jurisdiction over the dispute until such time as the court or courts designated in the agreement decline their jurisdiction.

The Commission's proposal was good. It is a reverse *lis pendens* mechanism ensuring that only the agreed court can determine the validity of the choice of court agreement if proceedings are instituted before that court. This solution, partly inspired by the doctrine of "competence over the competence", is well-known and well-functioning in international commercial arbitration.[33] However, it should be clarified that the reverse *lis pendens* mechanism only applies if the chosen court assumes jurisdiction on the basis of the choice of court agreement, and that the reverse mechanism should not apply where the chosen court sets the choice of court agreement aside, but takes jurisdiction on, for instance Article 5(1). In this case, the ordinary *lis pendens* mechanism in Article 27 should apply. Furthermore, Article 32(2) should only apply subject to Article 24 on tacit choice of court agreements. This criticism was accepted during the negotiations, and the provision adopted, Article 32(2), has this wording:[34]

> Without prejudice to Article 24, where a court of a Member State on which an agreement referred to in Article 23 confers exclusive jurisdiction is seized, any court of another Member State shall stay the proceedings until such time as the court seized on the basis of the agreement declares that it has no jurisdiction under the agreement.

During the 2010-2012 negotiations, the Commission also successfully proposed a choice of law rule for substantive validity of choice of court agreements; see *the Proposal* Article 23(1). Accordingly, this issue is governed by "the law of the Member State", whose courts are granted jurisdiction under the choice of court agreement. Formal validity of the choice of court agreement is still subject to the uniform standard in *Brussels I*, Article 23.

The choice of law rule on substantive validity of choice of court agreements is based on the similar solution in the Hague Choice of Court Convention, where a chosen court shall determine the validity of

---

33 Articles 8 and 16 of the Model Law on International Commercial Arbitration, as adopted by UNCITRAL on 21 June 1985 and amended on 4 December 2006.

34 During the 2010-2012 negotiations, it was with success also proposed to codify "the doctrine of separability" in Article 25. Thus, Article 25(5) states that a choice of court agreement that forms part of a contract shall be treated as an agreement independent of the other terms of the contract, so that the validity of the choice of court agreement cannot be contested solely on the ground that the contract is not valid. The doctrine is applied in the Hague Choice of Court Convention, Article 3(d), and recognised by the ECJ in Case C-269/95, *Benincasa*.

a choice of court agreement under "the law of that State".[35] However, the reference in the Hague Convention to "the law of that State" includes the choice of law rules of the Forum State.[36] It is not very clear from the new provision whether the reference to "the law of that Member State" includes the choice of law rules or not, but the intention was that this should be the case. Therefore, recital 20 makes it clear that the reference to "the law of that Member State", like the Hague Convention, includes the choice of law rules.

The Commission's proposal for a choice of law rule for substantive validity of choice of court agreements was presented as "a harmonised conflict of law rule on the substantive validity of choice of court agreements, thus ensuring a similar outcome on this matter whatever the court seized".[37] However, in reality this is not the case, because the provision does nothing but codifying status quo. At present, each Member State applies its own choice of law rules in respect of substantive validity of choice of court agreements; see Article 1(2)(d) of the Rome Convention and the Rome I Regulation.[38] Some Member States apply *lex fori*, others *lex contractus* and others a combination of these two laws.

Finally, during the 2010-2012 negotiations it was agreed that Article 23 shall apply regardless of the parties' domicile, thus replacing national law for cases where none of the parties have their domicile in a Member State.

7. Arbitration

Brussels I does not apply to arbitration; see Article 1(2)(d). The reason for this exclusion is that international commercial arbitration already was well regulated at the time when the Brussels Convention was negotiated by the New York Convention on Recognition and Enforcement of Arbitral Awards from 1958, which has been ratified or adhered to by all Member States of the EU.[39] *Brussels I* does not apply to the recognition and enforcement of arbitral awards; it does not apply for the purpose of determining the jurisdiction of courts and tribunals in respect of litigation relating to arbitration for example, proceedings to set aside an arbitral award; and, finally, it does not apply to the recognition of

35 The Proposal, p. 8.

36 Hartley, T. and Dougachi, M., "Explanatory Report on the 2005 Hague Choice of Court Agreements Convention", 2007, p. 43.

37 The Proposal, p. 8.

38 Regulation 593 of 17 June 2008 on Choice of Law for Contractual Obligations. The Regulation is in force in all Member States except Denmark.

39 Convention of 10 June 1958.

judgments given in such proceedings.[40] On the other hand, *Brussels I* applies when the main question of the dispute is within the scope of *Brussels I* and the arbitration issue is incidental, for instance where a party in reliance of an arbitration agreement claims that a court seized with the dispute declines its jurisdiction due to the agreement to arbitrate. Over the years, the ECJ has determined a few cases concerning the extent of the exclusion of arbitration.[41]

By and large, the exclusion of arbitration from the scope of *Brussels I* had not been controversial until 2009 where the ECJ delivered its judgment in the widely discussed West Tankers case.[42] West Tankers was sued in Italy in spite of an agreement to arbitrate in London. West Tankers brought proceedings in London seeking a declaration that the dispute between itself and the claimant in Italy was to be settled by arbitration pursuant to the arbitration agreement. West Tankers also sought an injunction restraining the claimants in Italy from pursuing any proceedings other than arbitration and requiring them to discontinue the proceedings commenced in Italy (an anti-suit injunction). The ECJ ruled that it is incompatible with *Brussels I* for a court of a Member State to make an order to restrain a person from commencing or continuing proceedings before the courts of another Member State on the ground that such proceedings would be contrary to an arbitration agreement. The Court also held that if, because of the subject-matter of the dispute, that is, the nature of the rights to be protected in proceedings, such as a claim for damages, those proceedings come within the scope of *Brussels I*, a preliminary issue concerning the applicability of an arbitration agreement, including in particular its validity, also comes within its scope of application.

The West Tankers judgment attracted significant criticism, especially from a British perspective, for allowing so-called "torpedo actions" where a party is attempting to avoid an arbitration agreement by instituting court proceedings.

During the negotiations in 2010-2012, various solutions were proposed. Some suggested an abolition of the exclusion for arbitration, while others, especially representatives of the arbitration sector, advocated an extended exclusion of arbitration from the scope of *Brussels I*. An abolition of the exception to exclude arbitration from the scope of

---

40 Jenard, *supra*, note 5, p. 13.

41 Case C-190/89, *Marc Rich*, and Case C-391/95, *Van Uden*.

42 Case C-185/09, *West Tankers*. See, for instance, Illmer, M., *Rabels Zeitschrift*, 2011, pp. 645-670; Grierson, J., *Journal of International Arbitration*, 2009, p. 891; Fentiman, R., *Cambridge Law Journal*, 2009, pp. 278-281 and Peel, E., *Law Quarterly Review*, 2009, p. 365.

Brussels I would mean that arbitration is to be governed by the Regulation. This solution would give the EU external competence in arbitration, which was unacceptable to most Member States. On the other hand, the proposal to extend the present exclusion of arbitration would mean that all cases where arbitration one way or the other is involved, either as main question or as an incidental question, would be outside the scope of *Brussels I*. As a consequence, such cases would be entirely governed by national law of the Member States, which would set back the clock till before 1968, where the Convention was signed. Therefore, this proposal was also unacceptable to most Member States.

Neither the former nor the latter solution seemed to have an impact on the "torpedo problem". And the proposal to exclude arbitration further from the scope of *Brussels I* would, on the contrary, create what has been named a "super torpedo", because all cases with arbitration aspects involved would be subject to national law.[43] Consequently, when preparing the recast negotiations of *Brussels I*, the Commission decided to place itself between the two solutions arguing that it is necessary to do something about litigants with abusive tactics. The Commission proposed a new Article 29(4).[44] The purpose of it was to "enhance the effectiveness of arbitration agreements in Europe, prevent parallel court and arbitration proceedings, and eliminate the incentive for abusive litigation tactics."[45] In substance, the proposal was a *lis pendens* mechanism based on the same principle proposed in order to improve the efficiency of exclusive choice of court agreements. The proposal, however, was not accepted. Instead, as a compromise, it was agreed to maintain status quo and adopt recital 12 explaining the "demarcation line" between arbitration and *Brussels I*.

8. *Lis Pendens* and Time of Seizure

The main purpose of the *lis pendens* provision in *Brussels I*, Article 27 is to avoid concurrent proceedings in disputes between the same parties in respect of the same legal relationship and thus to avoid irreconcilable judgments.[46] The provision is based on the principle that the court first seized should hear the case, provided it has jurisdiction. Consequently, a court in another Member State also seized of the matter is obliged to decline jurisdiction of its own motion, provided the court

43 Illmer, M., *Rabels Zeitschrift*, 2011, p. 666, and Fentiman, R., *International Journal of Procedural Law*, 2011, p. 151.

44 The Commission proposed Recital 11, which repeats the content of Jenard in this respect.

45 The Proposal, p. 9.

46 Jenard, *supra*, note 5, pp. 7 and 41.

first seized has jurisdiction. This is a harsh, but efficient provision obliging litigants to "race to the courts" for tactical or other reasons.

For the application of the *lis pendens* provision, it is essential to establish when a court is seized. Not surprisingly, the issue was submitted to the ECJ in the early 1980s. In light of the very different solutions applied under national law, the Court found that it was unable to come up with a uniform concept, and that national law should govern the issue.[47]

Very different solutions apply in the Member States. In some States, a court is seized when the document instituting the proceedings is lodged with the court. Service of that document takes place subsequently, and service is of no importance as far as the question of seizure is concerned. In other States, a court is seized when the document instituting the proceedings is lodged with the court and has been served on the defendant. Finally, in some States, the document instituting the proceedings has to be served on the defendant before it can be lodged with the court.

One of the main tasks facing the working group during the 1998-2000 negotiations was to come up with a uniform concept of seizure. The variety of national laws meant that litigants were at a very uneven footing. The working group examined several proposals, but it soon became clear that the uniform concept should be based on three considerations. First, an objective factor controlled by litigants; second, a flexible solution respecting national law; and third, the concept should encompass both the need to lodge the document instituting the proceedings with the court and the requirement in some States of service of that document before being lodged with the court.

The solution invented is *Brussels I*, Article 30: A court is deemed to be seized at the time when the document instituting the proceedings is lodged with the court, provided that the claimant has not subsequently failed to take the steps he was required to take to have service effected on the defendant. However, according to Article 30(2), if the document has to be served before being lodged with the court, the court is deemed to have been seized at the time when the document instituting the proceedings has been received by the authority responsible for service, provided that the claimant has not subsequently failed to take the steps he was required to take to have the document lodged with the court.

Both Article 30(1) and (2) rest on the principle that a court is seized as soon as the claimant has taken the first step which is registered by a

[47] Case 129/83, *Zelger*.

court or an authority responsible for service. Thus, litigants are on an equal footing with regard to the "race" to the courts.

9. International Jurisdiction

Under *Brussels I*, the Member States have the competence to determine the rules of jurisdiction where the defendant is domiciled in a third State, see *Brussels I*, Article 4. However, during the recast negotiations in 2010-2012, the Commission proposed that such defendants may be sued in the courts of a Member State only by virtue of the rules set out in *Brussels I*, Chapter II, Sections 2 to 8, see *the Proposal* Article 4(2). Consequently, the Member States' own rules of jurisdiction would have to be repealed, including their rules of exorbitant jurisdiction, and replaced by *Brussels I*. However, the Commission did not go as far as to propose that *Brussels I* also should govern recognition and enforcement of judgments from third States. Such a proposal would make sense in combination with the proposal to regulate jurisdiction where the defendant is domiciled in a third State, because in doing so *Brussels I* would become a complete instrument governing all external situations. As mentioned, such wide-ranging harmonization has been proposed by GEDIP. On the other hand, it is admitted that such a proposal would impair the international negotiation powers of the EU, for instance in the context of the Hague Conference for Private International Law.

The Commission justified the harmonisation of the rules of jurisdiction where the defendant is domiciled in a third State by referring to the need to protect weaker parties, ensure equal access to courts, and provide a level playing field for companies in the internal market.[48]

As part of the extension of the rules of jurisdiction in *Brussels I* to defendants domiciled in a third State, the Commission also proposed to introduce a provision on subsidiary jurisdiction and a rule on *forum necessitatis*, see *the Proposal*, Articles 25 and 26. Finally, the Commission proposed a discretionary *lis pendens* mechanism for parallel proceedings between the same parties in a Member State and a third State; see *the Proposal*, Article 34.

The Commission's proposals to extend the rules of jurisdiction in *Brussels I* to defendants domiciled in a third State etc. were very controversial. On the one hand, it makes sense to harmonise the rules of jurisdiction where the defendant is domiciled in a third State. The proposal would minimize the present possibilities for forum shopping under national law; it would provide uniform, transparent and coherent rules of jurisdiction regardless of the defendant's domicile, and it would

48 The Proposal, p. 2.

repeal the existing artificial and discriminatory distinction between defendants domiciled within and outside the EU.[49] On the other hand, there does not seem to be a need for the extension, because the present system functions reasonably well. At least, no economic data suggested the need for such harmonisation.[50]

As a large majority of the Member States – for political reasons – were against the proposal, it was not accepted in its entirety. However, as a compromise, it was agreed that Article on choice of court agreements and Articles 16 on consumer jurisdiction and Article 21(1)(G) on employer jurisdiction shall apply regardless of the domicile of the parties.

10. Recognition and Enforcement

A fundamental objective of both the 1998-2000 and the 2010-2012 revisions were to improve recognition and enforcement of judgments given that free movements of judgments is the overall objective of the Brussels system.

A. The 1998-2000 Negotiations

During the 1998-1999 revision, two major changes were made to the exceptions to recognition and enforcement, and the procedure for recognition and enforcement was expedited up.

First, for default judgments, the Convention, Article 27(2) was amended, so the requirement of due service was substituted with the requirement that service must have taken place "in such a way" as to enable the defendant to arrange for his defence, see *Brussels I*, Article 34(2). Another amendment was the introduction of the exception that a default judgment not entitled to recognition should nevertheless be recognized, if the defendant failed to commence proceedings to challenge the judgment when it was possible for him to do so.

Second, the Convention had a lacuna in respect of conflicting judgments, because it did not have a provision regulating irreconcilability between the judgment subject to recognition and a judgment from another Member State. That gap was closed in *Brussels I*, Article 34(4), which provides that a judgment shall not be recognized if it is irreconcilable with an earlier judgment given in another Member State involving the same cause of action between the same parties. "Earlier" refers

---

49 The Impact Assessment, p. 27. A proponent of total harmonisation is Weber, J., *Rabels Zeitschrift*, 2011, pp. 623-626. See also Basedow, J., *Common Market Law Review*, 2000, pp. 687-708.

50 The Impact Assessment, p. 25.

to the point in time when a judgment is delivered, not when proceedings were instituted. The practical need for this provision is probably modest due to the *lis pendens* provision.[51]

Under the Convention, the procedure for recognition and enforcement of judgments was governed partly by the Convention, partly by national law. This is still the case under *Brussels I*. However, under the Convention, a court could examine of its own motion, whether one or more of the grounds for denying recognition and enforcement were present or not. Reportedly, that possibility caused concern, because in some cases it resulted in lengthy examinations thwarting fast recognition and enforcement of judgments. Consequently, during the 1998-2000 negotiations, it was a clear goal to make the *exequatur* procedure for recognition and enforcement far more efficient.

The solution was *Brussels I*, Article 41. According to this provision, a judgment shall be declared enforceable immediately on completion of the formalities in Article 53 without any review under Articles 34 and 35 (the exceptions to recognition and enforcement). Under Article 53, the judgment holder is only required to produce a copy of the judgment satisfying the conditions necessary to establish its authenticity and the certificate introduced by Article 54. It follows from the prohibition in Article 41 that a court is not entitled to carry out any review of the judgment. The prohibition is general, and it covers all grounds for denying recognition and enforcement, even public policy. It also follows from Article 41 that at this stage the judgment debtor is not entitled to make any submissions on the application for recognition and enforcement. A full review can only be carried out if the judgment debtor appeals the decision of enforceability, see Articles 43-45.

B. The 2010-2012 Negotiations

Although the improvements made in 1998-2000 did speed up the *exequatur* procedure, the Commission in 2010-2012 proposed a total abolishment of it, see *the Proposal*, Article 38. The Commission justified the proposal to abolish *exequatur* by pointing out that "judicial cooperation and the level of trust among Member States have reached a degree of maturity which permits the move towards a simpler, less costly, and more automatic system of circulation of judgments, removing the existing formalities among Member States."[52] At the same time, the Commission proposed the introduction of procedural safeguards

51 It is surprising that priority is given to the judgment first delivered and not the judgment resulting from the proceedings first instituted. The latter solution is more in line with the *lis pendens* provision.

52 The Proposal, p. 5.

aiming at ensuring the defendant the right to a fair trial and his right to a defence, see *the Proposal*, Article 45, and abolishment of substantive public policy, see Article 46. In its justification for the latter proposal, the Commission referred to saving "the time and costs of the exequatur procedure while the necessary protection of defendants remains ensured."[53] In addition, the proposal could also be justified with the fact that public policy has only been applied a few times by the courts of the Member States and the ECJ.[54] However, a huge majority of Member States were against the Commission's radical proposals to abolish substantive public policy, but the proposal to abolish exequatur was accepted.

11. The Future

The revision of the Brussels and Lugano Conventions carried out in 1998-2000 resulted in a number of improvements. So did the recast negotiations from 2010-2012. Nevertheless, there is room for further improvements. Especially Article 5(1) on contract jurisdiction will remain controversial and continue to provoke case law, so it should be considered to abolish it. Another improvement would be to replace domicile for natural persons with habitual residence. A third improvement would be to set up a real uniform choice of law rule for substantive validity for choice of court agreements. Considering the need to enhance the efficiency of choice of court agreements, the choice of law rule should be based on the principle of alternative validity well known in the Rome Convention and the Rome I Regulation. The rule should be that the choice of court agreement is valid, provided it is so under either the law of the Member State in which the chosen court is (*lex fori*), or the law that governs the dispute (*lex causae*).[55] In the long-term perspective, one may hope that *Brussels I* will completely govern all external situations, and apply to defendants domiciled in non-Member States and apply to recognition and enforcement of judgments from such States.

---

[53] The Proposal, p. 6. This solution has been applied in the European Enforcement Order for Un-contested Claims, Regulation No. 805/2004 of 21 April 2004.

[54] For European and national case law, see The Heidelberg Report, pp. 241-252.

[55] The Rome Convention, Article 9, and the Rome I Regulation, Article 11.

The EU Water Framework Directive Twelve Years After

Legal Solutions for Water Problems?

Nicola NOTARO[1]

Deputy Head of the Unit "Protection of Water Resources", Directorate General Environment, European Commission

1. Introduction

The EU Water Framework Directive (WFD)[2] has reached a crucial phase in its implementation. The deadline for the achievement of its "good water status" objective by 2015 is approaching. The European Commission has just published a series of reports containing a detailed assessment of the Directive's implementation at Member States and European level in the framework of a new water strategy called the "Blueprint to Safeguard Europe's Water Resources".[3] Moreover, 2012 is the deadline for Member States to ensure that the Programmes of Measures (POMs) developed under their River Basin Management Plans (RBMPs) become operational.[4] This is therefore an appropriate

[1] The views expressed are the author's only. The author would like to express his gratitude to Rector Paul Demaret for the invaluable support and advice received when he was working as an assistant in the Department of Legal Studies at the College of Europe in Bruges (1996-1999).

[2] Directive 2000/60/EC of the European Parliament and of the Council establishing a framework for Community action in the field of water policy. OJ L327, 22 December 2000.

[3] The whole Blueprint package of policy papers was adopted on 14 November 2012. It is available at http://ec.europa.eu/environment/water/blueprint/index_en.htm. It is constituted by the Commission Communication on the Blueprint accompanied by an impact assessment; a Report on the implementation of the WFD, accompanied by a Commission Staff Working Document providing an analysis of the implementation of the Directive at European and Member State level; and a Report on the review of the EU policy on water scarcity and droughts, also accompanied by a Commission Staff Working Document providing additional detailed analysis.

[4] See WFD Art. 11.7.

time to take stock of the experience gained in implementing the WFD and to look into whether some key legal provisions of the Directive have proven suitable to the delivery of its policy objectives or need further clarification.

Due to space constraints, this piece will only provide a brief analysis of selected provisions of the WFD regarding the objectives and exemptions; the programmes of measures; quantitative aspects of water management and water pricing. After that, an overview of the new Commission proposals contained in the Blueprint to improve the implementation of the WFD will be provided.

2. No Deterioration and Good Status: Actions or Results?

Two key obligations for the Member States under the WFD concern the so called "no deterioration" of water status and the achievement of good water status by 2015. These notions reflect the need to prevent additional damage to the water ecosystems and to protect and restore them where necessary. These two obligations have raised questions concerning their exact scope and intensity.[5]

A. No Deterioration

Concerning "no deterioration", several questions have arisen: is this an obligation of means or result? As of when should it apply: upon the WFD entry into force in 2000 or upon the adoption of the RBMPs in 2009, or even later? Does it imply that water status should not deteriorate from, for example, high to good status or could a deterioration happen also within the same status category?

Article 4.1 of the WFD requires Member States to implement the necessary measures to prevent the deterioration of the status of all water bodies subject to the application of limited exemptions. While the language in this provision seems focused on the duty to take action ("implement the necessary measures"), it seems that Member States also have an obligation of result: they need to prevent water status deterioration through the "necessary measures" and if this is not achieved it means that they have not taken all the necessary measures. They would

---

5 See Andrea M. Keessen *et al.*, "European river basin districts: are they swimming in the same implementation pool?", *Journal of Environmental Law*, 2010, Vol. 22, No. 2, pp. 197-221, at pp. 206-207 and 210-211. See also Marleen van Rijswick, Herman Kasper Gilissen and Jasper van Kempen, "The need for international and regional transboundary cooperation in European river basin management as a result of new approaches in EC water law", *ERA-Forum: scripta iuris europaei*, 2010, Vol. 11, No. 1, pp. 129-157.

therefore be in breach of Article 4.1, unless they could rely on the exemptions provided under Articles 4.6 and 4.7.

Nowhere in the WFD is it specified that the principle of "no deterioration" should apply as of a specific date different from the date applicable to the other provisions of the Directive. Therefore, the only possible interpretation is that it applies as of the entry into force of the WFD in 2000. This is logical because every time the legislator wanted certain provisions of the WFD to take effect at a different time after the entry into force it specified that by providing a clear deadline (e.g. RBMPs to be adopted by 2009, good status to be achieved by 2015, etc.). Moreover, this is in line with the purpose of the WFD in Article 1, which refers to the prevention of deterioration, and with the idea that, while restoration of the aquatic ecosystem to good status may take time, at least deterioration should be immediately stopped.[6] In addition, this interpretation is supported by the general EU law principles of good faith and loyal cooperation according to which Member States should not take any action that risks undermining the attainment of the WFD objectives.

Regarding whether "no deterioration" only applies for deterioration from one status class to the other or within a status category, again the text of the Directive is not explicit. A very strict interpretation prohibiting all deterioration, including within the same status class, does not seems realistic. Even immediate actions aimed at stopping on going deterioration may need some time to produce their effects. Moreover, some minor deterioration may be due to temporary factors. Therefore, Member States should benefit from some flexibility, provided that they take action to counter trends showing a deterioration that may lead to a change of status of a water body. This is required by Article 11.5 and 17 for, respectively, surface and groundwater bodies.

B. Good Status

Also in relation to the achievement of "good water status" by 2015, the question has arisen of whether this is an obligation of means or result. The main reason for this is the language of Article 4.1 that requires Member States to protect, enhance and restore all water bodies "with the aim of" achieving good water status by 2015, subject to certain exemptions. In this case, the WFD language is very much fo-

6 In the river Acheloos case, (Case C-43/10, judgment of 11 September 2012) the Commission argued along these lines and was followed by the Advocate General. The Court did not rule specifically on this point but did recognise that the provision in art. 4.7 of the WFD should be applied by analogy also before 2009, the deadline for Member States to adopt their RBMPs.

cused on taking action to achieve the objective rather than on making its achievement a legal requirement.

Looking at how Member States have transposed this provision in their national law, it appears that, in most cases, they have interpreted it as an obligation of result.[7] This reading is confirmed by the general view held by the Member States and stakeholders involved in the Common Implementation Strategy (CIS) of the WFD who perceive the good status objective as an obligation.[8] This interpretation is also reinforced by the fact that a number of exemptions from "good status" obligation are provided for in Articles 4.5 to 4.7. Arguably, if the achievement of good status by 2015 was not an obligation of result, exemptions would not be essential.

However, another possible interpretation is that such exemptions are also relevant for an obligation of means as they may be relied upon by Member States that wish to delay taking measures, e.g. because of their costs.

Be that as it may, one wonders whether there is a big difference in practical terms between the two interpretations: After all, even under the weaker obligation, Member States must protect, enhance and restore all water bodies. This means that they are expected to put in place all necessary actions to achieve good status by 2015 or to explain why they have a possibility to lower their level of ambition and postpone this objective according to one of the exemptions.

3. Integration with other Policy Objectives: the Programmes of Measures (POMs)

The WFD brings together in a single Directive a number of previous water related directives, thereby streamlining EU water legislation.[9] Moreover, it also creates explicit links with other environment legislation by adopting a "combined approach" that requires Member States to check whether existing requirements under legislation on industrial emissions, nitrates, waste water treatment, chemicals, etc., are sufficient to achieve the WFD objectives. In case they are not, Member States are required to apply stricter emission controls. Therefore, this approach combines emission limits with environmental quality objectives.

---

7 See Andrea M. Keessen *et al.*, *supra*, note 5, at pp. 206-207.

8 The CIS is an open and participatory process that brings together the European Commission, Member States and stakeholders to cooperate in the implementation of the WFD. The author is directly involved in its work. See http://ec.europa.eu/environment/water/waterframework/objectives/implementation_en.htm.

9 See Art. 22 WFD for the list of legislation it repealed.

The integration of environment related directives under the WFD is enhanced by specific provisions on protected areas in Articles 4.1 and 6; on drinking water in Article 7; and by Article 4.9 which requires steps to be taken to guarantee that the WFD provides at least the same level of protection as the existing (in 2000) Union legislation.

But the central tool to bring together in a consistent implementation framework EU environmental legislation as well as – most importantly – legislation under other policy areas which affect water, is constituted by the RBMPs and, in particular, by the POMs developed thereunder. The latter, according to Article 11, must include "basic measures" and "supplementary measures" aimed at achieving the environmental objectives established under Article 4 on the basis of the analysis of pressures on each water body required under Article 5.

The basic measures are the minimum actions that Member States have to undertake. They cover efficient and sustainable water use, water pricing, protection of drinking water, controls over abstraction, impoundment and recharge; controls of point and diffuse sources of pollution and hydromorphological pressures as well as direct discharges into groundwater and chemical pollution. The supplementary measures are an open list of actions needed to achieve good status in addition to the basic measures.

Looking at the basic measures, it is clear that the WFD objectives cannot be achieved without actions taken under other policy areas such as land planning and use, agriculture, inland navigation, energy production, industrial emissions, etc.

In this respect, it has been argued[10] that the WFD lacks a policy integration legal requirement, e.g. because the RBMPs and the POMs are not legally binding under the Directive and therefore the measures they contains are not enforceable when they conflict with other policy objectives.

This reading seems to be based on a misunderstanding of Article 11.3 and its requirement for basic measures to be applied. The WFD is silent about the legal nature of the RBMPs or of the POMs developed thereunder. This is left for Member States to decide and, in fact, programmatic documents are most of the time not legally binding *per se*. They rather collect into a single plan or programme a number of measures of different nature ranging from legally binding to voluntary. However, Member States are legally required to implement the basic measures under the WFD. The fact that these may be included into a non-legally binding Programme of Measures cannot remove the obliga-

10 See Andrea M. Keessen *et al.*, *supra*, note 5, at pp. 212 ff.

tion for Member States to make these measures binding under national law. It is true that some of the basic measures are very clearly defined (e.g. prior authorisation for water abstraction) while others are more general in nature (e.g. controls of diffuse sources of pollution). However, in both cases, Member States must take measures and explain their actions in the RBMPs and in the POMs.

Therefore, the WFD contains powerful policy integration tools with respect to both other environment policies and to policies outside the environmental area and Member States should fully exploit these instruments.

4. WFD: Only Quality or also Quantity?

It is often maintained that the WFD, with respect to surface waters, focuses mostly on water quality and neglects water quantity aspects. This is based on the fact that good status for surface waters is composed of two elements – ecological and chemical status – while good status of groundwater comprises chemical and quantitative status. This has, for instance, occasionally pushed Mediterranean Member States to argue, in EU Council of Ministers' meetings, in favour of the development of a specific EU legislative instrument to tackle water scarcity and droughts, perceived as "their problems", which would not be adequately covered by the WFD.[11]

This view is partly supported by the Directive itself since its preambular paragraph 19 states that it is primarily concerned with the quality of water. However, it also goes on to recognise that quantity is an ancillary element in securing good water quality and therefore measures on quantity should also be established. This rather convoluted approach does not seem to clearly recognise that water quality and quantity are two sides of the same coin: they are co-essential since water flow (quantity) is necessary to ensure the functioning of the aquatic ecosystems (quality) which in turn provide ecosystem services such as water regulation and purification which are essential for both water quality and quantity.

A closer look at the text of the Directive reveals that the importance of water quantity aspects is better recognised than it would appear at first sight. Already preambular paragraph 20 recognises that the quantitative status of a groundwater body may have an influence on the ecological quality of associated surface waters. Preambular paragraphs 23 and 25 also acknowledge the need for common principles and common

[11] The author has witnessed this in discussions at the Working Party on Environment of the Council of Ministers.

definitions for the protection of water quality and quantity. In addition, Article 1 contains as one of the WFD objectives the promotion of sustainable water use, the mitigation of droughts and the provision of sufficient water supply. Water efficiency is also recognised both in Article 11, among the basic measures, and in Article 9 on water pricing. Moreover, one of the key basic measures required under Article 11 of the WFD concerns the prior authorisation of water abstraction and impoundments which are primarily related to water quantity management. Most importantly, Annex V mentions among the quality elements for the classification of ecological status the quantity and dynamics of water flow and the connection to groundwater bodies.

It is clear that the WFD reflects a certain reticence of the Member States to bind themselves too tightly under EU legislation to measures that may limit their sovereignty in water allocation. This sensitivity is also reflected in Article 192 of the TFEU, the legal basis for environment policy, under which the decision making procedure is usually qualified majority voting but quantitative aspects of water management are covered by one of the exceptions providing for unanimity.

In spite of the fact that water quantity is enshrined in the WFD, it does not provide management tools to facilitate quantitative water management at river basin level such as water accounts or water efficiency targets, nor does it clarify the notion of ecological water flow, i.e. the amount of water needed by the aquatic ecosystems to continue to be viable.

5. Article 9: Water Pricing and Cost-Recovery

No single provision of the WFD is a silver bullet that can ensure the achievement of the objectives of the Directive. However, a few provisions, if properly implemented, can provide a significant contribution. Article 9 is one of them. By requiring a water pricing policy and the internalisation of environmental costs, it aims at implementing the polluter pays principle.

These requirements can generate a more efficient use of water; increased water availability, including for environmental needs (ecological flow); and improved water quality, as polluting activities become more expensive and funds generated through pricing or taxation can be used to restore the aquatic ecosystems. Therefore, article 9 can, in principle, contribute to the achievement of all aspects of good water status as enshrined in the WFD.

Article 9 contains three main obligations for Member States to fulfil by 2010. First, they must put in place a water pricing policy that provides an adequate incentive to use water efficiently. Second, they must ensure that the main water using sectors (households, industry and agriculture) contribute adequately to the recovery of the costs of water services.

These two obligations are made more flexible by the possibility for Member States to take into account social, environmental and economic effects of the recovery as well as the geographic and climatic conditions of the regions affected. This limits enforcement action at EU level, particularly in relation to the level of pricing.

Under Article 9, Member States have a third obligation to report in their RBMPs on the actions taken to implement the two requirements above, including an explanation of how different sectors contribute to cost-recovery.

Lastly, Article 9 contains an exception clause in paragraph 4 which allows Member States to escape the implementation of the obligations on water pricing and cost-recovery in accordance with established practices, for a given water-use activity, where this does not compromise the achievement of the objectives of the WFD. An explanation on the use of this clause needs to be provided in the RBMPs.

The information provided by the Member States to the European Commission on the implementation of Article 9 in their RBMPs is often incomplete and scattered.[12] However, an assessment of the plans reveals that incentive and transparent water pricing is not applied across all Member States and water-using sectors, also due to the lack of metering. Only 49% of RBMPs plan to change the water pricing system to foster a more efficient use of water and only 40% include measures to improve water metering.

The text of Article 9 is not always clear and several interpretative questions have arisen.[13]

While Member States must put in place pricing policies that provide an incentive to efficient water use, an obligation to introduce water metering, a pre-condition for volumetric (incentive) water pricing, is not explicitly provided. In any event, Member States have a lot of flexibility in determining what an adequate incentive is and this will be assessed on a case by case base, taking into account local circumstances. The Commission control seems limited to whether an incentive pricing

---

12 See European Commission Report on the Implementation of the Water Framework Directive (2000/60/EC) – River Basin Management Plans, COM(2012)670 final, pp. 10-11, available at http://ec.europa.eu/environment/water/water-framework/pdf/COM-2012-670_EN.pdf.

13 See, e.g., the enlightening analysis in Herwig Unnerstall, "The principle of full cost recovery in the EU Water Framework Directive: genesis and content", *Journal of Environmental Law*, 2007, Vol. 19, No. 1, pp. 2-42.

policy is in place, if it covers all main uses and, in case it does not, if Member States have provided a convincing explanation for this in their RBMPs.

The notions of cost-recovery and water services are also controversial. The Commission has started infringement procedures against 9 Member States[14] who interpret water services as limited to water supply and treatment. It argues that this notion is much broader and includes many other services such as hydropower, flood protection, irrigation, self-abstraction, etc. This interpretation would make the principle of cost-recovery applicable to all such services, thereby giving a much broader scope to the application of the polluter pays principle under Article 9. The Court should clarify the interpretation of this notion in a case brought by the Commission.

On cost-recovery, it is generally understood that this covers the environmental and resource costs mentioned in Article 9.1. However, there is no common methodology agreed under the WFD to calculate such costs. In the implementation of cost-recovery Member States seem to have the same flexibility mentioned in relation to water pricing.

The exception clause in Article 9.4 may be seen as undermining all of the obligations in Article 9. It certainly further limits enforcement action by the Commission. However, a close reading shows that it would not be very easy for Member States to rely on it. They would have to demonstrate that there are established practices (presumably before the WFD or, at least, before 2010) that justify the non-respect of the obligations under Article 9. This should be limited to a given water-use activity and they should demonstrate that this does not compromise the objective of the WFD. Exemption clauses are interpreted restrictively by the Court but, once a Member State provides a plausible explanation, the burden of proof is reversed and it would be for the Commission to prove that the conditions for the application of the exception clause are not fulfilled.

All in all, Article 9 is not an easily enforceable provision due to the above ambiguities and flexibility. Other policy tools providing incentives to implementation may be more appropriate than enforcement.

6. The 2012 Water Blueprint: Taking the WFD Forward?

As mentioned above, the Blueprint is a package of policy documents including, in addition to the Blueprint Communication, an assessment of Member States' RBMPs and of EU policy on water scarcity and

---

14 These are Germany, Finland, Sweden, Belgium, The Netherlands, Austria, Denmark, Hungary and Ireland.

drought. These evaluations, together with reports from the European Environment Agency, show that, by 2015, 47% of the EU water bodies will fail to achieve good status.[15] This is obviously not in line with the Water Framework Directive goal of good water status everywhere, unless exemptions apply. Therefore, the European Commission has proposed in its new water strategy – the Blueprint – to renew efforts at all levels focusing on better implementation of the current legislation; more integration with relevant policies and filling few remaining legislative gaps.

First of all, the Commission proposes tools to improve the *implementation* of EU water policy. In this respect, the main Blueprint message is that, in spite of the progress achieved under water legislation such as on nitrates, waste water treatment, industrial emissions, priority substances and plant protection products; fuller implementation by the Member States is necessary. The Commission will continue its enforcement action and EU financial support will also be available but this can only complement, not replace, Member States' and private-sector long-term investment plans in these areas.

In order to facilitate implementation, the Commission proposes to integrate the notions of water balances, ecological flow and water efficiency targets into the implementation of the Water Framework Directive. It intends to develop, together with stakeholders and Member States, guidance documents under the Common Implementation Strategy that will allow the integration of those three elements into the next river basin management plans.

The Commission underlines the need to further develop the water accounts it developed together with the European Environment Agency in particular to improve the quality of the data and to reach a common understanding of the notion of ecological flow at EU level. This should be the basis to then develop a sound methodology to implement water efficiency targets in the river basins in which they are useful.

Another aspect tackled by the Blueprint is the issue of water pricing and cost recovery, including environmental costs. While these notions are enshrined in the Water Framework Directive, their practical application has faced methodological hurdles which have prevented improvements in water efficiency. The Commission proposes to develop a common methodology for cost-recovery calculation which should allow for comparable results throughout the Union taking duly into account ecosystem services. Volumetric water metering should be generalised and the Commission hopes that strides can be made in this respect under

---

15 See http://ec.europa.eu/environment/water/blueprint/index_en.htm.

the provisions on irrigation efficiency in the Rural Development Regulation.

Four additional implementation tools are proposed in the Blueprint. First, the establishment of a peer review process to allow river basin authorities to evaluate the management plans developed by others with a view to learning from each other and spreading good practices. Second, GMES (satellite) technology should be relied upon to fight illegal abstraction in the Member States where this is a real plague. Satellite mapping of river basins will allow a comparison between visibly irrigated areas and water abstraction permits. On this basis, inspections could be targeted to areas where problems have been identified. Third, the Commission proposes the development of guidance on water trading in order to facilitate the take up of this tool at river basin level when this would prove cost-effective. Fourth, the Commission plans to spread best practices to establish sustainable leakage levels for water infrastructure.

The second major objective of the Blueprint is to increase the *integration* of water policy objectives into other relevant policy areas. In this respect, agriculture plays a key role. The Blueprint identifies natural green infrastructures like floodplains, wetlands or buffer strips along river banks, as key measures to be mainstreamed into agricultural policy. The Commission proposals on the reform of the Common Agriculture Policy (CAP) offer good opportunities for this. Moreover, the addition of the WFD to cross-compliance would greatly reinforce the application of the Directive at farm level. Success in this area depends on a positive outcome in the on-going CAP negotiations in the Council and European Parliament but the Commission also proposes to develop guidance on green infrastructure to foster their take up.

Another area which is essential for integration is regional policy. Also in this case, the Blueprint highlights water management priorities to be mainstreamed in the spending of Cohesion and Structural Funds and loans of the European Investment Bank. In addition, the Commission has proposed some water related conditionalities for the Cohesion Fund. Member States who want to finance projects in the water sector from Cohesion funds ought to have a RBMP in place and a pricing policy in line with EU legislation.

The third objective of the Blueprint is to *identify possible gaps* in the current water policy and legislative framework to see if new action is needed. The Commission has identified some *lacunae* in two main areas: water efficiency in buildings and water re-use. It will add to the

Eco-design directive working plan[16] water related products. This means that it will look into all options to make products like taps and showers more water and energy efficient. This is expected to create market opportunities while achieving considerable water and energy savings. The Commission will also work on a regulation for setting EU quality standards for water re-use. The lack of such standards is an obstacle to water re-use, which instead would be very helpful in water stressed areas as the experience in some Member States clearly shows.

Finally, there are additional horizontal instruments proposed by the Commission in order to help deliver water policy objectives. First, and closely related to the Blueprint, is the Water Innovation Partnership which was launched in May 2012 and whose Strategic Implementation Plan, currently under development, should reflect the Blueprint priorities. The Partnership should facilitate the removal of obstacles to innovation in the water field by bringing together water managers and "innovators". Second, the Commission envisages formulating Member State specific recommendations, in the framework of the European Semester process, in relation to key aspects of water policy. This should identify win-win action for water protection and growth and jobs. Third, in the wider framework of inspections and surveillance in the implementation of EU environmental law, the Commission will look into options to reinforce inspections in the water field, for instance in relation to water abstraction permits. Fourth, the Blueprint also puts considerable emphasis on the knowledge base for water policy. The Commission Joint Research Centre has developed a hydro-economic model that will help water managers assess the cost-effectiveness of the measures included in their RBMPs. This tool should be further refined in order to become helpful for water managers in selecting cost-effective measures. The Blueprint also proposes to continue the development of the Water Information System for Europe (WISE) in order to make it more interoperable with national databases and to facilitate decision makers' access to essential information. Lastly, the Commission plans the simplification of reporting requirements in the water field by focusing, for instance, on water statistics that are most useful for water managers.

The Blueprint has shown the way for EU water policy to reach its objectives. It remains to be seen whether the political and financial commitment to achieve them will follow.

16 Directive 2009/125/EC of the European Parliament and of the Council establishing a framework for the setting of eco-design requirements for energy-related products, OJ L 285, 31 October 2009.

Modern Enforcement in the Single Market

Jacques PELKMANS

Senior Research Fellow at The Centre for European Policy Studies
Former Director of Economic Studies, College of Europe

In paying tribute to Paul Demaret as rector of the College of Europe for no less than 10 years and as a colleague (be it as Director of the Law department or as a widely respected EU lawyer), I have chosen to write about enforcement in the EU single market. More precisely, about modern enforcement methods and their empirically demonstrated effectiveness. As an economist also interested in EU law, I have long been amazed by the enormous efforts and dedication spent on formal enforcement methods, the more so when they end up as cases in the CJEU. Although professionally admirable, these great efforts beg the questions of cost / benefit and of effectiveness, the kind of questions economists tend to insist on. Paul has also been trained as an economist, be it that he eventually specialized on European law. I hope that the new and somewhat different angle of analyzing EU enforcement and the focus on *modern* enforcement will appeal to Paul's lingering interest in combining economics and law when studying European integration.

This essay[1] has five sections. First, the notion of modern EU enforcement and the drive behind it is set out, followed in section 2 by a survey (the landscape) of such enforcement efforts as compared with classical enforcement in the EU. Sections 3 and 4 zoom in on two major examples, namely SOLVIT and the 98/34 procedure preventing new technical barriers from arising in the Single Market, with some empirical underpinning. Section 5 concludes.

---

1 Much of the text and empirical evidence is based on Pelkmans, J. and Correia de Brito, A., *Enforcement in the EU Single Market*, Brussels, CEPS, 2012, p. 141.

1. The Drive behind Modern EU Enforcement

Given the Single Market *acquis*, the question asked is whether this *acquis* can be made to work for the proper functioning of the Single Market in a static as well as dynamic sense. This requires "*enforcement*": for the present purpose, the term "enforcement" comprises all activities, public and private, at EU and Member States' level, to ensure the proper transposition of EU law into national law, proper implementation and the best possible application of EU law governing the Single Market everywhere in the Union (and the EEA). It should be realized that good enforcement can not be taken for granted, for the simple reason that it is demanding. There is well-developed literature in law, political science and public administration providing many reasons why enforcement may fail, be weak, stay underdeveloped or is selective.[2] Without pretending to provide a survey of this literature, just consider reasons such as the bad "fit" in national regulation as it existed before, the inherent problems of a certain EU regulation or directive (some EU laws are internally inconsistent or can be characterized as "bad" regulation), capacity and interpretation issues in a national administration, heavy-handed bureaucratic traditions (irrespective of what EU law really requires), the neglect of European standards linked to the relevant directive(s), "goldplating" of directives in national law causing the requirements for business to be more onerous than justified by EU law, domestic political frictions about some EU laws, the lack of political legitimacy on a specific directive in domestic politics (rare, but disturbing when it does appear), and a lack of specialized expertise for highly technical directives (not least, their technical annexes or e.g. type-approval issues). This is far from exhaustive. Also note that this list does not even include the motive of a "protectionist" government. Broadly spoken, nowadays, Member States are accustomed to EU law and know that intra-EU protectionism, even when covert, is neither correct nor easy to achieve, given enforcement. Today's acceptance of the rigour of the internal market is greater than ever before and this is a significant, though "invisible", accomplishment. Nevertheless, there is always a temptation for some to be protectionist at the margin (especially before elections) or in the form of bureaucratic nuisance.

[2] Prominent examples from this literature include Siedentopf, H. and Ziller, J. (eds.), *Making European policies work: the implementation of Community legislation in the Member States*, London, Sage, 1988; Egan, M., "Single Market", in E. Jones *et al.*, *Handbook of EU Politics*, Oxford, OUP, 2011 and Falkner, G. and Trieb, O., "Three worlds of compliance or four? The EU-15 compared to new Member States", *Journal of Common Market Studies*, 2008, Vol. 46, No. 2, pp. 293-313.

This summary raises questions about the formal infringement approach of the EU. If there are many deep-seated reasons why EU law is not properly implemented and applied, the formal infringement procedures might not be very effective. No matter how many cases might be taken up by the Commission, it would not go to the roots of the problems. As a result, a steady stream of new infringements will be fed by mainly non-legal sources of Member States' conduct. Modern enforcement attempts to involve in a profound and permanent way the Member States because they are critical in reducing if not minimizing the problem. Moreover, there are at least two additional questions about EU enforcement: one is about costs & benefits of the formal procedures and another about effectiveness, indeed, effectiveness for what?

When considering the costs and benefits of formal infringement procedures, the principal benefit of solid enforcement is the credibility of EU law, here, for the better functioning of the Single Market. This benefit renders the formal infringement procedures indispensable. No matter how much criticism one might level on the formal approach, it must always remain prominent as a hardcore fall back option for recalcitrant Member States as well as for difficult issues of interpretation of EU law. To be sure, other methods should not necessarily be excluded, as NAFTA shows, where the threat of private litigation also generates a considerable degree of credibility. But even a superficial comparison with ASEAN, with its AFTA (ASEAN Free Trade Area) and the emerging AEC (ASEAN Economic Community), shows the severe limits of economic regionalism without any common system of detection and infringement procedures. This lack of credibility worsens exponentially with the shift from pure tariff removal to "deeper" economic integration based on the removal of regulatory and technical barriers in goods trade and the proper handling of regulatory questions in services markets, not to speak of IPRs or public procurement. The EU being a very "deep" instance of economic integration with a great deal of common regulation of market aspects, credible infringement resolution is and remains indispensable for economic agents in markets to rely on EU law in their decisions.

But the costs of formal infringement procedures are high. Although the total pecuniary costs of cases are not known (to the present author), telling indirect yardsticks are available. Figure 1 summarizes the recent experiences with formal infringement in the EU, including the periods used for moving to a next stage. It takes no less than 50 months (4 years), on average, before a case arrives at the CJEU followed by another two years for a judgment to be delivered. The costs of all parties involved in the litigation and the costs of lingering uncertainty over such long periods should not be taken lightly. They will undoubtedly act as a deterrent for many other parties before insisting on formal procedures via the Commission or via courts.

Figure 1: Formal Enforcement in case of infringement

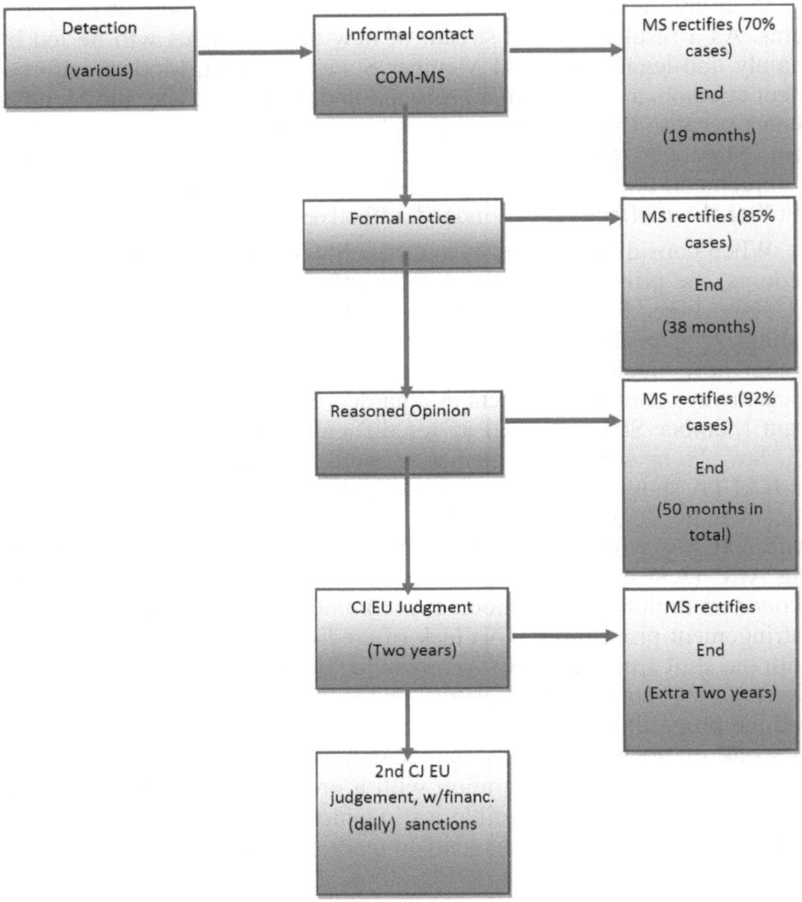

But Figure 1 and other indicators also make one wonder what the purpose is, or ought to be, of enforcement, beyond the general notion of credibility of the system. For European business and consumers, and also citizens more and more, the credibility of the system is more directly measured by the effectiveness of pre-empting, preventing or removing infringements right away. Indeed, formal infringement procedures cannot be very helpful for the proper functioning of the single market, if procedures can take up to 6 years. Stronger, there are very many infringements as signaled by Commission detection, complaints, national court cases and otherwise. Only a fraction of those end up in Luxembourg and many infringements remain unaddressed, often out of a disbelief that it will help (directly) or due to fears about long and costly procedures. Formal infringement procedures are therefore not an effective instrument to induce better enforcement of or compliance with Single Market rules. As a consequence, modern enforcement methods seek to avoid, as much as possible, to have to fall back on formal infringement approaches, whilst seeking to address violations of single market laws much more massively, directly and quickly.

2. The Landscape of EU Enforcement Efforts

Figure 2 shows the entire landscape of enforcement of Single Market law. Three of the five types of enforcement efforts have been available since the outset of the EEC: detection (via monitoring and complaints), pre-infringement initiatives and formal infringement procedures. However, as we shall see in the following sections, the scope of efforts in the former two has widened appreciably over time.

Figure 2: Enforcement of Single Market Law

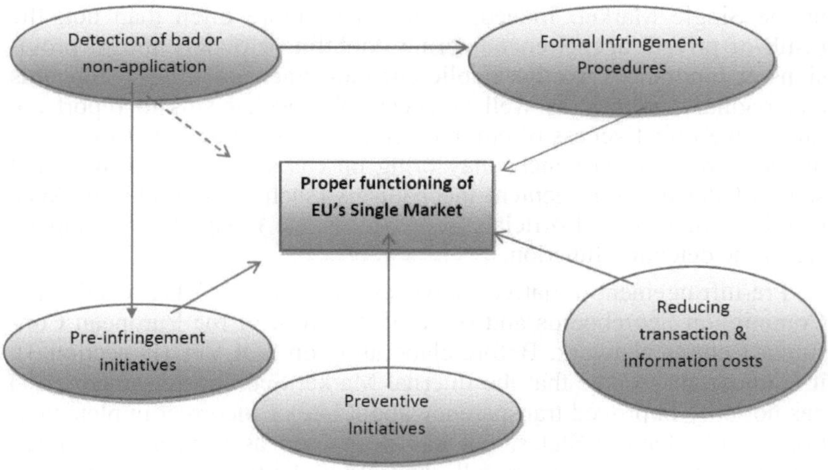

More recently, the emphasis is on effective prevention (in a number of ways). Lowering the transaction and information costs of business (and sometimes consumers) associated with perceived or actual "barriers" to intra-EU market access has also become far more important. These two types of efforts are not always clearly distinct – there can be some overlap for a few activities. The overall conclusion suggested strongly by Figure 2 is that complaints about insufficient or ineffective enforcement have been around for decades and that the EU level as well as Member States have responded (with some delays, to be sure) with more, and more differentiated, efforts. The *preventive* measures have expanded enormously, closely followed by much greater intensity of *pre-infringement* efforts, with the aim of pre-empting enforcement barriers or nipping them in the bud at low costs when detected.

Detection of incorrect implementation (transposition) and/or bad enforcement of Single Market law in the Member States long used to be a pure Commission activity, surrounded by confidentiality on the EU/Member States' interface. This was a consequence of the original emphasis on formal infringement efforts as spelled out in the Treaty. Of course, even in the formal approach, the Treaty encourages (after detection) informal moments on the Commission/Member States' interface with a view to resolve the problem immediately without further proceedings. As Figure 1 shows, no less than 70% of Commission detections are solved this way! Nowadays, however, detection and pre-infringement efforts have become ever more closely related and the initial secrecy has largely disappeared. The idea is probably that timely and effective detection is in the common interest of all economic agents in the Single Market. Indeed, detection is, more often than not, the result of private agents encountering doubtful or plainly illegal provisions or hindrances, so that public encouragement of filing complaints and regular publicity as well as accessible mechanisms to report are raising the effectiveness of enforcement. Thus, the Petitions Committee of the European Parliament may bring up cases reported to them and some of the pre-infringement mechanisms (such as SOLVIT, package meetings, networks of officials, scoreboards, etc.) may also be supportive of the detection function.

Pre-infringement initiatives nowadays include SOLVIT, two distinct Commission Scoreboards and some of the work of the European Consumer Centres Network. Before elaborating on SOLVIT (in section 3), it is important to note that the Internal Market Scoreboard (since 1997) has not only improved transparency about late or incorrect implementation of all Member States, but has been used as a basis of Council recommendations for successfully improving the track records of Member States such as lower transposition and compliance benchmarks for deficits.[3] The Consumers Scoreboard (since 2008) is helpful in tracking the (im)proper functioning of the internal market for retail services, a

3 See Pelkmans and Correia de Brito, *supra*, note 1, pp. 48 ff for details.

tool which supports a more targeted approach in addressing "malfunctioning" in value chains or direct consumer services.

As to formal infringement procedures, the early stages have also been transformed with a view to raise the effectiveness in addressing the insufficient working of the Single Market. The crux of the matter is to postpone the moment where the exchange between the Commission and the infringing Member State becomes an adversary one. Since the November 2007 Internal Market Review, the idea is to rely on the active *cooperation* of Member States, as a group as well as individually, in sharp contrast to later stages of the formal procedure where the Commission, as the guardian of the Treaty, *opposes* a Member States in a legal proceeding. This cooperative approach has been agreed in what is called "EU pilot", first in an experimental phase with 15 Member States, since 2010 in a second stage with 10 more Member States. Meanwhile, the success of EU Pilot is such that it is likely to replace the early stage of infringement procedures. EU Pilot is more informal and cooperative, leading frequently directly to better solutions of encountered problems and this with much greater speed. Rather than the legal period of one year in the formal approach, the benchmark for solving a problem is 10 weeks (in fact, taken over from the practice of SOLVIT). The actual record until September 2011 is less good, 102 days on average, yet still far better than the average of 19 months (!) in Figure 1. Some 80% of cases are resolved right away, the other 20% is shifted to the formal procedure. At least in part as a result of EU Pilot, the number of new infringement procedures launched has been falling conspicuously, from 536 in 2009 to only 206 in 2011.

Finally, a range of "preventive approaches" is employed nowadays. The aim is to alter in a structural way the conduct or administrative capacity of Member States in implementing and applying EU law. Space constraints make it impossible to discuss all but one of them, but we merely mention (i) regulatory impact assessment (forcing a solid analysis of incipient EU legislation and thereby preventing many problems), (ii) training officials and judges in EU law, (iii) disciplining Member States in respecting Mutual Recognition (based on Reg. 2008/764) and (iv) application of the new IMI system of inter-Member-States administrative cooperation (directly between – now – 11000 officials at national and regional level, with immediate translation of all languages) used for the services directive and recognition of regulated professions. Especially the IMI system is a resounding success, lowering transactions costs dramatically for officials and citizens, workers, professionals and others, whilst frequently achieving a speed of resolution of less than a week (as against months) and encountering fewer misunderstandings. A fifth means is a little noticed but remarkable trend, explicitly allowed by Member States recently in particular in the Single Market, of employing EU Regulations rather than directives. On 30 April 2011, the single market *acquis* consisted of 1,525 directives and 1,347 regulations. However, if one goes back ten years, the number of directives is more or less the same (1497) but EU Regulations add up to only 299! It is obvious that, other things equal, the implementation problems of EU Regulations are miniscule compared to directives and the fact that Member States have allowed this to happen so frequently is a clear sign of their greater cooperative attitude or "ownership" of the compliance issue in the Single Market. A sixth approach is the prevention of new technical barriers which will be dealt with in section 4.

Of course, all this does not claim to be exhaustive. For instance, there are perennial problems with the compliance of public procurement rules as well as with the national application of the procurement remedies directive 2007/66. However, space does not allow a further analysis (for a survey of the issues, see Pelkmans & Correia de Brito, 2012, chapter 7).

3. The SOLVIT System as a Low-Cost, High-Speed Practical Help

One of the ways in which the Commission has tried to solve problems that arise for citizens and businesses from the misapplication of internal market law is SOLVIT. SOLVIT, set up in 2002, is a network for settling cross-border disputes informally about the incorrect and inaccurate application of the single market rules arising between citizens or businesses and public administrations across EU Member States, to the extent that such disputes are not subject to legal proceedings at national or EU level. SOLVIT is meant as an informal alternative to other problem-solving mechanisms, such as national court procedures, formal complaints to the European Commission and petitions. The system is based on mutual cooperation[4] and online techniques, that allows for a decisional procedure, which is easily accessible, free of charge, and offers a quick solution to the internal market problems. SOLVIT is at same time an online alternative dispute resolution mechanism (ODR)[5] and a cooperation network between national administra-

4 The system is drawn up on the principle of mutual cooperation at three different levels: at cross-border level between the two centers involved in the decision procedure (the so-called "Home" center and the "Lead" center); at national level (between the Lead centre and the national administration, which allegedly acted in breach of EU law) and at European level (between the centers and the European Commission).

5 Compared with the infringement procedures as defined under Articles 258 and 260 TFEU, SOLVIT is an alternative complementary out-of-court dispute settlement mechanism.

tions, which contributes to improving the implementation capacity of EU law at national level, hence fostering the correct application of EU law. In fact, evaluation shows that SOLVIT Centres contribute to a "cultural change" in their own national civil service.[6]

Today, SOLVIT handles around 1300 cases a year (in 2011, SOLVIT handled a total of 3154 cases, of which 1306 fell within its mandate) and manages to find solutions for over 89% of its clients, with an average turnaround time of 70 days.[7] These are impressive figures compared to traditional infringement approaches which, one can safely assume, would never have been resorted to in the large majority of these cases. The trend has been upward over a decade and now reached a plateau. The levels of resolution rates remained high and stable at 89% (compared to 90% in 2010) (Figure 3).

Figure 3: Resolution rates of the SOLVIT cases during SOLVIT's mandate (2003-2011)

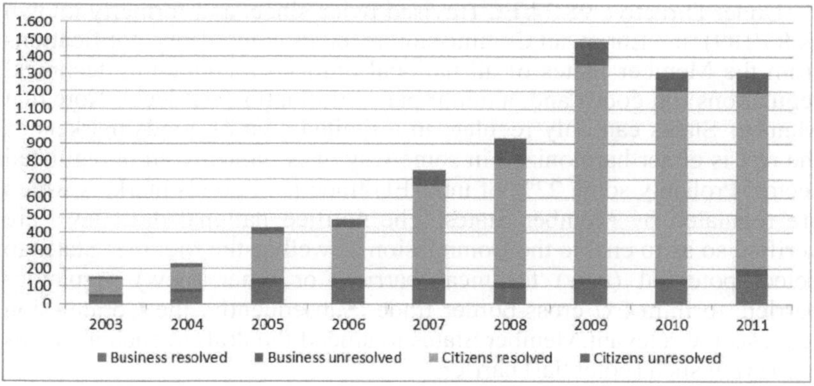

Source: European Commission working document, Making the Single Market deliver: Annual governance, check-up 2011.

SOLVIT intervention is particularly significant within specific areas of the internal market, where quick and/or cost-effective solutions are needed. In 2011, as in 2010, social security issues related to migrants generated the largest number of cases (39% in 2011, 34% in 2010). The proportion of cases concerning the recognition of professional qualifications remained at around 15%. The number of residence cases decreased to 12% (from 23% in 2010). Problems also occurred in relation to the

6 See European Commission Evaluation of SOLVIT, Final Report, November 2011.

7 See European Commission, "Making the Single Market deliver, Annual governance check-up 2011", 2012.

free movement of services and goods, taxation and motor vehicles registration and driving licenses. Cases involving the free movement of services and goods remained at 8%, while the number of taxation cases increased from 5% to 9% in relation to the last period.

One of the weaknesses of the SOLVIT network are scarce resources and limited legal expertise to carry out its tasks in a satisfactory way and enable them to deliver independent legal analysis of the cases. Ensuring an adequate level of staffing and legal expertise is even more pressing if we take into account the increasing variety of cases that SOLVIT is asked to address. Although, during 2011, staffing in some SOLVIT Centres improved, the overall staffing levels of the centres remain problematic.

4. Preventing New Technical Barriers from Arising in the Single Market

Under Directive 98/34/EC (revised twice since, and formerly known as 83/189), the European Commission receives compulsory notifications from the Member States of all national draft laws containing technical regulations (on goods and, a minor part, information services). Note that Member States can only regulate in a limited area of goods markets as the rest is either harmonized in some way or is typically an unregulated sector. Probably some 22% of intra-EU trade is in goods markets which are regulated by Member States. The notified national draft laws are verified so as to enable the Commission as well as the Member States to detect potential (new) technical barriers or other (new) regulatory barriers to intra-EU cross-border trade. Subsequently, the Commission requests the relevant Member States to amend the draft in such a way as to *prevent* such (potential) barriers.

This unique and most remarkable instrument has protected the internal goods market from becoming a mockery over time. The Directive 98/34/EC mechanism is remarkable for at least two reasons. First, Member States temporarily renounce their sovereign right and freedom to legislate as they want and when they want. A notification automatically postpones the conclusion of domestic pre-legislative procedures for three months, i.e. the draft cannot be adopted before the end of this standstill period. Normally, however, such standstill period is prolonged and takes four or six months. In case of a blockage (i.e. when the Commission announces that the proposal concerns a matter which is covered by a proposal for a directive, regulation or decision) it may reach twelve months. If the Council adopts a common position, the national legislative procedure is blocked for 18 months. This is a credible way to prevent new technical barriers from arising. Second, notification is not only compulsory but the CJEU has explicitly ruled (in CIA Security International, 1996) that non-notification renders the national law adopted subsequently "unenforceable". Again, a ruling that provides strong incentives to notify, thereby raising credibility of the Directive even further.

What is typically notified? The regular Commission reports on Directive 98/34/EC[8] speak of goods in the non-harmonized field as well as in the harmonized field. The latter refers to secondary national legislation which elaborates principles and specifications provided for in EU directives – the Member States have considerable discretion here, and in the 98/34 procedure it is verified whether that discretion is not used in ways which create unnecessary divergences or incompatibilities with the directive(s). In other words, it disciplines at EU level the national regulatory autonomy first received in the directive, such that no new barriers to internal market emerge.

Figure 4: Total number of notifications (1999-2010)

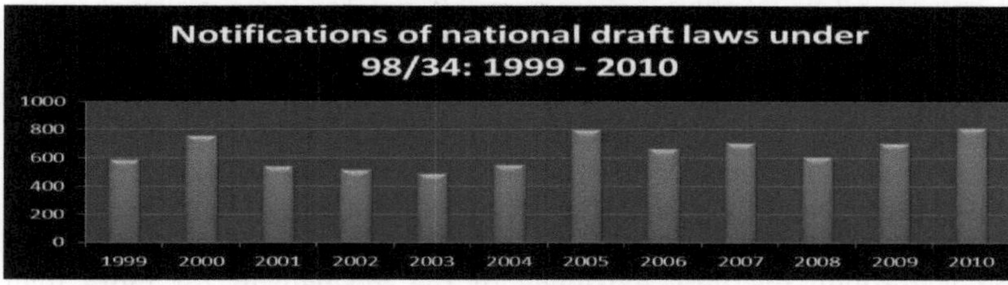

Notes: 2004: enlargement from EU-15 to EU-25; 2007: enlargement from EU-25 to EU-27. Sources: Pelkmans, 2007; SEC(2009) 1704 of 21 Dec. 2009 and SEC(2011) 1509 of 7 Dec. 2011.

How critical the 98/34 mechanism is for the protection of the internal goods market, can be read from Figure 4 showing the notifications over the period 1999-2010. The regulatory activity of Member States (on a limited part of goods trade) is considerable. In the period of the EU-12 (1988-1994) annual notifications hovered between 300 and 400 and many of these prompted observations from the Commission and/or Member States, suspecting potential barriers. During the period of the EU-15 (1995-2003), notifications start rising to (sometimes far) beyond 500 a year. A further structural increase can be observed after the first and second Eastern enlargement (2004-2010), approaching an annual average of around 700 a year.

8 Such as the latest ones: COM(2009)690 of 21 December 2009 (on 2006-2008) and COM(2011)853 of 7 December 2011 (on 2009 and 2010), for example.

In short, for already one and a half decade the notifications number more than 500, with a recent trend of 700 a year. This amounts to unique empirical evidence on the high, if not secularly increasing, regulatory activity of Member States. In Europe the shift to more and more EU regulation, at the expense of national regulation (at least in goods), is frequently discussed. What is rarely considered, however, is what Member States themselves do in the areas remaining under national regulatory autonomy, for the simple reason that there is no easy way to "observe" such trends. The 98/34 mechanism gives analysts unique (though partial, for goods only) empirical evidence about how Member States use their autonomy in goods markets. The inference is clear: Member States remain eager regulators. Yet, this eagerness creates serious risks of newly emerging technical or other regulatory barriers, which might be difficult, slow and costly to remove again. Hence, the justification of the intrusive 98/34 mechanism which does not reduce national regulatory autonomy but disciplines it for the sake of the internal goods market. It is important that the Member States jointly have assumed "ownership" since they all can (and do) make observations on the draft laws of other Member States, whilst being disciplined themselves as well.

The effectiveness of 98/34 in protecting the internal goods market can be appreciated once one "zooms in" on the actual working of the Commission. No less than some 12,500 notifications have been dealt with since 1988. The effectiveness of 98/34 is exerted in three ways. One is through the very existence of the mechanism for more than 25 years now, which is bound to have induced some degree of discipline and efforts to ensure EU legal compatibility in ministries in all EU Member States. The second way is via the working of the 98/34 notification procedure which has gradually engendered a greater "Europeanization" of domestic law making by the permanent machinery to comment on drafts of other EU countries, and to identify instances of potential and likely "barriers" springing from draft laws which have no mutual recognition clauses or comprise other (too) restrictive ways to pursue health, safety or environmental objectives. These two beneficial effects of 98/34 cannot be empirically verified in any meaningful fashion, although that does not mean that such impacts are not real.

A third effect can be verified empirically with the help of three proxy measures. We refer to *barriers which were actually prevented* via the comments and especially the detailed opinions. In the following we assume, for the sake of simplicity, that a detailed opinion is tantamount to "a barrier prevented" which is in actual practice very often the case. More generally, comments may also point to issues or a potential for later problems or overly complicated or heavy bureaucracy, etc., but comments may just as well provide advice or comparisons with solutions found elsewhere. By zooming in on comments and in particular, on detailed opinions, it is possible to calculate the "*proven prevention*" in the annual functioning of the 98/34 procedure. The empirical perspective can be provided with the help of three indicators. The first one is the "Gross Detection Rate" (=GDR), showing the reported activities (though not in substantive detail) of the procedure in detecting issues, problems and/or likely barriers. The GDR is the ratio of the sum of the comments and detailed opinions of one year, divided by the total number of notifications. The "Gross Prevention Indicator" (=GPI) focuses on prevention we are pretty sure about, that is, the share in percentages of all detailed opinions in all notifications in one year. However, the GPI is "gross" because, although it is relatively easy to calculate from the TRIS website, it cannot be fully precise in identifying how many new barriers have been prevented per year (assuming that one draft law is tantamount to one barrier). The reason is that more than one Member State can have a detailed opinion on the same notified draft law and/or that a Member State as well as the Commission may file a detailed opinion on the same draft law. The "Effective Prevention Indicator" (=EPI) filters such double counting from the calculation. The GPI is the share (in %) of the notifications which have attracted one or more detailed opinions. In Figure 5 this empirical perspective has been brought together for the last few years: the GDR for 2004-2011, the GPI for 2004-2011 and the EPI for 2010 and 2011.

Figure 5: Detection and effective prevention of barriers in 98/34

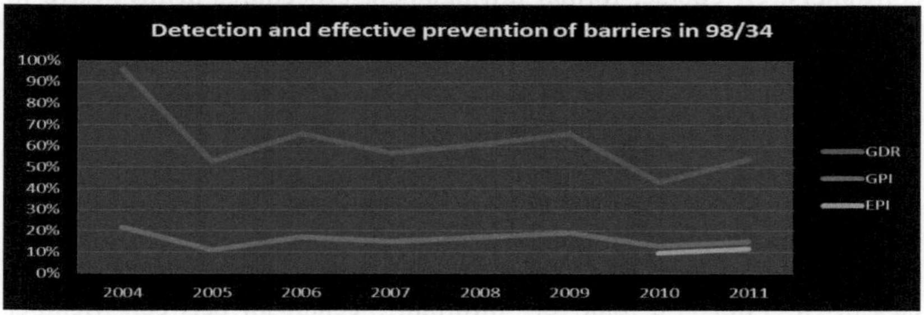

GDR = Gross Detection Rate; GPI = Gross Prevention Indicator; EPI = Effective Prevention Indicator

Figure 5 shows immediately that, after many years of relying on the Directive 98/34/EC and supporting CJEU case-law, such as Unilever and CIA-Security, the trend is that still around half of the notified draft laws lead to an issuance of either comments or detailed opinions or both (2004 was the first enlargement year and is an outlier). When it comes to identified (likely) barriers in national draft laws, the scores are much lower. Nonetheless, the GPI hoovers around 15% or so which is far from trivial. After filtering this, the EPI for 2010 and 2011 shows resp. 9.7% and 11.7%. These are good proxies of actually prevented barriers to intra-EU goods trade. Figure 5 is a firm proof of the value of a credible and intrusive mechanism such as procedure 98/34 to pre-empt the steady erosion of the internal market for goods.

5. Conclusions

Enforcement of and compliance with EU law, and in particular in the Single Market, is not only legally necessary but also of economic importance for business, consumers and the European economy at large. Only with reliable, permanent and effective enforcement will all the potential gains from the Single Market be fully reaped.

Modern enforcement assumes a broader, strategic view. It distinguishes five critical aspects: (i) good detection of bad implementation, a lack of implementation or bad or non-application, (ii) formal infringement procedures (the classical route), (iii) pre-infringement initiatives (ensuring that no infringement procedure will be necessary), (iv) preventive initiatives, and (v) reduction of transaction and information costs when exploiting the Single Market rights or laws.

Central to modern enforcement is that the classical route to the CJEU is costly and takes a lot of time. It is rarely suitable for European business confronted with suspected enforcement problems, let alone for consumers. Of course, formal infringement procedures always have to remain available for genuine interpretation issues or, more generally, for the credibility of the system. But it will never yield a proper functioning Single Market in and by itself and therefore has to be complemented by a host of other measures and initiatives.

Amongst the more important new instruments, the pre-infringement ones like SOLVIT and EU-Pilot have truly made a difference. SOLVIT is free of charge, easy to access (on line) and has accomplished a good record in terms of speed (10 weeks) and resolution (around 90% of the cases). EU-Pilot is a relatively informal mechanism between Member States and the Commission with a view to minimizing infringement cases and doing this rapidly. Started only in 2008, it has quickly become quite effective.

At least as important, if not more so, are the preventive approaches, including e.g. the inter-Member-States IMI on-line communication system between officials at national and regional level (which reduces transaction costs enormously, while enhancing trust between administrations and greatly increasing speed in many cases), the steady (selective) shift from directives to regulations for the internal market (thereby pre-empting numerous implementation problems) and the 98/34 procedures to prevent new technical barriers from arising in the Single Market (which works well).

It is crucial to appreciate that Member States' "ownership" of their EU obligations in the common interest is key to better and more effective enforcement. Almost equally important is it to see that modern enforcement is not primarily legal in nature but pays explicitly attention to e.g. the right incentives for complainants, speed of resolution, resources and the costs/benefit ratio of detection and resolution mechanisms. The point is to make the Single Market work better and to enhance the confidence and trust of business and consumers in that Single market.

This is not to say that EU enforcement in the Single Market has been resolved, far from it. It has improved and the net is cast much wider. Further improvement is nevertheless desirable, although perfect enforcement will of course always remain an illusion.

L'impact des instruments non contraignants (*soft-law*) dans l'interprétation du droit fiscal de l'Union européenne

Franco ROCCATAGLIATA*

Administrateur principal à la Commission européenne (DG TAXUD)

1. Introduction

Cette contribution n'a pas pour but d'analyser en détail le vaste sujet des différents types d'instruments juridiques non contraignants qui peuvent rentrer dans le concept de *soft-law*. L'intention est bien plus modeste : réfléchir aux différences – pour les instances institutionnelles de l'UE – entre l'approche *soft-law* et l'approche classique (ou *hard-law*) en matière fiscale, afin de mieux comprendre si les instruments non contraignants ont un impact réel dans l'interprétation du droit de l'UE.

Nous essayerons de définir les *instruments non contraignants* en vertu du TFUE et le rôle joué par les institutions européennes dans l'approche *soft-law* pour voir dans quelle mesure ceux-ci peuvent influencer les décisions de la Cour de justice de l'UE (ci-après : la Cour) et des juridictions nationales. Enfin, nous terminerons notre analyse avec quelques observations sur les limites de cette approche.

2. Les instruments non contraignants des institutions européennes

Dans la doctrine, la *soft-law* a été définie comme « *les règles de conduite énoncées dans des instruments auxquels n'a pas été conférée une force obligatoire en tant que telle, et qui peuvent néanmoins pro-*

* Un remerciement à l'ami Jean-Marc Van Leeuw pour son aide et ses précieuses suggestions.

duire certains effets juridiques – indirects – et dont l'objet est de potentiellement produire des effets pratiques ».[1] Si on se base sur les dispositions du TFUE, nous ne pouvons qu'agréer avec cette définition.

Selon une expression classique, la Commission européenne est *la gardienne des traités*. Elle est responsable de l'élaboration et de la proposition des politiques de l'UE et de la sauvegarde de leur efficacité et cohérence dans la mise en œuvre, jouant un rôle central de garante de l'intérêt général de l'UE. L'Article 288 du TFUE indique les instruments juridiques dont la Commission et les autres institutions UE disposent pour exercer leurs compétences et donne aussi une première définition de certains instruments de *soft-law* (*recommandations* et *avis*). Pour mieux dire, l'Article précise ce que ces instruments ne sont pas : « *la directive lie tout État membre destinataire quant au résultat à atteindre ... les recommandations et les avis ne lient pas* ». Cet élément négatif est la seule référence claire qu'on peut trouver dans le TFUE sur les instruments de *soft-law*. En fait, la doctrine juridique ne tient pas compte des termes *recommandations* ou *avis* comme *nomen juris* spécifiques mais, tout simplement, comme des termes génériques. En l'absence d'une notion bien définie de ce qu'on entend par *soft-law*, la liste des actes juridiques de l'UE n'ayant pas *force contraignante* – et, par conséquent, potentiellement inclus dans ce concept – est assez longue.

En matière fiscale, les *recommandations* (ou les *avis*) sont rares. Les *communications* de la Commission aux autres institutions européennes sont certainement les instruments non contraignants les plus fréquemment adoptés dans ce domaine. D'autres instruments juridiques de même nature existent, moins connus mais non moins importants, tels que les *livres blancs*, les *lignes directrices* ou les *codes de conduites*.[2]

Les *réponses* de la Commission aux questions posées par les membres du Parlement européen sont-elles des instruments de *soft-law*

---

1 Senden, L., « Soft Law, Self-Regulation and Co-Regulation in European Law : Where do they meet ? », *Electronic Journal of Comparative Law*, January 2005, *http://www.ejcl.org/91/art91-3.pdf* : « Rules of conduct that are laid down in instruments which have not been attributed legally binding force as such, but nevertheless may have certain – indirect – legal effects, and that are aimed at and may produce practical effects » (la traduction en français est reprise du Document PE 384.581v02-00, voir aussi http://www.europarl.europa.eu/meetdocs/2004_2009/documents/dt/653/653346/653346fr.pdf page 2). V. aussi : Snyder, F., « Soft Law and Institutional Practice in the European Community », dans *The Construction of Europe : Essays in Honour of Emile Noël*, 1994, p. 198 ; Christians, A., « Hard Law and Soft Law in International Taxation », *Wisconsin International Law Journal*, vol. 2, 2007, p. 3 (*http://ssrn.com/abstract=988782*).

2 Pour une liste complète : Parlement européen, *Document de travail n° PE 384.581*, 14 février 2007.

dans le sens qu'on vient d'énoncer ? À notre avis, la réponse est affirmative : ces *réponses* sont des actes officiels délivrés par la Commission à une autre institution de l'UE et elles ont un vrai impact externe : bien qu'elles restent formellement des instruments non contraignants, elles peuvent néanmoins avoir des conséquences importantes du point de vue juridique.[3]

En matière de fiscalité, les traités ne confèrent pas de pouvoirs autonomes à la Commission. Le cadre juridique est un peu plus favorable si nous considérons aussi les règles de la concurrence en matière d'*aides d'État*, étant donné que les mesures fiscales constituent presque un tiers du total des aides d'État aux entreprises. Or, dans ce domaine, le TFUE prévoit des pouvoirs importants pour la Commission afin de lui permettre de veiller à une correcte application des règles de la concurrence : les aides d'État relèvent d'un régime d'autorisation préalable de la Commission, sous le contrôle du juge de l'UE. Elles sont soumises, en application de l'Article 108 TFUE, à une procédure de notification obligatoire. Le rôle de la Commission en matière d'aides d'État est donc bien plus délicat que dans d'autres domaines où la Commission partage ses pouvoirs avec les autres institutions européennes.

Pour cette raison, les actes non contraignants de la Commission dans cette matière ont un impact externe important. Dans un souci de transparence et de prévisibilité, les *communications* ou les *lignes directrices* sont généralement publiées dans le Journal officiel afin d'expliquer quels sont les critères que la Commission adopte dans l'application de ses pouvoirs en matière de concurrence. C'est le cas, par exemple, de la Communication de la Commission *sur l'application des règles relatives aux aides d'État aux mesures fiscales.*[4]

Des remarques similaires peuvent être faites à propos de certains *actes de soft-law* du Conseil. Sur les questions fiscales, le Conseil (ECOFIN) adopte des *conclusions* et, parfois, prend des *résolutions*. L'exemple le plus significatif au cours de ces dernières années est probablement le *Code de conduite dans le domaine de la fiscalité des entreprises*. Ce *code de conduite* a été adopté par une *résolution* du

[3] La *Décision* de la Commission du 17 février 2003 *concernant le régime d'aide mis en œuvre par la Belgique en faveur des centres de coordination* confirme le principe de la *confiance légitime* pour les contribuables qui ont bénéficié des centres (point 62) ; J.O. L282, 30 octobre 2003, 25. Selon la Commission, cette confiance des contribuables était basée, *inter alia*, sur la réponse à une question parlementaire donnée par le commissaire à la concurrence en 1990 ; QE n° 1735/90 *de Vries*, 12 juillet 1990 ; J.O. C63, 11 mars 1991, 37.

[4] *Communication de la Commission sur l'application des règles relatives aux aides d'État aux mesures relevant de la fiscalité directe des entreprises* ; J.O. C384, 10 décembre 1998, 3.

Conseil de l'UE.[5] D'un point de vue purement formel, ce Code relève des *mesures atypiques*. Il est, en effet, formalisé par une *résolution* qui est une mesure qui ne trouve pas de mention explicite dans les traités.[6] En outre, cette *résolution* a été adoptée non seulement par le *Conseil*, mais aussi par « *les représentants des gouvernements des États membres, réunis au sein du Conseil* ». Il s'agit d'une formule plutôt énigmatique, probablement pour souligner que le Code de conduite affecte une matière relevant de la compétence des États membres. Ce n'est pas un instrument juridiquement contraignant, mais plutôt un engagement de nature politique pris par les gouvernements des États membres (*gentlemen's agreement*).

Les résolutions du Conseil ne sont pas, *per se*, des actes contraignants,[7] mais peuvent affecter de manière significative le comportement des États membres et même des institutions européennes.[8] Toutefois, l'absence formelle d'effets juridiquement contraignants – conformément à l'Article 263 TFUE – ne permet pas à la Cour d'effectuer un contrôle de la légalité des *codes de conduite* (ou plutôt des *résolutions* qui les adoptent), comme sur les autres actes de même nature.

Il existe encore d'autres actes non contraignants des institutions européennes, par exemple, les *documents de travail des services de la*

---

5 Résolution du Conseil et des Représentants des Gouvernements des États membres, réunis au sein du Conseil sur un code de conduite dans le domaine de la fiscalité des entreprises. Annexe I des Conclusions du Conseil ECOFIN du 1er décembre 1997 en matière de politique fiscale ; J.O. C2, 6 janvier 1998, 1.

6 V. Article 288 du TFUE. Dans ses conclusions dans l'affaire NIPFO, l'avocat général donne une définition de ce terme : « La résolution est … un de ces actes atypiques … auxquels le Conseil et la Commission ont parfois recours … afin d'exprimer leur volonté politique, en précisant les contours des accords de principe intervenus au sein de l'institution, afin d'éviter que ces accords puissent être remis en cause. En d'autres termes, les résolutions (surtout celles du Conseil) ne représentent, en principe, que des engagements politiques, dont on annonce, cependant, en même temps le développement futur dans les formes juridiquement efficaces visées par l'article [288] du traité » ; Conclusions de l'avocat général La Pergola du 30 septembre 1997, affaire C-4/96 (NIFPO), 56.

7 V. toutefois les conclusions de l'avocat général dans l'affaire NIPFO, *supra*, note 6, « … en raison de leur contenu et d'autres circonstances pertinentes, même les résolutions peuvent avoir un caractère juridiquement obligatoire. Il doit, cependant, s'agir d'actes ayant pour objet des questions que le Conseil est appelé à trancher de manière définitive, dans le cadre de sa compétence, grâce à une prise de position, plutôt que sous la forme et par le moyen d'un des actes définis à l'article [288] du traité » (57).

8 Particulièrement clair l'exemple du Code de conduite dans le domaine de la fiscalité des entreprises, que, au point J, reporte l'engagement de la Commission « d'examiner ou de réexaminer, au cas par cas, les régimes fiscaux en vigueur et les nouveaux projets des États membres … » à la lumière d'une interprétation (plus) rigoureuse des règles en matière d'aides d'État.

Commission[9] et les *documents de consultation.*[10] À notre avis, ces documents ont une nature encore différente et ne rentrent pas dans le concept de *soft-law*, comme nous l'avons délimité ci-avant. En fait, d'un point de vue formel, normalement, ils ne reçoivent pas une approbation politique explicite de la Commission.[11] Ils sont livrés directement par les services techniques de la Commission et le simple fait qu'ils soient publiés sur les sites internet des institutions européennes ne peut pas leur donner la valeur d'un acte officiel adopté par la Commission.

Voyons maintenant plus en détail les *recommandations* et les *communications* de la Commission.

Selon la Cour, les recommandations sont « *des actes qui, même à l'égard de leurs destinataires, ne visent pas à produire des effets contraignants* » et ne créent pas non plus de droits pour les particuliers.[12] Du point de vue institutionnel, les recommandations sont « *adoptées par les institutions de la Communauté lorsqu'elles ne détiennent pas, en vertu du traité, le pouvoir d'adopter des actes obligatoires ou lorsqu'elles estiment qu'il n'y a pas lieu d'édicter des règles plus contraignantes* ».[13] Bien que cela semble être exactement le cas de la matière fiscale au sein de l'UE, les *recommandations* dans ce domaine sont peu nombreuses : nous en avons trouvé seulement cinq.[14]

---

9 Il s'agit de documents préparés par les services de la Commission – par exemple, par la Direction générale Fiscalité et Union douanière (ou par des consultants) et qui, généralement, accompagnent une Communication. Par exemple, l'étude *La fiscalité des entreprises dans le marché intérieur* ; SEC(2001)1681 du 23 octobre 2001 publiée le même jour que la Communication de la Commission *Vers un marché intérieur sans entraves fiscales* ; COM(2001)582 ; ou le Staff Working Document *accompanying Commission Communication Removing cross-border tax obstacles for EU citizens* ; SEC(2010)1576, 20 décembre 2010.

10 La Commission lance de plus en plus de consultations publiques *on-line* pour avoir l'avis de la société civile et du monde des affaires avant de prendre des initiatives législatives ; pour un exemple récent : Document de consultation publique, *Marché intérieur : demande de contributions sur des exemples concrets de double non-imposition et sur les moyens de remédier à ce phénomène*, 29 février 2012 ; *http://ec.europa.eu/taxation_customs/common/consultations/tax/2012_double_non_taxation_fr.htm.*

11 Dans le sens du Collège des commissaires. L'expression *Commission européenne* désigne à la fois l'apparat administratif et le Collège des commissaires qui prennent des décisions collectives sur la base de propositions présentées par un ou plusieurs commissaires.

12 Arrêt de la CJCE du 13 décembre 1989 ; affaire C-322/88, *Grimaldi*, 16.

13 CJCE, C-322/88, *supra*, note 12, 13.

14 94/79/CE, 21 décembre 1993 *relative à l'imposition des non-résidents* ; 94/390/CE, 25 mai 1994, *concernant le mode d'imposition des PME* ; 2000/789/CE, 29 novembre 2000 fixant *des orientations sur les entrepositaires des produits soumis à accise* ; 2009/784/CE, 19 octobre 2009 *sur les procédures de réduction de la retenue*

Les *communications* sont certainement plus fréquentes. Une *communication* de la Commission européenne est un acte autonome de cette institution : sa validité ne dépend pas d'une décision du Parlement ou du Conseil et n'engage que la Commission.

Il existe une grande variété de *communications*, mais il n'y a pas de véritable classification officielle.[15] Certaines communications ont des noms particuliers : *livre vert, livre blanc* ou *plan d'action*, en fonction de leur objectif, leur stade de développement ou du destinataire final. Un cas particulier est la *communication interprétative*. Il s'agit encore une fois d'un acte autonome qui n'engage que la Commission, étant donné que l'interprétation contraignante du droit de l'UE est réservée à la Cour. Ce dernier type de communication n'est pas fréquent en matière fiscale. Il s'agit d'un document que la Commission adopte après un acte du Conseil pour expliquer les aspects techniques de l'acte et de son application. Vu que les *Directives* du Conseil en matière de fiscalité – notamment en matière de fiscalité directe – ne sont pas fréquentes, cela ne procure pas à la Commission beaucoup de travail supplémentaire pour interpréter ou compléter le droit fiscal secondaire.[16]

3. La politique fiscale européenne et la *soft-law*

Longtemps, la Commission a considéré que son rôle principal était de promouvoir une législation fiscale harmonisée proposant des *Projets de Directive* (ou des *Projets de Règlements*) et que c'était le seul moyen pour progresser en matière fiscale. Les Directives et Règlements ont l'avantage d'être des instruments contraignants qui bénéficient d'une longue discussion au sein des institutions européennes avant d'être adoptés et d'offrir une grande sécurité juridique grâce au contrôle de la Cour sur leur légalité et correcte application. Toutefois, en raison de la règle de l'unanimité en matière fiscale, il est assez difficile pour la Commission de mener à bien cette politique. En fait, à ce jour, le processus d'harmonisation fiscale a eu des résultats très limités. Ainsi, l'approche non contraignante, plus que l'effet d'une nouvelle stratégie,

---

à la source ; 2011/856/UE, 15 décembre 2011 *relative aux mesures permettant d'éviter la double imposition des successions.*

15 Une certaine doctrine a essayé de classifier les actes non contraignants sur la base de leur fonction et objectif ; v. Gribnau, H., « Improving the Legitimacy of Soft Law in EU Tax Law », *Intertax*, vol. 1, 2007, p. 33.

16 V., par exemple, le *Règlement d'exécution* (UE) n° 815/2012 de la Commission du 13 septembre 2012, d'application du règlement (UE) n° 904/2010 du Conseil sur les régimes particuliers de TVA applicables aux assujettis non établis dans l'UE ; J.O. L249, 14 septembre 2012, 3.

représente tout simplement la seule alternative possible si on veut que la Commission maintienne un rôle sur les questions fiscales.[17]

Un exemple plus récent de l'utilisation par la Commission de l'approche non contraignante en matière fiscale est la *coordination fiscale*. Dans sa communication intitulée *Coordination des systèmes de fiscalité directe des États membres dans le marché intérieur*[18] la Commission a estimé qu'il est extrêmement important de s'assurer que les 28 systèmes fiscaux nationaux, non harmonisés, travaillent bien ensemble, afin d'éviter des obstacles tels que la *discrimination fiscale* et la *double imposition* et de prévenir l'*érosion des assiettes fiscales* des États membres.[19] Souhaitant jouer un rôle actif dans la coordination des politiques fiscales des États membres, la Commission utilise à nouveau des instruments de *soft-law* pour lancer ce processus : les trois communications publiées par la Commission sur différents sujets de fiscalité[20] constituent un effort concret pour stimuler et traiter de manière cohérente, la coopération entre les États membres.

4. Impact des actes non contraignants de l'UE sur les décisions de la Cour

Voyons maintenant certaines « contaminations » – directes ou indirectes – de l'approche *soft-law* de l'UE sur les arrêts de la Cour ou sur les opinions des avocats généraux.

Il est rare – du moins en fiscalité – que la Cour prenne en compte, dans ses décisions, les instruments non contraignants des institutions de

---

17 « Le recours à des approches non législatives ou à des solutions juridiques non contraignantes pourrait être particulièrement efficace lorsqu'elles ont un fondement juridique solide, reposant sur le Traité et la jurisprudence de la Cour de justice. Dans ces cas, des instruments tels que des communications, des recommandations, des lignes directrices et des documents interprétatifs peuvent fournir aux États membres des orientations sur l'application des principes du Traité et favoriser l'élimination rapide des obstacles au marché intérieur » ; Communication du 23 mai 2001, Politique fiscale de l'Union européenne – Priorités pour les prochaines années ; COM(2001)260, 25.

18 « Une meilleure coopération entre les États membres et une meilleure coordination de leurs règles amélioreront considérablement les résultats de leurs systèmes fiscaux. … [qui] contribueront mieux au succès du marché intérieur … et au renforcement de la compétitivité des entreprises de l'Union au niveau mondial conformément à la stratégie de Lisbonne » ; COM(2006)823, du 19 décembre 2006, 3-4.

19 COM(2006)823, 19 décembre 2006, 4.

20 Commission européenne, Le traitement fiscal des pertes dans les situations transfrontalières ; COM(2006)824, 19 décembre 2006 ; Imposition à la sortie et nécessité de coordonner les politiques fiscales des États membres ; COM(2006)825 du 19 décembre 2006 ; L'application des mesures de lutte contre les abus dans le domaine de la fiscalité directe ; COM(2007)785, 10 décembre 2007.

l'UE. Les avocats généraux sont un peu plus « généreux » : parfois ils citent des instruments de *soft-law* de la Commission et les utilisent pour argumenter leurs *conclusions*. Nous en avons choisi quelques exemples en fiscalité directe et indirecte.

L'avocat général Sharpston dans une affaire de TVA concernant l'interprétation de l'Article 24 de la Sixième Directive TVA (77/388/CEE) qui autorise l'application de procédures simplifiées pour les petites entreprises[21] note que la notion de « *petite entreprise* » n'est pas définie dans la Directive. Par conséquent, elle estime raisonnable la position de la Commission, qui fait référence à ses recommandations concernant la définition des PME :[22] « *Bien que je ne pense pas qu'une définition formelle des petites entreprises doive nécessairement être appliquée au secteur de la TVA alors qu'elle n'a pas été élaborée spécifiquement pour ce domaine, une telle définition fournit néanmoins une indication utile de ce que le législateur communautaire considère comme une ... "petite entreprise"* ».[23]

Dans la célèbre affaire *Marks & Spencer*,[24] l'avocat général Poiares Maduro, dans ses *conclusions*, cite une communication de la Commission[25] pour souligner que l'absence de toute disposition relative à la compensation transfrontalière des pertes intragroupe dans l'UE constitue un obstacle au bon fonctionnement du marché intérieur. L'avocat général, avec une petite touche d'ironie, ajoute : « *le Conseil a probablement de fortes raisons pour ne point s'être engagé dans la voie* [législative] *préconisée par la Commission. Dans ces conditions, il n'appartient pas à la Cour de se substituer au législateur communautaire* ».[26]

D'autres références à des instruments non contraignants de la Commission peuvent être trouvées dans les affaires *Assurandør,*[27] *A.,*[28]

---

21 Arrêt de la CJCE, 28 septembre 2006 ; affaire C-128/05, *Commission / Autriche*.

22 Commission européenne, Recommandation 96/280/CE, 3 avril 1996 *concernant la définition des petites et moyennes entreprises* ; J.O. L107, 30 avril 1996, 4 ; Recommandation 2003/361/CE, 6 mai 2003 *concernant la définition des micro, petites et moyennes entreprises* ; J.O. L124, 20 mai 2003, 36.

23 Affaire C-128/05, *supra*, note 21 ; conclusions de l'avocat général du 27 avril 2006, 36.

24 Arrêt de la CJCE, 13.12.2005 ; affaire C-446/03, *Marks & Spencer*.

25 Communication *Un marché intérieur sans obstacle lié à la fiscalité des entreprises : réalisations, initiatives en cours et défis restants* ; COM(2003)726, 24 novembre 2003.

26 Affaire C-446/03, *supra*, note 24 ; conclusions de l'avocat général, 7 avril 2005, 4.

27 Affaire C-8/01, *Assurandør* ; conclusions de l'avocat général Micho, 3 octobre 2002, 81.

Sevic,[29] *Commission/Grèce,*[30] *FCE Bank,*[31] *Cobelfret*[32] et dans d'autres affaires fiscales.

Plus fréquemment, la Cour (ou l'avocat général) mentionne la *soft-law* du Conseil. Par exemple, dans les affaires *Cadbury,*[33] *Thin Cap,*[34] *ELISA*[35] et *Columbus*[36] quatre avocats généraux différents ont cité le *Code de conduite sur la fiscalité des entreprises,*[37] même s'ils l'ont fait seulement pour souligner la primauté des libertés fondamentales du traité sur les instruments de *soft-law*, même sur ceux qui sont adoptés à l'unanimité au sein du Conseil.

5. Impact des actes non contraignants de l'UE sur les décisions des tribunaux nationaux

En appliquant le droit national, les juges nationaux doivent, dans la mesure du possible, l'interpréter de manière conforme aux exigences du droit de l'UE.[38] Les tribunaux nationaux sont-ils obligés de prendre en compte les actes non contraignants des institutions européennes ? Quel effet peut avoir la *soft-law* sur leurs décisions ?

Selon la Cour, « [les] *recommandations* ... [sont] *des actes qui, même à l'égard de leurs destinataires, ne visent pas à produire des effets contraignants. Dès lors,* [elles] *ne sauraient créer des droits que les particuliers puissent invoquer devant un juge national* ».[39] Toutefois, dans le même arrêt, la Cour déclare : « *Cependant ... il convient de souligner que les actes en question ne peuvent être considérés pour*

28 Affaire C-101/05, *Skatteverket v A.* ; conclusions de l'avocat général Bot, 11 novembre 2007, 149.

29 Arrêt de la CJCE, 13 décembre 2005 ; affaire C-411/03, *Sevic* ; 25.

30 Arrêt de la CJCE, 20 septembre 2007 ; affaire C-74/06, *Commission / Grèce* ; 22.

31 Affaire C-210/04, *FCE Bank* ; conclusions de l'avocat général Léger, 29 septembre 2005, 45.

32 Affaire C-138/07, *Cobelfret NV* ; conclusions de l'avocat général Sharpston, 8 mai 2008, 28.

33 Affaire C-196/04, *Cadbury Schweppes* ; conclusions de l'avocat général Léger, 2 mai 2006, 56-57.

34 Affaire C-524/04, *Thin Cap Group Litigation* ; conclusions de l'avocat général Geelhoed, 29 juin 2006, 63.

35 Affaire C-455/05, *E.L.I.S.A.* ; conclusions de l'avocat général Mazák, 26 avril 2007, 114.

36 Affaire C-298/05, *Columbus Container* ; conclusions de l'avocat général Mengozzi, 29 mars 2007, 163.

37 V. *supra*, note 5.

38 Entre autres, arrêt de la CJCE, 26 septembre 2000 ; affaire C-262/97, *Engelbrecht*, 29.

39 C-322/88, *Grimaldi, supra*, note 12, 16.

autant comme dépourvus de tout effet juridique. En effet, les juges nationaux sont tenus de prendre les recommandations en considération en vue de la solution des litiges qui leur sont soumis, notamment lorsque celles-ci éclairent l'interprétation de dispositions nationales prises dans le but d'assurer leur mise en œuvre, ou encore lorsqu'elles ont pour objet de compléter des dispositions communautaires ayant un caractère contraignant ».[40]

En pratique, les citoyens ne peuvent pas invoquer la *soft-law* de la même façon que les dispositions contraignantes de l'UE, parce que la *soft-law* ne crée pas des droits subjectifs. Néanmoins, ils peuvent argumenter et mieux définir leurs droits avec l'aide des instruments juridiques non contraignants et les tribunaux nationaux, en décidant l'affaire, doivent en tenir compte.

Après une enquête rapide, il nous semble que, au moins en matière fiscale, les tribunaux nationaux ne prennent pas souvent en considération la *soft-law* de l'UE pour former leurs décisions.[41] Voyons quand même deux exceptions intéressantes de cours suprêmes des États membres.

Dans une décision du *Hoge Raad der Nederlanden* en matière de taux réduit de TVA sur les services,[42] la cour néerlandaise (après avoir répété le principe consolidé que l'interprétation du droit national donnée par les juridictions nationales doit toujours être conforme au droit de l'UE) expose dans ses argumentations d'autres éléments qui méritent notre attention. À ce propos, il est nécessaire de présenter les faits en question.

Le contribuable de cette affaire avait aussi déposé une plainte auprès de la Commission européenne contre les Pays-Bas, considérant que sa mise en œuvre de la Sixième directive TVA (77/388/CEE) était contraire au droit de l'UE. En réponse à cette plainte, la Commission avait envoyé une *lettre de mise en demeure*[43] aux autorités néerlandaises pour demander des informations sur l'application aux Pays-Bas des taux réduits de la TVA, indiquant de manière informelle, des lignes directrices pour faciliter l'identification des catégories spéciales pouvant en

40 C-322/88, *Grimaldi*, *supra*, note 12, 18.

41 Ils le font bien plus souvent en matière d'aides d'État. Et cela semble assez raisonnable si on tient compte des différents rôles couverts par la Commission dans ces deux domaines.

42 HR 43.169 (AZ3758) 10.8.2007 ; v. Weber, D., « Legal consequences of the applicability of Community law », *Legal Remedies in European Tax Law*, 2009, p. 61.

43 La *lettre de mise en demeure* représente la première phase de la *procédure d'infraction* ; elle permet aux États membres d'être informés sur le lancement de la procédure, de présenter leurs observations et, le cas échéant, de se conformer volontairement au droit primaire ou secondaire de l'UE évitant la suite du contentieux.

bénéficier selon la Directive en question.[44] Les observations formulées par la Commission aux autorités néerlandaises dans cette lettre ont été littéralement utilisées comme argumentation par la cour nationale pour rejeter l'appel du gouvernement néerlandais. La cour n'a fait aucune référence explicite à l'acte de la Commission, mais son influence indirecte sur la formulation de la décision finale de la cour est évidente.

Dans une demande de décision préjudicielle,[45] la *Corte suprema di cassazione* italienne s'est adressée à la Cour pour savoir si les avantages fiscaux italiens « *accordés aux sociétés coopératives ... sont compatibles avec le droit de la concurrence* » – en substance, si ces avantages sont qualifiables d'aides d'État au sens de l'Article 107 TFUE – et si « *l'utilisation de la forme juridique de la société coopérative ... peut être qualifiée d'abus de droit, lorsque le recours à cette forme sociale a lieu dans le but exclusif ou principal de réaliser une économie d'impôt* ». Dans son *ordinanza*, en motivant ses questions à la Cour, le juge de cassation italien ne fait pas seulement référence à la pratique de la Commission en matière d'aides d'État[46] – ce qui serait normal, compte tenu du rôle de la Commission dans cette matière – mais cite également une communication de la Commission pour promouvoir le recours aux coopératives en Europe.[47] Cette communication affirme : « *un traitement fiscal particulier peut être opportun, mais dans tous les aspects de la réglementation sur les coopératives, il conviendrait de respecter le principe selon lequel les protections ou avantages accordés à un type d'entité particulier doivent être proportionnés ... et ne devraient pas conduire à la concurrence déloyale. En plus, tout autre "avantage" accordé ne doit pas permettre le détournement de la forme coopérative par des coopératives fictives qui entendent échapper à leurs obligations en matière ... de gouvernance d'entreprise. La Commission invite les États membres, lorsqu'ils envisagent un traitement fiscal approprié et proportionné ... à veiller tout particulièrement à ce que ces dispositions ne créent pas de situations anticoncurrentielles* ». L'influence des actes non contraignants de la Commission sur la conduite du juge italien nous semble tout à fait évidente.

---

44 Sixième directive (77/388/CEE) ; Annexe H – *Liste des livraisons de biens et de prestations de services pouvant faire l'objet de taux réduit* (cat. 13).

45 Corte Suprema di Cassazione, *Ordinanze* n.3030-3033, 8 février 2008 ; demande ex article 267 TFUE ; affaires C-78-80/08, *Paint Graphos ; Adige Carni ; Franchetto*.

46 Commission européenne, *Décision sur les avantages fiscaux aux sociétés coopératives italiennes* ; CP 73/2006, citée par la demande de la Cour suprême italienne.

47 Commission européenne, *Communication sur la promotion des sociétés coopératives en Europe* ; COM(2004)18, 24 février 2004, point 3.2.6.

6. Limites de l'approche *soft-law*

Lorsque l'UE a une compétence législative, la seule façon de garantir la sécurité juridique et le respect des principes fondamentaux du droit, est d'assurer sa mise en œuvre suivant les procédures prévues par le traité, avec une participation active du Parlement européen et/ou du Conseil.[48]

Dans un document de travail, le Parlement européen a souligné que, dans le cadre de l'UE, les instruments juridiques non contraignants devraient être utilisés avec précaution étant donné qu'ils sont souvent « *équivoques, inefficaces et susceptibles d'exercer un effet négatif sur la législation communautaire et sur l'équilibre institutionnel, même lorsqu'ils sont inscrits dans le traité* ». En outre, le Parlement européen déplore l'utilisation des instruments de *soft-law* par la Commission « *lorsqu'ils se substituent à une législation européenne nécessaire en soi ... ou extrapolent la jurisprudence de la Cour de justice pour l'appliquer à des domaines inexplorés* ».[49]

Néanmoins, le Parlement européen – sans doute l'institution européenne la moins impliquée dans le processus législatif actuel en matière fiscale – reconnaît que « *cela ne signifie pas qu'il ne pourrait pas exister des domaines dans lesquels certains types limités d'instruments juridiques non contraignants pourraient être légitimement mis en œuvre pour concourir à la réalisation des objectifs de l'Union* ».[50] Les exemples donnés par le Parlement européen sont les communications et les lignes directrices publiées par la Commission pour expliquer l'application pratique de sa politique en matière d'aides d'État.

Le respect de l'équilibre institutionnel inscrit dans le traité n'est pas le seul obstacle à l'utilisation de l'approche *soft-law*. Il est clair que la *soft-law* ne peut pas être systématiquement utilisée pour remplacer les instruments contraignants du droit de l'UE si nous voulons assurer une complète transparence du processus décisionnel européen.

Enfin, la Commission elle-même, dans une communication sur la politique fiscale,[51] reconnaît les limites de cette approche qui nécessite des ressources importantes et, naturellement, est « *not directly enforceable in legal terms* ».

---

48 Parlement européen, Commission des affaires juridiques, Rapport sur les implications institutionnelles et juridiques du recours aux instruments juridiques non contraignants ; doc. PE 384.581v02-00 du 14 février 2007, 4.

49 Parlement européen, Commission affaires juridiques, Proposition de résolution sur les implications juridiques et institutionnelles du recours aux instruments juridiques non contraignants (soft law) ; doc. PE 386.366v02-00 du 28 juin 2007, 7.

50 Doc. PE 384.581v02-00, *supra*, note 48, 4.

51 COM(2001)260, *supra*, note 17, 4.3.

7. Conclusions

Si l'on peut reconnaître une certaine influence des instruments non contraignants de l'UE sur l'interprétation du droit par la Cour et les juridictions fiscales nationales, il ne faut pas, à notre avis, la surestimer.

Une comparaison intéressante peut être faite entre l'influence exercée sur les décisions de la Cour par les instruments UE de *soft-law* et celle exercée par un autre instrument non contraignant – très important en fiscalité internationale – le *Modèle OCDE.*[52]

Après avoir vu l'impact relativement rare de la *soft-law* UE sur les décisions de la Cour, on remarque que le Modèle OCDE est bien plus souvent cité dans les arrêts de la Cour en matière fiscale que la *soft-law* des institutions européennes.[53]

La Cour n'a pas toujours caractérisé de manière uniforme le Modèle OCDE comme source du droit.[54] Toutefois elle en reconnaît son autorité morale sur les principaux aspects de la fiscalité internationale, tels que, par exemple, la notion de résidence,[55] les prix de transfert[56] ou les gains en capital.[57] Une vérification rapide de la base donnée IBFD des arrêts des tribunaux nationaux[58] confirme la même attitude.

Cette approche plus favorable de la Cour envers un instrument non contraignant d'un organisme non-UE peut se justifier par le fait que l'OCDE délivre ses commentaires sur un sujet – la fiscalité internationale – principalement régi par des traités bilatéraux et du droit international coutumier. Aucune autre organisation internationale (ONU ou FMI) ne peut prétendre avoir la même expérience et savoir-faire sur le sujet. De plus, 21 États membres de l'UE sont aussi membres de l'OCDE. Dans la pratique, la *soft-law* de l'OCDE – par exemple, le

52 OCDE, *Modèle de convention fiscale concernant le revenu et la fortune.*

53 V les arrêts de la CJE dans les affaires C-337/08, *X Holding*, 3 ; C-311/08, *SGI*, 58 ; C-128/08, *Damseaux*, 33 ; C-105/08, *Commission / Portugal*, 5 ; C-138/07, *Cobelfret*, 56 ; C-114/06, *Lidl Belgium*, 22 ; C-101/05, *A.*, 54 ; C-379/05, *Amurta*, 72 ; C-524/04, *Thin Cap*, 47-49 ; C-150/04, *Commission c/ Danemark* 72 ; C-446/04, *FII* 66 ; C-470/04 *N.*, 45-46 ; C-346/04, *Conijn*, 17 ; C-210/04, *FCE Bank*, 39 ; C-513/03, *van Hilten*, 48 ; C-265/04, *Bouanich* 13-16 ; C-234/01, *Gerritse*, 45 ; C-385/00, *de Groot*, 98 ; C-324/00, *Lankhorst-Hohorst*, 39 ; C-436/00, *X et Y*, 54 ; C-136/00, *Danner*, 41 ; C-391/97, *Gschwind*, 24 ; C-336/96, *Gilly*, 24 et 31-32 ; C-107/94, *Asscher*, 47 ; C-80/94, *Wielockx*, 24 ; C-279/93, *Schumacker*, 32. Le Modèle OCDE est aussi cité dans plus de 25 conclusions des avocats généraux.

54 C-138/07, *Cobelfret*, 56, « pratique fiscale internationale » ; C-279/93, *Schumacker*, 32, « droit fiscal international ».

55 Case C-234/01, *Gerritse*, 45.

56 Case C-324/00, *Lankhorst-Hohorst*, 39.

57 Case C-265/04, *Bouanich*, 15.

58 Tax Treaties Case-Law Database (http://www.ibfd.org).

Modèle OCDE ou les lignes directrices sur les prix de transfert – sont formellement approuvés par une grande majorité des États membres de l'UE et leurs principaux partenaires internationaux. Alors que la *soft-law* de la Commission ne représente que le point de vue d'une institution européenne et, souvent, son point de vue n'est pas unanimement partagé par les États membres. En outre les instruments non contraignants de l'UE peuvent aborder un sujet – la sphère juridique européenne – sur lequel la seule interprétation contraignante revient à la Cour.

Malgré les limites de l'approche *soft-law* que nous venons de souligner, dans des matières comme la fiscalité, où il est impératif de trouver des alternatives à l'incapacité politique à légiférer, l'UE ne peut que continuer à soutenir ses politiques par des outils non législatifs. Seule une réforme des traités, qui compenserait la renonciation au droit de *veto* des États membres sur la politique fiscale européenne (avec un pouvoir de contrôle accru par le Parlement européen) pourrait rétablir un équilibre institutionnel correct et redonner aux instruments contraignants leur rôle régulateur, même en matière fiscale.

Pour évaluer l'impact des instruments de *soft-law*, il sera également utile de suivre les travaux du *Forum conjoint des prix de transfert*[59] qui, au cours des deux prochaines années, examineront comment les différents codes de conduite et lignes directrices adoptés depuis sa création en 2002 ont été mis en œuvre par les États membres. Cet exercice permettra de confirmer ou d'infirmer l'utilité des instruments de *soft-law* dans la mise en œuvre d'une politique fiscale européenne visant à faciliter le développement du marché unique en supprimant les obstacles fiscaux.

---

59 Le groupe d'experts dénommé « *Forum conjoint sur les prix de transfert* » assiste et conseille la Commission européenne sur les questions fiscales liées aux prix de transfert. Il s'agit d'un exemple intéressant de contribution à la régulation administrative en matière fiscale puisque l'ensemble des travaux a fait l'objet de propositions de *soft-law* de la Commission (*codes de conduite*), adoptées par le Conseil.

The Demise of the Principle of Equality of Economic Actors in Private Law

H.C. Stanisław SOŁTYSIŃSKI

Member of Poland's Legislative Council of Civil Law; former Professor of A. Mickiewicz University

1. The problem

In the 1990s, I was teaching a course at the College of Europe in Bruges on legal problems of economic reforms in the Central-Eastern European countries in transition. During those years, I also had an opportunity to debate many aspects of EU laws with other members of the College faculty, in particular Rector Demaret. He always had time to discuss various aspects of legal reforms in Poland. I also vividly remember our discussions about the future of the rapidly enlarged united Europe and the global economy. I was sharing with the new Rector my doubts regarding the super-optimistic vision of the future presented by many mainstream economists, mainly of the Chicago School and other futurologists who – like Fukuyama – were announcing the ultimate triumph of the inherited Western socio-economic model. I admit that although I harboured fewer illusions than the author of the "End of history", I did not expect that we would soon face a deep financial crisis, the crisis of the euro and the risk of insolvency of several old EU Members States that were viewed as models for new Member States, in particular Spain. Interestingly, this all occurred less than a few years after A. Greenspan repeatedly denied that there could be a housing crash in the US, assured that the macroeconomic risks are under effective control because such banks as JP Morgan scrutinize the balance sheet of Merrill Lynch before lending, and praised the innovation of credit default swaps that almost caused the collapse of AIG less than 12 months after publication of his "Adventures in a new World".[1]

1 Greenspan, A., *The Age of Turbulence*, London, 2007, pp. 233, 257, 371.

The main focus of this paper is the issue of growing departures from the principle of legal equality of economic actors in several important areas of private law and the rapid proliferation of special treatment granted to entities that are "too big to fail", "systemically important" or "too interconnected", to be treated equally. Such special treatment is usually bestowed on large-scale and sophisticated business players. As a result, legal inequality of participants of private law relations has deepened. Paradoxically, such unequal status of business actors has been introduced under the banner of freedom of contract, despite the fact that equality of business actors is still proclaimed to be one of the main foundations of a free-market economy and private law. Equally surprising is the fact that the growing list of exceptions from these principles have been achieved not by way of contract or self-regulation but as a result of lobbying aimed at "negotiating" legislative privileges, frequently orchestrated by way of secret negotiations.

Examples of deviations from the principle of equality will be illustrated by examples in the field of bankruptcy law, intellectual property and arbitration. Limited exceptions to the principle of equal treatment have been recognized in the past but principally in the form of special treatment of weaker parties (persons), such as victims of bodily injuries in tort actions, employees, minors entitled to alimony claims, consumers' rights against professional business actors, minority shareholders *vis-à-vis* dominant shareholders, etc. The principle of special treatment of the weaker party is dictated by the traditional postulate of fairness, one of the foundations of modern civil law heritage.

This Article focuses on the phenomenon of the growing role of special treatment and "bounties" granted to those business actors who are, by-and-large, economically strong and sophisticated market participants.

The Article analyses a few examples of departures from equality in private law. Because of a lack of uniform definition of civil law, I use this term throughout this paper to embrace such areas as bankruptcy law and intellectual property. Fortunately, in civil codes, the process of this curious affirmative action aimed at improving the status of the stronger parties in the field of substantive and procedural laws has been less visible to date. Privileged status bestowed to firms that are "systemically important" (for instance, in the domain of tax law) is beyond the scope of this essay but examples of tax cuts and preferential tax treatment for super-rich individuals are equally controversial. In the aftermath of the financial crisis, assumptions and socio-economic consequences of these modern bounties have been subjected to critical analyses by lawyers and economists, in particular in the United States. For instance, several recent studies illustrate the point that the bankruptcy priorities granted to netting agreements accelerated the financial crisis.[2]

I also illustrate the growing role of secret or at least non-transparent lobbying aimed at establishing special status for the most powerful industries. Lobbyists seek to obtain special legal status for their clients, try to limit their transparency obligations and scrutiny of regulators. Lobbying aimed at granting super priorities to parties of financial transactions, intellectual property owners and foreign investors illustrate this trend.

2. Special Treatment of Financial Transactions in Bankruptcy Law

A. The Objectives of Close-out Netting Legislation

During the last 25 years financial institutions have developed new legal instruments aimed at reducing their risk exposure when trading in derivatives, swaps, repurchase contracts ("repos") and other new financial instruments, in particular in the event of insolvency of a counterparty. Various types of netting transactions employ mechanisms similar to the traditional set-off but they are functionally and conceptually different from the latter concept. Close-out netting is usually described as an umbrella agreement covering a bundle of financial contracts between two parties, who have agreed that upon the occurrence of a predefined event (default), the party "in the money" (i.e. the non-defaulting party), all non-performed contracts covered by the netting agreement shall become due and the party which is "out of the money" shall pay a net amount to the non-defaulting party. Depending upon the terms and conditions of the umbrella agreement, often described as the "master agreement", close-out netting occurs automatically or at the election of the non-defaulting party. As a rule, the calculation of the net result of all unperformed obligations is performed by the party which is "in the money". The single net payment obligation constitutes the only obligation in lieu of all terminated contracts covered by the master agreement.[3]

---

2 Compare Roe, M.J., "The Derivatives Market's Payment Priorities as Financial Crisis Accelerator", *Stanford Law Review*, Vol. 63, 2011, pp. 539-590; Skeel, D., Jackson, T., "Transaction Consistency and the New Finance in Bankruptcy", *Columbia Law Review*, Vol. 112, No. 1, 2012, pp. 152-202, available at http//ssrn.com/ abstract=
1773631, pp. 1-18; Kacprzyk, M., Schnable, P., "When Safe Proved Risky", Commercial Paper During the Financial Crisis of 2007-2009, *Journal of Economic Perspective*, Vol. 29, No. 24, 2010, pp. 40-41.

3 Paech, P., "Preliminary Draft Principles regarding the Enforceability of Close-out Netting Provisions", UNIDROIT, Study LXXVIII L-Doc. 11, January 2012, at p. 3.

Netting is mainly a product of banks and other financial institutions that offer such agreements to other financial institutions or firms of the "real" economy. During the last two decades the denomination of "close-out netting" has become widely used in the standard agreements elaborated by market associations, such as International Swaps and Derivatives Association (ISDA), International Capital Market Association (ICMA) and European Banking Federation (EBF). This paper analyses the consequences of the special status of the close-out netting and its underlying transactions in the event of insolvency of a party to the umbrella (master) agreement.

B. *How and Why Financial Contracts have been insulated from Bankruptcy Disciplines?*

I. Arguments Pro and Contra Privileged Status of Financial Transactions (Eligible Parties and Eligible Transactions)

The prevailing model of bankruptcy law in the US and EU countries favours restructuring a failing firm's business and repayment of its debts, partially or wholly upon the firm's reorganization. Upon declaration of insolvency, creditors may not collect and set off their debts, even if they are due. The estate's administrator has broad powers. He may assume or reject outstanding obligations, recover pre-bankruptcy fraudulent conveyances when the debtor made payments or granted other benefits to its creditors for less than fair value, etc. The most fundamental principles of bankruptcy law are equal treatment of creditors and a directive of reorganization of the insolvent firm rather than its liquidation by selling separate assets of the state.

Banks and other financial institutions have long tried to receive special treatment in bankruptcy laws. In the United States, for instance, some financial transactions were insulated from the rigors of bankruptcy law in the Bankruptcy Code (1978). Despite a gradual expansion of the scope of the special status of financial transactions in the 1980s and 1990s, until the Bankruptcy Abuse Prevention and Consumer Protection Act 2005,[4] substantial uncertainty surrounded the range of transactions and parties eligible for such statutory "safe harbours". Also, judges sometimes applied a functional analysis of transactions upon which defendants claimed their insulation from such bankruptcy disciplines as

4 Pub. L. No. 109-8, §§, *et seq*., codified at 11 U.S.C. § 362(a) of 2000, here-and-after US Bankruptcy Reform Act 2005.

automatic stays, limitations on preferential and fraudulent transfers, and of *ipso facto* clauses.[5]

The US Bankruptcy Reform Act (2005) radically expanded the definition of protected financial transactions. The statutory list of contracts "liberated" from bankruptcy disciplines covers, *inter alia*, swaps, forwards, commodity contracts, repurchase agreements (repos) and securities contracts. Morrisson and Riegel opined that the concept of "protected parties" has become meaningless in the context of the "laundry list" of the names of popular financial transactions which were granted privileged status in the bankruptcy law.[6] The reform of 2005 granted the discussed privileges not only to banks and other regulated financial institutions such as commodity brokers, forward contract merchants, stockbrokers but to all "financial participants, defined as a clearing organization or an entity that entered protected financial transactions worth at least USD 1 billion in national value (or USS 100 million in mark-to-market value) anytime during the preceding 15 months.[7] This was just one example of the new principle that the big deserves should be treated with more respect than lower class creditors.

The "safe harbours" for financial transactions advocated by financial institutions and propagators of netting have been justified as necessary instruments for the protection of financial markets, including over the counter ("OTC") markets. Without these protections parties to derivatives transactions, swaps and close-out netting agreements would be subject to the automatic stays for extended periods and the bankruptcy administrator (trustee of a bankrupt entity) would be allowed to assume "in-the-money" contracts and reject "out-of-the-money" contracts in an effort to perform a successful restructuring the debtor. These characteristic powers of the bankruptcy administrator have been described ominously by the interested industry as "cherry picking". According to this view, losses from exposure to "cherry picking" and other bankruptcy rigors would undermine the stability of the financial markets.

5 See, Morrison, E.R., Riegel, J., "Financial Contracts and the New Bankruptcy Code: Insulating Market from Bankrupt Debtors and Bankruptcy Judges", Columbia Law School, The Center for Law and Economic Studies, Working Paper No. 291, 2006, http//ssrn.com/abstract=8783289. The authors cite, as example, in ReCrimi Mae, Inc., Bankruptcy Reports, No. 251, pp. 796, 801. The court was unwilling to agree, without solid evidence that a repurchase contract constituted a privileged sale of securities. Another example of judicial scepticism regarding special treatment of financial transactions was Lombard-Wall, Inc. v. Bankers Trust Co., Bankruptcy Reports, No. 23, p. 165 (Bankr. SNDY 1982). The Court held that a repo buyer should be considered a secured creditor rather than as a party to a transaction insulated from the impact of bankruptcy law.

6 *Ibid.*, at p. 28.

7 § 907(b) (i) (3), as codified at 11 USC § 01 (22A).

The second rationale for special treatment of parties to financial transactions is that repos, derivatives and, in particular, the netting agreements that may cover a dozen or more underlying contracts are too complex and too interconnected to be treated in the same way as other contracts. The complexity rationale is sometimes merged with the argument that many financial institutions function merely as middlemen. The whole clearing chain would become paralyzed if a broker were to be exposed to bankruptcy law restrictions.[8]

The third justification in favour of special treatment of parties to financial transactions has been that the application of the bankruptcy rules to financial transactions and netting would create a risk of market "grid-lock" and interfere with the handling monetary supply. US industry representatives and the Federal Reserve argued that without special treatment, the netting and swaps markets would be destabilised.[9]

The fourth rationale stresses the fact that netting reduces the risk arising under a cluster of transactions to the net amount, thus reducing the equity amount required by banks and other regulated financial institutions up to 85-97%.

The final rationale, which silenced "any lingering objections"[10] was the need to avoid systemic risks resulting from "domino failures" if the financial transactions were subject to the automatic stay and "cherry picking". Any delay to terminate a derivative contract or to net all contracts covered by a close-out netting agreement would have a crippling effect in the market due to the contagion effect.

The US Bankruptcy Reform Act (2005) was approved almost without any opposition although it dramatically enlarged the list of protected parties and eligible transactions, subject to special treatment. It insulated the counterparties to these contracts not only from the "cherry picking" and automatic stays but also from *ipso-facto* and constructive fraud rules (i.e. rules sanctioning debtor's payments and preferences granted on the eve of bankruptcy to related parties). Even the majority of US academics were silenced by the "systemic risk" rationale. However, in all fairness, some authors rightly observed that the policy underlying the overgenerous treatment of financial transactions by the Bankruptcy

---

8 Arguments presented in favour and against of special treatment of financial transactions are discussed by Skeel and Jackson, *supra*, note 2, pp. 8-11. See also Morrison and Riegel, *supra*, note 5, pp. 1-5.

9 Lubben, S.J., "Derivatives, Netting, Insolvency, and Users", *Banking Law Journal*, No. 112, 1995, pp. 638, 640; Krimminger, M., "Adjusting the Rules: What Bankruptcy Reform Will Mean for Financial Market Contracts", 11 October 2005, available at www.f.dic.gov. The debate in Congress in the 1980s and 1990s is summarized by Skeel and Jackson, *supra*, note 2, at pp. 8-11.

10 *Ibid.*, at p. 11.

Reform Act (2005) is slippery.[11] They pointed out that it is doubtful whether the new rules would assure market stability. Some critics expressed doubts as to whether drastic restrictions of the judicial functional analysis and granting special treatment to a "laundry list" of transactions that fit formal definitions developed by financial markets may actually reduce systemic risks. They observed, for instance, that protection for leveraged buy outs (LBOs) does little, if anything, to reduce systemic risks.[12] Finally, they also expressed concern that extending protection to any margin payments, settlements under a securities contract or any transfer under a derivative contract – even if made on the eve of bankruptcy and/or between related parties, except for cases involving actual proof of fraud – may result in pre-bankruptcy looting by insiders and make the task of the defrauded creditors more than troublesome.[13]

Following its success in the US, the financial institutions soon persuaded market regulators and policy makers in other jurisdictions to adopt similar "netting friendly" laws. The crusade orchestrated by the ISDA has resulted in a proliferation of "netting friendly" reforms of bankruptcy laws.[14] By the middle of 2011, the netting agreements and the underlying financial transactions had been "liberated" from the impact of bankruptcy laws in more than 40 countries. The EU Directive Amending the Settlement Finality Directive and the Financial Collateral Arrangements Directive provides that credit claims constitute an eligible type of collateral to financial collateral arrangements. However, the EU legal framework[15] making references to netting does not provide for substantive rules in the field of bankruptcy law.

A prominent executive of the ISDA explains that close-out netting is an essential component of the hedging activities of financial institutions and other users of derivatives.[16] He rightly stresses that swap dealers and

11 Morrisom and Riegel, *supra*, note 2, at p. 28.

12 *Ibid.*, at p. 28.

13 *Ibid.*, at p. 26. The authors illustrate their point by referring to transactions between Bear Stearns and Enron on the eve of the latter company's bankruptcy.

14 ISDA has over 830 members from 60 countries. They include the majority of dealers' associations that are in the business of privately negotiated derivatives and financial transactions, including transborder deals. The ISDA publishes standard contracts for users of close-out netting agreements and templates for transactions in OTC derivatives. See Werner, P.M., *Close-Out Netting and the World of Derivatives in Central and Eastern Europe and Beyond-ISDA's Perspective, Law in Transition*, 2012, at p. 49.

15 Directives on Settlement Finality 98/26/EC, Financial Collateral Arrangements 2002/37/EC and Insolvency Regulation 1246/2000.

16 Werner, *supra*, note 14, at p. 51.

other traders try to limit their exposure by maintaining a matched (balanced) book of offsetting transactions: "The result of this hedging activity is that, (...) the aggregate of derivatives activity includes a large number of inter-dealer and other hedge transactions that function largely to adjust risk positions and limit exposure to market movements".[17] The author points out that dealers do not wish to retain their exposures to unanticipated market movements. Legislative recognition of close-out netting that provides for insulation of such agreements from the intervention of an insolvency administrator's "cherry picking", "claw-back" claims in case of payments made by the insolvent entity on the eve of bankruptcy and other bankruptcy law rigors, radically limits the risk of the eligible parties (i.e. non-defaulting counterparties to financial transactions that obtained privileged status by "netting-friendly" laws).

According to the Bank for International Settlements close-out netting reduces risk exposure of the non-defaulting party up to 85%.[18] According to the British Bankers' Association, enforceable netting agreements would reduce the risk and capital requirements of their members for such transaction by 95-97%.[19] Thus, the objectives of the crusade aimed at assuring legal certainty for close-out netting master agreements elaborated by the ISDA are clear. Their main goals are twofold: (1) to minimise the risk of financial intermediators and (2) reduce the capital requirements of banks and other regulated financial institutions doing business in the field of netting (e.g. capital requirements under the Basel rules).

The result of close-out netting consisting in the reduction of risk and credit exposure from gross to net exposure under all contracts covered by the master agreement looks fine, as long as one forgets who bears the risk of insolvency (bankruptcy) of the defaulting party in the event of termination of the master agreement. But why only financial intermediators should be allowed to set off their claims under dozens of transactions when the remaining creditors are not allowed to exercise such right in the context of bankruptcy? Why do sophisticated financial dealers deserve special treatment and may avoid unwanted exposure when other creditors are subject to bankruptcy stay rules and should bear a higher risk? The propagators of netting usually do not discuss these issues or even reject the argument that the current status of eligible financial parties constitutes a case of unequal treatment of creditors.

---

17 *Ibid.*

18 Paech, P., Preliminary draft Report on the Need for an International Instrument on the Enforceability of Close-Out Netting, UNIDROIT 2011, Study LXXVIII C-Doc. 2, March 2011, at p. 17.

19 British Bankers' Association, Special Resolution Regime – Response to HM Treasury Consultation Document, 2009, p. 4.

The adverse macro-economic consequences associated with the growing privileges to eligible financial parties granted by Congress since 1978 were identified by a few legal scholars who expressed scepticism about the soundness of the policy of granting bankruptcy priorities. Several early studies alerted legislators that if the risk of one class of creditors is lowered by Congress, it would be transferred to passive and less sophisticated creditors such as consumers, tort claimants and employees.[20] These and other negative consequences of unequal treatment of creditors in bankruptcy laws materialized during the financial crisis. The frequently stressed rationale that special treatment of netting and other financial transactions in the insolvency law[21] is justified to keep systemic risk in check and avoid "fire sales", which could result from the application of the bankruptcy laws, looks rather unpersuasive, if not deeply discredited. The evidence from the crisis analysed in several legal and economic studies, published during last five years, demonstrates that the decisions to leave the market of derivatives largely unsupervised and special treatment of financial transactions in bankruptcy law did not contribute to keep systemic risk under control. On the contrary, solid data have been compiled which indicate that these legislative decisions constituted factors that had accelerated the crisis. Several scholars in the field of bankruptcy law presented evidence that the privileges granted to the "eligible parties" by the US bankruptcy law reform in 2005, that had been justified as keeping systemic risks in check, actually exacerbated the systemic risk. They triggered "fire sales" of collaterals of such defaulting parties as Bear Stearns, Lehman Brothers and A.I.G. by the parties "in the money" (e.g. J.P. Morgan and Goldman). Studies of the collapse of Bear Stearns and Lehman Brothers demonstrate how the statutory exclusions of the automatic stays first encouraged the non-defaulting parties to terminate their contracts and then to sell vast volumes of collaterals.[22] J.P. Morgan's actions on the eve of Lehman Brothers' bankruptcy are the best example of the effects of the statutory immunities from the automatic stay rule. The "party-in-the money" terminated the contract with Lehman, froze billions in securities and cash, and demanded an additional US 5 billion payment. Due to special treatment of derivatives, the party-out-of-money (Lehman) could not stop its privileged creditor from

---

20 See Schwarz, A., "Security Interests and Bankruptcy Priorities: A Review of Current Theories", *Journal of Legal Studies*, Vol. 10, 1981, pp. 1-3, 7-8, 11-13; Bebchuk, L.A. & Fried, J.M., "The Uneasy Case for the Priority of Secured Claims in Bankruptcy", *Yale Law Journal*, Vol. 105, 1996, pp. 857 *et seq*.

21 For the sake of brevity, I use the terms "bankruptcy law" and "insolvency law" as synonyms.

22 Roe, *supra*, note 2, at Skeel and Jackson, *supra*, note 2, pp. 12-13.

selling the assets by filing for bankruptcy and the bankruptcy administrator could not "claw-back" even if a transaction was made a few hours before bankruptcy, except in the case of actual fraud, which is almost impossible to prove.

The argument that the special treatment of the eligible financial transactions constitutes an effective mechanism reducing the contagion risk in case of insolvency of systematically important financial firms is also refuted by economic studies. A recent analysis of AIG's debacle concludes that the "safe harbours" replaced systemic risk in one segment of the market "*by another form of systemic risk involving 'fire' sales of qualified financial contracts and liquidity funding spirals*".[23]

According to recent studies, the main defect of the privileges granted to the eligible financial transactions consists in that they undermine market discipline because they offer the eligible parties super-priority rights. Unlike the other creditors, even many secured creditors, the privileged financial creditors can enforce their claims on the eve of bankruptcy,[24] in particular they can seize collaterals, whilst other creditors, subject to statutory stay rules, must wait for a decision of the bankruptcy administrator.[25] Their special status gives them, *inter alia*, a broadly defined set-off right. Finally, whilst they are insulated from the bankruptcy administrator's power to assume or reject the underlying contracts covered by master close-out netting templates, they usually can choose whether or not to terminate such agreement.[26]

The authors of these studies demonstrated that creditors of Lehman, AIG, Bear Stearns and other failed financial institutions displayed surprisingly low risk-awareness, if not negligence. They explain the surprisingly insufficient attention to the creditworthiness of their clients by such preeminent Wall Street investment banks as Goldman and J.P. Morgan. The bankruptcy privileges dampened their incentive to screen and monitor the risks associated with their transactions.[27] Mark J. Roe demonstrated that the super-priorities function as disincentives for market discipline and indirectly subsidize high risk derivatives and repurchase markets. He and other authors conclude that the US Bank-

23 Acharya, V., Adler, B., Richardson, M. & Roubini, N., "The Dodd Frank Act and the New Architecture of Global Finance" in V. Acharya, T. Coleym, M. Richardson, J. Walter (eds.), *Regulating Wall Street*, Wiley, 2011, at p. 298.

24 Compare the description of J.P. Morgan's tactics in Bear Stearn's insolvency, by Roe, *supra*, note 2, at p. 8.

25 Roe, *supra*, note 2, p. 7.

26 Netting agreements frequently give them a "wait and see" option.

27 *Ibid.*, at p. 16.

ruptcy Code privileges decrease the derivatives and repo players *ex ante* market discipline.[28]

There is ample evidence that the privileges granted to the eligible financial parties have neither increased the systemic stability of the financial markets nor reduced contagion effects. On the contrary, bankruptcy super-priorities contributed to the financial crisis, encouraged simultaneous liquidation of collaterals during the crisis, and exacerbated the information gap because the discussed special rights discourage counterparties from conducting solid financial audits. The disincentives to market discipline caused by these privileges encouraged knife-edge, systematically dangerous financing. This is illustrated, for instance, by Goldman's financing of AIG's and JP Morgan's overnight crediting of Bear Stearn. The latter firm's insolvency illustrates the problem. Bear's counterparties were willing to finance it for several years by way of overnight repos, until the debtor collapsed. Characteristically, both parties relied upon the Bankruptcy Code-created incentives and switched from traditional forms of financing (e.g. loans) to privileged repos. As a result, the percentage of Bear's repos financing climbed from 6% of its total liabilities in 1989 to 18% on the eve of its insolvency in 2008 (i.e. eight times its equity).[29]

Thus, the only assumption made by the advocates of special treatment of the eligible financial transactions have become "flash", namely, the forecast that the bankruptcy law reforms have contributed to the phenomenal growth of repo and derivatives market. In 2006 total financial sector debt was about twenty times larger than in 1981. During the same period, the interest rate derivatives market increased nearly forty times.[30] The rapidly growing asymmetry between the sluggish growth of the "real" economy and that of the financial sector raises serious questions about the social cost of the "pollution" caused by the systemic tail risk created by privileges granted to the financial actors and imperfections of the market regulatory schemes. Even "insiders" in the financial industry recommend examination of the costs of investment banking "pollution" and the role of regulations in tackling this externality.[31]

---

[28] Roe, *supra*, note 2, p. 5 *et seq.*; Skeel and Jackson, *supra*, note 2, pp. 16 *et seq.*; Acharya, V. and Bisin, A., "Counterparty Risk Externality: Centralized Versus Over-the-Counter Markets", 2011; http://ssrn.com/abstract=1788187, at p. 37.

[29] Roe, *supra*, note 2, at p. 20.

[30] Roe, *supra*, note 2, p. 3.

[31] See Haldane, A., "The US 100 Billion Question". Bank of England speech at the Institute of Regulation and Risk, Hong Kong, 30 March 2010. Some economists emphasize that welfare benefits of derivative markets are speculative and do not arise from fundamentals. See Singh, M., "Making OTC Derivatives Safe – A. Fresh

II. Post-Crisis Developments

The obvious fact that benefits granted to the eligible parties in bankruptcy law are bestowed at the cost of the other creditors is usually discreetly disregarded by the advocates of special treatment of close-out netting agreements in insolvency laws. But in 1999 Federal Deposit Insurance Company presented a reform proposal according to which the bankruptcy priorities for the eligible financial transactions were to be limited to 90% of the relevant debt. The proponent of the reform in the US Congress pointed out that, if enacted, the law would put pressure on lenders financing even large firms to check what sort of shape the firm is in, because no one was paying attention to Lehman.[32] This modest reform that required the privileged creditors to share only 10% of insolvency risk with all remaining creditors was effectively attacked by the ISDA and other advocates of the "too big to fail" fortress. They argued that the proposal would reduce leverage and liquidity in the repo market, destroy close-out netting and limit the growth of shadow banking.[33] These politically successful warnings that the derivatives and repos markets packed in close-out netting templates might collapse or shrivel without the powerful bankruptcy super-priorities show to what extent the rapid growth of these markets resulted from the privileged status and shifting of the risk onto other creditors rather than from their business ingenuity.

The financial crisis subjected the privileged status of the eligible financial transactions to a practical stress test. The basic assumptions of the policy makers and lobbyists of the special treatment of financial transactions have been, to put it mildly, undermined. However, the main reform passed by Congress "*demonstrates how remarkable the neglect of bankruptcy is*".[34] The Dodd-Frank Act established a new resolution regime for systematically important financial institutions that fall into insolvency but the new regulatory powers are outside the Bankruptcy Code. The Act borrowed a few provisions from the Bankruptcy Code (e.g. provisions modelled on fraudulent conveyances and preferences rules) but the new regulatory schemes that provide, *inter alia*, that swaps shall be traded by clearing houses, left the privileged status of the

---

Look", International Monetary Fund, WP/11/66, 2011, available at www.missing&imf.org at p. 17.

32 Braithwaite, T. & MacKenzie, M., "Creditors to Foot Bill in US Risk Regulation", *Financial Times*, 2 December 2009.

33 The opposition to this modest reform proposal is described in detail by Roe, *supra*, note 3, pp. 30-31.

34 Skeel and Jackson, *supra*, note 2, at p. 2. The authors comment refers to the Dodd-Frank Wall Street Reform and Consumer Protection Act, Publ. L. No. III-203, cited as "Dodd-Frank Act".

financial transactions in bankruptcy law largely untouched. It only provides for studies of bankruptcy law.[35]

Both the Dodd-Frank Act and the proposals made by the Financial Stability Board (FSB), a platform of international cooperation of financial institutions in Bern, provide that all systemically important financial market infrastructures should be subject to effective resolution regimes which provide, *inter alia*, that the resolution authority should have the power to order a short stay, for example for a period not exceeding two business day.[36] The FSB proposals recognise that termination rights under close-out netting could result "*in a disorderly rush for the exits that creates further market instability and frustrates the implementation of resolution measures aimed at achieving continuity*".[37] But it proposes cosmetic modifications of the privileged status of close-out netting. The modest competencies of the resolution authority include the powers to shortly stay such rights but only where they arise solely by reason of entry into resolution or in connection with the use of such resolution powers and provided that the substantive obligations under the contract and provision of collateral, continue to be performed.[38] The resolution authority would be permitted to transfer all contracts covered by a close-out netting agreement (no "cherry-picking" powers). After such transfer and a short period of stay, the early termination right of the netting counter party is preserved against the acquiring entity. If the contracts are not transferred to a "healthy" firm or a public entity, the early termination right may be exercised.[39]

In the event the resolution authority transfers a cluster of contracts covered by a netting template, the transferee will assume all the rights and obligations of the transferor. Paradoxically, the privileged counterparty will be in a more advantageous position than before the transfer because it will be able to enforce all its contractual rights to a commercially entity or the public authority burdened with the task of performing all obligations of a "systematically important" but insolvent financial institutions. The achievement of the objectives set forth in the FSB proposals is highly doubtful. The cosmetic limitations on early termination rights of "eligible financial transactions", combined with burdening the healthy "bridge" or public entities with all obligations of the insolvent entity, create a real risk of contagion when the privileged creditor

35 See §§ 202(e) and 216.

36 Financial Stability Board, Key Attributes of Effective Resolution Regimes for Financial Institutions, October 2011 at p. 42.

37 *Ibid.*, at p. 41.

38 *Ibid.*, at p. 41.

39 *Ibid.*, at p. 42.

rushes to enforce its contractual rights. The declarations of continuity of systemically important financial services, and assurances of an orderly exit of non-viable firms and fair allocation of losses without exposing taxpayers to loss,[40] set forth in the Preamble of the 2011 FSB proposals, are, putting it mildly, doubtful. The proposed powers for the resolution authority are much weaker than those of the insolvency administrator. The FSB proposals expressly adopted a key ISDA demand, namely, "no cherry-picking" powers should be granted to the resolution authority".[41]

It is tempting to imagine what would have happened if the FSB-promoted rules had been in place during the recent financial crisis. Imagine such resolution authority decisions made during a 48-hour stay on whether or to whom the super-priorities of creditors of AIG, Bear, and Lehman should be transferred. Also, consider the contagion effect of J.P. Morgan terminating its contractual rights and disposition of USD 25 billion collateral against Goldman just hours after the short stay. Imagine the consequences of enforcement of termination and other netting related rights by counterparties directed against a carefully selected "bridge" company that would have assigned such a risky portfolio as that which burdened AIG in 2008.

In all fairness, at least one essential objective elevated in the Preamble of the FSB 2011 document seems to be realistic. The Preamble emphasizes that losses of insolvent financial firms should be allocated to firm owners (shareholders) and "*creditors in a manner that respects the hierarchy of claims*".[42] Although, the privileged early termination rights granted to parties "in the money" by "netting friendly" laws are discretely not mentioned in the Preamble, privileges bestowed to financial contracts (collectively, early termination rights) retain their super-priority status in Annex IV of the FSB document. Thus, the quasi-feudal hierarchy of entitlements has been even strengthened, despite the lessons of the crisis.

III. Recent Efforts to Harmonize Close-out Netting Internationally: UNIDROIT Preliminary Draft Principles regarding the Enforceability of Close-out Netting Provisions

In 2008, the financial industry supported by the ISDA, approached UNIDROIT, the oldest UN organization specializing in the field of harmonization of private law, with a draft proposal for a convention on

[40] *Ibid.*, at p. 3 (preamble).
[41] *Ibid.*, at p. 42.
[42] *Ibid.*, at p. 3.

close-out netting. However, UNIDROIT decided to postpone the adoption of the project. Several members of its Governing Council expressed doubts regarding the proposed idea of supporting the concept of unconditional enforceability of a laundry list of derivatives and swaps in case of insolvency of a counter-party to a close-out netting agreement. When the Governing Council reconsidered the project at its 88th session in 2009, some members raised concerns but a study group on the netting of financial instruments was set up at the next session of UNIDROIT in 2010. In May 2012, the Draft Principles and Rules on the Netting of Financial Instruments[43] were presented to the Governing Council, along with the UNIDROIT Secretariat's proposal to submit the draft of a non-binding instrument to UNIDROIT Member States for further consideration.[44]

Whilst I share the proposition that harmonization of the close-out netting constitutes a reasonable objective and that the proposed rules are not ripe for elaborating an international convention, I had and I continue to have serious doubts regarding key proposed rules. My principal objections concern the proposed rules on enforceability of close-out netting and on formal requirements thereof.

Principles 4-6 of the UNIDROIT Draft Principles on Netting cover form requirements, use of standardized terms, and reporting obligations. They provide that the statutory formalities other than "in writing" requirements would hamper enforceability of netting provisions in a cross-jurisdictional context. Principle No. 6 proclaims that a failure to comply with a reporting duty "*should not affect the creation, validity, enforceability, effectiveness against third parties or admissibility in evidence of the contracts and the close-out netting provision*". I agree that the sanction of invalidity may be viewed as inappropriate, but the exclusion of all possible sanctions of enforceability and effectiveness against third parties of not only the netting agreements but also all the underlying contracts raises serious doubts. For instance, a sanction of ineffectiveness of certain high risk derivative instruments, until they are reported or registered in a public register, may undermine an effective supervision of the financial market by regulatory authorities. Furthermore, requirements of reporting and/or disclosure of such contracts, including those applicable to close-out netting provisions, *promote transparency and protect legitimate interests of third parties* (e.g. general creditors and customers of parties to close-out netting provi-

---

43 Here-and-after "UNIDROIT Draft Principles on Netting".

44 The following critical comments on the UNIDROIT Principles on Netting summarize my presentation during the UNIDROIT Governing Council session held in Rome on 7 May 2012. I served as Chairman of the Study Group on Netting.

sions). General creditors should be able to verify whether its current or future commercial counter-party is subject to a netting arrangement because this means that a cluster of its contracts is substantially exempt from *equal treatment of creditors* in the event of insolvency. Moreover, a netting provision may be concluded in breach of an earlier covenant.

During the works of the UNIDROIT Study Group on Netting, representatives of banks and the ISDA, and even some market regulators, argued that sanctions of ineffectiveness or inadmissibility in the event of a failure to comply with disclosure requirements would be inconsistent with the principle of speedy conclusion of financial transactions that are often made by phone or e-mail. In my opinion, "the deal done – bonus paid" canon of the current banking practice does not justify a recommendation that States should not introduce, for instance, a requirement of electronic reporting of certain high risk contracts to be recorded in a trade repository. Such requirements may be justified as a precondition of not the validity but only enforceability or effectiveness against third parties of some carefully selected high risk or large scale of transactions. The sweeping exemption proposed in *Principle 6 covers not only the netting provision but all contracts covered by a close-out netting provision.* The "no-formalities, deal done principle" is dangerous not only to third parties but also to the financial institutions. The myth of effective internal supervision by banks has been seriously undermined not only during the financial crisis but also recently.[45]

The UNIDROIT Draft Principles on Netting provide for very broad definitions of "eligible parties" and "eligible transactions". The latter term covers not only a long list of financial transactions but also contracts for the sale or delivery securities, money market instruments, units in a collective investment scheme, currency, any precious metal or any other fungible commodity, and any other type of contract designated to that effect under the relevant law (Principle 3d) and e)). This endless list goes well beyond "financial transactions". The main justification that "financial transactions" are systemically important disappears. UNIDROIT Principles, if adopted, would encourage parties to enter into two or three artificially connected transactions in order to assure the non-defaulting party special treatment in the event of insolvency. In all likelihood, they will need ISDA members to prepare a netting package.

---

45 Following the lessons of affairs of Nick Nelson of Barings, Jerome Kerviel of Société générale, Kweku Adoboli of UBS, J.P. Morgan lost more than 5 billion USD due to improper supervision of high risk transactions which resulted in the sharp fall of the value of the bank's shares until the discovery of the affair. So far, J.P. Morgan was viewed as a unique bank whose internal monitoring was almost perfect.

The enlarged list of eligible transactions set forth in Principle 3 speaks against the proposal proclaiming that States shall abstain from imposing sanctions of ineffectiveness and inadmissibility in evidence of certain derivative instruments and securities in the event of a failure of registration or disclosure of not only netting provisions but also the underlying contracts. Such sanctions may be justified for prudential reasons aimed at assuring transparency and protection of third parties. Publicly available information that a company is a party to a netting agreement is frequently more important to a potential counter-party than information that one or more of its assets are subject to a floating lien or mortgage. *Ineffectiveness is frequently imposed by laws of OECD countries in case of violation of reporting derivatives and specific capital market transactions.* Thus, for instance, a failure to disclose the transfer or acquisition of shares by a shareholder may even entail a sanction of invalidity of the transaction or the suspension of the right to exercise the voting rights from shares whose acquisition was not reported by the parties.[46] The ISDA also discovered that Slovakia passed a new law which provides that certain financial contracts entered into with Slovakian public entities shall be disclosed under the sanction of non-enforceability as of January 2012.[47] As a practicing lawyer, I was often confronted with clients' questions about what the sanctions are for disregarding a reporting obligation. Many companies accept the risk of a fine in order to benefit from hiding a transaction. It is widely reported that investment banks are frequently willing to devise equity derivatives to potential clients as tools for secretly acquiring shareholdings in listed companies.[48] Therefore, the sanction of invalidity or ineffectiveness is employed by legislators in order to assure observance of reporting/disclosure obligations.

During the works of the Study Group on Close-out Netting we have not analysed in depth the economic or systemic consequences of the proposal to recommend the elimination of the sanctions of ineffectiveness or a prohibition of any "*enforcement requirements beyond those specified in the close-out netting provision itself*" (Principle 7 a)). This sweeping exemption would disregard not only requirements of approvals by a judge during bankruptcy proceedings but also discourage the adoption of statutory rules providing that certain derivatives shall be traded by central counterparties (CCPs). Thus, UNIDROIT Principle

46 See, for instance, § 21(4) of the German Aktiengesetz and Article 6 § 3 of the Polish Code of Commercial Companies.

47 Werner, *supra*, note 18, at p. 54. Characteristically, the author, director of the ISDA, points out that such measures constitute a source of concern.

48 Compare Ferrarini, G., "Equity Derivatives and Transparency", in *Klaus Hopt Festschrift*, Berlin-New York, 2010, at p. 1822.

7(a) overlooks that regulators have been proposing, albeit with limited success so far, that a majority of derivatives should be moved to CCPs. The UNIDROIT draft seems to justify, subject to several conditions, that the competent authorities may only order a short "stay contractual acceleration or termination rights that may arise under a close-out netting provision" (Principle 8).

The UNIDROIT draft provides that "*the law should ensure that the close-out netting provision is enforceable in accordance with its terms, before and after the commencement of an insolvency proceeding in relation to one of the parties. Without the generality of the foregoing – a) the law should not impose enforcement requirements beyond those specified in the close-out netting provision itself.*" (Principle No. 7a). In the opinion of the financial industry and ISDA representatives, this is the most important principle. However, it raises difficult policy questions. A plain language interpretation of this principle implies that the basic function of the legislators is to enforce close-out netting arrangements in accordance with their terms. In other words, States should refrain from imposing any enforcement requirements or mandatory rules in this field. Such radical limitations of legislative powers is fully consistent with the ISDA Guide for Legislators that advise States to pass "netting friendly" laws that should remove obstacles to robust enforcement of the favoured contracts. These "primary obstacles" include insolvency laws, mandatory provisions enacted for the protection of debtors or certain categories of debtors outside insolvency laws, general principles of contract law and gaming laws.[49] Thus, ISDA legislative proposals not only treats some general principles contract law as "obstacles" but recommends that netting agreements and the underlying contract should be insulated from restrictions concerning gaming laws. Comments to the UNIDROIT Draft, Principle No. 7, try to qualify the textual interpretation of the proposed rule explaining that "*close-out netting is not shielded against every rule of commercial or insolvency law*".[50] Some official comments to the UNIDROIT draft note that close-out netting provisions would not be allowed to trump certain other fundamental rules, for instance, those relating to misrepresentation, fraud, or *actio Pauliana.*[51] However, Principle 7 expressly provides that the operation of the close-out netting should not be impaired by principles of equal treatment of creditors or the constructed fraud con-

[49] ISDA. A Guide for Legislators and Other Policy-Makers; March 2006, www.isda.org, at p. 3.

[50] UNIDROIT – C.D. (91) 5(c) Add. 1, p. 19.

[51] *Ibid.*, pp. 19-20.

cept when the defaulting party makes payment or gives preference on the eve of its insolvency.[52]

It is worth mentioning that leading restatements of *lex mercantoria* and the law of contracts stress the principle of freedom of contract but also contain an important qualification that the *autonomy of the parties is limited by the public policy mandatory laws and the parties may exclude or modify the application of the soft law principles, except as otherwise provided therein.*[53] Such limitations are totally disregarded in the UNIDROIT Principles on Netting. They emphasize only the freedom of contract principle because it is convenient to ISDA members but fail to encompass any rule aimed at protecting the public interest or eliminating practices which are basically unfair and have been held unenforceable in leading jurisdictions. Several members of the Study Group argued that the UNIDROIT Principles should address the issue of *walk-away clauses*[54] which provide that the net payment is payable only to the party that terminated the netting agreement but no payment at all should be paid to the bankrupt estate, even if it is a net creditor. Such a drastically unequal treatment of parties would be permissible under UNIDROIT DRAFT Principle 7. By contrast, US and EU laws treat "walk-away" clauses are unenforceable.[55] The majority of the Study Group has also decided to drop the issue of limiting a non-defaulting party's indefinite "*power to wait and see*". Certain netting agreements grant the non-defaulting party the right to withhold payments upon the default of its counterparty while at the same time not allowing the defaulting party to terminate the contract. It is worth contrasting this approach with the ISDA criticism of the bankruptcy administrator's powers to delay its decision to assume or reject contracts and its argument that a temporary stay ordered by a resolution authority should be limited to a maximum of two days, even in the case of insolvency of a systematically important financial institution.[56]

The ISDA frequently justifies its proposals aimed at assuring its members a right to "jump the queue" during insolvency and retain eve-of-bankruptcy fraudulent conveyances by pointing out that the powers of the administrator of the estate to assume or reject the debtor's con-

52 On the adverse consequences of insulating privileged parties from fraudulent conveyances payments or other benefits received during a suspect period, see Morrison and Riegel, *supra*, note 9, at pp. 25-26 and Roe, *supra*, note 2, at p. 588.

53 See, for instance, Articles 1.4 and 1.5 of the UNIDROIT Principles of International Contracts and Article 1.102 of the Principles of European Contract Law.

54 See, Doc. 4, p. 13.

55 § 210 (c) (8) (F) of the Dodd-Frank Act and Annex III, Section 3(b) iii of the EU Directive 2000/12/EC of 20 March 2000.

56 Compare Werner, *supra*, note 14, at p. 50.

tracts amount to arbitrary "cherry picking". But it is worth contrasting these powers of "cherry picking", exercised in the interest of the estate and all creditors, with the "netting friendly" laws that grant super-priorities principally in the interests of the financial industry. Indeed, ISDA lobbying efforts are basically not aimed at assuring "cherry-picking" privileges for its members but to secure them a whole "piece of the cake". To achieve this objective, the ISDA supported a long list of lucrative transactions, insulated from equal treatment of creditors. The UNIDROIT list of "eligible transactions" proposed by the ISDA extends beyond financial transactions and covers, *inter alia*, contracts for the sale or delivery of currency, gold, silver, platinum, palladium, or any other precious metal, and any other fungible commodity.[57] The forego-ing list of "mega-exceptions" to bankruptcy law disciplines, has little in common with the "systematically" important financial transactions. On 9th May 2013, the Governing Council approved the Draft Principles elaborated by the Committee of governmental experts subject to a few critical voices.

3. Patent and other Intellectual Property Rights

A. ACTA and the New EU Patent Package

Over the last 40 years, we have witnessed a significant strengthening of intellectual property rights. It was in the mid-1980s, particularly as a result of US pressure and subsequently due to the standards established under TRIPS, that the majority of its signatories had to incorporate laws ensuring effective protection of patent and other intellectual property rights. It soon turned out that the net beneficiaries of the new rules were firms from the US and a few other developed countries, whilst their markets have remained closed or difficult to penetrate by exporters of agricultural products and industrial goods from developed countries.[58] In the course of the last two decades Intellectual Property Alliance contin-ued its lobbying efforts aimed at extending the scope and duration of IP rights and sanctions for their violations. Recently, however, these repeated blanket extensions of patent and copyright terms have met with growing criticism in the US and EU. The phenomena of "patent thick-ets" and "patent trolls", coupled with a rapid increase in litigation, prompted even the Supreme Court of the United States to limit to some

57 Principle 3d.

58 Compare: Integrating Intellectual Property Rights and Development Policy Report of the Commission and Intellectual Property Rights, London, 2002, pp. 22 *et seq*.

extent the traditional "patent friendly" interpretation of patent laws.[59] Below, I will briefly discuss two interrelated questions: Do newest initiatives of the advocates of strengthening IP rights equally treat large firms and SMEs? Is the process of lobbying sufficiently transparent?

The Anti-Counterfeiting Trade Agreement ("ACTA") is a multilateral agreement. It was secretly negotiated and signed almost exclusively by developed countries.[60] Although ACTA is aimed at beefing up TRIPS, it was negotiated outside the WTO forum because the signatories were afraid that developing countries would this time demand trade concessions. Whilst the obligatory provisions of ACTA largely overlap with those of the EU directives, some of the ACTA provisions on criminal sanctions are not clear and conflict with freedom of information and privacy rights guaranteed by some Member States.[61] Numerous academics deplored the fact that the ACTA initiative was a "club approach of like-minded countries which excluded other globally important partners (e.g. Brazil, India, China and Russia) in the effort to impose agreed rules via bilateral agreements".[62]

ACTA unexpectedly triggered massive street protests of young people, first in Poland and the Baltic States and later on in "old" EU Member States. Soon afterwards, these protests were supported by hundreds of intellectual property and privacy experts leading to a rejection of the agreement by an overwhelming majority of the European Parliament in 2012. These massive and successful protests were prompted not so much by the substance of ACTA, but the lack of safeguards protecting privacy rights and, foremost, by the secrecy of negotiations during which stakeholders (i.e. internet users), critics of strengthening IP rights, and emerging market countries were not represented.

But the phenomena of secrecy, lack of transparency and proper representation of all interested parties during negotiations aimed at bestowing new economic privileges have continued apace. The current negotiations of a draft agreement for the unitary EU patent, and a draft agreement for a Unified Patent Court provide another illustration of this

---

59 See further Sołtysiński, S., "The Patent Reform Act and Recent US Supreme Court Decisions – A Correction of the Intellectual Property Policies? Patents and Technological Progress in a Globalized World", Liber Amicorum Joseph Straus, Berlin Heidelberg, 2009, pp. 856 *et seq*.

60 They are Australia, Canada, Korea, the US, Japan, Morocco, New Zealand, Singapore and the EU.

61 See Geiger, Ch., in Workshop on the Anti-Counterfeiting Trade Agreement (ACTA), Expo/B/Inta, FWC/2009-01/Lot 7/25 March 2012, pp. 55-60.

62 *Ibid.*, at pp. 53-55.

trend.[63] Basically, the long discussed idea of a unitary patent covering the entire EU market is sound, despite the fact that it will create new imbalances and strengthen the competitive positions of a few of the most developed EU economies, as well as innovative firms from the US and Japan.[64] New Member States ought to be prepared to make reasonable sacrifices in the interests of a long-term development of the single market. However, they should not be expected to support a new patent project which is deeply flawed and unduly favours mainly large patent owners.[65] First, inevitable imbalances will increase because the project provides that the new unitary European patents covering 25 EU Member States will be granted in English, French and German. Thus, the hitherto universally followed requirement that a monopoly right be granted in exchange for the disclosure of the best method of practicing the invention and that, in principle, its specification should be published in the official language of the jurisdiction where protection is sought will be abandoned in the interests of the most advanced EU Member States and third countries whose official language is English, French or German (e.g. the US, Canada and Australia).

Second, in principle, the same language requirements will apply during judicial proceedings before a new European Patent Court located in London, Paris and Munich. Thus, the owner of a medium-sized firm in Poland or the Czech Republic will have to study patent specifications in three foreign languages.

The third important principle respected in the EU conventions to date (namely, that a defendant shall be sued in a local court and may have to defend his/her case in the local language) will be also abandoned. The importance of the official language is illustrated by the fact that a compromise Spanish and Polish proposal suggesting the use of one official language (i.e. English) was rejected by those countries whose official languages are German and French.[66] The need to use a foreign language means that the patent system's information function will not be fully satisfied. It will also cause lack of legal transparency,

63 See European Commission, Proposal for a Regulation of the European Parliament and of the Council implementing enhanced cooperation in the area of the creation of unitary patent protection COM(2011)215 final.

64 The European Patent Office in Munich grants roughly half of its patents to US and German firms, and about 2% to applicants. Italian firms obtain about 3% of these grants. Polish firms received about 0.03% of such patents in 2011.

65 Italy and Spain, whose R&D potentials are much stronger than those of Poland and other new Member States, refused to join the new patent project and challenged it before the Court of Justice.

66 Ullrich, H., "Harmonizing Patent Law: The Untamable Union Patent", Max Planck Institute, Research Paper No. 12-03, pp. 13-15, http://ssrn.com/abstract=2027920.

which favours foreign patentees not only by giving them the said legal privileges but also forcing other market actors to operate at the risk of patent infringement. This is not only because the UK, France and Germany, the main beneficiaries of the new language regime, will be exempt from the traditional requirements of publication and conducting legal proceedings in the official language of the territory where the exclusive right is sought or enforced. The consequences of the new uniform patent package are best characterized by H. Ullrich: "*[T]he language regime produces direct and indirect costs over the lifetime of a patent for those who are not at full ease with its language, and it favours those who are familiar with it. [I]t distributes advantages and disadvantages (...) it enables the linguistic beneficiaries (...) to cover the entire EU-market, including the language territories of the non-beneficiaries by an exclusivity at no extra cost, extra effort of care and risk avoidance, which the non-beneficiaries seeking EU-wide act exclusion are asked to cover extra costs, which other members of the majority are not willing to make themselves*".[67] As in the case of the bankruptcy super-priorities, the new language regime not only bestows legal privileges for the strongest business actors but also shifts the costs of the reform to their weaker competitors.

Fourth, several prominent patent law experts demonstrated that the reduction of translation costs, advocated by the proponents of the uniform project, will mainly benefit a relatively small number of dominant firms which seek to obtain a large number of patent applications. These imbalances will be exacerbated on the level of Member States whose official language is English, French or German, in particular, those States where the three branches of the Unified Patent Court will be located (i.e. Paris, Munich and London).[68]

Hundreds of experts, including some Member States, criticized the new patent package, citing major gaps, lack of legal clarity and doubts regarding the process of recruitment of competent judges to be appointed to the new patent court. Even the basic rationale for the new patent system, namely lowering costs of obtaining patents, is being challenged. During the Polish Presidency (i.e. the second half of 2011), a promise was made "*to allow to all Member States that* they keep their current renewal fee income *while at the same time ensuring that those Member States which currently have a low renewal fee income will significantly*

---

67 *Ibid.*, at pp. 21-22.

68 *Ibid.*, pp. 13-14. The criticism that the largest firms will be the main beneficiaries of the project while advantages for SMEs are delusive was also expressed in the House of Commons of European Scrutiny Committee document: The Unified Patent Court: Help or Hindrance, HC 1799 (3 May, 2012), pp. 26-29, 39-41.

increase their renewal fee income".[69] Thus, if the patent renewal fees income of some Member States remain the same and fees of other EU countries significantly increase, the promise that the SMEs will pay less cannot be true. The majority of SMEs are interested in obtaining patent protection only in their domestic markets or in a few countries but they will bear the costs of obtaining patents and renewal fees in the whole European Community.

Fifth, the new EU patent package will multiply transaction costs resulting from the unclear coexistence of three types of patents in the uniform market: (i) the new European patents with unitary effects granted in 25 countries, (ii) the "old" European patents granted by the European Patent Office in Munich (the latter monopolies constitute a "bundle" of national patents designated by the applicant), and (iii) purely local patents issued by national patent offices. Such an unusual combination of exclusive rights will lead to a multiplication of the number of patents in every EU country, thus multiplying so-called "patent thickets", where "patent trolls" will be able to bring infringement suits also against SMEs. Many defendants will not be able to defend their rights in a foreign language and before a court located abroad. Even in countries where only one type of patent is available, the proliferation of patents due to unduly liberal standards of "novelty" and non-obviousness harms the public creating "innovation gridlock". Today, companies compete more in the courtroom than in the market place. Patent "thickets" are particularly harmful to start-ups.[70] A top European IP expert stresses "*that the unitary patent has been conceived of by interested circles mainly for the new forms of portfolio or pool based exploitation of patents as assets sold or licensed on standard terms by patent subsidiaries of large firms. The unitary patent virtually is not subject to any public interest lien (...)*".[71]

Not surprisingly, the negotiations of the European patent package were conducted largely in secrecy. Opinions of industry, especially SMEs, university circles and judges, were disregarded. Dr. J. Pagenberg, a member of the EU Commission's Committee of Experts, withdrew from this body at the end of 2011. He protested against negotiations behind "closed doors", the refusal to disclose drafts of the negotiated documents and refusal to address the questions and proposals

---

69 Pagenberg, J., *The EU Patent Package, Politics vs. Quality and the New Practice of Secret Legislation*, at p. 3.

70 IPhone, uCopy, iSue, "Not every innovation deserves a patent", *The Economist*, 1 September 2012, at p. 9.

71 Ullrich, *supra*, note 66, at p. 57.

made by future users of the system.[72] Pagenberg also concludes that, apart from numerous imperfections, the EU patent package takes into account the interest of the multinational corporations only, and disregards those of SMEs and individual inventors. The latter users of the new system should be able to apply for uniform protection in a few countries of their choice, "*combined with an efficient and affordable court system close to home and their local language*".[73] The EU patent package was adopted in 2013 when France, Germany and UK agreed that the Unitary Patent Court ("UPC") would be split into three central divisions located in Paris, Munich and London. Bulgaria, Poland and Spain have not joined the project. Spain instituted a challenge before the Court of Justice alleging that the EU patent project violates Art. 118 of the Lisbon Treaty. Whilst the doubts regarding the costs of the new EU patent system for stakeholders, in particular SMEs, are growing, benefits for the economies of the three countries that will host the branches of the UPC show an interesting distribution pattern. A recent publication of the UK Government indicates that the unitary patent will lead to direct benefits to the UK business of up to £40 million per year while the location of the UPC branch in London will benefit the economy up to £200 million per annum. The important point to note is that an inquisitive journalist discovered that the latter large sum represents additional income excpected by the UK legal profession which was generally critical of the EU project until London has become the host of the pharma division of the UPC.[74]

4. Bilateral Investment Protection Treaties and Arbitration (BITs)

I subscribe to the view that sees investor-protection institutions to be very important to industrial development. Judicial and administrative institutions that efficiently protect property rights and investments are prerequisites of sustainable development. But bestowing special privileges to foreign investors undermines the fundamental principle of equality of business actors and discriminates local business. Moreover,

---

[72] Pagenberg, *supra*, note 69, pp. 2 and 17-19. Professor Nowicka, who teaches intellectual property at A. Mickiewicz University (Poznań), showed me a reply from the EU Commission. The enclosed text of the uniform patent package contained only the Preamble and titles of all chapters, with the remaining contents deleted. Her criticism of the secrecy of the negotiation process echoes reservations made by Pagenberg and Ullrich.

[73] *Ibid.*, at. p. 22.

[74] J. Nurton, Managing Intellectual Property of 16 May, 2013, Unitary Patent Figures Don't Add Up, available at http://www.managingip.com/Blog/3206488/Unitary_patent_figures_dont_add_up.html.

it encourages the most efficient domestic firms to "emigrate" abroad at least by way of investing shares in their domestic companies in foreign held parent companies, thus obtaining a privileged status under the protective umbrella of BITs. It also transfers wealth from emerging markets to capital exporting countries.

In 1905, the US Secretary of State, E. Root, a Peace Prize Winner, argued that foreign investors cannot demand more rights that their local competitors: "*When a man goes into a foreign country to reside or to trade he submits himself, his rights, and interests to the jurisdiction of the courts of that country (...). It is very desirable that people who go into other countries shall realize that they are not entitled to have the laws and police regulations and methods of judicial procedure and customs of business made over to suit them, or to have any other or different treatment than that which is accorded to the citizens of the country into which they have gone; so long as the government of that country maintains, according to its own ideas and for the benefit of its own citizens (...).*"[75] The Calvo Doctrine provided that foreign investors may not seek protection abroad. A resolution of the General Assembly of United Nations of December 12, 1974 incorporated essential aspects of that doctrine in the Charter of Economic Rights and Obligations of States. But the BITs have completely reversed these legal standards. They have established preferential legal standards aimed at granting special status to foreign investors. Their privileges involve, *inter alia*:

– access to "friendly" arbitration fora after a short period of negotiations with the host State (usually six months). This privilege is described by arbitrators as "the best guarantee that the investment will be protected against undue infringement by the host state";[76]

– protection by a plethora of capacious and sweeping clauses such as "fair and equitable treatment", "the MFN treatment", "full protection and security" and assurances of "justified expectations of the investor". As admitted by the arbitral tribunal in EURECO v. Slovakia,[77] these concepts do not mirror protection available under EU Law. Several arbitral tribunals have held that the host country may not introduce legislative or other measures against "justified expectations" of the investor. Some courts of capital-exporting countries have issued decisions which have contributed to a deepening discrimination of host

75 Root, E., "The Basis of Protection of Citizens Abroad", *American Journal of International Law*, Vol. 4, 1910, pp. 526-527. The author argued that host states are liable only if they violate "the common standards of justice". *Ibid.*

76 Eastern Sugar v. Czech Republic, SCC No. 088/2004, http://ita.law.uvic.cg.

77 As reported by Peterson, L., "Investment Arbitration Reporter", Vol. 3, No. 17, at p. 7.

countries in arbitration fora. For instance, the Paris Court of Appeal gave a very broad meaning to the term of "foreign investment" as "any kind of asset invested in connection with economic activities".[78] Moreover, the court ruled that a legal action taken by the Czech Republic against the investor who concluded a lease contract in violation of Czech mandatory law amounts to a breach of a fundamental right of the foreign investor "*such as the right to legal security that the state must provide under fair and equitable treatment and under which investors' legitimate trust and expectations must be protected*".[79] This shocking decision amounts to a proclamation of a new investor's right consisting in dispensing him from respecting the host country's laws and imposing a duty on the host country to abstain from taking legal action against the investor.[80] The Paris Court of Appeal explained that filing a legal action violated the investor's "*legitimate trust and expectations*" protectable under the BIT, regardless of its legitimacy under Czech law.[81]

BITs are incompatible with the host country's constitutional principles of equality of business actors. Intra EU BITs are difficult to reconcile with Article 18 of the Treaty on the functioning of the European Union because they discriminate against firms from those Member States which do not benefit from such treatment in a given EU country. The Czech Republic brought a case before the EU Tribunal arguing that BITs are inconsistent with the Lisbon Treaty. Several authors and NGOs criticize the substantive law and procedural privileges granted to foreign investors.[82] Several World Bank and UNCTAD studies demonstrate that there is no evidence that the BITs materially increase foreign investment.[83] Critics of BITs point, *inter alia*, to the contrast in the economic

---

78 Czech Republic v. Pren Nreka, as reported by P. Duprey in *Journal of International Arbitration*, Vol. 26, No. 4, 2009, at p. 591.

79 As quoted by P. Duprey, at p. 603.

80 A commentator rightly stressed that enforcement of one's right is recognized by French courts as a fundamental constitutional right but it was refused to the host country because the Czech Republic failed to prove that the arbitral award violated international public policy.

81 *Ibid.*

82 Frank, S., "The Legitimacy Crisis in Investment Arbitration: Privatizing Public International Law Through Inconsistent Decisions", *Fordham Law Review*, 2005; M. Sornarajah, Evolution or Revolution in International Investment Arbitration? The Descent into Normlessness, in C. Brown and K. Miles, *Evolution in Investment Treaty Law and Arbitration*, Cambridge University Press, 2011, pp. 631 *et seq.*; P. Eberhardt, C. Oliver, *Profiting from Injustice. How Law Firms, Arbitrators and Financiers are Fuelling an Investment Arbitration Boom*, Brussels/Amsterdam, 2012, pp. 7 *et seq.*

83 Hollward-Dreimaier, "Do Bilateral Investment Treaties Attract FDI? Only a BIT but they Can Bite", *The World Bank*, 2003, pp. 3121 *et seq.*; UNCTAD, Bilateral Investment Treaties in the mid-1990s, United Nations, New York, 1998, pp. 6 *et seq.*

performance of Argentina, a country that was persuaded to execute more than 40 BITs and was exposed to dozens of foreign investment suits, and that of Brazil which has refused to sign such agreements.

5. Concluding Remarks

How can one explain the fact that policy decision makers are so easily "captured" by vested interests groups, despite the lesson of the recent financial crisis and evidence presented in studies that demonstrate the adverse consequences of departures from the principle of equal treatment of business actors? First, the power of lobbying organizations representing financial institutions, top intellectual property firms, and capital exporting countries, stems from their financial resources and political leverage. Thus, the invisible hand of the market has been gradually replaced by the visible hand of the lobbyist.

Second, general creditors, SME and other economic actors from emerging markets are not only weaker financially but usually badly organized. Paradoxically, the experience of recent patent negotiations in Brussels shows that the political leverage of young users of the Internet, who protested against ACTA, is much stronger than SMEs in old and new EU Member States.

Third, policy makers and executives of international organizations where economic reforms are prepared, and even market regulators, are usually inclined to approve proposals submitted by well-organized industries. My own hindsight teaches that the "gatekeepers" are usually recruited from the ranks of the supervised industries. Frequently, those officials dream of being hired by the industry they regulate. Moreover, officials of central banks and other market regulation authorities are often persuaded that granting privileges to firms in the sectors of economy subject to their control will assure a smooth functioning of the relevant sector.[84]

International organizations equipped with the task of preparing reform proposals and new conventions should try to avoid the trap or even avoid creating the impression that their fora are used to promote vested interests. When certain initiatives are financed by organizations representing vested interests and their recommended experts are paid from such sources, the host organization should at least assure the presence of reputable critics of the industry proposals. At a minimum, the opposing views should be considered and given thorough explanations in a final

84 During my chairmanship of the UNIDROIT Study Group on Netting, I was surprised that the majority of market regulators from the OECD countries and delegates of IMF, EIB and the European Commission usually approved ISDA proposals without asking difficult questions.

report. Unfortunately, both in the case of the recent EU patent package negotiations and works on UNIDROIT Principles on netting, these standards have not been observed. The subsequent studies, and the final explanatory memorandum accompanying the UNIDROIT Draft Principles on the Netting of Financial Instruments submitted to Member States do not contain a single reference to critical legal and economic studies of netting super-priorities, despite specific requests made during the works of the Study Group.[85] Such organizations like UNCITRAL and UNIDROIT are underfinanced and their executives are in a difficult situation. During the recent Uniform European Patent negotiations, the EU Commission explained that the opinions of hundreds of law professors, judges and SMEs were dismissed as the voice of alleged lobbyists or "interest parties".[86]

The problems with the close-out netting priorities, extensions of terms of protection of IP rights, and the recent uniforms European patent package is not that the two pertinent industries do not provide social benefits but that the new privileges are coupled with transferring costs to other business actors and consumers without solid cost analyses. Just like other critics of the bankruptcy superpriorities, I recognize the advantages of the close-out netting but I also see the pernicious effects of the sweeping bankruptcy privileges which enable sophisticated market actors to jump the queue of creditors in the event of their counterparty insolvency.[87] Whilst some special rules are justified (for instance, the treatment of a bundle of contracts covered by a netting agreement as a functional unity that should exempted from "cherry picking"), preferences on the eve of bankruptcy should be abolished and other privileges curtailed. Unfair covenants, such as "wait and see" and "walk away" clauses, should be prohibited. If the close-out netting agreements are equally important as the core banking business, then all repos and derivatives players should contribute to a special guaranty fund protecting taxpayers from the burden of bailing them out in case of insolvency. Without compelling evidence to the contrary, netting eligible transactions should be treated like other transactions. The list of "eligible transactions" shall be curtailed and sanctions for breach of transparency requirements should be effective.

Similarly, owners of intellectual property should learn from the lessons of ACTA and the EU unitary patent negotiations. Demanding

---

85 However, the UNIDROIT Governing Council recommended that the Chairman's critical observations be included in the materials submitted to UNIDROIT Member States.

86 Pagenberg, *supra*, note 69, at p. 2.

87 Roe, *supra*, note 2, at p. 38.

exclusive rights of unduly long duration and special remedies that are not available to holders of other property rights have already resulted in massive protests of consumers and the establishment of political parties promoting piracy. Criteria for granting patents shall be rigorously applied to avoid a proliferation of exclusive rights. Sham patents harm the public in many ways. They create innovation "gridlocks" and multiply costs by forcing firms to fight in courtrooms, instead of in the market place.[88]

A return to the principle of equal legal treatment of business players, subject to justified exceptions, constitutes an essential ingredient of a meaningful reform. Hitherto privileged segments of the economy, in particular the financial sector actors, should be most interested in such reform if they believe in free competition on an even playing ground and in diminishing the perverse incentives to make fast-and-hard deals without carefully checking the financial conditions of their counterparties relying on the bankruptcy super-priorities. For the financial industry, whose services and products are absolutely vital for the modern economy, it is also a prerequisite for recovering the confidence and respect of the public.

To date, meaningful reforms have stopped half-way and the elimination of the privileges constitutes the most difficult issue. Paradoxically, the UNIDROIT Close-Out Netting Project and the drafts of the EU uniform patent proposals demonstrate that industries having vested interests in the *status quo* try to "capture" the policy decision makers and obtain new privileges or "dilute" reforms. They defend the old privileges with the vigour of the French aristocracy that resisted reforms before the French Revolution and the Polish nobility that defended their privileged status before Poland's partition. Both groups were very much attached to their privileges and were also deeply convinced that they were "too powerful to fail" and "systemically important".

There are signals that some executives of the financial industry see the need to implement reforms that require sacrifices. Sandy Weil, the founder of the modern Citi Corporation, the largest global universal bank, publicly supports the Volcker rule that requires separation of investment banking from traditional core banking. Support has been growing for similar "ring-fencing" proposals in Europe (e.g. Vicker and Likkanen twin initiatives). Leaders of Citi (V. Pandit and M. Corbat) have been restructuring this universal bank with the aim of strengthening the role of the traditional banking and reducing the risky derivatives-trading.[89]

---

88 See iPhone, uCopy, iSue, *supra*, note 70, at p. 9.

89 *Financial Times*, 20 August 2012.

P. Singer, the Chairman of Elliot Associates (a lead US hedge fund) and a top contributor to Governor Romney's election fund, has recently outlined proposals for a deep reform of the banking system that goes beyond the Volcker rule.[90] He concluded that "conservatives who believe in free markets should also believe in sound fair markets".[91] N. Lawson, the UK's chancellor of the exchequer in the 1980s, also sees that the twin doctrines of "too big to fail" and "systemic importance" undermined market discipline, and fostered greed and incompetence in the financial sector. Industry leaders should realize that reforms imposed from outside are usually more painful and frequently implemented too late.

---

[90] *Financial Times*, 16 August 2012.

[91] *Ibid.*, Capitalism in Crisis, *Financial Times*, 6 February 2012.

Reflections on Equality

Substantive Values and Policy Outcomes

Takis TRIDIMAS

Sir John Lubbock Professor of Banking Law;
Deputy Director, Centre for Commercial Law Studies,
Queen Mary University of London

The principle of equality forms part of primary EU law and finds two legal bases. It is enshrined in the EU Charter of Fundamental Rights[1] and has also long been recognised as a general principle of law in the case law.[2] This paper seeks to explore some recent judgments of the ECJ applying the principle. Its judicial application brings to the fore the way the ECJ understands its function *vis-à-vis* the law-making institutions of both the EU and the Member States. A series of recent judgments illustrate an intensely policy-based and counter-majoritarian application of equality aiming at promoting substantive social and consumer values.

The ECJ understands the general principle of equal treatment as a substantive maxim of participation. Groups that are considered to be in comparable situations should be treated in a comparable manner unless there are objective reasons justifying differential treatment.[3] Whilst this understanding of the principle allows ample margin for legislative

---

1 See esp. Article 20 (equality before the law) and Article 21 (general principle of non-discrimination). Note that Chapter III of the Charter, headed "Equality", contains comprehensive and far-reaching provisions encompassing a number of positive and substantive rights whose normative content goes beyond the concept of equality strictly understood. It covers cultural, religious and linguistic diversity (Article 22); equality between men and women (Article 23); the rights of a child (Article 24); the rights of the elderly (Article 25); and integration of persons with disabilities (Article 26). The underlying premises of these stipulations are to honour human dignity and provide for equality of opportunity.

2 See e.g. Joined Cases 117/76 and 16/77, *Ruckdeschel v Hauptzollamt Hamburg-St. Annen*, 1977, ECR 1753, para. 7; Joined Cases C-27 & C-122/00, *Omega Air and Others*, 2002, ECR I-2569, para. 79.

3 See the cases cited in note 2.

discretion,[4] it does make for an activist court. The principle has two components. First, a determination must be made as to whether two groups are in a comparable situation. Secondly, if comparability is established, a determination must be made as to whether there might be objective reasons justifying differential treatment. Neither question however can be answered in an ideological vacuum. Answering them requires the Court to make a choice based on substantive values. Thus, answering the question whether two situations are comparable presupposes the adoption of a comparator on the basis of which the groups in issue are tested. The choice of the appropriate comparator entails in itself a judgment based on certain underlying values.[5] Furthermore, answering the question whether there is objective justification requires a balancing exercise juxtaposing the value of comparable treatment *vis-à-vis* certain objectives. Thus, both components of the equality principle are value-laden. In fact, more often than not the ECJ does not separate neatly the two components and applies them in combination.[6]

1. Equality as a principle of interpretation

An activist judgment is *Sturgeon.*[7] The case concerned the right of air passengers to compensation in the event of a flight delay under Regulation No. 261/2004.[8] The Regulation seeks to protect air passengers in the event that a flight is delayed or cancelled and provides for various forms of assistance and redress. The Court interpreted it as meaning that passengers are entitled to compensation not only where a flight is cancelled, which is expressly provided in Article 5, but also where a flight is delayed despite the absence of an express provision to that effect. The Court reasoned as follows. The avowed objective of the regulation was to strengthen passenger protection by redressing damage suffered by them during air travel. This was made clear in the preamble

4 See e.g. for unsuccessful invocation of the principle in the field of commercial freedom and economic regulation: Case C-127/07, *Société Arcelor Atlantique et Lorraine and Others v Premier minister*, 2008, ECR I-9895; Case C-210/03, *The Queen on the application of Swedish Match AB v Secretary of State for Health*, 2004, ECR I-11893.

5 See e.g. Case C-13/91, *P v S and Cornwall County Council*, 1996, ECR I-2143 where the ECJ and the British Government disagreed on the appropriate comparator in determining whether dismissal of a transsexual was sex discrimination.

6 See e.g. Case 8/82, *Wagner v BALM*, 1983, ECR 371, paras. 22-22; Joined Cases C-248-9/95, *SAM Schiffahrt and Stapf v Germany*, 1997, ECR I-4475, para. 55-56.

7 Joined Cases C-402/07 and C-432/07, *Sturgeon v Condor Flugdienst GmbH*, 2009, ECR I-10923.

8 Regulation No. 261/2004 establishing common rules on compensation and assistance to passengers in the event of denied boarding and of cancellation or long delay of flights (OJ 2004 L 46/1).

which expressly stated that the number of passengers affected by cancellations without prior warning and long delays remained too high.[9] In view of that objective, situations covered by the regulation must be compared by reference to the type and extent of the various types of damage suffered by the passengers concerned.[10] The regulation afforded a right to compensation to passengers whose flights were cancelled when they were re-routed and, as a result, suffered a loss of time equal to or in excess of three hours in relation to the duration of their scheduled journey. In the light of that choice, to deny the right to compensation to passengers who suffered a similar loss of time when their flight was delayed appeared unjustifiable.[11] The fact that Article 6 of the regulation expressly dealt with delays and gave passengers certain rights other than compensation was not seen as a barrier: these were autonomous forms of redress and did not exclude the right to compensation.[12]

From a majoritarian perspective, *Sturgeon* is a remarkable judgment. The Court appears to give little credit to the legislative process. It does not engage with the possible reasons which might have justified differential treatment between cancelled and delayed flights. Such differential treatment does not appear to be an irrational choice. It may be, for example, that the number of passengers whose flights are delayed is much larger than that those whose flights are cancelled. It would thus follow that the costs involved for the airline industry in the event that a right of compensation were recognized for delayed flights would be much larger. This would then have consequential effects on third parties such as their workforce or air travellers to whom the airlines would seek to pass the costs. One presumes that the legislature considered on a cost-benefit analysis that it would not be appropriate to impose such a burden on airliners. Furthermore, the judgment appears to depart from the language of the regulation. It would be difficult for airlines to predict on the basis of its wording that they would have to pay compensation in case of delayed flights.

There may be counterarguments. It may be said, for example, that airlines in fact have discretion in classifying a departure from schedule as a delay or a cancellation and could thus circumvent the requirements

9 Preamble, recital 3.

10 Para. 49.

11 Paras. 57-58.

12 Para. 66. Cf. the earlier judgment in Case C-344/04, *IATA and ELFAA*, 2006, ECR I-403 where the Court dismissed a challenge to the validity of Regulation No. 261/2004 stating that Articles 5 and 6 lay down "precisely and clearly" the obligations owed by an air carrier in the event of cancellation or long delay and that the preamble of a measure cannot be relied on as a ground for derogating from its provisions: see paras. 69 and 76 of that judgment.

of the regulation. But this argument is open to question. First, the ECJ did not base its finding on it. Secondly, were that to be the case, the mischief of the regulation would lie in its deficient drafting which would make it difficult for it to attain its objectives. The regulation would be vitiated not because of the breach of the principle of equality but because of internal inconsistency. In support of the Court's reasoning, it is correct to say that the regulation created a difference in treatment. It granted a right to compensation where rerouting of a cancelled flight led to a delay in excess of three hours but not where a similar delay occurred in the case of a delayed flight. Also, it does not appear from the judgment or the opinion of the Advocate General that the Council invoked any specific reasons to justify that difference. Furthermore, the Court did point out that, under the regulation, air carriers are not obliged to pay compensation if they can prove that the cancellation or long delay is caused by extraordinary circumstances beyond their control. Be this as it may, *Sturgeon* illustrates a heavily value-based application of equal treatment which does affect the allocation of property rights. It may be that the Court felt that the legislative process is not able to take account properly of the interests of consumers whilst it can properly take on board the interests of the airline industry. But it is unlikely that the judgment was motivated by a careful assessment of the participation opportunities afforded to competing interests in the decision-making process. The explanation lies in the emphasis placed by the legislature on consumer protection. A high level of consumer protection is the avowed objective of the regulation and, more generally, EU internal market competence.[13] This underlying objective led the Court to extend protection. Still, the case remains that legislative objectives operate at a level of abstraction and cannot be seen in isolation of the concrete provisions enacted to give effect to them. By invoking the principle of equal treatment, the Court in effect supplemented the legislation and changed an express legislative choice.

The importance of the ruling lies not only in establishing inconsistency of treatment but also in the consequences drawn from it. The Court did not annul the regulation. Invoking, instead, a presumption of constitutionality, it held that EU legislation should be interpreted as far as possible so as to comply with the general principle of equal treatment and procured such a compliant interpretation by extending the right to compensation to passengers whose flights were delayed. The procedural context of the case is here highly relevant. It came to the Court via a

---

[13] See Regulation No. 261/2004, *op. cit.*, preamble, recital 1 and Article 114(3) TFEU. The Regulation was based on Article 80(2) EC (now Article 100(2) TFEU) on transport and not on Article 114 TFEU. It is not denied, however, that a high level of consumer protection underpins, and can validly do so, EU transport policy.

reference for a preliminary ruling and the referring court only raised issues of interpretation without questioning the validity of the regulation. Absent such a question, it is highly uncertain whether the Court could legitimately annul it.[14] Be this as it may, the end result is that, whilst in a technical sense, the Court followed a milder form of intervention since it rescued the validity of legislation rather than annulling it, in terms of substance it asserted more power. Had the regulation been annulled, the issue of passenger rights would have been thrown open leaving it to the Council to reach another deal. By interpreting the legislation in accordance with the general principle of equality, the regulation remained in force incorporating in effect a policy choice co-written by the Court. It is true that it is still open to the EU legislature to revisit the issue but the judgment shifted the landscape as it placed the burden on those who might wish to unsettle it.

It is worth pointing out that the ECJ is by no means the only court to do so. The House of Lords has also been willing to interpret statute broadly and invite Parliament to reconsider if it does not agree.[15] The above analysis makes it clear that *Sturgeon* is by no means an arbitrary judgment. The choice made by the Court was helped by the objectives of the regulation, the perceived inconsistency of its provisions, and the procedural setting of the case which favoured interpretation rather than annulment. The important point for the present discussion however is that the Court exercised a value choice which placed less trust on the legislative process and used equality to procure concrete legislative outcomes different from those negotiated by the law-making institutions. Subsequently, in *Nelson*[16] the Court reiterated *Sturgeon* and dismissed the argument that its interpretation of Regulation No. 261/2004 runs counter to the principle of legal certainty and the

---

14 In an old case, the ECJ provided a ruling on the validity of a Community provision where the national court posed only a question of interpretation: see Case 16/65, *Schwarze*, 1965, ECR 877. That case however is wholly exceptional. As a general rule, the Court will only examine issues which expressly or by implication arise from the order for reference and on which interested parties have had the opportunity to submit their views. It will thus not rule on validity unless it has been asked to by the referring court: See Joined Cases 141 to 143/81, *Holdijk*, 1982, ECR 1299, para. 6; Joined Cases C-133, C-300 and C-362/93, *Crispoltoni II*, 1994, ECR I-4863, per Jacobs AG at paras. 87 *et seq.* of the Opinion.

15 See e.g. *Fitzpatrick v Sterling Housing Association Ltd*, 2001, 1 AC 27, where the House of Lords by a majority of three to two held that a same sex partner was capable of being a member of the original tenant's "family" within the meaning of the Rent Act 1977.

16 Joined Cases C-581/10 and C-629/10, *Nelson v Deutsche Lufthansa AG*, 23 October 2012, nyr.

principle of proportionality. The Court engaged in a valiant defence of its ruling following a more evidence-based approach.[17]

2. Equality and judicial review

An equally activist approach is illustrated by *Test-Achats*,[18] a rare example of successful judicial review of an EU legislative measure on grounds of discrimination. Directive 2004/113 was adopted on the basis of Article 13(1) EC (now Article 19(1) TFEU) and laid down a framework for combating discrimination based on sex in access to and supply of goods and services.[19] The Directive prohibits the long-standing practice of using gender as an actuarial factor in calculating insurance premiums. To ease its economic effects, the Directive introduced the prohibition with a time lag. Article 5(1) requires Member States to introduce it in new contracts concluded after 21 December 2007, i.e. three years after its coming into force.[20] Article 5(2) provides for an extensive derogation. It allows Member States to decide, before 21 December 2007, "to permit proportionate differences in individuals' premiums and benefits where the use of sex is a determining factor in the assessment of risk based on relevant and accurate actuarial and statistical data." The Court found Article 5(2) invalid on the ground that it allowed the derogation to persist indefinitely. It held that such a provision, which enables Member States to maintain without temporal limitation an exemption from the rule of unisex premiums and benefits, works against the achievement of the objective of equal treatment,

---

17 The Court held that (a) delayed passengers and passengers whose flight is cancelled are in the same situation in that members of both groups are in practice denied the opportunity to reorganise their travel arrangements freely; if they absolutely needed to reach their final destination at a particular time, they could not avoid the loss of time; (b) given the requirements arising from the principle of equal treatment, air carriers could not rely on the principle of legal certainty to avoid the obligation to compensate passengers of delayed flights; (c) there was no breach of proportionality as the interpretation provided by the Court reached a fair balance between the rights of air passengers and the obligations of airlines in light of the objective of consumer protection; (d) according to data provided to the Court, the proportion of flights for which delay confers entitlement to compensation was less than 0.15%.

18 Case C-236/09, *Test-Achats v Conseil des ministres*, 2011, EC R I-773.

19 Council Directive 2004/113/EC of 13 December 2004 implementing the principle of equal treatment between men and women in the access to and supply of goods and services (OJ 2004 L 373, p. 37).

20 The Directive came into force on 21 December 2004: see Article 18. Article 5(1) states as follows: "Member States shall ensure that in all new contracts concluded after 21 December 2007 at the latest, the use of sex as a factor in the calculation of premiums and benefits for the purposes of insurance and related financial services shall not result in differences in individuals' premiums and benefits".

which is the very purpose of Directive 2004/113.[21] It is therefore incompatible with Articles 21 and 23 of the Charter which enshrine the general principle of non discrimination and the principle of equal treatment between men and women respectively. Like *Sturgeon*, the judgment raises a number of issues pertaining both to its substantive findings and the consequences of illegality.

On the face of it, the Court intervened on procedural grounds carrying out a test of internal consistency. Allowing Member States to introduce a permanent derogation ran directly counter to the objective of the Directive, which was to implement the principle of equal treatment. It thus made for incoherent and self-contradictory policy making. The Court dismissed the Council's argument that, in some cases, the respective situations of men and women policyholders may not be regarded as comparable given that the levels of insured risk for the two sexes are different. Seen in that light, Article 5(2) does not provide for a real derogation but merely makes it possible not to treat different situations in the same way.

The Court's reasoning is based on the premise that Article 5(1) prohibits *simpliciter* the use of sex as a factor in the calculation of benefits and premiums. This is not however the only reading of the Directive. The purpose of Article 5(1) is to prohibit the use of sex as such a factor only where it is discriminatory i.e. in cases where men and women are in a comparable situation and there is no objective justification for their difference in treatment. The effect of Article 5(2) is to delineate the limits of the prohibition of Article 5(1) by indicating that the use of unisex premiums and benefits is not required where sex is an objective factor in differentiating risk. This interpretation is supported by the preamble to the Directive.[22] For one thing, as has been noted by Watson, Article 5 of the Directive could not prohibit the use of sex as a factor in calculating benefits or premiums unless such use constituted sex discrimination: if it went beyond this it would be *ultra vires* the competence of the Council under Article 19(1) TFEU.[23] For another, to prohib-

---

21 Para. 32.

22 Recital 19 of the Preamble states as follows: "Certain categories of risks may vary between the sexes. In some cases, sex is one but not necessarily the only determining factor in the assessment of risks insured. For contracts insuring those types of risks, Member States may decide to permit exemptions from the rule of unisex premiums and benefits, so long as they ensure that underlying actuarial and statistical date on which the calculations are based, are reliable, regularly updated and available to the public."

23 See Watson, P., "Equality, fundamental rights and the limits of legislative discretion: comment on Test-Achats", *European Law Review*, 2011, Vol. 36, p. 896 at pp. 901-2.

it the use of sex as a relevant factor even where it can objectively be linked to differential risk would amount to treating different situation in the same way which might in itself be a breach of the general principle of non discrimination.

The Opinion of Kokott AG casts a lot more light on the argument in favour of illegality. The Advocate General pointed out that, in relation to insurance products, it is much easier to implement distinctions on the basis of sex. By contrast, "[t]he correct recording and evaluation of economic and social conditions and of the habits of insured persons is much more complicated and is also more difficult to verify, particularly since those factors may be subject to changes over time."[24] Kokott AG continued that practical difficulties and reasons of convenience could not justify "[t]he use of a person's sex as a kind of *substitute criterion* for other distinguishing features."[25] It is difficult to disagree with those findings. As Watson states, however, there may be another way of looking at this issue: the use of a person's sex may not be a substitute criterion but merely a conclusion drawn from an assessment of a number of factors which shows as a result of an objective actuarial exercise that one or the other gender is more exposed to certain kinds of risk.[26]

A notable aspect of the judgment is the way the Court treated the consequences of incompatibility. It held that Article 5(2) must be declared invalid from the expiry of an "appropriate" transitional period which, in a rare but not unprecedented example of law-making, set on 21 December 2012.[27] It is however interesting that the Court did not annul the directive as a whole. Given the widespread economic repercussions of the ruling, one may entertain doubts as to whether the EU legislature would have agreed to adopt the directive if Member States were deprived of the derogation of Article 5(2). The contrast with the *First Tobacco Adverting case* on this issue is striking. It will be remembered that, in that case, the Court found that certain aspects of the directive prohibiting the sponsorship and advertising of tobacco products were beyond the scope of EU competence but annulled that di-

---

[24] Para. 66 of the Opinion.

[25] *Supra*, para. 67.

[26] *Supra*, at 899. As Watson points out, if it can be proved that a particular category of persons is less likely to be exposed to a specific risk than another category within the insured group why should it be prohibited for this to be reflected in the premium paid for coverage of that risk? See Watson, *supra*, note 23, at 904.

[27] Paras. 33-34. Kokott AG considered as appropriate a transitional period of three years commencing from the delivery of the judgment which would have expired on 1 March 2014. The AG however opined that after that transitional period existing tariffs, premiums and benefits should also be re-adapted: See paras. 80-81 of the Opinion. By contrast, the Court only granted prospective effect to its ruling.

rective as a whole since partial annulment would have entailed amendment of its provisions which was a matter for the Community legislature.[28] The intervention of the Court in *Test-Achats* amounted to such selective amendment. Its approach is all the more activist given that Directive 2004/113 regulates private law relations.

It is difficult to avoid the conclusion that the Court had an important input in shaping the metis of the policy. As in *Sturgeon*, it gave priority to the ultimate objectives of the directive disregarding its express provisions. In substantive terms, by disabling the derogation of Article 5(2) but leaving the prohibition of Article 5(1) intact, it chose a solution which is likely to minimize rather than maximize social welfare. By foreclosing the possibility of exceptions, it adds to societal costs since insurance companies are likely to equalize by increasing rather than decreasing premiums.

The judgment has in fact less to do with upholding the general principle of non-discrimination and more with giving effect to a specific policy. Article 19(1) TFEU grants the Council authority to take appropriate action to combat discrimination based on sex, racial or ethnic origin, religion or belief, disability, age or sexual orientation. It can readily be accepted that the Council does not have the obligation to act and much less the obligation to reach a specific legislative outcome. Whether legislation will be introduced and the specific contents of that legislation will depend on whether a consensus within the Council emerges and whether the Parliament grants its consent.[29] The specific provisions of the directive which may be adopted will be shaped by the vicissitudes of the political process and reflect the balance of powers among the political actors involved and the compromise that is eventually reached. Since Article 19(1) entrusts the combatting of discrimination to the legislative process, a range of outcomes could be presumed to be legal. The legislature can act with discretion subject to compatibility with constitutional norms including the general principles of law. In *Test-Achats*, however, the resulting solution of Article 5 did not run counter to the general principle of non discrimination. The Court in effect understood equality as consistency. It held that the compatibility of situations must be assessed in the light of the subject-matter and purpose of the EU measure which makes the distinction in question,[30] and proceeded to find the derogation of Article 5(2) invalid on the ground that it was directly at odds with the fundamental objective of the

---

28 Para. 117.

29 Under Article 19(1), the Council acts unanimously after obtaining the consent of the European Parliament.

30 Para. 29.

Directive. In *Test-Achats* as in *Sturgeon*, this understanding of equality as policy consistency enabled the Court to force a legislative solution which did not reflect the outcome of the legislative process. The justification of the judgment lies in the dynamic character of equality which has to be seen as a policy continuum. It is an ideal to be implemented incrementally and the judiciary should play its role.[31]

A number of consequential issues arise in this context. Since the Council enjoys discretion to introduce harmonization rules incrementally could the directive have validly been adopted if it excluded from its scope of application insurance contracts? The answer appears to be in the affirmative.[32] In exercising its legislative competence, the Council enjoys discretion whether to adopt a measure and also, if so, to determine the scope of its application. The principle of equality understood as policy consistency only kicks in once the Council has decided to regulate a specific area.[33]

The judgment favours the model of maximum harmonization and might perhaps raise questions about the arrangements made in other directives. As Watson points out,[34] other equality directives do provide for exceptions which are of indefinite duration and justify a direct difference in treatment.[35] Such exceptions also suffer from the same

---

31 See para. 20 of the judgment which refers to the "progressive achievement" of equality "having regard to the development of economic and social conditions within the European Union" and the analysis of N. Reich, Non-Discrimination and the Many Faces of Private Law in the Union – Some Thoughts After the "Test-Achats" Judgment 2011 EJRR 283 at 288.

32 This view was taken by Kokott AG. See para. 34 of the Opinion.

33 For the relative reliance of the Court on Articles 21 and 23 of the Charter and the inconsistency generated by the contradictory provisions of the Directive itself, see Tobler, C., "Case note on Test-Achats", *Common Market Law Review*, 2011, Vol. 48, p. 2041, at pp. 2053-54.

34 Watson, *supra*, note 23, at p. 903.

35 See e.g. Directive 2000/78 establishing a general framework of equal treatment in employment and occupation (2000) OJ L303/16, Article 6(1) of which allows Member States to provide for differences in treatment on grounds of age "if within the context of national law, they are objectively and reasonably justified by a legitimate aim including legitimate employment policy, labour market and vocational training opportunities"; see also Directive 2000/43 implementing the principle of equal treatment between persons irrespective of racial or ethnic origin [2000] OJ L180/22, Article 4 of which permits Member States to allow for differential treatment where a characteristic related to racial or ethnic origin constitutes a "genuine and determining occupational requirement" provided that such an objective is legitimate and proportionate. The same possibility is allowed by the Framework Directive, Article 4. Note also Directive 2006/54 on the implementation of the principle of equal opportunities and equal treatment of men and women in matters of employment and occupation (recast) (2006) OJ L204/23, Article 4 of which provides for positive measures "with a view to ensuring full equality in practice between men and women in working life".

deficiency identified by the Advocate General in *Test-Achats*, namely that they may lead to differences in treatment in the various Member States since the latter may take advantage of them to varying degrees. Similar issues may arise outside equality directives. The Thirteenth company law Directive on take-overs,[36] for example, allows so many opt outs, options and derogations for Member States that it brings hardly any coordination of national laws and it is not readily obvious how its objectives can be attained. The provisions of that directive stretch the requirements of policy consistency as understood in *Test-Achats* although the difference might be that it does not involve any constitutional issues.[37]

An interesting question which arises here is this. Assuming that Directive 2004/113 did not exist, would it be possible to argue that the practice of insurance companies to take gender into account in the calculation of risk would be contrary to the general principle of non-discrimination (Article 21 of the Charter) on the prohibition of discrimination on grounds of sex (Article 23 of the Charter)? Although this is not to be excluded, it would require a further extension in the understanding of general principles. So far, the Court's activism has been triggered by the existence, and built on, concrete legislation however tenuous the relationship between such legislation and the outcomes reached might be said to be. A bare bones horizontal application of equality has not been endorsed.

Test-Achats as *Sturgeon* illustrate that the Court is actively involved in supplementing or even amending the normative effect of EU instruments based on their ultimate objectives and the general principle of equal treatment. A different approach was followed in *Audiolux*[38] which demonstrates the limits of equality. The applicants were minority shareholders who argued essentially that they were entitled to sell their shares to the new owner of the corporation at the same price which it had paid previously to a substantial shareholder to acquire control. In the absence of a specific buy-out right, the applicants sought to rely on the general principle of equal treatment but their claim was squarely rejected. The Court held that establishing an obligation on a dominant shareholder to

---

Watson also points out that the strict approach in *Test Achats* contrasts sharply with *Richards v Secretary of State for Work and Pensions* (C-423/04, 2006, ECR I-3585) where the ECJ accepted the validity of long-standing derogations provided by Directive 79/7 (1987) OJ C309/1.

36 Directive 2004/25/EC on takeover bids (2004) OJ L 142/12.

37 See in this respect Case C-101/08, *Audiolux SA v Groupe Bruxelles Lambert SA (GBL)*, 2009, ECR I-9823 discussed below.

38 Case C-101/08, *Audiolux SA v Groupe Bruxelles Lambert SA (GBL)*, 2009, ECR I-9823.

treat all minority shareholders equally would require the determination of concrete circumstances where minority shareholders require specific protection and the articulation of specific conditions under which that obligation would apply. Such a decision would require the weighing of the interests of minority shareholders and those of dominant shareholders and would have far reaching consequences for corporate takeovers. It could thus only be done through the legislative process. Also, assuming the minority shareholders required special protection, various means of ensuring such protection could be envisaged. The principle of equality as a general principle of law could not determine the choice among them.[39] One might feel that the same could also be said about the claims in *Test-Achat* and *Sturgeon*. There are however two distinguishing factors. First, in *Audiolux* the Court suggested that there was no constitutional imperative which would justify judicial intervention. Secondly, in contrast to *Test-Achat* and *Sturgeon* where there was a concrete statutory setting, in *Audiolux* the claim was made in a statutory vacuum. Indeed, it would be difficult to see how a specific right could be based on the general principle of equal treatment in the absence of specific and detailed rules. If the Court accepted as a matter of principle the possibility of basing a right on the general principle of equality in the context of corporate law, it would risk opening the floodgates even if it did not entertain the specific claim of the applicants.

3. Equality and national policy choices

An assertive view of equality is also evidenced by *Mangold*.[40] In contrast to *Sturgeon* and *Test-Achats*, *Mangold* involved no policy inconsistency of the EU but a more overtly hierarchical application of the principle of non discrimination to national measures. The facts of the case are well-known. The issue was whether the German law which, by way of exception, allowed the conclusion of short-term contracts for workers above the age of 52 could be justified on the grounds of derogation stated in Article 6(1) of the Framework Directive. That article allows Member States to provide for differences in treatment on grounds of age if they are objectively and reasonable justified by a legitimate aim, including legitimate employment policy, labour market and vocational training objectives. The ECJ took the view that the exception of German law was too inflexible and too broad. It accepted that the legitimacy of its objective, i.e. to promote the vocational integration of unemployed older workers, could not be questioned and that

39 *Supra*, paras. 58-61.

40 Case C-144/04, *Werner Mangold v Rüdiger Helm*, 2005, ECR I-9981. See further Case C-555/07, *Seda Kücükdeveci v Swedex GmbH & Co. KG*, 2010, ECR I-0365.

Member States enjoy broad discretion in their choices.[41] It found however that the measure offended proportionality because it made it possible for all workers who had reached the age of 52 without distinction to be employed until the end of their working life on the basis of fixed-term contracts. The law did not take into account whether they were unemployed before the contract was concluded or the duration of any period of unemployment.[42] In finding that the law was disproportionate, the Court took into account, in particular, the following factors: (a) the law applied to a significant body of workers; (b) it risked excluding them from stable employment for a substantial part of their working life; (c) it was based solely on the criterion of age; (d) it ignored factors such as the structure of the labour market or the personal circumstances of the person concerned.[43]

It may be said that, in terms of the relationship among the branches of government and the relative position of the judiciary, the most important aspect in *Mangold* was not the elevation of the prohibition of non-discrimination on grounds of age to a general principle of EU law but the forceful application of proportionality to trump the choices of the German legislature. Notably, though, this aspect did not seem to trouble the *Bundesverfassungsgericht* when it was asked to decide whether the ECJ had exceeded its powers by delivering the judgment in *Mangold.*[44]

4. Conclusion

The above cases illustrate the counter-majoritarian effects of the general principle of equal treatment. The principle is at its best not when it is invoked in a statutory vacuum but when it is applied in the context of a specific legislative framework. In *Mangold* the Court applied it as part of a normative hierarchy determined by the principle of primacy. Based on a federalist perception of EU law, the case law posits that only the EU law-making bodies and not the national ones form a primary legislature. The Court therefore applied a high level of scrutiny even on a measure adopted by the national legislature. In *Test-Achat* and *Stur-*

---

41 See paras. 59-60 and 63.

42 *Id.*

43 Paras. 64-65.

44 BVERFG, 2 BvR 2661/06, 6 July 2010. For an English version, see http://www.bverfg.de/entscheidungen/rs20100706_2bvr266106en.html. In that case, following a deferential approach, the German Federal Constitutional Court rejected the complaint that the ECJ had acted ultra vires. The discussion in the judgment focused on the derivation of a general principle of non discrimination on grounds of age and the effects of the Framework Directive on individuals but not the findings of the ECJ that the German law was disproportionate.

geon the Court understood equal treatment as going well beyond a negative constitutional stipulation which constrains legislative discretion. It used the principle to promote specific policy outcomes in the economic and social sphere based on the putative intentions of the legislature rather than its actual dispositions. Showing constitutional empathy, the Court sees its role as being to contribute to the realisation of substantive values.

Europe in Crisis

Yet again, but now the Stakes are very High

Loukas TSOUKALIS

Jean Monnet Professor of European Integration at the University of Athens; President, Hellenic Foundation for European and Foreign Policy, Former Director of Economic Studies, College of Europe

1. The Background

Europe is in deep crisis: the statement sounds like a commonplace observation. It is the worst economic crisis for decades, with no end in sight as yet. It will shape Europe and European integration for years to come, but it also risks leading Europe down the road to disintegration.

The contrast with the mood prevailing at the turn of the new century is stark. Back then, Europe was riding on a wave of euro-enthusiasm, and many people were convinced that further integration was an unstoppable process. Three big and highly ambitious projects were expected to transform radically the economic and political scene in Europe: economic and monetary union (EMU), the biggest ever enlargement of the EU following the disintegration of the Soviet empire, and the turning of the European founding treaties into a constitution. It was meant to be yet another round of deepening and widening, as the European jargon goes, but on a much bigger scale than ever before.

Now, we are, of course, much wiser – lynched by reality, one might argue. We have learned, for example, that European citizens were no longer ready to give their leaders a *carte blanche* on the future of European integration. A yawning gap has opened between elected politicians and their electors on things European: parliamentary ratifications of the Lisbon Treaty (and its predecessor) were mostly comfortable, voted by large majorities, while referendum results revealed much unhappiness and also large amounts of ignorance on behalf of citizens. The elitist conspiracy of European integration, full of good intentions and with pretty remarkable results, probably reached its limits.[1] The so-called permissive consensus was no longer.

We have also learned that although enlargement may be indeed the most successful foreign policy of the EU, it inevitably comes with a price in terms of internal cohesion. Numbers also make a big difference. With twenty-seven (and soon twenty-eight), European Councils of different denominations are no longer a group. They have now come to resemble a mini-UN conference. And that makes a big difference on the way those councils are treated, especially by representatives of the bigger countries. On the other hand, more people now realize that the EU is not a modern incarnation of Saint Panteleimon, the all-merciful healer of all kinds of disease. The miracle of Europeanization has been cut down to size through experience.[2]

2. EMU as a Postmodern Construction

The creation of the single currency has been undoubtedly the most important act of integration. We always knew that the construction conceived at Maastricht was unbalanced, but that was all that was politically feasible at the time. Before the crisis, I used to compare EMU to a postmodern construction[3] that defied the laws of gravity. It did so successfully for more than ten years, and there were those who were lulled into believing that the good times would last forever. Alas, the laws of gravity (and the market) finally began to take their revenge – and they did so with great force. Was EMU a step too far in European integration? We are in the process of finding out the answer, and the stakes are very high indeed.

It all began with the bursting of the biggest financial bubble since the Great Depression. And most Europeans believed, or wanted to believe, that it was none of their business. With the benefit of hindsight, we, of course, know they were dead wrong. The crisis spread rapidly to the whole financial sector, the most globalized part of the world economy. And it then spilled over to the real economy leading to negative rates of growth in GDP in North America and Europe that had not been experienced since the 1920s and 1930s.[4]

1 Tsoukalis, L., *What Kind of Europe?*, Oxford, Oxford University Press, 2005 [2003].

2 The literature on Europeanization is rich and with a relatively long history. See, among others, Featherstone, K. and Radaelli, C.M. (eds.), *The Politics of Europeanization*, Oxford, Oxford University Press, 2003. It needs to be revisited with a critical eye.

3 *Supra*, note 1.

4 Hemerijck, A., Knapen, B. and van Doorne, E. (eds.), *Aftershocks: Economic Crisis and Institutional Choice*, Amsterdam, Amsterdam University Press, 2009; Roubini,

What had begun as a financial crisis of the West, only indirectly affecting the rest of the world, later turned into a European crisis, more specifically a crisis of the euro area, as people (and markets) began to realize what a currency without a state[5] really meant in difficult times. Greece served as the catalyst for this transformation, because it had at the time the worst combination of three different deficits: a large budget deficit, being added to an already sizeable public debt; an equally large, indeed unsustainable, deficit in its current account – a deficit of competitiveness, in other words; and a serious credibility deficit as people realized that Greek politicians had been repeatedly economical with the truth and creative with the use of statistics. Greece was not unique with respect to any of those three deficits among members of the euro area and the wider world. But it had, undoubtedly, the worst combination when markets began to panic again, while governments, and notably its own, took their time in trying to take a grip of an, admittedly, very difficult situation.[6]

There had been gross mismanagement and big policy errors in more than one country. Since the outbreak of the crisis, many people have engaged in the blame game. Yet, there is a broader issue at stake. The crisis is the result of colossal failures in markets and institutions. It also marks a big failure for economic science and its prophets.[7] The efficient market hypothesis, resting on the behaviour of rational actors armed with perfect information, which had provided the intellectual basis for

---

N. and Mihm, S., *Crisis Economics: A Crash Course in the Future of Finance*, New York, Penguin, 2010; Pisani-Ferry, J., *Le réveil des demons: La crise de l'euro et comment nous en sortir*, Paris, Fayard, 2011.

5 Padoa-Schioppa, T., *The Euro and Its Central Bank: Getting United after the Union*, Cambridge MA, MIT Press, 2004.

6 Tsoukalis, L., "Greece in the Euro Area: Odd Man Out, Or Precursor of Things to Come?" in W.R. Cline and G.B. Wolff (eds.), *Resolving the European Debt Crisis*, Washington DC, Peterson Institute for International Economics, 2012.

7 In *What Kind of Europe?*, *supra*, note 1, I wrote about the inherent instability of financial markets, the risk of systemic crisis in a deregulated environment, and raised the question about who will pay the costs, when the crisis does eventually break out: the finance industry, consumers, or taxpayers? Others, of course, expressed similar views, and more cogently: an old fashioned minority allegedly unable to understand, among other things, what a huge difference sophisticated computer models made in the functioning of financial markets. Now, we all do, although having drawn very different conclusions from the ones propagated by the economic orthodoxy at the time. In a remarkable piece of self criticism, the independent evaluation office of the IMF wrote about groupthink, intellectual capture and incomplete analytical approaches behind policies that had led to the crisis (Independent Evaluation Office of the International Monetary Fund (IEO), "IMF Performance in the Run-Up to the Financial and Economic Crisis: IMF Surveillance in 2004-07", IEO Evaluation Report, February 2011, Washington DC, IEO).

financial deregulation in the West, was shown to bear little resemblance to real life financial markets in which greed and moral hazard met in an explosive mix, with the old herd instinct being added for extra effect. One may indeed wonder what kind of world the authors of those theories inhabit, although some have been rewarded with Nobel prizes. Financial power often translates into political power: there were many instances of politicians having been hijacked by financial lobbies. And the academic profession was shown to be particularly prone to mainstream thinking – attachment to mainstream thinking was sometimes apparently related to pecuniary interest.

The crisis of the euro area has three main components: a banking crisis and a sovereign debt crisis, which are not unique to Europe but which acquire a totally different dimension because of the high degree of interdependence between countries, plus a competitiveness component which can no longer be dealt with through currency realignments. We still live with the consequences, including persistently low growth, high rates of unemployment, as well as a big increase in economic divergence inside Europe accompanied by the rise of populism within countries and a gradual loss of trust between them. European solutions to Europe-wide problems have become increasingly difficult as a result.

3. Lessons learned

When the crisis broke out, it dawned upon people that the EU had neither the institutions nor the instruments to deal with it. Some people suspected we did not have the political will either, and they bet accordingly. They have not won their bet, but the game is far from over.

We now know that the self regulation of financial markets had been a bad joke: alas, a joke that many politicians, including those of the centre-left, had taken seriously in trying to be modern. The cost in terms of political capital and credibility has been big, and it is still being paid. Now we know (or have just been reminded) that moral hazard, inherent in the "too big to fail" notion, is a real problem that needs to be addressed through regulation, or more drastic measures. We have also learned through bitter experience that retail banking needs to be insulated from high risk betting. Furthermore, pay compensations for those employed in the sector may be a matter of public concern, while the way the finance industry has so far been taxed (or not taxed) raises important questions of equity, and not only. There is a difference between democratically regulated markets and market driven democracies – and we have come very close to the latter. However, given the globalised nature of the financial sector, the effectiveness of regulation, supervision and taxation depends largely on the will and capacity to coordinate those functions at the level of G-20, EU-28 and Euro-17. But this should not be used as an excuse for doing nothing, while waiting for all tax havens and offshore centres, big and small, to concur.

Although almost all agree that over-indebtedness is a key factor behind the outbreak of the crisis, multiplied several times in a world where financial markets have tended to resemble the operations of a casino, deleveraging of the public and/or private sector needs careful monitoring. There is no doubt that fiscal consolidation is required in many EU countries and further afield. Ageing populations, rapidly rising health costs and a large increase of sovereign debt burdens as a result of the effort to deal with the consequences of the crisis do not leave governments with much of a choice. Yet, there is an open question about timing and aggregation. Much of Europe's periphery and beyond is now caught in a deadly trap of austerity and recession. Fiscal consolidation in a liquidity trap can be self-defeating, as Keynes would have said. The ECB may be trying to ease monetary policy, but interest rates in the beleaguered countries of the South remain too high because of country risk perceived by markets. Output lost today cannot easily be regained tomorrow. The unemployed become long-term unemployed. Economies implode and the risk of social explosion rises in the worst hit countries.

The bursting of financial bubbles leaves behind a debt overhang. History teaches us that some of it is usually written off, and some is eaten away through inflation. The sooner we draw the line between debt (public or private) that is sustainable and debt that is not, the better it will be for all concerned and also the quicker will economic recovery follow. The restructuring and recapitalisation of financial institutions is a necessary pre-condition for recovery. The moment of truth has been unduly delayed in Europe, in comparison to the United States for example, largely because of the highly decentralised nature of the European political system and the difficulties in reaching an agreement about how to distribute pain in the adjustment to a post-bubble world among debtors, bank stakeholders and taxpayers, even more so between countries. Not surprisingly, the most sensitive political issue is about who pays the bill.

We know from the negotiations in Bretton Woods and also from the early history of European monetary integration that it is difficult to agree about how to distribute the burden of adjustment between surplus and deficit countries in a world of fixed exchange rates. When there are no rules, the will of those with longer staying power in the game is likely to prevail. And these are usually surplus countries. In the earlier period of European monetary integration, preceding the creation of the euro, repeated attempts had been made to introduce rules that would ensure symmetry between surplus and deficit countries. Judging from experience, they have been apparently in vain. The problem is, of course, much bigger when exchange rates are irrevocably fixed.

Structural reforms are long overdue in many EU countries. Contrary to the expectations of those who had invested much political capital in the so-called open method of coordination, the Lisbon Strategy has not delivered much. It is not yet clear whether and how the strategy of Europe 2020 will fare any better. Insufficient progress in implementing reforms that had been officially endorsed at the European level matters even more for members of the euro area, because the exchange rate is no longer available. More flexible markets, especially the labour market, are needed for the proper functioning of a currency union. But reforms meet resistance, and we know from experience that structural reforms are politically very difficult when the economy is shrinking. In the short-term, they may also make the recession worse.

4. The Way Forward

While adopting rules, backed by the threat of sanctions, in order to strengthen fiscal discipline, we should also recognise that parts of Europe are already experiencing prolonged output and job contraction sustained by negative expectations. We must avoid at all costs a prolonged double-dip recession, with the weakest members of the euro area leading what may look like suicide dance.

We urgently need to restore confidence in the irreversibility of Europe's currency union: easier said than done, as the experience of recent years painfully demonstrates. This, in turn, presupposes that we design a set of conditions and measures that deal effectively with a dual problem: the fear of moral hazard prevalent in the creditor countries on the one hand, meaning that money lent to countries in difficulty may go into a bottomless pit, and the convertibility (or country) risk that has grown in debtor countries on the other, a risk translated into high interest rate premiums and fed by self sustaining market perceptions leading in turn to disintegration and the renationalisation of banking and financial sectors. A zero-sum mentality has taken over in Europe: the fear of "transfer union" in the creditor countries hits against the perception of the EU as the policeman of austerity in the South. It risks causing a big political explosion. Meanwhile, economic divergence grows between creditor and debtor countries.

Despite continuing differences about the appropriate mix of policies and the sequencing of measures, there is growing consensus that the survival of the euro requires a banking union, a kind of fiscal union including close and effective coordination of national policies coupled with a partial and gradual mutualisation of debt, as well as further advances in terms of political union.[8] Of course, the devil lies in the detail, and several politically difficult decisions seem to be left for later. A European guarantee for bank deposits and the issuing of Eurobonds are among them. Economics dictates, but the political appetite is lacking. We want to be virtuous, but not yet. Perhaps, it all boils down to lack of trust: we are reluctant to deliver our side of the bargain because we are not at all sure that others will do the same. But the stakes are high and time is running out. Piecemeal or half measures prolong the crisis and make exiting from it more costly. It is largely about restoring confidence in the capacity of our institutions, national as well as European, to take control of an admittedly very difficult situation. It is also about restoring trust between countries and regaining the conviction that there are benefits for all in this common project.

There are deep seated differences regarding the appropriate economic strategy to be adopted.[9] One side argues that the bursting of the bubble follows many years of high indebtedness, both private and public, with the mix varying from country to country. There is now need for deleveraging and fiscal consolidation accompanied by structural reforms, which should help to bring countries back to economic health and sustainability. This sounds like a plausible argument, with the qualification that what is good for one country may not necessarily be good for all countries at the same time. This is a familiar distinction that Keynes highlighted many years back. The counterargument therefore runs as follows: at a time when the private sector is trying to reduce its debt, any attempt by governments in most countries to do the same through budgetary contraction risks sending the European (and/or the global) economy down a deflationary spiral. The policy conclusion that follows from this argument is that countries with a margin of manoeuvre should boost domestic demand (and accept a higher rate of inflation?), while for those less fortunate or careless fiscal consolidation should not be excessively frontloaded. A growing number of analysts see the ECB as the crucial lender of last resort as market confidence sinks. But all this is still anathema to many Germans.

Provisions for closer coordination of national economic policies do not automatically resolve the problem of who actually sets the priorities for the euro area (and the EU as a whole). Germany has emerged,

8 For a very different view, see Sarrazin, T., *Europa braucht den Euro nicht: Wie uns politisches Wunschdenken in die Krise geführt hat*, Munich, Deutsche Verlags-Anstalt, 2012.

9 For a clear presentation of the academic underpinnings of the policy debate, see Wren-Lewis, S., "The Return of Schools of Thought in Macro-economics", 2012. Available at http://www.voxeu.org/article/return-schools-thought-macroeconomics, accessed 23 September 2012.

beyond any doubt, as the indispensable country inside the euro area, the lender of last resort in many ways. Thus, much of the politics of choosing the way to go about dealing with the crisis has been played out in Berlin, not Brussels. German political leaders have struggled to keep their French counterparts along with them, usually on their own terms. The Franco-German leadership (or hegemony) will be tested as economic differences between the two countries grow and so do their respective perceptions and policy preferences, especially after the election of President Hollande whose negotiating power will largely depend on his capacity to deliver internal reforms. Finding a working compromise between the two countries will be absolutely crucial for the survival of the euro.

The German example of sound public finances, wage moderation and structural reform should be imitated by other countries, but up to a point. What may be good medicine in the long term and under normal economic conditions, now risks killing the patient by throwing the economy into deep recession. When all economies in Europe do the same, the effect will be cumulative and the strategy self defeating. And there is another flaw with the argument that everybody should do like the Germans: if we all strive for current account surpluses, countries outside the euro area will have to provide the corresponding deficits. The United States are unlikely to accommodate. Do we have a better chance with China?

We need a differentiated approach to fiscal stabilisation and different sequencing. Adjustment should not be born disproportionately by deficit countries. Some have a wider margin of manoeuvre than others, and they should be encouraged to take advantage of it. We need a different package of structural reform, fiscal stabilisation and growth measures in Europe today, with more emphasis on growth as a necessary complement to the other two. Growth policies should be investment-led, with particular emphasis on education and infrastructure. This requires both a national and a European component.

We also need to address the fairness/equality deficit in our countries. Before the bubble burst, inequalities had grown rapidly within many countries, especially those where the finance dominated model of capitalism was strongest, such as the United States and the UK. The situation has deteriorated since then, because of the large increase in unemployment. Growing inequalities within our societies are undermining social cohesion and the political consequences are felt more intensely on the left side of the political spectrum. There is a strong feeling of unfairness as people recognise a small minority that became very rich while the party was on, and now the rest are being called upon to pay a heavy price in the name of adjustment. Distributional politics is back in a big way in our societies.

There is also a strong inter-generational dimension to the unequal distribution of gains and losses before and after the crisis. Having often been the "outsiders" in dual labour markets, young people are now the principal victims of recession and the rise in unemployment in several European countries. Young people become increasingly alienated from politics. Dealing more effectively with equity concerns and offering a credible vision for the future to young people, without resorting to populism, constitutes a major political challenge today.

Distributional issues are the preserve of national governments, and it can only remain so. Yet, in times of declining popular support for European integration, especially among those who perceive themselves as losers from the opening of markets and more competition at the European (and global) level, we need to address this problem at EU level as well. The European Globalisation Adjustment Fund was set up with losers from globalisation in mind. It remained mostly in the domain of symbolism, although its scope and the money spent have increased in recent years as a result of the crisis. What about enlarging its terms of reference by introducing an EU component of benefits paid to the unemployed linked to the crisis and with conditionality attached? It would be a redistributive and counter-cyclical measure, especially important in the context of monetary union. It would also serve as a political message addressed to those who feel left out of a Europe without borders: a good example of *intégration solidaire*, as the French would put it. Alternatively, countercyclical measures, with a redistributive dimension added to them, could be introduced within a separate budget especially designed for the countries of the euro area.

With the crisis, EMU has become a make or break issue for Europe. We have clearly reached a new integration frontier, and we are not at all sure what lies ahead. The measures required to deal comprehensively with the crisis form a tall order. The banking and sovereign debt problems need to be dealt with jointly, and half measures are unlikely to stabilize markets that exhibit simultaneously signs of panic and the behaviour of carnivores that smell blood. The financial firepower required will be very big, and so will be the ensuing risks for creditors, while national adjustment programmes will be stress testing political stability in the debtor countries, the flexibility of their economy as well as social endurance. A new balance will need to be found between stabilization and growth. The survival of EMU requires a new political bargain among member countries, as well as more effective common institutions and rules to back it up.

The stakes are very high indeed. The crisis is acting as a powerful catalyst for further integration in Europe. Admittedly, the appetite is not there. But necessity has often been a more powerful driver than good intentions or even desire. The alternative facing us today is disintegration at a very high cost; it is already gradually happening in the market.

More integration is not good for its own sake. And if it were so in the past, it is no longer: there are not enough buyers now. In some policy areas, however, Europe will require more not less coordination and integration. Financial markets are a prominent example, because interdependence in the market place has already gone very far. Interdependence needs joint management, and this has to be explained to people: there is an educational role for politicians as well. The same applies to the governance of the euro and also parts of the internal market. Can we seriously argue, for example, that in a single market with free movement of goods and capital, there is no need for coordination in the area of taxation, including corporate taxes? Unless we imply that taxes do not matter, or that free riding should be elevated into a high principle of the integration project. Of course, nobody is seriously talking about harmonized taxes, only for minimum rates that would put a floor underneath what now looks like a race to the bottom.[10]

Solidarity should remain an integral part of the overall European bargain. But it needs to be explained and defended against all kinds of populists and narrow nationalists. It also needs to be connected to common projects and common goods, in which most, if not all, see tangible benefits for them; and it has to be subject to conditions and rules.[11] No free lunch, in other words. This surely applies to the governance of the euro, and it should increasingly apply to immigration and free internal borders. Solidarity does not enjoy ample space in our increasingly atomized societies – and this is more true across borders. We shall need to rediscover the meaning of society and the value of public goods in the years to come, thus partly reversing a trend that has lasted for long and has gone too far.

One of the few good things about the crisis is that it has generated a lively public debate about ways and means of dealing with it at the European level. It has not been a mere juxtaposition of national debates

---

10 This is an argument put forward by Mario Monti, now Prime Minister of Italy, in his report to the President of the European Commission as part of a new European bargain for the re-launching of the internal market programme, Monti, M., "A New Strategy for the Single Market: Report to the President of the European Commission", 2010. Available at: http://ec.europa.eu/bepa/pdf/monti_report_final_10_05_2010_en.pdf.

11 Jacques Delors has repeatedly and convincingly argued the case for solidarity as a key part of the European bargain, and so has Helmut Schmidt.

going on almost independently of one another and limited to a small number of *cognoscenti*, which used to be the usual pattern with EU-related issues. As with so many other debates in a democracy, it has contained elements ranging all the way from the sublime to the ridiculous and nasty. There are signs of a European public forum emerging. We should nurture it.

How much adjustment is the European South willing or able to make? What is the appropriate mix for European macroeconomic policy? Should the ECB behave like a normal central bank, and should private banks be rescued or some of them at least be allowed to go under? And who stands to lose the most from an eventual disintegration? These are hot political issues that are now being aired in public.

We need to turn European integration again into a positive-sum game. And we need institutions to match the level of market integration (not only financial markets) already reached, and those institutions cannot be created simply by fiat. They must have legitimacy that can only be gained through democratic processes. It is expected that the big political families represented in the European Parliament will present joint candidates for President of the European Commission at the 2014 elections. They should be people with broader appeal beyond national borders. Their selection will require thinking out of the box. The 2014 elections could be a big step in the necessary transition from policy to politics in the EU.

The Property Aspects of the European Patent with Unitary Effect

A National Perspective for a European Prospect?

Hanns ULLRICH

Professor Dr. iur., MCJ NY University, Gräfelfing

1. Introduction

At present, patent protection in the European Union essentially rests on national law. Whether granted separately by national patent offices or centrally at uniform conditions by the European Patent Organization,[1] the terms of the exclusive right, which the patentees obtains, are defined by national law,[2] and so are its qualities as an object of property: whether and how it may be transferred, given as a security or become an object of levy in execution, what the position of a licensee is and whether and when the transactions involved deploy a patent law (*erga omnes*) effect *vis-à-vis* third parties.[3]

In the future, two new options of patent protection will additionally become available.[4] One is an option for an upgraded European patent:

1 As established by the Convention for the Grant of European Patents (European Patent Convention, EPC) of 5 October 1973, as amended by Revision Act of 29 November 2000, in force since 13 December 2007. Patents granted by the European Patent Office (Article 4 para. 2 EPC) are called "European patents" (Article 2 para. 1 EPC) as distinguished from national patents granted by national patent offices.

2 Article 2 para. 2, Article 64 para. 1 and 3 EPC; for exceptions see Articles 63, 64 para. 2, 69, 138 EPC.

3 See only § 15 German Patent Act (PatG); Articles L 613-8, L 619-9. French Code de la propriété intellectuelle (c.prop.int.); Sect. 30 *et seq.* U.K. Patents Act 1977. National rules tend to be rudimentary and dispersed or to follow from general principles (property law in general, civil procedure, bankruptcy law, etc.).

4 For details see Ullrich, "Harmonizing Patent Law: The Untamable Union Patent", in Janssens, van Overwalle (eds.), *Harmonization of European IP Law. From European Rules to Belgian Law and Practice* (Contributions in honour of F. Gotzen), Brussels,

As regards the terms of the exclusive patent right, the national patents, which the EPO grants as a "bundle"[5] under the name of European patents (Article 2 para. 1 EPC), will no longer be subject to national law as provided for by Article 2 para. 2, Article 64 para. 1 and 3 EPC, but by an international Agreement on a Unified Patent Court.[6] This Agreement, however, which is to be concluded among the Member States of the European Union only, does not provide for any rules governing the property aspects of this "UPCt-type" of a European patent. Rather, they remain a matter of the national laws of those Member States, which have been designated in the European patent application (Article 79 EPC). This is so because, on the one hand, the EPCt-type of European Patents still is a simple bundle of independent national patents. On the other, the Agreement provides for rules on the infringing acts and on exceptions only to enable the Unified Patent Court to exercise its jurisdiction, which precisely is limited to matters of infringement and of revocation.

The other option is for a territorially unitary form of patent protection. Following the failure of the project to create a European Union (ex Community) patent and the transition to enhanced cooperation in the area of unitary patent protection,[7] a Regulation on the European patent with unitary effect has been enacted.[8] It provides for that, upon registra-

---

2012, p. 243, *id.*, Select from Within the System: The European patent with unitary effect, in Geiger (ed.), *What Patent Law for Europe*, Paris, 2012, 207= ssrn, abstract=2159672).

5 The common qualification of the European patent as a "bundle" of (national) patents, see Beier, in Beier, Haertel, Schricker (eds.), "Europäisches Patentübereinkommen", Cologne, 1. Lfg., 1984, 53 (No. 9) 22. Lfg.1998, 112 (No. 90) is misleading. Once granted, the bundle falls apart in entirely independent, territorially separate patents, each following its individual legal fate as regards transfer, infringement, invalidation, abandonment or lapse. Nevertheless, the characterization of the European patent as a bundle of "national patents" is a convenient short term for that there is no European patent as such, but a number of territorially separate and independent exclusive rights, which have a common origin, the grant by the EPO, but which derive their substance from national law alone.

6 Article 25-29 Draft Agreement on a Unified Patent Court and Statute – of 19 February 2013, OJ EU 2013 C175, 1. This UPCt-Agreement will enter into force once it has been ratified by 13 EU Member States (Article 89).

7 See Jaeger, "Back to Square One? An Assessment of the Latest Proposals for a Patent and a Court for the Internal Market and Possible Alternatives", 43 IIC 286, 2012, and the references *supra*, note 4.

8 Regulation CEU/No 1257/2012 of the European Parliament and the Council of 17 December 2012 implementing enhanced cooperation in the area of the creation of unitary patent protection (UP Reg.), OJ EU 2012 L361, 1: for the substitution of a new Art. 5 to Art. 6-8 relating to the scope of the exclusive right see Ullrich, Enhanced cooperation in the area of unitary patent protection and European Integration, 13(4) ERA Forum 589, sub 2.3 (2013) = DOS 10, 1007/s 12027-013-0275-2.

tion made upon request by the patentee, "European patents granted with the same set of claims in respect of all the participating Member States shall benefit from unitary effect in the participating Member States" (Article 3 para. 1). Such European patent shall have a unitary character, provide uniform protection and shall have equal effect in all participating Member States. It may only be limited, transferred, revoked or lapse in respect of all the participating Member States (Article 3 para. 2). The Regulation does not the scope of the exclusivity of the unitary patent (direct and indirect infringement, exceptions, exhaustion), but instead indirectly refers to Art. 25-28 UPCt-Agreement (Art. 5). As to the unitary patent as an object of property, Article 10 determines that it "shall be treated in its entirety and in all the participating Member States as a national patent of the participating Member State …", in which the patent proprietor had, at the date of filing the application, his/her residence or principal place of business, or, by default, a place of business (Article 7 para. 1). In the absence of a "domicile" in a participating Member State, German law applies (Article 7 para. 3).

As many other features of the Regulation, such full reliance on national law as a way of defining the territorially unitary patent as a merchandisable object with respect to all the territories of enhanced cooperation comes as a surprise. All earlier projects of creating a Community patent provided for more or less detailed rules of their own governing the Community patent as an object of property,[9] and so do all the Regulations on Community industrial property.[10] The application of national law was residual and limited to the implementation of the property rules by transactional, in particular by contract law, this being a matter of non-harmonized general civil law.[11] Therefore, the question arises: Why the difference, what does it mean, which effect will it produce?

---

9 See Articles 39 – 44 Community Patent Convention of 15 December 1975, OJEC 1976 L 17, 1; Articles 38-43 Community Patent Convention of 15 December 1989, OJEC 1989 L 401, 9 (as incorporated into the Community Patent Agreement of 15 December 1989, OJEC 1989 L 401, 1); Articles 14-20 Proposal for a Council Regulation on the Community Patent of 1 August 2000, OJEC 2000 C 337, 278 as last revised by Council Doc. 16113/09 of 27 November 2009. These texts also deal with the Community patent application as an object of property, a matter which, with respect to the application for a European patent resulting in a unitary patent, cannot be dealt with here, see Ullrich, Select from Within the System, *loc. cit.*, text at note 104.

10 See *infra*, 2.B.2.I.

11 This state of non-harmonization was based on the assumption that general civil law is outside the competence of the EU. This may no longer hold true, but the matter is outside the scope of this paper, see for an introduction to the problems in the field of contracts relating to intellectual property Hilty, *Optionales europäisches Vertragsrecht* ("28. Modell"): "Geistiges Eigentum", RabelsZ 76, 2012, p. 339.

2. Markets and Market Rules for Patents

A. (Emerging) Markets for Trade in Patents

It is commonplace that patents are exploited not only "in-house" by the patentee through manufacturing and selling his/her products, but also through licensing out to third parties. At least in some fields of technology,[12] licensing out has even matured from a practice of seeking fringe benefits outside the patentee's main economic activities into a distinct, often important business, if not into the core business model of mere technology providers.[13] What is less well known is that there is also a market for the transfer of patents through change of ownership, be it by contractual assignment, be it by acquisition of corporate assets.[14] Leaving the latter case aside, the former has attracted the attention of economists analysing "secondary markets for intellectual property",[15] because these markets as well are expanding.[16] They relate to patents as assets rather than only as bargaining chips in negotiations for cooperation, joint ventures or mergers. As such, they may serve securisation purposes, but they are also traded for different other purposes.[17] They have come to the attention of lawyers, first, as patents bought up by "trolls" in view of – possibly predatory – licensing activities.[18] More

12 Typically in biotechnology with its RandD-focussed small firms, and in information/communication technologies.

13 See only WIPO, World intellectual Property Report 2011, The Changing Face of Innovation (WIPO Economics and Statistics Series), Geneva 2011 (WIPO Publication No. 944E/2011), sub. 1.3.2 *et passim*; Rapport Pietà, "Quel système de propriété intellectuelle pour la France d'ici 2020?, Paris, 2006, pp. 155 *et seq*.; Arora, Gambardella, "Ideas for rent: an overview of markets for technology", DIME Working Paper No. 87, June 2008, *passim*.

14 The recent Google/Motorola case (see Commission, IP/12/129: Commission approves acquisition of Motorola Mobility by Google, Press Release of 13 February 2012) is but a prominent example.

15 See Chesbrough, "Emerging Secondary Markets for Intellectual Property: US and Japanese Law Comparisons", Research Report to National Center for Industrial Property Information and Training (NCIPI), March 2006.

16 See Chesbrough, *supra*, Chapter 3 and 4 (covering "reassignments" in the US and Japan respectively; between 1980 and 2003 the number of reassignments has risen from 2,000 to 90,000); Serrano, "The Market for Intellectual Property: Evidence from the Transfer of Patents", JOB Market Paper, January 2005, noting that 20% of all patents granted to small innovators in the USA are traded by way of reassignment.

17 See Chesbrough, *supra*, Chapter 3 (intra-group transfer, transfer from individuals, research organizations; transfer may occur as stand alone transaction or bundled with other assets).

18 See only Layne-Farrar, Schmidt, "Licensing Complementary Patents: "Patent Trolls", Market Structure and "Excessive" Royalties", 25 Berkely Tech'y L.J. 1121, (2010).

generally, however, they essentially serve "non-producing entities" (NPE) of various types to put patents to use and to commercial value.[19] Just as licensing out or in, such transfer transactions simply mirror one purpose of patent protection, which is to transform inventive technology into a merchandisable good that may be valued at what the market yields, i.e. at what demand is willing to pay under conditions of competition.[20]

B. *Multiple, Diverse and Dispersed Rules for Unitary Patents as Property*

I. As any market, such markets for trade in patents will achieve their social purpose only if they are open, operate at conditions of undistorted competition and within a legal framework ensuring transparency of the transactions and legal certainty for all market actors. In the EU, such legal framework must serve the formation of the Internal Market. It is true that markets for intangibles do have inherent imperfections.[21] However, the law is called upon to mitigate them.[22] When establishing its own system of industrial property the EU legislator has tried to achieve exactly this. Thus, it is with an increasing degree of detailed regulation that the Regulations on Community Plant Variety Protection,[23] on Community Trade Marks,[24] and on Community Designs[25] have developed rules providing for the establishment of the respective titles of Union industrial property as assets in their own right. These rules follow a logic of a split system, the split being due to a division of competences. On the one hand, the Union legislator provides for the full and equal merchandisability of all Union titles[26] throughout the Internal

19 See *supra*, note 8 and already Chesbrough, *supra*, sub. 2.2.2.3.

20 See David, "Intellectual Property Institutions and the Panda's Thumb: Patents, Copyrights, and Trade Secrets in Economic Theory and History", in Wallerstein (ed.), *Global Dimensions of Intellectual Property Rights in Science and Technology*, Washington DC, 1993, pp. 19, 24 *et passim*.

21 See Arora, Gambardella, *supra*, sub. 4.

22 See McClure, "Commoditizing Intellectual Property Rights: The Practicability of a Commercialized and Transparent International IPR Market and the Need for International Standards", 6 Buff.Intell.Prop.J. 101, (2008).

23 Articles 22-28 Regulation (EC) 2100/94 of the Council of 27 July 1994 on Community Plant Variety Protection, OJEC 1994 L 227, 1, as amended.

24 Articles 16-24 Regulation (EC) 207/2009 of the Council of 26 February 2009 on the Community Trade Mark, OJ EU 2009 L 78, 1 (consolidated version of Reg. 40/94, as amended).

25 Articles 27-34 Regulation (EC) 6/2002 of the Council of 12 December 2001 on the Community Design, OJ EC 2002 L 3, 1.

26 Rather than providing only for uniform rules governing the merchandisability of a given, single title of protection, see *infra*).

Market by uniform rules qualifying the exclusive right as constituting property of the same kind as any (tangible) property. This concerns its transfer by way of assignment or other succession in title, but also its use as a security or its being the subject of rights in rem, its levy in execution, its subjection to bankruptcy, and the nature and (erga omnes) effects of restrictive licensing.[27] In addition to this guarantee of the quality and uniformity of industrial property titles of the Union, the legislator also took care of the invisible character of transactions regarding intangible property by limiting their effects *vis-à-vis* third parties by rules on transparency and good faith.[28]

On the other hand, given the limitation of its legislative powers to what is necessary for the functioning on the Internal Market,[29] the Union legislator carefully refrained from regulating more than the property characteristics of the respective titles of protection, thus avoiding both an undue interference with national civil (or common) law and an – at the time[30] – unreasonable workload of creating particular, possibly IP-type specific rules of property and contract law.[31] This prudent abstention is expressed in all the Regulations by a general rule of referral to national law.[32] As such, it does not mirror a principle/ exception relationship of national v. Union law nor does it represent a rule of conflicts of law, the Union title having a Union-wide territorial scope.[33] Rather, it

27 See the conclusive catalogue of license restrictions producing an erga omnes effect in Article 27 para. 2 Community Trade Mark Reg. and Article 32 para. 2 Community Design Reg. The catalogue corresponds to Article 8, para. 2 Directive 2008/95/EC of the European Parliament and the Council of 20 October 2008 on the approximation of the laws of Member States on trade marks, OJ EU 2008, L 299, 25 (consol. version of Dir. 89/104) aimed at harmonizing national law, see ECJ of 23 April 2009, case c-59/08, *Copad/Dior*, Rep. 2009 I 3421 at nos. 16 *et seq*. Dir. 98/71 of the European Parliament and the Council of 13 October 1998 on the legal protection of designs, OJ EC 1998 L 289, 28, does not harmonize the matter. Certainly by legislative inadvertence, Article 32 para. 2 Community Design Reg. does not list territorial restrictions. Article 20 Community Plant Variety Protection Reg. does not provide for a specific catalogue of license restrictions.

28 Article 23 para. 4 Community Plant Variety Protection Reg.; Article 17 para. 6, Article 23 Community Trade Mark Reg.; Article 28 para. 1 lit b), Article 33 Community Design Reg.

29 Article 118 para. 1 TFEU; formerly Article 94 *et seq*., Article 308 EC Treaty.

30 See *supra*, note 11.

31 Except for (mandatory) rules regarding form requirements (see for assignments Article 23 para. 2 Community Plant Variety Protection Reg.; Article 17 para. 2 Community Trade Mark Reg.), national contract law applies by default as regards the inter partes effects of the transaction.

32 Article 22 Community Plant Variety Protection Reg.; Article 16. Community Trade Mark Reg.; Article 27 Community Design Reg.

33 For a detailed analysis see Ruhl, *Gemeinschaftsgeschmacksmusterverordnung*, 2nd ed., Cologne 2010, Article 27, annot. 2 *et passim*.

precisely is a rule of referral to national law, the purpose of which essentially is to provide only for the implementation of the Union's rules regarding the status of Union titles of protection as property.[34]

Articles 14-19 and Article 23 of the proposed Community Patent Regulation closely followed the rules of the Regulations on the Community Trade Mark and the Community Design respectively.[35] There was an adaptation made to the particularities of patents as regards assignments[36] and as regards the catalogue of licensing restrictions producing *erga omnes* (patent law) effects.[37] No controversy has become apparent either in these particular respects or in general. Yet, instead of carrying these rules over to the Regulation on the European patent with unitary effect, the EU legislator decided to abstain from providing for any property rules of its own. The result is a fundamental change of the role and function of Article 7 of UP-Regulation, which provides for the application of one national to a unitary patent as an object of property. While by its wording similar to the rules on referral to national law contained in the Regulations on Community Plant Variety Protection, on Trade Marks and on Designs respectively, Article

---

34 See Ruhl, *supra*, Article 27, annot. 2, 10 (complementary, subsidiary function of national law regarding the property characteristics of the Union title). It follows that national law may not interfere with the regulatory purpose of the Regulations' rules determining the property status of Union titles. This holds true also for the erga-omnes-effects of restrictive licenses (*supra*, note 27). These may not be expanded or attributed to restrictions, which are not within the specific subject-matter of protection, because, inter alia, they affect the scope of potential intra-brand competition and of the free movement of goods downstream the distribution chain. Likewise, national law may not reinforce form requirements (*supra*, note 31; *contra*, Schennen in Eisenführ, Schennen, *Gemeinschaftsmarkenverordnung*, 3rd ed., Cologne 2010, Article 17 annot. 16). Moreover, the property rules governing Union titles of protection will be and must be interpreted consistently as part of a system. Where they are based on the same terms and principles, they may be read together so as to bridge lacunae, thus helping to overcome problems resulting from the application of divergent national laws, see *infra*, note 42.

35 In accordance with Article 26 Community Plant Variety Protection Reg., Article 24 Community Trade Mark Reg. and Article 34 Community Design Reg., Article 24 proposed Community Patent Regulation extended the property rules to applications for protection.

36 Article 14 of the Commission's original proposal of 2000 (*supra*, note 9) was a copy/paste text of Article 17 Community Trade Mark Reg., but has been rectified in later drafts by the Council. However, Article 16 on rights in rem (security interest) proposed Regulation on the Community patent has never been rectified by comparison to Article 19 Community Trade Mark Reg.

37 Article 19 para. 2 would have protected the patentee with *erga omnes*-effect against the breach of "any restriction in the licensing contract". Obviously, this was excessive by reference to the subject matter of patent protection (e.g. quality restrictions, customer restrictions), and would have needed to be limited in accordance with the requirements of Articles 34-36 TFEU.

7 gives a pivotal function to national law in that it is made the exclusive *sedes materiae*.

This means several things.

First, leaving the determination of the property aspects of unitary patents entirely to national law as it exists and evolves as a result of legislative activity and judicial practice will maintain non-transparency and uncertainty of the law. While it is true that existing secondary Union law governing Union titles of protection as an object of property is incomplete and in need of implementation by national law,[38] it nevertheless provides for the essential minimum of predictability of what the property aspect of these titles and their effects are. National law, by contrast, is not always easily accessible and understood, except possibly that of a few major jurisdictions. This may be less a problem for patentees, certainly not one for patentees domiciled within the Member States participating in enhanced cooperation.[39] However, trade in patents, whether by assignment, license or other uses of the patent as an asset, regards all market actors. They need to know what the law is as regards assignments, their form requirements and effects, as regards the position of the licensor and the licensee with respect to standing[40] and restrictive terms,[41] as regards the consequences of succession in title on pre-existing rights[42] or as regards the effects of property transactions on third parties in general.[43] Much of these matters is not to be found in

38 See *supra*.

39 Under Article 7 para. 1 UP-Reg., the main connecting factor for the applicable national law is the residence or the principal place of business of the patent applicant; see text *supra*, sub I. As to the problems arising from this determination of the applicable law see *infra*, note 53 and text sub 3.

40 See Article 22 para. 3 and 4 Community Trade Mark Reg.; Article 32 para. 3 and 4 Community Design Reg. With respect to both the European patent UPCt-type and the European patent with unitary effect, Article 47 UPCt-Agreement regulates the matter as one of procedural law. It is, however, one of substantive law as well, since standing in litigation implies that the licensee may dispose of the rights flowing from the patent, e.g. by way of settlement. This affects also the patent as an object of property. Therefore, the matter may not be regulated in the UPCt-Agreement alone, the less so as the Agreement may not interfere with the substance of the patent as established by EU law.

41 See *supra*, note 27, 34, 37.

42 See Article 23 para. 3 Community Plant Variety Protection Reg., Article 15 para. 2 proposed Union (ex Community) Patent Regulation. The Regulations on the Community Trade Mark and on the Community Design do not cover the issue. Comp. also Article L 613-8 para. 4 c.prop.int., and § 15 para. 3 PatG, the latter even containing a rule protecting a licensee from the effects of a subsequent grant of a license to another party.

43 See on the one hand Article 28 para. 2 Community Design Reg., Article 17 para. 6 Community Trade Mark Reg. providing that the assignee may not invoke his/her

national patent statutes but elsewhere in general property law, in procedural law, or in general principles of national law,[44] and often enough it is not written in a statutory text, but hidden in judicial practice. Whether sufficient and satisfactory or not,[45] this body of national law will have to be applied by the courts of other jurisdiction as well, and also by the Unified Patent Court.[46]

Second, subjecting the unitary patent as an object of property to one national law with effect throughout all territories of enhanced cooperation creates a wrong appearance of uniformity. While any given European patent with unitary effect will be subject to one law only and, thus, be unitary also as regards its property aspects, any other unitary patent may be subject to a different national law. In fact, as many as 25 different national laws may apply, the result being that, as an object of property, there will be up to 25 different types of unitary patents. This will be so, because under Article 7 para. 1 UP-Reg. the applicable national law will be that of the place where, at the time of filing the European patent application, the applicant had his/her residence or principal place of business or, by default, a place of business. Should none of these connecting factors exist, German law will apply.[47] This determination of

---

right before the transfer has been registered and, on the other, the complementary rules of Article 23 para. 4 Community Plant Variety Protection Reg., Article 33 para. 2 Community Design Reg., Article 23 Community Trade Mark Reg. protecting third parties from liability *vis-à-vis* the non-registered assignee or licensee, unless they are acting in bad faith. Article 15 para. 3, Article 23 proposed Community Patent Regulation were to the same effect.

44 See the sparse, yet different rules of Article L 613-8 *et seq*. c.prop.int., Sect. 30, 33 UK Patents Act, § 15 PatG, and as to the implementation for instance under German law Ullmann in Benkard, *Patentgesetz*, 10th ed., Munich, 2006, § 15 annot. 2 *et passim* (transfer), 42 (rights in rem), 43 *et passim* (levy in execution), 56 *et passim* (licenses)); for the UK see Cornish, Llewelyn, Aplin, *Intellectual Property*, 7th ed., London, 2010, sub. 7-15 *et passim*; for France Vivant, Navarro, *Code de la propriété intellectuelle*, 12e éd. Paris 2011, commentaires Article L 613-8, L 613-9. A detailed presentation of the national property law of patents in these (or in the other 22) jurisdictions is far beyond the purpose of this paper.

45 To the difference of property rules based on Union law, which national courts must implement by applying national law in accordance with effet utile-principles, a plain reference to national law means that it has to be taken as it is.

46 For instance, issues of entitlement, of good or bad faith of third parties (see *supra*, note 43), of breaches of licenses resulting in patent infringement etc. To the extent that matters of national law are outside the jurisdiction, which the ECJ would have under Article 267 TFEU, divergences of judicial interpretation of national law as applicable under Article 7 UP-Reg. may emerge both among national courts from different EU-Member States and between these courts and the UPCt. However marginal, this risk is inherent in the Article 7-approach.

47 According to Article 7 para. 3 UP-Reg. in case the patent applicant has no residence or place of business in an enhanced cooperation State, the law of the place applies,

the applicable national law does not mean a mere multiplicity of applicable laws, but a diversity.[48] National patent laws have never been harmonized in respect of the property aspects of patents by the EU or by an international agreement, but, if at all, are similar only due to some national legislation anticipating on the rules of the failed Community Patent Conventions.[49] There is, therefore, a lack of uniformity regarding an essential quality of patents as industrial property, which makes Article 7 UP-Reg. miss the requirement and the purpose of Article 118 para. 1 TFEU.[50]

Indeed, the combined effects of the multiplicity and diversity of applicable laws mean that building a portfolio of patents by acquisition or setting up independent pools will require dealing with various national property rules. Likewise, patents in an international joint venture relating to RandD or the like will follow different and divergent national laws. The implication always is an increase in transaction costs. In addition, the diversity of the applicable laws will impact on the value of patents as assets depending on which law applies,[51] and it will exacerbate legal uncertainty and non-transparency of the market. Finally, the purpose of Article 118 para. 1 TFEU is not merely to overcome a formal fragmentation of markets, but to stimulate their integration. Article 7 UP-Reg. does not satisfy this broader purpose. Typically, indeed, patents are not traded as single items, whose unitary character prevents

---

where the EPO has its headquarters pursuant to Article 6 para. 1 EPC, i.e. German law. While seemingly a default rule, Article 7 para. 3 UP-Reg. is of considerable importance. About 60% of all patent applications originate from outside EPO Contracting States, and even more from outside the Member States of the EU, see EPO, Annual Report 2011, Statistics and trends (www.epo.org/about-us/office/annual-report/2011/statistics-trends). How many of these applicants will have a place of business in an enhanced cooperation territory is an open question.

48 See *supra*, note 44.

49 See Kraßer in Beier, Haertel, Schricker, *supra*, 22. Lfg. 1998 at p. 119 *et passim*.

50 Article 7 para. 4 UP-Reg., which provides that "the acquisition of a right may not be dependent on any entry in a national patent register", does not establish uniformity either, except a negative one regarding the form of the acquisition of rights. Its reach is limited, indeed. Many national laws (not German law, see § 15 PatG), while requiring assignments and licences to be in writing, do not make registration of the acquisition a condition of its validity, but only of its full and immediate effectiveness *vis-à-vis* third parties, see Article L 613-8, last para. c.prop.int, Article 30 para. 6, Sect. 33 UK Patents Act 1977, and the references *supra*, note 44. This indirect incentive to registration ought to be maintained, albeit not with respect to national registers, but with respect to the EPO-Register (see Article 9 para. 1, lit. h) UP-Reg.). The need for rules on reasonable reliance/transparency and good faith is taken care of by all Union regulations, see *supra*, note 43.

51 For instance the different ease and effects of a transfer (see *supra*, note 50), the quality as a security or the status in insolvency directly affect the merchandisability of patents as a commodity or asset.

fragmentation. Rather, they are transferred or licensed as a package covering a technology.[52] Therefore, whenever such package does not only contain single source-patents, but patents acquired from or held by different applicants or owners,[53] problems of diversity of the applicable national laws are likely to arise. The UP-Regulation thus fails to put a major feature of unitary patent protection to full advantage, which would be the enhanced merchandisability of the European patent with unitary effect as compared to UPCt-type patents, which as objects of property are entirely national in character and territorially separate.

C. Indirect Discrimination

I. Yet another problem is that in its practical operation, Article 7 UP-Reg. will result in discrimination. To the difference of patent applicants having a residence or a principal place of business (or a place of business) in one of the EU Member States participating in enhanced cooperation, applicants, whose residence or place of business is in a non-participating Member State, may only obtain a unitary patent whose property aspects will always be governed by foreign law, be it the law of a place of business, which they have established in a participating Member State,[54] be it German law.[55] This preferential treatment of

52 In this respect, patents substantially differ from plant varieties, which are the product, or from trademarks, which identify products. Patents typically cover only parts or components of a technology, if not only aspects of such parts or components, see for the distinct operation of the patent system in this regard Ullrich, "Propriété intellectuelle, concurrence et régulation – limites de protection et limites de contrôle", *Revue international de droit économique*, 2009, pp. 399, 423 *et passim*.

53 In respect of the determination of the applicable national law ratione tempore, Article 7 para. 1 and 3 UP-Reg. differ from Article 22 Community Plant Variety Protection Reg., Article 27 Community Design Reg. and Article 16 Community Trade Mark Reg. Whereas under all the latter provisions the relevant date for determining the applicable law is that of the transaction (see Ruhl, *supra*, Article 27, annot. 6, 20, Schennen in Eisenführ, Schennen, *supra*, Article 16, annot. 7), with, as a result, a change over time of the applicable law as the proprietor and/or his/her domicile changes, Article 7 UP-Reg. apparently aims at determining an immovable status of the patent. The relevant date is that of the filing of the patent application, and the applicable law is that of the applicant's residence or place of business, and it so is once and forever.

54 At first glance, Article 7 para. 1 UP-Reg. seems to raise an issue of freedom of establishment (Article 49 TFEU). It may, indeed, have an impact on the choice of a residence or of a (principal) place of business as establishing a business in a Member State not participating in enhanced cooperation may become less attractive, given that its law will not apply to matters such as precisely assignments of unitary patents, succession in title, the in rem effects of licence restrictions etc. However, to the extent that Article 49 TFEU purports only to ensure full national treatment of nationals from other Member States, it will not apply. National treatment is not an issue under Article 7 UP-Reg. Rather, it is the fact of applicants from outside the enhanced cooperation group being subject to the various national laws of the participating States as

applicants domiciled in a Member State of the enhanced cooperation group amounts to an indirect discrimination on grounds of nationality, because the residence or the principal place of business of a patent applicant typically corresponds to his/her nationality. Such indirect discrimination comes under Article 18 TFEU.[56]

The concern about this indirect discrimination is not that EU firms, which are not domiciled in an enhanced cooperation State, may not rely on their domestic laws when it comes to the property aspects of their unitary patents. The unavailability of their national law is the result of the non-participation of their home countries in enhanced cooperation. Rather, the concern is about the preference, which firms domiciled in a participating Member State will enjoy by having their unitary patents governed by their domestic law. This preference matters, because it is their national law, which will determine the characteristics and the value of the patent as an object of property, and because differences of national law may be substantial.[57] For one thing, a given national regime may be more favorable to patentees than another, either generally or in view of the particular ways of patent exploitation existing for certain technologies or in certain industries. For another, differences of national laws

regards the property characteristics of their patents, which raises concern. For the same reason, there is no issue of protecting non-nationals of the cooperating Member States against their being invited to establish a business place in one of these States, at least not as long as the problem is not one of access to a more favourable law. The problem rather is the exposure to a foreign national law as regards the property aspects of an exclusive right, whose unitary effect, including the effects of its property characteristics, reaches beyond national territory to the entire territory of enhanced cooperation. In this respect, Article 18 TFEU has to complement the limited operation of Article 49 TFEU, see for the complementary and fundamental role of Article 18 TFEU, Holoubek in Schwarze, *EU-Kommentar*, 3rd ed., Baden-Baden, 2012, Article 18, annot. 1 *et seq*., 48 *et seq*. with references.

55 See *supra*, note 47.

56 See ECJ of 14 February 1995, case C-279/93, *Schumaker*, Rep. 1995 I 225, at Nos. 25 *et seq*., the recently ECJ of 20 January 2011, case C-155/09, Commission/Greece, Rep. 2011 I 65 at nos. 45 et seq.; of 25 January 2011, case C-382/08, Neukirchingen, Rep. 2011 I 139 at no. 34; also by *Holoubek* in *Schwarze*, *supra*, Article 18 AEUV, annot. 7, 15 *et seq*., 39. For an example of indirect discrimination in intellectual property protection resulting from the country of origin-principle of copyright law see ECJ of 30 June 2005, case C-28/04, *Tod's/Heyraud*, Rep. 2005 I 5781, Nos. 19 *et seq*. Whereas discrimination on grounds of nationality or equivalent connecting factors by Member States typically results from insufficient national treatment, discrimination by the EU Legislator or authorities mostly results from an unequal distribution of Union benefits between Member States and their respective nationals or more generally from an unequal treatment, see the references by Holoubek, *ibid*., at No. 39. Enhanced cooperation is conditional upon abiding to these rules of primary Union law and to non-discrimination in general, Article 326 TFEU.

57 See *supra*, sub 1. and 2., and the examples given in note 50.

produce costs of information and of adaptation for both patent applicants from Member States not participating in enhanced cooperation and for third parties in all EU Member States.[58]

These two consequences of subjecting the unitary patent as an object of property to a selective regime of national laws do not have the same effect of discrimination. As regards the differences of the applicable national laws, i.e. the legal advantages or disadvantages possibly benefitting or affecting patentees from inside the enhanced cooperation group in that he/she will always obtain a unitary patent which, as an object of property, will follow his/her domestic law, the discrimination does not alone affect patent applicants not domiciled in a Member State of the enhanced cooperation group. Patent applicants having a residence or a principal place of business within the territory of other enhanced cooperation States will be affected similarly. This simply follows from that different national laws apply depending on which is the Member State where the applicant is domiciled. There is, therefore, a problem of diversity[59] of the applicable laws, which originates from the fact that, as an object of property, the unitary patent is subject to national law rather than to a rule of uniform Union law.

This choice of national instead of Union law also entails the second mentioned discriminatory effect. It is due to the fact that the applicable national law can only be one of a Member State participating in enhanced cooperation. As a result, there will be a transaction cost differential regarding access to protection for applicants not domiciled within the territory of the enhanced cooperation group, as compared to applicants, who are domiciled within the territory of enhanced cooperation.[60]

58 See *supra*, sub 2.b)(i); Ullrich. Select from within the system, *supra*, sub III.1.a); generally Mankowski, *Interessenpolitik und europäisches Kollisionsrecht*, Baden-Baden, 2011, pp. 38 *et seq*. Market actors in all EU Member States are affected, because enhanced cooperation takes place within the Internal Market.

59 Whether and to what extent the rules on the free movement of goods (Articles 34 – 36 TFEU) may limit the diversity of the applicable national laws remains to be seen. Within the context of Article 10 UP-Reg. Member States might not remain as sovereign as they are under Article 36 TFEU when developing their national patent systems or else the UP-Regulation would introduce a dependency of the unitary patent on national patent policy.

60 See *supra*, note 58. Therefore, Article 7 para. 1 UP-Reg. is in conflict with recital 4 UP-Reg., as well as with recital 14 of Council Decision of 10 March 2011 authorizing enhanced cooperation in the area of the creation of unitary patent protection, OJEU 2011 L 76,53. It is also in contradiction with Statement 2 annexed to Council Doc. 6524/11 of 2 March 2011 "Proposal for a Council Decision authorizing enhanced cooperation in the area of the creation of unitary patent protection – Adoption of the Council Decision", which reads: "The place of establishment of an economic operator will be immaterial for the access to unitary patent protection to be created through enhanced cooperation in the area of unitary patent protection".

Whereas with respect to their property transactions the latter can always rely on "their" law, the former cannot.

II. As both discriminatory effects result from the choice of national law instead of the introduction of Union law rules defining the characteristics of the unitary patent as an object of property, this choice needs to rest on objective grounds in order to escape an Article 18 TFEU verdict.[61] If, as regards enhanced cooperation, the choice of national law is not reasonably related to the adequate operation of uniform patent protection by way of a European patent with unitary effect,[62] there will be no sufficient justification for access discrimination of patent applicants from EU Member States, who are not domiciled in an enhanced cooperation State.

In this regard, a first point is that under Article 7 para.1 lit.a) UP-Regulation the residence and the principal place of business of the patent applicant do not, like in a conflict-of-laws situation, serve as the connecting factors most suited to identify among various national laws the one which is the most closely related to the legal issue to be regulated. To the contrary, they only serve to make the national law regulate a matter, which by its nature is not national,[63] and which is not inherently linked to a particular national locus rei sitae, namely protection of the unitary patent as an object of property. Article 7 para. 1 lit.a) is not even intended to solve a territorial conflict between various potentially applicable national laws. Rather, its purpose is to select rules for a patent right of supra-national unitary effect, and to make them the uniform law governing this patent right throughout the entire territory of enhanced cooperation.[64] It is, therefore, a false conflicts rule, which by

---

61 Whereas the prohibition of discrimination directly connected to nationality is absolute, indirect discrimination may be justified by showing that the criterion indirectly connecting the discrimination to nationality is reasonably related and proportionate to a regulatory objective, which is legitimate under EU law, see e.g. ECJ of 30 June 2005, case C-28/04, *Tod's/Heyraud*, Rep. 2005 I 5781, nos. 28 *et seq*. with references; Holoubek in Schwarze, *supra*, Article 18 AEUV, annot. 21 *et seq*. with references.

62 Article 3 para. 2, subpara. 1, 2nd sent. UP-Reg. states that the European patent with unitary effect "shall provide uniform protection and shall have equal effect in all participating Member States".

63 Article 3 para. 2, subpara. 1, 1st sent. UP-Reg. expressly provides: "a European patent with unitary effect shall have unitary character". It thus does away with the link to a national territory and with the independent character of national protection as confirmed by Article 4 bis Paris Convention for the Protection of Industrial Property. The territory of reference is that of enhanced cooperation, see Article 3 para. 2, subpara. 2, UP-Reg.

64 Therefore, Article 7 para. 1 UP-Reg. may not be explained as a problem of non-use of a shared competence, Article 2 para. 2 TFEU. Once the European patent has been

elevating national law to the level of a supra-national regime serves to introduce a substitute for the regulation of the unitary patent as an object of property by Union law.[65]

Besides, at least as regards the qualification and the effects of the unitary patent as an object of transfer of rights and as a divisible good amenable to restrictive transactions, the geographic location of the residence or the principal place of business of the patent applicant in a particular Member State are no appropriate criteria for selecting the applicable law.[66] According to Article 3 UP-Regulation, upon registration of the unitary effect, all national patents resulting from the grant of a European patent merge into one non-national patent.[67] Correspondingly, the unitary patent's territory of protection, meaning the territory of its effects on market actors, is the entire market of enhanced cooperation. Therefore, the national "connecting factors" essentially serve only to favor local patentees by making their domestic laws apply. The result is a preferential regime for the unitary patent as an object of property rather than one of equal treatment.[68]

Moreover, the very choice of having a multiplicity of national laws control the property aspects of unitary patents is insufficiently related, if not in conflict with, the purpose of the UP-Regulation to establish patent protection with unitary effect throughout the area of enhanced cooperation. Under the general principles of conflict of laws, it is the law of the country providing for protection, which mandatorily applies at least to those characteristics of national intellectual property rights as objects of property, which result from their being constitutive of the

---

transformed into a unitary patent, it is no more subject to a residual national law, since it is no longer national in nature.

65 See *supra*, sub 2.b).

66 The combined effects of determining the applicable national law ratione tempore by reference to the filing date (*supra*, note 53) and of connecting the law applicable to the unitary patent as an object of property to the domicile of the applicant, will result in that, as the proprietor moves from his/her first Member State to others, he/she may have his/her patent portfolio composed of different varieties of the "unitary" patent. At least in the hypothesis of Article 7 para. 1, lit.b) UP-Reg. the problem may become serious.

67 See Ullrich, *Select from within the system*, *supra*, sub III.2.b)(i). The unitary patent does not remain for instance a "German law" or a "French law" object of property while being an exclusive right of the Union. It is only that German law or French law is made to apply by way of assimilation, if not simulation.

68 As has been established by all of the Community industrial property regulations, see *supra*, sub 2.a). Therefore, the question arises whether they represent a general principle of Union law.

exclusive right.[69] This follows from the principle of territoriality. The underlying rationale is that it is the country of protection, which, based on its needs and policy, defines the exclusivity, of which the property characteristics are an essential part.[70] As regards the European patent with unitary effect, however, it is not a Member State, which, with respect to its territory, determines its substance or scope. Rather, it is the EU legislator, which, with respect to the entire territory of enhanced cooperation and on the basis of its proper EU law, establishes the exclusive right. It is, therefore, for the EU legislator to determine the effects of the exclusivity in a uniform way for all unitary patents. If, as regards the property aspects of these unitary patents, the EU legislator relies on the application of national laws by extending their respective territorial reach so as to make each cover the territories of all Member States of the enhanced cooperation group, it establishes a regime, which, instead of ensuring uniformity of all unitary patents, results in that, as regards their property characteristics, there will be European patents with as many diverse unitary effects as there are diverse national laws of Member States of the enhanced cooperation group. As this referral to national law jeopardizes the attainment of the very objective of the creation of unitary patents,[71] the choice of a national law regime for the unitary patent as an object of property may not justify the discriminatory effects it entails.

Finally, as regards more particularly the discrimination of patent applicants domiciled in EU Member States not participating in enhanced cooperation, it may not be justified by any particularities of the operation or of the objective of enhanced cooperation. Enhanced cooperation is about advanced integration, not about exclusion. The system established by Article 7 para. 1, lit.a) UP-Regulation is to the mutual advantage of firms domiciled in participating Member States and to the detriment of EU firms from other Member States. It is not due to the particularities of creating a system of unitary patent protection within enhanced cooperation. Such a system also requires common and uniform rules for all unitary patents, as have been agreed upon since long,[72]

69 See European Max Planck Group on Conflicts of Laws in Intellectual Property (CLIP). "Principles of Conflicts of Laws in Intellectual Property", 2011, Article 3:301 (available at www.cl-ip.eu); Drexl, "Internationales Immaterialgüterrecht", in *Münchener Kommentar, Bürgerliches Gesetzbuch*, 5th ed., Vol. 11, Munich, 2010, pp. 1426 *et seq.* (annot. 155 *et seq.* (164), pp. 1444 *et seq.* (annot. 199 *et seq.*); Ahrens, Mc Guire, *Modellgesetz für Geistiges Eigentum*, Munich, 2011, Buch I, § 24 para. 1.

70 See *supra*, sub 1.2.a).

71 See Ullrich, *Select from within the system*, *supra*, sub III.2.a)(i).

72 See *supra*, sub 2.a)b).

and as logically follows from the principle of territoriality. The unity of the territory of protection, which the European patent with unitary effect is supposed to establish, may not be reduced to the unity of the patentee's territory of protection, i.e. to the unity of his/her market. The objective is the unity of the territory of all European patents with unitary effect, meaning the unity of the Internal Market or, for that matter, of the market of enhanced cooperation. It is precisely for this reason that the Union legislator has always taken care to subject the essential features of the EU industrial property rights as objects of property to its own rules and to attribute to national laws a complementary role only.[73] The rationale is that of a regime of equal treatment and of equal access to the full value of patents both as a means of defense against imitation and as a merchandisable asset.

In sum, Article 7 para. 1, lit.a) UP-Regulation does not represent an exception from the Union's principles of industrial property regulation, which is justified by enhanced cooperation, but an unjustified discrimination.

3. Conclusion

This should not be the concluding paper of a series of Articles on the "Untamable European Union Patent"[74] published since 2002.[75] The story is not over yet. All the papers were due to my teaching at the College of Europe. While critically examining and assessing the development, which legislative proposals have taken over so many years, I have always been inspired by the College's open, forward-looking spirit of European integration. It has, indeed, been an enormous privilege to serve as a visiting professor at the College, first, when Paul Demaret was a stimulating Director of European Legal Studies, then when he became an admirable Rector of the College. However, we met as colleagues long before, discussing and debating problems of European and international business law, and of the Community patent![76] The Community (now Union) patent thus stood at the beginning of "our" story. It should not stand also at its end. Our story, hopefully, will not be over

---

73 See *supra*, sub 2.a).

74 Ullrich, in Janssens, Van Overwalle (eds.), *supra*, at p. 243. The title prophetically has been chosen by the editors.

75 Starting with Ullrich, "Patent Protection in Europe: Integrating Europe into the Community or the Community into Europe?", *European Law Journal*, Vol. 8, 2002, p. 433.

76 See Demaret, "Le brevet communautaire après Centrafarm: un instrument dépassé ou inachevé?", *Revue trimestrielle de droit européen*, 1977, 1.

before a long time after we finally have seen a unitary patent truly serving the community within the Union.

L'émergence d'un droit social de la fonction publique dans l'Union européenne

Georges VANDERSANDEN

Professeur ordinaire émérite de la Faculté de Droit de l'Université libre de Bruxelles ; avocat honoraire au Barreau de Bruxelles

Depuis quelques années, la « physionomie » de la fonction publique de l'Union européenne a évolué en passant d'un régime essentiellement statutaire à une configuration dominée par des engagements de nature contractuelle. Ce processus a été accéléré du fait de la création de nombreux agences, offices et autres organes décentralisés au sein desquels le personnel contractuel a été nommé de façon prépondérante. Il en est résulté qu'un des attraits majeurs du statut, à savoir la perspective d'une stabilité d'emploi,[1] a progressivement cédé la place à un régime contractuel que l'on pourrait qualifier de « plus flexible » mais qui se révèle, en réalité, moins bien rémunéré, moins protecteur et plus aléatoire que le statut. La réforme administrative de 2004, qui a remodelé, par les modifications introduites, le statut et le régime applicable aux autres agents (RAA),[2] a traduit cette tendance en introduisant une nouvelle catégorie d'agents, dénommés assez curieusement « agents contractuels »[3] – alors que, par définition même, tous le sont –, qui s'est substituée aux agents auxiliaires et qui sont devenus, en quelque sorte, les agents « de droit commun » engagés au service des institutions, en particulier des agences.[4]

---

[1] Et qui, bien entendu, subsiste pour celles et ceux qui sont encore engagés comme « fonctionnaires ».

[2] Règlement (CE, Euratom) n° 723/2004 du Conseil, du 22 mars 2004, JO, L 124 du 27 avril 2004, p. 1.

[3] Articles 79 à 119 du RAA.

[4] Voy. Vandersanden, G. et Levi, L., « La réforme administrative de la Commission », *Cahiers de droit européen*, 2005, p. 285 et s.

Dès les premières années de son entrée en fonction,[5] le Tribunal de la Fonction publique de l'Union européenne – ci-après TFPUE – a été attentif à cette « restructuration », qui pourrait même s'apparenter, par certains aspects, à une « dénaturation », et s'est attaché à assouplir les effets d'un régime d'engagement contractuel qui pouvait, dans son application rigoureuse, aboutir à limiter les droits légitimes des agents.[6] Ce faisant, le TFPUE s'est placé résolument dans une optique qui s'apparente davantage aux paramètres du droit social que du droit administratif qui régit naturellement les rapports entre les institutions et leurs fonctionnaires. Si le nouvel éclairage ainsi donné à la jurisprudence en matière de fonction publique s'inspire d'une constatation factuelle, celle de l'importance accrue du nombre d'agents, il relève aussi d'une approche volontaire faite d'ouverture, de respect des droits fondamentaux et des droits sociaux, en particulier tels que reconnus aux plans international et européen, de la part du TFPUE.

Ainsi, la quasi absolue concomitance de l'avènement du TFPUE et de la réforme administrative a ouvert les portes d'une assise jurisprudentielle nouvelle qui a été habilement, de façon constructive, parfois même audacieuse, « exploitée » par le TFPUE qui a su saisir cette opportunité pour faire émerger les prémisses d'un droit social de la fonction publique à composante contractuelle.[7]

Sans prétendre à un relevé exhaustif, qui dépasserait le cadre de la présente contribution, nous analyserons brièvement ci-dessous les éléments saillants de cette évolution jurisprudentielle qui situe d'emblée le TFPUE dans la ligne de l'« activisme interprétatif » caractéristique, dès l'origine, de la manière de procéder de la Cour de justice.

Au stade actuel, nous retiendrons deux directions primordiales consistant, d'une part, dans la construction jurisprudentielle à partir de l'obligation de motivation et, d'autre part, dans l'extension de l'application de directives adressées aux États membres dans les relations entre les institutions et leur personnel contractuel.[8]

---

5 Le 1er octobre 2005.

6 Et aussi, peut-être, décourager celles et ceux qui voulaient entreprendre une carrière au sein de la fonction publique de l'Union européenne.

7 Exercice d'autant plus difficile et délicat qu'il devait s'accommoder du respect des règles du droit administratif qui est, depuis l'origine, la matrice en quelque sorte « naturelle » du droit de la fonction publique.

8 Il faudrait encore mentionner, parmi les avancées de caractère social dans ce type de contentieux, l'ouverture faite, tant dans le statut du TFPUE (annexe I au Protocole n° 3 au TFUE, Article 7, point 4) que dans son règlement de procédure (règlement du 25 juillet 2007 – JO L 225, p. 1 – chapitre quatrième, Articles 68 à 70), en vue de la recherche d'un *règlement amiable* susceptible, en cas de succès, de mettre fin au litige sans aboutir à un arrêt. La tentative de trouver un règlement amiable est coutu-

1. La construction jurisprudentielle à partir de l'obligation de motivation des décisions prises en cas de résiliation ou de non-renouvellement de contrats

Point n'est besoin de souligner l'importance capitale que revêt l'obligation de motivation. Cette exigence impérative trouve son fondement dans de multiples sources de droit[9] et a été reprise et soulignée de façon constante dans la jurisprudence.[10] Ainsi, l'obligation de motivation apparaît comme constituant « *un principe essentiel du droit communautaire auquel il ne saurait être dérogé qu'en raison de considérations impérieuses. Il a pour objectif, d'une part, de permettre à l'intéressé de vérifier le caractère fondé ou non de l'acte lui faisant*

mière dans le chef du juge de droit social. Cette procédure est même parfois obligatoire devant certaines juridictions, comme en Allemagne (voy. Kreppel, H., « The mediating function of Judges : the amicable settlement of cases before the Civil Service Tribunal of the EU », in *Les évolutions de la protection juridictionnelle des fonctionnaires internationaux et européens – Développements récents*, Bruxelles, Bruylant, coll. Pratique du contentieux européen, n° 2, 2012, pp. 145 et s.). Si nous avons choisi de ne pas lui consacrer des développements, c'est, d'une part, parce que nous avons déjà discuté ailleurs de sa portée et de son opportunité dans le régime des voies de recours ouvertes aux fonctionnaires et aux agents européens (Vandersanden, G., « Le contentieux de la fonction publique européenne : décision judiciaire ou règlement amiable ? », *Cahiers de droit européen*, 2010, pp. 569 et s.) mais aussi, et surtout, parce que nous avons expressément choisi de mettre, dans la présente analyse, l'accent sur la jurisprudence et donc sur l'approche « plus sociale » exercée par le juge dans sa mission première, qui est de statuer sur les litiges dont il est saisi et de les trancher par un arrêt.

9 Voy. not. Article 296, deuxième alinéa, du TFUE ; Article 41, par. 2, troisième tiret, de la Charte des droits fondamentaux de l'Union européenne, proclamée à Nice le 7 décembre 2000 (JO, C 364, p. 1) qui prévoit « *l'obligation pour l'administration de motiver ses décisions* » comme faisant partie du « *droit à une bonne administration* ». Voy. aussi l'Article 25, deuxième aliéna, du statut, selon lequel « *Toute décision faisant grief doit être motivée* ». Voy. aussi l'Article 90, par. 1 du statut, qui établit que l'autorité compétente doit, en réponse à une demande l'invitant à prendre une décision, notifier « *sa décision motivée à l'intéressé dans un délai de quatre mois à partir du jour de l'introduction de la demande* ». Il en est de même en cas de réponse à une réclamation (cf. Article 90, par. 2 du statut, deuxième alinéa).

10 En matière de fonction publique, voy. not. arrêts de la Cour du 26 novembre 1981, *Michel/Parlement*, aff. 195/80, *Rec.* p. 2861, point 22 ; du Tribunal de première instance du 20 mars 1991, aff. T-1/90, *Pérez-Minguez Casariego/Commission*, *Rec.* p. II-143, point 73 ; du 18 mars 1997, aff. jtes T-178/95 et T-179/95, *Picciolo et Calo/Comité des régions*, *RecFP* p. I-A-51 et II-155, point 33 ; du 20 juillet 2001, aff. T-351/99, *Brumter/Commission*, *RecFP* p. I-A-165 et II-757, point 28 ; du 16 mars 2004, aff. T-11/03, *Afari/BCE*, *RecFP* p. I-A-65 et II-267, point 37 ; du 6 juillet 2004, aff. T-281/01, *Huygens/Commission*, *RecFP* p. I-A-203 et II-903, point 105 et du 3 octobre 2006, aff. T-171/05, *Nijs/Cour des comptes*, point 36.

grief et d'apprécier l'opportunité d'introduire un recours et, d'autre part, de rendre possible le contrôle juridictionnel ».[11]

Néanmoins, en ce qui concerne les agents, l'Article 47 du RAA ne prévoit aucune obligation de motivation de la décision accompagnant, en ce qui concerne les agents temporaires,[12] le non-renouvellement d'un contrat à durée déterminée ou la résiliation d'un contrat à durée indéterminée, sous la seule réserve du respect du délai de préavis. Il s'en est suivi une jurisprudence, d'ailleurs constante, selon laquelle la résiliation unilatérale du contrat d'un agent temporaire, relevant d'un large pouvoir d'appréciation de l'autorité compétente et reconnue par l'agent, au moment même de son engagement, trouvait sa justification dans le contrat d'emploi et n'avait pas besoin, dès lors, d'être motivée. C'était sur ce point que la situation d'un agent temporaire se distinguait essentiellement de celle d'un fonctionnaire de manière à exclure l'application par analogie de l'Article 25 du statut, nonobstant le renvoi général de l'Article 11 du RAA aux Articles 11 à 26 du statut.[13]

La brèche était ainsi ouverte pour opérer, sinon un revirement de jurisprudence, du moins une clarification de l'exigence de motivation dans un tel contexte. L'occasion pour le TFPUE de préciser sa position lui fut d'abord offerte à l'occasion de contentieux visant des décisions de licenciement, soit de résiliation unilatérale de contrats à durée indéterminée (parfois aussi appelées « ruptures »), puis à l'occasion de litiges dirigés contre des décisions de non-renouvellement de contrats à durée déterminée arrivés à terme.

A. Le contentieux en matière de licenciement

La première affaire opposait un agent temporaire à son employeur, en l'occurrence la Fondation européenne pour la formation, à propos d'une décision de résiliation de son contrat à durée indéterminée pour raison d'insuffisance professionnelle.[14] Dans cette affaire, le TFPUE estime que « *compte tenu de l'évolution du droit concernant la protection du travailleur contre le licenciement et l'utilisation abusive de contrats ou de relations de travail à durée déterminée successifs, ainsi que de la jurisprudence communautaire elle-même concernant l'exigence de motivation formelle des actes susceptibles de faire grief,*

---

[11] Arrêt du 26 octobre 2006, aff. F-1/05, *Landgren/ETF*, point 61.

[12] Il en va de même pour les agents contractuels, l'Article 119 du RAA renvoyant, par analogie, à l'application de l'Article 47.

[13] Voy. not. arrêts de la Cour du 18 octobre 1977, aff. 25/68, *Schertzer/Parlement*, *Rec.* p. 1729, points 38 à 40 et du Tribunal de première instance du 28 janvier 1992, aff. T-45/90, *Speybrouck/Parlement*, *Rec.* p. II-33, point 90.

[14] Affaire Landgren, citée *supra*, note 11.

considérée...comme un principe essentiel du droit communautaire, il y a lieu d'examiner si la résiliation unilatérale d'un contrat à durée indéterminée d'un agent temporaire peut ne pas être motivée ».[15] À l'appui de son examen, qui s'apparente à une démonstration, le TFPUE se base sur les références suivantes :

- l'accord-cadre CES, UNICE et CEEP[16] sur le travail à durée déterminée, mis en œuvre par la directive 1999/70 du Conseil, du 28 juin 1999,[17] dont il ressort que les contrats à durée indéterminée constituent « *la forme générale de relations d'emploi entre employeurs et travailleurs* », se caractérisant par la stabilité de l'emploi ;
- l'existence de standards internationaux visant à éviter des licenciements abusifs de travailleurs, tels que l'Article 4 de la convention n° 158 de l'OIT et l'Article 24, sous a), de la Charte sociale européenne révisée du Conseil de l'Europe (n° 163), adoptée le 3 mai 1996, ces deux textes insistant sur l'interdiction de licencier des travailleurs sans motif valable lié à leur aptitude ou leur conduite ;
- l'Article 30 de la Charte des droits fondamentaux de l'Union européenne qui protège tout travailleur contre tout licenciement injustifié[18] et qui porte obligation, pour l'administration, de motiver ses décisions.[19]

De telles considérations peuvent parfaitement valoir au regard du libellé de l'Article 47 du RAA, sans s'y opposer, dans la mesure où cet Article se borne à prévoir la fixation d'un préavis sans aborder la question de la justification du licenciement. Il en résulte que la motivation est obligatoire dans le cas du licenciement d'un agent temporaire sous contrat à durée indéterminée afin de connaître les raisons qui fondent une telle décision, et que, même, celles-ci devraient, en règle générale, être « *clairement énoncées par écrit, de préférence dans le texte même de la décision concernée* ».[20]

Dans cette affaire, toutefois, l'intéressée, Mme Landgren, avait été dûment informée, avant que la décision de mettre fin à son contrat soit prise, à la suite d'entretiens avec le directeur de l'ETF, des raisons tirées

15 Point 65 de l'arrêt rendu dans l'affaire Landgren.

16 Soit Confédération européenne des syndicats, Union des confédérations de l'industrie et des employeurs et Centre européen des entreprises à participation publique.

17 JO, L 175, p. 43.

18 Article 30.

19 Article 41, par. 2, troisième tiret.

20 Point 81 de l'arrêt rendu dans l'affaire Landgren.

de son insuffisance professionnelle. De sorte que l'obligation de motivation était satisfaite.

Sans doute le TFPUE aurait-il pu s'arrêter là et constater que la décision de licenciement ayant été prise en conformité du droit et de la jurisprudence, le recours était rejeté.

Mais le Tribunal, et c'est même peut-être sous cet angle-là que son apport personnel à la solution du litige est la plus significative, va examiner si les motifs invoqués à l'appui de la décision de licenciement sont bien fondés, en particulier si l'appréciation portée par l'ETF est conforme à l'intérêt du service, c'est-à-dire si elle n'est pas entachée d'une erreur manifeste.[21]

D'emblée, le TFPUE souligne la nécessité, pour procéder à une telle évaluation, de « *prendre en considération l'ensemble des éléments qui sont susceptibles de déterminer la décision (de l'autorité compétente), et notamment l'intérêt de l'agent concerné. Cela résulte, en effet, du devoir de sollicitude de l'administration, qui reflète l'équilibre des droits et obligations réciproques que le statut et, par analogie, le RAA ont créé dans les relations entre l'autorité publique et ses agents* ».[22]

En procédant à cet examen, qui consistait en l'espèce à confronter les rapports d'évaluation défavorables et critiques à l'égard des prestations de la requérante et ceux qui pouvaient être considérés comme satisfaisants, le TFPUE, en substituant sa propre évaluation à celle de l'administration, arrive à la conclusion que « *la décision de licenciement est entachée d'une erreur manifeste d'appréciation et doit, en conséquence, être annulée* ».[23] On ne peut manquer de s'étonner quelque peu, toutefois, de cette conclusion qui devrait s'appuyer sur la démonstration d'erreurs flagrantes commises par l'ETF dans son évaluation des prestations de Mme Landgren, erreurs par lesquelles l'ETF aurait dépassé largement la marge d'appréciation qui est la sienne dans un tel contexte.[24] Sans doute le Tribunal a-t-il saisi l'opportunité que lui offrait

---

[21] En effet, s'agissant de décisions relevant, dans le chef de l'autorité compétente, d'un large pouvoir d'appréciation, le contrôle du juge doit se limiter, indépendamment du contrôle du respect de l'obligation de motivation, à la vérification de l'absence d'erreur manifeste ou de détournement de pouvoir : voy. not. arrêt de la Cour du 26 février 1981, 25/80, *De Briey/Commission*, *Rec.* p. 637, point 7 ; arrêts du Tribunal de première instance du 28 janvier 1992, aff. T-45/90, *Speybrouck/Parlement*, *Rec.* p. II-33, points 97 et 98 ; du 17 mars 1994, aff. T-51/91, *Hoyer/Commission*, *RecFP* p. I-A-103 et II-341, point 36 et du 14 juillet 1997, aff. T-123/95, *B/Parlement*, *RecFP* p. I-A-245 et II-697, point 70.

[22] Point 83 de l'arrêt.

[23] Point 91 de l'arrêt.

[24] En effet, étaient, en l'occurrence, en opposition, d'une part, de nombreux rapports d'évaluation défavorables et des appréciations fort négatives émises par des respon-

cette affaire pour se prononcer clairement, non seulement sur le caractère essentiel de l'obligation de motivation, mais aussi pour se donner le pouvoir de contrôler de façon extensive les motifs d'une décision de licenciement, une fois ces motifs donnés. En procédant à une réévaluation des motifs donnés par l'administration, par laquelle il substitue en réalité son appréciation à celle faite par l'administration, le Tribunal donne en particulier au moyen tiré de l'erreur manifeste, un contenu et une portée qui dépassent le sens habituellement reconnu à ce moyen en droit administratif et lui donne, par la combinaison du devoir de sollicitude qui s'impose à l'administration et de la mise en balance des intérêts tenant, d'une part, au fonctionnement du service et, d'autre part, à la prise en compte de la situation de l'intéressé, une portée élargie qui se veut plus égalitaire des droits respectifs de l'administration et de l'agent. Ce qui correspond à une approche que l'on pourrait qualifier de « plus sociale » du droit de la fonction publique et de la mission du juge.

Encore fallait-il tirer les conséquences de cette annulation. À cet égard aussi, le raisonnement du juge mérite d'être souligné. En l'espèce, la requérante avait déjà été licenciée et son état de santé s'était détérioré au point qu'elle n'était plus physiquement apte à reprendre l'exercice d'une activité au sein de l'ETF. Estimant que, dans ces circonstances, il n'y avait pas lieu de s'interroger sur l'existence, en faveur du travailleur, d'un éventuel droit à la réintégration en cas de licenciement illégal,[25] le TFPUE fait usage, « *afin d'assurer, dans l'intérêt de la requérante, un effet utile à l'arrêt, ... de la compétence de pleine juridiction qui lui est dévolue dans les litiges à caractère pécuniaire, en invitant la partie défenderesse à rechercher une solution amiable de nature à protéger adéquatement les droits de Mme Landgren* ».[26] Et le Tribunal d'inviter, en conséquence, les parties à rechercher un accord fixant une compensation pécuniaire équitable du licenciement illégal de la requérante, à en informer le Tribunal et à lui présenter, à défaut d'accord, les conclusions chiffrées échangées entre elles. Le Tribunal précise que, à cette fin, « *il conviendra de tenir compte, notamment, de ce que Mme Landgren a perçu des indemnités de chômage après son licenciement et*

---

sables de l'ETF et, d'autre part, des appréciations moins sévères, voire favorables émises par deux personnes, l'une d'elles étant faite peu de temps avant la décision de licenciement.

25 Il y a lieu de penser, toutefois, que le TFPUE reconnaît de la sorte implicitement un droit à la réintégration car c'est dans l'hypothèse où, comme en l'espèce, ce droit ne peut être appliqué qu'il convient d'évaluer, en guise de compensation, le montant d'un préjudice « équitable ».

26 Point 93 de l'arrêt.

de l'âge auquel elle aurait normalement pu, compte tenu de son état de santé, prétendre à une pension de retraite ».[27]

Ainsi, par un effet cumulatif associant de façon formelle l'obligation impérieuse de la motivation, son contrôle étendu portant sur l'examen des faits par une application extensive du moyen tiré de l'erreur manifeste d'appréciation, la substitution – au cours de cet examen – de sa propre évaluation à celle faite par l'administration, et le souci – en se reconnaissant une compétence de pleine juridiction qui vient compléter le contrôle de la légalité – de conférer à l'annulation prononcée un effet utile, au cas où la réintégration se révèle impossible pour assurer à l'agent concerné la réparation la plus adéquate de son préjudice, le TFPUE, dans cet arrêt rendu en assemblée plénière, a voulu marquer, sinon un revirement de jurisprudence, du moins sa volonté d'adapter le processus juridictionnel afin de le mettre de façon plus appropriée en relation avec la protection de la situation contractuelle des agents. Ce faisant, le Tribunal se donne, en quelque sorte, une dimension nouvelle qui l'assimile à une juridiction de droit social œuvrant néanmoins dans un cadre administratif.[28]

Évidemment, cette percée jurisprudentielle ne pouvait rester sans suite. Ce fut le cas et cela a permis au TFPUE à la fois de confirmer la jurisprudence Landgren et de la préciser.

Par deux arrêts du 9 décembre 2010,[29] le TFPUE a annulé les décisions de licenciement des requérantes motivées par le transfert des

---

27 Point 95 de l'arrêt.

28 Il est intéressant de noter, à ce propos, qu'à la suite du pourvoi introduit par l'ETF (à laquelle s'était jointe la Commission) contre cet arrêt, le Tribunal, par arrêt du 8 septembre 2009 (aff. T-404/06 P), d'une part, n'a pas suivi le TFPUE dans ses développements sur l'obligation de motivation mais a fondé celle-ci sur l'Article 25 de statut auquel renvoie, par analogie, l'article 11 du RAA (rejetant donc l'inclusion de la motivation dans l'*instrumentum* consistant dans la décision de licenciement), et, d'autre part, s'est abstenu de se prononcer sur la prise en compte des éléments matériels sur lesquels était fondée la décision de licenciement, au motif qu'il ne lui appartenait pas d'apprécier la force probante de documents, le contrôle du Tribunal dans le cadre d'un pourvoi étant limité aux questions de droit. Quant au moyen de pourvoi selon lequel le TFPUE aurait statué *ultra vires* en adressant à l'ETF une injonction quant à la réparation du préjudice encouru par la requérante, le Tribunal (tout en relevant au passage que le juge communautaire ne saurait ordonner à l'institution concernée de réintégrer la requérante dans ses fonctions), souligne qu'il s'agit en l'espèce d'un arrêt interlocutoire, le TFPUE ayant laissé aux parties le soin de rechercher un accord sur la compensation équitable à octroyer à la requérante sans définir de manière définitive et exhaustive les critères et modalités de calcul de cette compensation. L'arrêt du Tribunal, s'il conclut donc au rejet du pourvoi, ne suit pas pour autant le raisonnement « innovateur » du premier juge et contient même, tout en les accommodant, certaines « corrections » relevant de l'approche administrative plus traditionnelle.

29 Schuerings/ETF, F-87/08 et Vandeuren/ETF, F-88/08.

activités du programme « Tempus » qu'elles étaient chargées de mettre en œuvre, au sein de l'ETF, à une nouvelle agence, l'EACEA.[30] Après avoir rappelé, comme condition d'un motif valable, qu'à l'occasion du licenciement d'un agent temporaire sous contrat à durée indéterminée, « *l'autorité compétente doit tenir compte de l'intérêt du service, mais également, afin de satisfaire à son devoir de sollicitude, de l'intérêt de l'agent concerné* »,[31] le TFPUE estime que, dans les circonstances des affaires en cause, une décision de licenciement ne saurait être valable « *qu'à la condition...que ladite agence* (ETF) *n'ait pas disposé de poste sur lequel l'agent concerné aurait pu être réaffecté* ».[32] En réponse à l'objection faite par l'ETF qu'elle était tenue de respecter les procédures de sélection existantes et qu'elle devait disposer de postes disponibles, sous peine d'enfreindre le droit et de susciter des recours venant d'autres membres du personnel, le TFPUE relève que : « *il est indifférent que des règles internes prévoient des procédures particulières de sélection en cas de vacance d'emploi pour les mutations internes des agents. En effet, il convient de rappeler que, avant de publier une vacance d'emploi afin de pourvoir un poste par voie de mutation interne, l'administration a toujours la possibilité de procéder d'office à une réaffectation dans l'intérêt du service...et ce, sans méconnaître le principe de l'égalité de traitement... Est également indifférente... la circonstance que des mesures d'accompagnement aient été prises. En effet, si leur mise en place participe incontestablement au respect du devoir de sollicitude auquel une agence est par ailleurs tenue, cette circonstance ne saurait dispenser l'autorité compétente de fonder ses décisions de licenciement sur des motifs valables* ».[33] L'administration doit donc, au préalable, examiner si l'intéressé ne peut pas être réaffecté à un autre poste existant ou devant être prochainement créé à la suite, notamment, de l'attribution de nouvelles compétences à l'agence concernée. Le TFPUE précise même, en procédant à la mise en balance de l'intérêt du service et de celui de l'intéressé, que l'administration « *doit tenir compte, dans le cadre de son pouvoir d'appréciation, de différents critères parmi lesquels figurent les exigences du poste au regard des qualifications et du potentiel de l'agent, la circonstance que le contrat de travail de l'agent concerné précise ou non que ce dernier a été embauché pour occuper un poste déterminé, ses rapports d'évaluation, ainsi que son âge, l'ancienneté de service et le nombre d'années qui lui reste à cotiser avant de pouvoir faire valoir ses droits à la retraite* ».[34]

---

30 Agence exécutive « Éducation, audiovisuel et culture ».

31 Point 58 de l'arrêt Schuerings et point 59 de l'arrêt Vandeuren.

32 Point 59 de l'arrêt Schuerings et point 60 de l'arrêt Vandeuren.

33 Point 60 et 61 de l'arrêt Schuerings et points 61 et 62 de l'arrêt Vandeuren.

34 Point 63 de l'arrêt Schuerings et point 64 de l'arrêt Vandeuren.

Or, en l'espèce, non seulement l'ETF a procédé à de nombreuses mutations internes entre la date à laquelle elle a été informée du transfert des activités du programme « Tempus » l'EACEA et celle de la prise d'effet de la décision de licenciement de la requérante, mais elle n'a pas cherché à lui trouver un autre poste dans les conditions « prioritaires » qu'exigeait sa situation, se contentant de la faire participer, « *comme n'importe quel autre candidat, aux procédures internes de sélection mises en place afin de pourvoir aux postes vacants, et...dès lors, en agissant de la sorte, l'ETF a manqué à ses obligations* ».[35] Même si la requérante n'a montré aucun empressement pour chercher à occuper un poste vacant au sein de l'ETF, « *dès lors que c'est l'ETF qui a pris l'initiative de la licencier..., il ne saurait être pallié à l'absence de motif valable au licenciement par le reproche, formulé à l'égard de la requérante, de ne pas avoir postulé qu'à peu d'offres d'emploi au sein de l'EFT* ».[36]

En conséquence, le TFPUE prononce l'illégalité de la décision de licenciement et son annulation.

Mais, dans le souci de clarifier et de conforter sa position, le TFPUE ajoute, en soulignant qu'il le fait « *à titre surabondant* », que, « *pendant la période entourant le licenciement de la requérante, plusieurs postes parmi ceux libérés au sein de l'ETF correspondaient aux compétences de la requérante ou, à tout le moins, étaient susceptibles d'être occupés par elle après une rapide formation* ».[37] De plus, et également à titre surabondant, le TFPUE relève que le contrat de travail de la requérante « *ne faisait pas état de son affectation spécifique au département chargé de mettre en œuvre le programme "Tempus" auquel elle n'a été affectée que huit ans plus tard* », que ses rapports d'évaluation étaient, dans l'ensemble, élogieux, qu'elle était âgée au moment des faits de 53 ans et qu'elle aurait pu partir à la retraite à l'âge de 60 ans et qu'elle avait quatorze années d'ancienneté au sein de l'ETF.[38]

Quant aux conséquences indemnitaires de cette annulation, s'il est « normal » que la requérante soit rétablie dans son droit au traitement entre la date à laquelle la décision de licenciement a pris effet et celle à laquelle l'arrêt a été rendu, le TFPUE ajoute, s'agissant de l'avenir, qu'il appartient à l'ETF, selon la jurisprudence Landgren, « *qui impose*

---

[35] Point 64 de l'arrêt Schuerings et point 65 de l'arrêt Vandeuren.

[36] Point 65 de l'arrêt Schuerings et point 66 de l'arrêt Vandeuren.

[37] Point 67 de l'arrêt Schuerings.

[38] Point 68 de l'arrêt Schuerings. Quant à Mme Vandeuren, le point 68 de l'arrêt précise que ses rapports d'évaluation « *faisaient état d'un niveau élevé de performance* » et qu'à la date des faits, « *elle était âgée de 55 ans* », ce qui permet d'aboutir aux mêmes conclusions que dans l'affaire Schuerings.

la réintégration de l'intéressé en cas d'annulation de son licenciement...de réintégrer la requérante ». Le TFPUE confirme, ainsi, ce qu'il avait énoncé implicitement dans l'affaire Landgren,[39] à savoir que le droit de la requérante à obtenir la réparation d'un éventuel préjudice matériel futur se fonde sur la constatation qu'elle ne serait pas réintégrée ou ne pourrait l'être. Comme, en l'occurrence, l'éventualité d'une non-réintégration n'est, au jour de l'arrêt, qu'une supposition, « *il n'existe à l'heure actuelle aucun préjudice réel et certain dans le chef de la requérante* ».[40]

Quant au préjudice moral, il est inhérent à toute mesure de licenciement qui engendre dans le chef de la personne licenciée des sentiments de rejet, de frustration et d'incertitude pour l'avenir. Il ne saurait donc, en tant que tel, donner lieu à réparation sauf en cas de circonstances particulières.[41]

Bref, dans ces deux dernières affaires, le TFPUE confirme la jurisprudence inaugurée dans l'affaire Landgren et la renforce même, non seulement en substituant son propre raisonnement et ses propres critères à ceux de l'agence, mais aussi en dénonçant et sanctionnant le caractère insuffisant – voire le manque – des mesures prises par l'administration et qui auraient permis de maintenir les requérantes au sein de l'ETF. Cela, en dépit du fait que l'agence s'était trouvée confrontée à une situation indépendante de son fait et en dépit des solutions qu'elle avait cherché à trouver pour les requérantes dans le respect de la légalité et des droits de tous les intéressés. En l'occurrence, le TFPUE fait une application tout à fait extensive du devoir de sollicitude et, ce faisant, il fait de la protection de la situation des requérantes une préoccupation qui l'emporte sur l'intérêt du service. Protection qu'il étend dans l'évaluation du préjudice, en particulier matériel, au cas où la requérante

---

39 Voy. *supra*, note 25. Il convient, toutefois, de souligner que, dans son arrêt du 8 septembre 2009, le Tribunal, sur pourvoi, avait énoncé sans ambiguïté que le juge ne pouvait en aucun cas adresser à l'administration une injonction par laquelle il l'obligerait à réintégrer un agent à la suite d'un arrêt d'annulation : voy. *supra*, note 27. Voy. aussi, en ce sens, arrêt du Tribunal du 23 mars 2000, aff. T-197/98, *Rudolph/Commission*, *RecFP* p. I-A-55 et II-241, point 92.

40 Points 71 de l'arrêt Schuerings et de l'arrêt Vandeuren.

41 Ainsi en est-il si c'est le comportement de l'employeur qui a affecté moralement l'agent au-delà de ce qu'une personne licenciée ressent habituellement, notamment lorsque ledit employeur s'est fondé sur des motifs comportant une appréciation des capacités ou du comportement dudit agent susceptible de le blesser : points 73 des arrêts Schuerings et Vandeuren. Voy. aussi arrêt du Tribunal de première instance du 12 décembre 2000, aff. T-223/99, *Dejaiffe/OHMI*, *RecFP* p. I-A-277 et II-1267, point 91.

ne serait pas réintégrée, ce qui rendrait son préjudice « *réel et certain* ».[42]

B. Le contentieux en matière de non-renouvellement de contrats

La jurisprudence Landgren ne pouvait qu'inspirer, selon la même ligne de raisonnement, le TFPUE en cas de décision de non-renouvellement de contrats à durée déterminée.

Dans la première affaire, Bianchi/ETF,[43] le TFPUE, en faisant usage du moyen tiré de l'erreur manifeste, a examiné si la mesure entreprise prenait effectivement en considération l'ensemble des éléments qu'il appartenait à l'administration de mettre en balance, en vertu du devoir de sollicitude qui s'impose à elle, et notamment l'intérêt de l'agent concerné. À ce propos, il constate « *que la décision attaquée a été prise après consultation de services au sein desquels la requérante avait travaillé, ainsi que de celui auprès duquel elle aurait été affectée si son contrat avait été renouvelé. Compte tenu du large pouvoir d'appréciation dont jouit l'autorité compétente en matière de prolongation des contrats d'agent temporaire, il y a lieu de considérer que l'AHCC*[44] *n'a pas commis d'erreur manifeste d'appréciation en considérant que le jugement global... contenait des éléments négatifs...de telle sorte qu'il n'était pas dans l'intérêt du service de renouveler ledit contrat* ».[45] À cela s'ajoute le fait que les intérêts de la requérante ont été suffisamment pris en compte par l'administration puisqu'elle a pu les faire valoir au cours des entretiens qu'elle a eus avec la directrice de l'ETF, préalablement à l'adoption de la décision attaquée. Enfin, et cela mérite d'être souligné, le TFPUE rappelle « *que la requérante n'avait aucun droit au renouvellement de son contrat, ceci n'étant qu'une simple possibilité, subordonnée à la condition que ce renouvellement soit conforme à l'intérêt du service* ».[46]

---

42 Sur cette jurisprudence, voy. Vandersanden, G., « Le Tribunal de la Fonction Publique : un nouveau regard », in *Réalisations et défis de l'Union européenne. Mélanges en hommage à Panayotis Soldatos*, Bruxelles, Bruylant, 2012, pp. 385 et s. Voy. aussi Van Raepenbusch, S., « L'apport du Tribunal de la Fonction Publique européenne », in *Les évolutions de la protection juridictionnelle des fonctionnaires internationaux et européens*, Bruxelles, Bruylant, coll. Pratique du contentieux européen, 2012, n° 2, pp. 79 et s.

43 Aff. F-38/06, arrêt du 28 juin 2007.

44 Autorité habilitée à conclure les contrats.

45 Point 96 de l'arrêt.

46 Point 98. Cf. arrêt du 6 février 2003, aff. T-7/01, *Pyres/Commission, RecFP* p. I-A-37 et II-239, point 64.

Dans l'affaire Gheysens/Conseil de l'Union européenne,[47] le requérant avait été recruté d'abord comme agent auxiliaire, puis, comme agent contractuel auxiliaire, toujours dans le cadre de contrats à durée déterminée. Par note interne du 24 juin 2009, le directeur général de la DG A « Personnel et administration » a informé le requérant qu'il refusait de prolonger son contrat au-delà de la date d'expiration (30 septembre 2009) au motif que, en vertu des dispositions de l'Article 29 du statut, l'emploi occupé par le requérant devait être pourvu par voie de promotion, mutation d'un fonctionnaire ou par nomination d'un lauréat de concours. C'est donc contre cette note valant décision de non-renouvellement de son dernier contrat que le requérant a saisi le TFPUE. À l'appui de son recours, il faisait valoir une série de moyens tirés de la violation de l'Article 25 du statut (méconnaissance de l'obligation de motivation), des principes découlant de la directive 1999/70 du Conseil, du 28 juin 1999 et de l'accord-cadre dont elle avait pour objet d'assurer la mise en œuvre,[48] des règles fixant les conditions minimales pour éviter des licenciements abusifs des travailleurs, du devoir de sollicitude et du principe de bonne administration, ainsi que de la prétention que la décision litigieuse était dépourvue de base légale. À cela, le requérant ajoutait encore que la décision en question méconnaîtrait l'Article 3ter du RAA[49] ainsi que le principe d'exécution de bonne foi des contrats.

Si la plupart de ces moyens sont formulés en termes généraux et abstraits, ce qui les rend irrecevables, en revanche, le TFPUE examine attentivement le moyen tiré de la méconnaissance de l'Article 25 du statut et de l'obligation de motivation. À cette occasion, il souligne une fois encore le caractère essentiel que revêt l'obligation de motivation[50] et rappelle « *qu'une décision refusant de renouveler un contrat à durée déterminée est un acte faisant grief au sens de l'Article 25 du statut si elle est distincte du contrat en question, ce qui est le cas en particulier si elle est fondée sur des éléments nouveaux ou si elle constitue une prise de position de l'administration intervenant suite à une demande*

---

47 Aff. F-8/10, arrêt du 23 novembre 2010.

48 Cf. *supra*, note 17.

49 Au motif que le Conseil n'aurait pu légalement l'engager en qualité d'agent contractuel auxiliaire, dès lors que le poste qu'il occupait ne visait pas à couvrir des besoins passagers et occasionnels.

50 Ainsi, l'autorité compétente « est tenue de motiver ses décisions, à tout le moins, au plus tard, au stade du rejet de la réclamation » et « l'obligation de motiver doit, dans chaque cas, être appréciée en fonction des circonstances concrètes…en particulier, une décision est suffisamment motivée dès lors qu'elle est intervenue dans un contexte connu du fonctionnaire concerné, qui lui permet de comprendre la portée de la mesure prise à son égard » (point 63 de l'arrêt et références citées).

de l'agent intéressé et portant sur une possibilité, inscrite dans le contrat, de renouveler celui-ci…Une telle décision de refus doit être motivée… »[51] En l'espèce, il s'agit bien d'une décision distincte, puisque la note attaquée du 24 juin 2009 précisait que le contrat du requérant ne pourrait pas être renouvelé alors que, par ailleurs, ledit contrat prévoyait expressément une possibilité éventuelle de renouvellement. Dès lors, cette décision fait grief et doit être motivée. Le contrôle de la motivation exercé par le TFPUE fait apparaître que le requérant avait été effectivement informé du contexte dans lequel la décision litigieuse avait été prise par le Conseil de sorte que l'obligation de motivation avait été satisfaite.

Quant à une éventuelle erreur manifeste d'appréciation portant sur les motifs, le TFPUE se limite à en rappeler la portée limitée en raison du large pouvoir d'appréciation de l'autorité compétente, mais « tempérée » par le devoir de sollicitude qui pèse sur cette même autorité, pour conclure, sans entrer davantage dans leur discussion, qu'en l'espèce, « *les éléments avancés par le requérant ne permettent pas de démontrer que le Conseil aurait commis une erreur manifeste d'appréciation en adoptant la décision litigieuse* ».[52]

Enfin, les deux autres moyens encore examinés par le TFPUE, à savoir la méconnaissance de l'Article 3ter du RAA interprété à la lumière de la directive 1999/70 du Conseil et, d'autre part, la méconnaissance du principe d'exécution de bonne foi d'un contrat, sont tous deux brièvement rejetés par le TFPUE au motif qu'ils sont « *sans incidence sur la légalité de la décision litigieuse* ».[53]

Même si cette jurisprudence se base sur la même mécanique interprétative et sur les mêmes principes que ceux dégagés par l'arrêt rendu dans l'affaire Landgren, elle nous paraît se situer, si nous pouvons nous exprimer ainsi, un « cran en dessous ». Sans doute faut-il y voir, en effet, une différence essentielle et objective, tenant au fait que la rupture

---

51 Point 64 de l'arrêt. Si cela n'est pas contestable, il n'est pas sans intérêt de relever que, dans un arrêt du 4 juin 2009, le même TFPUE relève que : « …la fin d'un contrat de travail à durée déterminée, du simple fait de la survenance de son terme, ne constitue pas un licenciement à proprement parler, devant être spécialement motivé au regard de l'aptitude, de la conduite ou des nécessités de fonctionnement de l'institution » (aff. jtes, F-134/07 et F-8/08, *Vahan Adjemian e.a. et C. Renier/Commission*, point 104). Ce qui n'est pas contradictoire avec l'arrêt Gheysens qui rattache la notion d'acte faisant grief à des éléments nouveaux ou à une prise de position distincte du contrat et met, de plus, en exergue la différence fondamentale qui existe entre une mesure de licenciement qui, en elle-même, fait grief et le non-renouvellement d'un contrat qui ne fait pas grief en soi mais peut être contesté au regard du contexte entourant une telle fin de l'engagement.

52 Point 77 de l'arrêt.

53 Points 84 à 87 de l'arrêt.

d'un contrat à durée indéterminée est à la fois moins prévisible et plus grave que celle du non-renouvellement d'un contrat à durée déterminée, qui n'est que la conséquence « logique » de l'arrivée du terme et n'exige en soi aucune motivation spéciale[54] et parce qu'elle se heurte à l'espérance qui s'apparente à une garantie, celle de la sécurité de l'emploi. La référence à la stabilité de l'emploi comme élément protecteur de la situation contractuelle des agents a été particulièrement relevée et soulignée par le TFPUE dans sa jurisprudence concernant l'extension de l'application de certaines directives.

2. L'extension de l'application de directives adressées aux États membres dans les relations entre les institutions et leur personnel contractuel

Déjà, dans certaines des affaires citées ci-dessus, le TFPUE avait, de manière spontanée, à l'appui de son argumentation, fait état et application de l'accord-cadre annexé à la directive 1999/70 du Conseil. Mais la question de principe consistant à se demander si des directives, adressées aux États membres et non aux institutions, peuvent être considérées comme imposant en tant que telles des obligations auxdites institutions dans leurs rapports avec leur personnel, n'avait jamais été posée en ces termes. Cette question a été abordée et examinée par le TFPUE, qui lui a donné une interprétation extensive, sans pour autant méconnaître la nature juridique propre des directives, en insistant sur la nécessité d'une application « conforme » du contenu des directives dans des situations qui, si elles visent en premier lieu leurs destinataires naturels que sont les États, sont également « transposables » aux relations entre les institutions et leur personnel, qu'il s'agisse d'ailleurs tant des agents que des fonctionnaires.

Dès 2009, dans l'affaire Laleh Aayhan[55] et dans plusieurs arrêts ultérieurs,[56] et ce de façon constante, le TFPUE s'est fondé sur « l'invocabilité interprétative » de certaines directives[57] dont la finalité et le contenu étaient susceptibles de s'appliquer à des agents employés par

---

54 Voy. *supra*, notes 46 et 51.

55 Arrêt du 30 avril 2009, aff. F-65/07, *Laleh Aayhan/Parlement européen.*

56 Arrêt du 4 juin 2009, aff. jtes F-134/07 et F-8/08, *Vahan Adjemian e.a. et C. Renier/Commission* ; arrêt du 15 mars 2011, aff. F-120/07, *G. Strack/Commission ;* arrêt du 13 avril 2011, aff ; F-105/09, *S. Scheefer/Parlement européen.*

57 Il s'agissait, dans toutes ces affaires, de la directive 1999/70 du Conseil, du 28 juin 1999, concernant l'accord-cadre CES, UNICE et CEEP sur le travail à durée déterminée (JO, L 175 du 10 juillet 1999, p. 43), sauf dans l'affaire Strack où était invoquée la directive 2003/88/CE du Parlement européen et du Conseil, du 4 novembre 2003, concernant certains aspects de l'aménagement du temps de travail (JO, L 299 du 18 novembre 2003, p. 9).

les institutions afin de les faire bénéficier, par une sorte d'effet direct,[58] des dispositions desdites directives dans les circonstances et en conformité des mesures contenues dans de tels actes.

Le TFPUE rappelle, d'abord, que les dispositions d'une directive peuvent, en premier lieu, s'imposer indirectement à une institution si elles constituent l'expression d'un principe général de droit communautaire qu'il lui incombe alors d'appliquer comme tel.[59] En deuxième lieu, une directive peut lier une institution quand celle-ci a, dans le cadre de son autonomie institutionnelle et dans les limites du statut, entendu donner exécution à une obligation particulière énoncée dans une directive ou encore dans l'occurrence où un acte de portée générale d'application interne renvoie, lui-même, expressément aux mesures arrêtées par le législateur communautaire en application des traités.[60]

À ces deux hypothèses, le TFPUE, dans l'affaire Aayhan, en ajoute une troisième, à savoir que les institutions doivent, conformément au *devoir de loyauté*[61] qui pèse sur elles au titre de l'Article 10, deuxième alinéa, CE,[62] tenir compte dans leur comportement d'employeur, des dispositions législatives adoptées à l'échelle communautaire, imposant notamment des prescriptions minimales destinées à améliorer les conditions de vie et de travail des travailleurs dans les États membres au moyen d'un rapprochement des législations et pratiques nationales.[63]

S'agissant de la directive 1999/70 du Conseil mettant en œuvre l'accord-cadre CES, UNICE et CEEP sur le travail à durée indéterminée,[64] et même si la stabilité d'emploi à laquelle elle tend ne saurait être assimilée à un principe général de droit communautaire susceptible d'être érigé en règle de droit contraignante, il n'en demeure pas moins

---

58 Il nous semble qu'on puisse, en l'occurrence, parler d'effet direct dans la mesure où l'invocation des droits contenus dans les directives en question ne dépendent pas d'une transposition dans le chef des États et que les institutions, par ailleurs, n'en étant pas les destinataires, ne sauraient, de ce fait même, être astreintes à une telle transposition. C'est, d'une certaine manière, un « effet direct de substitution », les effets de la directive étant étendus aux institutions en sus de leurs destinataires « naturels » que sont les États membres. Ceci, en raison d'un critère « matériel » (auquel il faut ajouter la référence à la « finalité » dans la technique d'interprétation) tenant au contenu de l'acte qui trouve à s'appliquer à des situations internes existants tant dans les États qu'au sein des institutions dans les relations avec leur personnel, de façon comparable, sinon identique.

59 Arrêt de la Cour du 9 septembre 2003, aff. C-25/02, *Rinke*, *Rec*. p. I-8349, points 25 à 28.

60 Arrêt Ayhan, *supra*, points 113 et 116.

61 Souligné par nous.

62 Cet article a été abrogé et remplacé par l'article 4, par. E du TUE.

63 Arrêt Aayhan, *supra*, point 118.

64 Citée *supra*, note 57.

que la volonté du législateur de faire de cette finalité un objectif prééminent en matière de relations de travail au sein de l'Union européenne, est clairement affirmée. Dès lors, il incombe aux institutions communautaires, conformément au devoir de loyauté, d'interpréter, dans la mesure du possible, les dispositions du RAA à la lumière du texte et de la finalité de l'accord-cadre pour atteindre le résultat visé par celui-ci.[65]

Quant à l'existence de « *raisons objectives* », au sens de la clause 5, point 1, sous a), dudit accord-cadre, de nature à justifier le recours à des contrats d'agents auxiliaires à durée déterminée successifs, renouvelés à l'occasion de la tenue de chaque session parlementaire, tels que prévus par l'Article 78 du RAA, il y a lieu de reconnaître qu'elles sont en l'espèce justifiées en raison des besoins intermittents et massifs en ressources humaines du Parlement européen, pour la seule durée des sessions. De telles activités, en effet, si elles sont prévisibles, ne correspondent pas pour autant à un travail durable et permanent.[66]

Dans les affaires Vahan Adjemian e.a. et C. Renier,[67] le TFPUE reprend le raisonnement l'ayant conduit, dans l'affaire Aayhan, à reconnaître l'« invocabilité »[68] de la directive 1999/70 du Conseil.[69] Il examine également l'éventuelle méconnaissance de droits fondamentaux, en particulier les Articles 30[70] et 31, par. 1[71] de la Charte des droits fondamentaux. Après avoir souligné la signification particulière que le

---

65 Arrêt Aayhan, *supra*, points 117, 119, 120 et 122.

66 *Id.*, points 134 et 135. Sur la notion de « *raison objective* », voy. arrêt de la Cour du 4 juillet 2006, aff. C-212/04, *Adeneler e.a.*, *Rec.* p. I-6057, points 69 et 70.

67 Citées *supra*, note 56.

68 Par la méthode de l'interprétation par « invocabilité », le TFPUE agit, en quelque sorte, de la même manière que s'il était saisi d'une question préjudicielle que lui aurait renvoyée un juge national et qui porterait sur l'interprétation de l'une ou l'autre disposition de l'accord-cadre annexé à la directive. La Cour de justice a, quant à elle, été, à plusieurs reprises, appelée à se prononcer sur l'interprétation de la directive 1999/70 du Conseil. Ainsi, par exemple, sur la notion de « raison objective » permettant de justifier le renouvellement de contrats à durée déterminée, voy. arrêt du 26 janvier 2012, aff. C-586/10, *Bianca Kücük*. Il appartiendra au TFPUE d'aligner son interprétation – en cas d'identité de questions – sur celle dégagée par la Cour de justice dans le cadre de la procédure préjudicielle, tout en tenant compte des spécificités propres au régime de la fonction publique européenne.

69 Il est à noter que, dans ces affaires, les parties requérantes contestaient non seulement le non-renouvellement de contrats conclus pour une durée déterminée, mais aussi mettaient en cause la légalité de l'article 88 du RAA en ce qu'il limite la durée des contrats d'agents contractuels auxiliaires, tels que visés à l'article 3 ter du même RAA.

70 Selon lequel « *tout travailleur a droit à une protection contre tout licenciement injustifié* ». Voy. déjà affaire Landgren, *supra*, note 17.

71 Qui énonce le droit de tout travailleur à des conditions de travail respectant sa santé, sa sécurité et sa dignité.

Parlement européen, le Conseil et la Commission ont entendu donner à cette charte, le TFPUE en conclut qu'il convient d'en tenir compte pour l'interprétation des dispositions du statut et du RAA. Il rejette, toutefois, leur application en l'espèce car, d'une part, l'Article 30 ne condamne pas l'enchaînement de contrats à durée déterminée et ne contient aucun principe général de droit et car, d'autre part, l'Article 31, par. 1 n'apparaît pas pertinent pour être valablement invoqué à l'appui des revendications des parties requérantes.[72]

Mais sans doute le point le plus intéressant, dans ces affaires, consiste dans le développement auquel se livre le TFPUE à propos de l'examen du moyen avancé par les requérantes, tenant au *risque d'incohérence* qui résulterait de la clause 5 de l'accord-cadre qui s'imposerait dans ces États membres, au bénéfice de leurs travailleurs, sans lier pareillement les institutions et sans profiter, notamment, aux agents contractuels employés par ces dernières.[73]

Prenant appui sur le principe de coopération loyale, énoncé à l'Article 10, deuxième alinéa, CE, le TFPUE relève que celui-ci « *oblige non seulement les États membres à prendre toutes les mesures propres à garantir la portée et l'efficacité du droit communautaire... mais impose également aux institutions communautaires des devoirs réciproques de coopération loyale avec les États membres... À ce titre, il incombe aux institutions communautaires d'assurer, dans toute la mesure du possible, la cohérence entre leur conduite interne et leur action législative menée à l'échelle communautaire, notamment à destination des États membres* ».[74] S'agissant en particulier de l'accord-cadre qui poursuit une finalité de rapprochement des législations et des pratiques nationales en énonçant des prescriptions minimales relatives au travail à durée déterminée qui revêtent une importance particulière, « *il incombe à la Commission, conformément au devoir de loyauté qui pèse sur elle, d'interpréter, dans la mesure du possible, les dispositions du RAA à la lumière du texte et de la finalité de l'accord-cadre pour atteindre le résultat visé par celui-ci* ».[75] En sorte que « *la directive 1999/70 et l'accord-cadre sont, dans les circonstances de l'espèce et dans les limites tracées ci-dessus, invocables par les parties requérantes à l'encontre de la Commission aux fins d'une interprétation, dans la mesure du possible, des règles du RAA qui soit conforme aux finalités et*

---

[72] Points 103 à 107 de l'arrêt rendu dans les affaires Vahan Adjemian e.a. et C. Renier.

[73] Point 111.

[74] Points 112 et 113. Le TFPUE souligne, à ce propos, que cette obligation s'impose d'autant plus que la réforme administrative de 2004 a accentué une tendance à la contractualisation de la fonction publique européenne.

[75] Point 114. Voy. aussi arrêt Aayhan, *supra*, point 120.

aux prescriptions minimales dudit accord ».[76] Ce point de l'arrêt est essentiel en ce qu'il aboutit à soumettre l'application du RAA à une interprétation qui soit compatible avec les dispositions d'une directive (et de l'accord-cadre qui en est l'objet), rendant celle-ci de la sorte opposable, au moins en partie, à la Commission même si celle-ci n'en est pas destinataire. Certes, le TFPUE avance cette conclusion avec prudence : il ne s'agit que d'une interprétation « par voie d'invocation » et l'examen de la compatibilité ne peut se faire qu'au regard « des finalités et des prescriptions minimales de l'accord » et encore, « dans la mesure du possible ». Mais on ne saurait interpréter une disposition, de quelque nature qu'elle soit, sans la rendre applicable et donc opposable. Et cela, même si, comme en l'espèce, s'agissant d'une directive, les destinataires auxquels elle s'adresse sont les États membres et non la Commission ou d'ailleurs toute autre institution qui serait confrontée à un conflit identique ou semblable mettant en cause la compatibilité d'une disposition du RAA avec la directive. Ce raisonnement posé, le TFPUE procède à l'examen comparé du RAA avec la directive en question. Il constate que si l'accord-cadre pose le principe de la stabilité de l'emploi, et si, par conséquent, il vise à circonscrire le recours successif à des contrats à durée déterminée en raison des risques d'abus au détriment des travailleurs, il autorise aussi le renouvellement de tels contrats pour des « raisons objectives » qui doivent être fondées sur des circonstances précises et concrètes caractérisant une activité déterminée. Or, en l'espèce, il y a lieu de reconnaître que « *la création de la catégorie d'agents contractuels auxiliaires correspond à des besoins particuliers distincts de ceux couverts par la catégorie des agents contractuels visés à l'Article 3bis du RAA* ».[77] De tels agents, en effet, à la différence des agents contractuels « habituels » appelés à occuper des emplois, certes subalternes, mais durables, sont recrutés afin de répondre à des besoins en personnel passagers ou intermittents qui constituent des « raisons objectives » justifiant « *tant la durée déterminée des contrats d'agents auxiliaires que leur renouvellement en fonction de la survenance de ces besoins* ».[78] De plus, en l'absence d'une obligation générale en ce sens, on ne saurait exiger la transformation de contrats à durée déterminée, même renouvelés de façon successive, en un contrat à durée indéterminée.[79] Dès lors, comme dans l'affaire Aayhan examinée ci-dessus, le TFPUE conclut que « *l'accord-cadre ne saurait fonder des exceptions d'illégalité à l'encontre de l'Article 88 du RAA et de la*

[76] Point 117.
[77] Point 128.
[78] Point 132.
[79] Point 135.

décision du 28 avril 2004 ».[80] Remarquons qu'il s'agit, en l'espèce, à la différence de l'affaire Aayhan, d'une conclusion et non d'une position de principe. Le TFPUE utilise, d'ailleurs, les termes suivants : « *En tout état de cause, le RAA ne laisse pas apparaître qu'il porterait atteinte aux finalités et aux prescriptions minimales dudit accord-cadre* ».[81] *Quid* dans le cas contraire ? Faudrait-il se satisfaire d'une interprétation conforme ou de la reconnaissance de l'illégalité de la disposition du RAA en cause ou, à tout le moins, d'une mise à l'écart, sous la forme d'une non-application, de cette disposition pour défaut de compatibilité avec la directive et l'accord-cadre dont elle est le vecteur ? Sans doute la sanction devrait être celle d'une « mise à l'écart », la directive s'opposant à une norme de droit supérieur, en l'occurrence le règlement du Conseil fixant le statut et le RAA. En ce sens, le TFPUE, examinant par la suite la motivation de l'Article 88 du RAA, aborde cet examen pour « *savoir s'il y a lieu d'écarter l'application* » de cette disposition.[82] Mais tout doute n'est pas pour autant exclu, le TFPUE rejetant les exceptions d'irrecevabilité invoquées soit parce qu'elles sont irrecevables, soit parce qu'elles sont non fondées.[83] En tout état de cause, la constatation qu'une disposition du RAA serait non conforme à l'interprétation d'une directive rendue applicable au vu de cette jurisprudence, rendant de la sorte cette disposition inapplicable telle quelle – sans pour autant déclarer son illégalité – devrait aboutir à ce que le législateur européen en tire les conséquences et en modifie le texte afin d'en assurer la conformité.

L'arrêt rendu dans les affaires Adjemian et Renier a fait l'objet d'un pourvoi devant le Tribunal qui a rendu son arrêt le 21 septembre 2011.[84] Un des moyens invoqués par les requérants tenait en ce que le TFPUE aurait commis une erreur de droit en rejetant leurs exceptions d'illégalité portant sur l'Article 88 du RAA et sur la décision du 28 avril 2004, en ce que ceux-ci autorisent les institutions à conclure des contrats d'engagement à durée déterminée successifs, notamment sur le constat qu'une directive, en général, et la directive 1999/70, en particulier, ne pouvaient imposer, en tant que telles, des obligations aux institutions et, en l'espèce, à la Commission. Le Tribunal, après avoir souligné

80 Point 136. La décision de la Commission, du 28 avril 2004, fixait notamment à six années, décomptées sur une période de douze ans, la durée totale cumulée de prestation de services d'un agent non permanent, tous types de contrats ou d'affectations confondus.

81 Point 136. Souligné par nous.

82 Point 137. Souligné par nous. Le grief conclut, à la suite de cet examen, que le grief fondé sur l'absence de motivation n'est pas fondé.

83 Point 158.

84 Aff. T-325/09 P.

le caractère réglementaire du statut et du RAA et après avoir qualifié la décision du 28 avril 2004 comme étant une directive interne imposant une règle de conduite à la Commission et dont celle-ci ne peut s'écarter sans préciser les raisons qui l'y ont amenée, sous peine d'enfreindre le principe de l'égalité de traitement, rappelle que « *la directive 1999/70 est adressée aux États membres et non aux institutions. Par conséquent, les dispositions de cette directive ne peuvent être considérées comme imposant, en tant que telles, des obligations aux institutions, dans l'exercice de leurs pouvoirs législatifs ou décisionnels* ».[85] Cette directive ne saurait donc s'appliquer aux relations entre les institutions et leurs agents et ne saurait davantage fonder une exception d'illégalité. Quant au moyen tiré de la méconnaissance des finalités et des prescriptions minimales relatives au travail à durée déterminée de l'accord-cadre, mis en œuvre par la directive 1999/70, qui implique que celle-ci puisse être invoquée aux fins d'identifier l'existence ou de préciser la portée d'une obligation pesant sur les institutions, le Tribunal reconnaît que « *les règles ou principes édictés ou dégagés dans cette directive peuvent être invoqués à l'encontre de ces institutions lorsqu'ils n'apparaissent, eux-mêmes, que comme l'expression spécifique de règles fondamentales du traité CE et de principes généraux qui s'imposent directement auxdites institutions* ».[86] À cet égard, le Tribunal considère que le recours successif à des contrats à durée déterminée peut constituer une source potentielle d'abus au détriment des travailleurs et que, dans ces conditions, « *l'interdiction de l'abus de droit, en vertu duquel nul ne peut se prévaloir abusivement des normes de droit, fait partie des principes généraux du droit dont le juge assure le respect* ».[87] La prévention de tels abus est un objectif qui a été reconnu et encouragé par le législateur dans la directive 1999/70. En outre, ajoute le Tribunal, « *la poursuite des abus de droit en ce domaine répond...aux objectifs que la Communauté et les États membres, conscients des droits fondamentaux, tels ceux énoncés dans la charte sociale européenne signée à Turin le 18 octobre 1961 et dans la charte communautaire des droits sociaux fondamentaux des travailleurs de 1989, se sont fixés à l'Article 136 CE,*

---

[85] Points 49 à 52. Voy. aussi, en ce sens, par analogie, les arrêts de la Cour du 9 septembre 2003, aff. C-25/02, *Rinke*, *Rec.* p. I-8349, point 24 et du Tribunal du 21 mai 2008, aff. T-495/04, *Belfass*, *Rec.* p. II-781, point 43.

[86] Point 56.

[87] Point 59. Voy. aussi, en ce sens, les arrêts de la Cour du 22 mai 2008, aff. C-162/07, *Ampliscientifica et Amplifin*, *Rec.* p. I-4019, points 27, 30 et 32 (et jurisprudence citée) et du Tribunal du 8 mai 2007, aff. T-271/04, *Citymo*, *Rec.* p. II-1375, point 107 (et la jurisprudence citée). Voy. aussi Waelbroeck, D., « La notion d'abus de droit dans l'ordre juridique communautaire », in *Mélanges en hommage à Jean-Victor Louis*, Institut d'études européennes, éd. de l'Université de Bruxelles, 2003, vol. 1, pp. 595 et s.

au nombre desquels figurent l'amélioration des conditions de vie et de travail des travailleurs ainsi qu'une protection sociale adéquate de ces derniers ».[88] Il importe, dès lors, « *que le législateur, dans l'exercice du pouvoir législatif qu'il tire de l'Article 283 CE pour arrêter le RAA, et l'AHCC, dans l'exercice du large pouvoir d'appréciation dont elle dispose, dans le cadre fixé par les dispositions du RAA, sont tenus, lors de l'adoption ou de la mise en œuvre des règles qui régissent les relations entre les Communautés européennes et leurs agents, de prévenir les abus de droit pouvant résulter de l'utilisation de contrats d'engagement à durée déterminée successifs, conformément aux objectifs d'amélioration des conditions de vie et de travail des travailleurs ainsi que d'une protection sociale adéquate de ces derniers, visés à l'Article 136 CE* ».[89] Ainsi, le TFPUE était fondé à rechercher si l'Article 88 du RAA et la décision du 28 avril 2004 étaient conformes aux finalités et aux prescriptions minimales de l'accord-cadre et, finalement, au principe d'interdiction de l'abus de droit. Mais devait-il pour autant accueillir les exceptions d'illégalité soulevées par les requérants à l'encontre de ce même Article du RAA et de cette même décision en ce qu'ils fondaient les décisions individuelles portant refus de conclure des nouveaux contrats ou de renouveler leurs précédents contrats en qualité d'agents contractuels auxiliaires ? Ce qui signifie, pour le Tribunal, qu'il convient de rechercher s'il existe une obligation incombant au Conseil et à la Commission, dans l'exercice de leurs pouvoirs législatifs ou décisionnels, de prévenir les abus de droit résultant de l'utilisation de contrats d'engagement à durée déterminée successifs, consistant à imposer « *à l'AHCC de transformer en contrat à durée indéterminée une succession de contrats d'engagement à durée déterminée qui auraient eu pour objet l'exécution durable de tâches permanentes* ».[90] Or, il y a lieu de constater que l'AHCC dispose, en vertu de l'Article 249, deuxième alinéa, CE, « *d'une pleine liberté pour choisir les formes et les moyens les plus appropriés* » pour prévenir d'éventuels abus. Ainsi, elle peut adopter des mesures qui soit prévoient que le renouvellement de tels contrats doit être justifié par des raisons objectives, soit limitent la durée maximale totale des contrats à durée déterminée successifs, soit encore limitent le nombre de renouvellements de tels contrats. En revanche, il n'existe aucune règle imposant au législateur de prévoir la transformation des contrats de travail à durée déterminée en contrats à durée indéterminée, à tout le moins lorsque les abus de renouvellements successifs sont interdits et que de tels abus, s'ils ont été

[88] Point 60.
[89] Point 61. Souligné par nous.
[90] Point 65.

commis, puissent être sanctionnés par la réparation des dommages causés.[91] Cela dit, la caractéristique principale des contrats d'engagement en qualité d'agent contractuel auxiliaire « *est leur précarité dans le temps, correspondant à la finalité même de ces contrats qui est de faire remplir des tâches précaires, par nature ou en l'absence d'un titulaire, par du personnel occasionnel* ».[92] Dès lors, si l'AHCC a eu recours à une succession de contrats d'engagement à durée déterminée pour l'exécution durable de tâches permanentes, « *cet abus pourrait être corrigé et les conséquences négatives subies par l'intéressé pourraient être effacées en procédant à une requalification du contrat d'engagement conforme aux dispositions du RAA, laquelle peut notamment conduire à la transformation de contrats d'engagement à durée déterminée successifs en contrat à durée indéterminée* ».[93] Le TFPUE, en jugeant comme il l'a fait, n'a donc commis aucune erreur de droit.[94]

Toujours à propos du non-renouvellement de contrats à durée déterminée pour cause de survenance du terme, le TFPUE s'est prononcé, par arrêt rendu le 13 avril 2011, sur le cas de Mme Scheefer.[95] Celle-ci, engagée comme agent temporaire affecté en tant que médecin au cabinet médical de Luxembourg, a vu son contrat initial prorogé par deux avenants[96] pour une durée totale allant du 1er avril 2006 au 31 mars 2009. Entre-temps, la requérante s'était portée candidate à une procédure de sélection pour le recrutement d'un agent temporaire administrateur, mais sa candidature avait été rejetée pour défaut d'une expérience suffisante. Le 22 janvier 2009, elle avait interrogé le secrétaire général du Parlement européen sur la possibilité de poursuivre sa collaboration avec le service médical. Il lui fut répondu, par une note du 12 février 2009, qu'après un examen détaillé de sa situation, aucune solution juridiquement acceptable lui permettant de continuer son activité au sein du service médical n'avait pu être trouvée et a confirmé que le contrat de la requérante prendrait fin le 31 mars. Le TFPUE rejette, d'abord, la demande de requalification, faite par la requérante, de son contrat en engagement à durée indéterminée, au motif que cela constituerait une injonction empiétant sur les pouvoirs de l'autorité administrative. Ensuite, il précise le troisième chef de conclusions comme tendant à

---

91 Point 66 et jurisprudence citée.

92 Point 86.

93 Points 67 et 87.

94 L'arrêt du TFPUE est néanmoins partiellement annulé, sur la base d'un moyen de procédure, dans la mesure où il a prononcé un non-lieu à statuer sur les conclusions de certaines parties requérantes à l'encontre des décisions portant rejet de leurs réclamations et non pas à l'encontre des décisions faisant effectivement grief.

95 Aff. F-105/09, *Scheefer/Parlement européen*.

96 Datés respectivement du 26 février 2007 et du 26 mars 2008.

l'annulation du deuxième avenant en tant qu'il fixe au 31 mars 2009 le terme de l'engagement de la requérante. Conformément à la jurisprudence citée ci-avant, il aborde cette question de fond en faisant référence à la directive 1999/70 et à l'accord-cadre qui y est annexé. Ceci, en rappelant, de la façon déjà soulignée plus haut, l'obligation du Parlement européen, en sa qualité d'institution, d'interpréter et d'appliquer, « *conformément au devoir de loyauté qui pèse sur lui,... les dispositions du RAA à la lumière du texte et des finalités de l'accord-cadre. Or, cet accord-cadre fait de la stabilité d'emploi un objectif prééminent en matière de relations de travail au sein de l'Union européenne...Plus précisément, la clause 5, point 1, de celui-ci tend spécifiquement à "prévenir les abus résultant de l'utilisation de contrats ou de relations de travail à durée déterminée successifs"... en particulier, (elle) prescrit de fixer un nombre maximum de renouvellements de contrats ou de relations de travail à durée déterminée. La même clause prévoit, en son point 2, sous b), que les contrats à durée déterminée puissent, lorsque c'est approprié, être réputés conclus pour une durée indéterminée* ».[97] Il en découle qu'en ce qui concerne les institutions, « *l'Article 8, premier alinéa, du RAA,*[98] *doit recevoir une interprétation lui assurant une large portée et être strictement appliqué, dès lors qu'il tend précisément à limiter le recours à des contrats successifs d'agent temporaire à durée déterminée en réputant conclu pour une durée indéterminée le troisième contrat à durée déterminée qui viendrait à être conclu* ».[99] En conséquence, le TFPUE écarte les arguments avancés par la Parlement européen[100] et en conclut que la requérante remplissait les conditions d'application de l'Article 8, premier alinéa, du RAA. « *Il s'ensuit qu'il incombe au Tribunal de constater que l'avenant du 26 mars 2008 a été de plein droit requalifié en engagement à durée indéterminée par la seule volonté du législateur et que l'échéance du terme*

---

97 Point 54.

98 Selon cette disposition, « *L'engagement d'un agent temporaire...peut être conclu pour une durée déterminée ou indéterminée. Le contrat de cet agent engagé pour une durée déterminée ne peut être renouvelé qu'une fois pour une durée déterminée. Tout renouvellement ultérieur de cet engagement devient à durée indéterminée* ».

99 Point 55.

100 Le Parlement prétendait que sa réglementation interne l'aurait empêché de conclure un contrat à durée indéterminée alors qu'il convenait de garantir la sécurité du service assuré par le cabinet médical de Luxembourg. Argument rejeté car, même si la conclusion de contrats ne peut se faire qu'en attendant qu'il soit pourvu à des emplois dans l'attente d'un recrutement conforme à la procédure prévue par cette réglementation, cela n'exclut pas la conclusion de contrats à durée indéterminée auxquels il peut toujours être mis fin pour un motif légitime et moyennant un préavis. Par ailleurs, il n'existe pas, en l'espèce, une quelconque situation exceptionnelle que pourrait invoquer le Parlement.

fixé dans cet avenant ne pouvait entraîner l'engagement de la requérante ».[101] Dès lors, la note du 12 février 2009 contenant la prise de position du Parlement européen, sous la signature de son secrétaire général, fait grief à la requérante et ne constitue pas une décision purement confirmative, de sorte qu'elle doit être, pour les motifs relevés ci-dessus, annulée.[102]

Quant à la demande formulée par la requérante de l'octroi du « volet financier » qui constitue la « conséquence logique » de l'annulation de la décision attaquée, le TFPUE souligne la distinction qu'il y a lieu de faire entre « *une demande tendant au versement par une institution à un de ses agents d'une somme que celui-ci estime lui être due en vertu du RAA (et qui) entre dans la notion des "litiges de caractère pécuniaire" au sens de l'Article 91, paragraphe 1, du statut* » et « *des actions en responsabilité dirigées par les agents contre leur institution et tendant à l'obtention de dommages et intérêts* ».[103] Le TFPUE exerce donc, en l'occurrence, une compétence de pleine juridiction qui l'investit de la mission de donner à de tels litiges une solution complète et de statuer ainsi sur l'ensemble des droits et des obligations de l'agent. Se référant ensuite à la jurisprudence Landgren,[104] il rappelle « *que l'annulation d'un acte par le juge a pour effet d'éliminer rétroactivement cet acte de l'ordre juridique et que, lorsque l'acte annulé a déjà été exécuté, l'anéantissement de ses effets impose de rétablir la situation juridique dans laquelle la partie requérante se trouvait antérieurement à l'adoption de celui-ci* ».[105] En l'espèce, la requérante aurait dû se voir octroyer un contrat à durée indéterminée et son engagement n'a pas pu prendre fin le 31 mars 2009. « *Dans ces conditions, il convient de condamner le Parlement à verser à la requérante la différence entre, d'une part, le montant de la rémunération auquel elle aurait pu prétendre si elle était restée en fonction en son sein et, d'autre part, le montant de la rémunération, des honoraires, des indemnités de chômage ou de toute autre indemnité de substitution qu'elle a effectivement perçu, depuis le 1er avril 2009, en remplacement de la rémunération qu'elle percevait au Parlement* ».[106] Ainsi, la requérante se trouve, par rapport à la rémunération qui lui est due, en quelque sorte, « restituée » dans les liens du contrat à durée indéterminée auquel elle aurait eu droit en vertu des dispositions pertinentes de l'accord-cadre annexé à la

---

[101] Point 61.
[102] Point 62.
[103] Point 68.
[104] Cf. *supra*. Voy. aussi note 11.
[105] Point 69.
[106] Point 71.

directive 1999/70, qui s'appliquent à elle et qui, de ce fait, impliquent une « lecture conforme » de l'Article 8, premier alinéa, du RAA.

Alors que les trois affaires rapportées et commentées ci-dessus concernaient toutes l'application de la directive 1999/70 du Conseil, le TFPUE s'est référé, à l'appui de son argumentation, dans une affaire portant sur le report de jours de congé annuel, à la directive 2003/88/CE du Parlement européen et du Conseil, du 4 novembre 2003, concernant certains aspects de l'aménagement du temps de travail.[107] Ici encore, le TFPUE, sans reprendre pour autant l'argumentaire qui l'avait amené à conclure qu'une directive peut être invoquée dans les relations entre les institutions et leur personnel,[108] énonce sans discussion et, « *sans qu'il soit besoin, à ce stade, d'examiner la manière dont il y aurait lieu de résoudre un éventuel conflit entre une disposition statutaire et des prescriptions minimales de sécurité et de santé des travailleurs arrêtées à l'échelle de l'Union, (qu')il y a lieu de considérer qu'il incombait, en l'espèce, à la Commission de veiller à garantir le respect desdites prescriptions à l'égard du requérant dans l'application et l'interprétation des règles statutaires relatives, en particulier, au congé annuel* ».[109] Dans cette affaire, le requérant – qui était un fonctionnaire et non un agent – soulevait un moyen unique, tiré de la violation de l'Article 4, premier et deuxième alinéas, de l'annexe V au statut. Selon cette disposition, premier alinéa, « *Si un fonctionnaire, pour des raisons non imputables aux nécessités du service, n'a pas épuisé son congé annuel avant la fin de l'année civile en cours, le report de congé sur l'année suivante ne peut excéder douze jours* ». Et, deuxième alinéa, « *Si un fonctionnaire n'a pas épuisé son congé annuel au moment de la cessation de ses fonctions, il lui sera versé, à titre de compensation, par jour de congé dont il n'a pas bénéficié, une somme égale au trentième de sa rémunération mensuelle au moment de la cessation de ses fonctions* ».

---

[107] JO L 299 du 18 novembre 2003, p. 9.

[108] Cette absence d'argumentaire spécifique peut, en l'espèce, s'expliquer par le fait que le statut lui-même, en l'article 1er sexies, paragraphe 2, établit que « *Les fonctionnaires en activité bénéficient de conditions de travail qui respectent les normes de santé et de sécurité appropriées, au moins équivalentes aux prescriptions minimales applicables en vertu des mesures arrêtées dans ces domaines en application des traités* ». Cet article fait ainsi expressément référence à des actes prévoyant de telles mesures et qui relèveraient des traités, donc d'actes tels que la directive 2003/88 qui, précisément, ainsi qu'il ressort de l'article 1er, point 1, de celle-ci, énonce que « *La présente directive fixe des prescriptions minimales de sécurité et de santé en matière d'aménagement du temps de travail* ». Il y a ainsi, en quelque sorte, superposition de ces deux actes – statut et directive –, ce qui rend la directive quasi « directement invocable » à l'égard des institutions, même si, au moins formellement, elle ne s'adresse qu'aux États membres.

[109] Arrêt du 15 mars 2011, *G. Strack/Commission*, point 57.

En l'espèce, le requérant n'avait pas pris l'intégralité de son congé annuel pour des raisons de maladie, ce qui aurait dû l'autoriser à obtenir le report de son congé sur l'année suivante au-delà de douze jours, et ce qui avait aussi pour effet, du fait du refus opposé par la Commission à ses demandes, de limiter la somme versée au requérant, à titre de compensation, lors de la cessation de ses fonctions.

Le TFPUE va, dans un premier temps, examiner, à la lumière de la jurisprudence de la Cour, le contenu des prescriptions minimales pertinentes de la directive 2003/88, en particulier, de son Article 7.

Il souligne, d'abord, que « *le droit au congé annuel payé de chaque travailleur doit être considéré comme un principe de droit social de l'Union revêtant une importance particulière, auquel il ne saurait être dérogé et dont la mise en œuvre par les autorités nationales compétentes, ne peut être effectuée que dans les limites expressément énoncées par la directive elle-même* ».[110] Puis, il relève que, dans le même sens, l'Article 31, paragraphe 2, de la charte des droits fondamentaux, garantit le droit pour tout travailleur à une période annuelle de congés payés.[111] De son côté, l'Article 7, paragraphe 1 de la directive 2003/88 prévoit l'obligation pour les États membres de prendre les mesures nécessaires pour que tout travailleur bénéficie d'un congé annuel payé d'au moins quatre semaines. Il découle de ce même Article que le travailleur doit normalement pouvoir bénéficier d'un repos effectif, dans un souci de protection efficace de sa sécurité et de sa santé. Outre cela, la finalité du droit au congé annuel est aussi de permettre au travailleur de disposer d'une période de détente et de loisirs. Ce qui est différent du droit au congé de maladie qui est accordé au travailleur pour lui permettre de se rétablir. À ce sujet, le TFPUE relève que, selon l'Article 5, paragraphe 4, de la convention n° 132 de l'OIT, du 24 juin 1970, concernant les congés annuels payés, « *les absences de travail pour des motifs indépendants de la volonté de la personne employée intéressée, telles les absences dues à une maladie, [...] seront comptées dans la période de service* », disposition dont il faut tenir compte dans l'interprétation de la directive 2003/88.[112] Se fondant ensuite sur la jurisprudence Schultz-Hoff de la Cour,[113] qui énonce principalement que le droit au congé annuel payé conféré par la directive 2003/88 à tous les travailleurs ne peut être subordonné par un État membre à l'obligation

---

[110] Point 59. Voy., en ce sens, arrêts de la Cour du 26 juin 2001, aff. C-173/99, *BECTU*, point 43 ; du 18 mars 2004, aff. C-342/01, *Merino Gomez*, point 29 ; du 16 mars 2006, aff ; jtes C-131/04 et C-257/04, *Robinson-Steele e.a.*, point 48 et du 20 janvier 2009, aff. jtes C-350/06 et C-520/06, *Schultz-Hoff*, point 22.

[111] Point 59, *in fine*.

[112] Points 59 à 61.

[113] Citée *supra*, note 110.

d'avoir effectivement travaillé pendant la période de référence établie par la législation dudit État, le TFPUE en déduit que « *même si l'Article 7, paragraphe 1, de la directive 2003/88 ne s'oppose pas, en principe, à ce qu'une réglementation nationale prévoie la perte du droit au congé annuel payé à la fin d'une période de référence ou d'une période de report, encore faut-il que le travailleur ait eu effectivement la possibilité d'exercer, au cours de la période en cause, le droit que la directive lui confère. Tel n'est évidemment pas le cas d'un travailleur qui, durant tout ou partie de la période de référence et au-delà de la période de report fixée par le droit national, s'est trouvé en congé de maladie* ».[114] La Cour en a déduit, dans son arrêt Schultz-Hoff, « *qu'admettre que, dans de telles circonstances spécifiques d'incapacité de travail, les dispositions nationales pertinentes, et notamment celles fixant la période de report, puissent prévoir l'extinction du droit du travailleur au congé annuel payé garanti par l'Article 7, paragraphe 1, de la directive 2003/88, sans que le travailleur ait effectivement eu la possibilité d'exercer son droit au congé annuel payé, porterait atteinte au droit social directement conféré par l'Article 7 de ladite directive à chaque travailleur* ».[115] Enfin, lorsque la prise de congé annuel payé n'est plus possible, pour des raisons indépendantes de la volonté du travailleur, l'Article 7, paragraphe 2, de la directive 2003/88 prévoit que le travailleur a droit à une indemnité financière.[116]

Ces règles, appliquées à la situation du requérant, ont pour conséquence que celui-ci, ainsi qu'il découle de l'Article 7, paragraphe 2, de la directive 2003/88, ne saurait, en raison du fait que son incapacité de travail médicalement justifiée a perduré jusqu'à sa mise en invalidité, se voir privé de la possibilité de bénéficier d'une indemnité financière pour congé annuel non pris.[117] Quant au calcul de cette compensation, il ne saurait inclure uniquement, comme le prétendait la Commission, en invoquant l'Article 4, premier alinéa, de l'annexe V du statut, les jours de congé annuel non pris pour des raisons imputables aux seules « *nécessités de service* », cette expression n'excluant pas de prendre en considération l'absence de service justifiée par un congé de maladie et

---

114 Point 63.

115 Point 64.

116 Point 65. Cette indemnité doit, ainsi qu'en a décidé la Cour dans l'arrêt Schultz-Hoff (*supra*, note 110), être calculée de sorte que le travailleur soit placé dans une situation comparable à celle dans laquelle il aurait été s'il avait exercé le droit au congé pendant la durée de sa relation de travail. Ce qui signifie qu'il a non seulement droit à la rémunération pendant la période de repos correspondant au congé annuel payé, mais, en outre, cette rémunération est déterminante en ce qui concerne le calcul de l'indemnité financière de congé annuel non pris à la fin de la relation de travail.

117 Point 69.

ce, même en cas de maladie prolongée. Dès lors, le TFPUE estime que, « *dans ces conditions, il y a lieu de considérer que les prescriptions minimales de sécurité et de santé visées par l'Article 1er sexies du statut, et notamment les dispositions de l'Article 7 de la directive 2003/88, viennent compléter des dispositions proprement statutaires relatives aux congés* ».[118] Il n'est pas excessif d'en déduire, selon nous, que la finalité et le contenu de la directive 2003/88 s'intègrent en quelque sorte dans la rédaction de l'Article 1er sexies du statut, et que c'est la lecture ainsi éclairée et élargie de cette « disposition générale » qui sert de base pour une interprétation et une application conformes des dispositions « proprement statutaires » qui en précisent la portée. Même si l'Article 7 de la directive 2003/88 garantit une période minimale de congé annuel payé de quatre semaines, alors que le congé annuel auquel les fonctionnaires de l'Union peuvent prétendre s'élève à 24 jours au minimum, il n'en demeure pas moins que, ainsi que la Cour l'a interprété dans l'arrêt Schultz-Hoff, l'Article 7 de ladite directive « *reste pleinement transposable à la totalité du congé annuel tel que fixé par le statut* » pour le cas où un travailleur se trouve empêché de prendre son congé annuel en raison d'une absence pour maladie de longue durée.[119] En conséquence, le TFPUE annule la décision de la Commission par laquelle celle-ci a refusé, en application de l'Article 4, premier alinéa, de l'annexe V du statut, le report, au-delà des douze jours de plein droit, des jours de congé annuel non pris par le requérant pour cause de congé de maladie de longue durée.[120]

3. Considérations finales

À la lumière des arrêts rapportés et commentés ci-dessus, il semble pouvoir être avancé – avec la prudence qu'implique une jurisprudence qui devra encore être confirmée et précisée[121] – que le TFPUE a jeté un éclairage nouveau sur la fonction publique européenne en l'imprégnant

---

118 Point 75.

119 Point 77.

120 Point 79.

121 Trois arrêts du 13 juin 2012 sont venus confirmer et préciser cette jurisprudence. Il s'agit des affaires F-105/11, *Davids/Commission ;* F-63/11, *Macchia/Commission* et F-41/11, *Mocova/Commission*. Compte tenu des limites imposées à notre contribution, nous nous permettons de renvoyer au commentaire qui en a été fait par L. Poitvin-Solis et R. Schiano dans leur « Chronique de jurisprudence de la fonction publique de l'Union européenne », *Revue de l'Union européenne*, 2012, pp. 613-614.

d'une dimension qui relève du droit social tout en tenant compte de la structure réglementaire qui gouverne aussi bien le statut que le RAA.[122]

Il ne s'agit donc pas – et il importe, selon nous, de le souligner – d'un droit social qui prend appui et se modèle sur l'un ou l'autre régime de droit social national, mais qui se construit à partir de méthodes d'interprétation inspirées par des sources de droit relevant de la sphère du droit social international et européen, ainsi que par le recours à des droits fondamentaux et à des principes généraux de droit, comme le devoir de sollicitude, le devoir de loyauté, le principe de cohérence, l'exécution de bonne foi des contrats... La finalité déclarée étant d'assurer, autant que faire se peut, une certaine *sécurité de l'emploi* considérée comme constituant un objectif prioritaire – sans en faire pour autant une règle contraignante – et, surtout, de dénoncer certaines pratiques abusives qui aboutiraient à priver les agents des droits qu'ils tirent non seulement de leurs contrats mais aussi des dispositions du RAA et des directives européennes dont le contenu peut également trouver à s'appliquer dans les relations entre les institutions et leur personnel.

Il s'ensuit un certain rapprochement entre le régime contractuel auquel sont soumis les agents et celui, statutaire, s'appliquant aux fonctionnaires. Ce rapprochement, qui ne va pas jusqu'à la fusion, trouve à la fois son fondement dans les passerelles existant entre certaines dispositions du RAA et les dispositions du statut auxquelles elles renvoient et sa justification au regard d'une situation factuelle nouvelle, à savoir, la place grandissante occupée par les agents dans le personnel employé par les institutions européennes et, en particulier, par les agences et autres organes décentralisés. Cette nouvelle configuration de la fonction publique européenne, se traduisant par une tendance à la généralisation du recours au régime contractuel, a entraîné la prise de conscience, voire la nécessité, d'assurer à ces agents une protection tant juridique que juridictionnelle mieux adaptée au caractère souvent précaire de leur situation professionnelle.

---

122 Nous n'ignorons certes pas que le contentieux de la fonction publique traite aussi – et a toujours traité – de questions – outre celles relatives aux relations de travail proprement dites – concernant le régime de sécurité sociale : maladie, retraite, invalidité, accidents du travail, allocations familiales... Mais il l'a fait dans le cadre strict des règles du statut et de ses annexes en se basant, toutefois, également sur le respect des droits fondamentaux et des principes généraux de droit. Par la jurisprudence examinée ci-dessus, le TFPUE procède, selon nous, à un « basculement » de l'angle de vue et aussi d'attaque de ces questions en élargissant, à l'occasion d'un contexte contentieux différent, le champ matériel de son analyse à des sources de droit venant, d'une certaine manière, de l'« extérieur » et en amplifiant son champ d'investigation, voire en faisant parfois prévaloir l'application d'une directive de caractère social sur une disposition du RAA en soumettant cette dernière à une interprétation, sinon conforme, du moins compatible.

Par l'approche suivie, qui se démarque, dans une certaine mesure, de la rigidité du carcan du droit administratif, le TFPUE exprime le souci d'assurer une plus juste *égalité de traitement* entre les « employeurs » et leurs agents. Ce faisant, il se comporte davantage comme un juge de droit social, soupesant les droits des uns et des autres, que comme un juge de droit administratif qui veille au respect de règles impersonnelles et statutaires, l'assujettissement des fonctionnaires à ces règles étant la contrepartie des avantages que ces règles leur procurent, en particulier la stabilité de l'emploi.

Qu'il s'agisse de l'obligation de motivation des actes comme de l'« invocabilité » par voie d'interprétation de directives concernant des domaines susceptibles de s'appliquer, *mutatis mutandis*, aux relations de travail entre les institutions et leur personnel,[123] le souci constant manifesté par le TFPUE est de *mettre en balance l'intérêt du service et celui de l'intéressé*.

Aussi ne craint-il pas de faire prévaloir, à l'appui de son approche et de sa compréhension du litige qui lui est soumis, *sa propre évaluation des éléments factuels et du contexte juridique qui les entoure*, en substituant sa propre analyse à celle faite par l'administration et aux conclusions qu'elle en a tirées. Ce qui lui permet, par *une application extensive du moyen tiré de l'erreur manifeste*, d'encadrer, au point de la « corriger », la marge d'appréciation souvent discrétionnaire dont dispose l'autorité administrative dans de telles circonstances. À cela s'ajoute l'invocation fréquente du *devoir de sollicitude* qui renforce le contrôle effectué par le juge sur l'appréciation faite par l'administration. Cette jurisprudence, à la fois démonstrative et volontariste, peut aboutir à reconsidérer l'évaluation des faits telle qu'elle avait été faite sur le terrain par les responsables de l'administration et à lui donner une autre perception susceptible d'en changer l'issue en droit.[124]

---

123 En rendant de telles directives opposables aux institutions, en se basant sur l'argumentaire que nous avons relevé ci-dessus, le TFPUE situe son approche interprétative, d'une certaine façon, dans la ligne de l'arrêt Marleasing de la Cour de justice, dans lequel celle-ci a étendu l'obligation, pour les autorités nationales, y compris les autorités juridictionnelles, de tenir compte, lors de l'interprétation de leur droit national, de la lumière du texte et de la finalité de la directive (en l'occurrence, la directive 68/151/CEE du Conseil, du 9 mars 1968, tendant à coordonner, pour les rendre équivalentes, les garanties qui sont exigées, dans les États membres, des sociétés au sens de l'article 58, deuxième alinéa, du traité CEE pour protéger les intérêts tant des associés que des tiers), même en l'absence de mise en œuvre en droit interne, pour atteindre le résultat visé par celle-ci et assurer ainsi sa pleine efficacité : arrêt du 13 novembre 1990, aff. C-106/89, *Rec.* p. I-4135.

124 Cela nous a paru être particulièrement le cas, comme nous l'avons relevé, dans les affaires Landgren, d'une part, Schuerings et Vandeuren, d'autre part.

Ce qui est aussi remarquable, c'est la volonté affirmée du TFPUE, après avoir constaté une illégalité, de ne pas « rendre la main » à l'institution ou à l'agence défenderesse afin d'en tirer les conséquences, mais de se prononcer lui-même sur les suites à donner à l'arrêt rendu afin de donner à celui-ci un *effet utile* pour que l'intéressé soit effectivement rétabli dans ses droits de la façon la plus adéquate et la plus juste possible. À cette fin, le TFPUE, à partir du moment où le litige revêt un caractère pécuniaire, fait usage de la *compétence de pleine juridiction* que lui reconnaît le statut[125] et, si l'état du litige ne se prête pas à la fixation dans l'arrêt de la réparation du préjudice, matériel comme moral, subi, renvoie les parties à la recherche d'une solution amiable tout en se réservant le droit de se prononcer en définitive, à défaut d'accord.

Par cette façon de procéder, le TFPUE écarte certaines objections qui avaient été formulées à l'encontre du fonctionnement de la justice « administrative ».[126] Ainsi, en augmentant son contrôle juridictionnel par une application renforcée de l'obligation de motivation et par un recours extensif au moyen tiré de l'erreur manifeste. De même, en ouvrant le droit à réparation par l'utilisation de sa compétence de pleine juridiction et par la recherche d'une juste indemnisation, en particulier au cas où l'annulation prononcée serait empêchée de sortir ses effets.

Comme nous l'avons déjà relevé, le regard du juge, au fil de cette jurisprudence, a changé.[127] Il n'est plus celui qui est porté avec une certaine bienveillance sur l'administration qui bénéficiait souvent d'un préjugé favorable, notamment grâce à la marge d'appréciation discrétionnaire qui accompagnait souvent sa prise de décision, mais il se pose davantage sur le fonctionnaire, sur l'agent pour prendre en compte sa situation dans une optique plus équilibrée au regard de la notion d'intérêt du service et plus apte, au cas où il est jugé que son recours est bien fondé, à assurer la réintégration aussi complète que possible dans ses droits ou, à défaut, de lui octroyer une juste et équitable indemnisation, quitte à renvoyer la discussion sur ce point à une négociation préalable entre les parties à la cause.

Cette évolution jurisprudentielle opérée par le TFPUE, si elle a été accueillie avec une certaine réticence par le Tribunal à l'occasion du

---

125 Article 91, par. 1 du statut.

126 Voy. Vandersanden, G., « La procédure et les voies de recours », in *La fonction publique communautaire – Nouvelles règles et développements contentieux*, Bruxelles, Bruylant, coll. Pratique du droit communautaire, 2008, pp. 111 et s.

127 Voy. Vandersanden, G., « Le Tribunal de la Fonction Publique : un nouveau regard », *supra*, note 42.

pourvoi dirigé contre l'arrêt rendu dans l'affaire Landgren,[128] semble en tout cas, même si l'angle de l'évaluation juridique n'est pas nécessairement le même, ne pas rencontrer d'opposition de la part du Tribunal qui, de ce fait, se range aux côtés du juge spécialisé.[129]

Bref, au total, une présence plus affirmée du TFPUE dans ce genre de contentieux avec pour conséquence une emprise plus grande de celui-ci sur les diverses séquences du litige qui se trouve ainsi encadré de façon plus étroite dans ses tenants comme ses aboutissants. Il en résulte, selon nous, une analyse plus méticuleuse du procès portant sur les faits comme sur les conséquences à en tirer, ce qui en définitive permet de mieux appréhender le comportement de l'administration. L'accent est désormais mis sur les relations entre les parties, dans un contexte contractuel, donc plus égalitaire, mais qui reste influencé par la nature de droit public qui régit leurs rapports, et sur la protection sociale conférée par les instruments juridiques, de droit international et de droit européen, éclairés à la lumière des droits fondamentaux et des principes généraux de droit, au profit tant des fonctionnaires que des agents de l'Union européenne.

Par son activisme, le juge du TFPUE s'inscrit dans la continuité créative du droit – en l'occurrence, du droit social –, dont la Cour de justice, dès les premières années de son fonctionnement, a été l'initiatrice et est restée le plus bel exemple. En portant son contrôle sur l'application concrète des faits, sur des éléments matériellement vérifiables de l'espèce, il se donne les moyens pour évaluer, d'abord, le contexte factuel de l'espèce ainsi que la nature et l'ampleur des droits dont peut se prévaloir le requérant, puis, dans un deuxième temps, la manière dont l'administration a effectivement – ou non – tenu compte de ces droits et les a respectés au regard des faits préalablement établis. Dans chacune de ces étapes, le juge s'octroie les pouvoirs les plus larges pour assurer *in fine* la *protection sociale* la plus adéquate de l'intéressé(e). Il apparaît ainsi comme *le garant de l'effectivité des droits sociaux* tels que le droit de la fonction publique et le droit européen en général peuvent conférer aux fonctionnaires et aux agents.

Vers une politique jurisprudentielle de droit social ? L'avenir seul pourra le dire. Mais, en tout cas, la voie est tracée.

---

[128] Voy. *supra*, note 11.

[129] Voy. *supra*, note 28.

Has the European Union a Criminal Policy for the Enforcement of its Harmonised Policies?

John A.E. VERVAELE

Professor of Economic and European Criminal Law,
Utrecht School of Law

1. Introduction

The impact of Union Law on domestic criminal law goes hand in hand with the European integration process itself.[1] Professor Paul Demaret understood, at the eve of the coming into force of the Maastricht Treaty, very well the importance and included a course in the *curriculum* of the College on "*Le droit de l'Union et le droit répressif européen. Vers une justice repressive européenne, respecteuse des droits procéduraux fondamentaux*", combining European criminal law and human rights. In landmark rulings in the environmental case C-176/03[2] and in the ship source pollution case C-440/05[3] on the criminal law competence in the first pillar the ECJ clearly established a functional criminal law competence for the enforcement of community policies. Their importance was not limited to issues of competence, as they had consequences for the interactions with the Member States' legal order (community method versus third pillar method). Thanks to the rulings the first directives with criminal law substance were voted in the EU. However, their impact was limited as the type and level of criminal sanctions had to be defined in a second third pillar instrument. We cannot state that the rulings have resulted in a well-thought criminal policy for the enforcement of the harmonised EC policies, even in

1 Vervaele, J.A.E., "The Europeanisation of criminal law and the criminal law dimension of European integration", College Research Papers, 2005, http://www.coleurope.eu/sites/default/files/researchpaper/researchpaper_3_2005_vervaele.pdf.

2 Case C-176/03, Judgment of 15 September 2005.

3 Case C-440/05, Judgment of 23 October 2007.

policy areas of far-reaching integration, such as the internal market, the customs union, the monetary union or financial services. Why, for instance, does the Commission press for the criminal law harmonization of environmental law and criminal law protection of the financial interests of the EC, but fails to do the same in the field of competition or fisheries or the financing of terrorism? Why do the Member States press for the criminal law harmonization of terrorism, xenophobia, the protection of victims of crime, but not for the criminal law harmonization of serious violations of food safety rules, intellectual property infringements, or the financial management of businesses? Does this mean that there have been no thoughts at all about the constitutive elements of criminal policy at the Union before the entry into force of the Lisbon Treaty?

2. Council's Criminal Legislative Policy under the Amsterdam Treaty

From the Amsterdam Treaty on the Council/European Council were elaborating policy programmes (the Tampere Programme, the Hague Programme and the Stockholm Programme) for the area of freedom, security and justice. These Programmes did include criminal legislative policy. The Council did already accept in its Tampere Conclusions of 1999 that "*efforts to agree on common definitions, incriminations and sanctions should be focused in the first instance on a limited number of sectors of particular relevance*",[4] but the Tampere Programme[5] has clearly provided insufficient direction. Both Member States and the Council did feel the need to streamline the content of their legislative work in the criminal law field. Already in 2002 the Council does agree on an approach regarding approximation of penalties. In some cases, the Council states, that it may be sufficient to stipulate that the Member States shall provide that the offences concerned are punishable by effective, proportionate and dissuasive penalties and leave it to each Member State to determine the level and type of the penalties.[6] In other cases, the Council accepts the need for going further and agrees to establish a system of four penalty levels to be used in legislation:

Level 1: Penalties of a maximum of at least between 1 and 3 years of imprisonment

---

4 Conclusion No. 48.

5 Most recently updated by COM(2004)0401.

6 Doc. 914/02 DROIPEN 33, http://eurocrim.jura.unituebingen.de/cms/en/doc/1304.pdf.

Level 2: Penalties of a maximum of at least between 2 and 5 years of imprisonment

Level 3: Penalties of a maximum of at least between 5 and 10 years of imprisonment

Level 4: Penalties of a maximum of at least 10 years of imprisonment (cases where very serious penalties are required)

In practice the streamlining of the criminal law harmonization through minimum requirements for the maximum level of the penalties to be provided by national law in respect of specified offences has not been very successful and insufficient to elaborate a common approach of criminal law enforcement in the EU legislation.

This is certainly the reason why the Council adopted in 2009 conclusions on model provisions,[7] guiding the Council's criminal law deliberations. The Council was aiming at the following advantages: a/ guidelines and model provisions would facilitate negotiations by leaving room to focus on the substance of the specific provisions; b/ increased coherence would facilitate the transposition of EU provisions in national law and c/ legal interpretation would be facilitated when new criminal legislation is drafted in accordance with agreed guidelines which build on common elements. The main aim was however that the model provisions should guide future work of the Council on legislative initiatives that may include criminal provisions. The Council's model provisions do integrate the 2002 conclusion on penalties. Moreover the model provisions do refer explicitly to the Lisbon Treaty: "*If the approximation of criminal laws and regulations of the Member States proves essential to ensure the effective implementation of a Union policy in an area which has been subject to harmonisation measures, as under Article 83(2) of the Lisbon Treaty, it should follow the practice of setting the minimum level of maximum penalty*".

The conclusions on model provisions of 2009 are dealing with both the need for criminal provisions and the structure of criminal provisions itself. Concerning the necessity test, the conclusions insist that criminal law enforcement should be introduced only when it is considered essential for the protection of the legal interest, and, as a rule, be used only as a last resort. This double test (essential for the protection of the legal interest and *ultima ratio/ultimum remedium*) is further concretized be insisting on proportionality and subsidiarity. Criminal law provisions should address clearly defined and delimited conduct (*lex certa*), which cannot be addressed effectively by less severe measures. These criteria are applied in the model provisions to two areas:

7 http://eurocrim.jura.uni-tuebingen.de/cms/en/doc/1156.pdf.

– in the areas of particularly serious crime with a cross-border dimension resulting from the nature or impact of such offences or from a special need to combat them on a common basis, or

– if the approximation of criminal laws and regulations of the Member States proves essential to ensure the effective implementation of a Union policy in an area which has been subject to harmonisation measures.

Finally, when defining such a need, a final impact assessment should take into account the expected added value of criminal provisions compared to other enforcement measures, the serious and/or widespread and frequent the harmful conduct is and the impact on existing criminal provisions in EU legislation and on different legal systems within the EU. It is clear that these criteria of assessment of the need for criminal provisions contain general principles of criminal law and criminal policy issues and are addressed at the two substantive areas under Article 83 TFEU, the euro-offences under Article 83(1) TFEU and the criminal law enforcement of harmonised EU policies (annexe-competence) under Article 83(2) TFEU.

The second part of the model provisions is dealing with the structure of criminal provisions as such. The model provision's scheme is adressing *actus reus*, *mens rea*, inciting/aiding/abetting and attempt, penalties, liability of legal persons and penalties against legal persons. This means that provisions on jurisdiction or on mutual legal assistance or mutual recognition, dealt with in former EU conventions and framework decisions, have not been included in the model provisions. Concerning the definition of the *actus reus*, the following criteria are put forward: *lex certa*, foreseeability, conduct that causes actual harm or seriously threatens the right or essential interest to be protected. Abstracted danger to the protected right or interest is only possible if appropriate for the protection of interest or right. Concerning the *mens rea* element, as a general rule EU criminal legislation should only deal with intentionally committed conduct. However, negligence can be included when particularly appropriate for the protection of the interest or right. Strict liability is excluded explicitly. Concerning inciting, aiding and abetting, the model provisions impose the criminalization, following the criminalization of the main offence. When dealing with attempt the model rules are rather cautious. They refer to a necessity and proportionality test and to consideration of the different regimes under national law.

When it comes to penalties, the model rules provide for two regimes (let us call them model A and B). In some cases it can be sufficient to provide for effective, proportionate and dissuasive criminal penalties and leave it to each Member State to determine the level of the penalties (model A). In other cases there may be a need for going further in the approximation of the levels of penalties (model B). In these cases the Council conclusions of 2002 on penalties do apply. It is striking that the model provisions under model B do not deal with the type of criminal sanctions. When criminal law harmonisation under Article 83(2) TFEU is at stake, it will certainly not be sufficient to limit the harmonization to deprivation of liberty.

Finally, the model provisions contain extended provisions on liability of legal persons and penalties against legal persons. They introduce the obligation to ensure that a legal person can be held liable for criminal offences, but without imposing a criminal liability scheme. Attribution of liability is based on benefit for the legal person and attribution of (vicarious) liability of natural persons to the legal persons. A specific provision is dealing with the liability for lack of supervision or control, but also in this case there must be benefit for the legal person. The liability of legal persons shall not exclude criminal liability of the natural persons. Liability of legal persons is prescribed for entities having legal personality, except for states or public bodies in the exercise of state authority and for public international organizations. When it comes to penalties against legal persons, the model provisions do prescribe a list of different penalties (such as exclusion of public benefits, judicial winding-up, placing under judicial supervision, fines). However, these penalties of a criminal or non-criminal nature must meet the standard of effective, proportionate and dissuasive penalties. It is astonishing that the model provisions contain very detailed provisions on liability of legal persons, but stick to the practice under the Maastricht Treaty and Amsterdam Treaty and avoid the possibility of mandatory criminal liability in some areas of substantive criminal law.

Although the Council's model provisions were adopted one day before the Lisbon Treaty entered into force (30 November 2009) and were aimed at guiding the future work of the Council on legislative initiatives that may include criminal provisions, they are much more a systematization of the past performance, than a prospective criminal policy document. They do no take fully into account the substantive changes under the Treaty of Lisbon. The Lisbon Treaty does provide for a new legal framework for criminal legislation with the aim to prevent and punish crime in the common area of freedom, security and justice. Not only has the substance of criminal law harmonization and the applicable rules been changed by the Treaty of Lisbon, but also the objective of harmonization. Article 3 TEU clearly states that:

> The Union shall offer its citizens an area of freedom, security and justice without internal frontiers, in which the free movement of persons is ensured in conjunction with appropriate measures with respect to external border controls, asylum, immigration and the prevention and combating of crime.

Prevention and punishment of crime has become, compared to Article 2 of the Amsterdam TEU, an objective that is related to rights and duties of citizens, not only related to free movement of persons. Seen the wording of Article 82 TFEU, harmonization of criminal law and criminal procedure is also a necessary tool for strengthening judicial cooperation in criminal matters, based on mutual recognition and mutual trust. From this perspective the model provisions of the Council do not guide us as to the content of criminal policy choices. Which legal interests deserve criminal protection and to which extent? This is certainly the case for Article 83(2) TFEU, for which only very little *acquis* had been build up in the past, neither under the former third pillar, nor under the former first pillar. The criminal law protection directives in the environmental field are the exceptions to the rule. In light of Article 2 TFEU, which states that, in case of shared competence, the Member States shall exercise their competence to the extent that the Union has not exercised its competence, it becomes more and more necessary to know for which areas and to which extent the EU is willing to fill in its competence. As a mitigating factor we could say that the Council as such has no right of legislative initiative and is thus not very well placed to elaborate legislative policy. On the other hand the Council's model provisions are a policy document thoroughly discussed and adopted by the Member States in the Council, and the Member States do have legislative initiative.

3. A Criminal (Legislative) Policy under the Lisbon Treaty?

Since the coming into force of the Lisbon Treaty the European Commission has taken a proactive stand on the topic. On its website[8] DG Justice spells out three specific competences for criminal law in the TFEU. First, the EU can adopt directives providing for minimum rules regarding the definition (constituent elements and criminal sanctions) of Euro offences under Article 83(1) TFEU. Article 83(1) TFEU contains a list of particularly 10 serious areas of crime with a cross-border dimension. They include terrorism, trafficking in human beings and sexual exploitation of women and children, illicit drug trafficking, illicit arms trafficking, money laundering, corruption, counterfeiting of means of payment, computer crime and organised crime. Second the EU can also adopt directives, under Article 83(2) TFEU, providing for minimum rules on the definition of offences and criminal sanctions if they are essential for ensuring the effectiveness of a harmonised EU policy. Third, DG Justice refers to the duty to protect the financial interests of the EU, under Articles 310(6), 325, 85 and 86 TFEU, which might

8 http://ec.europa.eu/justice/criminal/criminal-law-policy/index_en.htm.

include, if necessary, by means of criminal law. This would mean that Article 325 TFEU could be used as a proper legal basis for criminal law protection of the financial interests of the EU. It remains unclear if DG Justice is of the opinion that this competence could also include regulations providing for criminal law provisions instead of directives.

The Commission published moreover in September 2011 a Communication entitled "*Towards an EU Criminal Policy – ensuring the effective implementation of EU policies through criminal law*",[9] dealing specifically with the competence under Article 83(2) TFEU. The Commission is aware of the fact that, for what is called lack of an explicit legal basis in this respect prior to the Lisbon Treaty, only very few measures have been taken for the purpose of strengthening the enforcement of EU policies. In a first part the Commission elaborates on the scope for EU criminal legislation. The Commission underlines that Article 83 (2) TFEU aims at strengthening mutual trust, ensuring effective enforcement and coherence and consistency in European criminal law itself. Article 83(2) TFEU does not list specific offences or areas of crime. For that reason the Commission elaborates this Communication as guidance for the policy choices of whether to use or not to use criminal law as an enforcement tool, also in relation to other enforcement tools, such as the administrative one. The Commission also adds Article 235(4) TFEU, referring to the protection of the financial interests of the EU:

> 4. The European Parliament and the Council, acting in accordance with the ordinary legislative procedure, after consulting the Court of Auditors, shall adopt the necessary measures in the fields of the prevention of and fight against fraud affecting the financial interests of the Union with a view to affording effective and equivalent protection in the Member States and in all the Union's institutions, bodies, offices and agencies.

However, the Commission is not making any explicit reference to directives or regulations with a criminal law substance. However, inserting it under the scope of criminal legislation in this document is considering the possibility to do so. Second, the Commission is dealing with the question of which principles should guide EU criminal law legislation. The Communication refers to general principles such as subsidiarity and respect for fundamental rights, referring explicitly to the EU Charter of Fundamental Rights and the ECHR, but not referring to Article 6 (3) TEU, and thus not referring explicitly to fundamental rights as guaranteed by the ECHR and "*as they result form the constitutional traditions common to the Member States*". It seems to me impossible to elaborate a criminal policy that would not take into account the

---

[9] COM(2011)573 final http://ec.europa.eu/justice/criminal/files/act_en.pdf.

constitutional traditions common to the Member States, and I do underline common, as they are a direct source for the general principles of EU law under Article 6(3) TEU. After the reference to the general principles, the Commission follows the two-step approach of the Council's model provisions. Step 1 is the decision on whether to adopt criminal law measures at all (last resort-*ultima ratio*/*ultimum remedium*). The proposed necessity and proportionality test is written in a negative way (restrain unless necessary and proportional) without taking into account that there might be positive duties under fundamental rights to investigate, prosecute and punish, also under Article 83(2) TFEU. Step 2 is dealing witch the principles guiding the decision on what kind of criminal law measures to adopt. The text refers to the concept of "minimum rules" and excludes full harmonisation, but underlines at the same time the need for legal certainty. The requirements for legal certainty are however not the same as for national criminal law legislation, as the directive has to be implemented in national law and cannot create or aggravate criminal liability as such. It is surprising that the Commission is not further elaborating on the concept of minimum rules, as this formulation was already used in the Amsterdam Treaty. These minimum rules are related to the Treaty objectives, including equivalent protection and common provisions when dealing with cross-border crime or enforcement of EU policies. This means that the concept of minimum rules is functional to the objectives of the Treaty and not an autonomous criterion. Regarding the sanctions the Commission is referring both to the type of sanctions and to the level of sanctions (taking into account aggravating or mitigating circumstances) that should be implemented in national law. The choice of sanctions must be evidence-driven and submitted to the necessity and proportionality test. Interesting is that the Commission insists on tailoring the sanctions to the crime, which has consequences for the choice of type of sanctions and consequences for the choice for criminal liability of legal persons. It thus becomes clear that the Commission does not exclude criminal liability of legal persons and criminal sanctions for legal persons of the competence under Article 83(2) TFEU. Finally, the minimum rules can also include provisions on jurisdiction, as well other aspects that are considered an essential part for the effective application of the legal provision.

Third, the Commission is dealing with the choice of policy areas where EU criminal law might be needed. Criteria are lack of effective enforcement or significant differences among Member States leading to inconsistent application of EU rules. Still in that case the Commission will have to assess case-by-case the specific enforcement problems and the choice for administrative and/or criminal enforcement. However, the Commission is already indicating in this Communication priority fields for criminal law harmonisation under Article 83(2) TFEU. Mentioned are three selected areas:

– The financial sector, e.g. concerning market manipulation and insider trading[10]

– The fight against fraud affecting the financial interest of the EU

– The protection of the euro against counterfeiting

The Commission mentions furthermore a set of areas (no exclusive list) in which criminal law enforcement might play a role:

– Illegal economy and financial criminality

– Road transport[11]

– Data protection[12]

– Customs rules

– Environmental protection

– Fisheries policy

– Internal market policies (counterfeiting, corruption, public procurement)

The assessment has to take into account a whole set of factors, including the seriousness and character of the breach and the efficiency of the enforcement system. The choice for administrative enforcement and or criminal enforcement is part of this assessment. The list of topics is not exclusive, but it is rather surprising that counterfeiting and piracy of products, feed and food safety and corruption are not in the prior list of already selected areas. There is already criminal law *acquis* for corruption.[13] The Commission had already submitted in 1995 a proposal for a directive on criminal measures aimed at ensuring the enforcement of intellectual property rights and a proposal for a framework decision to strengthen the criminal law framework to combat intellectual property offences.[14] The Commission had already tried in 2003,[15] in vain, to get

10 See "Communication on reinforcing sanctioning regimes in the financial sector", COM(2010)716 final of 08 December 2010.

11 See Commission Staff Working Paper SEC (2011) 391 of 28 March 2011, accompanying the White Paper "Roadmap to a Single European Transport Area – Towards a competitive and resource efficient transport system", COM(2011)144 of 28 March 2011.

12 See the Communication "A comprehensive approach on personal data protection in the European Union", COM(2010)609 of 04 November 2010.

13 Framework Decision 2003/568/JHA on combating corruption in the private sector.

14 COM(2005)276 final, http://eurlex.europa.eu/LexUriServ/site/en/com/2005/com-2005_0276en01.pdf.

15 COM(2003)52 final.

adopted a regulation containing criminal law enforcement obligations in the area of feed and food safety.

The Committee on Civil Liberties, Justice and Home Affairs of the EP adopted in May 2012 a "*Report on an EU approach on Criminal Law*" of rapporteur C. de Jong.[16] The report combines the tests of necessity, subsidiarity and proportionality with the general principles of criminal law (*lex certa, nulla poena sine culpa, lex mitior*, etc.) and does correspond fully to the 2011 Communication of the Commission. It does not contain any reference to the choice of policy areas that should deserve criminal law protection. More interesting is the procedural approach. It calls for an inter-institutional agreement on the principles and working methods governing proposals for future substantive criminal law provisions and invites the Commission and the Council to establish an inter-institutional working group in which these institutions and Parliament can draw up such an agreement and discuss general matters with a view to ensuring coherence in EU criminal law. As it stands there is a Council Working Party on substantive criminal law (DROIPEN) and a new inter-service coordination group on criminal law at the Commission. Furthermore the Commission has decided in February 2012 to set up a formal expert group on EU criminal policy.[17] At the EP there is no formal structure at all.

4. Criminal Harmonisation under the Lisbon Treaty in Practice

The directive 2011/36 on preventing and combating trafficking in human beings and protecting its victims[18] is the first directive that has been adopted under Article 83(1) TFEU. It contains the classic content as foreseen under the Council's model provisions and includes specific harmonization of the type and level of sanctions (model B of the Council's model provisions), but goes also beyond it, as it deals with aspects of jurisdiction, seizure and confiscation, and some aspects related to investigation and prosecution and of course many aspects of victim protection and victim rights. Directive 2011/92[19] on combating the sexual abuse and sexual exploitation of children and child pornography

16 http://www.europarl.europa.eu/sides/getDoc.do?type=REPORT&reference=A7-2012-0144&language=EN.

17 http://eurlex.europa.eu/LexUriServ/LexUriServ.do?uri=OJ:C:2012:053:0009:0010:EN:PDF.

18 Directive 2011/36 of 5 April 2011, http://eurlex.europa.eu/LexUriServ/LexUriServ.do?uri=OJ:L:2011:101:0001:0011:EN:PDF.

19 http://eur-lex.europa.eu/LexUriServ/LexUriServ.do?uri=OJ:L:2011:335:0001:0014:EN:PDF.

follows completely the same pattern. Meanwhile the Council did also reach a general agreement[20] on a proposal for a directive on attacks against information systems, replacing framework decision 2005/222/JHA. Also in this directive it has been opted for the harmonization of type and level of criminal sanctions (the B model). However, these directives do not always follow the four type levels of harmonization of custodial sanctions as elaborated in the 1992 agreement on criminal sanctions, as incorporated in the Council's model provisions. The influence of the EP as co-legislator has resulted, through amendments for more severe repression, in other sanction levels.

The first initiative under Article 83(2) TFEU is indeed in one of the three already selected areas in the Communication of September 2011, namely in the financial sector and on criminal sanctions for insider dealing and market manipulation. The Commission has used the policy criteria of the Communication of September 2011 for its assessment and has even produced in 2010 a Communication on "*Reinforcing sanctioning regimes in the financial service sector*",[21] based on comparative research by the three Committees of Supervisors (Committee of European Banking Supervisors-CEBS, Committee of European Insurance and Occupational Pensions Supervisors-CEIOPS and Committee of European Securities Regulators-CESR) on the equivalence of the sanctioning regimes in the financial sector in Member States. The review by the Commission in cooperation with the Committees of Supervisors spells out substantial divergences and weaknesses in national sanctioning regimes:

– Some competent authorities do not have at their disposal important types of sanctioning powers for certain violations

– Levels of administrative pecuniary sanctions vary widely across Member States and are too low in some Member States

– Some competent authorities cannot address administrative sanctions to both natural and legal persons

– Competent authorities do not take into account the same criteria in the application of sanctions

– Divergence exists in the nature (administrative or criminal) of sanctions provided for in national legislation

– The level of application of sanctions varies across Member States

As a consequence the Commission considers that a minimum common standard should be set and that this minimum common standard

20 http://register.consilium.europa.eu/pdf/en/11/st11/st11566.en11.pdf.

21 COM(2010)716 final.

might include criminal sanctions for the most serious violations. The proposed directive on criminal sanctions for insider dealing and market manipulation,[22] submitted in October 2011, is part of a legislative double text package, which includes also a proposal for a regulation on insider dealing and market manipulation (market abuse).[23] In fact the proposed regulation, based on Article 114 TFEU and aiming at replacing directive 2003/6/EC,[24] is the basic regulatory framework. The regulation proposal contains all definitions, obligations and prohibitions and does also regulate the applicable administrative enforcement regime, including administrative sanctions of a non-punitive and punitive character. This means that the proposed regulation contains very detailed provisions on the definition of the illicit behaviour and on the applicable administrative sanctions, including the type and level of sanctions (like for instance withdrawal of the authorisation or pecuniary sanctions for legal persons up to 10% of its total annual turnover in the preceding business year).[25] The proposed directive is the result of the assessment of the Commission on the need, proportionality and subsidiarity of criminal law enforcement in the financial sector. The Commission came to a positive result as far as serious market abuse offences are concerned. The proposed directive is surprising from different angles. Although the proposed regulation and the proposed directive are a regulatory package and contain quite some cross-references, the proposed directive refers only to the definitions of financial instruments and inside information in the proposed regulation, but strange enough reformulates the definition of insider dealing and market manipulation. These definitions in the proposed directive and regulation are not shaped in the same way; the ones in the proposed directive are written in a more precise style and do not contain further explanations and details. Second, seen the assessment of the necessity of criminal law harmonisation to ensure effective enforcement of Union policy against market abuse, it is also surprising that the proposed directive is choosing for what we have called model A of the Council's model provisions, this means that it is in this area sufficient to provide for effective, proportionate and dissuasive criminal penalties and leave it to each Member State to determine the type and level of the penalties. This type of criminal law harmonization was already possible under the 1st pillar of the Amsterdam Treaty, even after the ruling of the Court of Justice in

22 COM(2011)654 final, 20 October 2011.

23 COM(2011)651 final, 20 October 2011.

24 http://eur-lex.europa.eu/LexUriServ/LexUriServ.do?uri=OJ:L:2003:096:0016:00-16:EN:PDF.

25 Article 26 of the proposal.

the ship source pollution case.[26] And this brings me to the third point. The choice of Article 83(2) TFEU as legal basis is not discussed. There is no consideration as to which Article 83(2) TFEU is more appropriate than a legal basis linked to the substantial policy area (financial services). The consequence of the choice for Article 83(2) TFEU is at least that Denmark is not taking part in the adoption of this Directive[27] and that the UK and Ireland have an opting in choice, but no obligation to become part of and bound by the Directive.[28] In other words it is under Article 83(2) TFEU possible that criminal enforcement obligations, considered in line with proportionality and subsidiarity and considered necessary for the effective enforcement of a harmonised EU policy, will not be binding in three EU countries, including the EU country with the biggest centre of financial services. In this sense the proposal is rather a step backward than forward.

The second priority area under Article 83(2) TFEU concerns the protection of the financial interest of the EU. The *acquis* in this field dates from the Maastricht Treaty, being the 1995 regulation on administrative enforcement[29] and the 1995 Convention and two protocols[30] on criminal enforcement. The Commission did already submit in 2001 a proposal for a directive on the criminal-law protection of the Community's financial interests,[31] but the proposal was never thoroughly discussed at the Council. This file concerns not only the "*Lisbonisation*" of the Maastricht-*acquis*, but also some substantial new points, as the broadening of the material scope of the substantive offences, redefinition of jurisdiction criteria and the eventual criminal liability of legal persons. It is clear, in the light of the *acquis*, that this proposal will be a B model for the harmonisation of sanctions, so including harmonisation of type and level of the mandatory sanctions. The Commission has chosen for Article 325(4) TFEU instead of Article 83(2) TFEU as a legal basis, which means that it will be binding for all Member States, including Denmark, Ireland and the UK. However the Commission will elaborate a draft directive and not a regulation under Article 325(4) TFEU.

---

26 See Case C-176/03, Judgment of 15 September 2005.

27 In accordance with Articles 1 and 2 of Protocol No. 22.

28 In accordance with Articles 1, 2, 3, and 4 of Protocol 21.

29 Regulation 2988/95 on the protection of the EC's financial interest, http://eur-lex.europa.eu/LexUriServ/LexUriServ.do?uri=CELEX:31995R2988:EN:HTML.

30 Convention on the protection of the European Communities' financial interests of 26 July 1995, OJ C 316, 27.11.1995; First Protocol of 27.09.1996 to the Convention, OJ C 313, 23.10.1996 and Second Protocol to the Convention, OJ C 221, 19.07.1997.

31 COM(2001)272 final.

As far as the third priority area is concerned, the criminal protection of the counterfeiting of the single currency, the file concerns the "*Lisbonisation*" of the framework decision of 2000 on increasing protection by criminal penalties and other sanctions against counterfeiting in connection with the introduction of the euro.[32] For the moment being there is no legislative initiative in the pipeline yet. Concerning the other areas for which the Commission still has to decide if and to which extent harmonisation of criminal enforcement is necessary (like customs policy, illegal economy and financial criminality, data protection, etc.) there are no legislative proposals in the pipeline either. The Commission has published a communication on "*A Single Market for intellectual property rights. Boosting creativity and innovation to provide economic growth, high quality jobs and first class products and services in Europe*",[33] dealing also with enhanced fight against counterfeiting and piracy. However, until now there is no legislative proposal in the pipeline, although the Commission submitted already in 1995 a proposal for a directive on criminal measures aimed at ensuring the enforcement of intellectual property rights and a proposal for a framework decision to strengthen the criminal law framework to combat intellectual property offences.[34] Concerning corruption the Commission has published a communication on fighting corruption in the EU.[35] In some of the mentioned policy areas the Commission has tendered a study, like the one on sanctions in the field of commercial road transport.

5. Conclusion

Seen the shared competence[36] in the field of criminal law, based on shared sovereignty and common goals between the Member States and the EU, it is logic that both the EU and the Member States elaborate criminal policies, also in the area of European criminal law. But the shared competence also means that both European and national criminal policies must and should have a double dimension, a European and a national one. In fact, European criminal policy has to take account of common traditions in the Member States and the national criminal policies have to take into account the European dimension of their

---

32 http://europa.eu/legislation_summaries/fight_against_fraud/fight_against_counterfeiting/l33090_en.htm.

33 COM(2011)287 final, http://ec.europa.eu/internal_market/copyright/docs/ipr_strategy/COM_2011_287_en.pdf.

34 COM(2005)276 final, http://eur-lex.europa.eu/LexUriServ/site/en/com/2005/com2005_0276en01.pdf.

35 COM(2011)308 final http://ec.europa.eu/home-affairs/news/intro/docs/110606/308/1_EN_ACT_part1_v12[1].pdf.

36 Article 2 TFEU.

national criminal law enforcement. The prevention and punishment of market abuse, the commercialisation of dangerous food stuffs or of trafficking in human beings, just to give a couple of examples, can only be achieved through the integration of EU and national criminal policies.

This includes that EU criminal policy and national criminal policies should set the goals, taking into account the objectives of the EU Treaty. What is needed to offer EU citizens an area of freedom, security and justice in which free movement of persons is ensured in conjunction with prevention and combating of crime? It is quite clear that we cannot address only serious cross-border crime, but have to deal also with the criminal law enforcement of EU policies, if necessary. What type of legal interests do need and deserve criminal law protection? I think that we still can make a difference between

– Proper legal interest of the EU (counterfeiting of the single currency, protection of the financial interests of the EU, corruption of EU officials)

– Common legal interests in the area of freedom, security and justice (euro-crimes – Article 83(1) TFEU)

– Legal interest linked to harmonised EU policies (annex-competence – Article 83(2) TFEU).

Both EU as national criminal policy documents should deal with this three dimensions.

Criminal policy must be principle-based, combining the tests of necessity (*ultima ratio*), subsidiarity and proportionality and general principles of criminal law. But that is only a part of the story. Criminal policy is of course also about policy, this means that political choices must be made about the interests that do deserve and do need criminal law protection. This criminal law protection has to be defined in relation with other enforcement regimes, especially the punitive administrative enforcement. Criminal policy includes also the elaboration of instruments of integrated enforcement of EU policies, including prevention, administrative enforcement and criminal enforcement. Red flags to functional harmonisation were traditionally: prosecutorial discretion, criminal liability of legal persons, minimum penalties, sentencing discretion. Procedurally the emergency break under Article 83 TFEU can be used for this purpose, but this instrument is rather a political *ultima ratio*, although it could have a preventive effect during the negotiations. In my opinion national red flags can have only sense if they do not obstruct the European common goals in the area of freedom, security and justice.

Prevention and punishment of crime has become an objective that is related to rights and duties of citizens in the area of freedom, security and justice (Article 3 TEU). Seen the wording of Article 82 TFEU, harmonization of criminal law and criminal procedure is also a necessary tool for strengthening judicial cooperation in criminal matters, based on mutual recognition and mutual trust. From this perspective neither the model provisions of the Council, nor the report of the EP guides us as to the content of criminal policy choices. Which legal interests deserve criminal protection and to what extent? This is certainly the case for Article 83(2) TFEU, for which no or very little *acquis* had been build up in the past, neither under the former third pillar, nor under the first pillar. The Commission Communication of 2011 is going a step further and deals with the policy choices. This is clearly of added value, but it remains unclear on which basis and by which criteria policy areas have been selected or could be selected for criminal law protection.

The EU is sure about its competence, but still does not now when and how to deal with it: *certus an, incertus quando*.